MITSUBISHI

GALANT/MIRAGE/DIAMANTE
1990-00 REPAIR MANUAL

CHILTON'S

CEO	Rick Van Dalen
President	Dean F. Morgantini, S.A.E.
Vice President–Finance	Barry L. Beck
Vice President–Sales	Glenn D. Potere
Executive Editor	Kevin M. G. Maher, A.S.E.
Manager–Consumer Automotive	Richard Schwartz, A.S.E.
Manager–Professional Automotive	Richard J. Rivele
Manager–Marine/Recreation	James R. Marotta, A.S.E.
Production Specialist	Melinda Possinger
Project Managers	Tim Crain, A.S.E., Thomas A. Mellon, A.S.E., S.A.E., Eric Michael Mihalyi, A.S.E., S.T.S., S.A.E., Christine L. Sheeky, S.A.E., Richard T. Smith, Ron Webb
Schematics Editors	Christopher G. Ritchie, A.S.E., S.A.E., S.T.S., Stephanie A. Spunt
Editor	Eric Michael Mihalyi, A.S.E., S.T.S., S.A.E.

CHILTON Automotive Books

PUBLISHED BY **W. G. NICHOLS, INC.**

Manufactured in USA
© 2000 W. G. Nichols, Inc.
1025 Andrew Drive
West Chester, PA 19380
ISBN 0-8019-9315-6
Library of Congress Catalog Card No. 00-132514
2345678901 0987654321

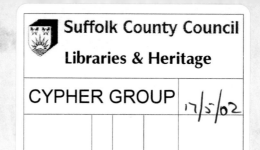
Contents

Contents

DRIVE TRAIN 7

SUSPENSION AND STEERING 8

BRAKES 9

BODY AND TRIM 10

TROUBLESHOOTING 11

GLOSSARY

MASTER INDEX

See last page for information on additional titles

SAFETY NOTICE

Proper service and repair procedures are vital to the safe, reliable operation of all motor vehicles, as well as the personal safety of those performing repairs. This manual outlines procedures for servicing and repairing vehicles using safe, effective methods. The procedures contain many NOTES, CAUTIONS and WARNINGS which should be followed, along with standard procedures to eliminate the possibility of personal injury or improper service which could damage the vehicle or compromise its safety.

It is important to note that repair procedures and techniques, tools and parts for servicing motor vehicles, as well as the skill and experience of the individual performing the work vary widely. It is not possible to anticipate all of the conceivable ways or conditions under which vehicles may be serviced, or to provide cautions as to all possible hazards that may result. Standard and accepted safety precautions and equipment should be used when handling toxic or flammable fluids, and safety goggles or other protection should be used during cutting, grinding, chiseling, prying, or any other process that can cause material removal or projectiles.

Some procedures require the use of tools specially designed for a specific purpose. Before substituting another tool or procedure, you must be completely satisfied that neither your personal safety, nor the performance of the vehicle will be endangered.

Although information in this manual is based on industry sources and is complete as possible at the time of publication, the possibility exists that some car manufacturers made later changes which could not be included here. While striving for total accuracy, Nichols Publishing cannot assume responsibility for any errors, changes or omissions that may occur in the compilation of this data.

PART NUMBERS

Part numbers listed in this reference are not recommendations by Nichols Publishing for any product brand name. They are references that can be used with interchange manuals and aftermarket supplier catalogs to locate each brand supplier's discrete part number.

SPECIAL TOOLS

Special tools are recommended by the vehicle manufacturer to perform their specific job. Use has been kept to a minimum, but where absolutely necessary, they are referred to in the text by the part number of the tool manufacturer. These tools can be purchased, under the appropriate part number, from your local dealer or regional distributor, or an equivalent tool can be purchased locally from a tool supplier or parts outlet. Before substituting any tool for the one recommended, read the SAFETY NOTICE at the top of this page.

ACKNOWLEDGMENTS

Nichols Publishing expresses appreciation to Mitsubishi Motors Corporation for their generous assistance.

Nichols Publishing would like to express thanks to all of the fine companies who participate in the production of our books:
- Hand tools supplied by Craftsman are used during all phases of our vehicle teardown and photography.
- Many of the fine specialty tools used in our procedures were provided courtesy of Lisle Corporation.
- Lincoln Automotive Products (1 Lincoln Way, St. Louis, MO 63120) has provided their industrial shop equipment, including jacks (engine, transmission and floor), engine stands, fluid and lubrication tools, as well as shop presses.
- Rotary Lifts (1-800-640-5438 or www.Rotary-Lift.com), the largest automobile lift manufacturer in the world, offering the biggest variety of surface and in-ground lifts available, has fulfilled our shop's lift needs.
- Much of our shop's electronic testing equipment was supplied by Universal Enterprises Inc. (UEI).
- Safety-Kleen Systems Inc. has provided parts cleaning stations and assistance with environmentally sound disposal of residual wastes.
- United Gilsonite Laboratories (UGL), manufacturer of Drylok® concrete floor paint, has provided materials and expertise for the coating and protection of our shop floor.

1

GENERAL INFORMATION AND MAINTENANCE

HOW TO USE THIS BOOK

Chilton's Total Car Care manual for the 1990–00 Mitsubishi Mirage, Galant and Diamante is intended to help you learn more about the inner workings of your vehicle while saving you money on its upkeep and operation.

The beginning of the book will likely be referred to the most, since that is where you will find information for maintenance and tune-up. The other sections deal with the more complex systems of your vehicle. Operating systems from engine through brakes are covered to the extent that the average do-it-yourselfer becomes mechanically involved. This book will not explain such things as rebuilding a differential for the simple reason that the expertise required and the investment in special tools make this task uneconomical. It will, however, give you detailed instructions to help you change your own brake pads and shoes, replace spark plugs, and perform many more jobs that can save you money, give you personal satisfaction and help you avoid expensive problems.

A secondary purpose of this book is a reference for owners who want to understand their vehicle and/or their mechanics better. In this case, no tools at all are required.

Where to Begin

Before removing any bolts, read through the entire procedure. This will give you the overall view of what tools and supplies will be required. There is nothing more frustrating than having to walk to the bus stop on Monday morning because you were short one bolt on Sunday afternoon. So read ahead and plan ahead. Each operation should be approached logically and all procedures thoroughly understood before attempting any work.

All sections contain adjustments, maintenance, removal and installation procedures, and in some cases, repair or overhaul procedures. When repair is not considered practical, we tell you how to remove the part and then how to install the new or rebuilt replacement. In this way, you at least save labor costs. "Backyard" repair of some components is just not practical.

Avoiding Trouble

Many procedures in this book require you to "label and disconnect . . . " a group of lines, hoses or wires. Don't be lulled into thinking you can remember where everything goes—you won't. If you hook up vacuum or fuel lines incorrectly, the vehicle may run poorly, if at all. If you hook up electrical wiring incorrectly, you may instantly learn a very expensive lesson.

You don't need to know the official or engineering name for each hose or line. A piece of masking tape on the hose and a piece on its fitting will allow you to assign your own label such as the letter A or a short

name. As long as you remember your own code, the lines can be reconnected by matching similar letters or names. Do remember that tape will dissolve in gasoline or other fluids; if a component is to be washed or cleaned, use another method of identification. A permanent felt-tipped marker or a metal scribe can be very handy for marking metal parts. Remove any tape or paper labels after assembly.

Maintenance or Repair?

It's necessary to mention the difference between maintenance and repair. Maintenance includes routine inspections, adjustments, and replacement of parts which show signs of normal wear. Maintenance compensates for wear or deterioration. Repair implies that something has broken or is not working. A need for repair is often caused by lack of maintenance. Example: draining and refilling the automatic transaxle fluid is maintenance recommended by the manufacturer at specific mileage intervals. Failure to do this can shorten the life of the transmission/transaxle, requiring very expensive repairs. While no maintenance program can prevent items from breaking or wearing out, a general rule can be stated: MAINTENANCE IS CHEAPER THAN REPAIR.

Two basic mechanic's rules should be mentioned here. First, whenever the left side of the vehicle or engine is referred to, it is meant to specify the driver's side. Conversely, the right side of the vehicle means the passenger's side. Second, screws and bolts are removed by turning counterclockwise, and tightened by turning clockwise unless specifically noted.

Safety is always the most important rule. Constantly be aware of the dangers involved in working on an automobile and take the proper precautions. See the information in this section regarding SERVICING YOUR VEHICLE SAFELY and the SAFETY NOTICE on the acknowledgment page.

Avoiding the Most Common Mistakes

Pay attention to the instructions provided. There are 3 common mistakes in mechanical work:

1. Incorrect order of assembly, disassembly or adjustment. When taking something apart or putting it together, performing steps in the wrong order usually just costs you extra time; however, it CAN break something. Read the entire procedure before beginning disassembly. Perform everything in the order in which the instructions say you should, even if you can't immediately see a reason for it. When you're taking apart something that is very intricate, you might want to draw a picture of how it looks when assembled at one point in order to make sure you get

everything back in its proper position. We will supply exploded views whenever possible. When making adjustments, perform them in the proper order. One adjustment possibly will affect another.

2. Overtorquing (or undertorquing). While it is more common for overtorquing to cause damage, undertorquing may allow a fastener to vibrate loose causing serious damage. Especially when dealing with aluminum parts, pay attention to torque specifications and utilize a torque wrench in assembly. If a torque figure is not available, remember that if you are using the right tool to perform the job, you will probably not have to strain yourself to get a fastener tight enough. The pitch of most threads is so slight that the tension you put on the wrench will be multiplied many times in actual force on what you are tightening. A good example of how critical torque is can be seen in the case of spark plug installation, especially where you are putting the plug into an aluminum cylinder head. Too little torque can fail to crush the gasket, causing leakage of combustion gases and consequent overheating of the plug and engine parts. Too much torque can damage the threads or distort the plug, changing the spark gap.

There are many commercial products available for ensuring that fasteners won't come loose, even if they are not torqued just right (a very common brand is Loctite®). If you're worried about getting something together tight enough to hold, but loose enough to avoid mechanical damage during assembly, one of these products might offer substantial insurance. Before choosing a threadlocking compound, read the label on the package and make sure the product is compatible with the materials, fluids, etc. involved.

3. Crossthreading. This occurs when a part such as a bolt is screwed into a nut or casting at the wrong angle and forced. Crossthreading is more likely to occur if access is difficult. It helps to clean and lubricate fasteners, then to start threading the bolt, spark plug, etc. with your fingers. If you encounter resistance, unscrew the part and start over again at a different angle until it can be inserted and turned several times without much effort. Keep in mind that many parts, especially spark plugs, have tapered threads, so that gentle turning will automatically bring the part you're threading to the proper angle. Don't put a wrench on the part until it's been tightened a couple of turns by hand. If you suddenly encounter resistance, and the part has not seated fully, don't force it. Pull it back out to make sure it's clean and threading properly.

Be sure to take your time and be patient, and always plan ahead. Allow yourself ample time to perform repairs and maintenance. You may find maintaining your car a satisfying and enjoyable experience.

TOOLS AND EQUIPMENT

▶ **See Figures 1 thru 15**

Naturally, without the proper tools and equipment it is impossible to properly service your vehicle. It would also be virtually impossible to catalog every tool that you would need to perform all of the operations in this book. Of course, it would be unwise for the amateur to rush out and buy an expensive set of tools on the theory that he/she may need one or more of them at some time.

The best approach is to proceed slowly, gathering a good quality set of those tools that are used most frequently. Don't be misled by the low cost of bargain tools. It is far better to spend a little more for better quality. Forged wrenches, 6 or 12-point sockets and fine tooth ratchets are by far preferable to their less expensive counterparts. As any good mechanic can tell you, there are few worse experiences than trying to work on a vehicle with bad tools. Your monetary

savings will be far outweighed by frustration and mangled knuckles.

Begin accumulating those tools that are used most frequently: those associated with routine maintenance and tune-up. In addition to the normal assortment of screwdrivers and pliers, you should have the following tools:

• Wrenches/sockets and combination open end/box end wrenches in sizes from $\frac{1}{8}$–$\frac{3}{4}$ in. or

3–19mm, as well as a ¹³/₁₆ in. or ⁵/₈ in. spark plug socket (depending on plug type).

➡**If possible, buy various length socket drive extensions. Universal-joint and wobble extensions can be extremely useful, but be** careful when using them, as they can change the amount of torque applied to the socket.

- Jackstands for support.
- Oil filter wrench.
- Spout or funnel for pouring fluids.

- Grease gun for chassis lubrication (unless your vehicle is not equipped with any grease fittings—for details, please refer to information on Fluids and Lubricants, later in this section).
- Hydrometer for checking the battery (unless equipped with a sealed, maintenance-free battery).
- A container for draining oil and other fluids.
- Rags for wiping up the inevitable mess.

In addition to the above items there are several others that are not absolutely necessary, but handy to have around. These include Oil Dry® (or an equivalent oil absorbent gravel—such as cat litter) and the usual supply of lubricants, antifreeze and fluids, although these can be purchased as needed. This is a basic list for routine maintenance, but only your personal needs and desire can accurately determine your list of tools.

After performing a few projects on the vehicle, you'll be amazed at the other tools and non-tools on

Fig. 1 All but the most basic procedures will require an assortment of ratchets and sockets

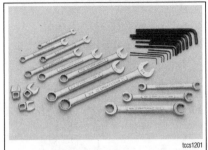

Fig. 2 In addition to ratchets, a good set of wrenches and hex keys will be necessary

Fig. 3 A hydraulic floor jack and a set of jackstands are essential for lifting and supporting the vehicle

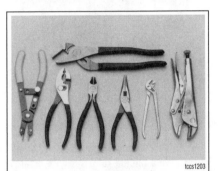

Fig. 4 An assortment of pliers, grippers and cutters will be handy for old rusted parts and stripped bolt heads

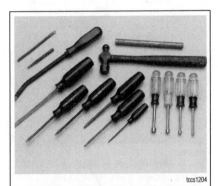

Fig. 5 Various drivers, chisels and prybars are great tools to have in your toolbox

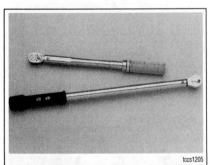

Fig. 6 Many repairs will require the use of a torque wrench to assure the components are properly fastened

Fig. 7 Although not always necessary, using specialized brake tools will save time

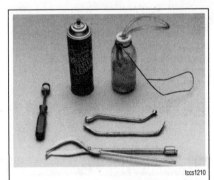

Fig. 8 A few inexpensive lubrication tools will make maintenance easier

Fig. 9 Various pullers, clamps and separator tools are needed for many larger, more complicated repairs

Fig. 10 A variety of tools and gauges should be used for spark plug gapping and installation

Fig. 11 Inductive type timing light

Fig. 12 A screw-in type compression gauge is recommended for compression testing

Fig. 13 A vacuum/pressure tester is necessary for many testing procedures

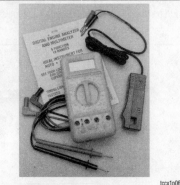

Fig. 14 Most modern automotive multimeters incorporate many helpful features

Fig. 15 Proper information is vital, so always have a Chilton Total Car Care manual handy

- Feeler gauges for valve adjustment.
- Timing light.

The choice of a timing light should be made carefully. A light which works on the DC current supplied by the vehicle's battery is the best choice; it should have a xenon tube for brightness. On any vehicle with an electronic ignition system, a timing light with an inductive pickup that clamps around the No. 1 spark plug cable is preferred.

In addition to these basic tools, there are several other tools and gauges you may find useful. These include:

- Compression gauge. The screw-in type is slower to use, but eliminates the possibility of a faulty reading due to escaping pressure.
- Manifold vacuum gauge.
- 12V test light.
- A combination volt/ohmmeter
- Induction Ammeter. This is used for determining whether or not there is current in a wire. These are handy for use if a wire is broken somewhere in a wiring harness.

As a final note, you will probably find a torque wrench necessary for all but the most basic work. The beam type models are perfectly adequate, although the newer click types (breakaway) are easier to use. The click type torque wrenches tend to be more expensive. Also keep in mind that all types of torque wrenches should be periodically checked and/or recalibrated. You will have to decide for yourself which better fits your pocketbook, and purpose.

Special Tools

Normally, the use of special factory tools is avoided for repair procedures, since these are not readily available for the do-it-yourself mechanic. When it is possible to perform the job with more commonly available tools, it will be pointed out, but occasionally, a special tool was designed to perform a specific function and should be used. Before substituting another tool, you should be convinced that neither your safety nor the performance of the vehicle will be compromised.

Special tools can usually be purchased from an automotive parts store or from your dealer. In some cases special tools may be available directly from the tool manufacturer.

your workbench. Some useful household items are: a large turkey baster or siphon, empty coffee cans and ice trays (to store parts), ball of twine, electrical tape for wiring, small rolls of colored tape for tagging lines or hoses, markers and pens, a note pad, golf tees (for plugging vacuum lines), metal coat hangers or a roll of mechanic's wire (to hold things out of the way), dental pick or similar long, pointed probe, a strong magnet, and a small mirror (to see into recesses and under manifolds).

A more advanced set of tools, suitable for tune-up work, can be drawn up easily. While the tools are slightly more sophisticated, they need not be outrageously expensive. There are several inexpensive tach/dwell meters on the market that are every bit as good for the average mechanic as a professional model. Just be sure that it goes to a least 1200–1500 rpm on the tach scale and that it works on 4, 6 and 8-cylinder engines. The key to these purchases is to make them with an eye towards adaptability and wide range. A basic list of tune-up tools could include:

- Tach/dwell meter.
- Spark plug wrench and gapping tool.

SERVICING YOUR VEHICLE SAFELY

♦ **See Figures 16, 17, 18, and 19**

It is virtually impossible to anticipate all of the hazards involved with automotive maintenance and service, but care and common sense will prevent most accidents.

The rules of safety for mechanics range from "don't smoke around gasoline," to "use the proper tool(s) for the job." The trick to avoiding injuries is to develop safe work habits and to take every possible precaution.

Do's

- Do keep a fire extinguisher and first aid kit handy.
- Do wear safety glasses or goggles when cutting, drilling, grinding or prying, even if you have 20–20 vision. If you wear glasses for the sake of vision, wear safety goggles over your regular glasses.

- Do shield your eyes whenever you work around the battery. Batteries contain sulfuric acid. In case of contact with the eyes or skin, flush the area with water or a mixture of water and baking soda, then seek immediate medical attention.
- Do use safety stands (jackstands) for any undervehicle service. Jacks are for raising vehicles; jackstands are for making sure the vehicle stays raised until you want it to come down. Whenever the vehicle is raised, block the wheels remaining on the ground and set the parking brake.
- Do use adequate ventilation when working with any chemicals or hazardous materials. Like carbon monoxide, the asbestos dust resulting from some brake lining wear can be hazardous in sufficient quantities.
- Do disconnect the negative battery cable when working on the electrical system. The secondary ig-

nition system contains EXTREMELY HIGH VOLTAGE. In some cases it can even exceed 50,000 volts.

- Do follow manufacturer's directions whenever working with potentially hazardous materials. Most chemicals and fluids are poisonous if taken internally.
- Do properly maintain your tools. Loose hammerheads, mushroomed punches and chisels, frayed or poorly grounded electrical cords, excessively worn screwdrivers, spread wrenches (open end), cracked sockets, slipping ratchets, or faulty droplight sockets can cause accidents.
- Likewise, keep your tools clean; a greasy wrench can slip off a bolt head, ruining the bolt and often harming your knuckles in the process.
- Do use the proper size and type of tool for the job at hand. Do select a wrench or socket that fits the nut or bolt. The wrench or socket should sit straight, not cocked.

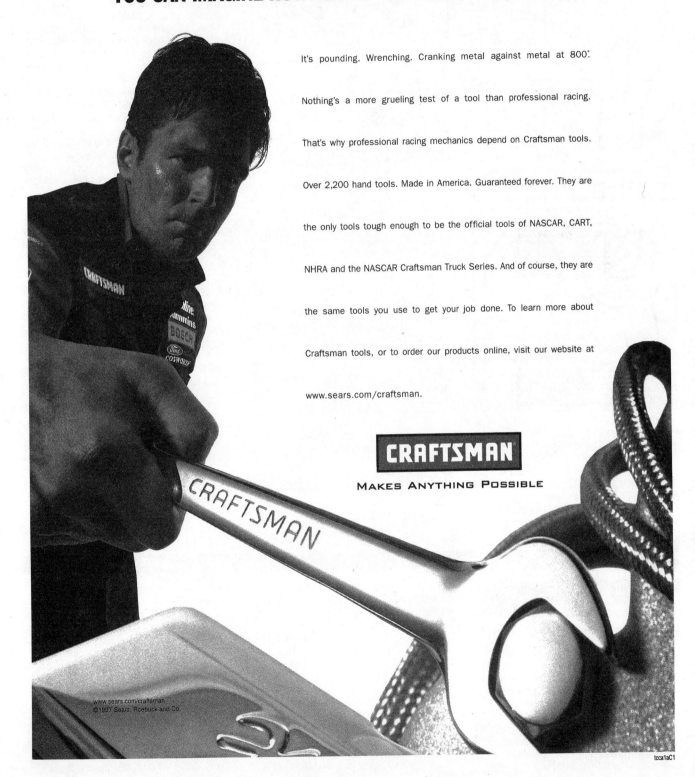
tcca1aC1

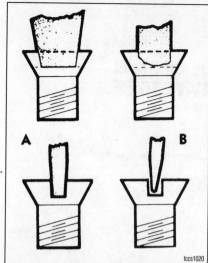

Fig. 16 Screwdrivers should be kept in good condition to prevent injury or damage which could result if the blade slips from the screw

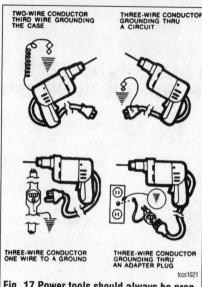

Fig. 17 Power tools should always be properly grounded

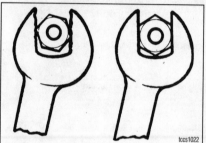

Fig. 18 Using the correct size wrench will help prevent the possibility of rounding off a nut

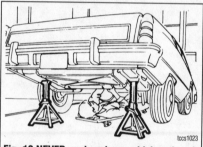

Fig. 19 NEVER work under a vehicle unless it is supported using safety stands (jackstands)

• Do, when possible, pull on a wrench handle rather than push on it, and adjust your stance to prevent a fall.

• Do be sure that adjustable wrenches are tightly closed on the nut or bolt and pulled so that the force is on the side of the fixed jaw.

• Do strike squarely with a hammer; avoid glancing blows.

• Do set the parking brake and block the drive wheels if the work requires a running engine.

Don'ts

• Don't run the engine in a garage or anywhere else without proper ventilation—EVER! Carbon

monoxide is poisonous; it takes a long time to leave the human body and you can build up a deadly supply of it in your system by simply breathing in a little every day. You may not realize you are slowly poisoning yourself. Always use power vents, windows, fans and/or open the garage door.

• Don't work around moving parts while wearing loose clothing. Short sleeves are much safer than long, loose sleeves. Hard-toed shoes with neoprene soles protect your toes and give a better grip on slippery surfaces. Jewelry such as watches, fancy belt buckles, beads or body adornment of any kind is not safe working around a vehicle. Long hair should be tied back under a hat or cap.

• Don't use pockets for toolboxes. A fall or bump can drive a screwdriver deep into your body. Even a rag hanging from your back pocket can wrap around a spinning shaft or fan.

• Don't smoke when working around gasoline, cleaning solvent or other flammable material.

• Don't smoke when working around the battery. When the battery is being charged, it gives off explosive hydrogen gas.

• Don't use gasoline to wash your hands; there are excellent soaps available. Gasoline contains dangerous additives which can enter the body through a cut or through your pores. Gasoline also removes all the natural oils from the skin so that bone dry hands will suck up oil and grease.

• Don't service the air conditioning system unless you are equipped with the necessary tools and training. When liquid or compressed gas refrigerant is released to atmospheric pressure it will absorb heat from whatever it contacts. This will chill or freeze anything it touches.

• Don't use screwdrivers for anything other than driving screws! A screwdriver used as a prying tool can snap when you least expect it, causing injuries. At the very least, you'll ruin a good screwdriver.

• Don't use an emergency jack (that little ratchet, scissors, or pantograph jack supplied with the vehicle) for anything other than changing a flat! These jacks are only intended for emergency use out on the road; they are NOT designed as a maintenance tool. If you are serious about maintaining your vehicle yourself, invest in a hydraulic floor jack of at least a $1\frac{1}{2}$ ton capacity, and at least two sturdy jackstands.

FASTENERS, MEASUREMENTS AND CONVERSIONS

Bolts, Nuts and Other Threaded Retainers

▶ See Figures 20, 21, 22, and 23

Although there are a great variety of fasteners found in the modern car or truck, the most commonly used retainer is the threaded fastener (nuts, bolts, screws, studs, etc.). Most threaded retainers may be reused, provided that they are not damaged in use or during the repair. Some retainers (such as stretch bolts or torque prevailing nuts) are designed to deform when tightened or in use and should not be reinstalled.

Whenever possible, we will note any special retainers which should be replaced during a procedure. But you should always inspect the condition of a retainer when it is removed and replace any that show signs of damage. Check all threads for rust or corro-

sion which can increase the torque necessary to achieve the desired clamp load for which that fastener was originally selected. Additionally, be sure that the driver surface of the fastener has not been compromised by rounding or other damage. In some cases a driver surface may become only partially rounded, allowing the driver to catch in only one direction. In many of these occurrences, a fastener may be installed and tightened, but the driver would not be able to grip and loosen the fastener again. (This could lead to frustration down the line should that component ever need to be disassembled again).

If you must replace a fastener, whether due to design or damage, you must ALWAYS be sure to use the proper replacement. In all cases, a retainer of the same design, material and strength should be used. Markings on the heads of most bolts will help determine the proper strength of the fastener. The same material, thread and pitch must be selected to assure

proper installation and safe operation of the vehicle afterwards.

Thread gauges are available to help measure a bolt or stud's thread. Most automotive and hardware stores keep gauges available to help you select the proper size. In a pinch, you can use another nut or bolt for a thread gauge. If the bolt you are replacing is not too badly damaged, you can select a match by finding another bolt which will thread in its place. If you find a nut which threads properly onto the damaged bolt, then use that nut to help select the replacement bolt. If however, the bolt you are replacing is so badly damaged (broken or drilled out) that its threads cannot be used as a gauge, you might start by looking for another bolt (from the same assembly or a similar location on your vehicle) which will thread into the damaged bolt's mounting. If so, the other bolt can be used to select a nut; the nut can then be used to select the replacement bolt.

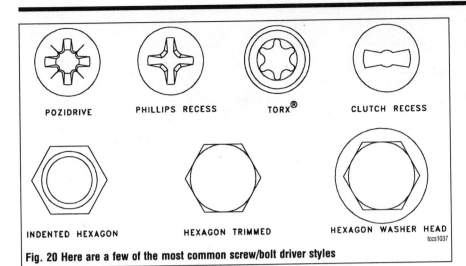

Fig. 20 Here are a few of the most common screw/bolt driver styles

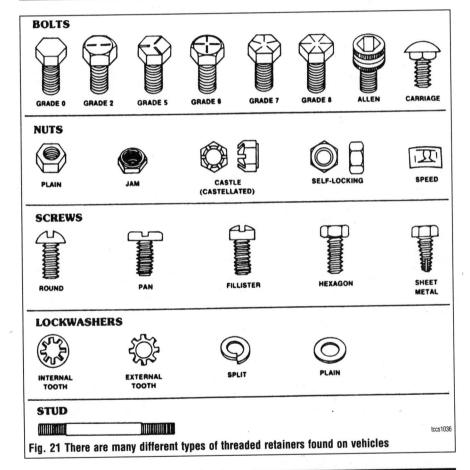

Fig. 21 There are many different types of threaded retainers found on vehicles

of the bolt head, screw head or nut face and the base material or washer (the surface on which the fastener is rotating). Approximately 40 percent of the applied torque is used in overcoming thread friction. This leaves only about 10 percent of the applied torque to develop a useful clamp load (the force which holds a joint together). This means that friction can account for as much as 90 percent of the applied torque on a fastener.

TORQUE WRENCHES

♦ See Figures 24 and 25

In most applications, a torque wrench can be used to assure proper installation of a fastener. Torque wrenches come in various designs and most automotive supply stores will carry a variety to suit your needs. A torque wrench should be used any time we supply a specific torque value for a fastener. A torque wrench can also be used if you are following the general guidelines in the accompanying charts. Keep in mind that because there is no worldwide standardization of fasteners, the charts are a general guideline

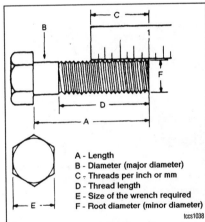

A - Length
B - Diameter (major diameter)
C - Threads per inch or mm
D - Thread length
E - Size of the wrench required
F - Root diameter (minor diameter)

Fig. 22 Threaded retainer sizes are determined using these measurements

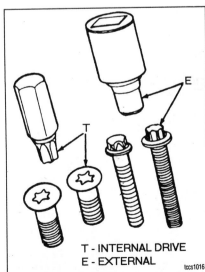

T - INTERNAL DRIVE
E - EXTERNAL

Fig. 23 Special fasteners such as these Torx® head bolts are used by manufacturers to discourage people from working on vehicles without the proper tools

In all cases, be absolutely sure you have selected the proper replacement. Don't be shy, you can always ask the store clerk for help.

✷✷ WARNING

Be aware that when you find a bolt with damaged threads, you may also find the nut or drilled hole it was threaded into has also been damaged. If this is the case, you may have to drill and tap the hole, replace the nut or otherwise repair the threads. NEVER try to force a replacement bolt to fit into the damaged threads.

Torque

Torque is defined as the measurement of resistance to turning or rotating. It tends to twist a body about an axis of rotation. A common example of this would be tightening a threaded retainer such as a nut, bolt or screw. Measuring torque is one of the most common ways to help assure that a threaded retainer has been properly fastened.

When tightening a threaded fastener, torque is applied in three distinct areas, the head, the bearing surface and the clamp load. About 50 percent of the measured torque is used in overcoming bearing friction. This is the friction between the bearing surface

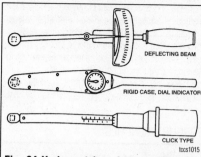

Fig. 24 Various styles of torque wrenches are usually available at your local automotive supply store

and should be used with caution. Again, the general rule of "if you are using the right tool for the job, you should not have to strain to tighten a fastener" applies here.

Beam Type

▶ See Figure 26

The beam type torque wrench is one of the most popular types. It consists of a pointer attached to the head that runs the length of the flexible beam (shaft) to a scale located near the handle. As the wrench is pulled, the beam bends and the pointer indicates the torque using the scale.

Click (Breakaway) Type

▶ See Figure 27

Another popular design of torque wrench is the click type. To use the click type wrench you pre-adjust it to a torque setting. Once the torque is reached, the wrench has a reflex signaling feature that causes a momentary breakaway of the torque wrench body, sending an impulse to the operator's hand.

Pivot Head Type

▶ See Figure 27 and 28

Some torque wrenches (usually of the click type) may be equipped with a pivot head which can allow it to be used in areas of limited access. BUT, it must be used properly. To hold a pivot head wrench, grasp the handle lightly, and as you pull on the handle, it should be floated on the pivot point. If the handle comes in contact with the yoke extension during the process of pulling, there is a very good chance the torque readings will be inaccurate because this could alter the wrench loading point. The design of the handle is usually such as to make it inconvenient to deliberately misuse the wrench.

➡It should be mentioned that the use of any U-joint, wobble or extension will have an effect on the torque readings, no matter what type of wrench you are using. For the most accurate readings, install the socket directly on the wrench driver. If necessary, straight extensions (which hold a socket directly under the wrench driver) will have the least effect on the torque reading. Avoid any extension that alters the length of the wrench from the handle to the head/driving point (such as a crow's foot). U-joint or wobble extensions can greatly affect the readings; avoid their use at all times.

U.S. Bolts

SAE Grade Number	1 or 2			5			6 or 7		
Number of lines always 2 less than the grade number.									
Bolt Size (Inches)—(Thread)	Maximum Torque			Maximum Torque			Maximum Torque		
	Ft./Lbs.	Kgm	Nm	Ft./Lbs.	Kgm	Nm	Ft./Lbs.	Kgm	Nm
¼ — 20	5	0.7	6.8	8	1.1	10.8	10	1.4	13.5
— 28	6	0.8	8.1	10	1.4	13.6			
⁵⁄₁₆ — 18	11	1.5	14.9	17	2.3	23.0	19	2.6	25.8
— 24	13	1.8	17.6	19	2.6	25.7			
⅜ — 16	18	2.5	24.4	31	4.3	42.0	34	4.7	46.0
— 24	20	2.75	27.1	35	4.8	47.5			
⁷⁄₁₆ — 14	28	3.8	37.0	49	6.8	66.4	55	7.6	74.5
— 20	30	4.2	40.7	55	7.6	74.5			
½ — 13	39	5.4	52.8	75	10.4	101.7	85	11.75	115.2
— 20	41	5.7	55.6	85	11.7	115.2			
⁹⁄₁₆ — 12	51	7.0	69.2	110	15.2	149.1	120	16.6	162.7
— 18	55	7.6	74.5	120	16.6	162.7			
⅝ — 11	83	11.5	112.5	150	20.7	203.3	167	23.0	226.5
— 18	95	13.1	128.8	170	23.5	230.5			
¾ — 10	105	14.5	142.3	270	37.3	366.0	280	38.7	379.6
— 16	115	15.9	155.9	295	40.8	400.0			
⅞ — 9	160	22.1	216.9	395	54.6	535.5	440	60.9	596.5
— 14	175	24.2	237.2	435	60.1	589.7			
1 — 8	236	32.5	318.6	590	81.6	799.9	660	91.3	894.8
— 14	250	34.6	338.9	660	91.3	849.8			

Metric Bolts

Relative Strength Marking	4.6, 4.8			8.8		
Bolt Markings						
Bolt Size Thread Size x Pitch (mm)	Maximum Torque			Maximum Torque		
	Ft./Lbs.	Kgm	Nm	Ft./Lbs.	Kgm	Nm
6 x 1.0	2–3	.2–.4	3–4	3–6	4–.8	5–8
8 x 1.25	6–8	.8–1	8–12	9–14	1.2–1.9	13–19
10 x 1.25	12–17	1.5–2.3	16–23	20–29	2.7–4.0	27–39
12 x 1.25	21–32	2.9–4.4	29–43	35–53	4.8–7.3	47–72
14 x 1.5	35–52	4.8–7.1	48–70	57–85	7.8–11.7	77–110
16 x 1.5	51–77	7.0–10.6	67–100	90–120	12.4–16.5	130–160
18 x 1.5	74–110	10.2–15.1	100–150	130–170	17.9–23.4	180–230
20 x 1.5	110–140	15.1–19.3	150–190	190–240	26.2–46.9	160–320
22 x 1.5	150–190	22.0–26.2	200–260	250–320	34.5–44.1	340–430
24 x 1.5	190–240	26.2–46.9	260–320	310–410	42.7–56.5	420–550

Fig. 25 Standard and metric bolt torque specifications based on bolt strengths—WARNING: use only as a guide

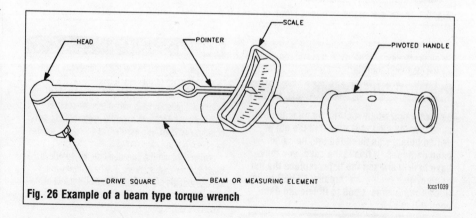

Fig. 26 Example of a beam type torque wrench

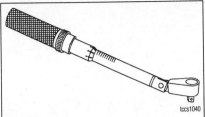

Fig. 27 A click type or breakaway torque wrench—note that this one has a pivoting head

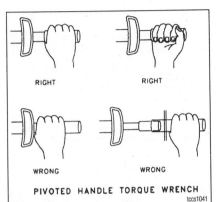

PIVOTED HANDLE TORQUE WRENCH

tccs1041

Fig. 28 Torque wrenches with pivoting heads must be grasped and used properly to prevent an incorrect reading

Rigid Case (Direct Reading)

♦ See Figure 29

A rigid case or direct reading torque wrench is equipped with a dial indicator to show torque values. One advantage of these wrenches is that they can be held at any position on the wrench without affecting accuracy. These wrenches are often preferred because they tend to be compact, easy to read and have a great degree of accuracy.

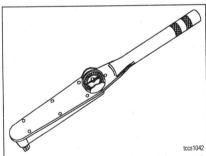

Fig. 29 The rigid case (direct reading) torque wrench uses a dial indicator to show torque

TORQUE ANGLE METERS

♦ See Figure 30

Because the frictional characteristics of each fastener or threaded hole will vary, clamp loads which are based strictly on torque will vary as well. In most applications, this variance is not significant enough to cause worry. But, in certain applications, a manufacturer's engineers may determine that more precise clamp loads are necessary (such is the case with

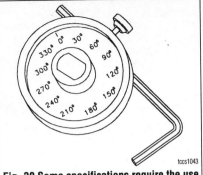

Fig. 30 Some specifications require the use of a torque angle meter (mechanical protractor)

many aluminum cylinder heads). In these cases, a torque angle method of installation would be specified. When installing fasteners which are torque angle tightened, a predetermined seating torque and standard torque wrench are usually used first to remove any compliance from the joint. The fastener is then tightened the specified additional portion of a turn measured in degrees. A torque angle gauge (mechanical protractor) is used for these applications.

Standard and Metric Measurements

♦ See Figure 31

Throughout this manual, specifications are given to help you determine the condition of various components on your vehicle, or to assist you in their installation. Some of the most common measurements include length (in. or cm/mm), torque (ft. lbs., inch lbs. or Nm) and pressure (psi, in. Hg, kPa or mm Hg). In most cases, we strive to provide the proper measurement as determined by the manufacturer's engineers.

Though, in some cases, that value may not be conveniently measured with what is available in your toolbox. Luckily, many of the measuring devices

CONVERSION FACTORS

LENGTH–DISTANCE

Inches (in.)	x 25.4	= Millimeters (mm)	x .0394	= Inches
Feet (ft.)	x .305	= Meters (m)	x 3.281	= Feet
Miles	x 1.609	= Kilometers (km)	x .0621	= Miles

VOLUME

Cubic Inches (in3)	x 16.387	= Cubic Centimeters	x .061	= in3
IMP Pints (IMP pt.)	x .568	= Liters (L)	x 1.76	= IMP pt.
IMP Quarts (IMP qt.)	x 1.137	= Liters (L)	x .88	= IMP qt.
IMP Gallons (IMP gal.)	x 4.546	= Liters (L)	x .22	= IMP gal.
IMP Quarts (IMP qt.)	x 1.201	= US Quarts (US qt.)	x .833	= IMP qt.
IMP Gallons (IMP gal.)	x 1.201	= US Gallons (US gal.)	x .833	= IMP gal.
Fl. Ounces	x 29.573	= Milliliters	x .034	= Ounces
US Pints (US pt.)	x .473	= Liters (L)	x 2.113	= Pints
US Quarts (US qt.)	x .946	= Liters (L)	x 1.057	= Quarts
US Gallons (US gal.)	x 3.785	= Liters (L)	x .264	= Gallons

MASS–WEIGHT

Ounces (oz.)	x 28.35	= Grams (g)	x .035	= Ounces
Pounds (lb.)	x .454	= Kilograms (kg)	x 2.205	= Pounds

PRESSURE

Pounds Per Sq. In. (psi)	x 6.895	= Kilopascals (kPa)	x .145	= psi
Inches of Mercury (Hg)	x .4912	= psi	x 2.036	= Hg
Inches of Mercury (Hg)	x 3.377	= Kilopascals (kPa)	x .2961	= Hg
Inches of Water (H_2O)	x .07355	= Inches of Mercury	x 13.783	= H_2O
Inches of Water (H_2O)	x .03613	= psi	x 27.684	= H_2O
Inches of Water (H_2O)	x .248	= Kilopascals (kPa)	x 4.026	= H_2O

TORQUE

Pounds–Force Inches (in–lb)	x .113	= Newton Meters (N·m)	x 8.85	= in–lb
Pounds–Force Feet (ft–lb)	x 1.356	= Newton Meters (N·m)	x .738	= ft–lb

VELOCITY

Miles Per Hour (MPH)	x 1.609	= Kilometers Per Hour (KPH)	x .621	= MPH

POWER

Horsepower (Hp)	x .745	= Kilowatts	x 1.34	= Horsepower

FUEL CONSUMPTION*

Miles Per Gallon IMP (MPG)	x .354	= Kilometers Per Liter (Km/L)	
Kilometers Per Liter (Km/L)	x 2.352	= IMP MPG	
Miles Per Gallon US (MPG)	x .425	= Kilometers Per Liter (Km/L)	
Kilometers Per Liter (Km/L)	x 2.352	= US MPG	

*It is common to covert from miles per gallon (mpg) to liters/100 kilometers (1/100 km), where mpg (IMP) x 1/100 km = 282 and mpg (US) x 1/100 km = 235.

TEMPERATURE

Degree Fahrenheit (°F) = (°C x 1.8) + 32
Degree Celsius (°C) = (°F – 32) x .56

tccs1044

Fig. 31 Standard and metric conversion factors chart

which are available today will have two scales so the Standard or Metric measurements may easily be taken. If any of the various measuring tools which are available to you do not contain the same scale as listed in the specifications, use the accompanying conversion factors to determine the proper value.

The conversion factor chart is used by taking the given specification and multiplying it by the necessary conversion factor. For instance, looking at the first line, if you have a measurement in inches such as "free-play should be 2 in." but your ruler reads only in millimeters, multiply 2 in. by the conversion factor of 25.4 to get the metric equivalent of 50.8mm. Likewise, if the specification was given only in a Metric measurement, for example in Newton Meters (Nm), then look at the center column first. If the measurement is 100 Nm, multiply it by the conversion factor of 0.738 to get 73.8 ft. lbs.

SERIAL NUMBER IDENTIFICATION

Vehicle Identification Number

◆ **See Figures 32, 33, and 34**

The Vehicle Identification Number (VIN) is located on a plate which is attached to the left top side of the instrument panel. These numbers are visible from the outside of the vehicle. All Vehicle Identification Numbers contain 17 digits. The vehicle number is a code which tells country, make, vehicle type, engine, body and many other important characteristics of that specific vehicle.

There is also a vehicle information code plate which is riveted to the bulkhead in the engine compartment. The plate shows the VIN, model code, engine model, transaxle model and body color codes. The engine code used on this plate differs from the code letter used in the 8th position of the Vehicle Identification Number (VIN). Either code can be used to identify the particular engine in the vehicle. Since the vehicle owners card is usually carried, it may be easier to use the code letter in the VIN for engine reference. A second reason for referring to the VIN for engine identification is that code 4G63, located on the vehicle information code plate, does identify the engine as a 2.0L DOHC engine, but does not tell you

if the engine is equipped with a turbocharger. If the 8th VIN number is a U, there is no doubt that the engine in question is a 2.0L DOHC engine equipped with a turbocharger.

The engine codes found on the vehicle information code plate are as follows:
- 4G15—1.5L SOHC engine
- 4G61—1.6L DOHC engine
- 4G93—1.8L SOHC engine
- 4G63—2.0L (SOHC or DOHC) engine
- 4G64—2.4L (SOHC or DOHC) engine
- 6G72—3.0L (SOHC or DOHC) engine
- 6G74—3.5L DOHC engine

A vehicle safety certification label is attached to the face of the left door pillar post. This label indicates the month and year of manufacture, Gross Vehicle Weight Rating (GRVW) front and rear, and Vehicle Identification Number (VIN).

Engine Identification Number

◆ **See Figure 35**

The engine model number is stamped at the front side on the top edge of the cylinder block. The same

4 character code as on the vehicle information code plate is used. The engine serial number is also stamped near the engine model number. As mentioned above, the engine can also be identified by the 8th digit in the VIN number.

Transaxle Identification

The transaxle model code is located on the vehicle information code plate. The transaxle identification number is etched on a boss located on the front upper portion of the case.

Drive Axle (AWD Galant Only)

The code for the drive axle is etched on a boss located on the case of the differential carrier.

Transfer Case (AWD Galant Only)

The transfer case has no separate model code, the code is located on the transaxle. The transfer case is only equipped on manual transaxle All Wheel Drive (AWD) models.

Fig. 32 The Vehicle Identification Number (VIN) plate is attached to the top left side of the instrument panel

Fig. 33 The vehicle model, engine model, transaxle model, and body color code are all noted on the vehicle information code plate

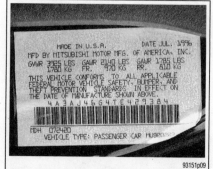

Fig. 34 Your car should have a vehicle safety certification label attached to the face of the left door pillar post

ENGINE AND VEHICLE IDENTIFICATION

Code ①	Liters (cc)	Cu. In.	Cyl.	Fuel Sys.	Type	Eng. Mfg.
4G15/A	1.5 (1468)	92	4	MFI	SOHC	Mitsubishi
4G61/Y	1.6 (1595)	98	4	MFI	DOHC	Mitsubishi
4G93/C	1.8 (1834)	112	4	MFI	SOHC	Mitsubishi
4G63/V	2.0 (1997)	122	4	MFI	SOHC	Mitsubishi
4G63/R	2.0 (1997)	122	4	MFI	DOHC	Mitsubishi
4G63/U	2.0 (1997)	122	4	MFI-Turbo	DOHC	Mitsubishi
4G64/G	2.4 (2351)	143	4	MFI	SOHC	Mitsubishi
4G64/L	2.4 (2351)	143	4	MFI	DOHC	Mitsubishi
6G72/H	3.0 (2972)	181	6	MFI	SOHC	Mitsubishi
6G72/J	3.0 (2972)	181	6	MFI	DOHC	Mitsubishi
6G72/L	3.0 (2972)	181	6	MFI	SOHC	Mitsubishi
6G74/P	3.5 (3497)	213	6	MFI	SOHC	Mitsubishi

Code ②	Year
L	1990
M	1991
N	1992
P	1993
R	1994
S	1995
T	1996
V	1997
W	1998
X	1999
Y	2000

MFI - Multiport fuel injection
SOHC - Single overhead camsh.
DOHC - Double overhead camshafts
① Engine ID / 8th digit of the VIN
② 10th digit of the VIN

93151c01

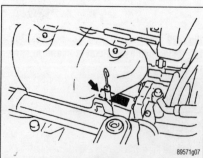

Fig. 35 Engine model number location— 4G63 (2.0L) engine shown

UNDERHOOD MAINTENANCE COMPONENT LOCATIONS—2.4L ENGINE

1. Power steering belt
2. Washer solvent bottle
3. Power steering reservoir
4. Oil fill cap
5. Brake master cylinder reservoir
6. Spark plug and plug wire

7. PCV valve
8. Distributor cap and rotor
9. Fuel filter (under air inlet tube)
10. Air filter housing
11. Engine compartment fuse box
12. Battery

13. Automatic transaxle fluid dipstick
14. Coolant recovery tank
15. Radiator cap
16. Engine oil dipstick

9315p01

UNDERHOOD MAINTENANCE COMPONENT LOCATIONS—1.8L ENGINE

1. Coolant recovery tank
2. Battery
3. Engine compartment fuse box
4. Air filter housing
5. Clutch fluid reservoir
6. Brake master cylinder reservoir
7. Spark plug and plug wire
8. PCV valve
9. Engine oil fill cap
10. Fuel filter
11. Engine compartment relay center
12. Washer solvent bottle
13. Power steering reservoir
14. Power steering belt
15. Engine oil dipstick
16. Radiator cap

93151p02

GENERAL ENGINE SPECIFICATIONS

Year	Model	Engine Displacement Liters (cc)	Engine ID/VIN	Engine Type	No. of Cyl.	Fuel System Type	Net Horsepower @ rpm	Net Torque @ rpm (ft. lbs.)	Bore x Stroke (in.)	Compression Ratio	Oil Pressure @ rpm
1990	Mirage	1.5 (1468)	4G15/A	SOHC	4	MFI	81@5500	91@3000	2.97x3.23	9.2:1	54@2000
	Galant	2.0 (1997)	4G63/V	SOHC	4	MFI	102@5000	116@4500	3.34x3.46	8.5:1	41@2000
	Galant	2.0 (1997)	4G63/R	DOHC	4	MFI	140@6000	125@5000	3.34x3.46	9.0:1	41@2000
1991	Mirage	1.5 (1468)	4G15/A	SOHC	4	MFI	92@6000	93@3000	2.97x3.23	9.4:1	54@2000
	Mirage	1.6 (1595)	4G61/Y	DOHC	4	MFI	123@6500	101@5000	3.24x2.95	9.2:1	54@2000
	Galant	2.0 (1997)	4G63/V	SOHC	4	MFI	102@5000	116@4500	3.34x3.46	8.5:1	41@2000
	Galant	2.0 (1997)	4G63/R	DOHC	4	MFI	140@6000	125@5000	3.34x3.46	9.0:1	41@2000
	Galant	2.0 (1997)	4G63/U	DOHC	4	MFI-T	195@6000	203@3000	3.34x3.46	7.8:1	41@2000
1992	Mirage	1.5 (1468)	4G15/A	SOHC	4	MFI	92@6000	93@3000	2.97x3.23	9.4:1	54@2000
	Mirage	1.6 (1595)	4G61/Y	DOHC	4	MFI	123@6500	101@5000	3.24x2.95	9.2:1	54@2000
	Galant	2.0 (1997)	4G63/V	SOHC	4	MFI	102@5000	116@4500	3.34x3.46	8.5:1	41@2000
	Galant	2.0 (1997)	4G63/R	DOHC	4	MFI	140@6000	125@5000	3.34x3.46	9.0:1	41@2000
	Galant	2.0 (1997)	4G63/U	DOHC	4	MFI-T	195@6000	203@3000	3.34x3.46	7.8:1	41@2000
	Diamante	3.0 (2972)	6G72/H	SOHC	6	MFI	175@5500	185@3000	3.59x2.99	10.0:1	30-80@2000
	Diamante	3.0 (2972)	6G72/J	DOHC	6	MFI	202@6000	201@3500	3.59x2.99	10.0:1	30-80@2000
1993	Mirage	1.5 (1468)	4G15/A	SOHC	4	MFI	92@6000	93@3000	2.97x3.23	9.2:1	54@2000
	Mirage	1.8 (1834)	4G93/C	SOHC	4	MFI	112@6000	116@4500	3.19x3.50	9.5:1	41@2000
	Galant	2.0 (1997)	4G63/V	SOHC	4	MFI	102@5000	116@4500	3.34x3.46	8.5:1	41@2000
	Galant	2.0 (1997)	4G63/R	DOHC	4	MFI	140@6000	125@5000	3.34x3.46	9.0:1	41@2000
	Diamante	3.0 (2972)	6G72/H	SOHC	6	MFI	175@5500	185@3000	3.59x2.99	10.0:1	30-80@2000
	Diamante	3.0 (2972)	6G72/J	DOHC	6	MFI	202@6000	201@3500	3.59x2.99	10.0:1	30-80@2000
1994	Mirage	1.5 (1468)	4G15/A	SOHC	4	MFI	92@6000	93@3000	2.97x3.23	9.2:1	54@2000
	Mirage	1.8 (1834)	4G93/C	SOHC	4	MFI	112@6000	116@4500	3.19x3.50	9.5:1	41@2000
	Galant	2.4 (2350)	4G64/G	SOHC	4	MFI	140@5500	148@3000	3.41x3.94	9.5:1	41@2000
	Galant	2.4 (2350)	4G64/L	DOHC	4	MFI	160@6000	160@4250	3.41x3.94	9.5:1	41@2000
	Diamante	3.0 (2972)	6G72/H	SOHC	6	MFI	175@5500	185@3000	3.59x2.99	10.0:1	30-80@2000
	Diamante	3.0 (2972)	6G72/J	DOHC	6	MFI	202@6000	201@3500	3.59x2.99	10.0:1	30-80@2000
1995	Mirage	1.5 (1468)	4G15/A	SOHC	4	MFI	92@6000	93@3000	2.97x3.23	9.2:1	54@2000
	Mirage	1.8 (1834)	4G93/C	SOHC	4	MFI	112@6000	116@4500	3.19x3.50	9.5:1	41@2000
	Galant	2.4 (2350)	4G64/G	SOHC	4	MFI	140@5500	148@3000	3.41x3.94	9.5:1	41@2000
	Galant	2.4 (2350)	4G64/L	DOHC	4	MFI	160@6000	160@4250	3.41x3.94	9.5:1	41@2000
	Diamante	3.0 (2972)	6G72/H	SOHC	6	MFI	175@5500	185@3000	3.59x2.99	10.0:1	30-80@2000
	Diamante	3.0 (2972)	6G72/J	DOHC	6	MFI	202@6000	201@3500	3.59x2.99	10.0:1	30-80@2000
1996	Mirage	1.5 (1468)	4G15/A	SOHC	4	MFI	92@6000	93@3000	2.97x3.23	9.2:1	54@2000
	Mirage	1.8 (1834)	4G93/C	SOHC	4	MFI	112@6000	116@4500	3.19x3.50	9.5:1	41@2000
	Galant	2.4 (2350)	4G64/G	SOHC	4	MFI	140@5500	148@3000	3.41x3.94	9.5:1	41@2000
	Galant	2.4 (2350)	4G64/L	DOHC	4	MFI	160@6000	160@4250	3.41x3.94	9.5:1	41@2000
	Diamante	3.0 (2972)	6G72/H	SOHC	6	MFI	175@5500	185@3000	3.59x2.99	10.0:1	30-80@2000
	Diamante	3.0 (2972)	6G72/J	DOHC	6	MFI	202@6000	201@3500	3.59x2.99	10.0:1	30-80@2000
1997	Mirage	1.5 (1468)	4G15/A	SOHC	4	MFI	92@6000	93@3000	2.97x3.23	9.2:1	54@2000
	Mirage	1.8 (1834)	4G93/C	SOHC	4	MFI	112@6000	116@4500	3.19x3.50	9.5:1	41@2000
	Galant	2.4 (2350)	4G64/G	SOHC	4	MFI	140@5500	148@3000	3.41x3.94	9.5:1	41@2000
	Diamante	3.5 (3497)	6G74/P	SOHC	6	MFI	214@5000	228@3000	3.66x3.38	9.5:1	30-80@2000
1998	Mirage	1.5 (1468)	4G15/A	SOHC	4	MFI	92@6000	93@3000	2.97x3.23	9.2:1	54@2000
	Mirage	1.8 (1834)	4G93/C	SOHC	4	MFI	112@6000	116@4500	3.19x3.50	9.5:1	41@2000
	Galant	2.4 (2350)	4G64/G	SOHC	4	MFI	140@5500	148@3000	3.41x3.94	9.5:1	41@2000
	Diamante	3.5 (3497)	6G74/P	SOHC	6	MFI	214@5000	228@3000	3.66x3.38	9.5:1	30-80@2000
1999	Mirage	1.5 (1468)	4G15/A	SOHC	4	MFI	92@6000	93@3000	2.97x3.23	9.2:1	54@2000
	Mirage	1.8 (1834)	4G93/C	SOHC	4	MFI	112@6000	116@4500	3.19x3.50	9.5:1	41@2000
	Galant	2.4 (2350)	4G64/G	SOHC	4	MFI	140@5500	148@3000	3.41x3.94	9.5:1	41@2000
	Galant	3.0 (2972)	6G72/L	SOHC	6	MFI	175@5500	185@3000	3.59x2.99	8.9:1	30-80@2000
	Diamante	3.5 (3497)	6G74/P	SOHC	6	MFI	214@5000	228@3000	3.66x3.38	9.5:1	30-80@2000
2000	Mirage	1.5 (1468)	4G15/A	SOHC	4	MFI	92@6000	93@3000	2.97x3.23	9.2:1	54@2000
	Mirage	1.8 (1834)	4G93/C	SOHC	4	MFI	112@6000	116@4500	3.19x3.50	9.5:1	41@2000
	Galant	2.4 (2350)	4G64/G	SOHC	4	MFI	140@5500	148@3000	3.41x3.94	9.5:1	41@2000
	Galant	3.0 (2972)	6G72/L	SOHC	6	MFI	175@5500	185@3000	3.59x2.99	8.9:1	30-80@2000
	Diamante	3.5 (3497)	6G74/P	SOHC	6	MFI	214@5000	228@3000	3.66x3.38	9.5:1	30-80@2000

MFI - Multiport fuel injection
MFI-T - Multiport fuel injection-turbocharged
SOHC - Single overhead camshaft
DOHC - Double overhead camshaft

93151c03

ROUTINE MAINTENANCE AND TUNE-UP

Proper maintenance and tune-up is the key to long and trouble-free vehicle life, and the work can yield its own rewards. Studies have shown that a properly tuned and maintained vehicle can achieve better gas mileage than an out-of-tune vehicle. As a conscientious owner and driver, set aside a Saturday morning, say once a month, to check or replace items which could cause major problems later. Keep your own personal log to jot down which services you performed, how much the parts cost you, the date, and the exact odometer reading at the time. Keep all receipts for such items as engine oil and filters, so that they may be referred to in case of related problems or to determine operating expenses. As a do-it-yourselfer, these receipts are the only proof you have that the required maintenance was performed. In the event of a warranty problem, these receipts will be invaluable.

The literature provided with your vehicle when it was originally delivered includes the factory recommended maintenance schedule. If you no longer have this literature, replacement copies are usually available from the dealer. A maintenance schedule is provided later in this section, in case you do not have the factory literature.

Air Cleaner (Element)

REMOVAL & INSTALLATION

Except 2.0L Turbocharged Engine

▶ **See Figures 36 thru 41**

1. Disconnect the negative battery cable.
2. Release the retaining clips from the air cleaner housing.
3. Loosen the clamp on the air outlet tube at the throttle body.
4. Detach the breather hose from the air inlet tube.
5. Unplug the MAF sensor connector.
6. Separate the upper and lower air cleaner housings and remove the air outlet tube and upper housing from the lower housing.
7. Remove the air cleaner element from the housing.

To install:

8. Clean the inside of the air cleaner housing of any dirt and debris that has collected inside.

9. Place a new air cleaner element inside the lower housing. Make sure the seal on the element is fully seated in the groove.
10. Install the upper air cleaner housing and inlet tube onto the lower housing.
11. Tighten the clamp on the inlet tube at the throttle body.
12. Attach the breather hose onto the air inlet tube.
13. Plug the connector into the MAF sensor.
14. Attach the air cleaner housing retaining clips.
15. Connect the negative battery cable.

2.0L Turbocharged Engine

▶ **See Figure 42**

1. Disconnect the negative battery cable.
2. Detach the air flow sensor connector.
3. Unfasten the boost hose.
4. Disconnect the solenoid valve with hoses.
5. Disconnect the air intake hose.
6. Unfasten the air cleaner retainer bolts and the air cleaner assembly.
7. Unclamp the cover and remove from the housing.

➡**Care must be taken when removing the air cleaner cover. The air flow sensor is attached and could be damaged during cover removal.**

8. Remove the air cleaner element. Thoroughly clean the air cleaner housing prior to replacing the air filter.

To install:

9. Install the new air cleaner element into the housing. Install and secure the cover in place.

Fig. 36 Release the retaining clips from the air cleaner housing

Fig. 37 Unplug the MAF sensor connector

Fig. 38 Detach the breather hose from the air inlet tube

Fig. 39 Loosen the clamp on the air outlet tube at the throttle body . . .

Fig. 40 . . . then remove the air outlet tube and upper housing from the lower housing

Fig. 41 Remove the air cleaner element from the housing

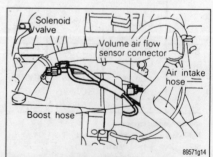

Fig. 42 Detach the air flow sensor connector, the boost hose and the solenoid valve connector

10. Install the air cleaner assembly and the retainer bolts.

11. Connect the air intake hose.

12. Attach the solenoid valve.

13. Connect the boost hose.

14. Attach the air flow sensor connector.

15. Connect the negative battery cable.

Fuel Filter

REMOVAL & INSTALLATION

▶ **See Figures 43 thru 48**

On most vehicles covered by this manual, the fuel filter is located in the engine compartment, mounted to the firewall.

✳✳ CAUTION

Do not use conventional fuel filters, hoses or clamps when servicing fuel injection systems. They are not compatible with the injection system and could fail, causing personal injury or damage to the vehicle. Use only hoses and clamps specifically designed for fuel injection systems.

1. Properly relieve the fuel system pressure as outlined in Section 5 of this manual.

2. If not already done, disconnect the negative battery cable.

3. On most models, the job is made easier if the air inlet hose and upper air cleaner housing is removed from the vehicle.

➡**Wrap shop towels around the fitting that is being disconnected to absorb residual fuel in the lines.**

4. Cover the hose connection with shop towels to prevent any splash of fuel that could be caused by residual pressure in the fuel pipe line. Hold the fuel filter nut securely with a backup wrench, then remove the banjo bolt on the engine feed line. Disconnect the high-pressure fuel line from the filter. Remove and discard the gaskets.

5. While holding the fuel filter nut securely with a back-up wrench, loosen the filter feed pipe flare nut on the bottom of the filter. Separate the flare nut connection from the filter. If equipped, remove and discard the gaskets.

6. Remove the mounting bolts and remove the fuel filter. If necessary, remove the fuel filter bracket.

To install:

7. Install the filter to its bracket only finger-tight. Movement of the filter will ease attachment of the fuel lines.

✳✳ WARNING

Ensure that the filter is installed with the flow arrow in the proper direction. The flow arrow typically points toward the engine side of the filter. Improper installation of the fuel filter will cause the vehicle to run poorly.

➡**Make sure new O-rings are installed prior to installation.**

8. Insert the filter feed pipe to the lower connection of the filter and manually screw in the main pipe's flare nut.

9. While holding the fuel filter nut with a back-up wrench, tighten the banjo bolt to 22 ft. lbs. (30 Nm). Tighten the flare nut to 25 ft. lbs. (35 Nm), with a back-up wrench on the nut.

10. Tighten the filter mounting bolts to 10 ft. lbs. (14 Nm).

11. Connect the negative battery cable. Turn the key to the **ON** position to pressurize the fuel system and check for leaks.

12. If repairs of a leak are required, remember to release the fuel pressure before opening the fuel system.

PCV Valve

REMOVAL & INSTALLATION

▶ **See Figures 49, 50, and 51**

1. Disconnect the negative battery cable.

2. If necessary for access, remove the air intake hose and air cleaner assembly.

3. If necessary, unfasten the retaining clamp, then disconnect the ventilation hose from the PCV valve.

4. Remove the PCV valve from the camshaft (rocker) cover.

To install:

5. Install the PCV valve into the rocker cover. If the valve is threaded, tighten the valve until snug.

6. Reconnect the ventilation hose to the valve.

7. If removed, install the air intake hose and the air cleaner assembly.

8. Connect the negative battery cable.

Fig. 43 Use a back-up wrench on the fuel filter nut when loosening the banjo-bolt on the engine feed line

Fig. 44 After the banjo-bolt is loose, remove from the fuel filter

Fig. 45 Make sure to replace the copper washers on the banjo-bolt fitting

Fig. 46 Make sure to use a back-up wrench when unfastening the main fuel pipe also

Fig. 47 Remove the two filter bracket retaining bolts . . .

Fig. 48 . . . then remove the filter from the vehicle

Fig. 49 Grasp the valve and gently remove it from the valve cover

Fig. 50 Twist and pull on the valve to remove it from the hose

Fig. 51 Inspect the grommet and replace if cracked or leaking oil

Evaporative Canister

SERVICING

▶ **See Figure 52**

The evaporative canister requires no periodic servicing. However, a careful inspection of the canister and hoses should be made frequently. Replace damaged components as required.

The canister is typically located under one of the front fenders, however on some later models it may be under the rear of the vehicle, near the gas tank.

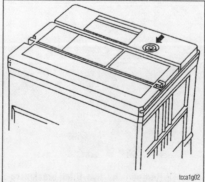

Fig. 52 The EVAP canister is typically located inside of the fender on most models covered by this manual

Battery

PRECAUTIONS

Always use caution when working on or near the battery. Never allow a tool to bridge the gap between the negative and positive battery terminals. Also, be careful not to allow a tool to provide a ground between the positive cable/terminal and any metal component on the vehicle. Either of these conditions will cause a short circuit, leading to sparks and possible personal injury.

Do not smoke, have an open flame or create sparks near a battery; the gases contained in the battery are very explosive and, if ignited, could cause severe injury or death.

All batteries, regardless of type, should be carefully secured by a battery hold-down device. If this is not done, the battery terminals or casing may crack from stress applied to the battery during vehicle operation. A battery which is not secured may allow acid to leak out, making it discharge faster; such leaking

corrosive acid can also eat away at components under the hood.

Always visually inspect the battery case for cracks, leakage and corrosion. A white corrosive substance on the battery case or on nearby components would indicate a leaking or cracked battery. If the battery is cracked, it should be replaced immediately.

GENERAL MAINTENANCE

▶ **See Figure 53**

A battery that is not sealed must be checked periodically for electrolyte level. You cannot add water to a sealed maintenance-free battery (though not all maintenance-free batteries are sealed); however, a sealed battery must also be checked for proper electrolyte level, as indicated by the color of the built-in hydrometer "eye."

Always keep the battery cables and terminals free of corrosion. Check these components about once a year. Refer to the removal, installation and cleaning procedures outlined in this section.

Keep the top of the battery clean, as a film of dirt can help completely discharge a battery that is not used for long periods. A solution of baking soda and water may be used for cleaning, but be careful to flush this off with clear water. DO NOT let any of the solution into the filler holes. Baking soda neutralizes battery acid and will de-activate a battery cell.

Batteries in vehicles which are not operated on a regular basis can fall victim to parasitic loads (small current drains which are constantly drawing current from the battery). Normal parasitic loads may drain a battery on a vehicle that is in storage and not used for 6–8 weeks. Vehicles that have additional accessories such as a cellular phone, an alarm system or other

Fig. 53 A typical location for the built-in hydrometer on maintenance-free batteries

devices that increase parasitic load may discharge a battery sooner. If the vehicle is to be stored for 6–8 weeks in a secure area and the alarm system, if present, is not necessary, the negative battery cable should be disconnected at the onset of storage to protect the battery charge.

Remember that constantly discharging and recharging will shorten battery life. Take care not to allow a battery to be needlessly discharged.

BATTERY FLUID

Check the battery electrolyte level at least once a month, or more often in hot weather or during periods of extended vehicle operation. On non-sealed batteries, the level can be checked either through the case on translucent batteries or by removing the cell caps on opaque-cased types. The electrolyte level in each cell should be kept filled to the split ring inside each cell, or the line marked on the outside of the case.

If the level is low, add only distilled water through the opening until the level is correct. Each cell is separate from the others, so each must be checked and filled individually. Distilled water should be used, because the chemicals and minerals found in most drinking water are harmful to the battery and could significantly shorten its life.

If water is added in freezing weather, the vehicle should be driven several miles to allow the water to mix with the electrolyte. Otherwise, the battery could freeze.

Although some maintenance-free batteries have removable cell caps for access to the electrolyte, the electrolyte condition and level on all sealed maintenance-free batteries must be checked using the built-in hydrometer "eye." The exact type of eye varies between battery manufacturers, but most apply a sticker to the battery itself explaining the possible readings. When in doubt, refer to the battery manufacturer's instructions to interpret battery condition using the built-in hydrometer.

➡ **Although the readings from built-in hydrometers found in sealed batteries may vary, a green eye usually indicates a properly charged battery with sufficient fluid level. A dark eye is normally an indicator of a battery with sufficient fluid, but one which may be low in charge. And a light or yellow eye is usually an indication that electrolyte supply has dropped below the necessary level for battery (and hydrometer) operation. In this last case, sealed batteries with an insufficient electrolyte level must usually be discarded.**

Fig. 54 On non-maintenance-free batteries, the fluid level can be checked through the case on translucent models; the cell caps must be removed on other models

Fig. 55 If the fluid level is low, add only distilled water through the opening until the level is correct

Fig. 56 Check the specific gravity of the battery's electrolyte with a hydrometer

Checking the Specific Gravity

▶ **See Figures 54, 55, and 56**

A hydrometer is required to check the specific gravity on all batteries that are not maintenance-free. On batteries that are maintenance-free, the specific gravity is checked by observing the built-in hydrometer "eye" on the top of the battery case. Check with your battery's manufacturer for proper interpretation of its built-in hydrometer readings.

❊❊ CAUTION

Battery electrolyte contains sulfuric acid. If you should splash any on your skin or in your eyes, flush the affected area with plenty of clear water. If it lands in your eyes, get medical help immediately.

The fluid (sulfuric acid solution) contained in the battery cells will tell you many things about the condition of the battery. Because the cell plates must be kept submerged below the fluid level in order to operate, maintaining the fluid level is extremely important. And, because the specific gravity of the acid is an indication of electrical charge, testing the fluid can be an aid in determining if the battery must be replaced. A battery in a vehicle with a properly operating charging system should require little maintenance, but careful, periodic inspection should reveal problems before they leave you stranded.

As stated earlier, the specific gravity of a battery's electrolyte level can be used as an indication of battery charge. At least once a year, check the specific gravity of the battery. It should be between 1.20 and 1.26 on the gravity scale. Most auto supply stores carry a variety of inexpensive battery testing hydrometers. These can be used on any non-sealed battery to test the specific gravity in each cell.

The battery testing hydrometer has a squeeze bulb at one end and a nozzle at the other. Battery electrolyte is sucked into the hydrometer until the float is lifted from its seat. The specific gravity is then read by noting the position of the float. If gravity is low in one or

more cells, the battery should be slowly charged and checked again to see if the gravity has come up. Generally, if after charging, the specific gravity between any two cells varies more than 50 points (0.50), the battery should be replaced, as it can no longer produce sufficient voltage to guarantee proper operation.

CABLES

▶ **See Figures 57, 58, 59, 60, and 61**

Once a year (or as necessary), the battery terminals and the cable clamps should be cleaned. Loosen

Fig. 57 Maintenance is performed with household items and with special tools like this post cleaner

Fig. 58 The underside of this special battery tool has a wire brush to clean post terminals

Fig. 59 Place the tool over the battery posts and twist to clean until the metal is shiny

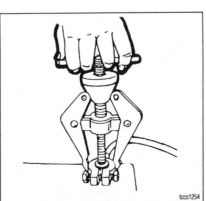

Fig. 60 A special tool is available to pull the clamp from the post

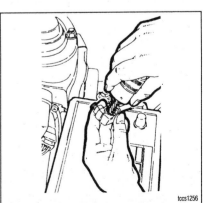

Fig. 61 The cable ends should be cleaned as well

the clamps and remove the cables, negative cable first. On batteries with posts on top, the use of a puller specially made for this purpose is recommended. These are inexpensive and available in most auto parts stores. Side terminal battery cables are secured with a small bolt.

Clean the cable clamps and the battery terminal with a wire brush, until all corrosion, grease, etc., is removed and the metal is shiny. It is especially important to clean the inside of the clamp thoroughly (an old knife is useful here), since a small deposit of foreign material or oxidation there will prevent a sound electrical connection and inhibit either starting or charging. Special tools are available for cleaning these parts, one type for conventional top post batteries and another type for side terminal batteries. It is also a good idea to apply some dielectric grease to the terminal, as this will aid in the prevention of corrosion.

After the clamps and terminals are clean, reinstall the cables, negative cable last; DO NOT hammer the clamps onto battery posts. Tighten the clamps securely, but do not distort them. Give the clamps and terminals a thin external coating of grease after installation, to retard corrosion.

Check the cables at the same time that the terminals are cleaned. If the cable insulation is cracked or broken, or if the ends are frayed, the cable should be replaced with a new cable of the same length and gauge.

CHARGING

> ※※ **CAUTION**
>
> **The chemical reaction which takes place in all batteries generates explosive hydrogen gas. A spark can cause the battery to explode and splash acid. To avoid serious personal injury, be sure there is proper ventilation and take appropriate fire safety precautions when connecting, disconnecting, or charging a battery and when using jumper cables.**

A battery should be charged at a slow rate to keep the plates inside from getting too hot. However, if some maintenance-free batteries are allowed to discharge until they are almost "dead," they may have to be charged at a high rate to bring them back to "life." Always follow the charger manufacturer's instructions on charging the battery.

REPLACEMENT

When it becomes necessary to replace the battery, select one with an amperage rating equal to or greater than the battery originally installed. Deterioration and just plain aging of the battery cables, starter motor, and associated wires makes the battery's job harder in successive years. The slow increase in electrical resistance over time makes it prudent to install a new battery with a greater capacity than the old.

Belts

INSPECTION

▶ **See Figures 62, 63, 64, 65, and 66**

Inspect the belts for signs of glazing or cracking. A glazed belt will be perfectly smooth from slippage, while a good belt will have a slight texture of fabric visible. Cracks will usually start at the inner edge of

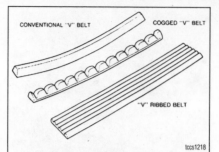

Fig. 62 There are typically 3 types of accessory drive belts found on vehicles today

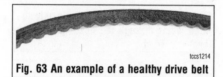

Fig. 63 An example of a healthy drive belt

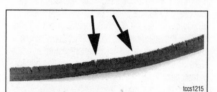

Fig. 64 Deep cracks in this belt will cause flex, building up heat that will eventually lead to belt failure

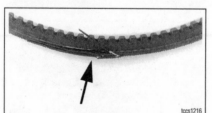

Fig. 65 The cover of this belt is worn, exposing the critical reinforcing cords to excessive wear

Fig. 66 Installing too wide a belt can result in serious belt wear and/or breakage

the belt and run outward. All worn or damaged drive belts should be replaced immediately. It is best to replace all drive belts at one time, as a preventive maintenance measure, during this service operation.

ADJUSTMENT

Excessive belt tension will cause damage to the alternator and water pump pulley bearings, while, on the other hand, loose belt tension will produce slip and premature wear on the belt. Therefore, be sure to adjust the belt tension to the proper level.

To adjust the tension on a drive belt, loosen the adjusting bolt or fixing bolt locknut on the alternator, alternator bracket or tension pulley. Then move the

alternator or turn the adjusting bolt to adjust belt tension. Once the desired value is reached, secure the bolt or locknut and recheck tension.

REMOVAL & INSTALLATION

1.5L, 1.6L, 1.8L, 2.0L and 2.4L Engines

ALTERNATOR BELT

▶ **See Figures 67, 68, and 69**

1. Loosen the alternator support nut.
2. Loosen the adjuster lock bolt.
3. Rotate the adjuster bolt counter clockwise to release the tension on the belt.
4. Remove the belt.

To install:

5. Install the belt on the pulleys.
6. Rotate the adjuster bolt clockwise until the proper tension is reached.
7. Tighten the adjuster lock bolt and the alternator support nut.

POWER STEERING BELT

▶ **See Figures 70 and 71**

1. Remove the alternator belt as described above.
2. Loosen the power steering pump adjusting bolts.
3. Remove the power steering pump fixed bolt on the rear of the bracket.
4. Rotate the pump toward the engine and remove the belt.

To install:

5. Install the belt on the pulleys.

Fig. 67 Loosen the adjuster lock bolt . . .

Fig. 68 . . . then remove the alternator belt from the engine

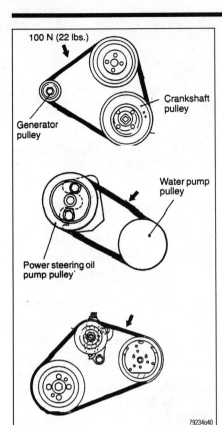

Fig. 69 Accessory V-belt routing—Mitsubishi 1.5L, 1.6L, 1.8L, 2.0L and 2.4L engines

Fig. 70 After the adjusting and fixed bolts are loosened, rotate the pump . . .

Fig. 71 . . . then remove the power steering belt from the engine

6. Rotate the pump until the proper tension is reached.
7. Tighten the adjusting bolts on the pump.
8. Tighten the fixed bolt on the rear of the bracket.
9. Install the alternator belt.

A/C COMPRESSOR BELT

1. Loosen the tension pulley and remove the belt.
2. The installation is the reverse of the removal.

3.0L DOHC, 3.0L SOHC (Galant models only) and 3.5L Engines

▶ See Figures 72 and 73

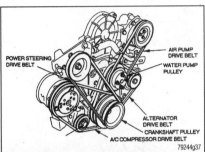

Fig. 72 Serpentine belt routing—Mitsubishi 3.0L engines (except 1998–00 Galant models)

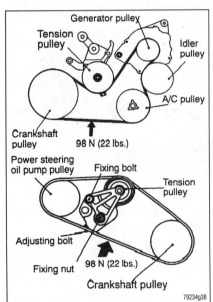

Fig. 73 Accessory V-belt routing—Mitsubishi 3.5L and 1998–00 3.0L SOHC Galant engines

✷✷ CAUTION

Wait at least 90 seconds after the negative battery cable is disconnected to prevent possible deployment of the air bag.

2. Raise and safely support the vehicle and remove the front undercover.
3. Loosen the tension pulley fixing nut and relieve the tension on the belt by turning the adjusting bolt.

4. Remove the belt.
To install:
5. Install the belt on the crankshaft and alternator pulleys.
6. Using the adjusting bolt on the tensioner, tighten the belt to the desired tension.
7. Tighten the fixing nut to hold the adjustment.
8. Install the undercover and lower the vehicle to the floor.
9. Connect the negative battery cable.

POWER STEERING BELT

1. Disconnect the negative battery cable.

✷✷ CAUTION

Wait at least 90 seconds after the negative battery cable is disconnected to prevent possible deployment of the air bag.

2. Raise and safely support the vehicle and remove the undercover.
3. Remove the alternator and A/C compressor belt.
4. Lower the vehicle and remove the cruise control pump link assembly.
5. Place the power steering hose under the oil reservoir.
6. Loosen the tension pulley fixing bolts and remove the power steering pump drive belt.
To install:
7. Install the power steering pump drive belt.
8. Insert an extension bar or equivalent into the opening at the end of the tension pulley bracket and pivot the pulley to apply tension to the belt.
9. Tighten the fixing bolts.
10. Raise the vehicle and install the alternator and A/C compressor belt.
11. Install the undercover and lower the vehicle.
12. Connect the negative battery cable.

3.0L SOHC (Diamante Models Only) Engine

1. Disconnect the negative battery cable.
2. Loosen the lockbolt on the face of the A/C tensioner pulley.
3. Turn the adjusting bolt of the A/C tensioner pulley to loosen the tension of the A/C belt.
4. Remove the A/C compressor belt.
5. Loosen the locknut on the face of the power steering/alternator tensioner pulley.
6. Turn the adjusting bolt of the tensioner pulley to loosen the tension of the belt.
7. Remove the power steering/alternator belt.
To install:
8. Install the power steering/alternator belt first and then the A/C compressor drive belt.
9. Adjust the belts to the proper tension by turning the adjusting bolts and tighten pulley fixing nut/bolt.
10. Tighten the mounting nut of the power steering/alternator tensioner pulley to 36 ft. lbs. (50 Nm).

➡**The manufacturer does not provide a torque specification for the bolt that secures A/C tensioner pulley.**

11. Connect the negative battery cable.

Timing Belts

INSPECTION

▶ **See Figures 74 thru 81**

All engines covered by this manual utilize timing belts to drive the camshaft from the crankshaft's turning motion and to maintain proper valve timing. Some manufacturer's schedule periodic timing belt replacement to assure optimum engine performance, to make sure the motorist is never stranded should the belt break (as the engine will stop instantly) and for some (manufacturer's with interference motors) to prevent the possibility of severe internal engine damage should the belt break.

Although the 1.5L and 1.8L engines are not listed as an interference motors (it is not listed by the manufacturer as a motor whose valves might contact the pistons if the camshaft was rotated separately from the crankshaft) the first 2 reasons for periodic replacement still apply and the timing belt should be replaced at 60,000 miles (96,000 km). The 1.6L, 2.0L, 2.4L, 3.0L, and 3.5L engines are listed as interference motors, so the timing belt MUST be replaced at 60,000 miles (96,000 km) to avoid severe engine damage if the belt should break.

But whether or not you decide to replace the timing belt in the manufacturers schedule, you would be wise to check it periodically to make sure it has not become damaged or worn. Generally speaking, a severely worn belt may cause engine performance to drop dramatically, but a damaged belt (which could give out suddenly) may not give as much warning. In general, any time the engine timing cover(s) is (are) removed you should inspect the belt for premature parting, severe cracks or missing teeth. Also, an access plug is provided in the upper portion of the timing cover so that camshaft timing can be checked without cover removal. If timing is found to be off, cover removal and further belt inspection or replacement is necessary.

For the timing belt removal and installation procedure, please refer to Section 3 of this manual.

Hoses

INSPECTION

▶ **See Figures 82, 83, 84, and 85**

Upper and lower radiator hoses, along with the heater hoses, should be checked for deterioration, leaks and loose hose clamps at least every 30,000 miles (48,000 km). It is also wise to check the hoses periodically in early spring and at the beginning of the fall or winter when you are performing other maintenance. A quick visual inspection could discover a weakened hose which might have left you stranded if it had remained unrepaired.

Whenever you are checking the hoses, make sure the engine and cooling system are cold. Visually inspect for cracking, rotting or collapsed hoses, and replace as necessary. Run your hand along the length of the hose. If a weak or swollen spot is noted when squeezing the hose wall, the hose should be replaced.

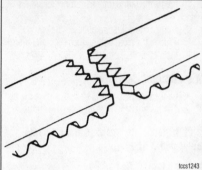
Fig. 74 Check for premature parting of the belt

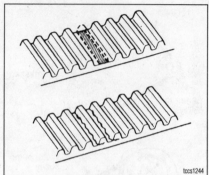
Fig. 75 Check if the teeth are cracked or damaged

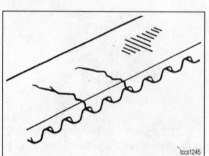
Fig. 76 Look for noticeable cracks or wear on the belt face

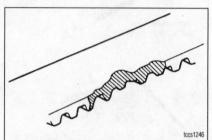
Fig. 77 You may only have damage on one side of the belt; if so, the guide could be the culprit

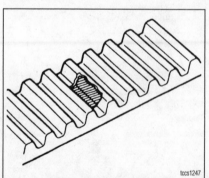
Fig. 78 Foreign materials can get in between the teeth and cause damage

Fig. 79 Inspect the timing belt for cracks, fraying, glazing or damage of any kind

Fig. 80 Damage on only one side of the timing belt may indicate a faulty guide

Fig. 81 ALWAYS replace the timing belt at the interval specified by the manufacturer

Fig. 82 The cracks developing along this hose are a result of age-related hardening

Fig. 83 A hose clamp that is too tight can cause older hoses to separate and tear on either side of the clamp

Fig. 84 A soft spongy hose (identifiable by the swollen section) will eventually burst and should be replaced

Fig. 85 Hoses are likely to deteriorate from the inside if the cooling system is not periodically flushed

REMOVAL & INSTALLATION

1. Remove the radiator pressure cap.

✳✴ CAUTION

Never remove the pressure cap while the engine is running, or personal injury from scalding hot coolant or steam may result. If possible, wait until the engine has cooled to remove the pressure cap. If this is not possible, wrap a thick cloth around the pressure cap and turn it slowly to the stop. Step back while the pressure is released from the cooling system. When you are sure all the pressure has been released, use the cloth to turn and remove the cap.

2. Position a clean container under the radiator and/or engine draincock or plug, then open the drain and allow the cooling system to drain to an appropriate level. For some upper hoses, only a little coolant must be drained. To remove hoses positioned lower on the engine, such as a lower radiator hose, the entire cooling system must be emptied.

✳✴ CAUTION

When draining coolant, keep in mind that cats and dogs are attracted by ethylene glycol antifreeze, and are quite likely to drink any that is left in an uncovered container or in puddles on the ground. This will prove fatal in sufficient quantity. Always drain coolant into a sealable container. Coolant may be reused unless it is contaminated or several years old.

3. Loosen the hose clamps at each end of the hose requiring replacement. Clamps are usually either of the spring tension type (which require pliers to squeeze the tabs and loosen) or of the screw tension type (which require screw or hex drivers to loosen). Pull the clamps back on the hose away from the connection.

4. Twist, pull and slide the hose off the fitting, taking care not to damage the neck of the component from which the hose is being removed.

➥**If the hose is stuck at the connection, do not try to insert a screwdriver or other sharp tool under the hose end in an effort to free it, as the connection and/or hose may become damaged. Heater connections especially may be easily damaged by such a procedure. If the hose is to be replaced, use a single-edged razor blade to make a slice along the portion of the hose which is stuck on the connection, perpendicular to the end of the hose. Do not cut deep so as to prevent damaging the connection. The hose can then be peeled from the connection and discarded.**

5. Clean both hose mounting connections. Inspect the condition of the hose clamps and replace them, if necessary.

To install:

6. Dip the ends of the new hose into clean engine coolant to ease installation.

7. Slide the clamps over the replacement hose, then slide the hose ends over the connections into position.

8. Position and secure the clamps at least $1/4$ in. (6.35mm) from the ends of the hose. Make sure they are located beyond the raised bead of the connector.

9. Close the radiator or engine drains and properly refill the cooling system with the clean drained engine coolant or a suitable mixture of ethylene glycol coolant and water.

10. If available, install a pressure tester and check for leaks. If a pressure tester is not available, run the engine until normal operating temperature is reached (allowing the system to naturally pressurize), then check for leaks.

✳✴ CAUTION

If you are checking for leaks with the system at normal operating temperature, BE EXTREMELY CAREFUL not to touch any moving or hot engine parts. Once temperature has been reached, shut the engine OFF, and check for leaks around the hose fittings and connections which were removed earlier.

CV-Boots

INSPECTION

◆ **See Figures 86 and 87**

The CV (Constant Velocity) boots should be checked for damage each time the oil is changed and any other time the vehicle is raised for service. These boots keep water, grime, dirt and other damaging matter from entering the CV-joints. Any of these could cause early CV-joint failure which can be expensive to repair. Heavy grease thrown around the inside of the front wheel(s) and on the brake caliper/drum can be an indication of a torn boot. Thoroughly check the boots for missing clamps and

Fig. 86 CV-boots must be inspected periodically for damage

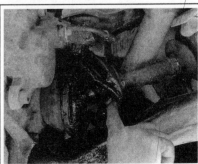

Fig. 87 A torn boot should be replaced immediately

tears. If the boot is damaged, it should be replaced immediately. Please refer to Section 7 for procedures.

Spark Plugs

♦ See Figure 88

A typical spark plug consists of a metal shell surrounding a ceramic insulator. A metal electrode extends downward through the center of the insulator and protrudes a small distance. Located at the end of the plug and attached to the side of the outer metal shell is the side electrode. The side electrode bends in at a 90° angle so that its tip is just past and parallel to the tip of the center electrode. The distance between these two electrodes (measured in thousandths of an inch or hundredths of a millimeter) is called the spark plug gap.

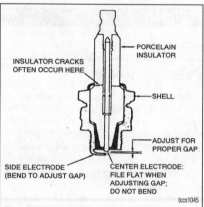

Fig. 88 Cross-section of a spark plug

The spark plug does not produce a spark, but instead provides a gap across which the current can arc. The coil produces anywhere from 20,000 to 50,000 volts (depending on the type and application) which travels through the wires to the spark plugs. The current passes along the center electrode and jumps the gap to the side electrode, and in doing so, ignites the air/fuel mixture in the combustion chamber.

SPARK PLUG HEAT RANGE

♦ See Figure 89

Spark plug heat range is the ability of the plug to dissipate heat. The longer the insulator (or the farther it extends into the engine), the hotter the plug will operate; the shorter the insulator (the closer the elec-

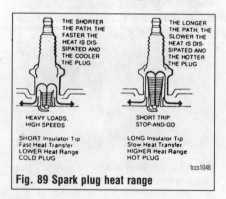

Fig. 89 Spark plug heat range

trode is to the block's cooling passages) the cooler it will operate. A plug that absorbs little heat and remains too cool will quickly accumulate deposits of oil and carbon since it is not hot enough to burn them off. This leads to plug fouling and consequently to misfiring. A plug that absorbs too much heat will have no deposits but, due to the excessive heat, the electrodes will burn away quickly and might possibly lead to preignition or other ignition problems. Preignition takes place when plug tips get so hot that they glow sufficiently to ignite the air/fuel mixture before the actual spark occurs. This early ignition will usually cause a pinging during low speeds and heavy loads.

The general rule of thumb for choosing the correct heat range when picking a spark plug is: if most of

Fig. 90 Carefully twist the boot end of the spark plug wire and withdraw the spark plug wire boot from the cylinder head

Fig. 92 A locking extension such as this is extremely helpful when removing spark plugs that are centrally located in the cylinder head such as on the 2.4L engine

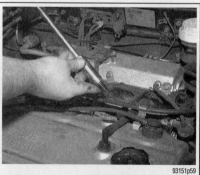

Fig. 94 . . . then carefully withdraw the spark plug from the engine

your driving is long distance, high speed travel, use a colder plug; if most of your driving is stop and go, use a hotter plug. Original equipment plugs are generally a good compromise between the 2 styles and most people never have the need to change their plugs from the factory-recommended heat range.

REMOVAL & INSTALLATION

♦ See Figures 90 thru 95

A set of spark plugs usually requires replacement after about 20,000–30,000 miles (32,000–48,000 km), depending on your style of driving. In normal operation plug gap increases about 0.001 in. (0.025mm) for every 2,500 miles (4,000 km). As the

Fig. 91 A special spark plug socket with a rubber insert is required to remove the spark plugs. Typically the spark plugs require a ⅝ spark plug socket

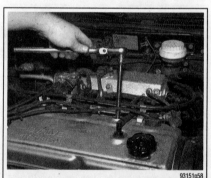

Fig. 93 Using the appropriate sized spark plug socket, necessary extensions and drive tools, loosen the spark plug . . .

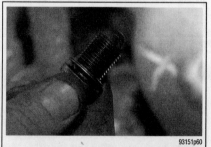

Fig. 95 After removing the plug from the engine, inspect it using the spark plug condition chart in this section to determine the running condition of your engine

gap increases, the plug's voltage requirement also increases. It requires a greater voltage to jump the wider gap and about two to three times as much voltage to fire the plug at high speeds than at idle. The improved air/fuel ratio control of modern fuel injection combined with the higher voltage output of modern ignition systems will often allow an engine to run significantly longer on a set of standard spark plugs, but keep in mind that efficiency will drop as the gap widens (along with fuel economy and power).

When you're removing spark plugs, work on one at a time. Don't start by removing the plug wires all at once, because, unless you number them, they may become mixed up. Take a minute before you begin and number the wires with tape.

1. Disconnect the negative battery cable, and if the vehicle has been run recently, allow the engine to thoroughly cool.

2. If equipped, remove the center cover.

3. On the 3.0L (SOHC and DOHC) and 3.5L engines, the upper intake manifold must be removed to access the rear spark plugs. Refer to Section 3 for the removal procedure.

4. Carefully twist the spark plug wire boot to loosen it, then pull upward and remove the boot from the plug. Be sure to pull on the boot and not on the wire, otherwise the connector located inside the boot may become separated.

5. Using compressed air, blow any water or debris from the spark plug well to assure that no harmful contaminants are allowed to enter the combustion chamber when the spark plug is removed. If compressed air is not available, use a rag or a brush to clean the area.

➡️**Remove the spark plugs when the engine is cold, if possible, to prevent damage to the threads. If removal of the plugs is difficult, apply a few drops of penetrating oil or silicone spray to the area around the base of the plug, and allow it a few minutes to work.**

6. Using a spark plug socket that is equipped with a rubber insert to properly hold the plug, turn the spark plug counterclockwise to loosen and remove the spark plug from the bore.

✳✳ WARNING

Be sure not to use a flexible extension on the socket. Use of a flexible extension may allow a shear force to be applied to the plug. A shear force could break the plug off in the cylinder head, leading to costly and frustrating repairs.

To install:

7. Inspect the spark plug boot for tears or damage. If a damaged boot is found, the spark plug wire must be replaced.

8. Using a wire feeler gauge, check and adjust the spark plug gap. When using a gauge, the proper size should pass between the electrodes with a slight drag. The next larger size should not be able to pass while the next smaller size should pass freely.

9. Carefully thread the plug into the bore by hand. If resistance is felt before the plug is almost completely threaded, back the plug out and begin threading again. In small, hard to reach areas, an old spark plug wire and boot could be used as a threading tool. The boot will hold the plug while you twist the end of the wire and the wire is supple enough to twist before it would allow the plug to crossthread.

✳✳ WARNING

Do not use the spark plug socket to thread the plugs. Always carefully thread the plug by hand or using an old plug wire to prevent the possibility of crossthreading and damaging the cylinder head bore.

10. Carefully tighten the spark plug. If the plug you are installing is equipped with a crush washer, seat the plug, then tighten about ¼ turn to crush the washer. If you are installing a tapered seat plug, tighten the plug to specifications provided by the vehicle or plug manufacturer.

11. Apply a small amount of silicone dielectric compound to the end of the spark plug lead or inside the spark plug boot to prevent sticking, then install the boot to the spark plug and push until it clicks into place. The click may be felt or heard, then gently pull back on the boot to assure proper contact.

12. On the 3.0L (SOHC and DOHC) and 3.5L engines, install the upper intake manifold. Refer to Section 3 for the installation procedure.

13. If equipped, install the center cover.

INSPECTION & GAPPING

▶ **See Figures 96, 97, 98, 99, and 100**

Check the plugs for deposits and wear. If they are not going to be replaced, clean the plugs thoroughly. Remember that any kind of deposit will decrease the efficiency of the plug. Plugs can be cleaned on a spark plug cleaning machine, which can sometimes be found in service stations, or you can do an acceptable job of cleaning with a stiff brush. If the plugs are cleaned, the electrodes must be filed flat. Use an ignition points file, not an emery board or the like, which will leave deposits. The electrodes must be filed perfectly flat with sharp edges; rounded edges reduce the spark plug voltage by as much as 50%.

Check spark plug gap before installation. The ground electrode (the L-shaped one connected to the body of the plug) must be parallel to the center electrode and the specified size wire gauge (please refer to the Tune-Up Specifications chart for details) must pass between the electrodes with a slight drag.

➡️**NEVER adjust the gap on a used platinum type spark plug.**

Always check the gap on new plugs as they are not always set correctly at the factory. Do not use a flat feeler gauge when measuring the gap on a used plug, because the reading may be inaccurate. A round-wire type gapping tool is the best way to check the gap. The correct gauge should pass through the electrode gap with a slight drag. If you're in doubt, try one size smaller and one larger. The smaller gauge

A normally worn spark plug should have light tan or gray deposits on the firing tip.

A physically damaged spark plug may be evidence of severe detonation in that cylinder. Watch that cylinder carefully between services, as a continued detonation will not only damage the plug, but could also damage the engine.

An oil fouled spark plug indicates an engine with worn poston rings and/or bad valve seals allowing excessive oil to enter the chamber.

This spark plug has been **left in the engine too long,** as evidenced by the extreme gap- Plugs with such an extreme gap can cause misfiring and stumbling accompanied by a noticeable lack of power.

A carbon fouled plug, identified by soft, sooty, black deposits, may indicate an improperly tuned vehicle. Check the air cleaner, ignition components and engine control system.

A bridged or almost bridged spark plug, identified by a build-up between the electrodes caused by excessive carbon or oil build-up on the plug.

Fig. 96 Inspect the spark plug to determine engine running conditions

tcca1p40

Fig. 97 A variety of tools and gauges are needed for spark plug service

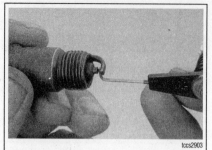

Fig. 98 Checking the spark plug gap with a feeler gauge

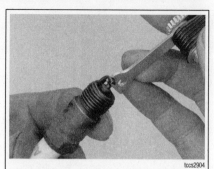

Fig. 99 Adjusting the spark plug gap

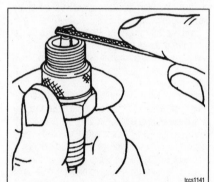

Fig. 100 If the standard plug is in good condition, the electrode may be filed flat— WARNING: do not file platinum plugs

should go through easily, while the larger one shouldn't go through at all. Wire gapping tools usually have a bending tool attached. Use that to adjust the side electrode until the proper distance is obtained. Absolutely never attempt to bend the center electrode. Also, be careful not to bend the side electrode too far or too often as it may weaken and break off within the engine, requiring removal of the cylinder head to retrieve it.

Spark Plug Wires

TESTING

▶ **See Figures 101 and 102**

At every tune-up/inspection, visually check the spark plug cables for burns cuts, or breaks in the insulation. Check the boots and the nipples on the distributor cap and/or coil. Replace any damaged wiring.

Every 50,000 miles (80,000 km) or 60 months, the resistance of the wires should be checked with an ohmmeter. Wires with excessive resistance will cause misfiring, and may make the engine difficult to start in damp weather.

To check resistance, an ohmmeter should be used on each wire to test resistance between the end connectors. Remove and install/replace the wires in order, one-by-one.

Resistance on these wires should be 4,000–6,000 ohms per foot. To properly measure this, remove the wires from the plugs and the coil pack. Do not pierce any ignition wire for any reason. Measure only from

the two ends. Take the length and multiply it by 6,000 to achieve the maximum resistance allowable in each wire, resistance should not exceed this value. If resistance does exceed this value, replace the wire.

➡ **Whenever the high tension wires are removed from the plugs, coil, or distributor, silicone grease must be applied to the boot before reconnection. Coat the entire interior surface with a suitable silicone grease.**

REMOVAL & INSTALLATION

▶ **See Figures 90, 103 and 104**

1. Remove the air cleaner inlet tube.
2. If equipped, remove the center cover from the valve cover.
3. Label each spark plug wire and make a note of its routing.

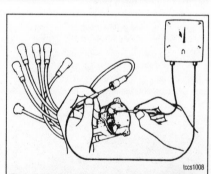

Fig. 101 Checking plug wire resistance through the distributor cap with an ohmmeter

Fig. 103 Remove the spark plug wires from the distributor cap or coil pack

➡ **Don't rely on wiring diagrams or sketches for spark plug wire routing. Improper arrangement of spark plug wires will induce voltage between wires, causing misfiring and surging. Be careful to arrange spark plug wires properly.**

4. Starting with the longest wire, disconnect the spark plug wire from the spark plug and then from the coil pack or distributor cap.

To install:

5. If replacing the spark plug wires, match the old wire with an appropriately sized wire in the new set.
6. Lubricate the boots and terminals with dielectric grease and install the wire on the coil pack. Make sure the wire snaps into place.
7. Route the wire in the exact path as the original and connect the wire to the spark plug.
8. Repeat the process for each remaining wire, working from the longest wire to the shortest.
9. Install the air cleaner inlet tube.

Fig. 102 Checking individual plug wire resistance with a digital ohmmeter

Fig. 104 Remove the plug wires from the wire dividers

Fig. 105 Loosen the distributor cap retaining screws . . .

Fig. 106 . . . then remove the cap from the distributor

Fig. 107 Grasp the rotor and pull it straight off of the distributor shaft

Fig. 108 The rotor must be aligned correctly to the distributor shaft before installation

Distributor Cap and Rotor

REMOVAL & INSTALLATION

▶ **See Figures 105, 106, 107, and 108**

1. Disconnect the negative battery cable.

➡**Depending on the reason for removing the distributor cap, it may make more sense to leave the spark plug wires attached. This is handy if you are testing spark plug wires, or if removal is necessary to access other components, and wire length allows you to reposition the cap out of the way.**

2. Label and disconnect the spark plug wires from the distributor cap.
3. Remove the distributor cap retaining screws or clips and remove the cap from the distributor.
4. Note its installed position, then remove the rotor from the distributor shaft.
5. The installation is the reverse of the removal.

INSPECTION

▶ **See Figures 109 and 110**

After removing the distributor cap and rotor, clean the components (both inside and outside of the cap) using soap and water. If compressed air is available, carefully dry the components (wearing safety goggles) or allow the parts to air dry. You can dry them with a clean, soft cloth, but don't leave any lint or moisture behind.

Once the cap and rotor have been thoroughly cleaned, check for cracks, carbon tracks, burns or other physical damage. Make sure the distributor cap's center button is free of damage. Check the cap terminals for dirt or corrosion. Always check the rotor blade and spring closely for damage. Replace any components where damage is found.

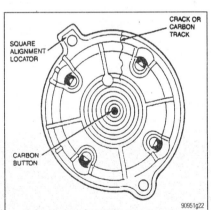

Fig. 109 Inspection points for the distributor cap

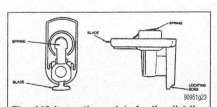

Fig. 110 Inspection points for the distributor rotor

Ignition Timing

GENERAL INFORMATION

▶ **See Figures 111 and 112**

Ignition timing is the measurement, in degrees of crankshaft rotation, of the point at which the spark plugs fire in each of the cylinders. It is measured in degrees before or after Top Dead Center (TDC) of the compression stroke.

Ideally, the air/fuel mixture in the cylinder will be ignited by the spark plug just as the piston passes

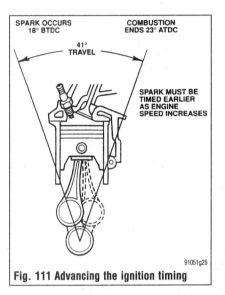

Fig. 111 Advancing the ignition timing

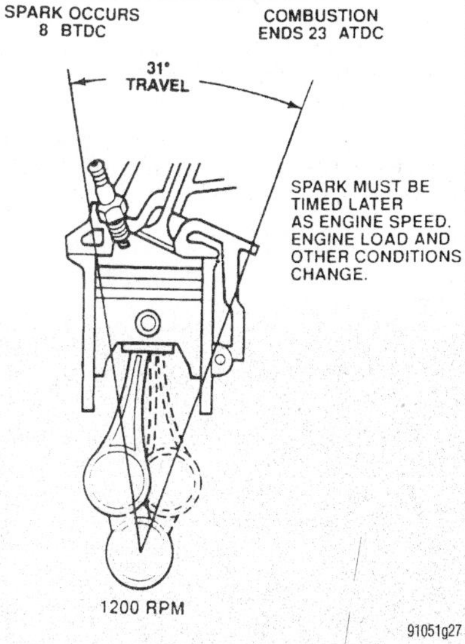

Fig. 112 Retarding the ignition timing

TDC of the compression stroke. If this happens, the piston will be at the beginning of the power stroke just as the compressed and ignited air/fuel mixture forces the piston down and turns the crankshaft. Because it takes a fraction of a second for the spark plug to ignite the mixture in the cylinder, the spark plug must fire a little before the piston reaches TDC. Otherwise, the mixture will not be completely ignited as the piston passes TDC and the full power of the explosion will not be used by the engine.

The timing measurement is given in degrees of crankshaft rotation before the piston reaches TDC (BTDC). If the setting for the ignition timing is 10° BTDC, each spark plug must fire 10 degrees before each piston reaches TDC. This only holds true, however, when the engine is at idle speed. The combustion process must be complete by 23°ATDC to maintain proper engine performance, fuel mileage, and low emissions.

As the engine speed increases, the pistons go faster. The spark plugs have to ignite the fuel even sooner if it is to be completely ignited when the piston reaches TDC. If the ignition is set too far advanced (BTDC), the ignition and expansion of the fuel in the cylinder will occur too soon and tend to force the piston down while it is still traveling up. This causes pre ignition or "knocking and pinging". If the ignition spark is set too far retarded, or after TDC (ATDC), the piston will have already started on its way down when the fuel is ignited. The piston will be forced down for only a portion of its travel, resulting in poor engine performance and lack of power.

Timing marks or scales can be found on the rim of the crankshaft pulley and the timing cover. The marks on the pulley correspond to the position of the piston in the No. 1 cylinder. A stroboscopic (dynamic) timing light is hooked onto the No. 1 cylinder spark plug wire. Every time the spark plug fires, the timing light flashes. By aiming the light at the timing marks while the engine is running, the exact position of the piston within the cylinder can be easily read (the flash of light makes the mark on the pulley appear to be standing still). Proper timing is indicated when the mark and scale are in specified alignment.

✳✳ WARNING

When checking timing with the engine running, take care not to get the timing light wires tangled in the fan blades and/or drive belts.

INSPECTION & ADJUSTMENT

1990–96 Models

▸ **See Figures 113 thru 119**

1. Set the parking brake, start and run the engine until normal operating temperature is obtained. Keep all lights and accessories OFF and the front wheels straight-ahead. Place the transaxle in **P** for automatic transaxle or Neutral for manual transaxle.
2. If not at specification, set the idle speed to the correct level.
3. Turn the engine **OFF**. Remove the waterproof cover from the ignition timing adjusting connector, and connect a jumper wire from this terminal

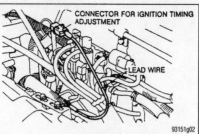
Fig. 113 Ignition timing adjustment connector—1990–92 Mirage with 1.5L engine

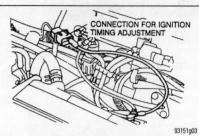
Fig. 114 Ignition timing adjustment connector—Mirage with 1.6L engine

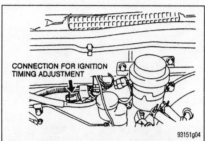
Fig. 115 Ignition timing adjustment connector—Galant with 2.0L engines

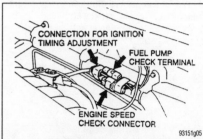
Fig. 116 Ignition timing adjustment connector—1992–96 Diamante

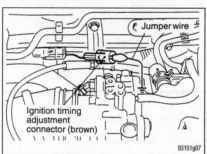
Fig. 117 Ignition timing adjustment connector—1994–96 Galant

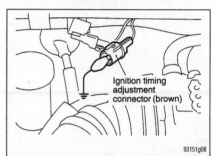
Fig. 118 Ignition timing adjustment connector—1993–96 Mirage with 1.5L engine

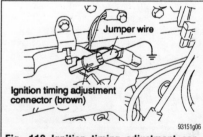
Fig. 119 Ignition timing adjustment connector—1993–96 Mirage with 1.8L engine

to a good ground. Refer to the corresponding illustrations for the correct location of the timing adjustment connector.

4. Connect a conventional power timing light to the No. 1 cylinder spark plug wire. Start the engine and run at idle.
5. Aim the timing light at the timing scale located near the crankshaft pulley.
6. Loosen the distributor or crank angle sensor hold-down nut just enough so the housing can be rotated.
7. Turn the housing in the proper direction until the specified timing is reached. Tighten the hold-down nut and recheck the timing. Turn the engine **OFF**.
8. Remove the jumper wire from the ignition timing adjusting terminal and install the water-proof cover.
9. Start the engine and check the actual timing (the timing without the terminal grounded). This reading should be approximately 5 degrees more than the basic timing. Actual timing may increase according to altitude. Also, actual timing may fluctuate because of slight variation accomplished by the ECU.

As long as the basic timing is correct, the engine is timed correctly.

10. Turn the engine **OFF**.
11. Disconnect the timing apparatus and tachometer.

1997–00 Models

The ignition timing is controlled by the Engine Control Module (ECM) and is not adjustable. However it can be inspected using a scan tool.

Valve Lash

ADJUSTMENT

◆ See Figures 120 and 121

The only engines that require periodic adjustment of the valves are the 1.5L engine in the 1990–95 Mirage and the 1.8L in the 1993–95 Mirage.

❊❊❊ WARNING

Incorrect valve clearance will cause noisy and/or unsteady engine operation, reduced engine output, and possible engine damage. Check the valve clearances and adjust as required while the engine is hot.

1. Warm the engine to operating temperature. Turn the engine **OFF**. Disconnect the negative battery cable.

2. Remove all spark plugs so engine can be easily turned by hand.

3. Remove the valve cover.

4. Turn the crankshaft clockwise until the notch on the pulley is aligned with the **T** mark on the timing belt lower cover. This brings both No. 1 and 4 cylinder pistons to Top Dead Center (TDC).

5. Wiggle the rocker arms on No. 1 and 4 cylinders up and down to determine which cylinder is at TDC on the compression stroke. Both rocker arms should move if the piston in that cylinder is at TDC on the compression stroke.

6. Measure the valve clearance with a feeler gauge. When the No. 1 piston is at TDC on the compression stroke, check No. 1 intake and exhaust; No. 2 intake and exhaust. Then turn the crankshaft clockwise 1 turn to bring No. 4 to TDC on its compression stroke. With No. 4 on TDC, compression stroke, check No. 2 exhaust and intake; and No. 4 intake and exhaust. Clearance is as follows:

1990–92 1.5L engine:

- Exhaust valve: 0.0098 in. (0.25mm)
- Intake valve: 0.0059 in. (0.15mm)

1993–95 1.5L engine:
- Exhaust valve: 0.0098 in. (0.25mm)
- Intake valve: 0.008 in. (0.20mm)

1993–95 1.8L engine:
- Exhaust valve: 0.012 in. (0.30mm)
- Intake valve: 0.008 in. (0.20mm)

7. If the valve clearance is out of specification, loosen the rocker arm locknut and adjust the clearance using a feeler gauge while turning the adjusting screw. When at specification, tighten the locknut. Be sure to hold the screw securely in place when tightening the locknut to prevent it from turning when tightening the locknut. Tightening torque of the locknut is as follows:
- 1.5L engine: 9–11 ft. lbs. (12–15 Nm)
- 1.8L engine: 7 ft. lbs. (9 Nm)

8. Recheck the clearance and readjust.

9. After adjusting the valves, install the valve cover and spark plugs, and connect the negative battery cable.

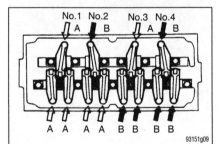

Fig. 120 Valve adjustment positions: (A) when engine is on TDC of cylinder 1 and (B) when engine is on TDC of cylinder 4

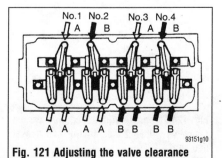

Fig. 121 Adjusting the valve clearance

ENGINE TUNE-UP SPECIFICATIONS

Year	Engine Displacement Liters (cc)	Engine ID/VIN	Spark Plugs Gap (in.)	Ignition Timing (deg.) MT	AT	Fuel Pump (psi)	Idle Speed (rpm) MT	AT	Valve Clearance In.	Ex.
1990	1.5 (1468)	4G15/A	0.040-0.043	3-7B	3-7B	48	700-800	700-800	0.015 ①	0.025 ①
	2.0 (1997)	4G63/V	0.039-0.043	3-7B	3-7B	48	650-850	650-850	HYD	HYD
	2.0 (1997)	4G63/R	0.039-0.043	3-7B	3-7B	48	650-850	650-850	HYD	HYD
1991	1.5 (1468)	4G15/A	0.040-0.043	3-7B	3-7B	48	700-800	700-800	0.015 ①	0.025 ①
	1.6 (1595)	4G61/Y	0.040-0.043	3-7B	3-7B	38	700-800	700-800	HYD	HYD
	2.0 (1997)	4G63/V	0.039-0.043	3-7B	3-7B	48	650-850	650-850	HYD	HYD
	2.0 (1997)	4G63/R	0.039-0.043	3-7B	3-7B	48	650-850	650-850	HYD	HYD
	2.0 (1997)	4G63/U	0.028-0.031	3-7B	3-7B	37	650-850	650-850	HYD	HYD
1992	1.5 (1468)	4G15/A	0.040-0.043	3-7B	3-7B	48	700-800	700-800	0.015 ①	0.025 ①
	1.6 (1595)	4G61/Y	0.040-0.043	3-7B	3-7B	38	700-800	700-800	HYD	HYD
	2.0 (1997)	4G63/V	0.039-0.043	3-7B	3-7B	48	650-850	650-850	HYD	HYD
	2.0 (1997)	4G63/R	0.039-0.043	3-7B	3-7B	48	650-850	650-850	HYD	HYD
	2.0 (1997)	4G63/U	0.028-0.031	3-7B	3-7B	37	650-850	650-850	HYD	HYD
	3.0 (2972)	6G72/H	0.039-0.043	—	3-7B	38	—	600-800	HYD	HYD
	3.0 (2972)	6G72/J	0.039-0.043	—	3-7B	38	—	600-800	HYD	HYD
1993	1.5 (1468)	4G15/A	0.040-0.043	3-7B	3-7B	38	650-850	650-850	0.015 ①	0.025 ①
	1.8 (1834)	4G93/C	0.039-0.043	3-7B	3-7B	38	650-850	650-850	0.008 ①	0.012 ①
	2.0 (1997)	4G63/V	0.039-0.043	3-7B	3-7B	48	650-850	650-850	HYD	HYD
	2.0 (1997)	4G63/R	0.039-0.043	3-7B	3-7B	48	650-850	650-850	HYD	HYD
	3.0 (2972)	6G72/H	0.039-0.043	—	3-7B	38	—	600-800	HYD	HYD
	3.0 (2972)	6G72/J	0.039-0.043	—	2-8B	38	—	600-800	HYD	HYD
1994	1.5 (1468)	4G15/A	0.040-0.043	3-7B	3-7B	48	700-800	700-800	0.015 ①	0.025 ①
	1.8 (1834)	4G93/C	0.039-0.043	5B	5B	38	600-800	650-850	0.008 ①	0.012 ①
	2.4 (2350)	4G64/G	0.039-0.043	3-7B	3-7B	38	650-850	650-850	HYD	HYD
	2.4 (2350)	4G64/L	0.039-0.043	2-8B	2-8B	38	700-800	700-800	HYD	HYD
	3.0 (2972)	6G72/H	0.039-0.043	—	3-7B	38	—	600-800	HYD	HYD
	3.0 (2972)	6G72/J	0.039-0.043	—	2-8B	38	—	600-800	HYD	HYD
1995	1.5 (1468)	4G15/A	0.039-0.043	5B	5B	38	650-850	650-850	0.008 ①	0.010 ①
	1.8 (1834)	4G93/C	0.039-0.043	5B	5B	38	600-800	650-850	0.008 ①	0.012 ①
	2.4 (2350)	4G64/G	0.039-0.043	3-7B	3-7B	38	650-850	650-850	HYD	HYD
	2.4 (2350)	4G64/L	0.039-0.043	2-8B	2-8B	38	700-800	700-800	HYD	HYD
	3.0 (2972)	6G72/H	0.039-0.043	—	3-7B	38	—	600-800	HYD	HYD
	3.0 (2972)	6G72/J	0.039-0.043	—	2-8B	38	—	600-800	HYD	HYD
1996	1.5 (1468)	4G15/A	0.039-0.043	5B	5B	38	650-850	650-850	0.008 ①	0.010 ①
	1.8 (1834)	4G93/C	0.039-0.043	5B	5B	38	600-800	650-850	0.008 ①	0.012 ①
	2.4 (2350)	4G64/G	0.039-0.043	3-7B	3-7B	38	650-850	650-850	HYD	HYD
	2.4 (2350)	4G64/L	0.039-0.043	2-8B	2-8B	38	700-800	700-800	HYD	HYD
	3.0 (2972)	6G72/H	0.039-0.043	—	3-7B	38	—	600-800	HYD	HYD
	3.0 (2972)	6G72/J	0.039-0.043	—	2-8B	38	—	600-800	HYD	HYD
1997	1.5 (1468)	4G15/A	0.039-0.043	5B	5B	38	650-850	650-850	0.008 ①	0.010 ①
	1.8 (1834)	4G93/C	0.039-0.043	5B	5B	38	600-800	650-850	0.008 ①	0.012 ①
	2.4 (2350)	4G64/G	0.039-0.043	3-7B	3-7B	38	650-850	650-850	HYD	HYD
	2.4 (2350)	4G64/L	0.039-0.043	2-8B	2-8B	38	700-800	700-800	HYD	HYD
	3.5 (3497)	6G74/P	0.039-0.043	—	2-8B	38	—	600-800	HYD	HYD
1998	1.5 (1468)	4G15/A	0.039-0.043	2-8B	2-8B	38	600-800	600-800	HYD	HYD
	1.8 (1834)	4G93/C	0.039-0.043	2-8B	2-8B	38	600-800	600-800	HYD	HYD
	2.4 (2350)	4G64/G	0.039-0.043	3-7B	3-7B	38	650-850	650-850	HYD	HYD
	2.4 (2350)	4G64/L	0.039-0.043	2-8B	2-8B	38	700-800	700-800	HYD	HYD
	3.5 (3497)	6G74/P	0.039-0.043	—	2-8B	38	—	600-800	HYD	HYD
1999	1.5 (1468)	4G15/A	0.039-0.043	2-8B	2-8B	38	600-800	600-800	HYD	HYD
	1.8 (1834)	4G93/C	0.039-0.043	2-8B	2-8B	38	600-800	600-800	HYD	HYD
	2.4 (2350)	4G64/G	0.039-0.043	2-8B	2-8B	38	650-850	650-850	HYD	HYD
	3.0 (2972)	6G72/L	0.039-0.043	2-8B	2-8B	38	600-800	600-800	HYD	HYD
	3.5 (3497)	6G74/P	0.039-0.043	—	2-8B	38	—	600-800	HYD	HYD
2000	1.5 (1468)	4G15/A	0.039-0.043	2-8B	2-8B	38	600-800	600-800	HYD	HYD
	1.8 (1834)	4G93/C	0.039-0.043	2-8B	2-8B	38	600-800	600-800	HYD	HYD
	2.4 (2350)	4G64/G	0.039-0.043	2-8B	2-8B	38	650-850	650-850	HYD	HYD
	3.0 (2972)	6G72/L	0.039-0.043	2-8B	2-8B	38	600-800	600-800	HYD	HYD
	3.5 (3497)	6G74/P	0.039-0.043	—	2-8B	38	—	600-800	HYD	HYD

NOTE: The Vehicle Emission Control Information label often reflects specification changes made during production. The label figures must be used if they differ from those in this chart.

B - Before top dead center
HYD - Hydraulic
① Hot engine

93151c05

Idle Speed

The idle speed is factory set and usually no adjustments are ever necessary. If an adjustment becomes necessary, first check that the spark plugs, injectors, idle air control servo and compression pressure are all normal.

Data from various sensors and switches are used by the ECU to determine the proper fuel/air mixture for optimal engine performance.

Air Conditioning System

SYSTEM SERVICE & REPAIR

▶ **See Figure 122**

➡**It is recommended that the A/C system be serviced by an EPA Section 609 certified automotive technician utilizing a refrigerant recovery/recycling machine.**

The do-it-yourselfer should not service his/her own vehicle's A/C system for many reasons, including legal concerns, personal injury, environmental damage and cost. The following are some of the reasons why you may decide not to service your own vehicle's A/C system.

According to the U.S. Clean Air Act, it is a federal crime to service or repair (involving the refrigerant) a Motor Vehicle Air Conditioning (MVAC) system for money without being EPA certified. It is also illegal to vent R-12 and R-134a refrigerants into the atmosphere. Selling or distributing A/C system refrigerant (in a container which contains less than 20 pounds of refrigerant) to any person who is not EPA 609 certified is also not allowed by law.

State and/or local laws may be more strict than the federal regulations, so be sure to check with your state and/or local authorities for further information. For further federal information on the legality of servicing your A/C system, call the EPA Stratospheric Ozone Hotline.

➡**Federal law dictates that a fine of up to $25,000 may be levied on people convicted of venting refrigerant into the atmosphere. Additionally, the EPA may pay up to $10,000 for information or services leading to a criminal conviction of the violation of these laws.**

When servicing an A/C system you run the risk of handling or coming in contact with refrigerant, which

Fig. 122 A label with information concerning the A/C system is typically located in the engine compartment

may result in skin or eye irritation or frostbite. Although low in toxicity (due to chemical stability), inhalation of concentrated refrigerant fumes is dangerous and can result in death; cases of fatal cardiac arrhythmia have been reported in people accidentally subjected to high levels of refrigerant. Some early symptoms include loss of concentration and drowsiness.

➡**Generally, the limit for exposure is lower for R-134a than it is for R-12. Exceptional care must be practiced when handling R-134a.**

Also, refrigerants can decompose at high temperatures (near gas heaters or open flame), which may result in hydrofluoric acid, hydrochloric acid and phosgene (a fatal nerve gas).

R-12 refrigerant can damage the environment because it is a Chlorofluorocarbon (CFC), which has been proven to add to ozone layer depletion, leading to increasing levels of UV radiation. UV radiation has been linked with an increase in skin cancer, suppression of the human immune system, an increase in cataracts, damage to crops, damage to aquatic organisms, an increase in ground-level ozone, and increased global warming.

R-134a refrigerant is a greenhouse gas which, if allowed to vent into the atmosphere, will contribute to global warming (the Greenhouse Effect).

It is usually more economically feasible to have a certified MVAC automotive technician perform A/C system service on your vehicle. Some possible reasons for this are as follows:

• While it is illegal to service an A/C system without the proper equipment, the home mechanic would have to purchase an expensive refrigerant recovery/recycling machine to service his/her own vehicle.

• Since only a certified person may purchase refrigerant—according to the Clean Air Act, there are specific restrictions on selling or distributing A/C system refrigerant—it is legally impossible (unless certified) for the home mechanic to service his/her own vehicle. Procuring refrigerant in an illegal fashion exposes one to the risk of paying a $25,000 fine to the EPA.

R-12 Refrigerant Conversion

If your vehicle still uses R-12 refrigerant, one way to save A/C system costs down the road is to investigate the possibility of having your system converted to R-134a. The older R-12 systems can be easily converted to R-134a refrigerant by a certified automotive technician by installing a few new components and changing the system oil.

The cost of R-12 is steadily rising and will continue to increase, because it is no longer imported or manufactured in the United States. Therefore, it is often possible to have an R-12 system converted to R-134a and recharged for less than it would cost to just charge the system with R-12.

If you are interested in having your system converted, contact local automotive service stations for more details and information.

PREVENTIVE MAINTENANCE

▶ **See Figures 123 and 124**

Although the A/C system should not be serviced by the do-it-yourselfer, preventive maintenance can be practiced and A/C system inspections can be per-

formed to help maintain the efficiency of the vehicle's A/C system. For preventive maintenance, perform the following:

• The easiest and most important preventive maintenance for your A/C system is to be sure that it is used on a regular basis. Running the system for five minutes each month (no matter what the season) will help ensure that the seals and all internal components remain lubricated.

➡**Some newer vehicles automatically operate the A/C system compressor whenever the windshield defroster is activated. When running, the compressor lubricates the A/C system components; therefore, the A/C system would not need to be operated each month.**

• In order to prevent heater core freeze-up during A/C operation, it is necessary to maintain proper antifreeze protection. Use a hand-held coolant tester (hydrometer) to periodically check the condition of the antifreeze in your engine's cooling system.

➡**Antifreeze should not be used longer than the manufacturer specifies.**

• For efficient operation of an air conditioned vehicle's cooling system, the radiator cap should have a holding pressure which meets manufacturer's specifications. A cap which fails to hold these pressures should be replaced.

• Any obstruction of or damage to the condenser configuration will restrict air flow which is essential to its efficient operation. It is, therefore, a good rule to keep this unit clean and in proper physical shape.

Fig. 123 A coolant tester can be used to determine the freezing and boiling levels of the coolant in your vehicle

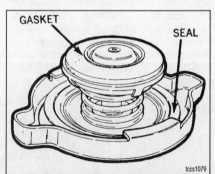

Fig. 124 To ensure efficient cooling system operation, inspect the radiator cap gasket and seal

➡️**Bug screens which are mounted in front of the condenser (unless they are original equipment) are regarded as obstructions.**

• The condensation drain tube expels any water which accumulates on the bottom of the evaporator housing into the engine compartment. If this tube is obstructed, the air conditioning performance can be restricted and condensation buildup can spill over onto the vehicle's floor.

SYSTEM INSPECTION

▶ **See Figure 125**

Although the A/C system should not be serviced by the do-it-yourselfer, preventive maintenance can be practiced and A/C system inspections can be performed to help maintain the efficiency of the vehicle's A/C system. For A/C system inspection, perform the following:

The easiest and often most important check for the air conditioning system consists of a visual inspection of the system components. Visually inspect the air conditioning system for refrigerant leaks, damaged compressor clutch, abnormal compressor drive belt tension and/or condition, plugged evaporator drain tube, blocked condenser fins, disconnected or broken wires, blown fuses, corroded connections and poor insulation.

A refrigerant leak will usually appear as an oily residue at the leakage point in the system. The oily residue soon picks up dust or dirt particles from the surrounding air and appears greasy. Through time, this will build up and appear to be a heavy dirt impregnated grease.

For a thorough visual and operational inspection, check the following:

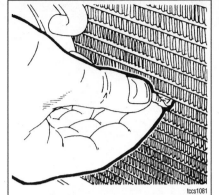

Fig. 125 Periodically remove any debris from the condenser and radiator fins

• Check the surface of the radiator and condenser for dirt, leaves or other material which might block air flow.
• Check for kinks in hoses and lines. Check the system for leaks.
• Make sure the drive belt is properly tensioned. When the air conditioning is operating, make sure the drive belt is free of noise or slippage.
• Make sure the blower motor operates at all appropriate positions, then check for distribution of the air from all outlets with the blower on **HIGH** or **MAX**.

➡️**Keep in mind that under conditions of high humidity, air discharged from the A/C vents may not feel as cold as expected, even if the system is working properly. This is because vaporized moisture in humid air retains heat more effectively than dry air, thereby making humid air more difficult to cool.**

• Make sure the air passage selection lever is operating correctly. Start the engine and warm it to normal operating temperature, then make sure the temperature selection lever is operating correctly.

Windshield Wipers

ELEMENT (REFILL) CARE & REPLACEMENT

▶ **See Figures 126 thru 135**

For maximum effectiveness and longest element life, the windshield and wiper blades should be kept clean. Dirt, tree sap, road tar and so on will cause streaking, smearing and blade deterioration if left on the glass. It is advisable to wash the windshield carefully with a commercial glass cleaner at least once a month. Wipe off the rubber blades with the wet rag afterwards. Do not attempt to move wipers across the windshield by hand; damage to the motor and drive mechanism will result.

To inspect and/or replace the wiper blade elements, place the wiper switch in the **LOW** speed position and the ignition switch in the **ACC** position. When the wiper blades are approximately vertical on the windshield, turn the ignition switch to **OFF**.

Examine the wiper blade elements. If they are found to be cracked, broken or torn, they should be replaced immediately. Replacement intervals will vary with usage, although ozone deterioration usually limits element life to about one year. If the wiper pattern is smeared or streaked, or if the blade chatters across the glass, the elements should be replaced. It is easiest and most sensible to replace the elements in pairs.

If your vehicle is equipped with aftermarket blades, there are several different types of refills and your vehi-

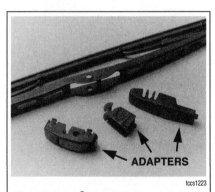

Fig. 126 Bosch® wiper blade and fit kit

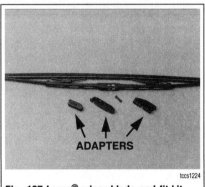

Fig. 127 Lexor® wiper blade and fit kit

Fig. 128 Pylon® wiper blade and adapter

Fig. 129 Trico® wiper blade and fit kit

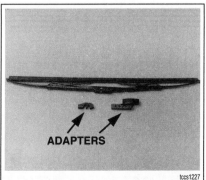

Fig. 130 Tripledge® wiper blade and fit kit

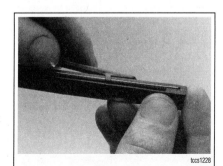

Fig. 131 To remove and install a Lexor® wiper blade refill, slip out the old insert and slide in a new one

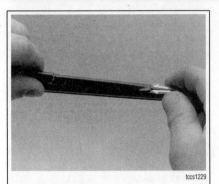

Fig. 132 On Pylon® inserts, the clip at the end has to be removed prior to sliding the insert off

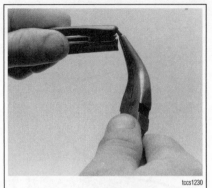

Fig. 133 On Trico® wiper blades, the tab at the end of the blade must be turned up . . .

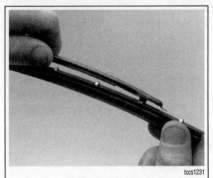

Fig. 134 . . . then the insert can be removed. After installing the replacement insert, bend the tab back

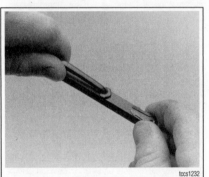

Fig. 135 The Tripledge® wiper blade insert is removed and installed using a securing clip

cle might have any kind. Aftermarket blades and arms rarely use the exact same type blade or refill as the original equipment. Here are some typical aftermarket blades; not all may be available for your vehicle:

The Anco® type uses a release button that is pushed down to allow the refill to slide out of the yoke jaws. The new refill slides back into the frame and locks in place.

Some Trico® refills are removed by locating where the metal backing strip or the refill is wider. Insert a small screwdriver blade between the frame and metal backing strip. Press down to release the refill from the retaining tab.

Other types of Trico® refills have two metal tabs which are unlocked by squeezing them together. The rubber filler can then be withdrawn from the frame jaws. A new refill is installed by inserting the refill into the front frame jaws and sliding it rearward to engage the remaining frame jaws. There are usually four jaws; be certain when installing that the refill is engaged in all of them. At the end of its travel, the tabs will lock into place on the front jaws of the wiper blade frame.

Another type of refill is made from polycarbonate. The refill has a simple locking device at one end which flexes downward out of the groove into which the jaws of the holder fit, allowing easy release. By sliding the new refill through all the jaws and pushing through the slight resistance when it reaches the end of its travel, the refill will lock into position.

To replace the Tridon® refill, it is necessary to remove the wiper blade. This refill has a plastic backing strip with a notch about 1 in. (25mm) from the end. Hold the blade (frame) on a hard surface so that the frame is tightly bowed. Grip the tip of the backing

strip and pull up while twisting counterclockwise. The backing strip will snap out of the retaining tab. Do this for the remaining tabs until the refill is free of the blade. The length of these refills is molded into the end and they should be replaced with identical types.

Regardless of the type of refill used, be sure to follow the part manufacturer's instructions closely. Make sure that all of the frame jaws are engaged as the refill is pushed into place and locked. If the metal blade holder and frame are allowed to touch the glass during wiper operation, the glass will be scratched.

Tires and Wheels

▶ **See Figure 136**

Common sense and good driving habits will afford maximum tire life. Fast starts, sudden stops and hard cornering are hard on tires and will shorten their useful life span. Make sure that you don't overload the vehicle or run with incorrect pressure in the tires. Both of these practices will increase tread wear.

➡ **For optimum tire life, keep the tires properly inflated, rotate them often and have the wheel alignment checked periodically.**

Inspect your tires frequently. Be especially careful to watch for bubbles in the tread or sidewall, deep cuts or underinflation. Replace any tires with bubbles in the sidewall. If cuts are so deep that they penetrate to the cords, discard the tire. Any cut in the sidewall of a radial tire renders it unsafe. Also look for uneven tread wear patterns that may indi-

Fig. 136 A label with information concerning the tires is typically located on one of the door pillars

cate the front end is out of alignment or that the tires are out of balance.

TIRE ROTATION

▶ **See Figures 137 and 138**

Tires must be rotated periodically to equalize wear patterns that vary with a tire's position on the vehicle. Tires will also wear in an uneven way as the front steering/suspension system wears to the point where the alignment should be reset.

Rotating the tires will ensure maximum life for the tires as a set, so you will not have to discard a tire early due to wear on only part of the tread. Regular rotation is required to equalize wear.

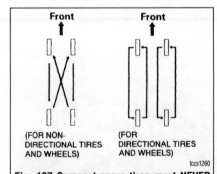

Fig. 137 Compact spare tires must NEVER be used in the rotation pattern

Fig. 138 Unidirectional tires are identifiable by sidewall arrows and/or the word "rotation"

When rotating "unidirectional tires," make sure that they always roll in the same direction. This means that a tire used on the left side of the vehicle must not be switched to the right side and vice-versa. Such tires should only be rotated front-to-rear or rear-to-front, while always remaining on the same side of the vehicle. These tires are marked on the sidewall as to the direction of rotation; observe the marks when reinstalling the tire(s).

Some styled or "mag" wheels may have different offsets front to rear. In these cases, the rear wheels must not be used up front and vice-versa. Furthermore, if these wheels are equipped with unidirectional tires, they cannot be rotated unless the tire is re-mounted for the proper direction of rotation.

➡**The compact or space-saver spare is strictly for emergency use. It must never be included in the tire rotation or placed on the vehicle for everyday use.**

TIRE DESIGN

▶ **See Figure 139**

For maximum satisfaction, tires should be used in sets of four. Mixing of different types (radial, bias-belted, fiberglass belted) must be avoided. In most cases, the vehicle manufacturer has designated a type of tire on which the vehicle will perform best. Your first choice when replacing tires should be to use the same type of tire that the manufacturer recommends.

When radial tires are used, tire sizes and wheel diameters should be selected to maintain ground clearance and tire load capacity equivalent to the original specified tire. Radial tires should always be used in sets of four.

✳✳ CAUTION

Radial tires should never be used on only the front axle.

When selecting tires, pay attention to the original size as marked on the tire. Most tires are described using an industry size code sometimes referred to as P-Metric. This allows the exact identification of the tire specifications, regardless of the manufacturer. If selecting a different tire size or brand, remember to

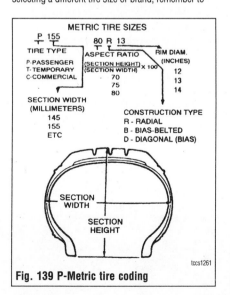

Fig. 139 P-Metric tire coding

check the installed tire for any sign of interference with the body or suspension while the vehicle is stopping, turning sharply or heavily loaded.

Snow Tires

Good radial tires can produce a big advantage in slippery weather, but in snow, a street radial tire does not have sufficient tread to provide traction and control. The small grooves of a street tire quickly pack with snow and the tire behaves like a billiard ball on a marble floor. The more open, chunky tread of a snow tire will self-clean as the tire turns, providing much better grip on snowy surfaces.

To satisfy municipalities requiring snow tires during weather emergencies, most snow tires carry either an M + S designation after the tire size stamped on the sidewall, or the designation "all-season." In general, no change in tire size is necessary when buying snow tires.

Most manufacturers strongly recommend the use of 4 snow tires on their vehicles for reasons of stability. If snow tires are fitted only to the drive wheels, the opposite end of the vehicle may become very unstable when braking or turning on slippery surfaces. This instability can lead to unpleasant endings if the driver can't counteract the slide in time.

Note that snow tires, whether 2 or 4, will affect vehicle handling in all non-snow situations. The stiffer, heavier snow tires will noticeably change the turning and braking characteristics of the vehicle. Once the snow tires are installed, you must re-learn the behavior of the vehicle and drive accordingly.

➡**Consider buying extra wheels on which to mount the snow tires. Once done, the "snow wheels" can be installed and removed as needed. This eliminates the potential damage to tires or wheels from seasonal removal and installation. Even if your vehicle has**

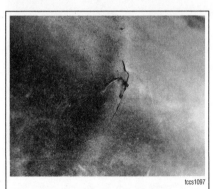

Fig. 140 Tires should be checked frequently for any sign of puncture or damage

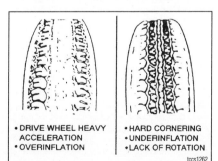

• DRIVE WHEEL HEAVY ACCELERATION
• OVERINFLATION

• HARD CORNERING
• UNDERINFLATION
• LACK OF ROTATION

Fig. 142 Examples of inflation-related tire wear patterns

styled wheels, see if inexpensive steel wheels are available. Although the look of the vehicle will change, the expensive wheels will be protected from salt, curb hits and pothole damage.

TIRE STORAGE

If they are mounted on wheels, store the tires at proper inflation pressure. All tires should be kept in a cool, dry place. If they are stored in the garage or basement, do not let them stand on a concrete floor; set them on strips of wood, a mat or a large stack of newspaper. Keeping them away from direct moisture is of paramount importance. Tires should not be stored upright, but in a flat position.

INFLATION & INSPECTION

▶ **See Figures 140 thru 147**

The importance of proper tire inflation cannot be overemphasized. A tire employs air as part of its structure. It is designed around the supporting strength of the air at a specified pressure. For this reason, improper inflation drastically reduces the tire's ability to perform as intended. A tire will lose some air in day-to-day use; having to add a few pounds of air periodically is not necessarily a sign of a leaking tire.

Two items should be a permanent fixture in every glove compartment: an accurate tire pressure gauge and a tread depth gauge. Check the tire pressure (including the spare) regularly with a pocket type gauge. Too often, the gauge on the end of the air hose at your corner garage is not accurate because it suffers too much abuse. Always check tire pressure when the tires are cold, as pressure increases with temperature. If you must move the vehicle to check the tire

Fig. 141 Tires with deep cuts, or cuts which bulge, should be replaced immediately

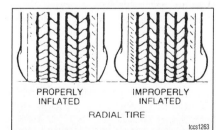

PROPERLY INFLATED
IMPROPERLY INFLATED
RADIAL TIRE

Fig. 143 Radial tires have a characteristic sidewall bulge; don't try to measure pressure by looking at the tire. Use a quality air pressure gauge

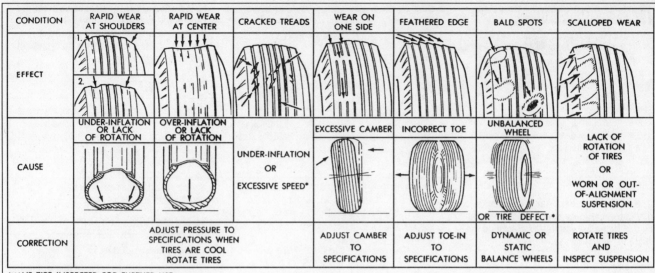

CONDITION	RAPID WEAR AT SHOULDERS	RAPID WEAR AT CENTER	CRACKED TREADS	WEAR ON ONE SIDE	FEATHERED EDGE	BALD SPOTS	SCALLOPED WEAR
EFFECT							
CAUSE	UNDER-INFLATION OR LACK OF ROTATION	OVER-INFLATION OR LACK OF ROTATION	UNDER-INFLATION OR EXCESSIVE SPEED*	EXCESSIVE CAMBER	INCORRECT TOE	UNBALANCED WHEEL OR TIRE DEFECT *	LACK OF ROTATION OF TIRES OR WORN OR OUT-OF-ALIGNMENT SUSPENSION.
CORRECTION		ADJUST PRESSURE TO SPECIFICATIONS WHEN TIRES ARE COOL ROTATE TIRES		ADJUST CAMBER TO SPECIFICATIONS	ADJUST TOE-IN TO SPECIFICATIONS	DYNAMIC OR STATIC BALANCE WHEELS	ROTATE TIRES AND INSPECT SUSPENSION

*HAVE TIRE INSPECTED FOR FURTHER USE.

tccs1267

Fig. 144 Common tire wear patterns and causes

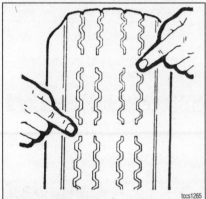

Fig. 145 Tread wear indicators will appear when the tire is worn

inflation, do not drive more than a mile before checking. A cold tire is generally one that has not been driven for more than three hours.

A plate or sticker is normally provided somewhere in the vehicle (door post, hood, tailgate or trunk lid) which shows the proper pressure for the tires. Never counteract excessive pressure build-up by bleeding off air pressure (letting some air out). This will cause the tire to run hotter and wear quicker.

✳✳ CAUTION

Never exceed the maximum tire pressure embossed on the tire! This is the pressure to be used when the tire is at maximum loading, but it is rarely the correct pressure for everyday driving. Consult the owner's manual or the tire pressure sticker for the correct tire pressure.

Once you've maintained the correct tire pressures for several weeks, you'll be familiar with the vehicle's braking and handling personality. Slight adjustments in tire pressures can fine-tune these characteristics,

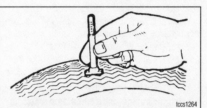

Fig. 146 Accurate tread depth indicators are inexpensive and handy

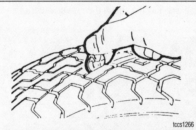

Fig. 147 A penny works well for a quick check of tread depth

but never change the cold pressure specification by more than 2 psi. A slightly softer tire pressure will give a softer ride but also yield lower fuel mileage. A slightly harder tire will give crisper dry road handling but can cause skidding on wet surfaces. Unless you're fully attuned to the vehicle, stick to the recommended inflation pressures.

All tires made since 1968 have built-in tread wear indicator bars that show up as 1/2 in. (13mm) wide smooth bands across the tire when 1/16 in. (1.5mm) of tread remains. The appearance of tread wear indicators means that the tires should be replaced. In fact, many states have laws prohibiting the use of tires with less than this amount of tread.

You can check your own tread depth with an inexpensive gauge or by using a Lincoln head penny. Slip the Lincoln penny (with Lincoln's head upside-

down) into several tread grooves. If you can see the top of Lincoln's head in 2 adjacent grooves, the tire has less than 1/16 in. (1.5mm) tread left and should be replaced. You can measure snow tires in the same manner by using the "tails" side of the Lincoln penny. If you can see the top of the Lincoln memorial, it's time to replace the snow tire(s).

CARE OF SPECIAL WHEELS

If you have invested money in magnesium, aluminum alloy or sport wheels, special precautions should be taken to make sure your investment is not wasted and that your special wheels look good for the life of the vehicle.

Special wheels are easily damaged and/or scratched. Occasionally check the rims for cracking, impact damage or air leaks. If any of these are found, replace the wheel. But in order to prevent this type of damage and the costly replacement of a special wheel, observe the following precautions:

• Use extra care not to damage the wheels during removal, installation, balancing, etc. After removal of the wheels from the vehicle, place them on a mat or other protective surface. If they are to be stored for any length of time, support them on strips of wood. Never store tires and wheels upright; the tread may develop flat spots.

• When driving, watch for hazards; it doesn't take much to crack a wheel.

• When washing, use a mild soap or non-abrasive dish detergent (keeping in mind that detergent tends to remove wax). Avoid cleansers with abrasives or the use of hard brushes. There are many cleaners and polishes for special wheels.

• If possible, remove the wheels during the winter. Salt and sand used for snow removal can severely damage the finish of a wheel.

• Make certain the recommended lug nut torque is never exceeded or the wheel may crack. Never use snow chains on special wheels; severe scratching will occur.

FLUIDS AND LUBRICANTS

Fluid Disposal

Used fluids such as engine oil, transaxle fluid, antifreeze and brake fluid are hazardous wastes and must be disposed of properly. Before draining any fluids, consult with your local authorities; in many areas, waste oil, antifreeze, etc. is being accepted as a part of recycling programs. A number of service stations and auto parts stores are also accepting waste fluids for recycling.

Be sure of the recycling center's policies before draining any fluids, as many will not accept different fluids that have been mixed together.

Fuel and Engine Oil Recommendations

ENGINE OIL

▶ See Figure 148

➡Mitsubishi recommends that SAE 5W-30 viscosity engine oil should be used for all climate conditions, however, SAE 10W-30 is acceptable for vehicles operated in moderate-to-hot climates.

Fig. 148 Look for the API oil identification label when choosing your engine oil

When adding oil to the crankcase or changing the oil or filter, it is important that oil of an equal quality to original equipment be used in your car. The use of inferior oils may void the warranty, damage your engine, or both.

The SAE (Society of Automotive Engineers) grade number of oil indicates the viscosity of the oil (its ability to lubricate at a given temperature). The lower the SAE number, the lighter the oil; the lower the viscosity, the easier it is to crank the engine in cold weather but the less the oil will lubricate and protect the engine in high temperatures. This number is marked on every oil container.

Oil viscosity's should be chosen from those oils recommended for the lowest anticipated temperatures during the oil change interval. Due to the need for an oil that embodies both good lubrication at high temperatures and easy cranking in cold weather, multi-grade oils have been developed. Basically, a multi-grade oil is thinner at low temperatures and thicker at high temperatures. For example, a 10W-40 oil (the W stands for winter) exhibits the characteristics of a 10 weight (SAE 10) oil when the car is first started and the oil is cold. Its lighter weight allows it to travel to the lubricating surfaces quicker and offer less resistance to starter motor cranking than, say, a straight 30 weight (SAE 30) oil. But after the engine reaches operating temperature, the 10W-40 oil begins acting like straight 40 weight (SAE 40) oil, its heavier weight providing greater lubrication with less chance of foaming than a straight 30 weight oil.

The API (American Petroleum Institute) designations, also found on the oil container, indicates the classification of engine oil used under certain given operating conditions. Only oils designated for use Service SJ heavy duty detergent should be used in your car. Oils of the SJ type perform may functions inside the engine besides their basic lubrication. Through a balanced system of metallic detergents and polymeric dispersants, the oil prevents high and low temperature deposits and also keeps sludge and dirt particles in suspension. Acids, particularly sulfuric acid, as well as other by-products of engine combustion are neutralized by the oil. If these acids are allowed to concentrate, they can cause corrosion and rapid wear of the internal engine parts.

❊❊ WARNING

Non-detergent motor oils or straight mineral oils should not be used in your engine.

Synthetic Oil

There are many excellent synthetic and fuel-efficient oils currently available that can provide better gas mileage, longer service life and, in some cases, better engine protection. These benefits do not come without a few hitches, however; the main one being the price of synthetic oil, which is significantly more expensive than conventional oil.

Synthetic oil is not for every car and every type of driving, so you should consider your engine's condition and your type of driving. Also, check your car's warranty conditions regarding the use of synthetic oils.

FUEL

All models equipped with a SOHC (Single Overhead Camshaft) engine are designed to operate using regular unleaded fuel with a minimum of 87 octane. All models equipped with a DOHC (Dual Overhead Camshaft) engine are designed to operate using regular unleaded fuel with a minimum of 91 octane. Mitsubishi warns that using gasoline with a lower octane rating can cause persistent and heavy knocking, and may cause internal engine damage.

If your vehicle is having problems with rough idle or hesitation when the engine is cold, it may be caused by low volatility fuel. If this occurs, try a different grade or brand of fuel.

OPERATION IN FOREIGN COUNTRIES

If you plan to drive your car outside the United States or Canada, there is a possibility that fuels will be too low in anti-knock quality and could produce engine damage. It is wise to consult with local authorities upon arrival in a foreign country to determine the best fuels available.

Engine

OIL LEVEL CHECK

▶ See Figures 149, 150, and 151

❊❊ CAUTION

The EPA warns that prolonged contact with used engine oil may cause a number of skin disorders, including cancer! You should make every effort to minimize your exposure to used engine oil. Protective gloves should be worn when changing the oil. Wash your hands and any other exposed skin areas as soon as possible after exposure to used engine oil. Soap and water, or waterless hand cleaner should be used.

The engine oil dipstick is typically located in the front of the engine near the exhaust manifold.

Fig. 150 Wipe the dipstick clean and reinsert it into the dipstick tube to get the correct oil level

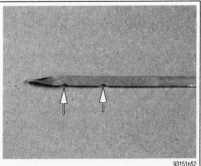

Fig. 151 The oil level should be between the marks/notches on the dipstick

Fig. 149 Grasp the oil level dipstick and pull upward to remove it from the dipstick tube

Engine oil level should be checked every time you put fuel in the vehicle or are under the hood performing other maintenance.

1. Park the vehicle on a level surface.

2. The engine may be either hot or cold when checking oil level. However, if it is hot, wait a few minutes after the engine has been turned **OFF** to allow the oil to drain back into the crankcase. If the engine is cold, do not start it before checking the oil level.

3. Open the hood and locate the engine oil dipstick. Pull the dipstick from its tube, wipe it clean, and reinsert it. Make sure the dipstick is fully inserted.

4. Pull the dipstick from its tube again. Holding it horizontally, read the oil level. The oil should be between the MIN and MAX marks or the notches on the dipstick. If the oil is below the MIN mark or lower notch, add oil of the proper viscosity through the capped opening of the valve cover.

5. Replace the dipstick, and check the level again after adding any oil. Be careful not to overfill the crankcase. Approximately one quart of oil will raise the level from the low mark to the high mark. Excess oil will generally be consumed at an accelerated rate even if no damage to the engine seals occurs.

OIL & FILTER CHANGE

▶ **See Figures 152 thru 163**

The oil and filter should be changed every 7,500 miles (12,000 km) under normal service and every 3,000 miles (5,000 km) under severe service.

✳✳ CAUTION

The EPA warns that prolonged contact with used engine oil may cause a number of skin disorders, including cancer! You should make every effort to minimize your exposure to used engine oil. Protective gloves should be worn when changing the oil. Wash your hands and any other exposed skin areas as soon as possible after exposure to used engine oil. Soap and water, or waterless hand cleaner should be used.

➡**The engine oil and oil filter should be changed at the recommended intervals on the Maintenance Chart. Though some manufacturers have at times recommended changing the filter only at every other oil change, Chilton recommends that you always change the filter with the oil. The benefit of fresh oil is quickly lost if the old filter is clogged and unable to do its job. Also, leaving the old filter in place leaves a significant amount of dirty oil in the system.**

The oil should be changed more frequently if the vehicle is being operated in a very dusty area. Before draining the oil, make sure that the engine is at operating temperature. Hot oil will hold more impurities in suspension and will flow better, allowing the removal of more oil and dirt.

It is a good idea to warm the engine oil first so it will flow better. This can be accomplished by 15–20

miles of highway driving. Fluid which is warmed to normal operating temperature will flow faster, drain more completely and remove more contaminants from the engine.

1. Raise and support the vehicle safely on jackstands. Make sure the oil drain plug is at the lowest point on the oil pan. If not, you may have to raise the vehicle slightly higher on one jackstand (side) than the other.

2. Before you crawl under the vehicle, take a look at where you will be working and gather all the necessary tools, such as a few wrenches or a ratchet and strip of sockets, the drain pan, some clean rags and, if the oil filter is more accessible from underneath the vehicle, you will also want to grab a bottle of oil, the new filter and a filter wrench at this time.

3. Position the drain pan beneath the oil pan drain plug. Keep in mind that the fast flowing oil, which will spill out as you pull the plug from the pan, will flow with enough force that it could miss the pan. Position the drain pan accordingly and be ready to move the pan more directly beneath the plug as the oil flow lessens to a trickle.

4. Loosen the drain plug with a wrench (or socket and driver), then carefully unscrew the plug with your fingers. Use a rag to shield your fingers from the heat. Push in on the plug as you unscrew it so you can feel when all of the screw threads are out of the hole (and so you will keep the oil from seeping past the threads until you are ready to remove the plug). You can then remove the plug quickly to avoid having hot oil run down your arm. This will also help assure that have the plug in your hand, not in the bottom of a pan of hot oil.

Fig. 152 Loosen the drain plug on the engine oil pan with a wrench. The drain plug's head is usually 17mm

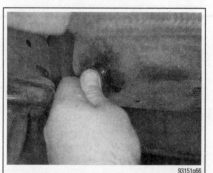

Fig. 153 When loosened sufficiently, slowly turn the drain plug by hand, keeping constant inward pressure on the plug to prevent oil from streaming out until you are ready

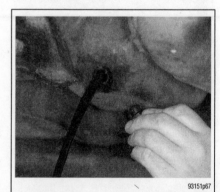

Fig. 154 When you are ready, carefully pull the drain plug out and to the side, out of the way of flowing oil

Fig. 155 Clean and inspect the threads on the oil pan

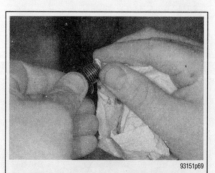

Fig. 156 Also inspect the drain plug threads before installing it back into the oil pan. Make sure the gasket on the drain plug is in place and does not require replacement

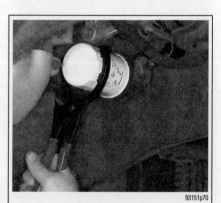

Fig. 157 A plier-type filter wrench is used here to loosen the filter

Fig. 158 When the filter is sufficiently loosened with the filter wrench, turn the filter by hand, but be careful, as oil will start to run out of the filter

Fig. 159 Once the oil filter is completely unthreaded, remove the filter from the engine

Fig. 160 Before installing a new oil filter, lightly coat the rubber gasket with clean oil

Fig. 161 Before installing a new oil filter, clean the gasket mounting surface of the oil filter housing and inspect the threads

Fig. 162 Loosen and remove the oil filler cap . . .

Fig. 163 . . . then insert a funnel, and pour oil directly into the engine

✳ CAUTION

Be careful of the oil; when at operating temperature, it is hot enough to cause a severe burn.

5. Allow the oil to drain until nothing but a few drops come out of the drain hole. Check the drain plug to make sure the threads and sealing surface are not damaged. Carefully thread the plug into position and tighten it snug, and give a slight additional turn. You don't want the plug to fall out (as you would quickly become stranded), but the pan threads are EASILY stripped from overtightening (and this can be time consuming and/or costly to fix).

6. To remove the filter, you may need an oil filter wrench since the filter may have been fitted too tightly and/or the heat from the engine may have made it even tighter. A filter wrench can be obtained at any auto parts store and is well-worth the investment. Loosen the filter with the filter wrench. With a rag wrapped around the filter, unscrew the filter from the boss on the side of the engine. Be careful of hot oil that will run down the side of the filter. Make sure that your drain pan is under the filter before you start to remove it from the engine; should some of the hot oil happen to get on you, there will be a place to dump the filter in a hurry and the filter will usually spill a good bit of dirty oil as it is removed.

7. Wipe the base of the mounting boss with a clean, dry cloth. When you install the new filter, smear a small amount of fresh oil on the gasket with your finger, just enough to coat the entire contact

surface. When you tighten the filter, rotate it about a quarter-turn after it contacts the mounting boss (or follow any instructions which are provided on the filter or parts box).

✳ WARNING

Operating the engine without the proper amount and type of engine oil will result in severe engine damage.

8. Remove the jackstands and carefully lower the vehicle, then IMMEDIATELY refill the engine crankcase with the proper amount of oil. DO NOT WAIT TO DO THIS because if you forget and someone tries to start the vehicle, severe engine damage will occur.

9. Refill the engine crankcase slowly, checking the level often. You may notice that it usually takes less than the amount of oil listed in the capacity chart to refill the crankcase. But, that is only until the engine is run and the oil filter is filled with oil. To make sure the proper level is obtained, run the engine to normal operating temperature, shut the engine **OFF**, allow the oil to drain back into the oil pan, and recheck the level. Top off the oil at this time to the fill mark.

➥**If the vehicle is not resting on level ground, the oil level reading on the dipstick may be slightly off. Be sure to check the level only when the vehicle is sitting level.**

10. Drain your used oil in a suitable container for recycling.

Manual Transaxle

FLUID RECOMMENDATIONS

For all vehicles with manual transaxles, use Hypoid gear oil SAE 75W-85W, or 75W-90W conforming to API specifications GL-4 or higher.

LEVEL CHECK

▶ **See Figures 164 and 165**

Inspect each component for leaking. Check the oil level by removing the filler plug. If the oil is contaminated, it is necessary to replace it with new oil. Check the oil level as follows:

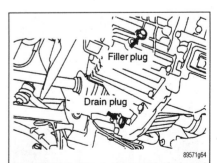

Fig. 164 Typical manual transaxle drain and filler plug location

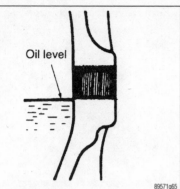

Fig. 165 Oil, when at the proper level, will reach the lower edge of the filler hole opening

1. Make sure the vehicle is parked on a level surface.
2. Remove the filler plug and make sure the oil level is up to the lower edge of the filler plug hole.
3. Check to be sure that the transaxle oil is not noticeably dirty and that it has a suitable viscosity.

DRAIN & REFILL

▶ **See Figures 166 and 167**

1. Make sure the vehicle is parked on a level surface.
2. Raise and safely support the vehicle. Place a suitable drain pan under the manual transaxle.
3. Remove the filler plug and the drain plug and allow the oil to drain completely.

Fig. 166 Use a box-end wrench to loosen the manual transaxle drain plug . . .

Fig. 167 . . . then withdraw the plug and drain the manual transaxle oil into a suitable container

4. Install the drain plug and tighten to 22 ft. lbs. (30 Nm).
5. Refill the transaxle to the proper level, as shown in the Capacities chart, with the appropriate fluid. The oil level should be at the bottom of the oil filler hole.
6. When the oil reaches the proper level, install the filler plug and tighten to 22 ft. lbs. (30 Nm).

Automatic Transaxle

FLUID RECOMMENDATIONS

Mitsubishi recommends the use of Mercon® automatic transmission fluid.

LEVEL CHECK

▶ **See Figures 168, 169, and 170**

The transaxle dipstick is located behind the air inlet hose, towards the firewall.
1. Park the vehicle on a level surface.
2. The transaxle should be at normal operating temperature when checking fluid level. To ensure the fluid is at normal operating temperature, drive the vehicle at least 10 miles.
3. With the selector lever in **P** and the parking brake applied, start the engine.
4. Open the hood and locate the transaxle fluid dipstick. Pull the dipstick from its tube, wipe it clean, and reinsert it. Make sure the dipstick is fully inserted.

Fig. 168 The automatic transaxle dipstick is typically located under the air cleaner inlet tube. Pull the dipstick up to remove it from the transaxle

Fig. 169 Wipe the dipstick clean and insert it into the transaxle again to get the correct fluid level reading

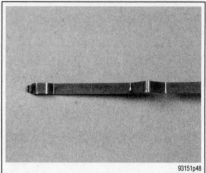

Fig. 170 The fluid level is OK if it is within the between the HOT and ADD areas on the dipstick. Do not overfill the transaxle or problems could occur

5. Pull the dipstick from its tube again. Holding it horizontally, read the fluid level. The fluid should be between the MIN and MAX mark. If the fluid is below the MIN mark, add fluid through the dipstick tube.
6. Insert the dipstick, and check the level again after adding any fluid. Be careful not to overfill the transaxle.

DRAIN & REFILL

▶ **See Figures 171 thru 177**

1. Raise and support the vehicle safely.
2. Place a suitable drain pan under the transaxle drain plug.
3. Remove the transaxle pan drain plug. Let the fluid completely drain out of the transaxle.
4. Install the drain plug and tighten it to 22–25 ft. lbs. (30–35 Nm).
5. If equipped, remove the drain plug on the differential of the transaxle.
6. Install the differential drain plug and tighten it to 22–25 ft. lbs. (30–35 Nm).
7. Remove the drain pan.
8. Lower the vehicle.
9. Fill the transaxle through the dipstick to the proper level.
10. Place the gear selector lever in **P** and start the engine. Run the engine at idle, engage the emergency brake and hold the brake pedal down. Move the gear selector lever through all transaxle ranges for approximately 5 minutes.
11. Return the selector lever to **P** and leave the engine running at idle.
12. Check the transaxle fluid level. The fluid level at normal operating temperature should read within the crosshatched area of the fluid level dipstick.
13. If the fluid level reads below the crosshatched area, adjust the level by adding fluid in small increments until the correct fluid level is obtained.

PAN & FILTER SERVICE

▶ **See Figures 178 thru 184**

The fluid should be changed according to the schedule in the Maintenance Intervals chart. If the car is normally used in severe service, such as stop and start driving, trailer towing, or the like, the interval should be halved. If the car is driven under especially nasty conditions, such as in heavy city traffic where the temperature normally reaches 90°F (32°C), or in very hilly or mountainous areas, or in police, taxi, or

Fig. 171 The transaxle drain plug is located on the bottom of the fluid pan. Typically the drain plug requires a 17mm wrench

Fig. 172 Carefully pull the transaxle drain plug out and to the side, out of the way of flowing transaxle oil

Fig. 173 The differential drain plug is located at the bottom of the transaxle, to the left of the fluid pan. Typically the drain plug requires a 17mm wrench

Fig. 174 Carefully pull the differential drain plug out and and to the side, out of the way of flowing transaxle oil

Fig. 175 A long, thin funnel is necessary to access the transaxle dipstick tube

Fig. 176 Place the funnel into the opening on the dipstick tube

Fig. 177 Pour the fluid directly into the funnel, periodically checking the fluid level to make sure you do not overfill the transaxle

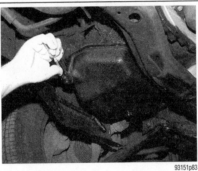

Fig. 178 Typically to remove the transaxle pan mounting bolts, a 10mm wrench is required. Remove the pan retaining bolts . . .

Fig. 179 . . . then carefully lower the fluid pan from the transaxle

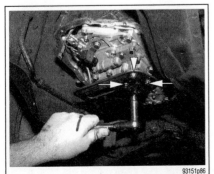

Fig. 180 Remove the four filter retaining bolts . . .

Fig. 181 . . . then remove the transaxle filter from the valve body

Fig. 182 Remove the transaxle pan gasket from the pan

Fig. 183 Thoroughly clean the mating surfaces of the pan and . . .

Fig. 184 . . . the transaxle case before installing the gasket and pan onto the case

delivery service, the fluid should be changed according to the severe service schedule.

The fluid must be hot before it is drained; a 20 minute drive should accomplish this.

1. Raise and safely support the vehicle.
2. Drain the fluid from the transaxle. See the procedure above.
3. Place a drain pan underneath the transaxle pan, then remove the pan attaching bolts.
4. If the pan is stuck on the transaxle, very carefully pry the pan loose on one corner. You can use a small prybar for this if you work CAREFULLY. Do not distort the pan flange, or score the mating surface of the transaxle case. You'll be very sorry later if you do.

➡**If the drained fluid is discolored (brown or black), thick, or smells burnt, serious transaxle troubles, probably due to overheating, should be suspected. Your car's transaxle should be inspected by a reliable transaxle specialist to determine the problem.**

5. Remove the pan and gasket.
6. Clean the pan with solvent and allow it to air dry. If you use a rag to wipe out the pan, you risk leaving bits of lint behind, which will clog the dinky hydraulic passages in the transaxle.
7. Remove the filter retaining bolts and remove the filter from the valve body.
To install:
8. Install a new filter, then install the retaining bolts and tighten them to 5 ft. lbs. (7 Nm).
9. Position the gasket on the pan, then install the pan. Tighten the bolts evenly and in rotation to 8–9 ft. lbs. (10–12 Nm.). Do not overtighten.
10. Lower the vehicle.

11. Add the recommended automatic transaxle fluid to the transaxle through the dipstick tube. You will need a long necked funnel, or a funnel and tube to do this. A quick check of the capacities chart later in this Section will reveal the capacity of the transaxle in your vehicle. On a first fill after removing the pan and filter, this number should be cut into a ⅓ and checked on the dipstick before refilling.
12. With the transaxle in **P**, put on the parking brake, block the front wheels, start the engine and let it idle. DO NOT RACE THE ENGINE. DO NOT MOVE THE LEVER THROUGH ITS RANGES.
13. With the lever in Park, check the fluid level. If it's OK, take the car out for a short drive, park on a level surface, and check the level again, as outlined earlier in this section. Add more fluid if necessary. Be careful not to overfill, which will cause foaming and fluid loss.

Transfer Case (AWD Galant Only)

FLUID RECOMMENDATIONS

When adding fluid or refilling the transfer case, use Hypoid gear oil SAE 75W-85W or 75W-90W conforming to API specifications GL-4 or higher.

LEVEL CHECK

▶ **See Figure 185**

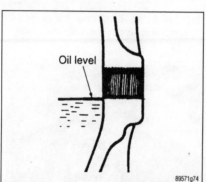

Fig. 185 Check to be sure the fluid reaches the bottom edge of the transfer case filler plug hole

Inspect each component for leaking. Check the oil level by removing the filler plug. If the oil is contaminated, it is necessary to replace it with new oil.

1. Park the vehicle on level surface.
2. Remove the filler plug and make sure the oil level reaches the lower edge of the filler plug hole.
3. Check to be sure that the oil is not noticeably dirty and that it has the proper viscosity.
4. If necessary, add oil through the filler hole until is runs out of the hole.

DRAIN & REFILL

▶ **See Figure 186**

1. Raise and safely support the vehicle, for access to the transfer case.
2. Place a suitable drain pan under the transfer case fluid drain plug.

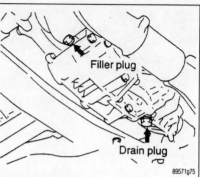

Fig. 186 Location of the transfer case filler and drain plugs

3. Remove the filler and the drain plug and allow the oil to drain into the drain pan.
4. After the fluid has drained completely, install the drain plug and tighten to 24 ft. lbs. (32 Nm).
5. Refill the transfer case to the proper level with Hypoid gear oil SAE 75W-85W/75W-90W conforming to API specifications GL-4 or higher. The oil level should reach the bottom edge of the oil filler hole.
6. Install the transfer case filler plug and tighten to 24 ft. lbs. (32 Nm).
7. Carefully lower the vehicle.

Rear Drive Axle (AWD Galant Only)

FLUID RECOMMENDATIONS

▶ **See Figure 187**

Since fluid viscosity range may vary depending on specific temperature range of operation, please refer

Lubricant	API classification GL-5 or higher	
Anticipated temperature range	Viscosity range	
Above −23°C (−10°F)	SAE 90 SAE 85W-90 SAE 80W-90	
−23°C to −34°C (−10°F to −30°F)	SAE 80W, SAE 80W-90	
Below −34°C (−30°F)	SAE 75W	

Fig. 187 Rear axle lubricant application chart

to the accompanying chart for the proper fluid for your vehicle.

LEVEL CHECK

1. Make sure the vehicle is parked on level ground.
2. Remove the oil fill plug to check the oil level.
3. The oil level is sufficient if it reaches the lower portion of the filler plug hole. If the fluid is low, add as required through the filler plug.

DRAIN & REFILL

▶ **See Figure 188**

1. Position the vehicle on a flat surface or raise and safely support the vehicle in a level position.
2. Place a suitable drain pan under the rear axle.

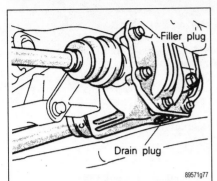

Fig. 188 Rear axle drain and filler plug locations—AWD models

3. Remove the filler and the drain plugs and allow the oil to drain completely into the pan.

4. Install the drain plug and tighten to 24 ft. lbs. (32 Nm).

5. Refill the rear axle with the proper type and amount of fluid. The level should reach the bottom of the oil filler hole.

6. Install the filler plug and tighten to 24 ft. lbs. (32 Nm).

7. If raised, carefully lower the vehicle.

Cooling System

FLUID RECOMMENDATIONS

A good quality ethylene glycol based or other aluminum compatible antifreeze is recommended for use in the vehicles covered by this manual. It is best to add a 50/50 mix of antifreeze and distilled water to avoid diluting the coolant in the system.

LEVEL CHECK

▶ **See Figure 189**

The coolant recovery tank is located in the engine compartment, typically on the fender well.

The proper coolant level is slightly above the **FULL COLD** marking on the recovery tank when the engine is cold. Top off the cooling system using the recovery tank and its marking as a guideline.

➡ **Never overfill the recovery tank.**

A coolant level that consistently drops is usually a sign of a small, hard to detect leak, although in the worst case it could be a sign of an internal engine

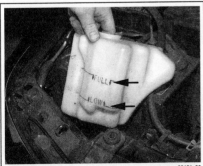

Fig. 189 The coolant level should be between the FULL and LOW levels on the coolant recovery tank

leak. In most cases, you will be able to trace the leak to a loose fitting or damaged hose.

Evaporating ethylene glycol antifreeze will have a sweet smell and leave small, white (salt-like) deposits, which can be helpful in tracing a leak.

✳ CAUTION

Never open, service or drain the radiator or cooling system when hot; serious burns can occur from the steam and hot coolant. Also, when draining engine coolant, keep in mind that cats and dogs are attracted to ethylene glycol antifreeze and could drink any that is left in an uncovered container or in puddles on the ground. This will prove fatal in sufficient quantities. Always drain coolant into a sealable container. Coolant should be reused unless it is contaminated or is several years old.

TESTING FOR LEAKS

▶ **See Figures 190 thru 195**

If a the fluid level of your cooling system is constantly low, the chances of a leak are probable. There are several ways to go about finding the source of your leak.

The first way should be a visual inspection. During the visual inspection, look around the entire engine area including the radiator and the heater hoses. The interior of the car should be inspected behind the

Fig. 190 A visual inspection for leaks will sometimes find a leak. This photo shows evidence of a leak at the upper radiator hose-to-thermostat housing junction

Fig. 192 This cooling system requires a threaded adapter for the recovery tank to allow the pressure tester to be connected

glove box and passenger side floorboard area, and check the carpet for any signs of moisture. The smartest way to go about finding a leak visually is to first inspect any and all joints in the system such as where the radiator hoses connect to the radiator and the engine. Another thing to look for is white crusty stains that are signs of a leak where the coolant has already dried.

If a visual inspection cannot find the cause of your leak, a pressure test is a logical and extremely helpful way to find a leak. A pressure tester will be needed to perform this and if one is not available they can be purchased or even rented at many auto parts stores. The pressure tester usually has a standard size radiator cap adapter on the pressure port, however, other adapters are available based on the size of the vehicle's radiator neck or recovery tank depending on where the pressure tester connects. when pressurizing the cooling system, make sure you do not exceed the pressure rating of the system, which can be found on the top of the radiator cap, however, if you have and aftermarket or replacement cap that does not have the rating on it, 16psi is a standard to use but some cars are higher. Overpressurizing the system can cause a rupture in a hose, or worse, in the radiator or heater core and possibly cause an injury or a burn if the coolant is hot. Overpressurizing is normally controlled by the radiator cap which has a vent valve in it which is opened when the system reaches it's maximum pressure rating. To pressure test the system:

➡ **The pressure test should be performed with the engine OFF.**

Fig. 191 Remove the recovery tank cap to allow the pressure tester to be connected to the system

Fig. 193 Thread the adapter onto the recovery tank

Fig. 194 Pump the cooling system with pressure, making sure not to overpressurize the system or damage can occur

Fig. 195 Watch the gauge on the system and observe the pressure reading

1. Remove the radiator or recovery tank cap.

2. Using the proper adapter, insert it onto the opening and connect the pressure tester,

3. Begin pressurizing the system by pumping the pressure tester and watching the gauge, when the maximum pressure is reached, stop.

4. Watch the gauge carefully and see if the pressure on the gauge drops, if it does, a leak is definitely present.

5. If the pressure stayed somewhat stable, visually inspect the system for leaks. If the pressure dropped, repressurize the system and then visually inspect the system.

6. If no signs of a leak are noticed visually, pressurize the system to the maximum pressure rating of the system and leave the pressure tester connected for about 30 minutes. Return after 30 minutes and verify the pressure on the gauge, if the pressure

dropped more than 20%, a leak definitely exists, if the pressure drop is less than 20%, the system is most likely okay.

Another way coolant is lost is by a internal engine leak, causing the oil to be contaminated or the coolant to be burned in the process of combustion and sent out the exhaust. To check for oil contamination, remove the dipstick and check the condition of the oil in the oil pan. If the oil is murky and has a white or beige "milkshake" look to it, the coolant is contaminating the oil through an internal leak and the engine must be torn down to find the leak. If the oil appears okay, the coolant can be burned and going out the tailpipe. A quick test for this is a cloud of white smoke appearing from the tailpipe, especially on start-up. On cold days, the white smoke will appear, this is due to condensation and the outside temperature, not a coolant leak. If the "smoke test"

does not verify the situation, removing the spark plugs one at a time and checking the electrodes for a green or white tint can verify an internal coolant leak and identify which cylinder(s) is the culprit and aiding your search for the cause of the leak. If the spark plugs appear okay, another method is to use a gas analyzer or emissions tester, or one of several hand-held tools that most professional shops possess. This tools are used to check the cooling system for the presence of Hydrocarbons (HC's) in the coolant.

DRAIN & REFILL

⬧ **See Figures 196 thru 205**

Ensure that the engine is completely cool prior to starting this service.

✳✳ CAUTION

Never open, service or drain the radiator or cooling system when hot; serious burns can occur from the steam and hot coolant. Also, when draining engine coolant, keep in mind that cats and dogs are attracted to ethylene glycol antifreeze and could drink any that is left in an uncovered container or in puddles on the ground. This will prove fatal in sufficient quantities. Always drain coolant into a sealable container. Coolant should be reused unless it is contaminated or is several years old.

1. Remove the recovery tank or radiator cap.

2. Raise and support the vehicle.

3. If necessary, remove the splash shield from under the front of the vehicle.

Fig. 196 The draincock is usually located at the bottom of the radiator

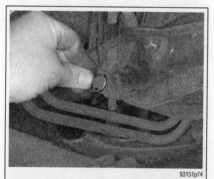

Fig. 197 Gently rotate the draincock counterclockwise to open the draincock . . .

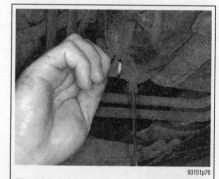

Fig. 198 . . . then allow the coolant to drain out of the radiator and cooling system

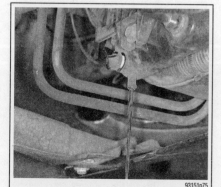

Fig. 199 Allow the fluid to drain until it stops and tighten the draincock hand tight

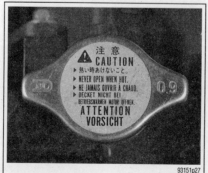

Fig. 200 Make sure to heed the caution on the radiator cap and NEVER open the cap when the engine is hot

Fig. 201 Grasp the radiator cap and rotate it counterclockwise . . .

Fig. 202 . . . to remove the cap from the radiator

Fig. 203 Pour the proper 50/50 coolant mixture into the radiator . . .

Fig. 204 . . . make sure to fill the coolant recovery tank to the proper level also

Fig. 205 Be sure the rubber gasket on the radiator cap has a tight seal

4. Place a drain pan of sufficient capacity under the radiator and open the petcock (drain) on the radiator.

➡Plastic petcocks easily bind. Before opening a plastic radiator petcock, spray it with some penetrating lubricant.

5. Drain the cooling system completely.
6. Close the petcock.
7. Remove the drain pan.
8. If necessary, install the splash shield under the vehicle.
9. Lower the vehicle.
10. Determine the capacity of the cooling system, then properly refill the system at the recovery tank and radiator with a 50/50 mixture of fresh coolant and distilled water until it reaches the **FULL COLD** line.
11. Leave the recovery tank or radiator cap off to aid in bleeding the system.
12. Start the engine and allow it to idle until the thermostat opens (the upper radiator hose will become hot). The coolant level should go down, this is normal as the system bleeds the air pockets out of the system.
13. Refill the system with coolant to the proper level.
14. Turn the engine **OFF** and check for leaks.

FLUSHING & CLEANING THE SYSTEM

1. Drain the cooling system completely as described earlier.
2. Close the petcock and fill the system with a cooling system flush (clean water may also be used, but is not as efficient).
3. Idle the engine until the upper radiator hose gets hot.

4. Allow the engine to cool completely and drain the system again.
5. Repeat this process until the drained water is clear and free of scale.
6. Flush the recovery tank with water and leave empty.

✳✳ CAUTION

Never open, service or drain the radiator or cooling system when hot; serious burns can occur from the steam and hot coolant. Also, when draining engine coolant, keep in mind that cats and dogs are attracted to ethylene glycol antifreeze and could drink any that is left in an uncovered container or in puddles on the ground. This will prove fatal in sufficient quantities. Always drain coolant into a sealable container. Coolant should be reused unless it is contaminated or is several years old.

7. Fill and bleed the cooling system as described earlier.

Brake Master Cylinder

The brake master cylinder reservoir is located under the hood, attached to the brake booster and firewall on the driver's side of the engine compartment.

FLUID RECOMMENDATIONS

✳✳ CAUTION

Brake fluid contains polyglycol ethers and polyglycols. Avoid contact with the eyes and wash your hands thoroughly after handling brake fluid. If you do get brake fluid in your eyes, flush your eyes with clean, running water for 15 minutes. If eye irritation persists, or if you have taken brake fluid internally, IMMEDIATELY seek medical assistance.

✳✳ WARNING

Clean, high quality brake fluid is essential to the safe and proper operation of the brake system. You should always buy the highest quality brake fluid that is available. If the brake fluid becomes contaminated, drain and flush the system, then refill the master cylinder with new fluid. Never reuse any brake

fluid. Any brake fluid that is removed from the system should be discarded. Also, do not allow any brake fluid to come in contact with a painted surface; it will damage the paint.

When adding fluid to the system, ONLY use fresh DOT 3 brake fluid from a sealed container. DOT 3 brake fluid will absorb moisture when it is exposed to the atmosphere, which will lower its boiling point. A container that has been opened once, closed and placed on a shelf will allow enough moisture to enter over time to contaminate the fluid within. If your brake fluid is contaminated with water, you could boil the brake fluid under hard braking conditions and lose all or some braking ability. Don't take the risk, buy fresh brake fluid whenever you must add to the system.

LEVEL CHECK

◆ **See Figures 206 thru 211**

✳✳ CAUTION

Brake fluid contains polyglycol ethers and polyglycols. Avoid contact with the eyes and wash your hands thoroughly after handling brake fluid. If you do get brake fluid in your eyes, flush your eyes with clean, running water for 15 minutes. If eye irritation persists, or if you have taken brake fluid internally, IMMEDIATELY seek medical assistance.

✳✳ WARNING

Be careful to avoid spilling any brake fluid on painted surfaces, because the paint coat will become discolored or damaged.

Observe the fluid level indicators on the master cylinder; the fluid level should be between the **MIN** and **MAX** lines.

Before removing the master cylinder reservoir cap, make sure the vehicle is resting on level ground and clean all dirt away from the top of the master cylinder. Unscrew the cap and fill the master cylinder until the level is between the **MIN** and **MAX** lines.

If the level of the brake fluid is less than half the volume of the reservoir, it is advised that you check the brake system for leaks. Leaks in a hydraulic brake system most commonly occur at the wheel cylinder and brake line junction points.

Fig. 206 The fluid level should be between the MAX and MIN lines; if the fluid level is low, be sure to check the brakes

Fig. 207 Wipe the master cylinder reservoir clean before opening the cap to ensure that no contamination enters the brake fluid

Fig. 208 Unscrew the master cylinder cap and remove it from the reservoir

Fig. 209 If the master cylinder cap gasket is swelled like such, it can be a sign of contamination. If the gasket is swelled . . .

Fig. 210 . . . make sure to push the gasket back to the normal position

Fig. 211 Carefully pour approved brake fluid from a fresh, sealed container directly into the reservoir

Clutch Master Cylinder

FLUID RECOMMENDATIONS

When adding or changing the fluid in the systems, use a quality brake fluid conforming to DOT 3 specifications from an sealed container. Never reuse old brake fluid.

LEVEL CHECK

▶ **See Figures 212, 213, and 214**

1. Wipe the clutch master cylinder reservoir cap and the surrounding area clean with a shop towel.

2. Inspect the fluid in the reservoir, making sure fluid is between the MAX and the MIN marks.

3. If required, remove the clutch master cylinder reservoir lid, then add fresh fluid to fill to the top full mark on the reservoir.

✳✳ WARNING

Be careful to avoid spilling any brake fluid on painted surfaces, because the paint coat will become discolored or damaged.

4. Reinstall the lid onto the clutch master cylinder.

5. If removed, install the air cleaner assembly.

Power Steering Pump

FLUID RECOMMENDATIONS

When adding or changing the power steering fluid, use Dexron®II ATF (Automatic Transmission Fluid).

LEVEL CHECK

▶ **See Figures 215, 216, 217, and 218**

Like all other general maintenance items, check every 3,000 miles (4,800 km) or once a month. Inspect the oil level in the reservoir by checking the po-

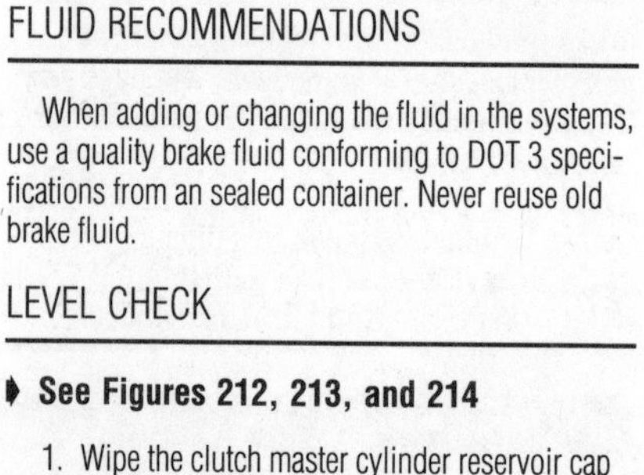

Fig. 212 The clutch master cylinder has MAX (A) and MIN (B) fill lines on the reservoir

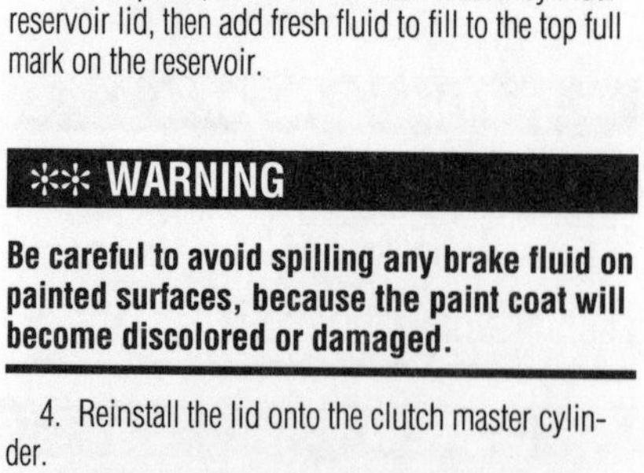

Fig. 213 Remove the clutch master cylinder lid by pulling it straight up and off the reservoir

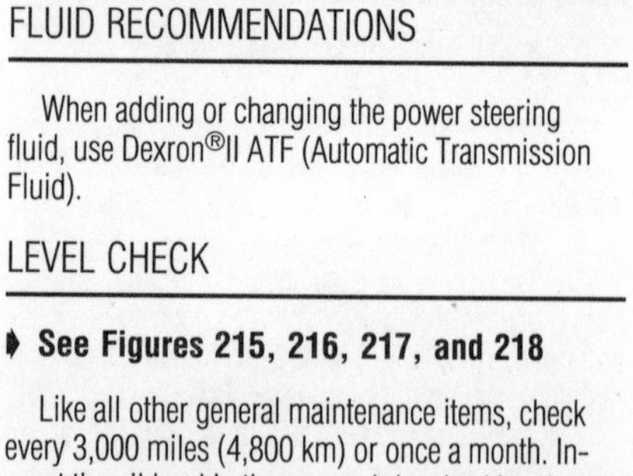

Fig. 214 If the fluid is low, add until it reaches the proper level on the side of the reservoir

Fig. 215 Twist the reservoir cap, then lift up on the integral cap/dipstick assembly

Fig. 216 Wipe the dipstick off, reinsert it into the reservoir and check the level

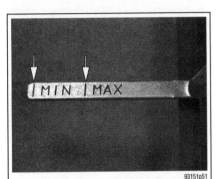

Fig. 217 Make sure the fluid lines are between the MIN and MAX lines on the dipstick

Fig. 218 If the power steering level is low, add fluid to the reservoir until the proper level is reached

sition of the fluid against the mark on the dipstick. Add fluid to the reservoir if the fluid does not reach the appropriate full line.

Chassis Greasing

On most models, the manufacturer doesn't install lubrication fittings on lube points on the steering linkage or suspension. However, if the lubrication point does have a grease fitting, lubricate with multi-purpose NLGI No. 2 (Lithium base) grease.

Body Lubrication and Maintenance

CAR WASHING

The car should be washed at regular intervals to remove dirt, dust, insects, and tar and other possibly damaging stains that can adhere to the paint and may cause damage. Proper exterior maintenance also helps in the resale value of the vehicle by maintaining its like-new appearance.

→It is particularly important to frequently wash the car in the wintertime to prevent corrosion, when salt has been used on the roads.

There are many precautions and tips on washing, including the following:
- When washing the car, do not expose it do direct sunlight.
- Use lukewarm water to soften the dirt before you wash with a sponge, and plenty of water, to avoid scratching.
- A detergent can be used to facilitate the softening of dirt and oil.

- A water-soluble grease solvent may be used in cases of sticky dirt. However, use a washplace with a drainage separator.
- Dry the car with a clean chamois and remember to clean the drain holes in the doors and rocker panels.
- If equipped with a power radio antenna, it must be dried after washing.

✳ CAUTION

Never clean the bumpers with gasoline or paint thinner, always use the same agent as used on the painted surfaces of the vehicle.

- Tar spots can be removed with tar remover or kerosene after the car has been washed.
- A stiff-bristle brush and lukewarm soapy water can be used to clean the wiper blades. Frequent cleaning improves visibility when using the wipers considerably.
- Wash off the dirt from the underside (wheel housings, fenders, etc.).
- In areas of high industrial fallout, more frequent washing is recommended.

✳ CAUTION

During high pressure washing the spray nozzle must never be closer to the vehicle than 13 inches (30cm). Do not spray into the locks.

- When washing or steam cleaning the engine, avoid spraying water or steam directly on the electrical components or near the distributor or ignition components. After cleaning the engine, the spark plug wells should be inspected for water and blown dry if necessary.

- Special car washing detergent is the best to use. Liquid dishwashing detergent can remove wax and leave the car's paint unprotected and in addition some liquid detergents contains abrasives which can scratch the paint.
- Bird droppings should be removed from the paintwork as soon as possible, otherwise the finish may be permanently stained.

✳ WARNING

When the car is driven immediately after being washed, apply the brakes several times in order to remove any moisture from the braking surfaces.

✳ WARNING

Engine cleaning agents should not be used when the engine is warm, a fire risk is present as most engine cleaning agents are highly flammable.

Automatic car washing is a simple and quick way to clean your car, but it is worth remembering that it is not as thorough as when you yourself clean the car. Keeping the underbody clean is vitally important, and some automatic washers do not contain equipment for washing the underside of the car.

When driving into an automatic was, make sure the following precautions have been taken:
- Make sure all windows are up, and no objects that you do not want to get wet are exposed.
- In some cases, rotating the side view mirrors in can help to avoid possible damage.
- If your car is equipped with a power antenna, lower it. If your vehicle has a solid mounted, non-power antenna, it is best to remove it, but this is not always practical. Inspect the surroundings to reduce the risk of possible damage, and check to see if the antenna can be manually lowered.

✳ WARNING

Most manufacturers do not recommend automatic car washing in the first six months due to the possibility of insufficient paint curing; a safe bet is to wait until after six months of ownership (when purchased new) to use an automatic car wash.

WAXING

→Before applying wax, the vehicle must be washed and thoroughly dried.

Waxing a vehicle can help to preserve the appearance of your vehicle. A wide range of polymer-based car waxes are available today. These waxes are easy to use and produce a long-lasting, high gloss finish that protects the body and paint against oxidation, road dirt, and fading.

Sometimes, waxing a neglected vehicle, or one that has sustained chemical or natural element damage (such as acid rain) require more than waxing, and a light-duty compound can be applied. For severely damaged surfaces, it is best to consult a professional to see what would be required to repair the damage.

Waxing procedures differ according to manufacturer, type, and ingredients, so it is best to consult the directions on the wax and/or polish purchased.

INTERIOR CLEANING

Upholstery

Fabric can usually be cleaned with soapy water or a proper detergent. For more difficult spots caused by oil, ice cream, soda, etc., use a fabric cleaner available at most parts stores. Be sure when purchasing the cleaner to read the label to ensure it is safe to use on your type of fabric. A safe method of testing the cleaner is to apply a small amount to an area usually unseen, such as under a seat, or other areas. Wait a while, perhaps even a day to check the spot for fading, discoloring, etc., as some cleaners will only cause these problems after they have dried.

Leather upholstery requires special care, it can be cleaned with a mild soap and a soft cloth. It is recommended that a special leather cleaner be used to clean but also treat the leather surfaces in your vehicle. Leather surfaces can age quickly and can crack if not properly taken care of, so it is vital that the leather surfaces be maintained.

Floor Mats and Carpet

The floor mats and carpet should be vacuumed or brushed regularly. They can be cleaned with a mild soap and water. Special cleaners are available to clean the carpeted surfaces of your vehicle, but take care in choosing them, and again it is best to test them in a usually unseen spot.

Dashboard, Console, Door Panels, Etc.

The dashboard, console, door panels, and other plastic, vinyl, or wood surfaces can be cleaned using a mild soap and water. Caution must be taken to keep water out of electronic accessories and controls to avoid shorts or ruining the components. Again special cleaners are available to clean these surfaces, as with other cleaners care must taken in purchasing and using such cleaners.

There are protectants available which can treat the various surfaces in your car giving them a "shiny new look", however some of these protectants can cause more harm than good in the long run. The shine that is placed on your dashboard attracts sunlight accelerating the aging, fading and possibly even cracking the surfaces. These protectants also attract more dust to stick to the surfaces they treat, increasing the cleaning you must do to maintain the appearance of your vehicle. Personal discretion is advised here.

Wheel Bearings

On most models covered by this manual, the wheel bearings used are sealed units and do not require routine maintenance. However on some Galant and Mirage models, the rear wheel bearing do require periodic repacking. For removal and installation instructions, please refer to Section 7 (for rear bearings) or Section 8 (for front bearings).

REPACKING

➡**Sodium based grease is not compatible with lithium based grease. Read the package labels and be careful not to mix the two types. If there is any doubt as to the type of grease used, completely clean the old grease from the bearing and hub before replacing.**

Before handling the bearings, there are a few things that you should remember to do and not to do.

DO the following:

- Remove all outside dirt from the housing before exposing the bearing.
- Treat a used bearing as gently as you would a new one.
- Work with clean tools in clean surroundings.
- Use clean, dry gloves, or at least clean, dry hands.
- Clean solvents and flushing fluids are a must.
- Use clean paper when laying out the bearings to dry.
- Protect disassembled bearings from rust and dirt. Cover them up.
- Use clean, lint-free rags to wipe the bearings.
- Keep the bearings in oil-proof paper when they are to be stored or are not in use.
- Clean the inside of the housing before replacing the bearing.

Do NOT do the following:

- Do not work in dirty surroundings.
- Do not use dirty, chipped or damaged tools.
- Do not work on wooden work benches or use wooden mallets.
- Do not handle bearings with dirty or moist hands.
- Do not use gasoline for cleaning. Use a safe solvent.
- Do not spin dry bearings with compressed air. They will be damaged.
- Do not use cotton waste or dirty cloths to wipe bearings.
- Do not scratch or nick bearing surfaces.
- Do not allow the bearing to come in contact with dirt or rust at any time.

The rear wheel bearings on some Galant and Mirage models require periodic maintenance. A premium high melting point grease meeting Grade Multipurpose Grease NLGI Grade #2 or equivalent must be used. Long fiber type greases must not be used. This service is recommended every 30,000 miles (48,000 km).

➡**For information on Wheel Bearing removal and installation, refer to Section 7 of this manual.**

1. Remove the wheel bearing.
2. Clean all parts in a non-flammable solvent and let them air dry.

➡**Only use lint-free rags to dry the bearings. Never spin-dry a bearing with compressed air, as this will damage the rollers.**

3. Check for excessive wear and damage. Replace the bearing as necessary.

➡**Packing wheel bearings with grease is best accomplished by using a wheel bearing packer (available at most automotive parts stores).**

4. If a wheel bearing packer is not available, the bearings may be packed by hand.
   a. Place a "healthy" glob of grease in the palm of one hand.
   b. Force the edge of the bearing into the grease so that the grease fills the space between the rollers and the bearing cage.
   c. Keep rotating the bearing while continuing to push the grease through.
   d. Continue until the grease is forced out the other side of the bearing.
5. Place the packed bearing on a clean surface and cover it until it is time for installation.
6. Install the wheel bearing.

TOWING THE VEHICLE

Front Wheel Drive Models

◆ **See Figures 219 and 220**

To prevent the bumper from deforming, these vehicles cannot be towed by a wrecker using sling-type equipment. If these vehicles require towing, use a wheel lift or flat bed equipment. It is recommended that the vehicle be towed from the front if a flat bed is not available.

Manual transaxle vehicles may be towed from the rear provided that the transaxle is in Neutral and the driveline has not been damaged. The steering wheel must be clamped in the straight-ahead position with a steering wheel clamping device designed for towing service use.

✳✳ CAUTION

Do not use the steering column lock to secure the front wheel position for towing.

Automatic transaxle vehicles may be towed on the front wheels at speeds not to exceed 30 mph (50 km/h) for a distance not to exceed 18 miles (30 km). If these limits can not be met, then the front wheels must be placed on a tow dolly.

All Wheel Drive Models

◆ **See Figure 221**

All Wheel Drive (AWD) vehicles should only be towed with all 4 wheels on the ground or lifted from the road surface. This means that the vehicle is to be towed either with flatbed equipment, with all wheels on dollies or flat towed. Damage to the viscous coupling may result if the vehicle is towed with only 2 wheels on the ground.

JUMP STARTING A DEAD BATTERY

◆ **See Figure 222**

Whenever a vehicle is jump started, precautions must be followed in order to prevent the possibility of

Fig. 219 Front towing position—FWD vehicles

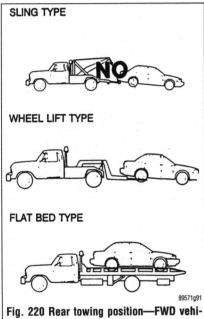

Fig. 220 Rear towing position—FWD vehicles

personal injury. Remember that batteries contain a small amount of explosive hydrogen gas which is a by-product of battery charging. Sparks should always be avoided when working around batteries, especially when attaching jumper cables. To minimize the possibility of accidental sparks, follow the procedure carefully.

※※ CAUTION

NEVER hook the batteries up in a series circuit or the entire electrical system will go up in smoke, including the starter!

Vehicles equipped with a diesel engine may utilize two 12 volt batteries. If so, the batteries are connected in a parallel circuit (positive terminal to positive terminal, negative terminal to negative terminal).

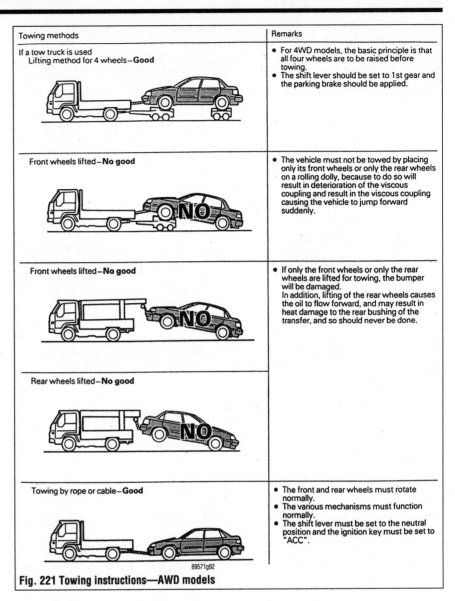

Towing methods	Remarks
If a tow truck is used Lifting method for 4 wheels—**Good**	• For 4WD models, the basic principle is that all four wheels are to be raised before towing. • The shift lever should be set to 1st gear and the parking brake should be applied.
Front wheels lifted—**No good**	• The vehicle must not be towed by placing only its front wheels or only the rear wheels on a rolling dolly, because to do so will result in deterioration of the viscous coupling and result in the viscous coupling causing the vehicle to jump forward suddenly.
Front wheels lifted—**No good**	• If only the front wheels or only the rear wheels are lifted for towing, the bumper will be damaged. In addition, lifting of the rear wheels causes the oil to flow forward, and may result in heat damage to the rear bushing of the transfer, and so should never be done.
Rear wheels lifted—**No good**	
Towing by rope or cable—**Good**	• The front and rear wheels must rotate normally. • The various mechanisms must function normally. • The shift lever must be set to the neutral position and the ignition key must be set to "ACC".

Fig. 221 Towing instructions—AWD models

Hooking the batteries up in parallel circuit increases battery cranking power without increasing total battery voltage output. Output remains at 12 volts. On the other hand, hooking two 12 volt batteries up in a series circuit (positive terminal to negative terminal, positive terminal to negative terminal) increases total battery output to 24 volts (12 volts plus 12 volts).

Jump Starting Precautions

• Be sure that both batteries are of the same voltage. Vehicles covered by this manual and most vehicles on the road today utilize a 12 volt charging system.

• Be sure that both batteries are of the same polarity (have the same terminal, in most cases NEGATIVE grounded).

• Be sure that the vehicles are not touching or a short could occur.

• On serviceable batteries, be sure the vent cap holes are not obstructed.

• Do not smoke or allow sparks anywhere near the batteries.

• In cold weather, make sure the battery electrolyte is not frozen. This can occur more readily in a battery that has been in a state of discharge.

• Do not allow electrolyte to contact your skin or clothing.

Jump Starting Procedure

1. Make sure that the voltages of the 2 batteries are the same. Most batteries and charging systems are of the 12 volt variety.

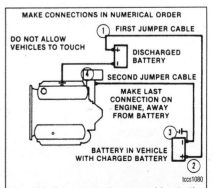

Fig. 222 Connect the jumper cables to the batteries and engine in the order shown

2. Pull the jumping vehicle (with the good battery) into a position so the jumper cables can reach the dead battery and that vehicle's engine. Make sure that the vehicles do NOT touch.

3. Place the transmissions/transaxles of both vehicles in **Neutral** (MT) or **P** (AT), as applicable, then firmly set their parking brakes.

➡**If necessary for safety reasons, the hazard lights on both vehicles may be operated throughout the entire procedure without significantly increasing the difficulty of jumping the dead battery.**

4. Turn all lights and accessories OFF on both vehicles. Make sure the ignition switches on both vehicles are turned to the **OFF** position.

5. Cover the battery cell caps with a rag, but do not cover the terminals.

6. Make sure the terminals on both batteries are clean and free of corrosion or proper electrical connection will be impeded. If necessary, clean the battery terminals before proceeding.

7. Identify the positive (+) and negative (−) terminals on both batteries.

8. Connect the first jumper cable to the positive (+) terminal of the dead battery, then connect the other end of that cable to the positive (+) terminal of the booster (good) battery.

9. Connect one end of the other jumper cable to the negative (−) terminal on the booster battery and the final cable clamp to an engine bolt head, alternator bracket or other solid, metallic point on the engine with the dead battery. Try to pick a ground on the engine that is positioned away from the battery in order to minimize the possibility of the 2 clamps touching should one loosen during the procedure. DO NOT connect this clamp to the negative (−) terminal of the bad battery.

✳✳ CAUTION

Be very careful to keep the jumper cables away from moving parts (cooling fan, belts, etc.) on both engines.

10. Check to make sure that the cables are routed away from any moving parts, then start the donor vehicle's engine. Run the engine at moderate speed for several minutes to allow the dead battery a chance to receive some initial charge.

11. With the donor vehicle's engine still running slightly above idle, try to start the vehicle with the dead battery. Crank the engine for no more than 10 seconds at a time and let the starter cool for at least 20 seconds between tries. If the vehicle does not start in 3 tries, it is likely that something else is also wrong or that the battery needs additional time to charge.

12. Once the vehicle is started, allow it to run at idle for a few seconds to make sure that it is operating properly.

13. Turn ON the headlights, heater blower and, if equipped, the rear defroster of both vehicles in order to reduce the severity of voltage spikes and subsequent risk of damage to the vehicles' electrical systems when the cables are disconnected. This step is especially important to any vehicle equipped with computer control modules.

14. Carefully disconnect the cables in the reverse order of connection. Start with the negative cable that is attached to the engine ground, then the negative

cable on the donor battery. Disconnect the positive cable from the donor battery and finally, disconnect the positive cable from the formerly dead battery. Be careful when disconnecting the cables from the positive terminals not to allow the alligator clips to touch any metal on either vehicle or a short and sparks will occur.

JACKING

▶ **See Figures 223, 224, 225, 226, and 227**

Your vehicle was supplied with a jack for emergency road repairs. This jack is fine for changing a flat tire or other short term procedures not requiring you to go beneath the vehicle. If it is used in an

Fig. 223 The easiest and most accessible place to place the jack when raising the rear of the vehicle is on the drip rail

Fig. 224 Place the jackstands also on the drip rail to support the rear of the vehicle once it is raised to the working position

Fig. 226 Place the jackstands also on the subframe to support the front of the vehicle once it is raised to the working position

emergency situation, carefully follow the instructions provided either with the jack or in your owner's manual. Do not attempt to use the jack on any portions of the vehicle other than specified by the vehicle manufacturer. Always block the diagonally opposite wheel when using a jack.

A more convenient way of jacking is the use of a garage or floor jack. You may use the floor jack to raise the front of the vehicle by placing it under the front subframe. The rear of the vehicle is most easily raised by using the lift points on the drip rail. All models are equipped with lift points located on the mid- crossmember in the front and a bracket located on the floorpan underneath the trunk.

Never place the jack under the radiator, engine or transaxle components. Severe and expensive damage will result when the jack is raised. Additionally, never jack under the floorpan or bodywork; the metal will deform.

Whenever you plan to work under the vehicle, you must support it on jackstands or ramps. Never use cinder blocks or stacks of wood to support the vehicle, even if you're only going to be under it for a few minutes. Never crawl under the vehicle when it is supported only by the tire-changing jack or other floor jack.

➡**Always position a block of wood or small rubber pad on top of the jack or jackstand to protect the lifting point's finish when lifting or supporting the vehicle.**

Small hydraulic, screw, or scissors jacks are satisfactory for raising the vehicle. Drive-on trestles or

Fig. 225 The most practical place to place the jack to raise the front of the vehicle is under the front subframe

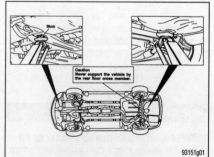

Fig. 227 All models covered by this manual are equipped with lift points on the mid-crossmember in the front and on a bracket on the floorpan in the rear

ramps are also a handy and safe way to both raise and support the vehicle. Be careful though, some ramps may be too steep to drive your vehicle onto without scraping the front bottom panels. Never support the vehicle on any suspension member (unless specifically instructed to do so by a repair manual) or by an underbody panel.

Jacking Precautions

The following safety points cannot be overemphasized:

• Always block the opposite wheel or wheels to keep the vehicle from rolling off the jack.

• When raising the front of the vehicle, firmly apply the parking brake.

• When the drive wheels are to remain on the ground, leave the vehicle in gear to help prevent it from rolling.

• Always use jackstands to support the vehicle when you are working underneath. Place the stands beneath the vehicle's jacking brackets. Before climbing underneath, rock the vehicle a bit to make sure it is firmly supported.

SCHEDULED MAINTENANCE INTERVALS
(MITSUBISHI DIAMANTE, GALANT, & MIRAGE)

TO BE SERVICED	TYPE OF SERVICE	VEHICLE MILEAGE INTERVAL (x1000)												
		7.5	15	22.5	30	37.5	45	52.5	60	67.5	75	82.5	90	97.5
Engine oil & filter	R	✓	✓	✓	✓	✓	✓	✓	✓	✓	✓	✓	✓	✓
Automatic transaxle fluid & filter	S/I		✓		✓		✓		✓		✓		✓	
Brake hoses	S/I		✓		✓		✓		✓		✓		✓	
Disc brake pads	S/I		✓		✓		✓		✓		✓		✓	
Driveshaft boots	S/I		✓		✓		✓		✓		✓		✓	
Valve clearance (Mirage)	S/I		✓		✓		✓		✓		✓		✓	
Air cleaner element	R				✓				✓				✓	
Engine coolant	R				✓				✓				✓	
Spark plugs (except Diamante w/platinum tip)	R				✓				✓				✓	
Spark plugs (Diamante w/platinum tip)	R								✓					
Ball joints & steering linkage seals	S/I				✓				✓				✓	
Drive belt(s)	S/I				✓				✓				✓	
Exhaust system	S/I				✓				✓				✓	
Fuel hoses	S/I				✓				✓				✓	
Manual transaxle oil (Mirage)	S/I				✓				✓				✓	
Manual transaxle oil (including transfer)	S/I				✓				✓				✓	
Manual transaxle oil (Galant)	S/I				✓				✓				✓	
Rear axle oil	S/I				✓				✓				✓	
Rear drum brake linings & rear wheel cylinders (Galant & Mirage)	S/I				✓				✓				✓	
Ignition cables	R								✓					
Timing belt(s)	R								✓					
Distributor cap & rotor	S/I								✓					
EVAP system (except canister)	S/I								✓					
Fuel system (tank, pipe line, connection & fuel tank filler tube cap)	S/I								✓					

R - Replace   S/I - Service or Inspect

FREQUENT OPERATION MAINTENANCE (SEVERE SERVICE)

If a vehicle is operated under any of the following conditions it is considered severe service:

- Extremely dusty areas.

- 50% or more of the vehicle operation is in 32°C (90°F) or higher temperatures, or constant operation in temperatures below 0°C (32°F).

- Prolonged idling (vehicle operation in stop and go traffic).

- Frequent short running periods (engine does not warm to normal operating temperatures).

- Police, taxi, delivery usage or trailer towing usage.

Oil & oil filter change - change every 3000 miles.

Disc brake pads - service or inspect ever 6000 miles.

Air filter element - service or inspect every 15,000 miles.

Automatic transaxle fluid & filter - replace every 15,000 miles.

Rear drum brake linings & rear wheel cylinders (Galant & Mirage).

Spark plugs (except Diamante w/platinum tip) - replace every 15,000 miles.

Manual transaxle oil (including transfer) (Galant & Mirage) - replace every 30,000 miles.

93151c09

CAPACITIES

Year	Model	Engine Displacement Liters (cc)	Engine ID/VIN	Engine Oil with Filter (qts.)	Transmission (qts.) Manual	Transmission (qts.) Auto.	Transfer Case (qts.)	Drive Axle Front (qts.)	Drive Axle Rear (qts.)	Fuel Tank (gal.)	Cooling System (qts.)
1990	Mirage	1.5 (1468)	4G15/A	3.4	1.8	6.5	—	—	—	13.2	5.3
	Galant	2.0 (1997)	4G63/V	4.1	1.9	6.4	—	—	—	15.9	7.6
	Galant	2.0 (1997)	4G63/R	4.6	2.4	6.4	—	—	—	15.9	7.6
1991	Mirage	1.5 (1468)	4G15/A	3.4	1.8	6.5	—	—	—	13.2	5.3
	Mirage	1.6 (1595)	4G61/Y	4.6	1.9	6.5	—	—	—	13.2	5.3
	Galant	2.0 (1997)	4G63/V	4.1	1.9	6.4	—	—	—	15.9	7.6
	Galant	2.0 (1997)	4G63/R	4.6	2.4	6.4	—	—	—	15.9	7.6
	Galant	2.0 (1997)	4G63/U	4.6	2.4	6.9	—	—	0.74	15.9	7.6
1992	Mirage	1.5 (1468)	4G15/A	3.4	1.8	6.5	—	—	—	13.2	5.3
	Mirage	1.6 (1595)	4G61/Y	4.6	1.9	6.5	—	—	—	13.2	5.3
	Galant	2.0 (1997)	4G63/V	4.1	1.9	6.4	—	—	—	15.9	7.6
	Galant	2.0 (1997)	4G63/R	4.6	2.4	6.4	—	—	—	15.9	7.6
	Galant	2.0 (1997)	4G63/U	4.6	2.4	6.9	—	—	0.74	15.9	7.6
	Diamante	3.0 (2972)	6G72/H	4.5	—	7.9	—	—	—	19.0	8.5
	Diamante	3.0 (2972)	6G72/J	4.5	—	7.9	—	—	—	19.0	8.5
1993	Mirage	1.5 (1468)	4G15/A	3.5	2.2	6.3	—	—	—	13.2	5.3
	Mirage	1.8 (1834)	4G93/C	4.0	2.3	6.3	—	—	—	13.2	6.3
	Galant	2.0 (1997)	4G63/V	4.1	1.9	6.4	—	—	—	15.9	7.6
	Galant	2.0 (1997)	4G63/R	4.6	2.4	6.4	—	—	—	15.9	7.6
	Diamante	3.0 (2972)	6G72/H	4.5	—	7.9	—	—	—	19.0	8.5
	Diamante	3.0 (2972)	6G72/J	4.5	—	7.9	—	—	—	19.0	8.5
1994	Mirage	1.5 (1468)	4G15/A	3.5	2.2	6.3	—	—	—	13.2	5.3
	Mirage	1.8 (1834)	4G93/C	4.0	2.3	6.3	—	—	—	13.2	6.3
	Galant	2.4 (2350)	4G64/G	4.5	2.2	6.3	—	—	—	16.9	7.4
	Galant	2.4 (2350)	4G64/L	4.5	2.2	7.9	—	—	—	16.9	7.4
	Diamante	3.0 (2972)	6G72/H	4.5	—	7.9	—	—	—	19.0	8.5
	Diamante	3.0 (2972)	6G72/J	4.5	—	7.9	—	—	—	19.0	8.5
1995	Mirage	1.5 (1468)	4G15/A	3.5	2.2	6.3	—	—	—	13.2	5.3
	Mirage	1.8 (1834)	4G93/C	4.0	2.3	6.3	—	—	—	13.2	6.3
	Galant	2.4 (2350)	4G64/G	4.5	2.2	6.3	—	—	—	16.9	7.4
	Galant	2.4 (2350)	4G64/L	4.5	2.2	7.9	—	—	—	16.9	7.4
	Mirage	1.8 (1834)	4G93/C	4.0	2.3	6.3	—	—	—	13.2	6.3
	Galant	2.4 (2350)	4G64/G	4.5	2.2	6.3	—	—	—	16.9	7.4
	Galant	2.4 (2350)	4G64/L	4.5	2.2	7.9	—	—	—	16.9	7.4
	Diamante	3.0 (2972)	6G72/H	4.5	—	7.9	—	—	—	19.0	8.5
	Diamante	3.0 (2972)	6G72/J	4.5	—	7.9	—	—	—	19.0	8.5
1997	Mirage	1.5 (1468)	4G15/A	3.5	2.2	8.2	—	—	—	13.2	5.3
	Mirage	1.8 (1834)	4G93/C	4.0	2.3	8.2	—	—	—	13.2	6.3
	Galant	2.4 (2350)	4G64/G	4.5	2.2	6.0	—	—	—	16.9	7.4
	Diamante	3.5 (3497)	6G74/P	4.5	—	9.0	—	—	—	18.7	10.0
1998	Mirage	1.5 (1468)	4G15/A	3.5	2.2	8.2	—	—	—	13.2	5.3
	Mirage	1.8 (1834)	4G93/C	4.0	2.3	8.2	—	—	—	13.2	6.3
	Galant	2.4 (2350)	4G64/G	4.5	2.3	6.3	—	—	—	16.9	7.4
	Diamante	3.5 (3497)	6G74/P	4.5	—	9.0	—	—	—	18.7	10.0
1999	Mirage	1.5 (1468)	4G15/A	3.5	2.2	8.2	—	—	—	13.2	5.3
	Mirage	1.8 (1834)	4G93/C	4.0	2.3	8.2	—	—	—	13.2	6.3
	Galant	2.4 (2350)	4G64/G	4.5	2.3	8.2	—	—	—	16.3	7.4
	Galant	3.0 (2972)	6G72/L	4.5	2.3	9.0	—	—	—	16.3	7.4
	Diamante	3.5 (3497)	6G74/P	4.5	—	9.0	—	—	—	18.7	10.0
2000	Mirage	1.5 (1468)	4G15/A	3.5	2.2	8.2	—	—	—	13.2	5.3
	Mirage	1.8 (1834)	4G93/C	4.0	2.3	8.2	—	—	—	13.2	6.3
	Galant	2.4 (2350)	4G64/G	4.5	2.3	8.2	—	—	—	16.3	7.4
	Galant	3.0 (2972)	6G72/L	4.5	2.3	9.0	—	—	—	16.3	7.4
	Diamante	3.5 (3497)	6G74/P	4.5	—	9.0	—	—	—	18.7	10.0

NOTE: All capacities are approximate. Add fluid gradually and ensure a proper fluid level is obtained.

93151c07

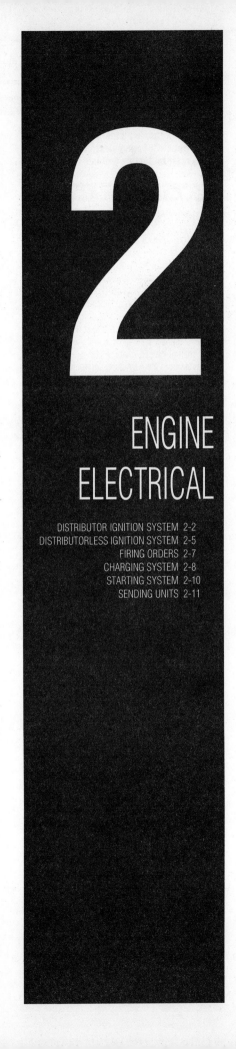

2

ENGINE
ELECTRICAL

DISTRIBUTOR IGNITION SYSTEM

➡ For information on understanding electricity and troubleshooting electrical circuits, please refer to Section 6 of this manual.

General Information

The ignition system on the 1.5L, 1993–96 1.8L, 2.0L SOHC, 1994–98 2.4L SOHC, 3.0L SOHC, and 3.5L engines uses a pointless type distributor, whose advance mechanism is controlled by the Engine Control Unit (ECU). On the 1.5L, 1.8L, 2.4L and 3.5L engines, the distributor houses a built in ignition coil and ignition power transistor. The 2.0L SOHC and 3.0L SOHC engines utilize a separate coil and transistor assembly.

When the ignition switch is turned **ON**, battery voltage is applied to the ignition coil primary winding. As the shaft of the distributor rotates, signals are transmitted from the powertrain control module to the ignition power transistor. These signals activate the power transistor to cause ignition coil primary winding current flow from the ignition coil negative terminal through the power transistor to ground repeatedly. This interruption induces high voltage in the ignition coil secondary windings, which is diverted through the distributor, spark plug cable and spark plug to ground, thus causing ignition in each cylinder.

Diagnosis and Testing

SECONDARY SPARK TEST

♦ See Figures 1 thru 6

The best way to perform this procedure is to use a spark tester (available at most automotive parts stores). Three types of spark testers are commonly available. The Neon Bulb type is connected to the spark plug wire and flashes with each ignition pulse. The Air Gap type must be adjusted to the individual spark plug gap specified for the engine. The last type of spark plug tester looks like a spark plug with a grounding clip on the side, but there is no side electrode for the spark to jump to. The last two types of testers allows the user to not only detect the presence of spark, but also the intensity (orange/yellow is weak, blue is strong).

1. Disconnect a spark plug wire at the spark plug end.
2. Connect the plug wire to the spark tester and ground the tester to an appropriate location on the engine.
3. Crank the engine and check for spark at the tester.
4. If spark exists at the tester, the ignition system is functioning properly.
5. If spark does not exist at the spark plug wire, perform diagnosis of the ignition system using individual component diagnosis procedures.

CYLINDER DROP TEST

♦ See Figures 7, 8, and 9

The cylinder drop test is performed when an engine misfire is evident. This test helps determine which cylinder is not contributing the proper power. The easiest way to perform this test is to remove the plug wires one at a time from the cylinders with the engine running.

Fig. 1 This spark tester looks just like a spark plug, attach the clip to ground and crank the engine to check for spark

Fig. 3 Attach the clip to ground and crank the engine to check for spark

Fig. 5 A tool used by many professionals to check the secondary ignition pattern is an oscilloscope, similar to this one from UEI

1. Place the transaxle in **P**, engage the emergency brake, and start the engine and let it idle.
2. Using a spark plug wire removing tool, preferably the plier type, carefully remove the boot from one of the cylinders.

✳✳ WARNING

Make sure your body is free from touching any part of the car which is metal. The secondary voltage in the ignition system is high

Fig. 2 This spark tester has an adjustable air-gap for measuring spark strength and testing different voltage ignition systems

Fig. 4 This spark tester is the easiest to use just place it on a plug wire and the spark voltage is detected and the bulb on the top will flash with each pulse

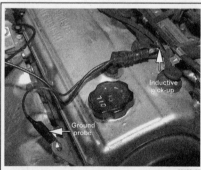
Fig. 6 The setup of the oscilloscope is quite easy, just connect the ground lead and place the inductive pick-up on one of the plug wires

and although it cannot kill you, it will shock you and it does hurt.

3. The engine will sputter, run worse, and possibly nearly stall. If this happens reinstall the plug wire and move to the next cylinder. If the engine runs no differently, or the difference is minimal, shut the engine off and inspect the spark plug wire, spark plug, and if necessary, perform component diagnostics as covered in this section. Perform the test on all cylinders to verify the which cylinders are suspect.

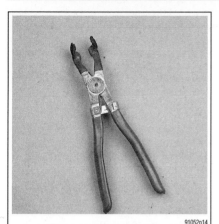

Fig. 7 These pliers are insulated and help protect the user from shock as well as the plug wires from being damaged

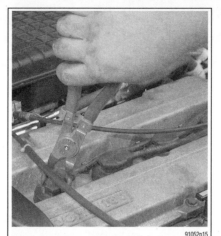

Fig. 8 To perform the cylinder drop test, remove one wire at a time and . . .

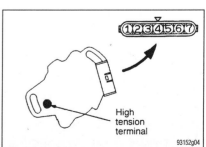

Fig. 9 . . . note the idle speed and idle characteristics of the engine. The cylinder(s) with the least drop is the non-contributing cylinder(s)

Adjustments

There are no adjustments to the distributor ignition system other than the ignition timing adjustment. Refer to section 1 for ignition timing adjustment.

Ignition Coil

TESTING

1.5L, 1.8L, 2.4L, and 3.5L Engines

▶ **See Figures 10, 11, and 12**

➡**The ignition coil is an integral part of the distributor.**

1. Measure the resistance of the primary ignition coil as follows:

a. Unplug the electrical connector at the distributor. Using an ohmmeter, measure the resistance between the two terminals of the distributor, **NOT THE WIRE HARNESS**, except for the 3.5L engine, in which you test across terminals **1** and **2** of the distributor.

b. Measure the resistance and compare to the desired specifications of:
- 0.9–1.2 ohms on the 1.5L, 1.8L, and 2.4L engines
- 0.5–0.7 ohms on the 3.5L engine

c. If the actual reading differs from the desired specification, replace the ignition coil.

d. If the measured value is within standard allowance, there are no broken wires or short circuits.

2. Measure the resistance of the secondary ignition coil as follows:

a. Insert one of the test leads into the secondary ignition coil terminal on top of the distributor cap.

b. Touch the second test lead to terminal **1** or terminal **2** of the distributor connector.

c. Measure the resistance and compare to the desired specifications of:
- 20–29 kilo-ohms on the 1.5L, 1.8L, and 2.4L engines
- 9–13 kilo-ohms on the 3.5L engine

d. If the measured value is within standard allowance, there are no broken wires or short circuits.

e. If the actual reading differs from the desired specification, replace the ignition coil!.

2.0L SOHC and 3.0L SOHC Engines

▶ **See Figure 13**

1. Measure the resistance of the primary ignition coil as follows:

a. Unplug the electrical connector at the coil. Using an ohmmeter, measure the resistance between the two terminals of the coil, **NOT THE WIRE HARNESS**.

b. Measure the resistance and compare to the desired specifications of:
- 0.9–1.2 ohms on the 2.0L SOHC engine
- 0.72–0.88 ohms on the 3.0L SOHC engine

c. If the actual reading differs from the desired specification, replace the ignition coil.

d. If the measured value is within standard allowance, there are no broken wires or short circuits.

2. Measure the resistance of the secondary ignition coil as follows:

a. Insert one of the test leads into the secondary ignition coil terminal on top of the distributor cap.

b. Touch the second test lead to terminal **1** or terminal **2** of the distributor connector.

c. Measure the resistance and compare to the desired specifications of:
- 20–29 kilo-ohms on the 2.0L SOHC engine
- 10.29–13.92 kilo-ohms on the 3.0L SOHC engine

d. If the measured value is within standard allowance, there are no broken wires or short circuits.

e. If the actual reading differs from the desired specification, replace the ignition coil!.

REMOVAL & INSTALLATION

1.5L, 1.8L, 2.4L, and 3.5L Engines

➡**The ignition coil is an integral part of the distributor.**

2.0L SOHC and 3.0L SOHC Engines

▶ **See Figure 14**

1. Disconnect the negative battery cable.
2. Remove the coil wire from the ignition coil by gripping the boot and not the cable.
3. Detach the electrical connectors for the coil.

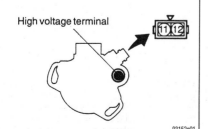

Fig. 10 Distributor connector pins and location—1.5L and 1.8L engines

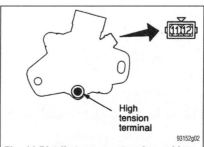

Fig. 11 Distributor connector pins and location—2.4L SOHC engine

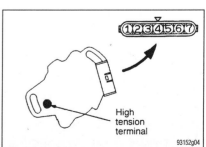

Fig. 12 Distributor connector pins and location—3.5L engine

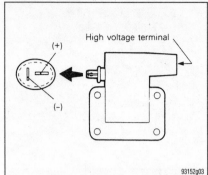

Fig. 13 Distributor connector pins and location—3.0L SOHC engine

4. Remove the retaining screws and coil from engine.

5. Installation is the reverse of the removal procedure.

Power Transistor (Ignition Module)

REMOVAL & INSTALLATION

1.5L, 1.8L, 2.4L, and 3.5L Engines

The power transistor (ignition module) is an integral part of the distributor.

2.0L SOHC and 3.0L SOHC Engines

▶ **See Figure 14**

1. Disconnect the negative battery cable.
2. Detach the electrical connectors for the power transistor.
3. Remove the retaining screws and power transistor from engine.
4. Installation is the reverse of the removal procedure.

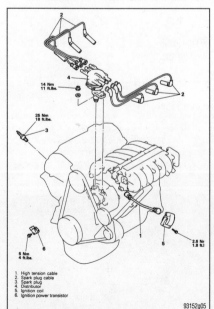

Fig. 14 Ignition system component locations—3.0L SOHC engine

Distributor

REMOVAL & INSTALLATION

▶ **See Figures 14, 15, 16, 17, and 18**

Before removing the distributor, position No. 1 cylinder at Top Dead Center (TDC) on the compression stroke and align the timing marks.

1. Disconnect the negative battery cable.
2. Remove the ignition wire cover, if equipped.
3. Detach the distributor harness connector.
4. Remove the distributor cap with all ignition wires still connected. Remove the coil wire, if necessary.
5. Matchmark the rotor to the distributor housing and the distributor housing to the engine.
6. Remove the hold-down nut.
7. Carefully remove the distributor from the engine.

INSTALLATION

▶ **See Figures 19 and 20**

Timing Not Disturbed

1. Install a new distributor housing O-ring and lubricate with clean oil.

Fig. 15 Detach the connectors from the distributor

Fig. 17 Remove the distributor hold-down nuts . . .

2. Install the distributor in the engine so the rotor is aligned with the matchmark on the housing and the housing is aligned with the matchmark on the engine. Be sure the distributor is fully seated and the distributor shaft is fully engaged.

3. Install the hold-down nut.
4. Attach the distributor harness connectors.
5. Install the distributor cap.
6. Connect the negative battery cable.
7. Adjust the ignition timing and tighten the hold-down nut to 8 ft. lbs. (11 Nm).

Timing Disturbed

1. Install a new distributor housing O-ring and lubricate with clean oil.

2. Position the engine so the No. 1 piston is at Top Dead Center (TDC) of its compression stroke and the mark on the vibration damper is aligned with **0** on the timing indicator.

3. Align the distributor housing and gear mating marks. Install the distributor in the engine so the slot or groove of the distributor's installation flange aligns with the distributor installation stud in the engine block. Be sure the distributor is fully seated. Inspect alignment of the distributor rotor making sure the rotor is aligned with the position of the No. 1 ignition wire in the distributor cap.

Fig. 16 Remove the bolt holding the wire harness and capacitor, then move the harness and capacitor to the side

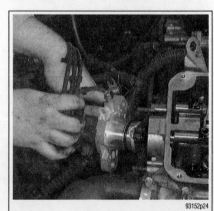

Fig. 18 . . . then slide the distributor from the engine

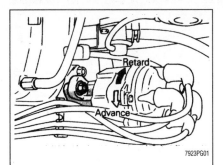

Fig. 19 Adjusting the distributor—1.5L engine shown, others similar

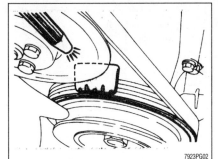

Fig. 20 Checking the ignition timing—1.5L engine, others similar

4. Install the hold-down nut.
5. Attach the distributor harness connectors.
6. Install the distributor cap.
7. Connect the negative battery cable.
8. Adjust the ignition timing and tighten the hold-down nut to 8 ft. lbs. (11 Nm).

Crankshaft and Camshaft Position Sensors

For procedures on the position sensors, please refer to Section 4 in this manual.

DISTRIBUTORLESS IGNITION SYSTEM

General Information

The ignition system found on the 1.6L, 1997–00 1.8L, 2.0L DOHC, 1999–00 2.4L SOHC, 2.4L DOHC, and 3.0L DOHC engines is a distributorless type. The advance of this system, like the distributor type ignition, is controlled by the Engine Control Unit (ECU) or Powertrain Control Module (PCM). The distributorless ignition system contains a crank angle/position sensor which detects the crank angle or position to each cylinder and converts this data into pulse signals. These signals are sent to the ECU/PCM, which calculates the engine rpm and regulates the fuel injection and ignition timing accordingly. The system also contains a top dead center sensor which detects the top dead center position of each cylinder and converts this data into pulse signals. These signals are then sent to the ECU/PCM, which calculates the sequence of fuel injection and engine rpm.

When the ignition switch is turned **ON**, battery voltage is applied to the ignition coil primary winding. As the crank angle sensor shaft rotates, ignition signals are transmitted from the multi port injection control unit to the power transistor. These signals activate the power transistor to cause ignition coil primary winding current to flow from the ignition coil negative terminal through the power transistor to ground or be interrupted, repeatedly. This action induces high voltage in the secondary winding of the ignition coil. From the ignition coil, the secondary winding current produced flows through the spark plug to ground, thus causing ignition in each cylinder.

Diagnosis and Testing

Refer to Diagnosis and Testing under Distributor Ignition in this section.

Adjustments

There are no adjustments to the distributorless ignition system other than the ignition timing adjustment. Refer to section 1 for ignition timing adjustment.

Ignition Coil(s)

TESTING

1.6L and 1990 2.0L DOHC Engines

♦ See Figures 21 and 22

1. Disconnect the negative battery cable and ignition coil harness connector.
2. Measure the primary coil resistance as follows:
  a. Measure the resistance between terminals of the coil pack, **NOT THE WIRE HARNESS**, between **4** and **2** (coils at the No. 1 and No. 4 cylinder sides) of the ignition coil, and between terminals **4** and **1** (coils at the No. 2 and No. 3 cylinder sides).

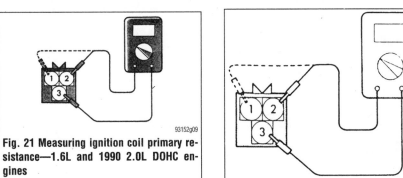

Fig. 21 Measuring ignition coil primary resistance—1.6L and 1990 2.0L DOHC engines

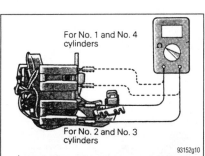

For No. 1 and No. 4 cylinders

For No. 2 and No. 3 cylinders

Fig. 22 Measuring ignition coil secondary resistance—1.6L and 1990 2.0L DOHC engines

  b. Compare reading to the desired primary coil resistance of 0.77–0.95 ohms.
3. Measure the coil secondary resistance as follows:
  c. Detach the connector from the ignition coil.
  d. Measure the resistance between the high-voltage terminals for the No. 1 and No. 4 cylinders, and between the high-voltage terminals for the No. 2 and No. 3 cylinders.
  e. Compare the measured resistance to the desired secondary coil resistance of 10.3–13.9 kilo-ohms.
4. If the readings are not within the specified value, replace the ignition coil.

1991–93 2.0L DOHC Engines

♦ See Figures 23 and 24

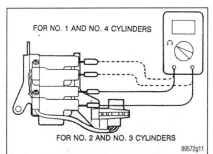

Fig. 23 Measuring the primary ignition coil resistance—1991–93 2.0L DOHC engines

FOR NO. 1 AND NO. 4 CYLINDERS

FOR NO. 2 AND NO. 3 CYLINDERS

Fig. 24 Measuring ignition coil secondary resistance—1991–93 2.0L DOHC engines

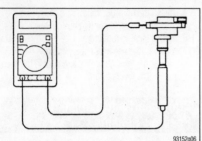

Fig. 25 Measuring ignition coil secondary resistance—1997–00 1.8L and 1999–00 2.4L SOHC engines

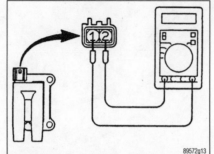

Fig. 26 Measure the primary coil resistance between the connector terminals—2.4L DOHC engine

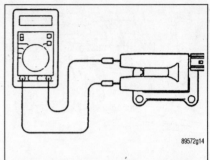

Fig. 27 Measure the secondary resistance between the towers of the coil—2.4L DOHC engine

1. Disconnect the negative battery cable and ignition coil harness connector.

2. Measure the primary coil resistance as follows:

   a. Measure the resistance between terminals **3** and **2** (coils at the No. 1 and No. 4 cylinder sides) of the ignition coil, and between terminals **3** and **1** (coils at the No. 2 and No. 3 cylinder sides).

   b. Compare reading to the desired primary coil resistance of 0.70–0.86 ohms.

3. Measure the coil secondary resistance as follows:

   c. Detach the connector from the ignition coil.

   d. Measure the resistance between the high-voltage terminals for the No. 1 and No. 4 cylinders, and between the high-voltage terminals for the No. 2 and No. 3 cylinders.

   e. The desired secondary coil resistance is 11.3–15.3 kilo-ohms.

4. If the readings are not within the specified value, replace the ignition coil.

1997–00 1.8L and 1999–00 2.4L SOHC Engines

♦ **See Figure 25**

1. Measure the resistance of the secondary ignition coil as follows:

   a. Insert one of the test leads into the secondary ignition coil terminal of the coil.

   b. Touch the second test lead to terminal **1** or terminal **2** of the coil connector.

   c. Measure the resistance and compare to the desired specifications of 9.4–12.8 kilo-ohms.

   d. If the measured value is within standard allowance, there are no broken wires or short circuits.

   e. If the actual reading differs from the desired specification, replace the ignition coil.

2.4L DOHC Engines

♦ **See Figures 26 and 27**

1. Disconnect the negative battery cable.
2. To check the primary coil resistance, perform the following:

   a. Detach the electrical connector from the coil pack.

   b. Using an ohmmeter, measure the resistance between the two terminals of the coil, **NOT THE WIRE HARNESS**.

   c. If the resistance is not between 0.74–0.90 ohms, replace the ignition coil.

3. To check the secondary coil resistance, perform the following:

   a. Tag and disconnect the spark plug wires from the ignition coil.

   b. Measure the secondary resistance of the coil between the towers of each individual coil.

   c. If the resistance is not between 20.1–27.3 kilo-ohms, replace the ignition coil.

3.0L DOHC Engine

♦ **See Figures 28 and 29**

1. Measure the resistance of the primary ignition coil as follows:

   a. Unplug the electrical connector at the coil pack. Using an ohmmeter, measure the resistance between the terminals of the coil pack, **NOT THE WIRE HARNESS**. Measure the resistance between terminals:

   - **2–3** for Coil **A**
   - **1–3** for Coil **B**
   - **4–3** for Coil **C**

   b. Measure the resistance and compare to the desired specifications of 0.67–0.81 ohms.

   c. If the actual reading differs from the desired specification, replace the ignition coil.

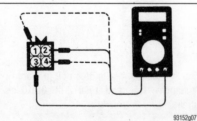

Fig. 28 Measuring ignition coil primary resistance—3.0L DOHC engine

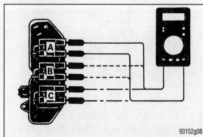

Fig. 29 Measuring ignition coil secondary resistance—3.0L DOHC engine

   d. If the measured value is within standard allowance, there are no broken wires or short circuits.

2. Measure the resistance of the secondary ignition coil as follows:

3. Insert the lead of the ohmmeter between coil pack cylinder terminals:

   - Between coil terminals **1–4** for Coil **A**
   - Between coil terminals **2–5** for Coil **B**
   - Between coil terminals **3–6** for Coil **C**

   e. Measure the resistance and compare to the desired specifications of 11.3–15.3 kilo-ohms.

   f. If the measured value is within standard allowance, there are no broken wires or short circuits.

   g. If the actual reading differs from the desired specification, replace the ignition coil pack.

REMOVAL & INSTALLATION

1.6L, 2.0L DOHC, and 2.4L DOHC Engines

♦ **See Figure 30**

1. Disconnect the negative battery cable.
2. Tag and remove the spark plug wires from the ignition coil by gripping the boot and not the cable.

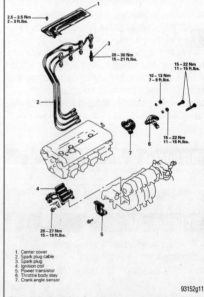

Fig. 30 Ignition system component locations—1.6L and 2.0L DOHC engines

3. Detach the electrical connectors for the coil.

4. Remove the retaining screws and coil from engine.

5. Installation is the reverse of the removal procedure.

1997–00 1.8L and 1999–00 2.4L Engines

▶ See Figure 31

1. Disconnect the negative battery cable.

2. Detach the electrical connector(s) for the coil(s).

3. Remove the spark plug wire(s) to the companion cylinder(s).

4. Remove the coil retaining bolts and lift the coil from the cylinder head.

5. The installation is the reverse of the removal.

3.0L DOHC Engine

▶ See Figure 32

1. Disconnect the negative battery cable.

2. Remove the intake manifold plenum (upper intake manifold). Refer to Section 3.

3. Tag and remove the spark plug wires from the ignition coil by gripping the boot and not the cable.

4. Detach the electrical connectors for the coil.

5. Remove the retaining screws and coil from engine.

6. Installation is the reverse of the removal procedure.

Power Transistor (Ignition Module)

REMOVAL & INSTALLATION

1.6L, 2.0L DOHC, and 2.4L DOHC Engines

▶ See Figure 30

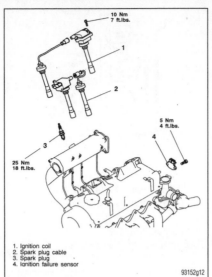

1. Ignition coil
2. Spark plug cable
3. Spark plug
4. Ignition failure sensor

93152g12

Fig. 31 Ignition system component locations—1997–00 1.8L engine shown, 1999–00 2.4L engine similar

1. Disconnect the negative battery cable.

2. Detach the electrical connectors for the transistor.

3. Remove the retaining screws and remove the transistor from engine.

4. Installation is the reverse of the removal procedure.

1.8L and 1999–00 2.4L Engines

The power transistor (ignition module) is an integral part of the powertrain control module.

3.0L DOHC Engine

▶ See Figure 32

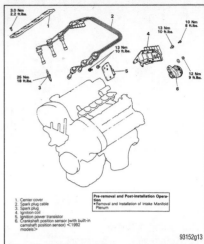

1. Center cover
2. Spark plug cable
3. Spark plug
4. Ignition coil
5. Ignition power transistor
6. Crankshaft position sensor (with built-in camshaft position sensor) <1992 models>

Pre-removal and Post-installation Operation
• Removal and Installation of Intake Manifold Plenum

93152g13

Fig. 32 Ignition system component locations—3.0L DOHC engine

1. Disconnect the negative battery cable.

2. Remove the intake manifold plenum (upper intake manifold). Refer to Section 3.

3. Detach the electrical connectors for the transistor.

4. Remove the retaining screws and remove the transistor from engine.

5. Installation is the reverse of the removal procedure.

Crankshaft and Camshaft Position Sensors

For procedures on the position sensors, please refer to Section 4 in this manual.

FIRING ORDERS

▶ See Figures 33 thru 40

➡To avoid confusion, remove and tag the spark plug wires one at a time, for replacement.

If a distributor is not keyed for installation with only one orientation, it could have been removed previously and rewired. The resultant wiring would hold the correct firing order, but could change the relative placement of the plug towers in relation to the engine. For this reason it is imperative that you label all wires before disconnecting any of them. Also, before removal, compare the current wiring with the accompanying illustrations. If the current wiring does not match, make notes in your book to reflect how your engine is wired.

79233g21

Fig. 33 1.5L (4G15) and 1993–96 1.8L (4G93) engines
Firing order: 1–3–4–2
Distributor rotation: Counterclockwise

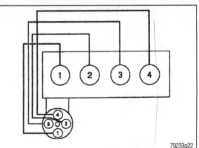

79233g22

Fig. 34 2.0L (4G63) SOHC engine
Firing order: 1–3–4–2
Distributor rotation: Clockwise

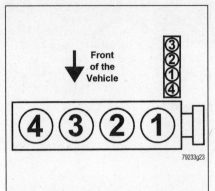

Fig. 35 1.6L (4G61) and 2.0L (4G63) DOHC engines
Firing order: 1–3–4–2
Distributorless ignition system

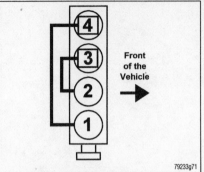

Fig. 36 1997–00 1.8L (4G93) and 1999–00 2.4L (4G64) Engines with distributorless ignition
Firing order: 1–3–4–2
Distributorless ignition system

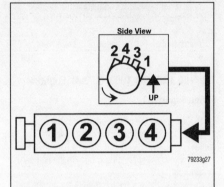

Fig. 37 2.4L (4G64) engine with distributor ignition
Firing order: 1–3–4–2
Distributor rotation: Counterclockwise

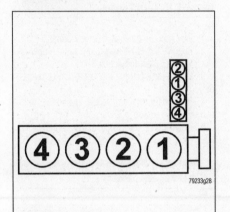

Fig. 38 2.4L (4G64) DOHC engine with distributorless ignition
Firing order: 1–3–4–2
Distributorless ignition system

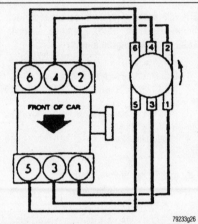

Fig. 39 3.0L (6G72) SOHC and 3.5L (6G74) engines
Firing order: 1–2–3–4–5–6
Distributor rotation: Counterclockwise

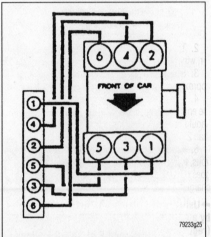

Fig. 40 3.0L (6G72) DOHC engine
Firing order: 1–2–3–4–5–6
Distributorless ignition system

CHARGING SYSTEM

General Information

The automobile charging system provides electrical power for operation of the vehicle's ignition and starting systems and all the electrical accessories. The battery serves as an electrical surge or storage tank, storing (in chemical form) the energy originally produced by the engine driven alternator. The system also provides a means of regulating generator output to protect the battery from being overcharged and to avoid excessive voltage to the accessories.

The storage battery is a chemical device incorporating parallel lead plates in a tank containing a sulfuric acid/water solution. Adjacent plates are slightly dissimilar, and the chemical reaction of the 2 dissimilar plates produces electrical energy when the battery is connected to a load such as the starter motor. The chemical reaction is reversible, so that when the generator is producing a voltage (electrical pressure) greater than that produced by the battery, electricity is forced into the battery, and the battery is returned to its fully charged state.

The vehicle's alternator is driven mechanically, by a belt(s) that is driven by the engine crankshaft. In an alternator, the field rotates while all the current produced passes only through the stator winding. The brushes bear against continuous slip rings rather than a commutator. This causes the current produced to periodically reverse the direction of its flow creating alternating current (A/C). Diodes (electrical one-way switches) block the flow of current from traveling in the wrong direction. A series of diodes is wired together to permit the alternating flow of the stator to be converted to a pulsating, but unidirectional flow at the alternator output. The alternator's field is wired in series with the voltage regulator.

The regulator consists of several circuits. Each circuit has a core, or magnetic coil of wire, which operates a switch. Each switch is connected to ground through one or more resistors. The coil of wire responds directly to system voltage. When the voltage reaches the required level, the magnetic field created by the winding of wire closes the switch and inserts a resistance into the generator field circuit, thus reducing the output. The contacts of the switch cycle open and close many times each second to precisely control voltage.

Alternator Precautions

Several precautions must be observed when performing work on alternator equipment.

• If the battery is removed for any reason, make sure that it is reconnected with the correct polarity. Reversing the battery connections may result in damage to the one-way rectifiers.

• Never operate the alternator with the main circuit broken. Make sure that the battery, alternator, and regulator leads are not disconnected while the engine is running.

• Never attempt to polarize an alternator.

• When charging a battery that is installed in the vehicle, disconnect the negative battery cable.

• When utilizing a booster battery as a starting aid, always connect it in parallel; negative to negative, and positive to positive.

• When arc (electric) welding is to be performed on any part of the vehicle, disconnect the negative battery cable and alternator leads.

• Never unplug the PCM while the engine is running or with the ignition in the **ON** position. Severe and expensive damage may result within the solid state equipment.

Alternator

TESTING

Voltage Test

1. Make sure the engine is **OFF**, and turn the headlights on for 15–20 seconds to remove any surface charge from the battery.

2. Using a DVOM set to volts DC, probe across the battery terminals.

3. Measure the battery voltage.

4. Write down the voltage reading and proceed to the next test.

No-Load Test

1. Connect a tachometer to the engine.

✳✳ CAUTION

Ensure that the transmission is in Park and the emergency brake is set. Blocking a wheel is optional and an added safety measure.

2. Turn off all electrical loads (radio, blower motor, wipers, etc.)

3. Start the engine and increase engine speed to approximately 1500 rpm.

4. Measure the voltage reading at the battery with the engine holding a steady 1500 rpm. Voltage should have raised at least 0.5 volts, but no more than 2.5 volts.

5. If the voltage does not go up more than 0.5 volts, the alternator is not charging. If the voltage goes up more than 2.5 volts, the alternator is overcharging.

➡ Usually under and overcharging is caused by a defective alternator, or its related parts (regulator), and replacement will fix the problem; however, faulty wiring and other problems can cause the charging system to malfunction. Further testing, which is not covered by this book, will reveal the exact component failure. Many automotive parts stores have alternator bench testers available for use by customers. An alternator bench test is the most definitive way to determine the condition of your alternator.

6. If the voltage is within specifications, proceed to the next test.

Load Test

1. With the engine running, turn on the blower motor and the high beams (or other electrical accessories to place a load on the charging system).

2. Increase and hold engine speed to 2000 rpm.

3. Measure the voltage reading at the battery.

4. The voltage should increase at least 0.5 volts from the voltage test. If the voltage does not meet specifications, the charging system is malfunctioning.

➡ Usually under and overcharging is caused by a defective alternator, or its related parts (regulator), and replacement will fix the problem; however, faulty wiring and other problems can cause the charging system to malfunction. Further testing, which is not covered by this book, will reveal the exact component failure. Many automotive parts stores have alternator bench testers avail-

able for use by customers. An alternator bench test is the most definitive way to determine the condition of your alternator.

REMOVAL & INSTALLATION

1.5L, 1.6L, 1.8L, 2.0L and 2.4L Engines

▸ **See Figures 41 thru 48**

1. Disconnect the negative battery cable.
2. Remove the left side cover panel under the vehicle.
3. On turbocharged Galant models, remove the air intake hose.
4. Remove the drive belts.
5. Remove the water pump pulleys.
6. Remove the alternator upper bracket/brace.

7. On the 1.6L engine remove the battery, windshield washer reservoir and battery tray.

8. On the 1.6L engine, remove the attaching bolts at the top of the radiator and lift up the radiator. Do not disconnect the radiator hoses.

9. Detach the alternator wiring connectors.

10. Remove the alternator mounting bolts and remove the alternator.

To install:

11. Position the alternator on the lower mounting fixture and install the lower mounting bolt and nut. Tighten nut just enough to allow for movement of the alternator.

12. On the 1.6L engine, lower the radiator and reinstall the upper attaching bolts.

13. On the 1.6L engine, install the battery, windshield washer reservoir and battery tray.

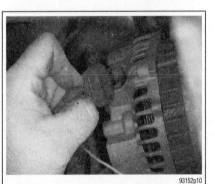

Fig. 41 Detach the regulator connector from the alternator

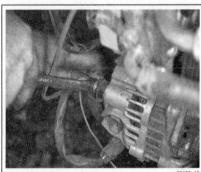

Fig. 42 Remove the nut retaining the battery cable to the alternator . . .

Fig. 43 . . . then remove the battery cable from the alternator

Fig. 44 Remove the nut retaining the wire harness to the alternator, and remove the harness from the alternator

Fig. 45 Remove the nut for the pivot bolt on the rear of the alternator . . .

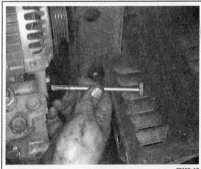

Fig. 46 . . . then remove the pivot bolt from the alternator

Fig. 47 Remove the alternator adjusting bolt . . .

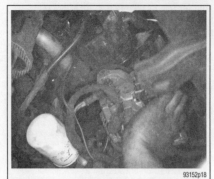

Fig. 48 . . . then remove the alternator from the vehicle

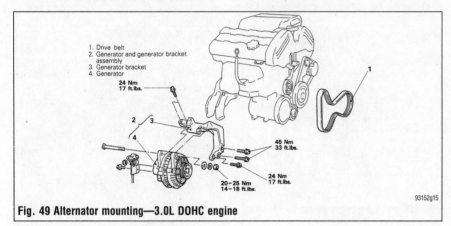

1. Drive belt
2. Generator and generator bracket assembly
3. Generator bracket
4. Generator

24 Nm
17 ft.lbs.

45 Nm
33 ft.lbs.

24 Nm
17 ft.lbs.

20–25 Nm
14–18 ft.lbs.

Fig. 49 Alternator mounting—3.0L DOHC engine

14. Install the alternator upper bracket/brace and connect the alternator electrical harness.

15. Install the water pump pulleys.

16. Install the drive belts and adjust to the proper tension.

17. On turbocharged Galant models, install the air intake hose.

18. Install the left side cover panel under the vehicle as required.

19. Connect the negative battery cable and check for proper operation.

3.0L DOHC Engine

▶ See Figure 49

1. Disconnect the negative battery cable.
2. Remove the headlamp washer reservoir tank.
3. Remove the condenser fan and upper radiator insulator.
4. Loosen the tensioner pulley and remove the alternator drive belt.
5. Remove the alternator upper and lower mounting bolts.
6. Remove the alternator support bracket mounting bolts.
7. Remove the alternator support bracket from the vehicle.
8. Disconnect the alternator wiring harness.
9. Remove the alternator from the vehicle.

To install:

10. Install the alternator to the vehicle and connect the wiring harness.

11. Install the alternator support bracket to the vehicle and tighten the bracket mounting bolts to specifications.

12. Position the alternator on the mounting bracket. Install and tighten the mounting bolt and nut to 17 ft. lbs. (24 Nm).

13. Reinstall the drive belt and adjust the tensioner until the proper belt tension is achieved.

14. Install the upper radiator insulator and condenser fan.

15. Install the headlamp washer reservoir tank.

16. Connect the negative battery cable and check the charging system for proper operation.

3.0L SOHC and 3.5L Engines

▶ See Figures 50 and 51

1. Disconnect the negative battery cable.

2. Disconnect and remove the air intake hose.

3. Loosen the tensioner pulley and remove the alternator drive belt.

4. On California models, remove the rear bank converter assembly.

5. Remove the engine roll stopper stay bracket assembly.

6. On the 3.0L SOHC engine, disconnect the EGR temperature sensor wire and remove the EGR pipe assembly.

7. On the 3.0L SOHC engine, remove the intake plenum stay bracket assembly.

8. Detach the alternator wiring harness connectors.

9. Remove the alternator upper and lower mounting bolts.

10. From beneath the vehicle, remove the alternator.

To install:

11. Position the alternator on the lower mounting fixture. Install and tighten the mounting bolt and nut to 14–18 ft. lbs. (20–25 Nm).

12. Connect the alternator wiring harness.

13. On the 3.0L SOHC engine, install the intake plenum stay bracket and tighten the mounting bolt to 13 ft. lbs. (18 Nm).

14. On the 3.0L SOHC engine, install the EGR pipe and tighten the fitting connections to 43 ft. lbs. (60 Nm).

15. On the 3.0L SOHC engine, connect the EGR temperature sensor wire.

16. Connect the engine roll stopper stay and tighten the mounting bolt to 35 ft. lbs. (45 Nm) and the nut to 36–43 ft. lbs. (50–60 Nm).

17. Install the rear converter assembly, if removed.

18. Reinstall the drive belt and adjust the tensioner until the proper belt tension is achieved.

19. Connect the air intake hose.

20. Connect the negative battery cable and check the charging system for proper operation.

Regulator

REMOVAL & INSTALLATION

The voltage regulator on models covered by this manual is an integral part of the alternator. If the regulator is defective, replace the alternator assembly.

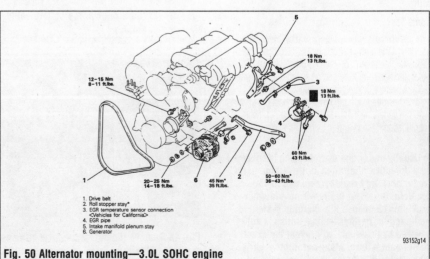

12–15 Nm
8–11 ft.lbs.

18 Nm
13 ft.lbs.

18 Nm
13 ft.lbs.

60 Nm
43 ft.lbs.

20–25 Nm
14–18 ft.lbs.

45 Nm*
35 ft.lbs.

50–60 Nm*
36–43 ft.lbs.

1. Drive belt
2. Roll stopper stay
3. EGR temperature sensor connection <Vehicles for California>
4. EGR pipe
5. Intake manifold plenum stay
6. Generator

Fig. 50 Alternator mounting—3.0L SOHC engine

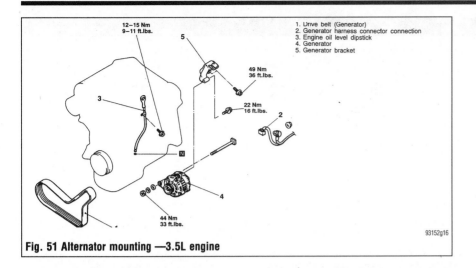

1. Drive belt (Generator)
2. Generator harness connector connection
3. Engine oil level dipstick
4. Generator
5. Generator bracket

12–15 Nm
9–11 ft.lbs.

49 Nm
36 ft.lbs.

22 Nm
16 ft.lbs.

44 Nm
33 ft.lbs.

93152g16

Fig. 51 Alternator mounting —3.5L engine

STARTING SYSTEM

General Information

The starting system includes the battery, starter motor, solenoid, ignition switch, circuit protection and wiring connecting the components. An inhibitor switch located in the park/neutral safety switch or Transmission Range (TR) sensor is included in the starting system to prevent the vehicle from being started with the vehicle in gear.

When the ignition key is turned to the **START** position, current flows and energizes the starter's solenoid coil. The solenoid plunger and clutch shift lever are activated and the clutch pinion engages the ring gear on the flywheel. The switch contacts close and the starter cranks the engine until it starts.

To prevent damage caused by excessive starter armature rotation when the engine starts, the starter incorporates an over-running clutch in the pinion gear.

Starter

TESTING

Voltage Drop Test

➡**The battery must be in good condition and fully charged prior to performing this test.**

1. Disable the ignition system by unplugging the coil pack. Verify that the vehicle will not start.

2. Connect a voltmeter between the positive terminal of the battery and the starter **B+** circuit.

3. Turn the ignition key to the **START** position and note the voltage on the meter.

4. If voltage reads 0.5 volts or more, there is high resistance in the starter cables or the cable ground, repair as necessary. If the voltage reading is ok proceed to the next step.

5. Connect a voltmeter between the positive terminal of the battery and the starter **M** circuit.

6. Turn the ignition key to the **START** position and note the voltage on the meter.

7. If voltage reads 0.5 volts or more, there is high resistance in the starter. Repair or replace the starter as necessary.

➡**Many automotive parts stores have starter bench testers available for use by customers. A starter bench test is the most definitive way to determine the condition of your starter.**

REMOVAL & INSTALLATION

▶ **See Figures 52 and 53**

1. Disconnect the negative battery cable.
2. Detach the air-flow sensor assembly connector and remove the breather hose.

3. Remove the resonator retaining nuts and remove the air intake hose and resonator assembly as required.

➡**Use care when removing the air cleaner cover because the air-flow sensor is attached and is a sensitive component.**

4. If equipped with Active-ECS suspension, remove the air compressor as follows:
   a. Detach the two electrical connectors, from the compressor.
   b. Disconnect the air line at the compressor.
   c. Remove the three mounting bolts, securing the compressor to the chassis.
5. Raise the vehicle and support safely.
6. Remove the engine undercover.
7. Remove the heat shield from beneath the intake manifold on the 1.5L engine.
8. If necessary, detach the speedometer cable connector at the transaxle end.
9. Detach the starter motor electrical connections.
10. Remove the starter motor mounting bolts and remove the starter.
11. The installation is the reverse of the removal procedure. Tighten the starter mounting bolts to 22 ft. lbs. (31 Nm).
12. Connect the negative battery cable and check the starter for proper operation.

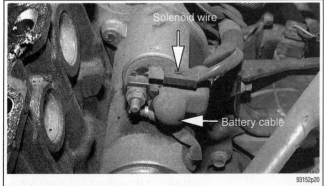

Solenoid wire

Battery cable

93152p20

Fig. 52 Remove the starter electrical connections, noting their locations

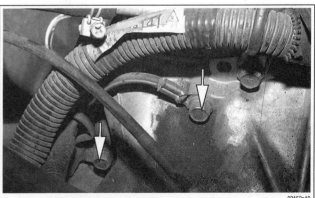

93152p19

Fig. 53 Location of the two starter retaining bolts

SENDING UNITS

➡This section describes the operating principles of sending units, warning lights and gauges. Sensors which provide information to the Engine Control Unit (ECU) or Electronic or Powertrain Control Module (ECM/PCM) are covered in Section 4 of this manual.

Instrument panels contain a number of indicating devices (gauges and warning lights). These devices are composed of two separate components. One is the sending unit, mounted on the engine or other remote part of the vehicle, and the other is the actual gauge or light in the instrument panel.

Several types of sending units exist, however most can be characterized as being either a pressure type or a resistance type. Pressure type sending units convert liquid pressure into an electrical signal which is sent to the gauge. Resistance type sending units are most often used to measure temperature and use variable resistance to control the current flow back to the indicating device. Both types of sending units are connected in series by a wire to the battery (through the ignition switch). When the ignition is turned **ON**, current flows from the battery through the indicating device and on to the sending unit.

Engine Coolant Temperature Sending Unit

TESTING

The coolant temperature sending unit is used to operate the temperature gauge. Do not confuse this sending unit with the other switches or sensors used to signal the engine control unit or air conditioning regarding temperature of the coolant. Usually, these other units are mounted near the coolant temperature sensor used for engine control.

Gauge Check

1. Detach the engine coolant gauge sending unit electrical connector.
2. Connect a suitable test light (12V–3.4W) between the harness side connector and the ground.
3. Turn the ignition switch to the **ON** position.
4. Check the condition of the test light and gauge as follows:

   a. If all components are operating properly, the test light should illuminate and the gauge needle should move.

   b. If the test light is illuminated and the gauge needle does not move, replace the coolant temperature gauge.

   c. If the test light is illuminated and the gauge needle does not move, check the fuse for a broken wire, or resistance between the gauge terminals

   d. If the test light is not illuminated and the gauge is not moving, check, then replace the wiring harness, if necessarly.

Sender Check

♦ **See Figure 54**

1. Drain the engine coolant to a level below the coolant temperature sending unit.

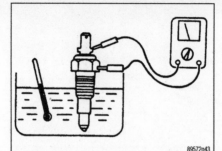

Fig. 54 Place the sending unit in water and measure the resistance

2. Disconnect the sending unit wiring harness and remove the coolant temperature sending unit.
3. Place the sending unit tip in a pan of warm water. Use a thermometer to measure the water temperature.
4. Measure the resistance across the sending unit terminals while the sending unit is in the water.
5. Note the ohm reading and compare to the following specifications:
   - Water temperature of 68°F (20°C)—2.21–2.69 kilo-ohms resistance
   - Water temperature of 158°F (70°C)—90.5–117.5 ohms resistance
   - Water temperature of 176°F (80°C)—264–328 ohms resistance.

If the resistance is not approximately accurate for the temperature, the sending unit must be replaced.

Fig. 55 Detach the connector from the coolant temperature sending unit

Fig. 57 . . . then remove the sending unit from the thermostat housing

REMOVAL & INSTALLATION

♦ **See Figures 55, 56, 57, and 58**

1. Disconnect the negative battery cable.
2. Position a suitable drain pan under the radiator.
3. Drain the engine coolant a level below the coolant temperature sending unit.
4. Disconnect the sending unit wiring harness, then remove the coolant temperature sending unit from the engine.

   To install:

5. Coat the sending unit threads with a suitable thread sealant.
6. Install the engine coolant temperature gauge sending unit into the bore in the engine and tighten to 7–8 ft. lbs. (10–12 Nm).
7. Attach the electrical harness connector to the sending unit.
8. Fill the cooling system to the proper level. Connect the negative battery cable.

Oil Pressure Sending Unit

TESTING

Gauge Check

♦ **See Figure 59**

Fig. 56 Using a suitable size socket and drive tool, loosen the sending unit . . .

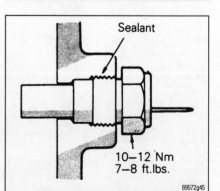

Fig. 58 Before installing the sending unit, coat the threads with a suitable sealant

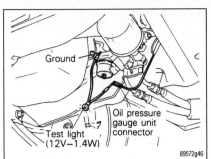

Fig. 59 Testing the oil pressure sending unit and gauge

1. Detach the oil pressure gauge unit electrical connector.

2. Use a suitable test light (12V–3.4W) to ground the harness side connector.

3. Turn the ignition to the **ON** position.

4. Check the condition of the test light and gauge as follows:

   a. If all components are operating properly, the test light will flash or light steadily and the oil pressure gauge needle will move.

   b. If the test light flashes or lights steadily but the gauge does not move, the gauge must be replaced.

   c. If neither the test light or the gauge operate, check the oil pressure gauge circuit and replace, if necessary.

Sending Unit Check

1. Remove the electrical harness connector from the sending unit and remove the sending unit from the oil filter head.

2. Connect an ohmmeter between the terminal and the sending unit body cavity and check for conductivity. If there is no conductivity, replace the sending unit.

3. Next, insert a very thin wedge through the oil hole in the end of the sending unit. Push the wedge in slightly and measure resistance. There should be no conductivity.

4. If there is conductivity, even when wedge is pushed, replace the sending unit.

5. If there is no conductivity when a 71 psi pressure is placed through the oil hole, the sending unit is operating properly.

6. Check to see that there is no air pressure leakage through the sending unit. If there is air pressure leakage, the diaphragm is broken and the sending unit will require replacement.

REMOVAL & INSTALLATION

▶ **See Figures 60 thru 65**

1. Disconnect the negative battery cable.

2. Raise and support the vehicle safely.

3. Detach the electrical harness connector from the sending unit, then remove the unit from the oil filter head.

To install:

4. Apply a thin bead of sealant to the threaded portion of the oil pressure sending unit. Do not allow sealer to contact the end of the threaded portion of the sending unit.

5. Install the sending unit and tighten to 8 ft. lbs. (12 Nm). Do not overtighten the sending unit.

6. Attach the electrical harness connector to the sending unit.

7. Carefully lower the vehicle, then connect the negative battery cable.

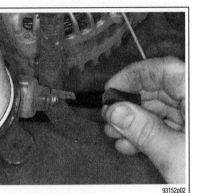

Fig. 60 Detach the connector from the oil pressure sending unit

Fig. 61 The body of the sending unit has a unique shape . . .

Fig. 62 . . . and the use of an oil pressure sending unit socket greatly aids the removal and installation

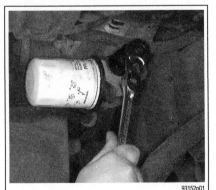

Fig. 63 Using the socket and a suitable drive tool, loosen the sending unit . . .

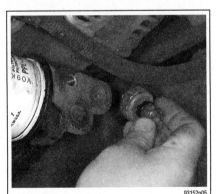

Fig. 64 . . . then remove the sending unit from the oil filter head

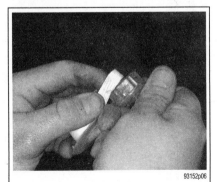

Fig. 65 Before installing the sending unit, it is a good idea to place Teflon® tape on the threads

Troubleshooting Basic Starting System Problems

Problem	Cause	Solution
Starter motor rotates engine slowly	· Battery charge low or battery defective · Defective circuit between battery and starter motor · Low load current · High load current	· Charge or replace battery · Clean and tighten, or replace cables · Bench-test starter motor. Inspect for worn brushes and weak brush springs. · Bench-test starter motor. Check engine for friction, drag or coolant in cylinders. Check ring gear-to-pinion gear clearance.
Starter motor will not rotate engine	· Battery charge low or battery defective · Faulty solenoid · Damaged drive pinion gear or ring gear · Starter motor engagement weak · Starter motor rotates slowly with high load current · Engine seized	· Charge or replace battery · Check solenoid ground. Repair or replace as necessary. · Replace damaged gear(s) · Bench-test starter motor · Inspect drive yoke pull-down and point gap, check for worn end bushings, check ring gear clearance · Repair engine
Starter motor drive will not engage (solenoid known to be good)	· Defective contact point assembly · Inadequate contact point assembly ground · Defective hold-in coil	· Repair or replace contact point assembly · Repair connection at ground screw · Replace field winding assembly
Starter motor drive will not disengage	· Starter motor loose on flywheel housing · Worn drive end busing · Damaged ring gear teeth · Drive yoke return spring broken or missing	· Tighten mounting bolts · Replace bushing · Replace ring gear or driveplate · Replace spring
Starter motor drive disengages prematurely	· Weak drive assembly thrust spring · Hold-in coil defective	· Replace drive mechanism · Replace field winding assembly
Low load current	· Worn brushes · Weak brush springs	· Replace brushes · Replace springs

tcs2c01

Troubleshooting Basic Charging System Problems

Problem	Cause	Solution
Noisy alternator	· Loose mountings · Loose drive pulley · Worn bearings · Brush noise · Internal circuits shorted (High pitched whine)	· Tighten mounting bolts · Tighten pulley · Replace alternator · Replace alternator · Replace alternator
Squeal when starting engine or accelerating	· Glazed or loose belt	· Replace or adjust belt
Indicator light remains on or ammeter indicates discharge (engine running)	· Broken belt · Broken or disconnected wires · Internal alternator problems · Defective voltage regulator	· Install belt · Repair or connect wiring · Replace alternator · Replace voltage regulator/alternator
Car light bulbs continually burn out—battery needs water continually	· Alternator/regulator overcharging	· Replace voltage regulator/alternator
Car lights flare on acceleration	· Battery low · Internal alternator/regulator problems	· Charge or replace battery · Replace alternator/regulator
Low voltage output (alternator light flickers continually or ammeter needle wanders)	· Loose or worn belt · Dirty or corroded connections · Internal alternator/regulator problems	· Replace or adjust belt · Clean or replace connections · Replace alternator/regulator

tcs2c02

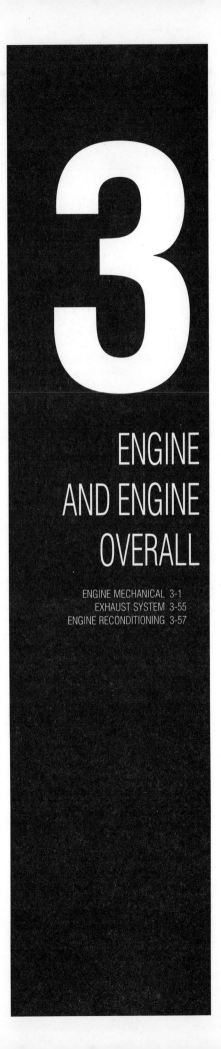

3

ENGINE
AND ENGINE
OVERALL

ENGINE MECHANICAL

Engine

REMOVAL & INSTALLATION

▶ **See Figure 1**

In the process of removing the engine, you will come across a number of steps which call for the removal of a separate component or system, such as "disconnect the exhaust system" or "remove the radiator." In most instances, a detailed removal procedure can be found elsewhere in this manual.

It is virtually impossible to list each individual wire and hose which must be disconnected, simply because so many different model and engine combinations have been manufactured. Careful observation and common sense are the best possible approaches to any repair procedure.

Removal and installation of the engine can be made easier if you follow these basic points:
- If you have to drain any of the fluids, use a suitable container.
- Always tag any wires or hoses and, if possible, the components they came from before disconnecting them.
- Because there are so many bolts and fasteners involved, store and label the retainers from components separately in muffin pans, jars or coffee cans. This will prevent confusion during installation.
- After unbolting the transmission or transaxle, always make sure it is properly supported.
- If it is necessary to disconnect the air conditioning system, have this service performed by a qualified technician using a recovery/recycling station. If the system does not have to be disconnected, unbolt the compressor and set it aside.
- When unbolting the engine mounts, always make sure the engine is properly supported. When removing the engine, make sure that any lifting devices are properly attached to the engine. It is recommended that if your engine is supplied with lifting hooks, your lifting apparatus be attached to them.
- Lift the engine from its compartment slowly, checking that no hoses, wires or other components are still connected.
- After the engine is clear of the compartment, place it on an engine stand or workbench.
- After the engine has been removed, you can perform a partial or full teardown of the engine using the procedures outlined in this manual.

1. Relieve fuel system pressure.

✳✳ CAUTION

Observe all applicable safety precautions when working around fuel. Whenever servicing the fuel system, always work in a well ventilated area. Do not allow fuel spray or vapors to come in contact with a spark or open flame. Keep a dry chemical fire extinguisher near the work area. Always keep fuel in a container specifically designed for fuel storage; also, always properly seal fuel containers to avoid the possibility of fire or explosion.

2. Disconnect the negative battery cable.
3. Remove the engine undercover if equipped.

4. Matchmark the hood and hinges and remove the hood assembly.
5. Remove the air cleaner assembly and all adjoining air intake duct work.
6. Drain the engine coolant, remove the radiator hoses, and remove the radiator assembly, coolant reservoir, and intercooler, as equipped.

✳✳ CAUTION

Never open, service or drain the radiator or cooling system when hot; serious burns can occur from the steam and hot coolant. Also, when draining engine coolant, keep in mind that cats and dogs are attracted to ethylene glycol antifreeze and could drink any that is left in an uncovered container or in puddles on the ground. This will prove fatal in sufficient quantities. Always drain coolant into a sealable container. Coolant should be reused unless it is contaminated or is several years old.

7. Remove the transaxle and transfer case as equipped.
8. Tag and detach the following electrical connections:
- Accelerator cable
- Heater hoses
- Brake booster vacuum hose
- Vacuum hoses
- Fuel lines
- Engine ground cables
- Any applicable sensors
- Coolant temperature and oil pressure sending units
- Exhaust Gas Recirculation (EGR) temperature sensor
- Connection for the idle speed control motor
- Fuel injectors
- Power transistor
- Ignition coil and any applicable distributor connections
- The connections for the alternator
- Power steering pressure switch
- A/C compressor
- Refrigerant temperature switch
- Condenser

9. Remove the air conditioner drive belt and the air conditioning compressor. Leave the hoses attached. Do not discharge the system. Place the compressor aside and secure it using a suitable device.
10. Remove the power steering pump and place the pump aside and secure it using a suitable device.
11. Remove the exhaust manifold-to-exhaust pipe nuts. Discard the gasket.
12. Install the engine hoist equipment and make certain the attaching points on the engine are secure.
13. Raise the hoist enough to support the engine.
14. Remove the front and rear engine roll stoppers.
15. Remove the left engine mount and support bracket.

✳✳ WARNING

Double check that all cables, hoses, harness connectors, etc., are disconnected from the engine.

16. Slowly lift the engine and remove it from the vehicle.

To install:
17. Install the engine and secure all control brackets and mounts.
18. Install the transaxle, and transfer case if equipped.
19. The balance of the installation is the reverse of removal with the addition of the following notes:
  a. Use new clamps or O-rings to connect the high pressure fuel line and the fuel return line.
  b. Use new gaskets to connect the exhaust system to the engine.
  c. Fill the engine with the proper amount of engine oil and coolant.
  d. Start the engine, allow it to reach normal operating temperature.
  e. Check for leaks.
  f. Check the ignition timing and adjust if necessary.
  g. Road test the vehicle and check all fluid levels and functions for proper operation.

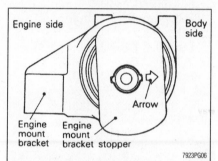

Fig. 1 Alignment of the engine mount stopper bracket—Diamante shown

Rocker Arm (Valve) Cover

REMOVAL & INSTALLATION

Except 3.0L (SOHC and DOHC) and 3.5L Engines

▶ **See Figures 2 thru 11**

1. Disconnect the negative battery cable.
2. If necessary, remove the air intake hose.
3. If necessary, remove the throttle cable from the cable routing clips.

Fig. 2 If necessary, remove the throttle cable from the cable routing clips

Fig. 3 Remove the breather hose from the valve cover

Fig. 4 Remove the PCV valve and hose from the valve cover

Fig. 5 Twist each spark plug wire to remove it from the spark plug . . .

Fig. 6 . . . then position the wires out of the way

Fig. 7 The upper timing cover is retained by three bolts. Unfasten the bolts . . .

Fig. 8 . . . then carefully remove the cover from the engine

Fig. 9 Remove the valve cover retaining bolts . . .

Fig. 10 . . . then lift the valve cover off of the cylinder head

Fig. 11 Remove the valve cover gasket, thoroughly clean the valve cover and cylinder head, and replace the gasket

4. If equipped, remove the breather hose from the valve cover.

5. Remove the crankcase ventilation tube from the valve cover.

6. On the 1.6L and 2.0L (DOHC) engines, remove the ignition wire cover.

7. Label and remove the ignition wires and separators.

8. Remove the upper timing belt cover.

9. Remove the valve cover retaining bolts, starting from the outside and working in.

10. Remove the valve cover and gasket from the cylinder head.

To install:

11. Clean the valve cover gasket sealing surfaces.

12. Install new valve cover gaskets and if equipped, O-rings onto the valve covers.

13. Place the valve cover into position and beginning in the center of the valve cover and working outward, tighten the retaining bolts as follows:

- 1.5L engine: 12–18 inch lbs. (1–2 Nm)
- 1.6L, 1.8L, 2.0L DOHC, and 2.4L engines: 24–36 inch lbs. (2–3 Nm)
- 2.0L SOHC engine: 48–60 inch lbs. (4–5 Nm)

14. Install the crankcase ventilation tube.

15. Install the ignition wire separators and the ignition wires.

16. On the 1.6L and 2.0L (DOHC) engines, install the ignition wire cover.

17. Install the air intake hose.

18. Connect the negative battery cable.

19. Run the engine and check for leaks and proper operation.

3.0L and 3.5L Engines

▶ See Figure 12

1. Disconnect the negative battery cable.

2. Remove the upper intake manifold as described in this section.

3. On the 3.0L DOHC engine, remove the ignition wire cover.

4. Remove the ignition wires and spark plugs.

5. Remove the crankcase ventilation tubes from both valve covers.

6. Remove the retaining nuts and engine wiring from both valve covers and move aside.

7. Remove the valve cover retaining bolts and studs.

8. Remove both valve covers from the engine.

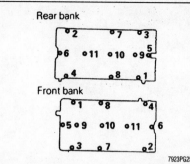

Fig. 12 Rocker cover bolt torque sequence—3.0L DOHC engine

To install:

9. Clean the valve cover gasket sealing surfaces.

10. Install new valve cover gaskets onto the valve covers.

11. Place the valve covers into position.

12. Reinstall the valve cover retaining bolts and studs and tighten in sequence to:
- 3.0L SOHC engine: 7 ft. lbs. (9 Nm)
- 3.0L DOHC engine: 42–54 inch lbs. (4–5 Nm)
- 3.5L engine: 30 inch lbs. (3 Nm)

13. Install the engine wiring and tighten the retaining nuts.

14. Install the crankcase ventilation tubes into both valve covers.

15. Install the ignition wire separators, the ignition wires, and the spark plugs.

16. On the 3.0L DOHC engine, install the ignition wire cover.

17. Install the upper intake manifold as described in this section.

18. Connect the negative battery cable.

19. Run the engine and check for leaks and proper operation.

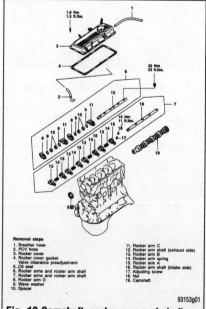

Removal steps
1. Breather hose
2. PCV hose
3. Rocker cover
4. Rocker cover gasket
   Valve clearance preadjustment
5. Oil seal
6. Rocker arms and rocker arm shaft
7. Rocker arms and rocker arm shaft
8. Rocker arm D
9. Wave washer
10. Spacer
11. Rocker arm C
12. Rocker arm shaft (exhaust side)
13. Rocker arm B
14. Rocker arm spring
15. Rocker arm A
16. Rocker arm shaft (intake side)
17. Adjusting screw
18. Nut
19. Camshaft

Fig. 13 Camshaft, rocker arm and shaft assemblies—1.5L engine

Rocker Arm/Shafts

REMOVAL & INSTALLATION

1.5L and 1.8L Engines

♦ **See Figures 13 and 14**

1. Disconnect the negative battery cable.

2. For 1.8L engines, label and disconnect the spark plug cables.

3. Disconnect the accelerator cable, breather hose and PCV hose connections.

4. Remove the rocker cover.

5. Loosen both rocker arm shaft assemblies gradually and evenly and remove the rocket shafts from the vehicle.

6. If disassembly is required, keep all parts in the exact order of removal.

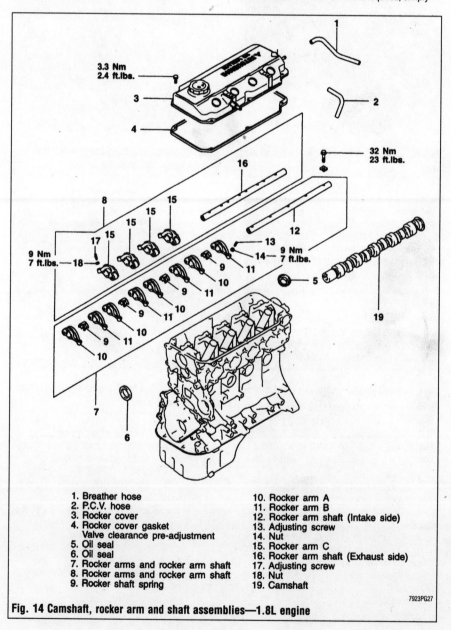

1. Breather hose
2. P.C.V. hose
3. Rocker cover
4. Rocker cover gasket
   Valve clearance pre-adjustment
5. Oil seal
6. Oil seal
7. Rocker arms and rocker arm shaft
8. Rocker arms and rocker arm shaft
9. Rocker shaft spring
10. Rocker arm A
11. Rocker arm B
12. Rocker arm shaft (Intake side)
13. Adjusting screw
14. Nut
15. Rocker arm C
16. Rocker arm shaft (Exhaust side)
17. Adjusting screw
18. Nut
19. Camshaft

Fig. 14 Camshaft, rocker arm and shaft assemblies—1.8L engine

To install:

7. Lubricate the rocker shaft with clean engine oil and install the rockers and springs.

8. Install the rocker arm and shaft assemblies. Tighten the rocker arm shaft retainer bolts to 23 ft. lbs. (32 Nm).

9. Check valve adjustment and install the valve cover. Tighten the valve cover bolts to 16 inch lbs. (1.8 Nm) for the 1.5L engine or to 29 inch lbs. (3.3 Nm) for the 1.8L engine.

10. If detached, connect the spark plug cables.

11. Connect the accelerator cable, breather hose and PCV hose.

12. Connect the negative battery cable.

2.0L SOHC Engine

♦ **See Figure 15**

On this engine, the hydraulic lifters are built into the rocker arms. If lifter service is required, simply

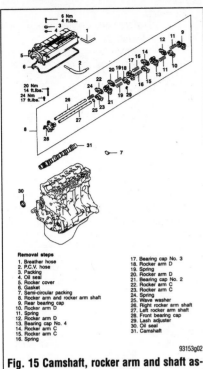

Removal steps

1. Breather hose
2. P.C.V. hose
3. Packing
4. Oil seal
5. Rocker cover
6. Gasket
7. Semi-circular packing
8. Rocker arm and rocker arm shaft
9. Rear bearing cap
10. Rocker arm D
11. Spring
12. Rocker arm D
13. Bearing cap No. 4
14. Rocker arm C
15. Rocker arm C
16. Spring
17. Bearing cap No. 3
18. Rocker arm D
19. Spring
20. Rocker arm D
21. Bearing cap No. 2
22. Rocker arm C
23. Rocker arm C
24. Spring
25. Wave washer
26. Right rocker arm shaft
27. Left rocker arm shaft
28. Front bearing cap
29. Lash adjuster
30. Oil seal
31. Camshaft

93153g02

Fig. 15 Camshaft, rocker arm and shaft assemblies—2.0L SOHC engine

remove the lifter from the bore in the rocker arm. It is recommended that all of the rocker arms and lash adjusters be replaced at the same time.

1. Disconnect the negative battery cable.
2. Remove the valve cover.
3. Matchmark the distributor to the cylinder head and remove the distributor.
4. Remove camshaft timing belt.
5. Working in a crisscross pattern from the center outward, loosen the camshaft bearing caps in gradual steps.
6. Remove the rocker arms, shafts and bearing caps as an assembly.

➡ **It is essential that all parts be kept in the same order and orientation for reinstallation. Be sure to mark and separate parts, so parts will not be mixed during reassembly.**

7. Disassemble rocker shaft assembly. Starting at rear bearing cap, slide each piece off shafts.

➡ **Inspect the roller surfaces of the rockers. Replace if there are any signs of damage or if the roller does not turn smoothly. Check the inside bore of the rockers and lifter for wear.**

To install:

8. Apply a drop of sealant to the rear edges of the end caps.
9. Install the assembly into the front bearing cap, making sure the notches in the rocker shafts are facing up. Insert the installation bolt, but do not tighten at this point.
10. Install the remaining cap bolts. Tighten all bolts evenly and gradually to 15 ft. lbs. (20 Nm). Remove the lash adjuster retainers.
11. Install the timing belt as required.
12. Align the matchmarks and install the distributor.
13. Remove the lash adjuster retaining tools.

14. Install the valve cover, with a new gasket and semi-circular packing in place.
15. Connect the negative battery cable.
16. Run the engine and check ignition timing.

1.6L and 2.0L DOHC (Turbo and Non-turbo) Engines

▶ **See Figure 16**

1. Disconnect the negative battery cable.
2. Remove the valve cover and discard the gasket.
3. Install lash adjuster retainer tools MD998443 or equivalent, to the rocker arm.
4. Remove the rocker shaft hold-down bolts gradually and evenly and remove the rocker shaft/arm assemblies.
5. If disassembly is required, keep all parts in the exact order of removal. Inspect the roller surfaces of the rockers. Replace if there are any signs of damage or if the roller does not turn smoothly. Check the inside bore of the rockers and the adjuster tip for wear.

To install:

6. Lubricate the rocker shaft with clean engine oil and install the rockers and springs in their proper places.
7. Install the rocker shaft assemblies on the engine. Tighten the bolts gradually and evenly to 21–25 ft. lbs. (29–35 Nm).

➡ **When installing the rocker arm shaft, make certain the notch is properly located.**

8. Remove the lash adjuster retaining tools.
9. Install the valve cover with a new gasket.
10. Connect the negative battery cable.

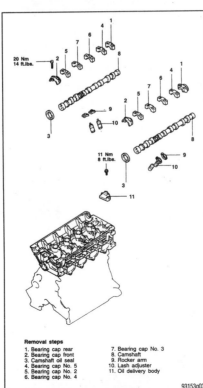

Removal steps

1. Bearing cap rear
2. Bearing cap front
3. Camshaft oil seal
4. Bearing cap No. 5
5. Bearing cap No. 2
6. Bearing cap No. 4
7. Bearing cap No. 3
8. Camshaft
9. Rocker arm
10. Lash adjuster
11. Oil delivery body

93153g03

Fig. 16 Camshaft, rocker arm and shaft assemblies—1.6L and 2.0L DOHC engines

2.4L Engine

▶ **See Figures 17, 18, and 19**

1. Disconnect the negative battery cable.
2. Remove the accelerator cable from the retaining clamps and position the accelerator cable out of the way.
3. Remove the air intake hose.
4. Disconnect the breather hose and the PCV hose.
5. Disconnect the spark plug cables from the spark plugs.
6. Remove the rocker cover and gasket.
7. Install lash adjuster retainer tools MD998443 or equivalent, to the rocker arm.
8. Remove the rocker shaft hold-down bolts gradually and evenly and remove the rocker shaft/arm assemblies.
9. Disassemble the rockers and the rocker shaft springs from the rocker shafts. If they are to be reused, note the location and positioning of all rocker shaft components. It is recommended that all lash adjusters and rockers be replaced as a complete set.

To install:

10. Immerse the lash adjusters in clean diesel fuel, and using a small wire, move the plunger up and down four or five times. while pushing down lightly on the check ball in order to bleed the air from the adjuster.
11. Install the lash adjusters to the rocker arms and attach the special holding tool.
12. Lubricate the rocker shaft with clean engine oil and install the rocker arms.
13. Temporarily tighten the rocker shaft assembly with the mounting bolts so that all rocker arms on the inlet valve side do not push on the valves.
14. Fit the rocker shaft springs from above and position them so that they are at right angles to the plug side. Install the rocker springs before installing the exhaust side rocker shaft and rocker arm assembly.
15. Install the exhaust side rocker shaft assembly in the engine. Tighten the rocker shaft mounting bolts gradually and evenly to 23 ft. lbs. (32 Nm).
16. Remove the lash adjuster retaining tools.
17. Install the rocker cover and tighten the mounting bolts to 30 inch lbs. (3 Nm).
18. Reinstall the spark plug wires to the spark plugs.
19. Reconnect the PCV and breather hoses.
20. Install the air intake hose.
21. Reattach the accelerator cable brackets and reconnect the accelerator cable.
22. Connect the negative battery cable.

3.0L SOHC Engine

▶ **See Figures 20 and 21**

On this engine, the hydraulic lash adjusters are built into the rocker arms.

1. Disconnect the negative battery cable.
2. Remove the valve cover. Install lash adjuster retainer tools MD998443 or equivalent, to prevent the auto-lash adjuster from falling out of the rocker arm.
3. Loosen rocker arm and shaft assembly evenly in several steps. Remove the rocker arm and shaft assembly as a complete unit.
4. Remove the rear camshaft bearing cap and slide the rocker arms, springs and washers from the shaft. If they are to be reused, note the location and positioning of all rocker shaft components. It is rec-

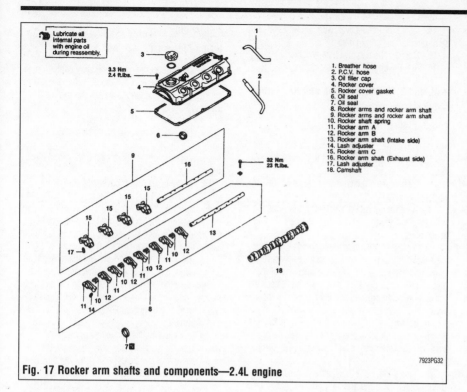

Lubricate all internal parts with engine oil during reassembly.

3.3 Nm
2.4 ft.lbs.

32 Nm
23 ft.lbs.

1. Breather hose
2. P.C.V. hose
3. Oil filler cap
4. Rocker cover
5. Rocker cover gasket
6. Oil seal
7. Oil seal
8. Rocker arms and rocker arm shaft
9. Rocker arms and rocker arm shaft
10. Rocker shaft spring
11. Rocker arm A
12. Rocker arm B
13. Rocker arm shaft (Intake side)
14. Lash adjuster
15. Rocker arm C
16. Rocker arm shaft (Exhaust side)
17. Lash adjuster
18. Camshaft

7923PG32

Fig. 17 Rocker arm shafts and components—2.4L engine

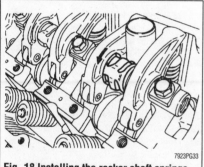

7923PG33

Fig. 18 Installing the rocker shaft springs—2.4L (4G64) engines

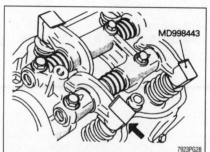

MD998443

7923PG28

Fig. 19 Install the auto lash adjuster holder to prevent them from falling out—2.4L (4G64) engines

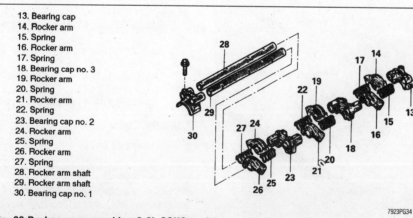

13. Bearing cap
14. Rocker arm
15. Spring
16. Rocker arm
17. Spring
18. Bearing cap no. 3
19. Rocker arm
20. Spring
21. Rocker arm
22. Spring
23. Bearing cap no. 2
24. Rocker arm
25. Spring
26. Rocker arm
27. Spring
28. Rocker arm shaft
29. Rocker arm shaft
30. Bearing cap no. 1

7923PG34

Fig. 20 Rocker arm assembly—3.0L SOHC engine

ommended that all lash adjusters and rockers be replaced as a complete set.

To install:

5. Immerse the lash adjusters in clean diesel fuel. Using a small wire, move the plunger of the lash adjuster up and down 4 or 5 times while pushing down lightly on the check ball in order to bleed out the air. Install the lash adjusters in the rocker arms.

6. Using a light coat of engine oil, assemble the rocker arms to the shaft. Install the rear camshaft bearing cap.

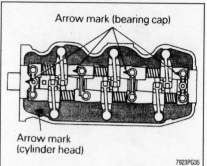

Arrow mark (bearing cap)

Arrow mark (cylinder head)

7923PG35

Fig. 21 When installing the rocker arm/shaft assemblies, ensure that the arrow marks point in the same direction as the arrow stamped into the cylinder head—3.0L SOHC engine

7. Lubricate the camshaft and rocker shaft with clean engine oil and position on the cylinder head.

8. Apply a drop of sealant to the rear edges of the end caps.

9. Install the assembly making sure the notches in the rocker shafts are facing up.

10. Install the cap bolts and tighten evenly and gradually to 14 ft. lbs. (20 Nm). Remove the lash adjuster retainers.

11. Install the valve cover.

12. Connect the negative battery cable.

3.0L DOHC Engine

♦ See Figure 22

1. Relieve the fuel system pressure.

✳✳ CAUTION

Observe all applicable safety precautions when working around fuel. Whenever servicing the fuel system, always work in a well ventilated area. Do not allow fuel spray or vapors to come in contact with a spark or open flame. Keep a dry chemical fire extinguisher near the work area. Always keep fuel in a container specifically designed for fuel storage; also, always properly seal fuel containers to avoid the possibility of fire or explosion.

2. Disconnect battery negative cable.

3. Remove the timing belt cover and timing belt. Refer to the timing belt procedure in this section.

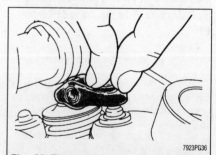

7923PG36

Fig. 22 The rocker arms sit beneath the camshaft and are supported on one end by the valve stem and on the other end by the hydraulic lash adjuster—Diamante with 3.0L DOHC engine

4. Remove the center cover, breather and PCV hoses, and spark plug cables.

5. Remove the rocker cover.

6. Remove the throttle body stay, both camshaft sprockets, and oil seals.

7. Remove the Camshaft Position (CMP) sensor and adapter from the rear of the camshaft.

8. Remove the intake and exhaust camshafts.

9. Remove rocker arms and lash adjusters from the head. It is recommended that all lash adjusters and rockers be replaced as a complete set.

To install:

10. Immerse the lash adjusters in clean diesel fuel. Using a small wire, move the plunger of the lash adjuster up and down four or five times while pushing down lightly on the check ball in order to bleed out the air. Lubricate and install the lash adjusters in the cylinder head.

11. Lubricate the camshafts with clean engine oil and position the camshafts on the cylinder head.

12. Install the bearing caps. Tighten the caps in sequence, in 2 or 3 steps. Caps 2, 3 and 4 have a front mark. Install with the mark aligned with the front mark on the cylinder head. Intake caps have **I** stamped on the cap and exhaust caps have **E**. Also, be sure the rocker arm is correctly mounted on the lash adjuster and the valve stem end. Torque the front and rear retaining cap bolts to 14 ft. lbs. (20 Nm) and tighten the center 3 retaining cap bolts to 8 ft. lbs. (11 Nm).

13. Apply a coating of engine oil to the oil seals and install.

14. Install the timing belt, valve cover and all related parts. Refer to the timing belt procedure in this section.

15. Connect the negative battery cable and check for leaks.

3.5L Engine

♦ **See Figure 23**

1. Disconnect the negative battery cable.
2. Remove the rocker arm cover.

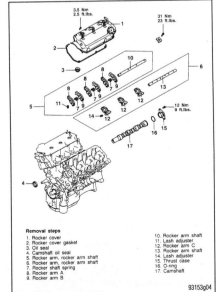

Fig. 23 Camshaft, rocker arm and shaft assemblies—3.5L engine

3. Install the lash adjuster clips on the rocker arms, then loosen the bearing cap bolts. Do not remove the bolts from the bearing caps.

4. Remove the rocker arms, shafts and bearing caps as an assembly.

To install:

5. Install the bearing caps/rocker arm assemblies. Tighten the bolts to 23 ft. lbs. (31 Nm).

6. Remove the lash adjuster clips.

7. Install the rocker arm cover using a new gasket.

8. Connect the negative battery cable.

Thermostat

REMOVAL & INSTALLATION

♦ **See Figures 24, 25, 26, and 27**

1. Disconnect the negative battery cable.
2. Drain the cooling system.

✻✻ CAUTION

Never open, service or drain the radiator or cooling system when hot; serious burns can occur from the steam and hot coolant. Also, when draining engine coolant, keep in mind that cats and dogs are attracted to ethylene glycol antifreeze and could drink any that is left in an uncovered container or in puddles on the ground. This will prove fatal in sufficient quantities. Always drain coolant into a sealable container. Coolant should be reused

Fig. 24 Remove the thermostat housing retaining bolts

Fig. 26 Remove the thermostat from the thermostat housing, noting the location of the relief valve

unless it is contaminated or is several years old.

3. Remove any necessary components to access the thermostat.

4. Remove the thermostat housing retaining bolts.

5. Lift the housing from the engine.

6. Remove the thermostat taking note of its original position in the housing.

To install:

➡**In order to prevent leakage, make sure both mating surfaces are clean and free of any old gasket material.**

7. Install the thermostat so its flange seats tightly in the machined groove in the intake manifold or thermostat case. Refer to its location prior to removal. Align the relief valve with the alignment mark on the thermostat housing.

8. Use a new gasket or O-ring and reinstall the thermostat housing. Torque the housing mounting bolts to the following specifications:

- 1.8L engine: 16 ft. lbs. (22 Nm)
- 1.5L, 1.6L, 2.0L DOHC, and 1990–92 2.0L SOHC engines: 12–14 ft. lbs. (17–20 Nm)
- 1993 2.0L SOHC engine: 7–10 ft. lbs. (10–15 Nm)
- 2.4L engine: 10 ft. lbs. (14 Nm)
- 3.0L and 3.5L engines: 12–14 ft. lbs. (17–20 Nm)

9. Fill the system with coolant.

10. Install the removed air intake plumbing.

Fig. 25 Carefully lift the housing from the engine

Fig. 27 If reusing the thermostat, always replace the O-ring

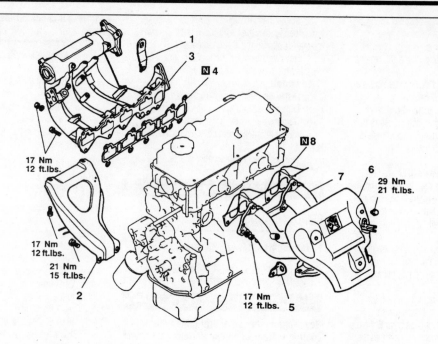

1. Engine hanger
2. Intake manifold stay
3. Intake manifold
4. Intake manifold gasket

5. Engine hanger
6. Exhaust manifold cover
7. Exhaust manifold
8. Exhaust manifold gasket

7923PG38

Fig. 28 Exploded view of the intake and exhaust manifold mounting—1.5L (4G15) engine

11. Connect the negative battery cable, run the vehicle until the thermostat opens and fill the radiator completely.

12. Once the vehicle has cooled, recheck the coolant level.

Intake Manifold

REMOVAL & INSTALLATION

1.5L Engine

♦ See Figure 28

1. Relieve the fuel system pressure.

✳✳ CAUTION

Observe all applicable safety precautions when working around fuel. Whenever servicing the fuel system, always work in a well ventilated area. Do not allow fuel spray or vapors to come in contact with a spark or open flame. Keep a dry chemical fire extinguisher near the work area. Always keep fuel in a container specifically designed for fuel storage; also, always properly seal fuel containers to avoid the possibility of fire or explosion.

2. Disconnect battery negative cable and drain the cooling system.

✳✳ CAUTION

Never open, service or drain the radiator or cooling system when hot; serious burns can occur from the steam and hot coolant. Also,

when draining engine coolant, keep in mind that cats and dogs are attracted to ethylene glycol antifreeze and could drink any that is left in an uncovered container or in puddles on the ground. This will prove fatal in sufficient quantities. Always drain coolant into a sealable container. Coolant should be reused unless it is contaminated or is several years old.

3. Disconnect the upper radiator hose, heater hose and water bypass hose.

4. Remove the thermostat housing from intake manifold.

5. Disconnect the accelerator cable, breather hose and air intake hose.

6. Remove all vacuum hoses and pipes as necessary, including the brake booster vacuum line.

7. Remove the throttle body assembly.

8. Disconnect the high pressure fuel line and the fuel return hose.

9. Tag and detach the electrical connectors from the oxygen sensor, coolant temperature sensor, intake air temperature, idle speed control assembly, EGR temperature sensor, spark plug wires and distributor.

10. Remove the fuel rail, fuel injectors, pressure regulator and insulators.

11. Remove the EGR valve from the intake manifold.

12. Remove the intake manifold support bracket and remove the engine mount support bracket.

13. Remove the intake manifold mounting bolts and remove the intake manifold assembly.

To install:

14. Clean all gasket material from the cylinder head intake mounting surface and intake manifold assembly. Check both surfaces for cracks or other dam-

age. Check the intake manifold water passages and jet air passages for clogging. Clean if necessary.

15. Using a straight edge, measure the distortion of the intake manifold-to-cylinder head. Total distortion or warpage should be 0.006 inches (0.15mm or less).

16. Install a new intake manifold gasket to the head and install the manifold. Torque the manifold in a crisscross pattern, starting from the inside and working outwards to 13 ft. lbs. (18 Nm).

17. Install the intake manifold support bracket and torque the mounting bolts to 16 ft. lbs. (22 Nm).

18. Install the engine mount support bracket and torque the mounting bolts to 26 ft. lbs. (36 Nm).

19. Using a new gasket, install the EGR valve and torque the mounting bolts to 15 ft. lbs. (21 Nm).

20. Using new insulators and O-rings, install the fuel delivery pipe, injectors and pressure regulator to the engine. Torque the retaining bolts to 7–9 ft. lbs. (10–14 Nm).

21. Attach the electrical connectors to the oxygen sensor, coolant temperature sensor, intake air temperature, idle speed control assembly, EGR temperature sensor, spark plug wires and distributor.

22. Using a new O-ring for the feed pipe and a new clamp for the return pipe, install the fuel hoses.

23. Install the throttle body assembly.

24. Install the vacuum hoses and pipes as necessary, including the brake booster vacuum line.

25. Install and adjust the accelerator cable. Install the breather and air intake hose.

26. Using a new gasket, install the thermostat housing to the intake manifold and tighten the mounting bolts to 13 ft. lbs. (18 Nm).

27. Connect the upper radiator hose, heater hose and water bypass hose. Be sure to use new hose clamps.

28. Fill the system with coolant.

29. Connect the negative battery cable, run the vehicle until the thermostat opens, fill the radiator completely.

30. Check and adjust the idle speed and ignition timing.

31. Once the vehicle has cooled, recheck the coolant level.

1.8L Engine

♦ **See Figures 29 and 30**

1. Relieve the fuel system pressure.

> ⁂ **CAUTION**
>
> **Observe all applicable safety precautions when working around fuel. Whenever servicing the fuel system, always work in a well ventilated area. Do not allow fuel spray or vapors to come in contact with a spark or open flame. Keep a dry chemical fire extinguisher near the work area. Always keep fuel in a container specifically designed for fuel storage; also, always properly seal fuel containers to avoid the possibility of fire or explosion.**

2. Disconnect battery negative cable and drain the cooling system.

> ⁂ **CAUTION**
>
> **Never open, service or drain the radiator or cooling system when hot; serious burns can occur from the steam and hot coolant. Also, when draining engine coolant, keep in mind that cats and dogs are attracted to ethylene glycol antifreeze and could drink any that is left in an uncovered container or in puddles on the ground. This will prove fatal in sufficient quantities. Always drain coolant into a sealable container. Coolant should be reused unless it is contaminated or is several years old.**

3. Disconnect the accelerator cable and the air intake hose.

4. Tag and detach the electrical connectors from the oxygen sensor, coolant temperature sensor, idle speed control assembly, EGR temperature sensor, oil pressure switch, spark plug wires and distributor.

5. Disconnect the wiring from the throttle position sensor, fuel injectors and disconnect the ground cables.

6. Remove all vacuum hoses and pipes as necessary, including the brake booster and PCV vacuum lines.

7. Disconnect the upper radiator hose, heater hose and water bypass hose.

8. Disconnect the high pressure fuel line and the fuel return hose.

9. Remove the fuel rail, fuel injectors, pressure regulator and insulators.

10. Remove the intake manifold support bracket.

11. If the thermostat housing is preventing removal of the intake manifold, remove it.

12. Remove the intake manifold mounting bolts/nuts and remove the intake manifold assembly.

To install:

13. Clean all gasket material from the cylinder head intake mounting surface and intake manifold assembly. Check both surfaces for cracks or other damage. Check the intake manifold water passages and jet air passages for clogging. Clean if necessary.

14. Using a straight edge, measure the distortion of the intake manifold-to-cylinder head. Total distortion or warpage should be 0.006 inches (0.15mm or less).

15. Install a new intake manifold gasket to the head and install the manifold. Torque the manifold in a crisscross pattern, starting from the inside and working outwards to 14 ft. lbs. (20 Nm).

16. If removed, install the thermostat housing.

17. Install the intake manifold brace bracket.

18. Install the fuel delivery pipe, injectors and pressure regulator to the engine. Torque the retaining bolts to 108 inch lbs. (12 Nm).

19. Using a new O-ring for the feed pipe and a new clamp for the return pipe, install the fuel hoses.

20. Connect the upper radiator hose, heater hose and water bypass hoses.

21. Install the vacuum hoses and pipes as necessary. Be sure to connect the brake booster and PCV vacuum lines.

22. Connect the wiring to the throttle position sensor, fuel injectors and connect the ground cables.

23. Attach the electrical wiring to the oxygen sensor, coolant temperature sensor, idle speed control assembly, EGR temperature sensor, oil pressure switch, spark plug wires and distributor.

24. Connect and adjust the accelerator cable and install the air intake hose.

25. Fill the system with coolant.

26. Connect the negative battery cable, run the vehicle until the thermostat opens, fill the radiator completely.

27. Check and adjust the idle speed and ignition timing.

28. Once the vehicle has cooled, recheck the coolant level.

2.0L SOHC Engine

♦ **See Figure 31**

1. Relieve the fuel system pressure.

> ⁂ **CAUTION**
>
> **Observe all applicable safety precautions when working around fuel. Whenever servicing the fuel system, always work in a well ventilated area. Do not allow fuel spray or vapors to come in contact with a spark or open flame. Keep a dry chemical fire extinguisher near the work area. Always keep fuel in a container specifically designed for fuel storage; also, always properly seal fuel containers to avoid the possibility of fire or explosion.**

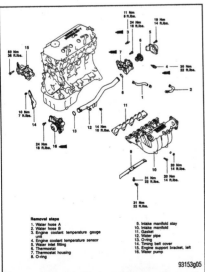

Removal steps
1. Water hose A
2. Water hose B
3. Engine coolant temperature gauge unit
4. Engine coolant temperature sensor
5. Water inlet fitting
6. Thermostat
7. Thermostat housing
8. O-ring
9. Intake manifold stay
10. Intake manifold
11. Gasket
12. Water pipe
13. O-ring
14. Timing belt cover
15. Engine support bracket, left
16. Water pump

93153g05

Fig. 29 Exploded view of the intake manifold mounting—1993 1.8L engine

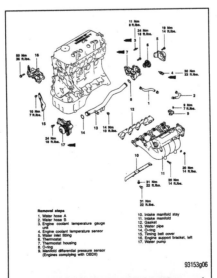

Removal steps
1. Water hose A
2. Water hose B
3. Engine coolant temperature gauge unit
4. Engine coolant temperature sensor
5. Water inlet fitting
6. Thermostat
7. Thermostat housing
8. O-ring
9. Manifold differential pressure sensor (Engines complying with OBDII)
10. Intake manifold stay
11. Intake manifold
12. Gasket
13. Water pipe
14. O-ring
15. Timing belt cover
16. Engine support bracket, left
17. Water pump

93153g06

Fig. 30 Exploded view of the intake manifold mounting—1994–00 1.8L engine

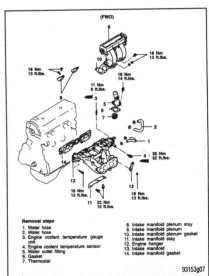

Removal steps
1. Water hose
2. Water hose
3. Engine coolant temperature gauge unit
4. Engine coolant temperature sensor
5. Water outlet fitting
6. Gasket
7. Thermostat
8. Intake manifold plenum stay
9. Intake manifold plenum
10. Intake manifold plenum gasket
11. Intake manifold stay
12. Engine hanger
13. Intake manifold
14. Intake manifold gasket

93153g07

Fig. 31 Exploded view of the intake manifold mounting—2.0L SOHC engine

2. Disconnect the battery negative cable.
3. Drain the cooling system.

✳✳ CAUTION

Never open, service or drain the radiator or cooling system when hot; serious burns can occur from the steam and hot coolant. Also, when draining engine coolant, keep in mind that cats and dogs are attracted to ethylene glycol antifreeze and could drink any that is left in an uncovered container or in puddles on the ground. This will prove fatal in sufficient quantities. Always drain coolant into a sealable container. Coolant should be reused unless it is contaminated or is several years old.

4. Disconnect the accelerator cable and air intake hose.
5. Disconnect the upper radiator hose, heater hose and water bypass hose.
6. Unplug the vacuum connection at the power brake booster and the PCV valve if still connected. Disconnect all remaining vacuum hoses and pipes as necessary.
7. Disconnect the high pressure fuel line, fuel return hose and remove throttle control cable brackets.
8. Tag and detach the electrical connectors from the oxygen sensor, coolant temperature sensor, thermo switch, idle speed control assembly, EGR temperature sensor, distributor, fuel injectors and spark plug wires. Position the engine wiring harness aside.
9. Matchmark the distributor housing to the intake manifold, and remove the distributor.
10. Remove the intake manifold bracket and the engine hanger.
11. If the thermostat housing is preventing removal of the intake manifold, remove it.
12. Remove the intake manifold mounting bolts and remove the intake manifold assembly. Disassemble manifold from the intake plenum on a work bench as required.
To install:
13. Clean all gasket material from the cylinder head intake mounting surface and intake manifold assembly. Check both surfaces for cracks or other damage. Check the intake manifold water passages and jet air passages for clogging. Clean if necessary.
14. Assemble the intake manifold assembly using all new gaskets. Torque air intake plenum bolts to 11–14 ft. lbs. (15–19 Nm).
15. Install a new intake manifold gasket to the head and install the manifold. Torque the manifold in a crisscross pattern, starting from the inside and working outwards to 11–14 ft. lbs. (15–19 Nm).
16. Install the fuel delivery pipe, injectors and pressure regulator to the engine. Torque the retaining bolts to 4 ft. lbs. (6 Nm).
17. Install the thermostat housing, intake manifold brace bracket, and engine hanger bracket.
18. Connect or install all hoses, cables and electrical connectors that were removed or disconnected during the removal procedure.
19. Align the distributor matchmarks and install the distributor.
20. Fill the system with coolant.
21. Connect the negative battery cable, run the vehicle until the thermostat opens, fill the radiator completely.

22. Adjust the accelerator cable. Check and adjust the idle speed and ignition timing.
23. Once the vehicle has cooled, recheck the coolant level.

1.6L and 2.0L DOHC Engines

▸ **See Figure 32**

1. Relieve the fuel system pressure.

✳✳ CAUTION

Observe all applicable safety precautions when working around fuel. Whenever servicing the fuel system, always work in a well ventilated area. Do not allow fuel spray or vapors to come in contact with a spark or open flame. Keep a dry chemical fire extinguisher near the work area. Always keep fuel in a container specifically designed for fuel storage; also, always properly seal fuel containers to avoid the possibility of fire or explosion.

2. Disconnect battery negative cable and drain the cooling system.

✳✳ CAUTION

Never open, service or drain the radiator or cooling system when hot; serious burns can occur from the steam and hot coolant. Also, when draining engine coolant, keep in mind that cats and dogs are attracted to ethylene glycol antifreeze and could drink any that is left in an uncovered container or in puddles on the ground. This will prove fatal in sufficient quantities. Always drain coolant into a sealable container. Coolant should be reused unless it is contaminated or is several years old.

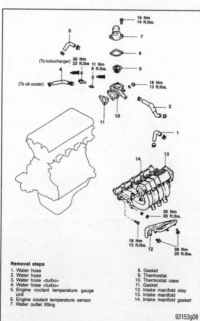

Fig. 32 Exploded view of the intake manifold and related components—1.6L and 2.0L DOHC engine

3. Disconnect the accelerator cable and air intake hose.
4. Disconnect the coolant hose from the throttle housing.
5. Detach the vacuum connection at the power brake booster and the PCV valve if still connected. Disconnect all remaining vacuum hoses and pipes as necessary.
6. Disconnect the high pressure fuel line, fuel return hose and remove throttle control cable brackets.
7. Tag and detach the electrical connectors from the oxygen sensor, coolant temperature sensor, thermo switch, throttle position sensor, idle speed control assembly, EGR temperature sensor, distributor, fuel injectors and spark plug wires. Position the engine wiring harness aside.
8. Remove the intake manifold bracket.
9. Remove the intake manifold mounting bolts and remove the intake manifold assembly. Disassemble manifold on a work bench as required.
To install:
10. Clean all gasket material from the cylinder head intake mounting surface and intake manifold assembly. Check both surfaces for cracks or other damage. Check the intake manifold water passages and jet air passages for clogging. Clean if necessary.
11. Assemble the intake manifold assembly using all new gaskets.
12. Install a new intake manifold gasket to the head and install the manifold. Torque the manifold in a crisscross pattern, starting from the inside and working outwards to 11–14 ft. lbs. (15–20 Nm).
13. Install the fuel delivery pipe, injectors and pressure regulator to the engine. Torque the retaining bolts to 4 ft. lbs. (6 Nm).
14. Install the intake manifold brace bracket and tighten bolts to 13–18 ft. lbs. (18–25 Nm).
15. Connect or install all hoses, cables and electrical connectors that were removed or disconnected during the removal procedure.
16. Fill the system with coolant.
17. Connect the negative battery cable, run the vehicle until the thermostat opens, fill the radiator completely.
18. Adjust the accelerator cable.
19. Check and adjust the idle speed and ignition timing.
20. Once the vehicle has cooled, recheck the coolant level.

2.4L Engine

▸ **See Figures 33 thru 51**

Fig. 33 Detach the A/C temp electrical connector

Fig. 34 Unplug the connector from the Throttle Position (TP) sensor

Fig. 35 Detach the connectors from all of the fuel injectors

Fig. 36 Unplug the main engine harness junction electrical connector

Fig. 37 Detach the Camshaft Position (CMP) sensor connector

Fig. 38 Unplug the connector from the Manifold Absolute Pressure (MAP) sensor

Fig. 39 Detach the connector for the Idle Air Control (IAC) motor

Fig. 40 Remove the engine harness retaining bracket bolts, then move the harness out of the way

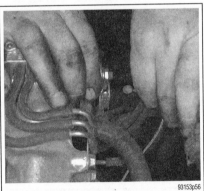

Fig. 41 Remove the accelerator cable end from the throttle lever

Fig. 42 Remove the accelerator cable bracket retaining bolts . . .

Fig. 43 . . . then position the accelerator cable out of the way

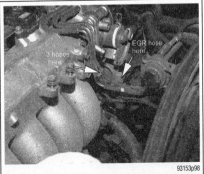

Fig. 44 Disconnect the EGR hose and the three vacuum hoses on the back of the intake manifold

Fig. 45 Remove the hose shown here from the throttle body

Fig. 46 Remove the brake booster vacuum hose from the back of the intake manifold

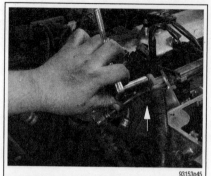

Fig. 47 Remove the fuel feed line-to-fuel rail retaining fitting bolts . . .

Fig. 48 . . . then remove the fuel feed line from the fuel injector rail

Fig. 49 From underneath the vehicle, remove the two intake manifold support bracket bolts

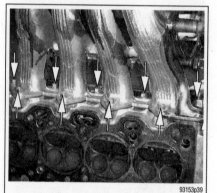

Fig. 50 Remove the intake manifold retaining bolts . . .

Fig. 51 . . . then remove the manifold from the cylinder head

1. Relieve the fuel system pressure.

✳✳ CAUTION

Observe all applicable safety precautions when working around fuel. Whenever servicing the fuel system, always work in a well ventilated area. Do not allow fuel spray or vapors to come in contact with a spark or open flame. Keep a dry chemical fire extinguisher near the work area. Always keep fuel in a container specifically designed for fuel storage; also, always properly seal fuel containers to avoid the possibility of fire or explosion.

2. Disconnect battery negative cable and drain the cooling system.

✳✳ CAUTION

Never open, service or drain the radiator or cooling system when hot; serious burns can occur from the steam and hot coolant. Also, when draining engine coolant, keep in mind that cats and dogs are attracted to ethylene glycol antifreeze and could drink any that is left in an uncovered container or in puddles on the ground. This will prove fatal in sufficient quantities. Always drain coolant into a sealable container. Coolant should be reused unless it is contaminated or is several years old.

3. Disconnect the accelerator cable, breather hose and air intake hose.

4. Disconnect the coolant hose from the throttle housing.

5. Detach the vacuum connection at the power brake booster and the PCV valve if still connected. Disconnect all remaining vacuum hoses and pipes as necessary.

✳✳ CAUTION

Fuel injection systems remain under pressure after the engine has been turned OFF. Properly relieve fuel pressure before disconnecting any fuel lines. Failure to do so may result in fire or personal injury.

6. Disconnect the high pressure fuel line, fuel return hose and remove throttle control cable brackets.

7. Tag and unplug the electrical connectors from the coolant temperature sensor, coolant temperature gauge, IAC valve, ignition coil, EGR temperature sensor, knock sensor, oxygen sensor, throttle position sensor, distributor, A/C temperature sensor, fuel injectors and ignition power transistor. Position the engine wiring harness aside.

8. Label and disconnect the spark plug wires from the spark plugs.

9. Remove the intake manifold stay bracket.

10. Remove the intake manifold mounting bolts and remove the intake manifold assembly. Disassemble manifold on a work bench as required.

To install:

11. Clean all gasket material from the cylinder head intake mounting surface and intake manifold assembly. Check both surfaces for cracks or other damage. Check the intake manifold water passages and

jet air passages for clogging. Clean if necessary.

12. Assemble the intake manifold assembly using all new gaskets.

13. Position a new intake manifold gasket on the head, then install the manifold. Torque the manifold in a crisscross pattern, starting from the inside and working outwards to 15 ft. lbs. (20 Nm) for bolts, and to 26 ft. lbs. (35 Nm) for nuts on 1994 vehicles or 15 ft. lbs. (20 Nm) for nuts on 1995–00 vehicles.

14. Install the fuel delivery pipe, injectors and pressure regulator to the engine. Torque the retaining bolts to 4 ft. lbs. (6 Nm).

15. Install the intake manifold brace bracket and tighten bolts to 21 ft. lbs. (29 Nm).

16. Connect or install all hoses, cables and electrical connectors that were removed or disconnected during the removal procedure.

17. Fill the system with coolant.

18. Connect the negative battery cable, run the vehicle until the thermostat opens, fill the radiator completely.

19. Adjust the accelerator cable. Check and adjust the idle speed and ignition timing.

20. Once the vehicle has cooled, recheck the coolant level.

3.0L and 3.5L Engines

◆ See Figures 52 thru 57

1. Relieve the fuel system pressure.

✳✳ CAUTION

Observe all applicable safety precautions when working around fuel. Whenever servic-

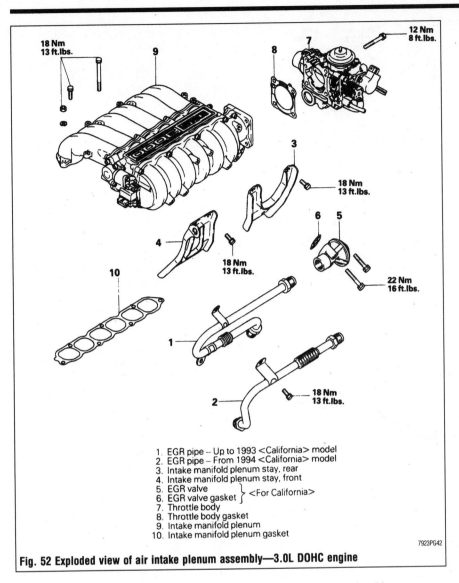

1. EGR pipe -- Up to 1993 <California> model
2. EGR pipe – From 1994 <California> model
3. Intake manifold plenum stay, rear
4. Intake manifold plenum stay, front
5. EGR valve }<For California>
6. EGR valve gasket }
7. Throttle body
8. Throttle body gasket
9. Intake manifold plenum
10. Intake manifold plenum gasket

7923PG42

Fig. 52 Exploded view of air intake plenum assembly—3.0L DOHC engine

ing the fuel system, always work in a well ventilated area. Do not allow fuel spray or vapors to come in contact with a spark or open flame. Keep a dry chemical fire extinguisher near the work area. Always keep fuel in a container specifically designed for fuel storage; also, always properly seal fuel containers to avoid the possibility of fire or explosion.

2. Disconnect battery negative cable and drain the cooling system.

✳✳ CAUTION

Never open, service or drain the radiator or cooling system when hot; serious burns can occur from the steam and hot coolant. Also, when draining engine coolant, keep in mind that cats and dogs are attracted to ethylene glycol antifreeze and could drink any that is left in an uncovered container or in puddles on the ground. This will prove fatal in sufficient quantities. Always drain coolant into a sealable container. Coolant should be reused unless it is contaminated or is several years old.

3. Remove the air intake hose(s).
4. Disconnect the accelerator control cables from the throttle body.
5. Tag and disconnect the vacuum hoses including the brake booster hose.
6. Tag and detach the wire harness connectors.
7. Disconnect the high pressure and return fuel hoses.
8. Disconnect EGR pipe and remove the EGR valve and EGR temperature sensor from the intake plenum assembly.
9. If equipped, remove the manifold pressure sensor.
10. Remove the plenum retaining bracket.
11. Remove the plenum retaining nuts and bolts and remove the air intake plenum from the intake manifold. Discard the gasket.
12. Remove the upper timing belt covers.
13. Remove the water pump stay bracket.

➡**It is not necessary to remove the fuel injectors from the intake unless the manifold assembly is being replaced.**

14. Remove the fuel rail with the injectors attached.

15. Disconnect the coolant hoses from the intake manifold. Be sure to note the connections.
16. Remove the intake manifold mounting nuts and remove the intake manifold.
17. Clean the gasket mounting surfaces.
To install:
18. Check all items for cracks, clogging and warpage. Maximum warpage is 0.0059 inches (0.15mm). Replace any questionable parts.
19. Thoroughly clean and dry the mating surfaces of the heads, intake manifold and air intake plenum.
20. Install new intake manifold gaskets to the cylinder heads with the adhesive side facing up.
21. Place the manifold on the cylinder heads.
22. Lubricate the studs lightly with oil and install the nuts.
23. For vehicles produced up to and including November of 1993, tighten the mounting nuts as follows:
   a. Front bank nuts: 27–43 inch lbs. (3–5 Nm)
   b. Rear bank nuts: 9–11 ft. lbs. (12–15 Nm)
   c. Front bank nuts: 9–11 ft. lbs. (12–15 Nm)
24. For vehicles produced after November of 1993, tighten the mounting nuts as follows:
   a. Front bank nuts: 48–72 inch lbs. (5–8 Nm)
   b. Rear bank nuts to: 14–17 ft. lbs. (20–23 Nm)
   c. Front bank nuts to: 14–17 ft. lbs. (20–23 Nm)
25. Using new clamps, connect the coolant hoses to the intake manifold.
26. Using new O-rings, install the fuel rail assembly, if removed. Tighten the mounting bolts to 7–9 ft. lbs. (10–13 Nm).
27. Install a new intake air plenum gasket and install the plenum. Tighten the retaining nuts and bolts evenly and gradually to 13 ft. lbs. (18 Nm).
28. Install the retaining bracket and tighten the retaining bolts to 13 ft. lbs. (18 Nm).
29. If removed, install the manifold pressure sensor.
30. Using a new gasket, install the EGR valve and tighten the bolts to 16 ft. lbs. (22 Nm).
31. Install the EGR temperature sensor and tighten the fitting to 7–9 ft. lbs. (10–12 Nm).
32. Connect the EGR pipe and tighten the fittings to 43 ft. lbs. (60 Nm).
33. Replace the O-ring and connect the high pressure fuel hose. Tighten the retaining bolts to 48 inch lbs. (5 Nm).
34. Using a new hose clamp, connect the fuel return hose.
35. Install the water pump stay bracket.
36. Install the upper timing belt covers.
37. Connect the harness connector and vacuum hoses.
38. Connect and adjust the accelerator cables.
39. Install the air intake hose(s).
40. Fill the system with coolant.
41. Connect the negative battery cable, run the vehicle until the thermostat opens, fill the radiator completely.
42. Check and adjust the idle speed and ignition timing.
43. Once the vehicle has cooled, recheck the coolant level.

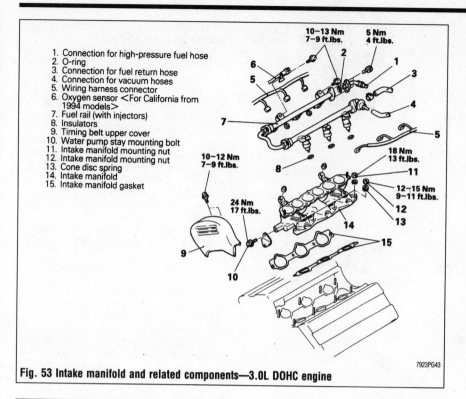

1. Connection for high-pressure fuel hose
2. O-ring
3. Connection for fuel return hose
4. Connection for vacuum hoses
5. Wiring harness connector
6. Oxygen sensor <For California from 1994 models>
7. Fuel rail (with injectors)
8. Insulators
9. Timing belt upper cover
10. Water pump stay mounting bolt
11. Intake manifold mounting nut
12. Intake manifold mounting nut
13. Cone disc spring
14. Intake manifold
15. Intake manifold gasket

Fig. 53 Intake manifold and related components—3.0L DOHC engine

7923PG43

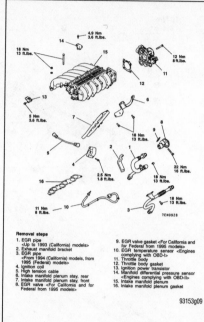

Removal steps
1. EGR pipe <Up to 1993 (California) models>
2. Exhaust manifold bracket
3. EGR pipe <From 1994 (California) models, from 1995 (Federal) models>
4. Ignition coil
5. High tension cable
6. Intake manifold plenum stay, rear
7. Intake manifold plenum stay, front
8. EGR valve <For California and for Federal from 1995 models>
9. EGR valve gasket <For California and for Federal from 1995 models>
10. EGR temperature sensor <Engines complying with OBD-I>
11. Throttle body
12. Throttle body gasket
13. Ignition power transistor
14. Manifold differential pressure sensor <Engines complying with OBD-II>
15. Intake manifold plenum
16. Intake manifold plenum gasket

93153g09

Fig. 54 Exploded view of air intake plenum assembly—3.0L SOHC engine

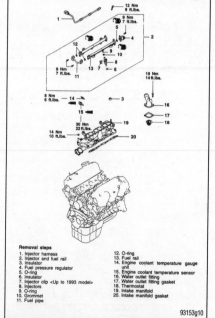

Removal steps
1. Injector harness
2. Injector and fuel rail
3. Insulator
4. Fuel pressure regulator
5. O-ring
6. Insulator
7. Injector clip <Up to 1993 model>
8. Injectors
9. O-ring
10. Grommet
11. Fuel pipe
12. O-ring
13. Fuel rail
14. Engine coolant temperature gauge unit
15. Engine coolant temperature sensor
16. Water outlet fitting
17. Water outlet fitting gasket
18. Thermostat
19. Intake manifold
20. Intake manifold gasket

93153g10

Fig. 55 Exploded view of the intake manifold mounting—3.0L SOHC engine

Removal steps
1. Engine cover
2. Clamp
3. Accelerator cable bracket
4. Intake plenum stay, front
5. Intake plenum stay, rear
6. EGR valve
7. EGR valve gasket
8. EGR pipe
9. EGR pipe gasket
10. Connector bracket
11. Vacuum pipe
12. Throttle body
13. Throttle body gasket
14. Intake plenum
15. Intake plenum gasket

93153g11

Fig. 56 Exploded view of air intake plenum assembly—3.5L engine

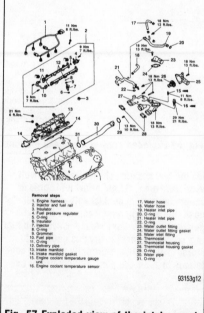

Removal steps
1. Engine harness
2. Injector and fuel rail
3. Insulator
4. Fuel pressure regulator
5. O-ring
6. Insulator
7. Injector
8. O-ring
9. Grommet
10. Fuel pipe
11. O-ring
12. Delivery pipe
13. Intake manifold
14. Intake manifold gasket
15. Engine coolant temperature gauge unit
16. Engine coolant temperature sensor
17. Water hose
18. Water hose
19. Heater inlet pipe
20. O-ring
21. Heater inlet pipe
22. O-ring
23. Water outlet fitting
24. Water outlet fitting gasket
25. Water inlet fitting
26. Thermostat
27. Thermostat housing
28. Thermostat housing gasket
29. O-ring
30. Water pipe
31. O-ring

93153g12

Fig. 57 Exploded view of the intake manifold mounting—3.5L engine

Exhaust Manifold

REMOVAL & INSTALLATION

1.5L and 1.8L Engine

♦ See Figures 58 and 59

1. Disconnect battery negative cable.
2. Raise the vehicle and support safely.
3. Remove the exhaust pipe to exhaust manifold nuts and separate exhaust pipe. Discard gasket.

4. Lower vehicle.
5. Remove electric cooling fan assembly, if necessary.
6. If the oxygen sensor is located in the manifold, remove the sensor.
7. Disconnect necessary EGR components.
8. Remove outer exhaust manifold heat shield and engine hanger. Detach the electrical connector and remove the oxygen sensor.
9. Remove the exhaust manifold mounting bolts, the inner heat shield and the exhaust manifold.

To install:
10. Clean all gasket material from the mating surfaces and check the manifold for damage.
11. Using a new gasket, install the manifold. For 1.5L engines, tighten the nuts in a crisscross pattern to 13 ft. lbs. (18 Nm). For 1.8L engines, tighten the inner nuts in a crisscross pattern to 13 ft. lbs. (18 Nm) and tighten the two outer (larger) nuts to 22 ft. lbs. (30 Nm).
12. Install the heat shields.
13. Connect EGR components.
14. If removed, install the oxygen sensor.

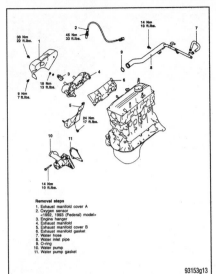

Removal steps
1. Exhaust manifold cover A
2. Oxygen sensor
   <1992, 1993 (Federal) model>
3. Engine hanger
4. Exhaust manifold cover B
5. Exhaust manifold cover B
6. Exhaust manifold
7. Water hose
8. Water inlet pipe
9. O-ring
10. Water pump
11. Water pump gasket

93153g13

Fig. 58 Exploded view of the exhaust manifold —1.5L engine

15. Install the electric cooling fan assembly as required.

16. Install a new flange gasket and connect the exhaust pipe.

17. Connect the negative battery cable and check for exhaust leaks.

1.6L and 2.0L Engines

♦ **See Figures 60, 61, and 62**

1. Disconnect the negative battery cable.
2. Raise the vehicle and support safely.
3. Remove the front exhaust pipe to exhaust manifold nuts and separate exhaust pipe. Discard the gasket.
4. Lower the vehicle.
5. If equipped with air conditioning, remove condenser cooling fan assembly.
6. Using special tool MD998703 or equivalent, disconnect and remove the oxygen sensor.

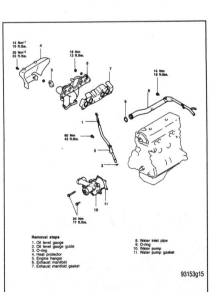

Removal steps
1. Oil level gauge
2. Oil level gauge guide
3. O-ring
4. Heat protector
5. Engine hanger
6. Exhaust manifold
7. Exhaust manifold gasket
8. Water inlet pipe
9. O-ring
10. Water pump
11. Water pump gasket

93153g15

Fig. 60 Exhaust manifold exploded view— 2.0L SOHC engine

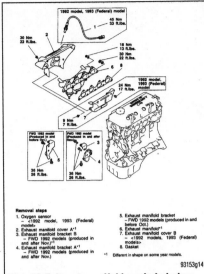

Removal steps
1. Oxygen sensor
   – <1992 model, 1993 (Federal) model>
2. Exhaust manifold cover A*1
3. Exhaust manifold bracket B
   – FWD 1992 models (produced in and after Nov.)*1
4. Exhaust manifold bracket A*1
   – FWD 1992 models (produced in and after Nov.)
5. Exhaust manifold bracket
   – FWD 1992 models (produced in and before Oct.)
6. Exhaust manifold*1
7. Exhaust manifold cover B
   – <1992 models, 1993 (Federal) models>
8. Gasket

*1 Different in shape on some year models.

93153g14

Fig. 59 Exhaust manifold exploded view— 1.8L engine

7. Remove outer exhaust manifold heat shield and the engine hanger.

8. Remove the exhaust manifold mounting nuts, the inner heat shield and the exhaust manifold from the engine.

To install:

9. Clean all gasket material from the mating surfaces and check the manifold for damage or cracking.

10. Using a new gasket, install the exhaust manifold, to the engine. Tighten the nuts to in a crisscross pattern to 11–14 ft. lbs. (15–20 Nm) for 2.0L SOHC engine or to 18–22 ft. lbs. (25–30 Nm) for 1.6L and 2.0L DOHC engine.

11. Install the outer heat shield and tighten the mounting bolts to 10 ft. lbs. (14 Nm).

12. Install the electric cooling fan assembly, if removed.

13. Using a new flange gasket, connect the exhaust pipe and tighten the mounting nuts to 29–36 ft. lbs. (40–50 Nm).

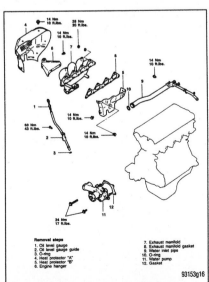

Removal steps
1. Oil level gauge
2. Oil level gauge guide
3. O-ring
4. Heat protector "A"
5. Heat protector "B"
6. Engine hanger
7. Exhaust manifold
8. Exhaust manifold gasket
9. Water inlet pipe
10. O-ring
11. Water pump
12. Gasket

93153g16

Fig. 61 Exhaust manifold exploded view— 1.6L and 2.0L (non-turbo) DOHC engine

---

14. Connect the negative battery cable and check for exhaust leaks.

2.4L Engine

♦ **See Figures 63 thru 71**

1. Disconnect battery negative cable.
2. Raise the vehicle and support safely.
3. Remove the exhaust pipe-to-exhaust manifold nuts, the hanger retaining bolt, then separate the exhaust pipe. Discard the gasket.
4. Remove the outer exhaust manifold heat shield and engine hanger.
5. Remove the exhaust manifold mounting nuts and the exhaust manifold from the engine.

To install:

6. Clean all gasket material from the mating surfaces and check the manifold for damage or cracking.

7. Install a new gasket and install the manifold. Tighten the nuts to in a crisscross pattern to 18–21 ft. lbs. (25–29 Nm).

8. Install the heat shields and tighten the mounting bolts 10 ft. lbs. (14 Nm).

9. Install a new flange gasket and connect the exhaust pipe. Tighten the mounting nuts to 32 ft. lbs. (44 Nm).

10. Connect the negative battery cable and check for exhaust leaks.

3.0L Engines

♦ **See Figures 72 and 73**

> ✺✺✺ **CAUTION**
>
> **Do not attempt the work on the exhaust system until it has completely cooled.**

1. Disconnect battery negative cable.
2. Raise the vehicle and support safely.
3. Remove the exhaust pipe to exhaust manifold nuts and remove the front exhaust pipe.
4. Lower the vehicle.
5. If removing the front manifold, remove condenser electric cooling fan assembly.

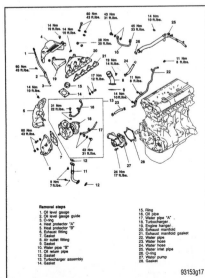

Removal steps
1. Oil level gauge
2. Oil level gauge guide
3. O-ring
4. Heat protector "A"
5. Heat protector "B"
6. Exhaust fitting
7. Gasket
8. Air outlet fitting
9. Gasket
10. Water pipe "B"
11. Oil return pipe
12. Gasket
13. Turbocharger assembly
14. Gasket
15. Ring
16. Oil pipe
17. Water pipe "A"
18. Turbocharger
19. Engine hanger
20. Exhaust manifold
21. Exhaust manifold gasket
22. Water pipe
23. Water hose
24. Water pipe
25. Water inlet pipe
26. O-ring
27. Water pump
28. Gasket

93153g17

Fig. 62 Exhaust manifold exploded view— 2.0L (turbo) DOHC engine

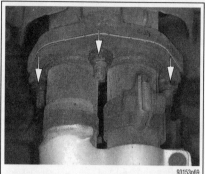

Fig. 63 Remove the exhaust pipe-to-exhaust manifold nuts

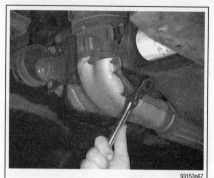

Fig. 64 Remove the hanger retaining bolt . . .

Fig. 65 . . . then separate the pipe from the manifold

Fig. 66 Remove the heat shield retaining bolts . . .

Fig. 67 . . . then remove the heat shield from the exhaust manifold

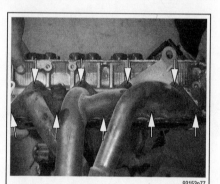

Fig. 68 Remove the exhaust manifold retaining nuts

Fig. 69 Remove the engine lifting eye from the manifold . . .

Fig. 70 . . . then remove the manifold from the cylinder head

Fig. 71 Remove the exhaust manifold gasket, thoroughly clean the mounting surfaces, and replace the gasket

6. For the DOHC engine, if removing the front manifold, remove the alternator and mounting bracket from the vehicle.

7. For the DOHC engine, separate the A/C compressor from the mounting bracket. Leaving the hoses connected, position the compressor aside.

8. If removing the front manifold, remove the oil dipstick and tube from the engine.

9. For the DOHC engine, if removing the front manifold, remove the heat protector.

10. If removing the rear manifold, disconnect the EGR tube.

11. For the SOHC engine, if removing the rear manifold, remove the intake plenum stay and the roll stopper bracket.

12. Unplug the electrical connector and remove the oxygen sensor.

13. Remove the exhaust manifold mounting bolts the manifold.

To install:

14. Clean all gasket material from the mating surfaces and check the manifold for damage.

15. Install a new gasket and install the manifold. Tighten the nuts in a crisscross pattern to 21 ft. lbs. (30 Nm) for the SOHC engine or to 14 ft. lbs. (19 Nm) for the DOHC engine.

16. Install the heat shields.

17. Connect the EGR tube and intake plenum stay and roll stopper bracket, if removed.

18. Install the oxygen sensor.

19. Install the electric cooling fan assembly, A/C compressor, dipstick tube and alternator, as required.

20. Install a new flange gasket and connect the exhaust pipe or converter assembly.

21. Install the drive belt(s) and adjust for proper tension.

22. Connect the negative battery cable and check for exhaust leaks.

3.5L Engine

♦ See Figure 74

✳✳ CAUTION

Do not attempt the work on the exhaust system until it has completely cooled.

1. Disconnect battery negative cable.
2. Raise the vehicle and support safely.
3. Remove the exhaust pipe to exhaust manifold nuts and remove the front exhaust pipe.

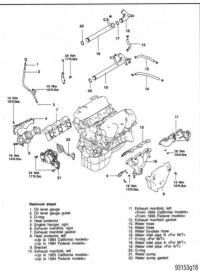

Fig. 72 Exploded view of the exhaust manifold and related components—3.0L SOHC engine

Removal steps
1. Oil level gauge
2. Oil level gauge guide
3. O-ring
4. Heat protector
5. Engine hanger, right
6. Exhaust manifold, right
7. Exhaust manifold gasket
8. Heat protector, left
   <Up to 1993 California models>
   <Up to 1994 Federal models>
9. Bracket
10. Exhaust manifold, left
    <Up to 1993 California models>
    <Up to 1994 Federal models>
11. Exhaust manifold, left
    <From 1994 California models>
    <From 1995 Federal models>
12. Exhaust manifold gasket
13. Water hose
14. Water hose
15. Water by-pass hose
16. Water inlet pipe B <For M/T>
17. O-ring <For M/T>
18. Water inlet pipe A <For M/T>
19. Water inlet pipe <For A/T>
20. O-ring
21. Water pump
22. Water pump gasket

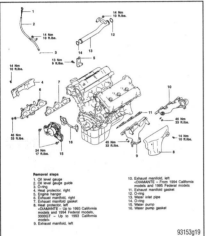

Fig. 73 Exploded view of the exhaust manifold —3.0L DOHC engine

Removal steps
1. Oil level gauge
2. Oil level gauge guide
3. O-ring
4. Heat protector, right
5. Engine hanger
6. Exhaust manifold, right
7. Exhaust manifold gasket
8. Heat protector, left
   <DIAMANTE – Up to 1993 California models and 1994 Federal models, 3000GT – Up to 1993 California models>
9. Exhaust manifold, left
10. Exhaust manifold, left
    <DIAMANTE – From 1994 California models and 1995 Federal models>
11. Exhaust manifold gasket
12. O-ring
13. Water inlet pipe
14. O-ring
15. Water pump
16. Water pump gasket

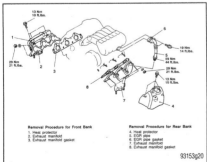

Fig. 74 Exhaust manifold exploded view—3.5L engine

Removal Procedure for Front Bank
1. Heat protector
2. Exhaust manifold
3. Exhaust manifold gasket

Removal Procedure for Rear Bank
4. Heat protector
5. EGR pipe
6. EGR pipe gasket
7. Exhaust manifold
8. Exhaust manifold gasket

4. Lower the vehicle.
5. If removing the front manifold, remove the radiator and cooling fan assembly.
6. If removing the front manifold, remove the alternator.
7. Remove the heat protector(s).

8. If removing the rear manifold, disconnect the EGR tube.
9. Remove the exhaust manifold mounting bolts the manifold.

To install:
10. Clean all gasket material from the mating surfaces and check the manifold for damage.
11. Install a new gasket and install the manifold. Tighten the nuts in a crisscross pattern to 21 ft. lbs. (30 Nm).
12. Install the heat protector(s).
13. If installing the rear manifold, replace the gasket and connect the EGR tube.
14. If installing the front manifold, install the radiator and cooling fan assembly.
15. If installing the front manifold, install the alternator.
16. Install the drive belt(s) and adjust for proper tension.
17. Raise and safely support the vehicle securely on jackstands.
18. Install a new flange gasket and connect the exhaust pipe or converter assembly.
19. Lower the vehicle.
20. Connect the negative battery cable and check for exhaust leaks.

Turbocharger

REMOVAL & INSTALLATION

2.0L DOHC Engine (1990–93 Galant Only)

▶ See Figures 75 and 76

Many turbocharger failures are due to oil supply problems. Heat soak after hot shutdown can cause the engine oil in the turbocharger and oil lines to "coke." Often the oil feed lines will become partially or completely blocked with hardened particles of carbon, blocking oil flow. Check the oil feed pipe and oil return line for clogging. Clean these tubes well. Always use new gaskets above and below the oil feed eyebolt fitting. Do not allow particles of dirt or old gasket material to enter the oil passage hole and that no portion of the new gasket blocks the passage.
1. Disconnect the negative battery cable.
2. Drain the engine oil, cooling system and remove the radiator. On vehicles equipped with A/C, remove the condenser fan assembly with the radiator.

✺✺ CAUTION

The EPA warns that prolonged contact with used engine oil may cause a number of skin disorders, including cancer! You should make every effort to minimize your exposure to used engine oil. Protective gloves should be worn when changing the oil. Wash your hands and any other exposed skin areas as soon as possible after exposure to used engine oil. Soap and water, or waterless hand cleaner should be used.

✺✺ CAUTION

Never open, service or drain the radiator or cooling system when hot; serious burns can occur from the steam and hot coolant. Also, when draining engine coolant, keep in mind that cats and dogs are attracted to ethylene

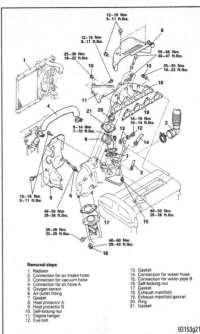

Fig. 75 Exploded view of the turbocharger mounting (1 of 2)

Removal steps
1. Radiator
2. Connection for air intake hose
3. Connection for vacuum hose
4. Connection for air hose A
5. Oxygen sensor
6. Air outlet fitting
7. Gasket
8. Heat protector A
9. Heat protector B
10. Self-locking nut
11. Engine hanger
12. Eye bolt
13. Gasket
14. Connection for water hose
15. Connection for water pipe B
16. Self-locking nut
17. Gasket
18. Exhaust manifold
19. Exhaust manifold gasket
20. Ring
21. Gasket

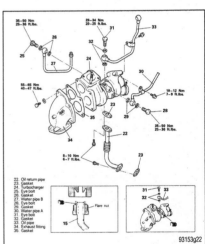

Fig. 76 Exploded view of the turbocharger mounting (2 of 2)

22. Oil return pipe
23. Gasket
24. Turbocharger
25. Eye bolt
26. Gasket
27. Eye bolt
28. Gasket
29. Water pipe A
30. Water pipe B
31. Eye bolt
32. Gasket
33. Oil pipe
34. Exhaust fitting
35. Gasket

glycol antifreeze and could drink any that is left in an uncovered container or in puddles on the ground. This will prove fatal in sufficient quantities. Always drain coolant into a sealable container. Coolant should be reused unless it is contaminated or is several years old.

3. Detach the oxygen sensor connector and remove the sensor.
4. Remove the oil dipstick and tube.
5. Remove the air intake bellows hose, the wastegate vacuum hose, the connections for the air outlet hose, and the upper and lower heat shield.
6. Unbolt the power steering pump and bracket assembly and leaving the hoses connected, wire it aside.
7. Remove the self-locking exhaust manifold nuts, the triangular engine hanger bracket, the eye-

bolt and gaskets that connect the oil feed line to the turbo center section and the water cooling lines. The water line under the turbo has a threaded connection.

8. Remove the exhaust pipe nuts and gasket and lift off the exhaust manifold. Discard the gasket.

9. Remove the 2 through bolts and 2 nuts that hold the exhaust manifold to the turbocharger.

10. Remove the 2 capscrews from the oil return line (under the turbo). Discard the gasket. Separate the turbo from the exhaust manifold. The 2 water pipes and oil feed line can still be attached.

11. Visually check the turbine wheel (hot side) and compressor wheel (cold side) for cracking or other damage. Check whether the turbine wheel and the compressor wheel can be easily turned by hand. Check for oil leakage. Check whether or not the wastegate valve remains open. If any problem is found, replace the part. Inspect oil passages for restriction or deposits and clean as required.

12. The wastegate can be checked with a pressure tester. Apply approximately 9 psi to the actuator and make sure the rod moves. Do not apply more than 10.3 psi or the diaphragm in the wastegate may be damaged. Vacuum applied to the wastegate actuator should be maintained, replace if leaks vacuum. Do not attempt to adjust the wastegate valve.

To install:

13. Prime the oil return line with clean engine oil. Replace all locking nuts. Before installing the threaded connection for the water inlet pipe, apply light oil to the inner surface of the pipe flange. Assemble the turbocharger and exhaust manifold.

14. Install the exhaust manifold using a new gasket.

15. Connect the water cooling lines, oil feed line and engine hanger.

16. If removed, install the power steering pump and bracket.

17. Install the heat shields, air outlet hose, wastegate hose and air intake bellows.

18. Install the oil dipstick tube and dipstick. Install the oxygen sensor.

19. Install the radiator assembly.

20. Fill the engine with oil, fill the cooling system and reconnect the negative battery cable.

※※ WARNING

Operating the engine without the proper amount and type of engine oil will result in severe engine damage.

Radiator

REMOVAL & INSTALLATION

▸ **See Figures 77 thru 91**

1. Disconnect the negative battery cable.
2. Drain the cooling system when safe.

※※ CAUTION

Never open, service or drain the radiator or cooling system when hot; serious burns can occur from the steam and hot coolant. Also, when draining engine coolant, keep in mind that cats and dogs are attracted to ethylene glycol antifreeze and could drink any that is left in an uncovered container or in puddles on the ground. This will prove fatal in suffi-

cient quantities. Always drain coolant into a sealable container. Coolant should be reused unless it is contaminated or is several years old.

3. Disconnect the overflow tube. Some vehicles may also require removal of the overflow tank.

4. Disconnect upper and lower radiator hoses.

5. Detach the electrical connectors from the cooling fan and air conditioning condenser fan, if equipped.

6. For Mirage and Diamante models, remove the fan assembly.

7. Disconnect the thermo sensor wires.

8. If equipped with an automatic transaxle, disconnect and plug the automatic transaxle cooler lines.

9. Remove the upper radiator mounts and lift out the radiator assembly or radiator/fan assembly, as applicable.

To install:

10. Install the radiator or radiator and fan, if removed as an assembly.

11. Connect the automatic transaxle cooler lines, if disconnected.

12. Connect the thermo sensor wires.

13. Install the fan, if removed separately.

14. Install the radiator hoses.

15. Install the air cleaner support bracket, if removed.

16. Install the overflow tube and reservoir, if removed.

17. Fill the system with coolant.

18. Connect the negative battery cable, run the vehicle until the thermostat opens, fill the radiator

Fig. 77 Use a pair of pliers to remove the hose clamp . . .

Fig. 78 . . . then disconnect the overflow hose from the radiator

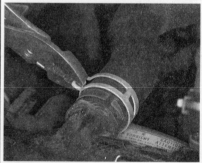
Fig. 79 Use pliers to release the hose clamp tension . . .

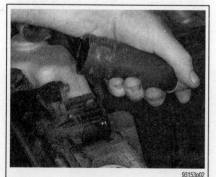
Fig. 80 . . . then remove the upper radiator hose from the radiator

Fig. 81 From underneath the vehicle, remove the hose clamp . . .

Fig. 82 . . . then disconnect the lower radiator hose

Fig. 83 Remove the transaxle hose clamp

Fig. 84 Disconnect the transaxle cooler lines on the passenger side . . .

Fig. 85 . . . and the cooler lines from underneath the radiator assembly

Fig. 86 After the transaxle cooler lines are removed, place a plug over the fitting on the radiator to prevent contamination

Fig. 87 Detach the connectors for the electric fans. The connectors are located on the driver's side top . . .

Fig. 88 . . . there is also a connector on the lower passenger side of the radiator

Fig. 89 Remove the radiator mount bolts . . .

Fig. 90 . . . then remove the mounts from the radiator and radiator support panel

Fig. 91 Carefully grasp the radiator and fan assembly and lift it out of the vehicle

completely and check the automatic transaxle fluid level, if equipped.

19. Once the vehicle has cooled, recheck the coolant level.

Engine Fan

REMOVAL & INSTALLATION

Except Diamante

▶ See Figures 77 thru 93

1. Disconnect the negative battery cable.
2. Drain and recycle the engine coolant.

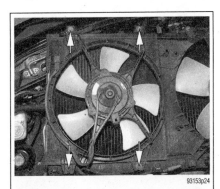

Fig. 92 The fans are retained to the radiator by four retaining bolts. Remove the retaining bolts . . .

Fig. 93 . . . then carefully lift the fan from the radiator

> ⁂ **CAUTION**
>
> Never open, service or drain the radiator or cooling system when hot; serious burns can occur from the steam and hot coolant. Also, when draining engine coolant, keep in mind that cats and dogs are attracted to ethylene glycol antifreeze and could drink any that is left in an uncovered container or in puddles on the ground. This will prove fatal in sufficient quantities. Always drain coolant into a sealable container. Coolant should be reused unless it is contaminated or is several years old.

3. Remove the overflow hose and disconnect the upper radiator hose.

➡It is recommended that each clamp be matchmarked to the hose. Observe the marks and reinstall the clamps exactly when reinstalling the radiator.

4. If equipped with an automatic transaxle, remove and plug the fluid cooler hoses.
5. Unplug the electrical connector(s) from the coolant fan motor.
6. Remove the mounting bolts, then remove the fan and shroud assembly from the vehicle.
7. Remove the fan blade retainer nut from the shaft on the fan motor and separate the fan from the motor.
8. Remove the motor to shroud attaching screws and the motor from the shroud.
To install:
9. Install the motor to the shroud and secure with the mounting bolts.
10. Install the remaining components in the reverse order of removal.
11. Fill the cooling system. Connect the negative battery cable and check the cooling fan for proper operation.

Diamante

♦ See Figure 94

1. Disconnect the negative battery cable.

2. Drain the cooling system only when the radiator and the engine are at safe temperatures.

> ⁂ **CAUTION**
>
> Never open, service or drain the radiator or cooling system when hot; serious burns can occur from the steam and hot coolant. Also, when draining engine coolant, keep in mind that cats and dogs are attracted to ethylene glycol antifreeze and could drink any that is left in an uncovered container or in puddles on the ground. This will prove fatal in sufficient quantities. Always drain coolant into a sealable container. Coolant should be reused unless it is contaminated or is several years old.

3. Unplug the cooling fan and radiator sensor connector(s). Most of these connectors employ a waterproof connector. When disconnecting, make sure all parts of the connector remain intact.
4. Disconnect the upper radiator hose from the radiator and remove overflow tank.
5. Remove the fan mounting screws. The radiator and condenser cooling fans are separately removable.
6. Remove the fan assembly and disassemble as required.
To install:
7. Position the fan and install the mounting screws.
8. Install the electrical connectors and the upper radiator hose.
9. Refill the cooling system.
10. Connect the negative battery cable and check the fan for proper operation.

Water Pump

REMOVAL & INSTALLATION

1.5L and 1.8L Engine

♦ See Figures 95 and 96

1. Disconnect the negative battery cable.
2. Drain the cooling system.

> ⁂ **CAUTION**
>
> Never open, service or drain the radiator or cooling system when hot; serious burns can occur from the steam and hot coolant. Also, when draining engine coolant, keep in mind that cats and dogs are attracted to ethylene glycol antifreeze and could drink any that is left in an uncovered container or in puddles on the ground. This will prove fatal in sufficient quantities. Always drain coolant into a sealable container. Coolant should be reused unless it is contaminated or is several years old.

3. Remove the engine undercover.
4. Disconnect the clamp bolt from the power steering hose.
5. Remove the engine drive belts.
6. Support the engine with the appropriate equipment and remove the engine mount bracket.
7. Remove the timing belt. Refer to the timing belt procedure in this section.
8. Remove the power steering pump bracket.
9. Remove the alternator brace.

➡The water pump mounting bolts are different in length, note their positioning for reassembly.

10. Remove the water pump, gasket and O-ring where the water inlet pipe(s) joins the pump.
To install:
11. Thoroughly clean both gasket surfaces of the water pump and block.
12. For 1.5L engines, install a new O-ring into the groove on the front end of the water inlet pipe. Do not apply oils or grease to the O-ring. Wet the O-ring with water only.
13. For 1.8L engines, apply a 0.09–0.12 in. (2.5–3.0mm) continuous bead of sealant to water pump and install the pump assembly. Install the water pump within 15 minutes of the application of the

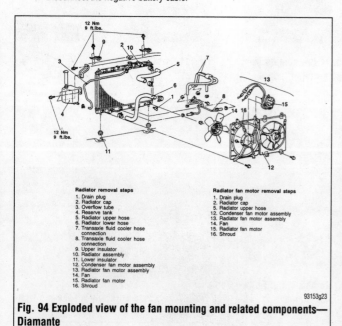

Radiator removal steps
1. Drain plug
2. Radiator cap
3. Overflow tube
4. Reserve tank
5. Radiator upper hose
6. Radiator lower hose
7. Transaxle fluid cooler hose connection
8. Transaxle fluid cooler hose connection
9. Upper insulator
10. Radiator assembly
11. Lower insulator
12. Condenser fan motor assembly
13. Radiator fan motor assembly
14. Fan
15. Radiator fan motor
16. Shroud

Radiator fan motor removal steps
1. Drain plug
2. Radiator cap
5. Radiator upper hose
12. Condenser fan motor assembly
13. Radiator fan motor assembly
14. Fan
15. Radiator fan motor
16. Shroud

93153g23

Fig. 94 Exploded view of the fan mounting and related components—Diamante

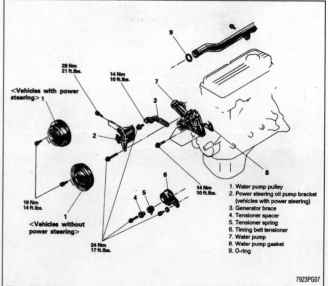

1. Water pump pulley
2. Power steering oil pump bracket (vehicles with power steering)
3. Generator brace
4. Tensioner spacer
5. Tensioner spring
6. Timing belt tensioner
7. Water pump
8. Water pump gasket
9. O-ring

7923PG07

Fig. 95 Water pump and related components—Mirage with 1.5L (4G15) engine

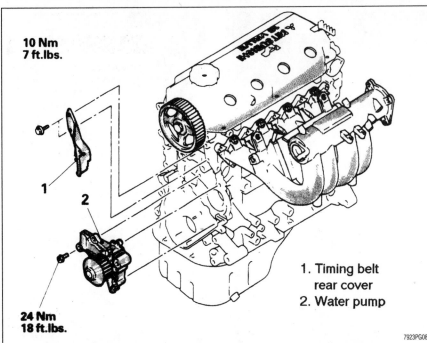

**10 Nm
7 ft.lbs.**

1

2

**24 Nm
18 ft.lbs.**

1. Timing belt
   rear cover
2. Water pump

7923PG08

Fig. 96 Water pump and related components—Mirage with 1.8L (4G93) engines

sealant. Wait 1 hour after installation of the water pump to refill the cooling system or start the engine.

14. Install the gasket and pump assembly and tighten the bolts to 17 ft. lbs. (24 Nm). Use care when aligning the water pump with the water inlet pipe.

15. Install the remaining components in the reverse order of removal.

16. Fill the system with coolant.

17. Connect the negative battery cable, run the vehicle until the thermostat opens and fill the radiator completely.

18. Once the vehicle has cooled, recheck the coolant level.

1.6L and 2.0L (SOHC and DOHC) Engines

♦ See Figure 97

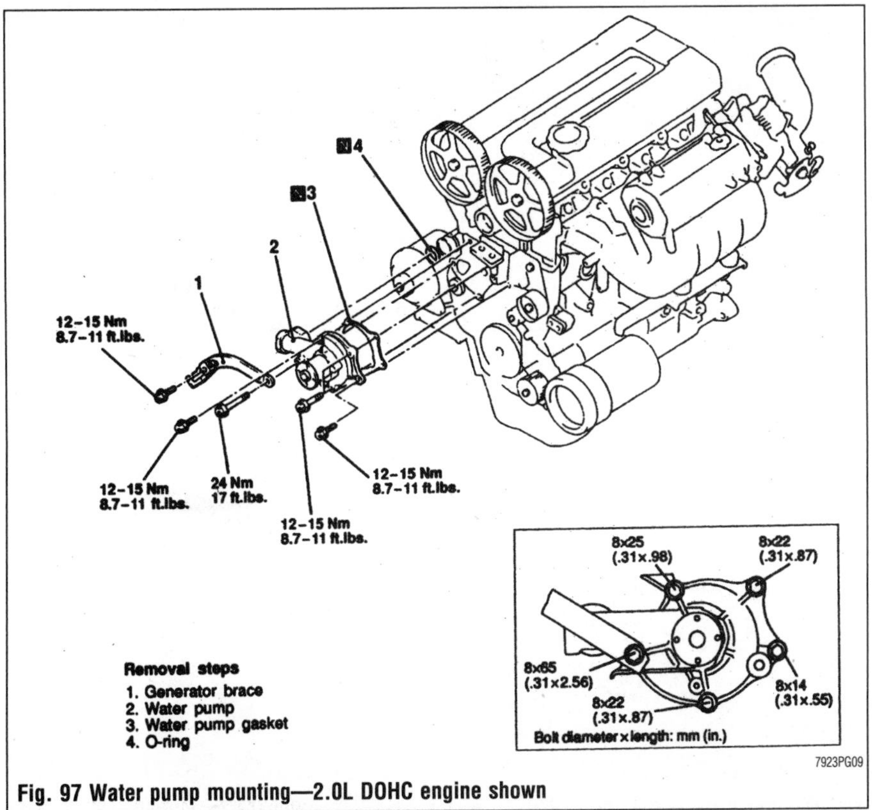

1. Disconnect the negative battery cable.
2. Drain the engine coolant.

✳✳ CAUTION

Never open, service or drain the radiator or cooling system when hot; serious burns can occur from the steam and hot coolant. Also, when draining engine coolant, keep in mind that cats and dogs are attracted to ethylene glycol antifreeze and could drink any that is left in an uncovered container or in puddles on the ground. This will prove fatal in sufficient quantities. Always drain coolant into a sealable container. Coolant should be reused unless it is contaminated or is several years old.

3. Remove the timing belt. Refer to the timing belt procedure in this section.

4. If necessary, remove the alternator brace from the water pump.

5. If necessary, remove the timing belt rear cover.

6. Remove the water pump mounting bolts.

7. Remove the water pump, gasket and O-ring.

To install:

8. Install a new O-ring on the water inlet pipe. Coat the O-ring with water or coolant. Do not allow oil or other grease to contact the O-ring.

9. Use a new gasket and install the water pump to the engine block. Torque the mounting bolts to 8.7–11 ft. lbs. (12–15 Nm). Install the alternator brace on the water pump. Torque the brace pivot bolt to 17 ft. lbs. (24 Nm).

10. If removed, install the timing belt rear cover.

11. Install the timing belt. Refer to the timing belt procedure in this section.

12. Install the remaining components.

13. Refill the engine with coolant.

14. Connect the negative battery cable, start the engine and check for leaks.

2.4L Engine

♦ See Figures 98 thru 108

1. Disconnect the negative battery cable.
2. Drain the cooling system.

✳✳ CAUTION

Never open, service or drain the radiator or cooling system when hot; serious burns can occur from the steam and hot coolant. Also, when draining engine coolant, keep in mind that cats and dogs are attracted to ethylene glycol antifreeze and could drink any that is left in an uncovered container or in puddles on the ground. This will prove fatal in sufficient quantities. Always drain coolant into a sealable container. Coolant should be reused unless it is contaminated or is several years old.

3. Remove the engine undercover.

4. Disconnect the clamp bolt from the power steering hose.

5. Support the engine with the appropriate equipment and remove the engine mount bracket.

6. Remove the engine drive belts and the A/C tensioner bracket.

7. Remove the timing belt covers from the front of the engine.

■4

■3

2

1

**12–15 Nm
8.7–11 ft.lbs.**

**12–15 Nm
8.7–11 ft.lbs.**

**24 Nm
17 ft.lbs.**

**12–15 Nm
8.7–11 ft.lbs.**

**12–15 Nm
8.7–11 ft.lbs.**

8x25
(.31x.98)

8x22
(.31x.87)

8x65
(.31x2.56)

8x22
(.31x.87)

8x14
(.31x.55)

Bolt diameter×length: mm (in.)

Removal steps
1. Generator brace
2. Water pump
3. Water pump gasket
4. O-ring

7923PG09

Fig. 97 Water pump mounting—2.0L DOHC engine shown

Fig. 98 Remove the water pump pulley retaining bolts . . .

Fig. 99 . . . then remove the pulley from the pump

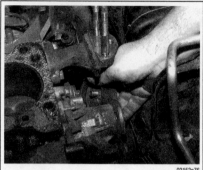

Fig. 100 Remove the A/C belt idler pulley

Fig. 101 Remove the A/C belt idler pulley bracket retaining bolt . . .

Fig. 102 . . . then remove the idler pulley retaining bracket

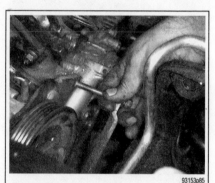

Fig. 103 Remove the alternator brace from the engine

Fig. 104 Remove the water pump retaining bolts on the top . . .

Fig. 105 . . . then remove the bolts on the bottom of the pump assembly

Fig. 106 Grasp the water pump and remove it from the engine block

Fig. 107 If the impeller fins on the water pump show any signs of wear, it is advisable to replace the water pump rather than reuse it

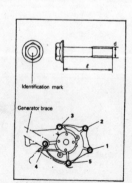

No.	Identification mark	Bolt diameter (d) x length (ℓ) mm (in.)	Torque Nm (ft.lbs.)
1	4	8 x 14 (.31 x .55)	
2	4	8 x 22 (.31 x .87)	12–15 (9–10)
3	4	8 x 30 (.31 x 1.18)	
4	7	8 x 65 (.31 x 2.56)	20–27 (15–19)
5	4	8 x 28 (.31 x 1.10)	12–15 (9–10)

Fig. 108 Water pump bolt identification—2.4L Engine

8. Remove the camshaft and silent shaft timing belts. Refer to the timing belt procedure in this section.

9. Remove the A/C belt idler pulley and pulley bracket.

10. Remove the alternator brace.

11. Remove the water pump, gasket and O-ring where the water inlet pipe(s) joins the pump.

To install:

12. Thoroughly clean both gasket surfaces of the water pump and block.

13. Install a new O-ring into the groove on the front end of the water inlet pipe and wet with clean antifreeze only. Do not apply oils or grease to the O-ring.

14. Using a new gasket, install the water pump assembly. Tighten bolts with the head mark **4** to 10 ft. lbs. (14 Nm) and bolts with the head mark **7** to 18 ft. lbs. (24 Nm).

15. Install the A/C pulley and pulley bracket.

16. Install the timing belts. Refer to the timing belt procedure in this section.

17. Install the engine drive belts.

18. Install the engine mount bracket.

19. Install the engine undercover.

20. Fill the system with coolant.

21. Connect the negative battery cable, run the vehicle until the thermostat opens and fill the radiator completely.

22. Once the vehicle has cooled, recheck the coolant level.

3.0L and 3.5L Engines

♦ See Figure 109

1. Disconnect the negative battery cable.
2. Drain the cooling system.

✳✳ CAUTION

Never open, service or drain the radiator or cooling system when hot; serious burns can occur from the steam and hot coolant. Also, when draining engine coolant, keep in mind that cats and dogs are attracted to ethylene glycol antifreeze and could drink any that is left in an uncovered container or in puddles on the ground. This will prove fatal in sufficient quantities. Always drain coolant into a sealable container. Coolant should be reused unless it is contaminated or is several years old.

3. Remove the engine undercover.

4. Disconnect the clamp bolt from the power steering hose.

5. Support the engine with the appropriate equipment and remove the engine mount bracket.

6. Remove the timing belt. Refer to the timing belt procedure in this section.

7. Disconnect the coolant hoses from the pump, if equipped.

8. Remove the alternator brace.

➡**The water pump bolts are different in size. Note their locations for installation.**

9. Remove the water pump, gasket and O-ring where the water inlet pipe joins the pump.

To install:

10. Thoroughly clean both gasket surfaces of the water pump and block.

11. Install a new O-ring into the groove on the front end of the water inlet pipe. Do not apply oils or grease to the O-ring. Wet with water only.

12. Using a new gasket, install the water pump assembly to the engine block. Torque the mounting bolts to 17 ft. lbs. (24 Nm).

13. Connect the hoses to the pump.

14. Install the timing belt. Refer to the timing belt procedure in this section.

15. Install the engine drive belts.

16. Fill the system with coolant.

17. Connect the negative battery cable, run the vehicle until the thermostat opens and fill the radiator completely.

18. Once the vehicle has cooled, recheck the coolant level.

Cylinder Head

REMOVAL & INSTALLATION

1.5L Engine

♦ See Figures 110 and 111

1. Relieve the fuel system pressure.

✳✳ CAUTION

Observe all applicable safety precautions when working around fuel. Whenever servicing the fuel system, always work in a well ventilated area. Do not allow fuel spray or vapors to come in contact with a spark or open flame. Keep a dry chemical fire extinguisher near the work area. Always keep fuel in a container specifically designed for fuel storage; also, always properly seal fuel containers to avoid the possibility of fire or explosion.

2. Disconnect the negative battery cable.
3. Drain the cooling system.

✳✳ CAUTION

Never open, service or drain the radiator or cooling system when hot; serious burns can occur from the steam and hot coolant. Also, when draining engine coolant, keep in mind that cats and dogs are attracted to ethylene glycol antifreeze and could drink any that is left in an uncovered container or in puddles on the ground. This will prove fatal in sufficient quantities. Always drain coolant into a sealable container. Coolant should be reused unless it is contaminated or is several years old.

4. Remove the air intake hose and the air cleaner assembly.

5. Disconnect the ground cable connection and the accelerator cable.

6. Disconnect the PCV and the breather hose connection.

7. Label and disconnect the vacuum hoses from the intake and throttle body.

8. Disconnect the vacuum line for the brake booster.

9. Remove the upper radiator hose, throttle body hoses, bypass hose and heater hose connections.

10. Disconnect the fuel feed and return lines.

11. Remove the spark plug wires.

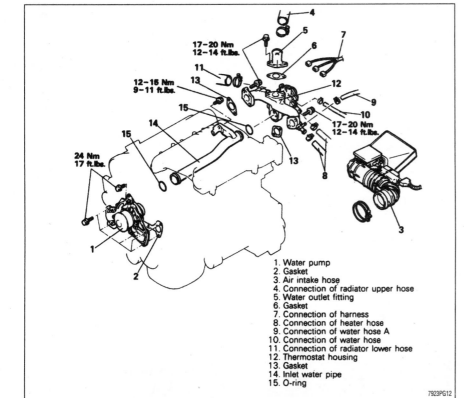

17-20 Nm
12-14 ft.lbs.

12-15 Nm
9-11 ft.lbs.

17-20 Nm
12-14 ft.lbs.

24 Nm
17 ft.lbs.

1. Water pump
2. Gasket
3. Air intake hose
4. Connection of radiator upper hose
5. Water outlet fitting
6. Gasket
7. Connection of harness
8. Connection of heater hose
9. Connection of water hose A
10. Connection of water hose
11. Connection of radiator lower hose
12. Thermostat housing
13. Gasket
14. Inlet water pipe
15. O-ring

7923PG12

Fig. 109 Water pump and related components—3.0L DOHC shown

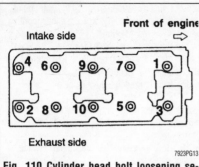

Fig. 110 Cylinder head bolt loosening sequence—Mirage with 1.5L (4G15) engine

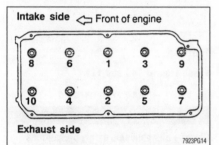

Fig. 111 Cylinder head bolt tightening sequence—Mirage with 1.5L (4G15) engine

12. Disconnect the electrical harness plugs from the following:
  • Crankshaft Position (CKP) and Camshaft Position (CMP) sensors
  • Heated Oxygen (HO₂S) sensor
  • Engine Coolant Temperature (ECT) sensor and gauge sender
  • Idle Speed Control (ISC) motor
  • Throttle Position (TP) sensor
  • Intake Air Temperature (IAT) sensor
  • Exhaust Gas Recirculation (EGR) temperature sensor

13. Disconnect electrical harness plugs from the ignition distributor, fuel injectors, power transistor and ground cable.

14. Disconnect the engine control wiring harness.

15. Remove the clamp that holds the power steering pressure hose to the engine mounting bracket.

16. Place a jack and wood block under the oil pan and carefully lift just enough to take the weight off the engine mounting bracket and remove the bracket.

17. Remove the valve cover.

18. Remove the timing belt upper cover.

19. Rotate the crankshaft clockwise and align the timing marks.

20. Attach the timing belt to the camshaft sprocket with cord or a wire tie.

21. Secure the camshaft from turning and remove the camshaft sprocket with the timing belt attached.

22. Remove the timing belt rear upper cover.

23. Remove the exhaust pipe from the exhaust manifold.

24. Loosen the cylinder head mounting bolts in sequence using three steps.

25. Remove the cylinder head.

To install:

26. Thoroughly clean the mating surfaces of the head and block.

27. Place a new head gasket on the cylinder block with the identification marks facing upward. Do not use sealer on the gasket.

28. Carefully install the cylinder head on the block. Tighten the cylinder head bolts as outlined in the following steps:
  a. Tighten the bolts to 36 ft. lbs. (49 Nm) in the correct sequence
  b. Loosen the bolts completely in the reverse of the tightening order.
  c. Tighten the bolts, in sequence, to 14 ft. lbs. (20 Nm)
  d. Tighten each bolt, in sequence, 90 degrees
  e. Tighten each bolt, in sequence, an additional 90 degrees

29. Install a new exhaust pipe gasket and connect the exhaust pipe to the manifold.

30. Install the upper rear timing cover.

31. Align the timing marks and install the cam sprocket. Torque the retaining bolt to 51 ft. lbs. (70 Nm). Check the belt tension and adjust, if necessary. Install the outer timing cover.

32. Install the valve cover and torque the retaining bolts to 16 inch lbs. (1.8 Nm).

33. Install the engine mount bracket and remove the support jack.

34. Install the clamp that holds the power steering pressure hose to the engine mounting bracket.

35. Attach the following electrical connectors:
  • CKP and CMP sensors
  • HO₂S sensor
  • ECT sensor and gauge sender
  • ISC motor
  • TP sensor
  • IAT sensor
  • EGR temperature sensor

36. Connect wiring for the ignition distributor, fuel injectors, power transistor and ground cable.

37. Connect the engine control wiring harness.

38. Replace the O-rings and connect the fuel lines.

39. Install the air cleaner assembly. Connect the breather hose.

40. Fill the system with coolant.

41. Connect the negative battery cable.

1.8L Engine

♦ **See Figures 112 and 113**

1. Relieve fuel system pressure. Disconnect the negative battery cable.

2. Remove the air cleaner assembly.

3. Drain the cooling system.

> ✷✷ **CAUTION**
>
> **Never open, service or drain the radiator or cooling system when hot; serious burns can occur from the steam and hot coolant. Also, when draining engine coolant, keep in mind that cats and dogs are attracted to ethylene glycol antifreeze and could drink any that is left in an uncovered container or in puddles on the ground. This will prove fatal in sufficient quantities. Always drain coolant into a sealable container. Coolant should be reused unless it is contaminated or is several years old.**

4. Disconnect the brake booster vacuum hose and PVC valve connection.

5. Note the locations, then disconnect the vacuum hoses from the intake and throttle body.

6. Remove the upper radiator hose, overflow tube and the water hose from the thermostat to the throttle body.

7. Disconnect the fuel feed and return lines.

8. Unplug the accelerator cable connection from the throttle body.

9. Detach the wiring from the oil pressure switch.

10. Disconnect the wiring from the following components:
  • Heated Oxygen (HO₂S) sensor
  • Engine Coolant Temperature (ECT) sensor and gauge sender
  • Idle Air Control (IAC) motor
  • Exhaust Gas Recirculation (EGR) temperature sensor
  • Throttle Position (TP) sensor
  • Knock sensor
  • Fuel injectors

11. Remove the spark plug wires.

12. Unbolt the control harness assembly and position aside.

13. Remove the thermostat housing, thermostat and the thermostat case with O-ring from the engine.

14. Remove the rocker cover.

15. Remove the timing belt upper cover.

16. Rotate the crankshaft clockwise and align the timing marks.

17. Attach the timing belt to the camshaft sprocket with cord or a wire tie.

18. Secure the camshaft from turning and remove the camshaft sprocket with the timing belt attached.

19. Remove the timing belt rear upper cover.

20. Loosen the cylinder head bolts in two or three steps in the proper sequence.

21. Remove the cylinder head from the engine.

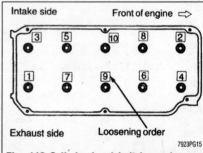

Fig. 112 Cylinder head bolt loosening sequence—1.8L engine

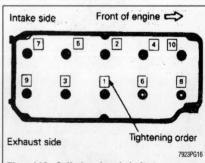

Fig. 113 Cylinder head bolt torque sequence—1.8L engine

✳✳ CAUTION

When removing the cylinder head, take care not to bend or damage the plug guide. The plug guide can not be replaced.

To install:

22. Thoroughly clean the mating surfaces of the head and block.

23. Place a new head gasket on the cylinder block with the identification marks facing upward. Do not use sealer on the gasket.

24. Carefully install the cylinder head on the block.

25. Measure the cylinder head bolts prior to installation. Replace any that exceed 3.795 in. (96.4mm).

26. Apply a small amount of engine oil to the thread section of the bolt and install so the chamfer of the washer faces upward.

27. Tighten the cylinder head bolts as follows:
   a. In the proper tightening sequence, torque bolts to 54 ft. lbs. (75 Nm).
   b. In the reverse order of the tightening sequence, fully loosen all bolts.
   c. In the proper tightening sequence, torque bolts to 14 ft. lbs. (20 Nm).
   d. In the proper tightening sequence, tighten bolts $1/4$ turn (90 degrees).
   e. In the proper tightening sequence, tighten bolts an additional $1/4$ turn (90 degrees).

28. Install the camshaft sprocket and tighten the bolt to 65 ft. lbs. (90 Nm), while holding the sprocket in place using the appropriate wrench. Confirm proper timing mark alignment.

29. Install the upper timing belt cover and rocker cover. Torque the rocker cover bolts to 29 inch lbs. (3 Nm).

30. Loosen the water pipe mounting bolt for ease of thermostat housing installation.

31. Apply a thin bead of sealant MD970389 or equivalent, to the water tube connection on the thermostat case.

32. Apply a small amount of water to the O-ring of the water inlet pipe and press the thermostat case assembly onto the water inlet pipe. Install the thermostat case assembly mounting bolt tightening to 16 ft. lbs. (22 Nm).

33. Tighten the water pipe mounting bolt.

34. Install the thermostat into the housing so the jiggle valve is located at the top. Tighten the housing bolts to 10 ft. lbs. (14 Nm).

35. Attach the wiring to the following components:
   - HO$_2$S sensor
   - ECT sensor and gauge sender
   - IAC motor
   - EGR temperature sensor
   - TP sensor
   - Knock sensor
   - Fuel injectors

36. Connect the upper radiator hose to the thermostat housing.

37. Connect the accelerator cable connection to the throttle body.

38. Connect the oil pressure switch.

39. Install the spark plug wires.

40. Connect the control harness assembly.

41. Replace the O-ring for the high pressure hose and install a new clamp on the return hose and reconnect the fuel lines.

42. Install the air intake hose. Connect the breather hose and air cleaner case cover.

43. Reconnect the brake booster and the PCV vacuum hoses.

44. Fill the system with coolant.

45. Connect the negative battery cable

2.0L SOHC Engine

▶ **See Figures 114 and 115**

1. Disconnect the negative battery cable.
2. Drain the cooling system.

✳✳ CAUTION

Never open, service or drain the radiator or cooling system when hot; serious burns can occur from the steam and hot coolant. Also, when draining engine coolant, keep in mind that cats and dogs are attracted to ethylene glycol antifreeze and could drink any that is left in an uncovered container or in puddles on the ground. This will prove fatal in sufficient quantities. Always drain coolant into a sealable container. Coolant should be reused unless it is contaminated or is several years old.

3. Remove the air intake hose.
4. Disconnect the accelerator cable and remove the bracket.
5. Disconnect the high pressure fuel line and remove the O-ring.

✳✳ CAUTION

Observe all applicable safety precautions when working around fuel. Whenever servicing the fuel system, always work in a well ventilated area. Do not allow fuel spray or vapors to come in contact with a spark or open flame. Keep a dry chemical fire extinguisher near the work area. Always keep fuel in a container specifically designed for fuel storage; also, always properly seal fuel containers to avoid the possibility of fire or explosion.

6. Disconnect the upper radiator hose, the coolant by-pass hose and the heater hose from the head and/or intake manifold.

7. Disconnect the brake booster vacuum hose.

8. Remove the fuel return hose.

9. Label and detach the vacuum hose(s) running to the manifold. Disconnect the PCV hose at the valve cover.

10. Tag and disconnect the spark plug wires from the distributor cap.

11. Label and detach each electrical connector, including the distributor lead and the injector connectors. Note that some of the wiring must be disconnected at the firewall. When all the connectors are loose, remove the bracket bolts holding the control wiring harness in place and move the harness to an out-of-the-way location.

12. Remove the clamp holding the power steering and air conditioning hoses to the top of the left engine mount bracket. Move the hoses out of the way but don't disconnect either hose from its system.

13. Position a floor jack and a broad piece of lumber under the engine. Elevate the jack just enough to support the engine without raising it.

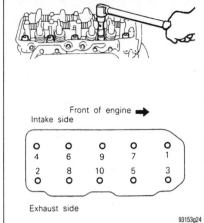

Fig. 114 Cylinder head bolt loosening sequence—2.0L SOHC engine

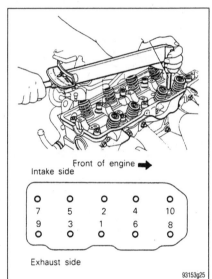

Fig. 115 Cylinder head bolt tightening sequence—2.0L SOHC engine

14. Remove the through-bolt from the left side engine mount. It may be necessary to adjust the jack slightly to allow the bolt to come free. When the bolt has been removed, disconnect the nuts and bolts holding the mounting bracket to the engine and remove the bracket.

15. Remove the valve cover and gasket. Remove the half-circle plug from the head.

16. Remove the upper timing belt cover. Turn the crankshaft clockwise until all the timing marks align, setting the engine to TDC/compression for No. 1 cylinder.

17. Remove the bolt holding the camshaft sprocket to the camshaft. Remove the camshaft sprocket, with the belt attached, and place it on the lower timing belt cover. Do NOT allow the belt to come off the sprocket.

✳✳ WARNING

Do not rotate the crankshaft once the camshaft sprocket is removed.

18. Remove the self-locking nuts and the small retaining bolt holding the exhaust pipe to the bottom of the exhaust manifold. Separate the pipe from the manifold and remove the gasket.

19. Remove the bolts holding the support brace to the bottom of the intake manifold.

20. Use the special hex wrench (MB 998051-01) and loosen the head bolts in the order shown in 2 or 3 passes. When all are finger loose, remove the bolts.

21. Rock the head gently to break it loose; if tapping is necessary, do so with a rubber or wooden mallet at the corners of the head. DO NOT pry the head up by wedging tools between the head and the block.

22. Lift the head free of the engine. It is coming off with both manifolds and the intake plenum attached; the help of an assistant is recommended for lifting. Support the head assembly on wooden blocks on a suitable workbench. Refer to Cleaning and Inspection in this section for work to be done before installing the head. If the head has been removed for work other than gasket replacement, the rocker assembly and camshaft or other components may be removed.

Before reinstallation, the head should be completely assembled on the bench. This allows proper location and tightening of all the external items.

To install:

23. Place a new gasket on the engine so that the identifying mark faces up (towards the head) and is at the timing belt end of the block. Install a new gasket on the exhaust pipe.

✳✳ WARNING

Do not apply sealant to the head gasket or mating surfaces.

24. Install the head straight down onto the block. Try to eliminate most of the side–to–side adjustments as this may move the gasket out of position. Install the bolts by hand and just start each bolt 1 or 2 turns on the threads.

25. The head bolt torque specification is 68 ft. lbs. (92 Nm) for a cold engine. The bolts must be tightened in the order shown in 3 steps. On the first pass, tighten all the bolts to about 22 ft. lbs. (30 Nm), then proceed through the order tightening each bolt to about 45 ft. lbs. (61 Nm). The final torque is achieved on the third pass.

26. Install the intake manifold support brace to the manifold and tighten the bolts to 16 ft. lbs. (22 Nm).

27. Making sure the gasket is still in place, connect the exhaust pipe to the base of the exhaust manifold. Use new self-locking nuts; tighten the nuts and the small bracket bolt to 26 ft. lbs. (35 Nm).

28. Make sure the camshaft has not changed position during repairs. Carefully install the camshaft sprocket and belt onto the camshaft. Tighten the retaining bolt to 66 ft. lbs. (91 Nm).

29. Install the upper timing belt cover, then tighten the bolts to 8 ft. lbs. (11 Nm).

30. Apply sealant to the contact surfaces of the half-circle plug and install the plug in the head. Install the valve cover and gasket.

31. Install the engine mount bracket to the engine. Tighten the mounting nuts and bolts to 42 ft. lbs. (57 Nm).

32. Adjust the jack (if necessary) so that the engine mount bushing aligns with the bodywork bracket. Install the through-bolt and tighten the nuts snug.

33. Slowly release tension on the floor jack so that the weight of the engine bears fully on the mount. Tighten the through-bolt to 52 ft. lbs. (71 Nm) and the small safety nut to 26 ft. lbs. (36 Nm).

34. Install the bracket holding the power steering hose and air conditioning hose to the top of the engine mount.

35. Position the control wiring harness and install the retaining bolts. Attach each electrical connector to its proper location, making sure the wires are properly routed and firmly connected.

36. Install the spark plug wires in the distributor cap.

37. Connect the PCV hose and the vacuum hose(s).

38. Connect the fuel return line. Connect the brake booster vacuum hose.

39. Install the heater hose, the coolant by-pass hose and the upper radiator hose. Pay close attention to the position and routing of these hoses and insure that they are not crimped or constricted. Install the clamps in the same location as before removal.

40. Install a new O-ring on the high pressure fuel line and lubricate it with a coating of gasoline. Carefully connect the high pressure fuel line to the fuel rail, taking care not to damage the O-ring. Tighten the bolts only to 4 ft. lbs. (6 Nm).

41. Connect the accelerator cable and adjust it as necessary.

42. Install the air intake hose.

43. Fill the cooling system with coolant.

44. Changing the oil and filter is recommended to eliminate pollutants in the oil.

✳✳ WARNING

Operating the engine without the proper amount and type of engine oil will result in severe engine damage.

45. Connect the negative battery cable.

46. Start the engine and check for leaks of fuel, vacuum or oil.

47. Check the operation of all engine electrical systems as well as dashboard gauges and lights.

48. Perform necessary adjustments to the accelerator cable, drive belts and engine specifications. Adjust the coolant level after the engine has cooled off.

1.6L and 2.0L DOHC Engines

♦ See Figures 116, 117, and 118

1. Relieve fuel system pressure.
2. Disconnect the negative battery cable.
3. Drain the cooling system.

✳✳ CAUTION

Never open, service or drain the radiator or cooling system when hot; serious burns can occur from the steam and hot coolant. Also, when draining engine coolant, keep in mind that cats and dogs are attracted to ethylene glycol antifreeze and could drink any that is left in an uncovered container or in puddles on the ground. This will prove fatal in sufficient quantities. Always drain coolant into a sealable container. Coolant should be reused unless it is contaminated or is several years old.

4. Disconnect the accelerator cable. There will be 2 cables if equipped with cruise-control.

5. Remove the air cleaner with the air intake hose.

6. Detach the electrical connectors from the the oxygen sensor, engine coolant temperature sensor, the engine coolant temperature gauge unit and the engine coolant temperature switch on vehicles with air conditioning.

7. Disconnect the wiring from the ISC motor, throttle position sensor, crankshaft angle sensor, fuel injectors, ignition coil, power transistor, noise filter, knock sensor on turbocharged engines, EGR temperature sensor (California vehicles), ground cable and engine control wiring harness.

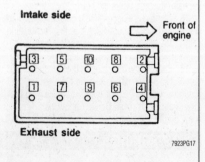

Fig. 116 Cylinder head bolt removal sequence—1.6L and 2.0L DOHC engines

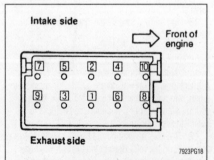

Fig. 117 Cylinder head bolt torque sequence—1.6L and 2.0L DOHC engines

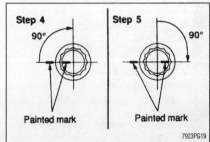

Fig. 118 To ensure that the bolts are tightened exactly 180 total degrees, mark the head bolt and cylinder head as shown—1.6L and 2.0L DOHC engines

8. Remove the upper radiator hose and the overflow tube.

9. Remove the spark plug cable center cover, then remove the spark plug cables.

10. Disconnect and plug the high pressure fuel line.

11. Disconnect the small vacuum hoses.

12. Remove the heater hose and water bypass hose.

13. Remove the PCV hose.

14. If turbocharged, remove the vacuum hoses, water line and eyebolt connection for the oil line for the turbo.

15. Disconnect and plug the fuel return hose.

16. Disconnect the brake booster vacuum hose.

17. Remove the timing belt.

18. Remove the valve cover and the half-round seal.

19. On non-turbocharged engines, remove the exhaust pipe self-locking nuts and separate the exhaust pipe from the exhaust manifold. Discard the gasket.

20. On turbocharged engines, remove the sheet metal heat protector and remove the bolts that attach the turbocharger to the exhaust manifold.

21. Loosen the cylinder head mounting bolts in 3 steps, starting from the outside and working inward. Lift off the cylinder head assembly and remove the head gasket.

To install:

22. Thoroughly clean and dry the mating surfaces of the head and block. Check the cylinder head for cracks, damage or engine coolant leakage. Remove scale, sealing compound and carbon. Clean oil passages thoroughly. Check the head for flatness. End to end, the head should be within 0.002 in. (0.05mm) normally, with 0.008 in. (0.2mm) the maximum allowed out of true. The total thickness allowed to be removed from the head and block is 0.008 in. (0.2mm) maximum.

23. Place a new head gasket on the cylinder block with the identification marks at the front top (upward) position. Make sure the gasket has the proper identification mark for the engine. Do not use sealer on the gasket. Replace the turbo gasket and ring, if equipped.

24. Carefully install the cylinder head on the block. Using 3 even steps, torque the head bolts, in sequence, to 65–72 ft. lbs. (90–100 Nm). This torque applies to a cold engine. If checking cylinder head bolt torque on hot engine, the desired specification is 72–80 ft. lbs. (100–110 Nm).

25. On turbocharged engine, install the heat shield. On non-turbocharged engines, install a new exhaust pipe gasket and connect the exhaust pipe to the manifold.

26. Apply sealer to the perimeter of the half-round seal and to the lower edges of the half-round portions of the belt-side of the new gasket. Install the valve cover.

27. Install the timing belt and all related items.

28. Connect or install all previously disconnected hoses, cables and electrical connections. Adjust the throttle cable(s).

29. Install the spark plug cable center cover.

30. Replace the O-rings and connect the fuel lines.

31. Install the air cleaner and intake hose. Connect the breather hose.

32. Change the engine oil and oil filter.

33. Fill the system with coolant.

34. Connect the negative battery cable.

35. Run the vehicle until the thermostat opens, and fill the radiator completely.

36. Check and adjust the idle speed and ignition timing.

37. Once the vehicle has cooled, recheck the coolant level.

2.4L Engine

▶ **See Figures 119 thru 131**

1. Relieve the fuel system pressure.
2. Disconnect the negative battery cable.
3. Remove the air cleaner with all air intake hoses.
4. Drain the cooling system.

> ✳✳ **CAUTION**
>
> **Never open, service or drain the radiator or cooling system when hot; serious burns can occur from the steam and hot coolant. Also, when draining engine coolant, keep in mind that cats and dogs are attracted to ethylene glycol antifreeze and could drink any that is left in an uncovered container or in puddles on the ground. This will prove fatal in sufficient quantities. Always drain coolant into a sealable container. Coolant should be reused unless it is contaminated or is several years old.**

Fig. 119 Remove the upper radiator hose . . .

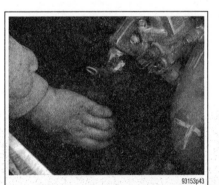

Fig. 120 . . . and also the lower radiator hoses from the thermostat housing

Fig. 121 Remove the heater hose from the cylinder head

Fig. 122 Remove the three thermostat housing retaining bolts . . .

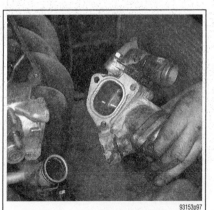

Fig. 123 . . . then remove the thermostat housing from the cylinder head

Fig. 124 Using a suitable device, such as a breaker bar and the appropriate socket, loosen the cylinder head bolts in the proper sequence

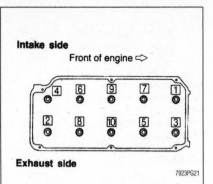

Intake side
Front of engine ⇨

Exhaust side

7923PG21

Fig. 125 Cylinder head bolt removal sequence—2.4L (4G64) engine

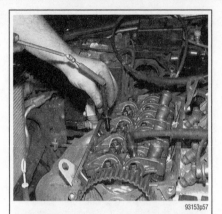

93153p57

Fig. 126 A magnet can be extremely helpful when removing the cylinder head bolts

93153p99

Fig. 127 Grasp the cylinder head and lift it off the engine block with the manifolds attached. It is a good idea to use a helper for this, as the assembly is very heavy

93153p00

Fig. 128 Remove the cylinder head gasket from the block

93153p40

Fig. 129 Thoroughly clean the gasket surfaces of the cylinder head

93153p75

Fig. 130 Also, make sure to thoroughly clean the engine block mating surfaces before reassembling the engine

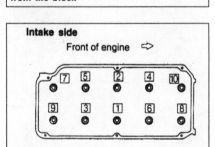

Intake side
Front of engine ⇨

Exhaust side

7923PG22

Fig. 131 Cylinder head bolt installation sequence—2.4L (4G64) engine

5. Disconnect the accelerator cable. Remove the cable mounting brackets and position the cable aside.
6. Remove the breather hose.
7. Label and disconnect the vacuum lines at the throttle body.
8. Disconnect and plug the high pressure fuel line.
9. Disconnect and plug the fuel return hose.
10. Label and detach the connectors from the following components:
   - A/C compressor
   - Power steering pressure switch
   - Heated Oxygen (HO2S) sensor
   - Engine Coolant Temperature (ECT) gauge sender
   - ECT sensor
   - Manifold Absolute Pressure (MAP) sensor

- Intake Air Temperature (IAT) sensor
- Throttle Position (TP) sensor
- Idle Air Control (IAC) motor
- Injector harness
- Ignition coil
- Camshaft Position (CMP) sensor
- Exhaust Gas Recirculation (EGR) solenoid valve

11. Remove the spark plug wire cover and wires.
12. At the thermostat case assembly, remove the coolant hoses and unbolt the thermostat case from the engine.
13. Remove the upper timing belt cover.
14. Align all timing marks.
15. Secure the timing belt to the camshaft sprocket with cord or a wire tie.
16. Remove the camshaft sprocket.
17. Remove the valve cover and the half-round seal.
18. Disconnect the intake manifold stay bracket from the intake manifold.
19. Remove the exhaust pipe self-locking nuts and separate the exhaust pipe from the exhaust manifold. Discard the gasket.
20. Loosen the cylinder head mounting bolts in 3 steps, starting from the outside and working inward. Lift off the cylinder head assembly and remove the head gasket.

To install:
21. Thoroughly clean the mating surfaces of the head and block.
22. Place a new head gasket on the cylinder block with the identification marks at the front top (upward) position. Do not use sealer on the gasket.

23. Inspect the cylinder head bolt length prior to installation. If the length exceeds 3.91 in. (99.4mm), the bolt must be replaced. Install the washer onto the bolt so the chamfer on the washer faces towards the head of the bolt.
24. Carefully install the cylinder head on the block and tighten the cylinder head bolts as follows:
   a. Following the proper tightening sequence, tighten the cylinder head bolts to 58 ft. lbs. (78 Nm).
   b. Loosen all bolts completely.
   c. Torque bolts to 15 ft. lbs. (20 Nm).
   d. Tighten bolts an additional 1/4 turn.
   e. Tighten bolts an additional 1/4 turn.
25. Install the new exhaust pipe gasket and connect the exhaust pipe to the manifold. Tighten the bolts to 33 ft. lbs. (44 Nm).
26. Install the thermostat case and tighten the mounting bolts to 18 ft. lbs. (24 Nm).
27. Connect the coolant hoses to the thermostat case.
28. Apply sealer to the perimeter of the half-round seal and to the lower edges of the half-round portions of the belt-side of the new gasket. Install the valve cover.
29. Install the camshaft sprocket with the timing belt attached. Remove the cord or wire tie.
30. Install the upper timing belt cover.
31. Connect the intake manifold stay and tighten the mounting bolts to 22 ft. lbs. (30 Nm).
32. Attach the connectors to the following components:
   - A/C compressor
   - Power steering pressure switch

- HO$_2$S sensor
- ECT gauge sender
- ECT sensor
- MAP sensor
- IAT sensor
- TP sensor
- IAC motor
- Injector harness
- Ignition coil
- CMP sensor
- EGR solenoid valve

33. Install the spark plug wires and cover.
34. Replace the O-rings and connect the fuel lines.
35. Install the air cleaner and intake hose. Connect the breather hose.
36. Fill the cooling system.
37. Connect the negative battery cable

3.0L DOHC Engine

♦ See Figures 132 and 133

1. Relieve fuel system pressure. Disconnect the negative battery cable.
2. Drain the cooling system.

✳✳ CAUTION

Never open, service or drain the radiator or cooling system when hot; serious burns can occur from the steam and hot coolant. Also, when draining engine coolant, keep in mind that cats and dogs are attracted to ethylene glycol antifreeze and could drink any that is left in an uncovered container or in puddles on the ground. This will prove fatal in sufficient quantities. Always drain coolant into a sealable container. Coolant should be reused unless it is contaminated or is several years old.

3. Remove the air intake hoses.
4. Remove air intake plenum and intake manifold.
5. Remove the exhaust manifold.
6. Remove the timing belt. Refer to the timing belt procedure in this section.
7. Remove the breather hose.
8. Remove the spark plug wire center cover and remove the spark plug wires.
9. Remove the rocker covers.
10. Remove the intake camshaft sprockets.
11. Remove the rear timing belt cover.
12. Remove the ignition coil assembly.
13. Disconnect all water hoses from the thermostat housing and remove the housing.
14. Disconnect the water inlet from the front head.
15. Loosen the cylinder head mounting bolts in the reverse of the torque sequence and loosen the bolts in three steps. Lift off the cylinder head assembly and remove the head gasket.
To install:
16. Thoroughly clean the sealing surfaces of the head and block.
17. Place a new head gasket on the cylinder block with the identification marks in the front top (upward) position. Do not use sealer on the gasket.
18. Carefully install the cylinder head on the block. Be sure the head bolt washers are installed with the chamfered edge upward. Using three even steps, torque the head bolts in sequence, to 76–83 ft. lbs. (105–115 Nm).

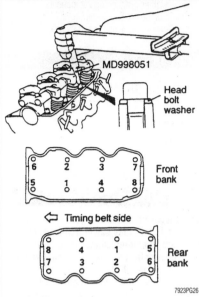

Fig. 132 Tighten the cylinder head bolts according to the sequence shown—3.0L (SOHC and DOHC) engines

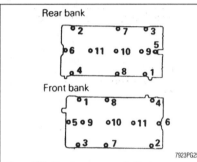

Fig. 133 Rocker cover bolt torque sequence—Diamante 3.0L DOHC engine

19. Install new O-ring and connect the water inlet to the head. Tighten the mounting bolt to 9–11 ft. lbs. (12–15 Nm).
20. Replace the gaskets and install the thermostat housing. Tighten the mounting bolts to 12–14 ft. lbs. (17–20 Nm).
21. Using new hose clamps, connect the hoses to the thermostat housing.
22. Install the ignition coil and torque the mounting bolts to 7 ft. lbs. (10 Nm).
23. Install the rear timing belt cover and torque the mounting bolts to 17 ft. lbs. (24 Nm).
24. Install the intake camshaft sprockets. Tighten the retaining bolt to 65 ft. lbs. (90 Nm).
25. Apply sealer to the lower edges of the valve cover. Tighten the bolts in the proper sequence to 44–51 inch lbs. (5–6 Nm).
26. Connect the spark plug wires and install the center cover. Tighten the bolts that secure the center cover to 27 inch lbs. (3 Nm)
27. Install the breather hose.
28. Install the timing belt. Refer to the timing belt procedure in this section.
29. Install the exhaust manifold assembly.
30. Using all new gaskets, install the intake manifold and air intake plenum.
31. Install the air intake hoses.
32. Change the engine oil and oil filter.

33. Fill the system with coolant.
34. Connect the negative battery cable.
35. Adjust the accelerator cable.
36. Start the engine.
37. Check and adjust the idle speed and ignition timing.
38. Once the vehicle has cooled, recheck the coolant level.

3.0L SOHC Engine

♦ See Figure 132

1. Relieve the fuel system pressure.
2. Disconnect the negative battery cable.
3. Drain the cooling system.

✳✳ CAUTION

Never open, service or drain the radiator or cooling system when hot; serious burns can occur from the steam and hot coolant. Also, when draining engine coolant, keep in mind that cats and dogs are attracted to ethylene glycol antifreeze and could drink any that is left in an uncovered container or in puddles on the ground. This will prove fatal in sufficient quantities. Always drain coolant into a sealable container. Coolant should be reused unless it is contaminated or is several years old.

4. Remove the air intake hose.
5. Remove the exhaust manifold.
6. Remove the air intake plenum and intake manifold.
7. Remove the timing belt. Refer to the timing belt procedure in this section.
8. Remove the camshaft sprockets and the rear timing belt cover.
9. Remove the power steering pump bracket. If removing the rear head, remove the alternator brace.
10. Disconnect the water inlet pipe.
11. Remove the purge pipe assembly.
12. Remove the valve cover.
13. Using the reverse sequence of the installation sequence, loosen the cylinder head mounting bolts in three steps. Lift off the cylinder head assembly and remove the head gasket.
To install:
14. Thoroughly clean the sealing surfaces of the head and block.
15. Place a new head gasket on the cylinder block making sure the identification mark on the cylinder head gasket is in the front top (upward) location. Do not use sealer on the gasket.
16. Carefully install the cylinder head on the block. Be sure the head bolt washers are installed with the chamfered edge upward. Using three even steps, torque the head bolts in sequence, to 76–83 ft. lbs. (105–115 Nm).
17. Apply sealer to the lower edges of the half-round portions and install the valve cover. Tighten valve cover bolts to 7 ft. lbs. (9 Nm).
18. Install the purge pipe assembly.
19. Connect the water inlet pipe.
20. Install the power steering pump bracket and alternator brace.
21. Install the rear timing belt cover and camshaft sprockets. Torque the retaining bolt to 65 ft. lbs. (90 Nm).
22. Install the timing belt. Refer to the timing belt procedure in this section.

23. Using all new gaskets, install the intake manifold, air intake plenum and exhaust manifold.

24. Install the air intake hose.

25. Fill the system with coolant.

26. Connect the negative battery cable.

27. Start the engine.

28. Check and adjust the idle speed and ignition timing.

29. Once the vehicle has cooled, recheck the coolant level.

3.5L Engine

▶ **See Figure 134**

1. Disconnect the negative battery cable.
2. Drain the engine coolant

❊❊ CAUTION

Never open, service or drain the radiator or cooling system when hot; serious burns can occur from the steam and hot coolant. Also, when draining engine coolant, keep in mind that cats and dogs are attracted to ethylene glycol antifreeze and could drink any that is left in an uncovered container or in puddles on the ground. This will prove fatal in sufficient quantities. Always drain coolant into a sealable container. Coolant should be reused unless it is contaminated or is several years old.

3. Remove the timing belt. Refer to the timing belt procedure in this section.

4. Remove the intake and exhaust manifolds.

5. Remove the spark plug wires.

6. Remove the cylinder head covers.

7. Remove the timing belt rear center cover.

8. Loosen the cylinder head bolts gradually in three stages, in the opposite of the installation sequence.

9. Remove the cylinder head.

To install:

10. Clean the cylinder head and mounting surface on the engine block.

11. Install the cylinder head using a new gasket.

12. Tighten the bolts in sequence using three stages to 76–83 ft. lbs. (103–113 Nm).

13. Install the timing belt rear center cover.

14. Install the cylinder head covers using new gaskets. Tighten the bolts to 2–3 ft. lbs. (3–4 Nm).

15. Install the spark plug wires.

16. Install the intake and exhaust manifolds.

17. Install the timing belt. Refer to the timing belt procedure in this section.

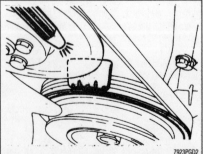

Fig. 134 Cylinder head bolt tightening sequence—3.5L engine

18. Install any remaining components.

19. Refill the cooling system.

20. Connect the negative battery cable.

Oil Pan

REMOVAL & INSTALLATION

1.5L Engine

▶ **See Figure 135**

1. Disconnect the negative battery cable.
2. Drain the engine oil.

❊❊ CAUTION

The EPA warns that prolonged contact with used engine oil may cause a number of skin disorders, including cancer! You should make every effort to minimize your exposure to used engine oil. Protective gloves should be worn when changing the oil. Wash your hands and any other exposed skin areas as soon as possible after exposure to used engine oil. Soap and water, or waterless hand cleaner should be used.

3. Remove the bell housing lower cover.

4. Remove the oil pan retainer bolts. Tap the oil pan with a rubber mallet to break seal.

➡**Do not use a prytool when removing the oil pan. If available, oil pan remover tool MD998727 or equivalent may be used to break the seal.**

To install:

5. Clean all gasket surfaces of the cylinder block and the oil pan.

6. Apply sealant to the gasket surfaces of the oil pan.

7. Install the oil pan onto the cylinder block within 15 minutes after applying sealant. Install the fasteners and tighten to 60 inch lbs. (7 Nm).

8. Install the bell housing cover.

9. Install the oil drain plug with a new seal and tighten to 29 ft. lbs. (40 Nm).

10. Lower the vehicle and fill the crankcase to the proper level with clean engine oil.

❊❊ WARNING

Operating the engine without the proper amount and type of engine oil will result in severe engine damage.

11. Connect the negative battery cable. Start the engine and check for leaks.

1.8L Engine

▶ **See Figure 136**

1. Disconnect the negative battery cable.
2. Raise the vehicle and support safely.
3. Remove the oil pan drain plug and drain the engine oil.

❊❊ CAUTION

The EPA warns that prolonged contact with used engine oil may cause a number of skin disorders, including cancer! You should make every effort to minimize your exposure to used engine oil. Protective gloves should

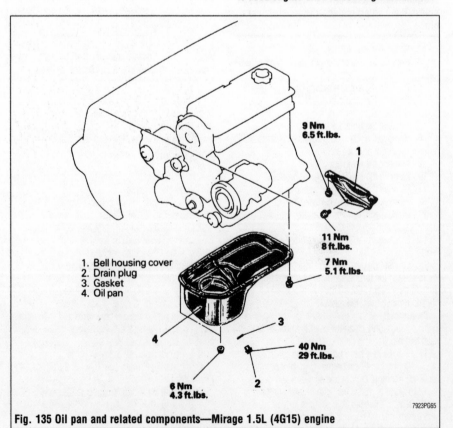

1. Bell housing cover
2. Drain plug
3. Gasket
4. Oil pan

9 Nm
6.5 ft.lbs.

11 Nm
8 ft.lbs.

7 Nm
5.1 ft.lbs.

40 Nm
29 ft.lbs.

6 Nm
4.3 ft.lbs.

Fig. 135 Oil pan and related components—Mirage 1.5L (4G15) engine

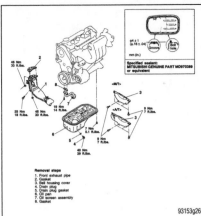

Fig. 136 Oil pan and related components—
1.8L engine

be worn when changing the oil. Wash your
hands and any other exposed skin areas as
soon as possible after exposure to used engine oil. Soap and water, or waterless hand
cleaner should be used.

4. Disconnect and lower the exhaust pipe from
the engine manifold.
5. Remove the bell housing lower cover.
6. Remove the oil pan retainer bolts and remove
the oil pan.

➡️**Do not use a prytool when removing the oil
pan. If available, oil pan remover tool
MD998727 or equivalent may be used break
the seal.**

To install:
7. Clean all gasket surfaces of the cylinder
block and the oil pan.
8. Apply sealant around the gasket surfaces of
the oil pan.
9. Install the oil pan onto the cylinder block
within 15 minutes after applying sealant. Install the
fasteners and tighten to 60 inch lbs. (5 Nm).
10. Install the bell housing cover.
11. Connect the exhaust pipe to the engine manifold with new gasket in place. Tighten the exhaust
pipe to manifold flange nuts to 33 ft. lbs. (45 Nm).
Install and tighten the support bolt to 18 ft. lbs. (25
Nm).
12. Install the oil drain plug and tighten to 29 ft.
lbs. (40 Nm).
13. Fill the crankcase to the proper level.

✳✳ WARNING

**Operating the engine without the proper
amount and type of engine oil will result in
severe engine damage.**

14. Connect the negative battery cable. Start the
engine and check for leaks.

1.6L and 2.0L Engines

FRONT WHEEL DRIVE

◆ **See Figures 137 and 138**

1. Disconnect the negative battery cable.
2. Raise the vehicle and support safely.
3. Remove the oil pan drain plug and drain the
engine oil.

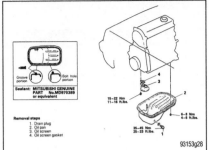

Fig. 137 Oil pan and related components—
2.0L SOHC engine

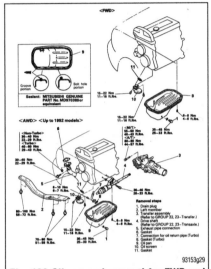

Fig. 138 Oil pan and removal for FWD and
AWD 1.6L and 2.0L DOHC engines

✳✳ CAUTION

**The EPA warns that prolonged contact with
used engine oil may cause a number of skin
disorders, including cancer! You should
make every effort to minimize your exposure
to used engine oil. Protective gloves should
be worn when changing the oil. Wash your
hands and any other exposed skin areas as
soon as possible after exposure to used engine oil. Soap and water, or waterless hand
cleaner should be used.**

4. Disconnect and lower the exhaust pipe from
the engine manifold.
5. Using the appropriate equipment, support the
weight of the engine.
6. Remove the retainer bolts and the center
crossmember.
7. Remove the oil pan bolts. Using special tool
MD998727, tap in between the engine block and the
oil pan.

➡️**Do not use a chisel, screwdriver or similar
tool when removing the oil pan. Damage to
engine components may occur.**

8. Inspect the oil pan for damage and cracks.
Replace if faulty. While the pan is removed, inspect
the oil screen for clogging, damage and cracks. Replace if faulty.

To install:
9. Using a wire brush or other tool, scrape clean
all gasket surfaces of the cylinder block and the oil
pan so that all loose material is removed. Clean sealing surfaces of all dirt and oil.
10. Apply sealant around the gasket surfaces of
the oil pan in such a manner that all bolt holes are
circled and there is a continuous bead of sealer
around the entire perimeter of the oil pan.

➡️**The continuous bead of sealer should be
applied in a bead approximately 0.16 in.
(4mm) in diameter.**

11. Install the oil pan onto the cylinder block
within 15 minutes after applying sealant. Install the
fasteners and tighten to 4–6 ft. lbs. (6–8 Nm).
12. Install the crossmember and tighten the
mounting bolts to 72 ft. lbs. (100 Nm).
13. Connect the exhaust pipe to the engine manifold with new gasket in place. Tighten the exhaust
pipe to manifold flange nuts to 29 ft. lbs. (40 Nm).
14. Install the oil drain plug and tighten to 33 ft.
lbs.
15. Lower the vehicle and fill the crankcase to the
proper level with clean engine oil.

✳✳ WARNING

**Operating the engine without the proper
amount and type of engine oil will result in
severe engine damage.**

16. Connect the negative battery cable.
17. Start the engine and check for leaks.

ALL WHEEL DRIVE

◆ **See Figure 138**

1. Disconnect the negative battery cable.
2. Raise the vehicle and support safely.
3. Remove the oil pan drain plug and drain the
engine oil.

✳✳ CAUTION

**The EPA warns that prolonged contact with
used engine oil may cause a number of skin
disorders, including cancer! You should
make every effort to minimize your exposure
to used engine oil. Protective gloves should
be worn when changing the oil. Wash your
hands and any other exposed skin areas as
soon as possible after exposure to used engine oil. Soap and water, or waterless hand
cleaner should be used.**

4. Disconnect and lower the exhaust pipe from
the engine manifold.
5. Remove the transfer assembly and right driveshaft.
6. Using the appropriate equipment, support the
weight of the engine and remove the center crossmember.
7. Disconnect the return pipe for the turbocharger from the side of the oil pan.
8. Remove the oil pan bolts. Using special tool
MD998727, tap in between the engine block and the
oil pan.

➡️**Do not use a chisel, screwdriver or similar
tool when removing the oil pan. Damage to
engine components may occur.**

9. Inspect the oil pan for damage and cracks. Replace if faulty. While the pan is removed, inspect the oil screen for clogging, damage and cracks. Replace if faulty.

To install:

10. Using a wire brush or other tool, scrape clean all gasket surfaces of the cylinder block and the oil pan so that all loose material is removed. Clean sealing surfaces of all dirt and oil.

11. Apply sealant around the gasket surfaces of the oil pan in such a manner that all bolt holes are circled and there is a continuous bead of sealer around the entire perimeter of the oil pan.

➡️**The continuous bead of sealer should be applied in a bead approximately 0.16 in. (4mm) in diameter.**

12. Install the oil pan onto the cylinder block within 15 minutes after applying sealant. Install the fasteners and tighten to 4–6 ft. lbs. (6–8 Nm).

13. Install the oil return pipe using a new gasket, if removed. Tighten retainers to 5–7 ft. lbs. (7–10 Nm).

14. Install the left member and tighten the forward retainer bolts to 72 ft. lbs. (100 Nm). Tighten the rearward left member bolts to 58 ft. lbs. (80 Nm).

15. Install the transfer assembly and right driveshaft.

16. Connect the exhaust pipe from the engine manifold with new gasket in place. Tighten the exhaust pipe to manifold flange nuts to 29 ft. lbs. (40 Nm).

17. Install the oil drain plug and tighten to 33 ft. lbs.

18. Lower the vehicle and fill the crankcase to the proper level with clean engine oil.

❊❊ WARNING

Operating the engine without the proper amount and type of engine oil will result in severe engine damage.

19. Connect the negative battery cable. Start the engine and check for leaks.

2.4L Engine

▶ **See Figure 139**

1. Disconnect the negative battery cable.

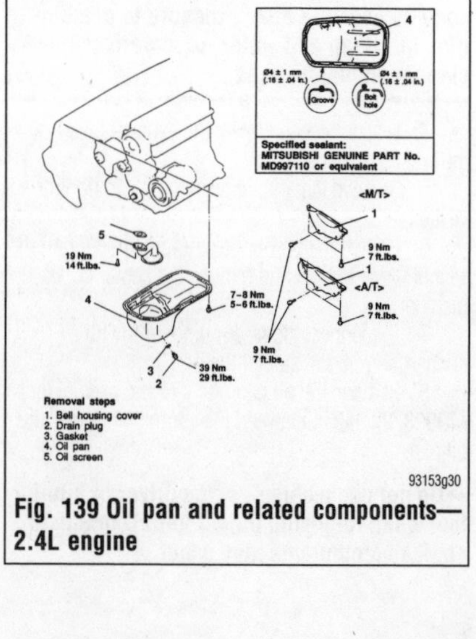

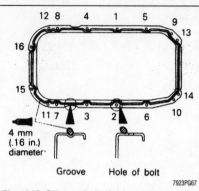

Fig. 139 Oil pan and related components—2.4L engine

2. Remove the oil pan drain plug and drain the engine oil.

❊❊ CAUTION

The EPA warns that prolonged contact with used engine oil may cause a number of skin disorders, including cancer! You should make every effort to minimize your exposure to used engine oil. Protective gloves should be worn when changing the oil. Wash your hands and any other exposed skin areas as soon as possible after exposure to used engine oil. Soap and water, or waterless hand cleaner should be used.

3. Remove the oil dipstick and tube assembly.
4. Detach the Heated Oxygen (HO₂S) sensor connector.
5. Remove the front exhaust pipe from the vehicle.
6. Remove the bell housing cover.
7. Remove the oil pan retainer bolts. Using special tool MD998727 or equivalent, tap in between the engine block and the oil pan.

➡️**Do not use a prytool when removing the oil pan. Damage to engine components may occur.**

To install:

8. Apply sealant around the gasket surfaces of the oil pan.
9. Install the oil pan onto the cylinder block within 15 minutes after applying sealant. Install the fasteners and tighten to 6 ft. lbs. (8 Nm).
10. Install the oil drain plug and tighten to 29 ft. lbs. (39 Nm).
11. Install the bell housing cover, and tighten the mounting bolts to 7 ft. lbs. (9 Nm).
12. Install the front exhaust pipe and tighten the bolts at the catalytic converter to 36 ft. lbs. (49 Nm). Tighten the nuts at the exhaust manifold to 32 ft. lbs. (44 Nm).
13. Reconnect the HO₂S sensor connector.
14. Fill the crankcase to the proper level.

❊❊ WARNING

Operating the engine without the proper amount and type of engine oil will result in severe engine damage.

15. Connect the negative battery cable. Start the engine and check for leaks.

3.0L Engines

▶ **See Figure 140**

1. Disconnect the negative battery cable.
2. Remove the oil pan drain plug and drain the engine oil.

❊❊ CAUTION

The EPA warns that prolonged contact with used engine oil may cause a number of skin disorders, including cancer! You should make every effort to minimize your exposure to used engine oil. Protective gloves should be worn when changing the oil. Wash your hands and any other exposed skin areas as soon as possible after exposure to used en-

Fig. 140 Oil pan bolt tightening sequence and application of sealant to the pan—Diamante 3.0L engines

gine oil. Soap and water, or waterless hand cleaner should be used.

3. Remove the left side crossmember. If equipped with 4WS, it will also be necessary to remove the right side crossmember.
4. Remove the starter motor.
5. Disconnect the roll stopper stay bracket, from the rear transaxle stay bracket. Remove the both transaxle stay brackets.
6. Remove the bell housing lower cover,
7. Remove the oil pan mounting bolts. Using special tool MD998727 or equivalent, separate and remove the engine oil pan.

To install:

8. Apply a 0.16 in. (4mm) continuous bead of sealer around the surface of the oil pan.

➡️**Assemble the oil pan to the cylinder block within 15 minutes after applying the sealant.**

9. Install the oil pan mounting bolts. Following proper sequence, tighten mounting bolts to 48 inch lbs. (6 Nm).
10. Install lower bell housing cover and the starter motor.
11. Install the transaxle stay brackets and connect the roll stopper bracket.
12. Install the crossmember(s) and tighten the mounting bolts to 43–51 ft. lbs. (60–70 Nm).
13. Fill the engine with the proper amount of oil.

❊❊ WARNING

Operating the engine without the proper amount and type of engine oil will result in severe engine damage.

14. Connect the negative battery cable and check for leaks.

3.5L Engine

▶ **See Figures 141, 142, and 143**

1. Disconnect the negative battery cable.
2. Drain the engine oil.

❊❊ CAUTION

The EPA warns that prolonged contact with used engine oil may cause a number of skin disorders, including cancer! You should make every effort to minimize your exposure

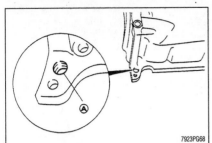

Fig. 141 Install a bolt in the threaded hole to force the oil pan from the engine block—3.5L engine

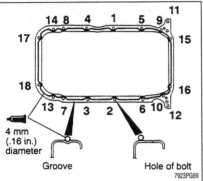

4 mm (.16 in.) diameter • Groove • Hole of bolt

7923PG69

Fig. 142 Apply sealant and tighten the bolts in the order shown—3.5L engine, upper oil pan shown

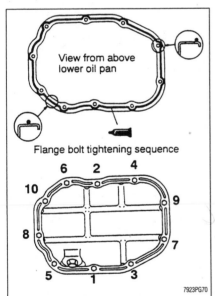

View from above lower oil pan

Flange bolt tightening sequence

7923PG70

Fig. 143 Apply sealant and tighten the bolts in the order shown—3.5L engine, lower oil pan shown

to used engine oil. Protective gloves should be worn when changing the oil. Wash your hands and any other exposed skin areas as soon as possible after exposure to used engine oil. Soap and water, or waterless hand cleaner should be used.

3. Remove the mounting bolts from the lower oil pan.

4. Place a block of wood against the side of the pan and tap the block with a hammer to break the seal and remove the lower pan.
5. Remove the starter.
6. Remove the dipstick tube.
7. Unbolt the upper oil pan.

✳✳ WARNING

Do not pry or use seal breaker tool to remove the oil pan. Damage to the aluminum surface can result.

8. Screw a bolt into the threaded hole to force the oil pan from the engine block and remove the pan.
9. Remove the bolt used to remove the pan.
To install:
10. Clean and degrease the sealing surfaces of the upper oil pan and engine block.
11. Apply a bead of silicone sealant along the mounting surface of the upper oil pan.
12. Install the upper oil pan. Tighten the bolts in sequence to 4 ft. lbs. (6 Nm).
13. Install the dipstick tube using a new O-ring.
14. Install the starter assembly.
15. Clean and degrease the sealing surface of the lower oil pan.
16. Place a bead of sealant on the mounting surface of the lower oil pan. Install the lower pan. Tighten the bolts in sequence to 7–9 ft. lbs. (10–12 Nm).
17. Install the drain plug using a new washer. Tighten the drain plug to 29 ft. lbs. (39 Nm).
18. Lower the vehicle and fill the crankcase to the correct level.

✳✳ WARNING

Operating the engine without the proper amount and type of engine oil will result in severe engine damage.

19. Connect the negative battery cable.
20. Start the engine and check for leaks.

Oil Pump

REMOVAL & INSTALLATION

1.5L and 1.8L Engines

♦ See Figures 144 and 145

➡Whenever the oil pump is disassembled or the cover removed, the gear cavity must be filled with petroleum jelly to seal the pump and act as a prime. Do not use grease.

1. Disconnect the negative battery cable.
2. Raise and support the vehicle.
3. Drain the engine oil.

✳✳ CAUTION

The EPA warns that prolonged contact with used engine oil may cause a number of skin disorders, including cancer! You should make every effort to minimize your exposure to used engine oil. Protective gloves should be worn when changing the oil. Wash your

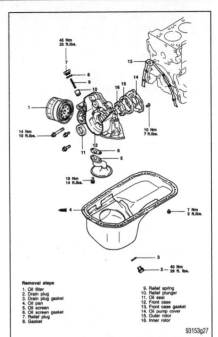

Removal steps
1. Oil filter
2. Drain plug
3. Drain plug gasket
4. Oil pan
5. Oil screen
6. Oil screen gasket
7. Relief plug
8. Gasket
9. Relief spring
10. Relief plunger
11. Oil seal
12. Front case
13. Front case gasket
14. Oil pump cover
15. Outer rotor
16. Inner rotor

93153g27

Fig. 144 Exploded view of the oil pump mounting—1.5L engine

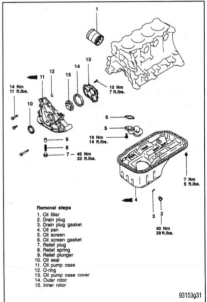

Removal steps
1. Oil filter
2. Drain plug
3. Drain plug gasket
4. Oil pan
5. Oil screen
6. Oil screen gasket
7. Relief plug
8. Relief spring
9. Relief plunger
10. Oil seal
11. Oil pump case
12. O-ring
13. Oil pump case cover
14. Outer rotor
15. Inner rotor

93153g31

Fig. 145 Exploded view of the oil pump mounting—1.8L engine

hands and any other exposed skin areas as soon as possible after exposure to used engine oil. Soap and water, or waterless hand cleaner should be used.

4. Support the engine using a suitable device
5. Remove the front engine mount bracket and accessory drive belts.
6. Remove timing belt upper and lower covers.
7. Remove the timing belt and crankshaft sprocket. Refer to the timing belt procedure in this section.
8. Remove the oil pan and remove the oil screen.

9. Remove the front cover mounting bolts. Note the lengths of the mounting bolts as they are removed for proper installation.

10. Remove the front case assembly and oil pump assembly.

11. Remove the oil pump cover.

12. Remove the inner and outer gears from the front case.

To install

13. Remove all gasket material from the mating surfaces and clean all parts.

14. Thoroughly coat both oil pump gears with clean engine oil and install them in the correct direction of rotation.

15. Install the pump cover and tighten the bolts to 84 inch lbs. (10 Nm).

16. Coat the relief valve and spring with clean engine oil. Install them and tighten the plug to 33 ft. lbs. (45 Nm).

17. Install a new front crankshaft seal and coat the lips of the seal with clean engine oil.

18. Install the front case and oil pump assembly to the engine block using a new gasket. Tighten the bolts to 10 ft. lbs. (14 Nm).

19. Install the oil screen with new gasket. Torque the screen bolts to 14 ft. lbs. (19 Nm).

20. Install the oil pan.

21. Install the crankshaft sprocket and timing belt. Refer to the timing belt procedure in this section.

22. Fill the crankcase to the proper level.

✳✳ WARNING

Operating the engine without the proper amount and type of engine oil will result in severe engine damage.

23. Connect the negative battery cable.

1.6L, 2.0L and 2.4L Engines

◆ See Figures 146, 147, 148, and 149

➡**Whenever the oil pump is disassembled or the cover removed, the gear cavity must be filled with petroleum jelly to seal the pump and act as a prime. Do not use grease.**

1. Disconnect the negative battery cable.

2. Rotate the engine so No. 1 cylinder is on Top Dead Center (TDC) of its compression stroke.

3. Drain the engine oil.

✳✳ CAUTION

The EPA warns that prolonged contact with used engine oil may cause a number of skin disorders, including cancer! You should make every effort to minimize your exposure to used engine oil. Protective gloves should be worn when changing the oil. Wash your hands and any other exposed skin areas as soon as possible after exposure to used engine oil. Soap and water, or waterless hand cleaner should be used.

4. Using the proper equipment, support the weight of the engine. Remove the front engine mount bracket and accessory drive belts.

5. Remove timing belt upper and lower covers.

6. Remove the timing belt and crankshaft sprocket. Refer to the timing belt procedure in this section.

7. Detach the electrical connector from the oil pressure sending unit and remove the oil pressure sensor. Remove the oil filter and the oil filter bracket.

8. Remove the oil pan, oil screen and gasket.

9. Using special tool MD998162, remove the plug cap in the engine front cover.

10. Remove the plug on the side of the engine block. Insert a Phillips screwdriver with a shank diameter of 0.32 in. (8mm) into the plug hole. This will hold the silent shaft.

11. Remove the driven gear bolt that secures the oil pump driven gear to the silent shaft.

12. Remove the front cover mounting bolts. Note the lengths of the mounting bolts as they are removed for proper installation.

13. Remove the front case cover and oil pump assembly. If necessary, the silent shaft can come out with the cover assembly.

14. Remove the oil pump cover, located on the back of the engine front cover. Remove the oil pump drive and driven gears.

15. After disassembling the oil pump, clean all components and remove gasket material from mating surfaces.

16. Assemble the oil pump gears into the front case and rotate it to ensure smooth rotation and no looseness. Be sure there is no ridge wear on the contact surface between the front case and the gear surface of the oil pump front cover.

To install

17. Align the timing mark on the oil pump drive gear with that on the driven gear and install them into the engine front case. Apply engine oil to the gears.

18. Install the oil pump cover and tighten the retainer bolts to 13 ft. lbs. (18 Nm).

19. Using the appropriate driver, install a new crankshaft seal into the front case.

20. Position new front case gasket in place. Set seal guide tool MD998285 on the front end of the crankshaft to protect the seal from damage. Apply a thin coat of oil to the outer circumference of the seal pilot tool.

21. Install the front case assembly through a new front case gasket and temporarily tighten the flange bolts.

22. Mount the oil filter on the bracket with new oil filter bracket gasket in place. Install the bolts with washers and tighten to 14 ft. lbs. (19 Nm).

23. Insert a Phillips screwdriver into the hole in the left side of the engine block to lock the silent shaft in place.

24. Install the oil pump drive gear onto the left silent shaft. Tighten the driven gear bolt to 27 ft. lbs. (37 Nm).

25. Install a new O-ring to the groove in the front case and install the plug cap. Using the special tool MD998162, tighten the cap to 17 ft. lbs. (24 Nm).

26. Install the oil screen in position with new gasket in place.

27. Clean both mating surfaces of the oil pan and the cylinder block. Apply sealant in the groove in the oil pan flange.

➡**After applying sealant to the oil pan, do not exceed 15 minutes before installing the oil pan.**

28. Install the oil pan to the engine and secure with the retainers. Tighten bolts to 5 ft. lbs. (7 Nm).

29. Install the oil pressure gauge unit and the oil pressure switch. Connect the electrical harness connector.

30. Install the oil cooler. Secure with oil cooler bolt tightened to 31 ft. lbs. (43 Nm).

31. Refill the crankcase.

32. Install new oil filter.

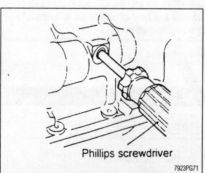

Fig. 146 Holding the silent shaft for oil pump gear removal—2.0L engine

Phillips screwdriver

7923PG71

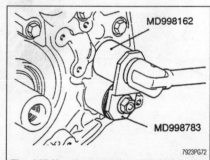

MD998162

MD998783

7923PG72

Fig. 147 Use the special socket and holder to remove the balance shaft plug—2.0 engine

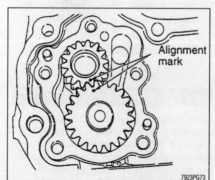

Alignment mark

7923PG73

Fig. 148 Aligning oil pump timing marks— 2.0L engine

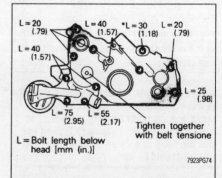

L = 20 (.79) L = 40 (1.57) •L = 30 (1.18) L = 20 (.79)

L = 40 (1.57)

L = 75 (2.95) L = 55 (2.17)

L = 25 (.98)

Tighten together with belt tensione

L = Bolt length below head [mm (in.)]

7923PG74

Fig. 149 Front case bolt identification— 2.0L and 2.4L engines

✳✳ WARNING

Operating the engine without the proper amount and type of engine oil will result in severe engine damage.

33. Connect the negative battery cable and start the engine.
34. Verify correct oil pressure.
35. Inspect for leaks.

3.0L Engines

♦ **See Figure 150**

➡Whenever the oil pump is disassembled or the cover removed, the gear cavity must be filled with petroleum jelly to seal the pump and act as a prime. Do not use grease.

1. Disconnect the negative battery cable.
2. Drain the engine oil.

✳✳ CAUTION

The EPA warns that prolonged contact with used engine oil may cause a number of skin disorders, including cancer! You should make every effort to minimize your exposure to used engine oil. Protective gloves should be worn when changing the oil. Wash your hands and any other exposed skin areas as soon as possible after exposure to used engine oil. Soap and water, or waterless hand cleaner should be used.

3. Remove the front engine mount bracket and accessory drive belts.
4. Remove timing belt upper and lower covers.
5. Remove the timing belt and crankshaft sprocket. Refer to the timing belt procedure in this section.
6. Remove the oil pan.
7. Remove the oil screen and gasket.
8. Remove the front cover mounting bolts. Note the lengths of the mounting bolts as they are removed for proper installation.
9. Remove the front case cover and oil pump assembly.

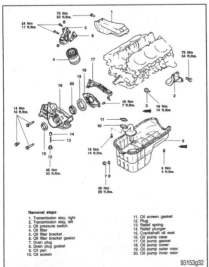

Fig. 150 Exploded view of the oil pump mounting—3.0L engines

To install:
10. Thoroughly clean all gasket material from all mounting surfaces.
11. Apply engine oil to the entire surface of the gears or rotors.
12. Assemble the front case cover and oil pump assembly to the engine block.
13. Install the oil screen with new gasket.
14. Install the oil pan.
15. Install the crankshaft sprocket and timing belt. Refer to the timing belt procedure in this section.
16. Install the timing belt covers.
17. Install the drive belts and the front engine mount bracket.
18. Connect the negative battery cable, refill the crankcase and check for adequate oil pressure.

✳✳ WARNING

Operating the engine without the proper amount and type of engine oil will result in severe engine damage.

3.5L Engine

♦ **See Figures 151 and 152**

1. Disconnect the negative battery cable.
2. Remove the timing belt. Refer to the timing belt procedure in this section.
3. Drain the engine oil.

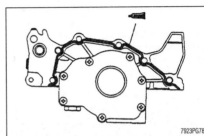

Fig. 151 Apply sealant to the rear of the oil pump case—3.5L engine

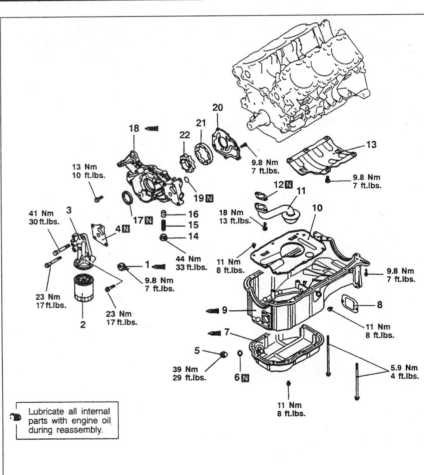

Lubricate all internal parts with engine oil during reassembly.

Removal steps

1. Oil pressure gauge unit	12. Oil screen gasket
2. Oil filter	13. Baffle plate
3. Oil filter bracket	14. Plug
4. Oil filter bracket gasket	15. Relief spring
5. Drain plug	16. Relief plunger
6. Drain plug gasket	17. Crankshaft oil seal
7. Oil pan, lower	18. Oil pump case
8. Cover	19. O-ring
9. Oil pan, upper	20. Oil pump cover
10. Baffle plate	21. Oil pump outer rotor
11. Oil screen	22. Oil pump inner rotor

Fig. 152 Exploded view of the oil pump mounting—3.5L engine

4. Remove the splash shield from the wheel well.
5. Remove the oil filter adapter.
6. Remove the lower and upper oil pans.
7. Remove the lower baffle, oil pump pick-up and upper baffle.
8. Remove the oil pump case mounting bolts and the oil pump case.
9. Remove the oil pump gear cover.
10. Make matchmarks on the oil pump rotors before removing them.
11. Remove the crankshaft seal from the oil pump case.

To install:
12. Install a new crankshaft seal in the oil pump cover.
13. Apply engine oil to the rotors, then align the matchmarks and install the rotors in the oil pump case.
14. Install the rotor cover. Tighten the bolts to 7 ft. lbs. (10 Nm).
15. Apply a 0.113 in. (3mm) bead of sealant to the back of the oil pump case. Install the case on the engine and tighten the bolts to 10 ft. lbs. (14 Nm).
16. Install the upper baffle plate and oil pump pick-up using a new gasket. Tighten the baffle bolts to 7 ft. lbs. (10 Nm) and the pick-up bolts to 13 ft. lbs. (18 Nm).
17. Install the lower baffle in the upper oil pan. Tighten the bolts to 8 ft. lbs. (11 Nm).
18. Install the oil pans.
19. Install the oil filter adapter using a new gasket. Tighten the larger bolt to 30 ft. lbs. (41 Nm) and the smaller bolt to 17 ft. lbs. (23 Nm).
20. Install the timing belt and remaining components. Refer to the timing belt procedure in this section.
21. Fill the engine with the correct amount of oil.

22. Connect the negative battery cable.
23. Start the engine and check for leaks.

Crankshaft Damper

REMOVAL & INSTALLATION

▶ See Figures 153 and 154

1. Disconnect the negative battery cable.
2. Remove the accessory drive belts from around the crankshaft pulley. Refer to Section 1.

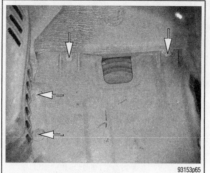

93153p65

Fig. 153 Remove the fasteners, then remove the side inner fender splash shield

3. Raise and support the vehicle.
4. Remove the passenger side front wheel.
5. Remove the passenger side inner fender splash shield to gain access to the crankshaft damper.
6. On the 1.5L, 1.6L, 2.0L and 2.4L engines, remove the pulley-to-sprocket bolts.
7. On the 1.5L, 1.8L, 3.0L and 3.5L engines, remove the crankshaft pulley center retaining bolt.
8. Remove the damper from the crankshaft using a suitable puller.

To install:
9. Place the damper onto the crankshaft, ensuring the key-way is aligned.
10. On the 1.5L, 1.8L, 3.0L and 3.5L engines, install the crankshaft pulley center retaining bolt and tighten the bolt as follows:
   • 1.5L engine: 51–72 ft. lbs. (70–100 Nm)
   • 1.8L and 3.5L engines: 134 ft. lbs. (185 Nm)
   • 3.0L engines: 108–116 ft. lbs. (150–160 Nm)
11. On the 1.5L, 1.6L, 2.0L and 2.4L engines, install the pulley-to-sprocket bolts and tighten the bolts as follows:
   • 1.5L engine: 10 ft. lbs. (14 Nm)
   • 1.6L and 2.0L engines: 14–22 ft. lbs. (20–30 Nm)
   • 2.4L engine: 18 ft. lbs. (25 Nm)
12. On the 1.6L and 2.0L engines, install the pulley-to-sprocket bolts and tighten them to 14–22 ft. lbs. (20–30 Nm).
13. Install the splash shield.
14. Install the wheel, then carefully lower the vehicle.
15. Install the accessory drive belts. Refer to Section 1.
16. Connect the negative battery cable.

Timing Cover and Belt

REMOVAL & INSTALLATION

➡ Refer to Section 1 for the proper timing belt service interval.

1.5L Engine

1990—94 MODELS

▶ See Figures 155 and 156

93153p60

Fig. 154 Unfasten the crankshaft pulley retaining bolts, then remove the pulley

1. Disconnect the negative battery cable.
2. Remove the engine under cover.
3. Raise and safely support the weight of the engine using the appropriate equipment. Remove the front engine mount bracket and accessory drive belts.
4. If necessary, remove the coolant reservoir tank.
5. Using the proper equipment, slightly raise the engine to take the weight off the side engine mount. Remove the engine mount bracket.
6. Remove the drive belts, tension pulley brackets, water pump pulley and crankshaft pulley.
7. Remove all attaching screws and remove the upper and lower timing belt covers.
8. Make a mark on the back of the timing belt indicating the direction of rotation so it may be reassembled in the same direction if it is to be reused. Loosen the timing belt tensioner and remove the timing belt.

➡ If coolant or engine oil comes in contact with the timing belt, they will drastically shorten its life. Also, do not allow engine oil or coolant to contact the timing belt sprockets or tensioner assembly.

9. Remove the tensioner spacer, tensioner spring and tensioner assembly.
10. Inspect the timing belt for cracks on back surface, sides, bottom and check for separated canvas. Check the tensioner pulley for smooth rotation.

To install:
11. Position the tensioner, tensioner spring and tensioner spacer on engine block.
12. Align the timing marks on the camshaft sprocket and crankshaft sprocket. This will position No. 1 piston on TDC on the compression stroke.
13. Position the timing belt on the crankshaft sprocket and keeping the tension side of the belt tight, set it on the camshaft sprocket.
14. Apply counterclockwise force to the camshaft sprocket to give tension to the belt and make sure all timing marks are aligned.
15. Loosen the pivot side tensioner bolt and the slot side bolt. Allow the spring to take up the slack.
16. Tighten the slot side tensioner bolt and then the pivot side bolt. If the pivot side bolt is tightened first, the tensioner could turn with bolt, causing over tension.
17. Turn the crankshaft clockwise. Loosen the pivot side tensioner bolt and then the slot side bolt to allow the spring to take up any remaining slack.

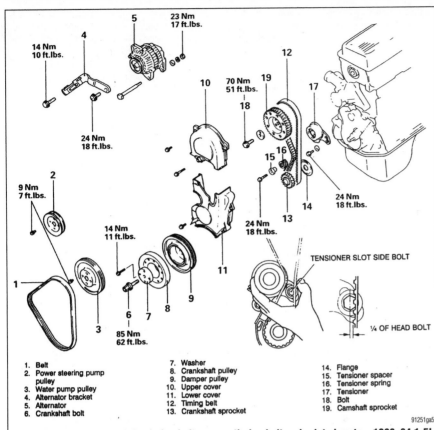

Fig. 155 Exploded view of the timing belt covers, timing belt and related parts—1990–94 1.5L engine

1. Belt	7. Washer
2. Power steering pump pulley	8. Crankshaft pulley
3. Water pump pulley	9. Damper pulley
4. Alternator bracket	10. Upper cover
5. Alternator	11. Lower cover
6. Crankshaft bolt	12. Timing belt
	13. Crankshaft sprocket

14. Flange	
15. Tensioner spacer	
16. Tensioner spring	
17. Tensioner	
18. Bolt	
19. Camshaft sprocket	

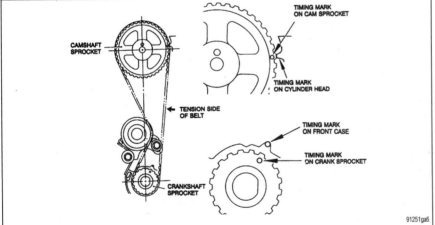

Fig. 156 Camshaft and crankshaft sprocket mark alignment for proper timing belt installation—1990–94 1.5L engine

Tighten the slot bolt and then the pivot side bolt to 14–20 ft. lbs. (20–27 Nm).

18. Check the belt tension by holding the tensioner and timing belt together by hand and give the belt a slight thumb pressure at a point level with tensioner center. Make sure the belt cog crest comes as deep as about $1/4$ of the width of the slot side tensioner bolt head. Do not manually overtighten the belt or it will make a howling noise.

19. Install the timing belt covers and all related items.

20. Connect the negative battery cable.

1995–00 MODELS

▶ **See Figure 157**

1. Disconnect the negative battery cable.
2. Remove the engine undercover.
3. Rotate the crankshaft clockwise and position the engine at TDC of the compression stroke.
4. Raise and safely support the weight of the engine using the appropriate equipment. Remove the A/C clamp, front engine mount bracket and accessory drive belts.
5. Remove the crankshaft pulley.

6. Remove timing belt upper and lower covers.
7. Make a mark on the back of the timing belt indicating the direction of rotation so it may be reassembled in the same direction if it is to be reused. Loosen the timing belt tensioner and move the tensioner to provide slack to the timing belt. Tighten the tensioner in this position.
8. Remove the timing belt.

✳✳ WARNING

Coolant and engine oil will damage the rubber in the timing belt, drastically reducing its life. Do not allow engine oil or coolant to contact the timing belt, the sprockets or tensioner assembly.

9. If defective, remove the tensioner spacer, tensioner spring and tensioner assembly.
To install:
10. Position the tensioner, tensioner spring and tensioner spacer on engine block.
11. Align the timing marks on the camshaft sprocket and crankshaft sprocket. This will position No. 1 piston on TDC on the compression stroke.
12. Position the timing belt on the crankshaft sprocket and keeping the tension side of the belt tight, set it on the camshaft sprocket, then the tensioner.
13. Apply slight counterclockwise force to the camshaft sprocket to give tension to the belt and be sure all timing marks are aligned.
14. Loosen the pivot side tensioner bolt and the slot side bolt. Allow the spring to remove the slack.
15. Tighten the slot side tensioner bolt, then the pivot side bolt. If the pivot side bolt is tightened first, the tensioner could turn with bolt, causing over tension.
16. Turn the crankshaft clockwise. Loosen the pivot side tensioner bolt, then the slot side bolt to allow the spring to take up any remaining slack. Tighten the slot bolt, then the pivot side bolt to 17 ft. lbs. (24 Nm).
17. Install the timing belt covers and tighten the cover bolts to 84–96 inch lbs. (10–11 Nm). Install all other applicable components.

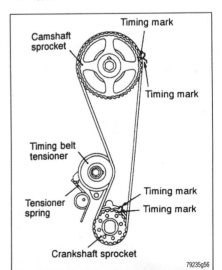

Fig. 157 Align the timing belt sprockets as indicated before removing the timing belt—1995–00 1.5L engine

1.6L & 2.0L (Non-Turbo) DOHC Engines

♦ **See Figure 158**

➡️**The 1.6L engine is not equipped with silent shafts. Disregard all instructions pertaining to silent shafts if working on that engine.**

1. Disconnect the negative battery cable.
2. Remove the engine undercover.
3. If necessary, remove the coolant reservoir.
4. Using the proper equipment, slightly raise the engine to take the weight off the side engine mount. Remove the engine mount bracket.
5. Remove the drive belts, tension pulley brackets, water pump pulley and crankshaft pulley.
6. Remove all attaching screws and remove the upper and lower timing belt covers.
7. Rotate the crankshaft clockwise and align the timing marks so No. 1 piston will be at TDC of the compression stroke. At this time the timing marks on the camshaft sprocket and the upper surface of the cylinder head should coincide, and the dowel pin of the camshaft sprocket should be at the upper side.

➡️**Always rotate the crankshaft in a clockwise direction. Make a mark on the back of the timing belt indicating the direction of rotation so it may be reassembled in the same direction if it is to be reused.**

8. Remove the auto tensioner and remove the outermost timing belt.
9. Remove the timing belt tensioner pulley, tensioner arm, idler pulley, oil pump sprocket, special washer, flange and spacer.
10. Remove the silent shaft (inner) belt tensioner and remove the belt.

To install:

11. Align the timing marks on the crankshaft sprocket and the silent shaft sprocket. Fit the inner timing belt over the crankshaft and silent shaft sprocket. Ensure that there is no slack in the belt.
12. While holding the inner timing belt tensioner with your fingers, adjust the timing belt tension by applying a force towards the center of the belt, until the tension side of the belt is taut. Tighten the tensioner bolt.

➡️**When tightening the bolt of the tensioner, ensure that the tensioner pulley shaft does not rotate with the bolt. Allowing it to rotate with the bolt can cause excessive tension on the belt.**

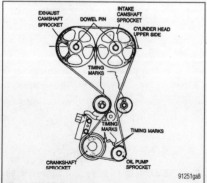

Fig. 158 Camshaft and crankshaft timing belt sprocket alignment marks—1990–94 Mitsubishi 1.6L and 2.0L DOHC engines

13. Check belt for proper tension by depressing the belt on it's long side with your finger and noting the belt deflection. The desired reading is 0.20–0.28 in. (5–7mm). If tension is not correct, readjust and check belt deflection.
14. Install the flange, crankshaft and washer to the crankshaft. The flange on the crankshaft sprocket must be installed towards the inner timing belt sprocket. Tighten bolt to 80–94 ft. lbs. (110–130 Nm).
15. To install the oil pump sprocket, insert a Phillips screwdriver with a shaft 0.31 in. (8mm) in diameter into the plug hole in the left side of the cylinder block to hold the left silent shaft. Tighten the nut to 36–43 ft. lbs. (50–60 Nm).
16. Using a wrench, hold the camshaft at it's hexagon between journal No. 2 and 3, then tighten the bolt to 58–72 ft. lbs. (80–100 Nm). If no hexagon is present between journal No. 2 and 3, hold the sprocket stationary with a spanner wrench while tightening the retainer bolt.
17. Carefully push the auto tensioner rod in until the set hole in the rod aligns with the hole in the cylinder. Place a wire into the hole to retain the rod.
18. Install the tensioner pulley onto the tensioner arm. Locate the pinhole in the tensioner pulley shaft to the left of the center bolt. Then, tighten the center bolt finger-tight.
19. When installing the timing belt, turn the 2 camshaft sprockets so their dowel pins are located on top. Align the timing marks facing each other with the top surface of the cylinder head. When you let go of the exhaust camshaft sprocket, it will rotate 1 tooth in the counterclockwise direction. This should be taken into account when installing the timing belts on the sprocket.

➡️**Both camshaft sprockets are used for the intake and exhaust camshafts and are provided with 2 timing marks. When the sprocket is mounted on the exhaust camshaft, use the timing mark on the right with the dowel pin hole on top. For the intake camshaft sprocket, use the 1 on the left with the dowel pin hole on top.**

20. Align the crankshaft sprocket and oil pump sprocket timing marks.
21. After alignment of the oil pump sprocket timing marks, remove the plug on the cylinder block and insert a Phillips screwdriver with a shaft diameter of 0.31 in. (8mm) through the hole. If the shaft can be inserted 2.4 in. deep, the silent shaft is in the correct position. If the shaft of the tool can only be inserted 0.8–1.0 in. (20–25mm) deep, turn the oil pump sprocket 1 turn and realign the marks. Reinsert the tool making sure it is inserted 2.4 in. deep. Keep the tool inserted in hole for the remainder of this procedure.

➡️**The above step assures that the oil pump socket is in correct orientation to the silent shafts. This step must not be skipped or a vibration may develop during engine operation.**

22. Install the timing belt as follows:
    a. Install the timing belt around the intake camshaft sprocket and retain it with 2 spring clips or binder clips.
    b. Install the timing belt around the exhaust sprocket, aligning the timing marks with the cylinder head top surface using 2 wrenches. Retain the belt with 2 spring clips.

c. Install the timing belt around the idler pulley, oil pump sprocket, crankshaft sprocket and the tensioner pulley. Remove the 2 spring clips.
    d. Lift upward on the tensioner pulley in a clockwise direction and tighten the center bolt. Make sure all timing marks are aligned.
    e. Rotate the crankshaft ¹/₄ turn counterclockwise. Then, turn in clockwise until the timing marks are aligned again.
23. To adjust the timing (outer) belt, turn the crankshaft ¹/₄ turn counterclockwise, then turn it clockwise to move No. 1 cylinder to TDC.
24. Loosen the center bolt. Using tool MD998738 or equivalent and a torque wrench, apply a torque of 22–25 inch. lbs. (2.6–2.8 Nm). Tighten the center bolt.
25. Screw the special tool into the engine left support bracket until its end makes contact with the tensioner arm. At this point, screw the special tool in some more and remove the set wire attached to the auto tensioner, if the wire was not previously removed. Then remove the special tool.
26. Rotate the crankshaft 2 complete turns clockwise and let it sit for approximately 15 minutes. Then, measure the auto tensioner protrusion (the distance between the tensioner arm and auto tensioner body) to ensure that it is within 0.15–0.18 in. (3.8–4.5mm). If out of specification, repeat Step 1–4 until the specified value is obtained.
27. If the timing belt tension adjustment is being performed with the engine mounted in the vehicle, and clearance between the tensioner arm and the auto tensioner body cannot be measured, the following alternative method can be used:
    a. Screw in special tool MD998738 or equivalent, until its end makes contact with the tensioner arm.
    b. After the special tool makes contact with the arm, screw it in some more to retract the auto tensioner pushrod while counting the number of turns the tool makes until the tensioner arm is brought into contact with the auto tensioner body. Make sure the number of turns the special tool makes conforms with the standard value of 2¹/₂–3 turns.
    c. Install the rubber plug to the timing belt rear cover.
28. Install the timing belt covers and all related items.
29. Connect the negative battery cable.

1.8L & 2.0L SOHC Engines

♦ **See Figures 159, 160, and 161**

1. Position the engine so the No. 1 piston is at TDC of the compression stroke.
2. Disconnect the negative battery cable.
3. Remove the engine undercover.
4. Using the proper equipment, slightly raise the engine to take the weight off the side engine mount. Remove the engine mount bracket.
5. Remove the drive belts, tension pulley brackets, water pump pulley and crankshaft pulley.
6. Remove all attaching screws and remove the upper and lower timing belt covers.
7. Remove the timing belt covers.
8. Remove the outer crankshaft sprocket and flange.
9. Remove the silent shaft (inner) belt tensioner and remove the belt.

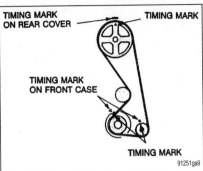

Fig. 159 Camshaft and crankshaft sprocket alignment for proper timing belt replacement—1.8L and 2.0L SOHC engines

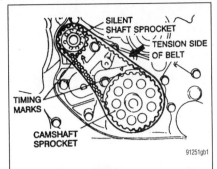

Fig. 160 Silent shaft sprocket alignment marks for belt replacement—1.8L and 2.0L SOHC engines

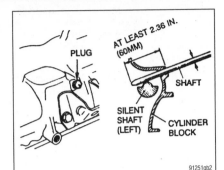

Fig. 161 Checking the rear silent shaft for proper positioning—1.8L and 2.0L SOHC engines

To install:

10. Align the timing marks of the silent shaft sprockets and the crankshaft sprocket with the timing marks on the front case.

11. Wrap the timing belt around the sprockets so there is no slack in the upper span of the belt and the timing marks are still aligned.

12. Install the tensioner pulley and move the pulley by hand so the long side of the belt deflects about $1/4$ in. (6mm).

13. Hold the pulley tightly so the pulley cannot rotate when the bolt is tightened. Tighten the bolt to 15 ft. lbs. (20 Nm) and recheck the deflection amount.

14. Install the timing belt tensioner fully toward the water pump and tighten the bolts. Place the upper end of the spring against the water pump body.

15. Align the timing marks of the camshaft, crankshaft and oil pump sprockets with their corresponding marks on the front case or rear cover.

➡**There is a possibility to align all timing marks and have the oil pump sprocket and silent shaft out of time, causing an engine vibration during operation. If the following step is not followed exactly, there is a 50 percent chance that the silent shaft alignment will be 180 degrees off.**

16. Before installing the timing belt, ensure that the left side (rear) silent shaft (oil pump sprocket) is in the correct position as follows:

a. Remove the plug from the rear side of the block and insert a tool with shaft diameter of 0.31 in. (8mm) into the hole.

b. With the timing marks still aligned, the shaft of the tool must be able to go in at least $2^1/3$ in. (59mm). If the tool can only go in about 1 in. (25mm), the shaft is not in the correct orientation and will cause a vibration during engine operation. Remove the tool from the hole and turn the oil pump sprocket 1 complete revolution. Realign the timing marks and insert the tool. The shaft of the tool must go in at least $2^1/3$ in. (59mm).

c. Recheck and realign the timing marks.

d. Leave the tool in place to hold the silent shaft while continuing.

17. Install the belt to the crankshaft sprocket, oil pump sprocket, then camshaft sprocket, in that order. While doing so, make sure there is no slack between the sprocket except where the tensioner is installed.

18. Recheck the timing marks' alignment. If all are aligned, loosen the tensioner mounting bolt and allow the tensioner to apply tension to the belt.

19. Remove the tool that is holding the silent shaft and rotate the crankshaft a distance equal to 2 teeth on the camshaft sprocket. This will allow the tensioner to automatically apply the proper tension on the belt. Do not manually overtighten the belt or it will howl.

20. Tighten the lower mounting bolt first, then the upper spacer bolt.

21. To verify correct belt tension, check that the deflection at the longest span of the belt is about $1/2$ in. (13mm).

22. The installation of the timing belt covers and all related items, is the reverse of the removal procedure. Make sure all pieces of packing are positioned in the inner grooves of the covers when installing.

23. Connect the negative battery cable.

2.0L (Turbo) DOHC Engine

♦ See Figures 162 and 163

1. Disconnect the negative battery cable.
2. Remove the engine undercover.
3. Remove the engine mount bracket.
4. Remove the drive belts.
5. Remove the belt tensioner pulley.
6. Remove the water pump pulleys.
7. Remove the crankshaft pulley.
8. Remove the stud bolt from the engine support bracket and remove the timing belt covers.
9. Rotate the crankshaft clockwise to line up the camshaft timing marks. Always turn the crankshaft in the normal direction of rotation only.
10. Loosen the tension pulley center bolt.

➡**If the timing belt is to be reused, mark the direction of rotation on the flat side of the belt with an arrow.**

11. Move the tension pulley towards the water pump and remove the timing belt.

12. Remove the crankshaft sprocket center bolt using special tool MB9g67 to hold the crankshaft sprocket while removing the center bolt. Then, use MB998778 or equivalent puller to remove the sprocket.

13. Mark the direction of rotation on the timing belt B with an arrow.

14. Loosen the center bolt on the tensioner and remove the belt.

❋❋ **WARNING**

Do not rotate the camshafts or the crankshaft while the timing belt is removed.

To install:

15. Place the crankshaft sprocket on the crankshaft. Use tool MB9g67 or equivalent to hold the crankshaft sprocket while tightening the center bolt. Tighten the center bolt to 80–94 ft. lbs. (108–127 Nm).

16. Align the timing marks on the crankshaft sprocket B and the balance shaft.

17. Install timing belt B on the sprockets. Position the center of the tensioner pulley to the left and above the center of the mounting bolt.

18. Push the pulley clockwise toward the crankshaft to apply tension to the belt and tighten the mounting bolt to 14 ft. lbs. (19 Nm). Do not let the pulley turn when tightening the bolt because it will cause excessive tension on the belt. The belt should deflect 0.20–0.28 in. (5–7mm) when finger pressure is applied between the pulleys.

19. Install the crankshaft sensing blade and the crankshaft sprocket. Apply engine oil to the mounting bolt and tighten the bolt to 80–94 ft. lbs. (108–127 Nm).

20. Use a press or vise to compress the auto-tensioner pushrod. Insert a set pin when the holes are lined up.

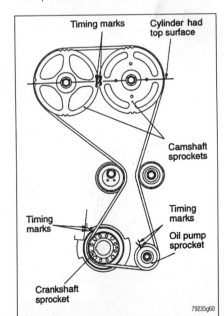

Fig. 162 Camshaft and crankshaft timing belt sprocket TDC alignment mark positioning for timing belt removal and installation— 2.0L turbo engine

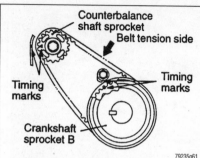

Fig. 163 Timing belt B installation mark alignment— 2.0L turbo

※※ **WARNING**

Do not compress the pushrod too quickly, damage to the pushrod can occur.

21. Install the auto-tensioner on the engine.
22. Align the timing marks on the camshaft sprocket, crankshaft sprocket and the oil pump sprocket.
23. After aligning the mark on the oil pump sprocket, remove the cylinder block plug and insert a prytool in the hole to check the position of the counterbalance shaft. The prytool should go in at least 2.36 in. (60mm) or more, if not, rotate the oil pump sprocket once and realign the timing mark so the prytool goes in. Do not remove the prytool until the timing belt is installed.
24. Install the timing belt on the intake camshaft and secure it with a clip.
25. Install the timing belt on the exhaust camshaft.
26. Align the timing marks with the cylinder head top surface using two wrenches. Secure the belt with another clip.
27. Install the belt around the idler pulley, oil pump sprocket, crankshaft sprocket and the tensioner pulley.
28. Turn the tensioner pulley so the pinholes are at the bottom. Press the pulley lightly against the timing belt.
29. Screw the special tool into the left engine support bracket until it contacts the tensioner arm, then screw the tool in a little more and remove the pushrod pin from the auto-tensioner. Remove the special tool and tighten the center bolt to 35 ft. lbs. (48 Nm).
30. Turn the crankshaft $1/4$ turn counterclockwise, then clockwise until the timing marks are aligned.
31. Loosen the center bolt. Install Mitsubishi Special Tool MD998767, or equivalent, on the tensioner pulley. Turn the tensioner pulley counterclockwise with a torque of 2.6 ft. lbs. (3.5 Nm) and tighten the center bolt to 35 ft. lbs. (48 Nm). Do not let the tensioner pulley turn when tightening the bolt.
32. Turn the crankshaft clockwise two revolutions and align the timing marks.
33. After 15 minutes, measure the protrusion of the pushrod on the auto-tensioner. The standard measurement is 0.150–0.177 in (3.8–4.5mm). If the protrusion is out of specification, loosen the tensioner pulley, apply the proper torque to the belt and retighten the center bolt.
34. Install the timing belt covers and all applicable components.

2.4L Engine

▶ See Figures 164 thru 182

1. Be sure that the engine's No. 1 piston is at TDC in the compression stroke.

※※ **CAUTION**

Wait at least 90 seconds after the negative battery cable is disconnected to prevent possible deployment of the air bag.

2. Disconnect the negative battery cable.
3. Remove the spark plug wires from the tree on the upper cover.
4. Drain the cooling system.

※※ **CAUTION**

Never open, service or drain the radiator or cooling system when hot; serious burns can occur from the steam and hot coolant. Also, when draining engine coolant, keep in mind that cats and dogs are attracted to ethylene glycol antifreeze and could drink any that is left in an uncovered container or in puddles on the ground. This will prove fatal in sufficient quantities. Always drain coolant into a sealable container. Coolant should be reused unless it is contaminated or is several years old.

5. Remove the shroud, fan and accessory drive belts.
6. Remove the radiator as required.

Fig. 164 Remove the upper engine mount-to-mount bracket nuts

Fig. 166 . . . then remove the engine mount from the vehicle

7. Remove the power steering pump, alternator, air conditioning compressor, tension pulley and accompanying brackets, as required.
8. Remove the upper front timing belt cover.
9. Remove the water pump pulley and the crankshaft pulley(s).
10. Remove the lower timing belt cover mounting screws and remove the cover.
11. If the belt(s) are to be reused, mark the direction of rotation on the belt.
12. Remove the timing (outer) belt tensioner and remove the belt. Unbolt the tensioner from the block and remove.
13. Remove the outer crankshaft sprocket and flange.
14. Remove the silent shaft (inner) belt tensioner and remove the inner belt. Unbolt the tensioner from the block and remove it.
15. To remove the camshaft sprockets, use SST MB9g67–01 and MIT308239, or their equivalents.
To install:
16. Install the camshaft sprockets and tighten the center bolt to 65 ft. lbs. (90 Nm).
17. Align the timing mark of the silent shaft belt sprockets on the crankshaft and silent shaft with the marks on the front case. Wrap the silent shaft belt around the sprockets so there is no slack in the upper span of the belt and the timing marks are still in line.
18. Install the tensioner initially so the actual center of the pulley is above and to the left of the installation bolt.
19. Move the pulley up by hand so the center span of the long side of the belt deflects about $1/4$ in. (6mm).

Fig. 165 Remove the upper engine mount through-bolt . . .

Fig. 167 Remove the three upper timing cover retaining bolts . . .

Fig. 168 . . . then remove the upper timing cover

Fig. 169 Remove the A/C belt tensioner pulley and bracket assembly

Fig. 170 Loosen the bolt on the tensioner pulley and slide the pulley to the left to relieve the tension on the timing belt

Fig. 171 Make sure you mark the rotation of the timing belt if you plan on reusing the belt

Fig. 172 Remove the timing belt from the engine by lifting it out the top

Fig. 173 Unfasten the two timing belt tensioner retaining bolts . . .

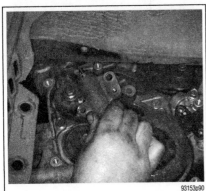

Fig. 174 . . . then remove the tensioner from the engine block

Fig. 175 Remove the bolt and remove the crankshaft timing belt pulley

Fig. 176 After unfastening the retainer, remove the CKP trigger wheel from the crankshaft

Fig. 177 Remove the silent shaft tensioner retaining bolt . . .

Fig. 178 . . . then remove the tensioner from the engine block

Fig. 179 Remove the silent shaft belt from the engine

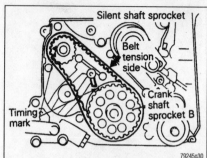

Fig. 180 Silent shaft alignment marks. Notice the tension side of the inner (silent shaft) belt—2.4L engine

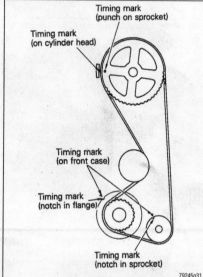

Fig. 181 Timing belt pulley alignment marks—2.4L engine

20. Hold the pulley tightly so it does not rotate when the bolt is tightened. Tighten the bolt to 15 ft. lbs. (20 Nm). If the pulley has moved, the belt will be too tight.

21. Install the timing belt tensioner fully toward the water pump and temporarily tighten the bolts. Place the upper end of the spring against the water pump body. Align the timing marks of the cam, crankshaft and oil pump sprockets with the corresponding marks on the front case or head.

➡️**If the following steps are not followed exactly, there is a chance that the silent shaft alignment will be 180 degrees off. This will cause a noticeable vibration in the engine and the entire procedure will have to be repeated.**

22. Before installing the timing belt, ensure that the left side silent shaft is in the correct position.

➡️**It is possible to align the timing marks on the camshaft sprocket, crankshaft sprocket and the oil pump sprocket with the left balance shaft out of alignment.**

23. With the timing mark on the oil pump pulley aligned with the mark on the front case, check the alignment of the left balance shaft to assure correct shaft timing.

a. Remove the plug located on the left side of the block in the area of the starter.

b. Insert a tool having a shaft diameter of 0.3 in. (8mm) into the hole.

c. With the timing marks still aligned, the tool must be able to go in at least $2\frac{1}{3}$ in. (59mm). If it can only go in about 1 in. (25mm), turn the oil pump sprocket one complete revolution.

d. Recheck the position of the balance shaft with the timing marks realigned. Leave the tool in place to hold the silent shaft while continuing.

24. Install the belt to the crankshaft sprocket, oil pump sprocket and the camshaft sprocket, in that order. While doing so, be sure there is no slack between the sprockets except where the tensioner will take it up when released.

25. Recheck the timing marks' alignment.

26. If all are aligned, loosen the tensioner mounting bolt, and allow the tensioner to apply tension to the belt.

27. Remove the tool that is holding the silent shaft in place and turn the crankshaft clockwise a distance equal to two teeth of the camshaft sprocket. This will allow the tensioner to automatically tension the belt the proper amount.

✳️✳️ WARNING

Do not manually apply pressure to the tensioner. This will overtighten the belt and will cause a howling noise.

28. First tighten the lower mounting bolt and then tighten the upper spacer bolt.

✳️✳️ WARNING

If any binding is felt when adjusting the timing belt tension by turning the crankshaft, STOP turning the engine, because the pistons may be hitting the valves.

29. To verify that belt tension is correct, check that the deflection of the longest span (between the camshaft and oil pump sprockets) is $\frac{1}{2}$ in. (13mm).

30. Install the lower timing belt cover. Be sure the packing is properly positioned in the inner grooves of the covers when installing.

31. Install the water pump pulley and the crankshaft pulley(s).

32. Install the upper front timing belt cover.

33. Install the power steering pump, alternator, air conditioning compressor, tension pulley and accompanying brackets, as required.

34. Install the radiator, shroud, fan and accessory drive belts.

35. Install the spark plug wires to the tree on the upper cover.

36. Refill the cooling system.

37. Connect the negative battery cable. Start the engine and check for leaks.

3.0L SOHC Engine

1992–94 MODELS

▶ **See Figures 182 and 183**

1. Disconnect the negative battery cable.
2. Remove the engine undercover.
3. Remove the cruise control actuator.
4. Remove the accessory drive belts.

5. Remove the air conditioner compressor tension pulley assembly.

6. Remove the tension pulley bracket.

7. Using the proper equipment, slightly raise the engine to take the weight off the side engine mount. Remove the engine mounting bracket.

8. Detach the power steering pump pressure switch connector. Remove the power steering pump and wire aside.

9. Remove the engine support bracket.

10. Remove the crankshaft pulley.

11. Remove the timing belt cover cap.

12. Remove the timing belt upper and lower covers.

13. If the same timing belt will be reused, mark the direction of the timing belt's rotation for installation in the same direction. Make sure the engine is positioned so the No. 1 cylinder is at the TDC of its compression stroke and the sprockets' timing marks are aligned with the engine's timing mark indicators.

14. Loosen the timing belt tensioner bolt and remove the belt. If the tensioner is not being removed, position it as far away from the center of the engine as possible and tighten the bolt.

15. If the tensioner is being removed, paint the outside of the spring to ensure that it is not installed backwards. Unbolt the tensioner and remove it along with the spring.

To install:

16. Install the tensioner, if removed, and hook the upper end of the spring to the water pump pin and the lower end to the tensioner in exactly the same position as originally installed. If not already done, position both camshafts so the marks align with those on the rear. Rotate the crankshaft so the timing mark aligns with the mark on the oil pump.

17. Install the timing belt on the crankshaft sprocket and while keeping the belt tight on the tension side, install the belt on the front camshaft sprocket.

18. Install the belt on the water pump pulley, then the rear camshaft sprocket and the tensioner.

19. Rotate the front camshaft counterclockwise to tension the belt between the front camshaft and the crankshaft. If the timing marks became misaligned, repeat the procedure.

20. Install the crankshaft sprocket flange.

21. Loosen the tensioner bolt and allow the spring to apply tension to the belt.

22. Turn the crankshaft 2 full turns in the clockwise direction until the timing marks align again. Now that the belt is properly tensioned, torque the tensioner lock bolt to 21 ft. lbs. (29 Nm). Measure the belt tension between the rear camshaft sprocket and the crankshaft with belt tension gauge. The specification is 46–68 lbs. (210–310 N).

23. Install the timing covers. Make sure all pieces of packing are positioned in the inner grooves of the covers when installing.

24. Install the crankshaft pulley. Tighten the bolt to 108–116 ft. lbs. (150–160 Nm).

25. Install the engine support bracket.

26. Install the power steering pump and reconnect wire harness at the power steering pump pressure switch.

27. Install the engine mounting bracket and remove the engine support fixture.

28. Install the tension pulleys and drive belts.

29. Install the cruise control actuator.

30. Install the engine undercover.

1. Engine support bracket
2. Bolt
3. Washer
4. Crankshaft pulley
5. Access cover
6. Right side upper front cover
7. Cap
8. Left side upper front cover
9. Front lower cover
10. Flange

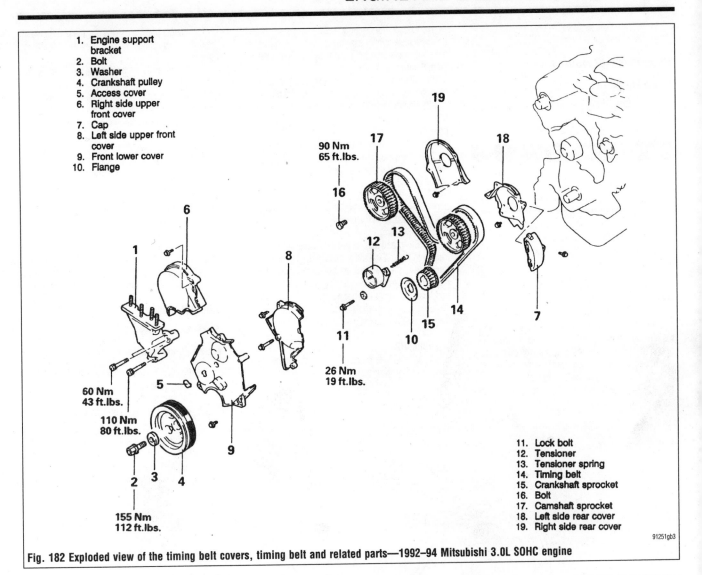

90 Nm
65 ft.lbs.

60 Nm
43 ft.lbs.

110 Nm
80 ft.lbs.

155 Nm
112 ft.lbs.

26 Nm
19 ft.lbs.

11. Lock bolt
12. Tensioner
13. Tensioner spring
14. Timing belt
15. Crankshaft sprocket
16. Bolt
17. Camshaft sprocket
18. Left side rear cover
19. Right side rear cover

91251gb3

Fig. 182 Exploded view of the timing belt covers, timing belt and related parts—1992–94 Mitsubishi 3.0L SOHC engine

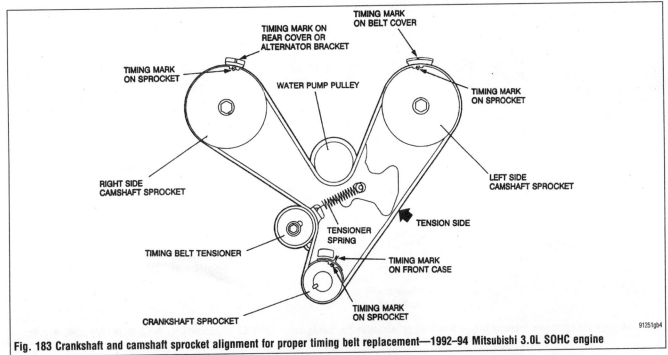

TIMING MARK
ON BELT COVER

TIMING MARK ON
REAR COVER OR
ALTERNATOR BRACKET

TIMING MARK
ON SPROCKET

WATER PUMP PULLEY

TIMING MARK
ON SPROCKET

RIGHT SIDE
CAMSHAFT SPROCKET

LEFT SIDE
CAMSHAFT SPROCKET

TENSION SIDE

TIMING BELT TENSIONER

TENSIONER
SPRING

TIMING MARK
ON FRONT CASE

CRANKSHAFT SPROCKET

TIMING MARK
ON SPROCKET

91251gb4

Fig. 183 Crankshaft and camshaft sprocket alignment for proper timing belt replacement—1992–94 Mitsubishi 3.0L SOHC engine

31. Connect the negative battery cable.
32. Road test the vehicle.

EXCEPT 1992–94 MODELS

▶ See Figure 184

1. Position the engine so the No. 1 cylinder is at TDC of its compression stroke.
2. Disconnect the negative battery cable.

✳ CAUTION

Wait at least 90 seconds after the negative battery cable is disconnected to prevent possible deployment of the air bag.

3. Remove the engine undercover.
4. Remove the front undercover panel.
5. Remove the cruise control pump and the link assembly.
6. Remove the alternator.
7. Raise and suspend the engine so that force is not applied to the engine mount.
8. Remove the timing covers from the engine.
9. If the same timing belt will be reused, mark the direction of the timing belt's rotation for installation in the same direction. Make sure the engine is positioned so the No. 1 cylinder is at the TDC of its compression stroke and the timing marks are aligned with the engine's timing mark indicators on the valve covers or head.

10. Loosen the center bolt of tensioner pulley and unbolt auto-tensioner assembly. The auto-tensioner assembly must be reset to correctly adjust belt tension. Remove the timing belt.

11. Using a wrench, hold the camshaft at its hexagon and remove the camshaft sprocket bolt.

12. Remove and position the auto-tensioner into a vise with soft jaws. The plug at the rear of tensioner protrudes, be sure to use a washer as a spacer to protect the plug from contacting vise jaws.

13. Slowly push the rod into the tensioner until the set hole in rod is aligned with set hole in the auto-tensioner.

14. Insert a 0.055 in. (1.4mm) wire into the aligned set holes. Unclamp the tensioner from the vise and install it on the engine. Tighten tensioner to 17 ft. lbs. (24 Nm).

15. Clean and inspect both auto tensioner mounting bolts. Coat the threads of the old bolts with thread sealer. If new bolts are installed, inspect the heads of the new bolts. If there is white paint on the bolt head, no sealer is required. If there is no paint on the head of the bolt, apply a coat of thread sealer to the bolt. Install both bolts and tighten to 17 ft. lbs. (24 Nm).

To install:

16. Install the tensioner, if removed, and hook the upper end of the spring to the water pump pin and the lower end to the tensioner in exactly the same position as originally installed.

17. Ensure both camshafts are still positioned so the timing marks align with those on the rear timing covers.

18. Rotate the crankshaft so the timing mark aligns with the mark on the front cover.

19. Install the timing belt on the crankshaft sprocket and while keeping the belt tight on the tension side, install the belt on the front (left) camshaft sprocket.

20. Install the belt on the water pump pulley, then the rear (right) camshaft sprocket and the tensioner.

21. Loosen the bolt that secures the adjustment of the tensioner and lightly press the tensioner against the timing belt.

22. Check that the timing marks are in alignment.

23. Rotate the crankshaft 2 full turns in the clockwise direction only, then realign the timing marks.

24. Tighten the bolt that secures the tensioner to 19 ft. lbs. (26 Nm).

25. Install the lower and the upper timing belt covers, along with all other applicable components.

3.0L DOHC Engine

1992–94 MODELS

▶ See Figure 185

1. Position the engine so the No. 1 cylinder is at TDC of its compression stroke.
2. Disconnect the negative battery cable.
3. Remove the engine undercover.

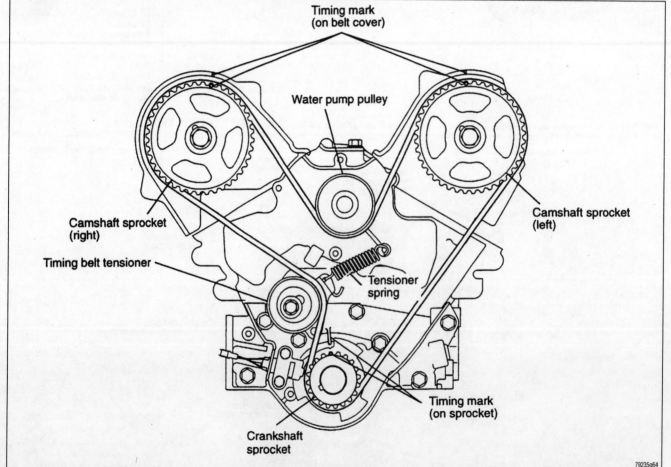

Fig. 184 Align the sprockets properly before removing or installing the timing belt—1995–96 Diamante with the 3.0L (6G72) SOHC engine

79235g64

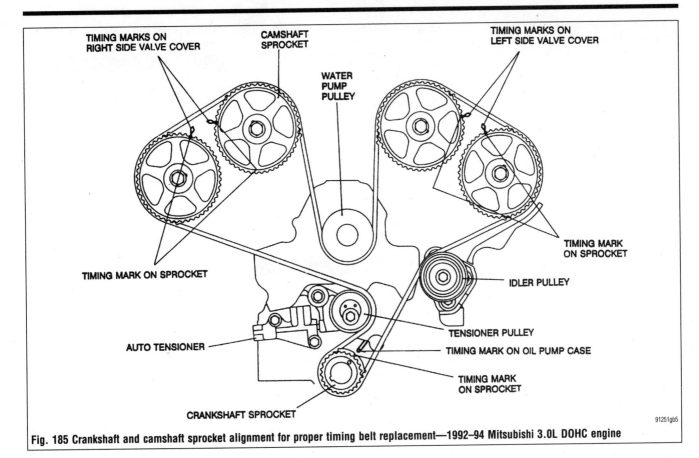

Fig. 185 Crankshaft and camshaft sprocket alignment for proper timing belt replacement—1992–94 Mitsubishi 3.0L DOHC engine

4. Remove the cruise control actuator.

5. Remove the alternator. Remove the air hose and pipe.

6. Remove the belt tensioner assembly and the power steering belt.

7. Remove the crankshaft pulley.

8. Disconnect the brake fluid level sensor.

9. Remove the timing belt upper cover.

10. Using the proper equipment, slightly raise the engine to take the weight off the side engine mount. Remove the engine mount bracket.

11. Remove the alternator/air conditioner idler pulley.

12. Remove the engine support bracket. The mounting bolts are different lengths; mark them for proper installation.

13. Remove the timing belt lower cover. Timing bolt cover mounting bolts are different in length, note their position during removal.

14. If the same timing belt will be reused, mark the direction of the timing belt's rotation for installation in the same direction. Make sure the engine is positioned so the No. 1 cylinder is at the TDC of its compression stroke and the sprockets' timing marks are aligned with the engine's timing mark indicators on the valve covers or head.

15. Loosen the timing belt tensioner bolt and remove the belt.

16. Remove the tensioner assembly.

To install:

17. If the auto tensioner rod is fully extended, reset it as follows:

   a. Clamp the tensioner in a soft-jaw vice in level position.

   b. Slowly push the rod in with the vice until the set hole in the rod is aligned with the hole in the cylinder.

   c. Insert a stiff wire into the set holes to retain the position.

   d. Remove the assembly from the vice.

18. Leave the retaining wire in the tension and install to the engine.

19. If the timing marks of the camshaft sprockets and crankshaft sprocket are not aligned at this point, proceed as follows:

➡**Keep fingers out from between the camshaft sprockets. The sprockets may move unexpectedly because of valve spring pressure and could pinch fingers.**

   a. Align the mark on the crankshaft sprocket with the mark on the front case. Then move the sprocket 2 teeth clockwise to lower the piston so the valve can't touch the piston when the camshafts are being moved.

   b. Turn each camshaft sprocket 1 at a time to align the timing marks with the mark on the valve cover or head. If the intake and exhaust valves of the same cylinder are opened simultaneously, they could interfere with each other. Therefore, if any resistance is felt, turn the other camshaft to move the valve.

   c. Align the timing mark of the crankshaft sprocket, then continue 1 tooth farther in the counterclockwise direction to facilitate belt installation.

20. Using 4 spring loaded paper clips to hold the belt on the cam sprockets, install the belt to the sprockets in the following order:

- **1st**—exhaust camshaft sprocket for the front head
- **2nd**—intake camshaft sprocket for the front head
- **3rd**—water pump pulley

- **4th**—intake camshaft sprocket for the rear head
- **5th**—exhaust camshaft sprocket for the rear head
- **6th**—idler pulley
- **7th**—crankshaft sprocket
- **8th**—tensioner pulley

21. Turn the tensioner pulley so its pin holes are located above the center bolt. Then press the tensioner pulley against the timing belt and simultaneously tighten the center bolt.

22. Make certain that all timing marks are still aligned. If so, remove the 4 clips.

23. Turn the crankshaft $1/4$ turn counterclockwise, then turn it clockwise until all timing marks are aligned.

24. Loosen the center bolt on the tensioner pulley. Using tool MD998767 or equivalent and a torque wrench, apply a torque of 7 ft. lbs. (10 Nm). Tighten the tensioner bolt; make sure the tensioner doesn't rotate with the bolt.

25. Remove the set wire attached to the auto tensioner, if the wire was not previously removed.

26. Rotate the crankshaft 2 complete turns clockwise and let it sit for approximately 5 minutes. Then, make sure the set pin can easily be inserted and removed from the hole in the tensioner.

27. Measure the auto tensioner protrusion (the distance between the tensioner arm and auto tensioner body) to ensure that it is within 0.15–0.18 in. (3.8–4.5mm). If out of specification, repeat Steps 1–4 until the specified value is obtained.

28. Make sure all pieces of packing are positioned in the inner grooves of the lower cover, position cover on engine and install mounting bolts in their original location.

29. Install the engine support bracket and secure using mounting bolts in their original location. Lubricate the reaming area of the reamer bolt and tighten slowly.

30. Install the idler pulley.

31. Install the engine mount bracket. Remove the engine support fixture.

32. Make sure all pieces of packing are positioned in the inner grooves of the upper cover and install.

33. Connect the brake fluid level sensor.

34. Install the crankshaft pulley. Tighten the bolt to 130–137 ft. lbs. (180–190 Nm).

35. Install the belt tensioner assembly and the power steering belt.

36. Install the air hose and pipe.

37. Install the alternator.

38. Install the cruise control actuator.

39. Install the engine undercover.

40. Connect the negative battery cable.

1995–96 MODELS

▶ **See Figure 186**

1. Position the engine so the No. 1 cylinder is at TDC of its compression stroke.

2. Disconnect the negative battery cable.

3. Remove the engine undercover.

4. Remove the cruise control actuator.

5. Remove the alternator. Remove the air hose and pipe.

6. Remove the belt tensioner assembly and the power steering belt.

7. Remove the crankshaft pulley.

8. Disconnect the brake fluid level sensor.

9. Remove the timing belt upper cover.

10. Using the proper equipment, slightly raise the engine to take the weight off the side engine mount. Remove the engine mount bracket.

11. Remove the alternator/air conditioner idler pulley.

12. Remove the engine support bracket. The mounting bolts are different lengths; mark them for proper installation.

13. Remove the timing belt lower cover. Timing bolt cover mounting bolts are different in length, note their position during removal.

✳✳ CAUTION

Be sure to disconnect the negative battery cable. Wait at least 90 seconds after the negative battery cable is disconnected to prevent possible deployment of the air bag.

14. If the same timing belt will be reused, mark the direction of the timing belt's rotation for installation in the same direction. Be sure the engine is positioned so the No. 1 cylinder is at the TDC of its compression stroke and the timing marks are aligned with the engine's timing mark indicators on the rear timing covers.

✳✳ WARNING

Turning the camshaft sprocket when the timing belt is removed could cause the valves to contact with the pistons, resulting in severe engine damage.

15. Remove the bolts that secure the auto-tensioner to the engine block and remove the tensioner.

To install:

➡**The auto-tensioner assembly must be reset to correctly adjust belt tension.**

16. Loosen the center bolt of tensioner pulley to provide timing belt slack.

17. Remove the timing belt assembly.

18. Position the auto-tensioner into a vise with soft jaws. The plug at the rear of tensioner protrudes, be sure to use a washer as a spacer to protect the plug from contacting vise jaws.

19. Slowly push the rod into the tensioner until the set hole in rod is aligned with set hole in the auto-tensioner.

20. Insert a 0.055 in. (1.4mm) wire into the aligned set holes. Remove the tensioner from the vise and install it on the engine.

21. Tighten tensioner mounting bolts to 17 ft. lbs. (24 Nm).

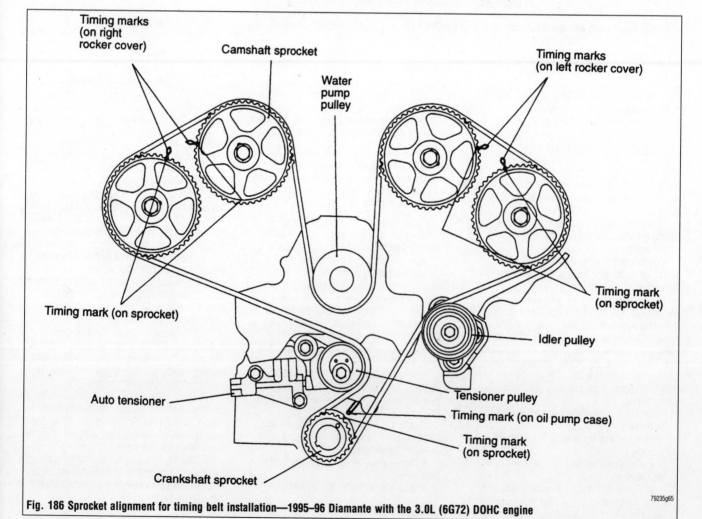

Fig. 186 Sprocket alignment for timing belt installation—1995–96 Diamante with the 3.0L (6G72) DOHC engine

79235g65

✲✲ WARNING

DO NOT rotate or turn the camshafts when removing the sprockets or severe engine damage will result from internal component interference.

22. Align the mark on the crankshaft sprocket with the mark on the front case. Then, move the crankshaft sprocket 1 tooth counterclockwise.

23. Align the timing marks of the camshafts with the marks on the rear covers.

24. Using large paper clips to secure the timing belt to the sprockets, install the timing belt in the following order. Be sure camshafts-to-cylinder heads and crankshaft-to-front cover timing marks are aligned. Install the timing belt around the pulleys in the following order:

    a. Exhaust camshaft sprocket (front bank).
    b. Intake camshaft sprocket (front bank).
    c. Water pump pulley.
    d. Intake camshaft sprocket (rear bank).
    e. Exhaust camshaft sprocket (rear bank).
    f. Tensioner pulley.
    g. Crankshaft pulley.
    h. Idler pulley.

➡**Since the camshaft sprockets turn easily, secure them with box wrenches when installing the timing belt.**

25. Align all timing marks on the crankshaft and raise the tensioner pulley against the belt to remove slack, snug tensioner bolt.

26. Check the alignment of all the timing marks and remove the clips that secure the timing belt to the camshaft sprockets.

27. Rotate the engine $1/4$ turn counterclockwise, then rotate the engine clockwise to align the timing marks. Check that all the timing marks are in alignment.

28. Loosen the center bolt on the tensioner pulley.

29. Using tool MD998752 or equivalent and a torque wrench, apply 84 inch lbs. (10 Nm) to the tool on the tensioner. Tighten the tensioner bolt to 35 ft. lbs. (49 Nm) and be sure the tensioner does not rotate with the bolt.

30. Rotate the crankshaft two complete turns clockwise and let it sit for approximately five minutes. Then, check that the set pin can easily be inserted and removed from the hole in the auto-tensioner.

31. Remove the set wire attached to the auto-tensioner.

32. Measure the auto-tensioner protrusion (the distance between the tensioner arm and auto-tensioner body) to ensure that it is within 0.15–0.18 in. (3.8–4.5mm). If out of specification, repeat adjustment procedure until the specified value is obtained.

33. Check again that the timing marks on all sprockets are in proper alignment.

34. Install the timing belt covers and all other applicable components.

3.5L Engine

◆ **See Figure 187**

1. Disconnect the negative battery cable.
2. Drain the cooling system.

✲✲ CAUTION

Never open, service or drain the radiator or cooling system when hot; serious burns can occur from the steam and hot coolant. Also, when draining engine coolant, keep in mind that cats and dogs are attracted to ethylene glycol antifreeze and could drink any that is left in an uncovered container or in puddles on the ground. This will prove fatal in sufficient quantities. Always drain coolant into a sealable container. Coolant should be reused unless it is contaminated or is several years old.

3. Remove the drive belts.
4. Remove the upper radiator shroud.
5. Remove the fan and fan pulley.
6. Without disconnecting the lines, remove the power steering pump from its bracket and position it to the side. Remove the pump brackets.
7. Remove the belt tensioner pulley bracket.
8. Without releasing the refrigerant, remove the air conditioning compressor from its bracket and position it to the side.
9. Remove the bracket.

10. Remove the cooling fan bracket.
11. On some vehicles it may be necessary to remove the pulley from the crankshaft to access the lower cover bolts.
12. Remove the timing belt cover bolts and the upper and lower covers from the engine.
13. Detach the crankshaft position sensor connector.
14. Using SST MB9g67–01 and MD998754, or their equivalents, remove the crankshaft pulley from the crankshaft.
15. Use a shop rag to clean the timing marks to assist in properly aligning the timing marks.
16. Loosen the center bolt on the tension pulley and remove the timing belt.

➡**If the same timing belt will be reused, mark the direction of timing belt's rotation, for installation in the same direction. Be sure engine is positioned so No. 1 cylinder is at the TDC of it's compression stroke and the sprockets timing marks are aligned with the engine's timing mark indicators.**

17. Remove the auto-tensioner, the tension pulley and the tension arm assembly.
18. Remove the sprockets by holding the hexagonal portion of the camshaft with a wrench while removing the sprocket bolt.

To install:
19. Install the crankshaft pulley and turn the crankshaft sprocket timing mark forward (clockwise) three teeth to move the piston slightly past No. 1 cylinder top dead center.
20. If removed, install the camshaft sprockets and tighten the bolts to 64 ft. lbs. (88 Nm).
21. Align the timing mark of the left bank side camshaft sprocket.
22. Align the timing mark of the right bank side camshaft sprocket, and hold the sprocket with a wrench so that it doesn't turn.
23. Set the timing belt onto the water pump pulley.
24. Check that the camshaft sprocket timing mark of the left bank side is aligned and clamp the timing belt with double clips.
25. Set the timing belt onto the idler pulley.

✲✲ WARNING

If any binding is felt when adjusting the timing belt tension by turning the crankshaft, STOP turning the engine, because the pistons may be hitting the valves.

26. Turn the crankshaft one turn counterclockwise and set the timing belt onto the crankshaft sprocket.
27. Set the timing belt on the tension pulley.
28. Place the tension pulley pin hole so that it is towards the top. Press the tension pulley onto the timing belt, and then provisionally tighten the fixing bolt. Tighten the bolt to 35 ft. lbs. (48 Nm).
29. Slowly turn the crankshaft two full turns in the clockwise direction until the timing marks align. Remove the four double clips.
30. Install the crankshaft position sensor connector.
31. Install the upper and lower covers on the engine and secure them with the retaining screws. Be sure the packing is properly positioned in the inner grooves of the covers when installing.

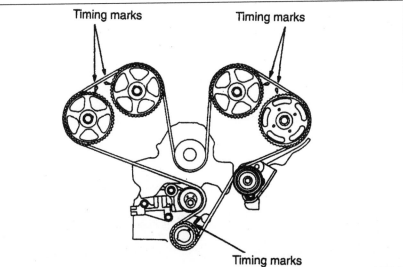

Fig. 187 Clean the timing marks to verify their position when aligning—3.5L engine

79245g34

32. Install the crankshaft pulley if it was removed. Tighten the bolt to 110 ft. lbs. (150 Nm).

33. Install the air conditioning bracket and compressor on the engine. Install the belt tensioner.

34. Install the power steering pump into position. Install the fan pulley and fan.

35. Install the fan shroud on the radiator.

36. Refill the cooling system.

37. Connect the negative battery cable.

38. Start the engine and check for fluid leaks.

INSPECTION

▶ **See Figures 188 thru 195**

An inspection of the timing belt should be performed at least any time the upper timing belt cover is off. If the timing belt shows any signs of failure, it should be replaced. Recommended timing belt replacement intervals can be found in Section 1 of this manual.

Front Crankshaft Seal

REMOVAL & INSTALLATION

▶ **See Figure 196**

On all engines, the camshaft oil seal requires the removal of the timing belt(s). It is advised to replace the seal while replacing the timing belts.

➡ **The seal is located behind the crankshaft timing sprocket.**

1. To remove the seal use a suitable seal removal tool and pry it out of the cover.

2. Thoroughly clean the sealing area of the front cover.

3. Using a suitable installation tool (a large socket works well if none is available), install the seal into the front cover.

❋❋ WARNING

Make sure to install the seal to the correct depth, if the seal is installed too far, an oil leak will occur.

Camshaft, Bearings and Lifters

REMOVAL & INSTALLATION

1.5L Engine

▶ **See Figures 197 and 198**

1. Disconnect the negative battery cable.

2. Rotate the engine and position the No. 1 piston to TDC of its compression stroke.

3. Disconnect the accelerator cable, breather hose and PCV hose connections.

4. Matchmark the positioning of the distributor housing and the positioning of the distributor rotor to the engine block and remove the distributor.

5. Remove the valve cover and discard the gasket.

6. Loosen both rocker arm assemblies gradually and evenly, and remove the rocker shafts from the vehicle.

7. Remove the timing belt covers.

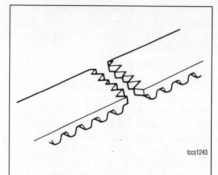

Fig. 188 Check for premature parting of the belt

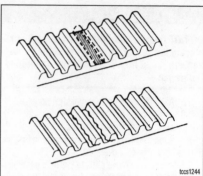

Fig. 189 Check if the teeth are cracked or damaged

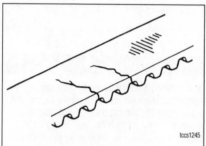

Fig. 190 Look for noticeable cracks or wear on the belt face

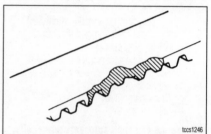

Fig. 191 You may only have damage on one side of the belt; if so, the guide could be the culprit

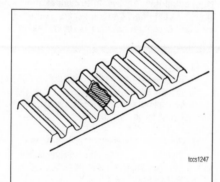

Fig. 192 Foreign materials can get in between the teeth and cause damage

Fig. 193 Inspect the timing belt for cracks, fraying, glazing or damage of any kind

Fig. 194 Damage on only one side of the timing belt may indicate a faulty guide

Fig. 195 ALWAYS replace the timing belt at the interval specified by the manufacturer

➡ **DO NOT allow the camshaft or the crankshaft to rotate after the timing belt is removed.**

8. Remove the timing belt assembly.

9. Holding the camshaft sprocket from turning, loosen and remove the bolt that secures the sprocket.

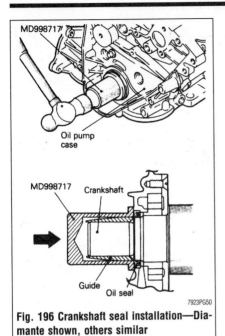

Fig. 196 Crankshaft seal installation—Diamante shown, others similar

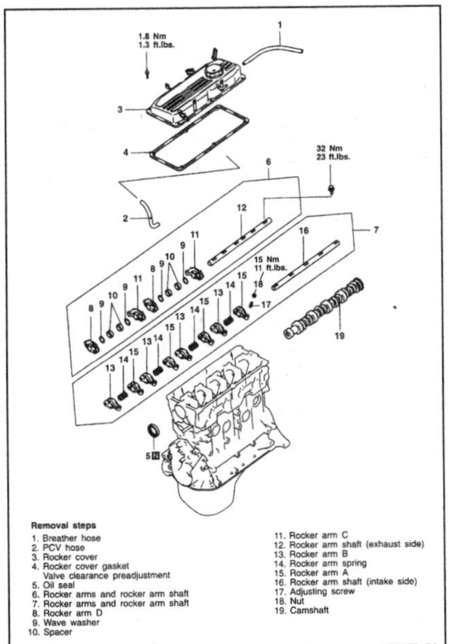

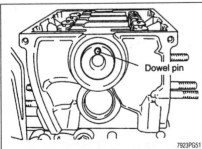

Removal steps
1. Breather hose
2. PCV hose
3. Rocker cover
4. Rocker cover gasket
   Valve clearance preadjustment
5. Oil seal
6. Rocker arms and rocker arm shaft
7. Rocker arms and rocker arm shaft
8. Rocker arm D
9. Wave washer
10. Spacer

11. Rocker arm C
12. Rocker arm shaft (exhaust side)
13. Rocker arm B
14. Rocker arm spring
15. Rocker arm A
16. Rocker arm shaft (intake side)
17. Adjusting screw
18. Nut
19. Camshaft

Fig. 197 Camshaft, rocker arm and shaft assemblies—1.5L engine

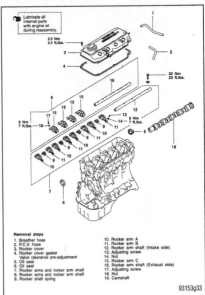

Fig. 198 Positioning of the camshaft dowel pin—Mirage 1.5L (4G15) engine

10. Remove the camshaft sprocket from the camshaft. Note the positioning of the dowel pin at the end of the camshaft.

11. Remove the camshaft oil seal from the front of the cylinder head.

12. Remove the camshaft from the head.

13. Carefully check all parts for damage and wear.

To install:

14. Lubricate the camshaft with heavy engine oil and slide it into the head. Be sure to position the dowel pin at the 12 o'clock position.

15. Check the camshaft end-play between the thrust case and camshaft. The camshaft end-play should be 0.002–0.008 in. (0.05–0.20mm). If the end-play is not within specification, replace the camshaft thrust bearing.

16. Install a new camshaft oil seal. Be sure to lubricate the lips of the seal with clean engine oil.

17. Install the camshaft sprocket and install the mounting bolt. Tighten the bolt to 51 ft. lbs. (70 Nm) while holding the camshaft from turning.

18. Install the timing belt assembly.

19. Install the timing belt covers.

20. Install the rocker shaft assemblies. Torque the bolts gradually and evenly to 23 ft. lbs. (32 Nm).

21. Check valve adjustment and install the valve cover with a new gasket. Tighten the valve cover bolt to 16 inch lbs. (1.8 Nm).

22. Align the distributor marks and install the distributor.

23. Connect the accelerator cable, breather hose and PCV hose.

24. Connect the negative battery cable and check the ignition timing.

1.8L Engine

▶ **See Figure 199**

1. Disconnect the negative battery cable.

2. Rotate the engine and position the No. 1 piston to TDC of its compression stroke.

3. Label and disconnect the spark plug cables.

4. Matchmark the positioning of the distributor housing and the positioning of the distributor rotor to the engine block and remove the distributor.

5. Detach the air flow sensor connector and remove the air cleaner case cover.

6. Disconnect the accelerator cable, breather hose and PCV hose connections.

7. Remove the rocker cover and discard the gasket.

8. Loosen both rocker arm shaft assemblies gradually and evenly and remove the rocket shafts from the vehicle. Do not disassembly rocker arms and rocker arm shaft assemblies.

9. Remove the timing belt covers.

✳✳ WARNING

DO NOT allow the camshaft or the crankshaft to rotate after the timing belt is removed!

10. Remove the timing belt assembly.

11. Holding the camshaft sprocket from turning, loosen and remove the bolt that secures the sprocket.

12. Remove the camshaft sprocket from the camshaft. Note the positioning of the dowel pin at the end of the camshaft.

13. Remove the camshaft oil seal from the front of the cylinder head.

14. Remove the camshaft from the head.

Removal steps
1. Breather hose
2. P.C.V. hose
3. Rocker cover
4. Rocker cover gasket
   Valve clearance pre-adjustment
5. Oil seal
6. Oil seal
7. Rocker arms and rocker arm shaft
8. Rocker arms and rocker arm shaft
9. Rocker shaft spring

10. Rocker arm A
11. Rocker arm B
12. Rocker arm shaft (intake side)
13. Adjusting screw
14. Nut
15. Rocker arm C
16. Rocker arm shaft (exhaust side)
17. Adjusting screw
18. Nut
19. Camshaft

Fig. 199 Camshaft, rocker arm and shaft assemblies—1.8L engine

15. Carefully check all parts for damage and wear.

To install:

16. Lubricate the camshaft journals and camshaft with clean engine oil and install the camshaft in the cylinder head. Be sure to position the dowel pin at the end of the camshaft as noted during the removal procedure.

17. Check the camshaft end-play between the thrust case and camshaft. The camshaft end-play should be 0.002–0.008 in. (0.05–0.20mm). If the end-play is not within specification, replace the camshaft thrust bearing.

18. Install a new camshaft oil seal. Be sure to lubricate the lips of the seal with clean engine oil.

19. Install camshaft sprocket and torque the retainer bolt to 65 ft. lbs. (90 Nm). Be sure to secure the sprocket while tightening the bolt.

20. Install the timing belt assembly.

21. Install the timing belt covers.

22. Install the rocker arm and shaft assemblies. Tighten the rocker arm shaft retainer bolts to 23 ft. lbs. (32 Nm).

23. Check the valve adjustment and install the valve cover with a new gasket. Tighten the valve cover bolts to 29 inch lbs. (3.3 Nm).

24. Align the distributor marks and install the distributor.

25. Connect the spark plug cables.

26. Connect the accelerator cable, breather hose and PCV hose.

27. Attach the air flow sensor connector and install the air cleaner case cover.

28. Connect the negative battery cable.

29. Run the engine at idle until normal operating temperature is reached.

30. Check idle speed and ignition timing and adjust as required.

2.0L SOHC Engine

▶ **See Figure 200**

1. Disconnect the negative battery cable.

2. Disconnect the breather and the PCV hoses.

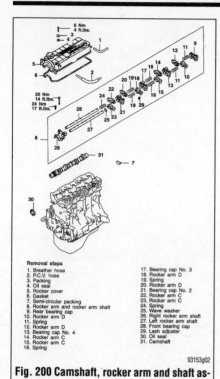

Removal steps

1. Breather hose
2. P.C.V. hose
3. Packing
4. Oil seal
5. Rocker cover
6. Gasket
7. Semi-circular packing
8. Rocker arm and rocker arm shaft
9. Rear bearing cap
10. Rocker arm D
11. Spring
12. Rocker arm D
13. Bearing cap No. 4
14. Rocker arm C
15. Rocker arm C
16. Spring

17. Bearing cap No. 3
18. Rocker arm D
19. Spring
20. Rocker arm D
21. Bearing cap No. 2
22. Rocker arm C
23. Rocker arm C
24. Spring
25. Wave washer
26. Right rocker arm shaft
27. Left rocker arm shaft
28. Front bearing cap
29. Lash adjuster
30. Oil seal
31. Camshaft

93153g02

Fig. 200 Camshaft, rocker arm and shaft assemblies—2.0L SOHC engine

3. Remove the accelerator cable bracket and position the cable aside.

4. Install lash adjuster retainer tools MD998443 or equivalent, to the rocker arm.

5. Remove the valve cover and semi-circular packing.

6. Matchmark the distributor housing to the cylinder head, and remove the distributor.

7. Remove the timing belt covers and the timing belt.

8. Remove the camshaft sprocket.

9. Remove the carrier bolts and remove the rocker arms, rocker shafts and bearing caps from the engine as an assembly.

10. Remove the camshaft from the cylinder head.

11. Inspect the bearing journals on the camshaft for excess wear or damage.

12. Measure the cam lobe height and compare to the desired readings.

13. Inspect the bearing surfaces in the cylinder head.

14. Replace any components that are damaged or show signs of excess wear.

To install:

15. Lubricate the camshaft journals and camshaft with clean engine oil and install the camshaft in the cylinder head.

16. Align the camshaft bearing caps with the arrow marks (depending on cylinder numbers) and install in numerical order.

17. Install the rocker shaft assembly to the cylinder head. Torque the bearing cap bolts from the center outward, in three steps, until a final torque of 15 ft. lbs. (20 Nm) is reached.

18. Apply a coating of engine oil to the oil seal. Using the proper size driver, press-fit the seal into the cylinder head.

19. Install the camshaft sprocket and torque retaining bolt to 65 ft. lbs. (90 Nm).

20. Install the timing belt.

21. Align the matchmarks and install the distributor.

22. Remove the lash adjuster retaining tools.

23. Install the valve cover and all related parts.

24. Connect the negative battery cable and run engine to check for leaks.

25. Check and adjust ignition timing, if necessary.

1.6L and 2.0L DOHC Engines

♦ See Figures 201 and 202

1. Disconnect the negative battery cable.

2. Remove the accelerator cable bracket and position the cable aside.

3. Remove the breather hose and disconnect the PCV hose.

4. Label and disconnect the spark plug cables.

5. Matchmark the distributor housing to the cylinder head, and remove the distributor.

6. Remove the rocker cover.

7. Install lash adjuster retainer tools MD998443 or equivalent, to the rocker arm.

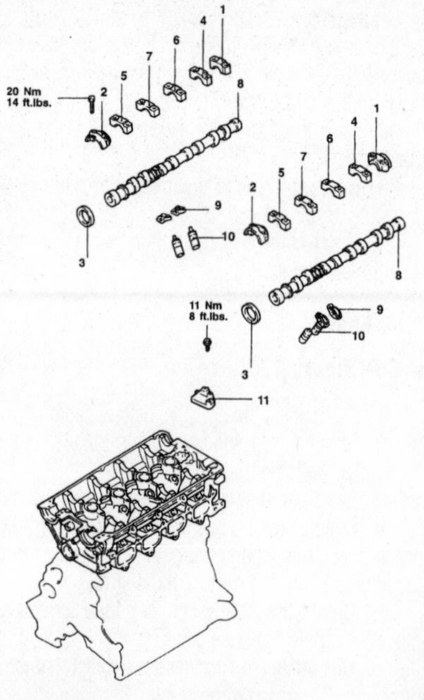

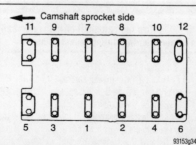

Removal steps

1. Bearing cap rear
2. Bearing cap front
3. Camshaft oil seal
4. Bearing cap No. 5
5. Bearing cap No. 2
6. Bearing cap No. 4

7. Bearing cap No. 3
8. Camshaft
9. Rocker arm
10. Lash adjuster
11. Oil delivery body

93153g03

Fig. 201 Camshaft and rocker arms—1.6L and 2.0L DOHC engines

Fig. 202 Camshaft bearing cap tightening sequence—1.6L and 2.0L DOHC engines

8. Remove the timing belt covers and the timing belt assembly.

9. Remove the camshaft sprocket retainer bolt while holding shaft stationary with an appropriate wrench. Remove the sprocket from the shaft.

10. Remove the camshaft oil seal.

11. Remove both rocker arm shaft assemblies from the head. Do not disassemble the rocker arms and rocker arm shaft assemblies.

12. Remove the camshaft from the cylinder head.

13. Inspect the bearing journals on the camshaft, cylinder head, and bearing caps.

To install:

14. Lubricate the camshaft journals and camshaft with clean engine oil and install the camshaft in the cylinder head.

15. Install the rocker arm and shaft assemblies. Tighten the rocker arm shaft retainer bolts to 21–25 ft. lbs. (29–35 Nm).

16. Apply a coating of engine oil to the oil seal. Using the proper size driver, press-fit the seal into the cylinder head.

17. Install camshaft sprocket and retainer bolt. Tighten the bolts to 65 ft. lbs. (90 Nm).

18. Install the timing belt and belt covers.

19. Align the matchmarks and install the distributor.

20. Remove the lash adjuster retaining tools.

21. Install the rocker cover using new gasket material on mating surfaces.

22. Connect the spark plug cables.

23. Install the breather hose and connect the PCV hose.

24. Connect the negative battery cable.

25. Run the engine at idle until normal operating temperature is reached. Check idle speed and ignition timing; adjust as required.

2.4L Engine

♦ See Figures 203 and 204

1. Relieve the fuel system pressure following proper procedure.

2. Disconnect the negative battery cable.

3. Disconnect the accelerator cable, PCV hoses, breather hoses, spark plug cables and the remove the valve cover.

➡**Always rotate the crankshaft in a clockwise direction. Make a mark on the back of the timing belt indicating the direction of rotation so it may be reassembled in the same direction if it is to be reused.**

4. Rotate the crankshaft clockwise and align the timing marks so that the No. 1 piston will be at TDC of the compression stroke. At this time the timing marks on the camshaft sprocket and the upper surface of the cylinder head should coincide, and the dowel pin of the camshaft sprocket should be at the upper side.

5. Remove the timing belt upper and lower covers.

6. Remove the camshaft timing belt.

7. Use a wrench between the No. 2 and No. 3 journals to hold the camshaft; remove the camshaft sprockets.

8. Loosen the bearing cap bolts in 2–3 steps. Label and remove all camshaft bearing caps.

➡**If the bearing caps are difficult to remove, use a plastic hammer to gently tap the rear part of the camshaft.**

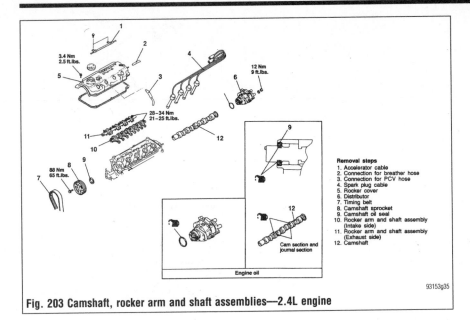

Fig. 203 Camshaft, rocker arm and shaft assemblies—2.4L engine

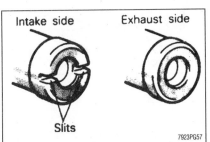

Fig. 204 Camshaft identification—2.4L engine

9. Remove the intake and exhaust camshafts.
10. Remove the rocker arms and lash adjusters.

➡️**It is essential that all parts be kept in the same order and orientation for reinstallation. In order to prevent confusion during installation, be sure to mark and separate all parts.**

To install:

11. Install the lash adjusters and rocker arms into the cylinder head. Lubricate lightly with clean oil prior to installation.
12. Lubricate the camshafts with heavy engine oil and position the camshafts on the cylinder head.
13. Check the camshaft journals and lobes for wear or damage. Also, check the cylinder head oil holes for clogging. Visually inspect the rocker arm roller and replace if dented, damaged or evidence of seizure is evident. Check the roller for smooth rotation. Replace if excess play or binding is present. Also, inspect the valve contact surface for possible damage or seizure. It is recommended that all rocker arms and lash adjusters be replaced together.

➡️**Do not confuse the intake camshaft with the exhaust camshaft. The intake camshaft has a split on the rear face for driving the crank angle sensor.**

14. Make sure the dowel pin on both camshaft sprocket ends are located on the top.
15. Install the bearing caps. Tighten the caps in sequence and in 2 or 3 steps. No. 2 and 5 caps are of the same shape. Check the markings on the caps to identify the cap number and intake/exhaust symbol.

Only **L** (intake) or **R** (exhaust) is stamped on No. 1 bearing cap. Also, make sure the rocker arm is correctly mounted on the lash adjuster and the valve stem end. Torque the retaining bolts to 15 ft. lbs. (20 Nm).

16. Apply a coating of engine oil to the oil seal. Using the proper size driver, press-fit the seal into the cylinder head.
17. Install the camshaft sprockets. While holding the camshaft at its hexagon, between number 2 and 3 journals tighten sprocket bolts to 58–72 ft. lbs. (80–100 Nm).
18. Install the timing belt, covers and related components.
19. Install the valve cover, using new gasket, and reconnect all related components.
20. Reconnect the negative battery cable.

3.0L DOHC Engine

◆ See Figures 205 and 206

1. Relieve the fuel system pressure.
2. Disconnect negative battery cable.
3. Remove the intake manifold plenum.
4. Remove the timing belt cover and the timing belt.

⁂ WARNING

DO NOT rotate the crankshaft or camshafts after the timing belt has been removed. If rotated, severe internal engine damage will result from the pistons hitting the valves.

5. Remove the center cover, breather, PCV hoses, and the spark plug cables.
6. Remove the rocker cover and the semi-circular packing.
7. Matchmark the position of the crankshaft position sensor at the rear of the camshaft, then remove the sensor.
8. If equipped with a camshaft sensor, remove the sensor from the front of the engine.
9. Being sure to hold the flats of the camshaft, loosen the camshaft sprocket bolts.
10. Noting the positioning and location of the sprockets, remove the sprockets from the camshafts.

➡️**Be sure to note the positioning of the knock pin at the end of the camshafts for reinstallation purposes.**

➡️**Be sure to keep the valve train components labeled and in proper order for reassembly.**

11. Loosen the bearing cap bolts in 2–3 steps.
12. Label and remove all camshaft bearing caps.

➡️**If the bearing caps are difficult to remove, use a plastic hammer to gently tap the components.**

13. Mark the components and remove the intake and the exhaust camshafts.
14. Remove the rocker arms and the lash adjusters. Be sure to note the location of the valve train components for reinstallation purposes.

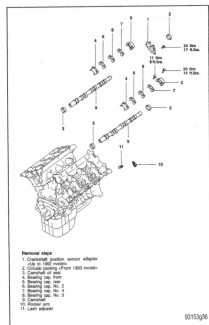

Fig. 205 Camshaft, rocker arm and shaft assemblies—3.0L DOHC engine

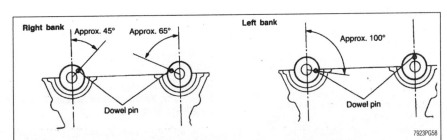

Fig. 206 Proper positioning of the camshaft knock pins—3.0L DOHC engine

15. Check the camshaft journals for wear or damage. Check the cam lobes for damage. Also, check the cylinder head oil holes for clogging.

To install:

➡ **Lubricate the valve train components with clean engine oil.**

16. Bleed and install the lash adjusters to the to the original bores in the cylinder head.
17. Install the rocker arms to the cylinder head.
18. Lubricate the camshafts with clean engine oil and position the camshafts on the cylinder head.

✶✶ WARNING

Be sure to properly position the knock pins of the camshaft to prevent valve to piston interference.

➡ **Do not confuse the intake camshaft with the exhaust camshaft. The intake camshaft on the Diamante has a B or J stamped on the hexagon depending on the application. The exhaust camshaft on the Diamante has a D or K stamped on the hexagon depending on application.**

➡ **Install the bearing caps according to the identification mark and cap number. Bearing caps No. 2, 3 and are marked as such. The caps also are marked I for intake or E for exhaust.**

19. Install the bearing caps. Tighten the caps in sequence, gradually in 2 or 3 steps. Caps 2, 3 and 4 have a front mark. Install with the mark aligned with the front mark on the cylinder head. Torque the retaining bolts for caps No. 2, 3 and 4 to 8 ft. lbs. (11 Nm) and torque the retaining bolts for the front and rear caps to 14 ft. lbs. (20 Nm).
20. Apply a coating of engine oil to the oil seals and install the oil seals to the front and rear of the camshafts.
21. Holding the flats of the camshaft, install and tighten the sprocket bolts to 65 ft. lbs. (90 Nm).
22. If removed, install the camshaft position sensor and tighten the mounting bolts to 78 inch lbs. (9 Nm).
23. Aligning the matchmark, install the crankshaft position sensor at the rear of the camshaft and tighten the mounting nut to 7 ft. lbs. (12 Nm).
24. Align the marks on the camshaft and crankshaft sprockets. Install the timing belt assembly.
25. Install the rocker cover and the semi-circular packing.
26. Install the intake manifold plenum.
27. Install the spark plug cables, center cover, breather and PCV hoses.
28. Connect the negative battery cable and check for leaks.

3.0L SOHC Engine

▶ **See Figures 207, 208, 209, and 210**

1. Disconnect the negative battery cable.
2. Rotate and position the engine to TDC of compression stroke.
3. If removing the right side (front) camshaft, matchmark the distributor rotor and distributor housing to the engine block and remove the distributor.
4. Remove the intake manifold plenum stay bracket.

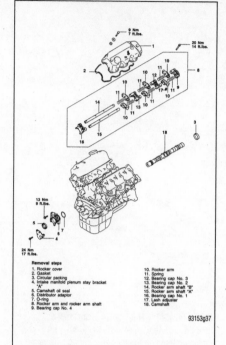

Fig. 207 Camshaft, rocker arm and shaft assemblies—3.0L SOHC engine

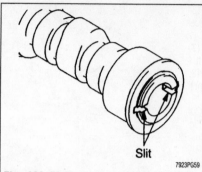

Fig. 208 Right bank camshaft identification—3.0L SOHC engine

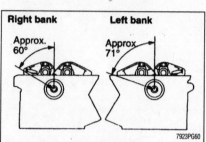

Fig. 209 Proper positioning of the camshafts—3.0L SOHC engine

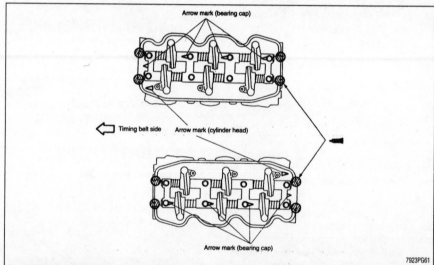

Fig. 210 Alignment of the rocker shafts and application of sealant—3.0L SOHC engine

5. Remove the distributor housing adapter and discard the O-ring.
6. Remove the valve covers and the timing belt.
7. Using camshaft sprocket holding tool MB9g67 and MD998719 or equivalent, hold the sprocket and loosen the bolt.
8. Remove the bolt and note the positioning of the of the knock pin at the end of the camshaft and remove the sprocket.
9. Install auto lash adjuster retainer tools MD998443 or equivalent, on the rocker arms.

➡ **Be sure to note the position of the rocker arms, rocker shafts and bearing caps for re-installation purposes.**

10. Remove the camshaft bearing caps but do not remove the bolts from the caps.

11. Remove the rocker arms, rocker shafts and bearing caps, as an assembly.
12. Remove the camshaft from the cylinder head.
13. Inspect the bearing journals on the camshaft, cylinder head, and bearing caps.

To install:

➡ **The right bank camshaft is identified by a 4mm slit at the rear end of the camshaft.**

14. Lubricate the camshaft journals and camshaft with clean engine oil and install the camshaft in the cylinder head. Be sure to properly position the knock pin of the camshaft as noted during removal.
15. Apply sealer at the ends of the bearing caps and install the rocker arms, rocker shafts and bearing caps as an assembly. Properly position the arrows on the bearing caps.

16. Torque the bearing cap bolts in the following sequence: No. 3, No. 2, No. 1 and No. 4 to 85 inch lbs. (10 Nm).

17. Repeat the sequence increasing the torque to 14 ft. lbs. (20 Nm).

18. Remove the auto lash adjuster retainer tools from the rocker arms.

19. Install the camshaft sprocket and bolt.

20. Using camshaft sprocket holding tool MB9g67 and MD998719 or equivalent, hold the sprocket and tighten the bolt to 65 ft. lbs. (90 Nm).

21. Install the timing belt and valve covers.

22. Using a new O-ring, install the distributor extension housing.

23. Install the intake manifold plenum stay bracket.

24. Install the distributor assembly. Be sure to align the rotor and distributor housing matchmarks.

25. Connect the negative battery cable and check for leaks.

3.5L Engine

▶ **See Figures 211 and 212**

1. Disconnect the negative battery cable.

2. Remove the timing belt. Refer to the timing belt procedure in this section.

3. Remove the rocker arm cover.

4. Install the lash adjuster clips on the rocker arms, then loosen the bearing cap bolts. Do not remove the bolts from the bearing caps.

5. Remove the rocker arms, shafts and bearing caps as an assembly.

6. Remove the camshafts.

To install:

7. Lubricate the camshafts with engine oil and position them on the cylinder heads.

8. Position the dowel pins as shown in the drawing.

9. Install the bearing caps/rocker arm assemblies. Tighten the bolts to 23 ft. lbs. (31 Nm).

10. Install the rocker arm cover using a new gasket.

11. Install the timing belt and remaining components. Refer to the timing belt procedure in this section.

12. Connect the negative battery cable.

INSPECTION

Camshaft Lobe Lift

Camshaft lobe lift is the amount (measured in inches or millimeters) that the camshaft is capable of LIFTING the valve train components in order to open the valves. The lobe lift is a measure of how much taller the "egg shaped" portion of the camshaft lobe is above the base or circular portion of the shaft lobe. Lift is directly proportional to how far the valves can open and a worn camshaft (with poor lobe lift) cannot fully open the valves. The lobe lift therefore can be directly responsible for proper or poor engine performance.

Lobe lift can be measured in 2 ways, depending on what tools are available and whether or not the camshaft has been removed from the engine. A dial gauge can be used to measure the lift with the camshaft installed, while a micrometer is normally only used once the shaft has been removed from the engine.

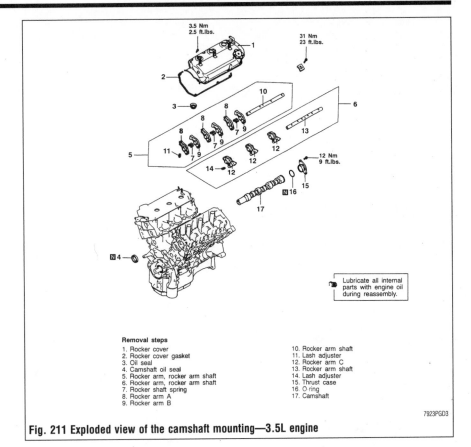

Removal steps
1. Rocker cover
2. Rocker cover gasket
3. Oil seal
4. Camshaft oil seal
5. Rocker arm, rocker arm shaft
6. Rocker arm, rocker arm shaft
7. Rocker shaft spring
8. Rocker arm A
9. Rocker arm B
10. Rocker arm shaft
11. Lash adjuster
12. Rocker arm C
13. Rocker arm shaft
14. Lash adjuster
15. Thrust case
16. O-ring
17. Camshaft

Lubricate all internal parts with engine oil during reassembly.

7923PGD3

Fig. 211 Exploded view of the camshaft mounting—3.5L engine

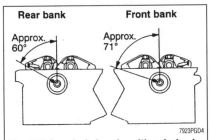

Fig. 212 Camshaft dowel position during installation—3.5L engine

7923PGD4

DIAL GAUGE METHOD

Lobe lift may be checked with the camshaft installed. In all cases, a dial gauge is positioned somewhere on the valve train (pushrod, lifter, or camshaft itself) and the camshaft is then turned to measure the lift.

Check the lift of each lobe in consecutive order and make a note of the reading.

1. Remove the valve cover for access to the camshaft.

2. Install a dial indicator so that the actuating point of the indicator is directly placed on the camshaft.

➡**A remote starter can be used to turn the engine over during the next steps. If a remote starter is not available, remove the spark plugs in order to relieve engine compression, and turn the engine over using a large wrench or socket on the crankshaft damper bolt. BE SURE to only turn the engine in the normal direction of rotation.**

3. Turn the crankshaft over until the tappet is on the base circle of the camshaft lobe.

4. Zero the dial indicator. Continue to rotate the crankshaft slowly until the pushrod (or camshaft lobe) is in the fully raised position.

5. Compare the total lift recorded on the dial indicator with the elevation specification shown in the Engine Specification chart.

To check the accuracy of the original indicator reading, continue to rotate the crankshaft until the indicator reads zero. If the lift on any lobe is below specified wear limits listed, the camshaft and the valve tappets must be replaced.

6. Install the valve cover(s).

MICROMETER

▶ **See Figure 213**

A micrometer may used to measure camshaft lobe lift, but this is usually only after it has been removed from the engine. Once the valve cover is removed

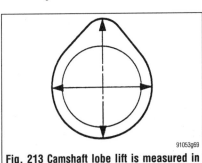

Fig. 213 Camshaft lobe lift is measured in two places

91053g69

from the, access may be possible (though a little awkward) to measure the camshaft lobes using a micrometer.

In any case, two measurements are necessary for each lobe. Measurement **Y** or the total LOBE HEIGHT and measurement **X** or the total LOBE WIDTH. To find the lobe lift, you simply subtract **X** from **Y** (subtract the width from the height).

Note each measurement, then make your calculation to determine the lift. Note the final results and repeat the process on the remaining camshaft lobes. Finally, you should compare your results to the specifications charts and decide if a new camshaft is in your future.

Balance Shaft

REMOVAL & INSTALLATION

2.0L and 2.4L Engines

▶ See Figure 214

➡A special oil seal guide tool, MD998285, and a plug cap socket tool, MD998162, or exact equivalents are needed to complete this operation.

1. Disconnect the negative battery cable.
2. Raise and safely support the vehicle.
3. Drain the engine oil.

✳✳ CAUTION

The EPA warns that prolonged contact with used engine oil may cause a number of skin disorders, including cancer! You should make every effort to minimize your exposure to used engine oil. Protective gloves should be worn when changing the oil. Wash your hands and any other exposed skin areas as soon as possible after exposure to used engine oil. Soap and water, or waterless hand cleaner should be used.

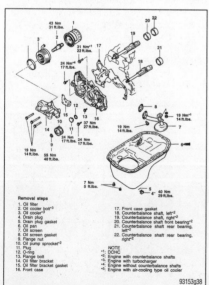

Removal steps
1. Oil filter
2. Oil cooler bolt*³
3. Oil cooler*³
4. Drain plug
5. Drain plug gasket
6. Oil pan
7. Oil screen
8. Oil screen gasket
9. Flange nut
10. Oil pump sprocket*²
11. Plug
12. O-ring
13. Flange bolt
14. Oil filter bracket
15. Oil filter bracket gasket
16. Front case

17. Front case gasket
18. Counterbalance shaft, left*²
19. Counterbalance shaft, right*²
20. Counterbalance shaft front bearing*²
21. Counterbalance shaft rear bearing, left*²
22. Counterbalance shaft rear bearing, right*²

NOTE
*¹: DOHC
*²: Engine with counterbalance shafts
*³: Engine with turbocharger
*⁴: Engine without counterbalance shafts
*⁵: Engine with air-cooling type oil cooler

93153g38

Fig. 214 Exploded view of the balance shaft assemblies—2.0L and 2.4L engines

4. Remove the oil filter, oil pressure switch, oil gauge sending unit, oil filter mounting bracket and gasket.
5. Remove engine oil pan, oil screen and gasket.
6. Remove the relief plug, gasket, relief spring and relief plunger.
7. Lower the vehicle.
8. Using the proper equipment, support the weight of the engine.
9. Remove the front engine mount bracket and accessory drive belt.
10. Remove the timing belts and sprockets.
11. Using special tool MD998162, remove the plug cap in the engine front cover.
12. Remove the plug on the side of the engine block. Insert a Phillips screwdriver with a shank diameter of 0.32 in. (8mm) into the plug hole. This will hold the silent shaft.
13. Remove the driven gear bolt that secures the oil pump driven gear to the silent shaft.
14. Remove and tag the front cover mounting bolts. Note the lengths of the mounting bolts as they are removed for proper installation.
15. Remove the front case cover and oil pump assembly. If necessary, the silent shaft can come out with the cover assembly.
16. Remove the silent shaft oil seals, the crankshaft oil seal and front case gasket.
17. Remove the silent shafts and inspect as follows:
   a. Check the oil holes in the shaft for clogging.
   b. Check journals of the shaft for seizure, damage and contact with bearing. If there is anything wrong with the journal, replace the silent shaft bearing, silent shaft or front case.
   c. Check the silent shaft oil clearance. If the clearance is beyond the specifications, replace the silent shaft bearing, silent shaft or front case. The specifications for oil clearances are as follows:

Right shaft
- Front—0.0012–0.0024 in. (0.03–0.06mm)
- Rear—0.0008–0.0021 in. (0.02–0.05mm)

Left shaft
- Front—0.0020–0.0036 in. (0.05–0.09mm)
- Rear—0.0017–0.0033 in. (0.04–0.08mm)

To install:
18. Lubricate the bearing surface of the shaft and the bearing journals with clean engine oil. Carefully install the silent shafts to the block.
19. Clean the gasket material from the mating surface of the cylinder block and the engine front cover. Install new gasket in place.
20. Install the oil pump drive gear and driven gear to the front case, lining up the timing marks.
21. Lubricate the gears with clean engine oil. Install the oil pump cover, with new gasket in place and tighten the mounting bolts to 13 ft. lbs. (18 Nm).
22. Using proper size driver, install the crankshaft oil seal into the front engine case.
23. Using the proper size socket wrench, press in the silent shaft oil seal into the front case.
24. Place pilot tool MD998285 or equivalent, onto the nose of the crankshaft. Apply clean engine oil to the outer circumference of the pilot tool.
25. Install the front case onto the engine block and temporarily tighten the flange bolts (other than those for tightening the filter bracket).

26. Mount the oil filter bracket with new gasket in place. Install the 4 bolts with washers and tighten to 16 ft. lbs. (22 Nm).
27. Insert the Phillips screwdriver into the hole on the side of the engine block.
28. Secure the oil pump driven gear onto the left silent shaft by tightening the driven gear flange bolt to 29 ft. lbs. (40 Nm).
29. Install a new O-ring onto the groove in the front case. Using special socket tool, install and tighten the plug cap to 20 ft. lbs. (27 Nm).
30. Install the oil pump relief plunger and spring into the bore in the oil filter bracket and tighten to 36 ft. lbs. (50 Nm). Make sure a new gasket is in place.
31. Clean both mating surfaces of the oil pan and the cylinder block.
32. Apply sealant in the groove in the oil pan flange, keeping towards the inside of the bolt holes. The width of the sealant bead applied is to be about 0.16 in. (4mm) wide.

➡After applying sealant to the oil pan, do not exceed 15 minutes before installing the oil pan.

33. Install the oil pan to the engine and secure with the retainers. Tighten bolts to 6 ft. lbs. (8 Nm).
34. Install the oil pressure gauge unit and the oil pressure switch. Attach the electrical harness connector.
35. Install new oil filter and fill engine with clean engine oil.
36. Install the timing belts and all related items.

➡The timing of the oil pump sprocket and connected silent shaft can be incorrect, even with the timing mark aligned. Make certain that all special timing belt installation procedures are followed to ensure proper orientation of the silent shafts.

37. Install any remaining components removed during disassembly.
38. Connect the negative battery cable and start the engine.
39. Check for proper timing and inspect for leaks.

Rear Main Seal

REMOVAL & INSTALLATION

▶ See Figure 215

1. Disconnect the negative battery cable.
2. Remove the transaxle from the vehicle, as outlined in Section 7.
3. Remove the flywheel/driveplate assembly.
4. Remove the rear engine plate and the bell-housing cover.
5. If the crankshaft rear oil seal case is leaking, remove it. Otherwise, just remove the oil seal. Some engines have a separator that should also be removed.

To install:
6. Lubricate the inner diameter of the new seal with clean engine oil.
7. Install the oil seal in the crankshaft rear oil seal case using tool MD998376 or equivalent. Press the seal all the way in without tilting it. Force the oil separator into the oil seal case so the oil hole in the separator is downward.

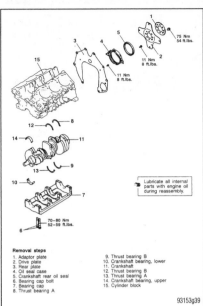

Removal steps
1. Adaptor plate
2. Drive plate
3. Rear plate
4. Oil seal case
5. Crankshaft rear oil seal
6. Bearing cap bolt
7. Bearing cap
8. Thrust bearing A
9. Thrust bearing B
10. Crankshaft bearing, lower
11. Crankshaft
12. Thrust bearing B
13. Thrust bearing A
14. Crankshaft bearing, upper
15. Cylinder block

93153g39

Fig. 215 Typical drive plate and rear main seal mounting

8. Run a bead of sealer along any seams between the seal case and block. Install the seal case with a new gasket.

9. Install the flywheel/driveplate and transaxle.

10. Connect the negative battery cable and check for leaks.

11. Adjust oil level as necessary.

Flywheel/Driveplate

REMOVAL & INSTALLATION

♦ **See Figure 215**

1. Disconnect the negative battery cable.

2. Remove the transaxle, as outlined in Section 7.

3. If equipped with a manual transaxle, remove the clutch disc and pressure plate. Refer to Section 7.

4. Mark the position of the flywheel/driveplate on the crankshaft and remove the retaining bolts.

5. On automatic transaxle equipped models, remove the driveplate adapter.

6. Remove the flywheel/driveplate from the engine.

To install:

7. Coat the threads of the driveplate/flywheel retaining bolts with thread locking compound.

8. Position the driveplate/flywheel on the crankshaft flange.

9. On automatic transaxle equipped models, install the driveplate adapter.

10. Install and tighten the bolts, in a alternating star pattern, to the following specifications:
   - 1.5L engine: 98 ft. lbs. (135 Nm)
   - 1.6L, 2.0L and 2.4L engines: 94–101 ft. lbs. (130–140 Nm)
   - 1.8L engine: 72 ft. lbs. (100 Nm)
   - 3.0L and 3.5L engines: 53–56 ft. lbs. (72–76 Nm)

11. If equipped with a manual transaxle, install the clutch and pressure plate.

12. Install the transaxle. Refer to Section 7.

13. Connect the negative battery cable.

EXHAUST SYSTEM

Inspection

♦ **See Figures 216 thru 222**

➡**Safety glasses should be worn at all times when working on or near the exhaust system. Older exhaust systems will almost always be covered with loose rust particles which will shower you when disturbed. These particles are more than a nuisance and could injure your eye.**

❊❊ CAUTION

DO NOT perform exhaust repairs or inspection with the engine or exhaust hot. Allow the system to cool completely before attempting any work. Exhaust systems are noted for sharp edges, flaking metal and rusted bolts. Gloves and eye protection are required. A

healthy supply of penetrating oil and rags is highly recommended.

Your vehicle must be raised and supported safely to inspect the exhaust system properly. Placing 4 safety stands under the vehicle for support should provide enough room for you to slide under the vehicle and inspect the system completely. Start the inspection at the exhaust manifold or turbocharger pipe where the header pipe is attached and work your way

to the back of the vehicle. On dual exhaust systems, remember to inspect both sides of the vehicle. Check the complete exhaust system for open seams, holes loose connections, or other deterioration which could

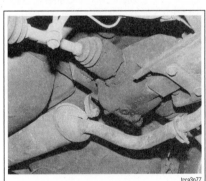

tcca3p77

Fig. 218 Make sure the exhaust components are not contacting the body or suspension

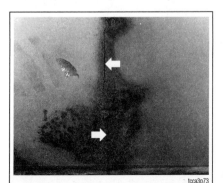

tcca3p73

Fig. 216 Cracks in the muffler are a guaranteed leak

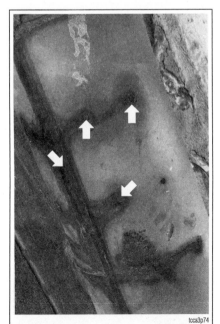

tcca3p74

Fig. 217 Check the muffler for rotted spot welds and seams

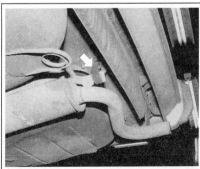

tcca3p78

Fig. 219 Check for overstretched or torn exhaust hangers

Fig. 220 Example of a badly deteriorated exhaust pipe

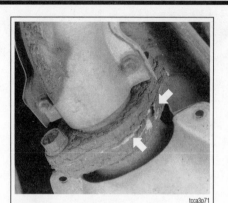

Fig. 221 Inspect flanges for gaskets that have deteriorated and need replacement

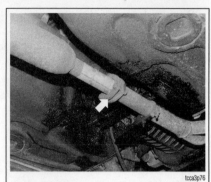

Fig. 222 Some systems, like this one, use large O-rings (doughnuts) in between the flanges

permit exhaust fumes to seep into the passenger compartment. Inspect all mounting brackets and hangers for deterioration, some models may have rubber O-rings that can be overstretched and non-supportive. These components will need to be replaced if found. It has always been a practice to use a pointed tool to poke up into the exhaust system where the deterioration spots are to see whether or not they crumble. Some models may have heat shield covering certain parts of the exhaust system , it will be necessary to remove these shields to have the exhaust visible for inspection also.

REPLACEMENT

♦ See Figure 223

There are basically two types of exhaust systems. One is the flange type where the component ends are attached with bolts and a gasket in-between. The other exhaust system is the slip joint type. These components slip into one another using clamps to hold them together.

❋❋ CAUTION

Allow the exhaust system to cool sufficiently before spraying a solvent exhaust fasteners. Some solvents are highly flammable and could ignite when sprayed on hot exhaust components.

Before removing any component of the exhaust system, ALWAYS squirt a liquid rust dissolving agent onto the fasteners for ease of removal. A lot of knuckle skin will be saved by following this rule. It may even be wise to spray the fasteners and allow them to sit overnight.

Flange Type

♦ See Figure 224

❋❋ CAUTION

Do NOT perform exhaust repairs or inspection with the engine or exhaust hot. Allow the system to cool completely before attempting any work. Exhaust systems are noted for sharp edges, flaking metal and rusted bolts. Gloves and eye protection are required. A healthy supply of penetrating oil and rags is highly recommended. Never spray liquid rust dissolving agent onto a hot exhaust component.

Before removing any component on a flange type system, ALWAYS squirt a liquid rust dissolving agent onto the fasteners for ease of removal. Start by unbolting the exhaust piece at both ends (if required). When unbolting the headpipe from the manifold, make sure that the bolts are free before trying to remove them. if you snap a stud in the exhaust manifold, the stud will have to be removed with a bolt ex-

tractor, which often means removal of the manifold itself. Next, disconnect the component from the mounting; slight twisting and turning may be required to remove the component completely from the vehicle. You may need to tap on the component with a rubber mallet to loosen it. If all else fails, use a hacksaw to separate the parts. An oxy-acetylene cutting torch may be faster but the sparks are DANGEROUS near the fuel tank, and at the very least, accidents could happen, resulting in damage to the under-car parts, not to mention yourself.

Slip Joint Type

♦ See Figure 225

Before removing any component on the slip joint type exhaust system, ALWAYS squirt a liquid rust dissolving agent onto the fasteners for ease of removal. Start by unbolting the exhaust piece at both ends (if required). When unbolting the headpipe from the manifold, make sure that the bolts are free before trying to remove them. if you snap a stud in the exhaust manifold, the stud will have to be removed with a bolt extractor, which often means removal of the manifold itself. Next, remove the mounting U-bolts from around the exhaust pipe you are extracting from the vehicle. Don't be surprised if the U-bolts break while removing the nuts. Loosen the exhaust pipe from any mounting brackets retaining it to the floor pan and separate the components.

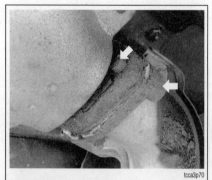

Fig. 223 Nuts and bolts will be extremely difficult to remove when deteriorated with rust

Fig. 224 Example of a flange type exhaust system joint

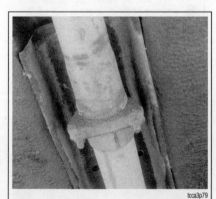

Fig. 225 Example of a common slip joint type system

ENGINE RECONDITIONING

Determining Engine Condition

Anything that generates heat and/or friction will eventually burn or wear out (for example, a light bulb generates heat, therefore its life span is limited). With this in mind, a running engine generates tremendous amounts of both; friction is encountered by the moving and rotating parts inside the engine and heat is created by friction and combustion of the fuel. However, the engine has systems designed to help reduce the effects of heat and friction and provide added longevity. The oiling system reduces the amount of friction encountered by the moving parts inside the engine, while the cooling system reduces heat created by friction and combustion. If either system is not maintained, a break-down will be inevitable. Therefore, you can see how regular maintenance can affect the service life of your vehicle. If you do not drain, flush and refill your cooling system at the proper intervals, deposits will begin to accumulate in the radiator, thereby reducing the amount of heat it can extract from the coolant. The same applies to your oil and filter; if it is not changed often enough it becomes laden with contaminates and is unable to properly lubricate the engine. This increases friction and wear.

There are a number of methods for evaluating the condition of your engine. A compression test can reveal the condition of your pistons, piston rings, cylinder bores, head gasket(s), valves and valve seats. An oil pressure test can warn you of possible engine bearing, or oil pump failures. Excessive oil consumption, evidence of oil in the engine air intake area and/or bluish smoke from the tailpipe may indicate worn piston rings, worn valve guides and/or valve seals. As a general rule, an engine that uses no more than one quart of oil every 1000 miles is in good condition. Engines that use one quart of oil or more in less than 1000 miles should first be checked for oil leaks. If any oil leaks are present, have them fixed before determining how much oil is consumed by the engine, especially if blue smoke is not visible at the tailpipe.

COMPRESSION TEST

♦ **See Figure 226**

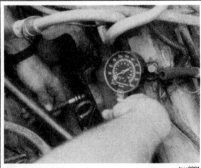

Fig. 226 A screw-in type compression gauge is more accurate and easier to use without an assistant

A noticeable lack of engine power, excessive oil consumption and/or poor fuel mileage measured over an extended period are all indicators of internal engine wear. Worn piston rings, scored or worn cylinder bores, blown head gaskets, sticking or burnt valves, and worn valve seats are all possible culprits. A check of each cylinder's compression will help locate the problem.

➡**A screw-in type compression gauge is more accurate than the type you simply hold against the spark plug hole. Although it takes slightly longer to use, it's worth the effort to obtain a more accurate reading.**

1. Make sure that the proper amount and viscosity of engine oil is in the crankcase, then ensure the battery is fully charged.
2. Warm-up the engine to normal operating temperature, then shut the engine **OFF**.
3. Disable the ignition system.
4. Label and disconnect all of the spark plug wires from the plugs.
5. Thoroughly clean the cylinder head area around the spark plug ports, then remove the spark plugs.
6. Set the throttle plate to the fully open (wide-open throttle) position. You can block the accelerator linkage open for this, or you can have an assistant fully depress the accelerator pedal.
7. Install a screw-in type compression gauge into the No. 1 spark plug hole until the fitting is snug.

☼ WARNING

Be careful not to crossthread the spark plug hole.

8. According to the tool manufacturer's instructions, connect a remote starting switch to the starting circuit.
9. With the ignition switch in the **OFF** position, use the remote starting switch to crank the engine through at least five compression strokes (approximately 5 seconds of cranking) and record the highest reading on the gauge.
10. Repeat the test on each cylinder, cranking the engine approximately the same number of compression strokes and/or time as the first.
11. Compare the highest readings from each cylinder to that of the others. The indicated compression pressures are considered within specifications if the lowest reading cylinder is within 75 percent of the pressure recorded for the highest reading cylinder. For example, if your highest reading cylinder pressure was 150 psi (1034 kPa), then 75 percent of that would be 113 psi (779 kPa). So the lowest reading cylinder should be no less than 113 psi (779 kPa).
12. If a cylinder exhibits an unusually low compression reading, pour a tablespoon of clean engine oil into the cylinder through the spark plug hole and repeat the compression test. If the compression rises after adding oil, it means that the cylinder's piston rings and/or cylinder bore are damaged or worn. If the pressure remains low, the valves may not be seating properly (a valve job is needed), or the head gasket may be blown near that cylinder. If compression

in any two adjacent cylinders is low, and if the addition of oil doesn't help raise compression, there is leakage past the head gasket. Oil and coolant in the combustion chamber, combined with blue or constant white smoke from the tailpipe, are symptoms of this problem. However, don't be alarmed by the normal white smoke emitted from the tailpipe during engine warm-up or from cold weather driving. There may be evidence of water droplets on the engine dipstick and/or oil droplets in the cooling system if a head gasket is blown.

OIL PRESSURE TEST

Check for proper oil pressure at the sending unit passage with an externally mounted mechanical oil pressure gauge (as opposed to relying on a factory installed dash-mounted gauge). A tachometer may also be needed, as some specifications may require running the engine at a specific rpm.

1. With the engine cold, locate and remove the oil pressure sending unit.
2. Following the manufacturer's instructions, connect a mechanical oil pressure gauge and, if necessary, a tachometer to the engine.
3. Start the engine and allow it to idle.
4. Check the oil pressure reading when cold and record the number. You may need to run the engine at a specified rpm, so check the specifications.
5. Run the engine until normal operating temperature is reached (upper radiator hose will feel warm).
6. Check the oil pressure reading again with the engine hot and record the number. Turn the engine **OFF**.
7. Compare your hot oil pressure reading to that given in the chart. If the reading is low, check the cold pressure reading against the chart. If the cold pressure is well above the specification, and the hot reading was lower than the specification, you may have the wrong viscosity oil in the engine. Change the oil, making sure to use the proper grade and quantity, then repeat the test.

Low oil pressure readings could be attributed to internal component wear, pump related problems, a low oil level, or oil viscosity that is too low. High oil pressure readings could be caused by an overfilled crankcase, too high of an oil viscosity or a faulty pressure relief valve.

Buy or Rebuild?

Now that you have determined that your engine is worn out, you must make some decisions. The question of whether or not an engine is worth rebuilding is largely a subjective matter and one of personal worth. Is the engine a popular one, or is it an obsolete model? Are parts available? Will it get acceptable gas mileage once it is rebuilt? Is the car it's being put into worth keeping? Would it be less expensive to buy a new engine, have your engine rebuilt by a pro, rebuild it yourself or buy a used engine from a salvage yard? Or would it be simpler and less expensive to buy another car? If you have considered all these matters and more, and have still decided to rebuild the engine, then it is time to decide how you will rebuild it.

➡The editors at Chilton feel that most engine machining should be performed by a professional machine shop. Don't think of it as wasting money, rather, as an assurance that the job has been done right the first time. There are many expensive and specialized tools required to perform such tasks as boring and honing an engine block or having a valve job done on a cylinder head. Even inspecting the parts requires expensive micrometers and gauges to properly measure wear and clearances. Also, a machine shop can deliver to you clean, and ready to assemble parts, saving you time and aggravation. Your maximum savings will come from performing the removal, disassembly, assembly and installation of the engine and purchasing or renting only the tools required to perform the above tasks. Depending on the particular circumstances, you may save 40 to 60 percent of the cost doing these yourself.

A complete rebuild or overhaul of an engine involves replacing all of the moving parts (pistons, rods, crankshaft, camshaft, etc.) with new ones and machining the non-moving wearing surfaces of the block and heads. Unfortunately, this may not be cost effective. For instance, your crankshaft may have been damaged or worn, but it can be machined undersize for a minimal fee.

So, as you can see, you can replace everything inside the engine, but, it is wiser to replace only those parts which are really needed, and, if possible, repair the more expensive ones. Later in this section, we will break the engine down into its two main components: the cylinder head and the engine block. We will discuss each component, and the recommended parts to replace during a rebuild on each.

Engine Overhaul Tips

Most engine overhaul procedures are fairly standard. In addition to specific parts replacement procedures and specifications for your individual engine, this section is also a guide to acceptable rebuilding procedures. Examples of standard rebuilding practice are given and should be used along with specific details concerning your particular engine.

Competent and accurate machine shop services will ensure maximum performance, reliability and engine life. In most instances it is more profitable for the do-it-yourself mechanic to remove, clean and in-spect the component, buy the necessary parts and deliver these to a shop for actual machine work.

Much of the assembly work (crankshaft, bearings, piston rods, and other components) is well within the scope of the do-it-yourself mechanic's tools and abilities. You will have to decide for yourself the depth of involvement you desire in an engine repair or rebuild.

TOOLS

The tools required for an engine overhaul or parts replacement will depend on the depth of your involvement. With a few exceptions, they will be the tools found in a mechanic's tool kit (see Section 1 of this manual). More in-depth work will require some or all of the following:
- A dial indicator (reading in thousandths) mounted on a universal base
- Micrometers and telescope gauges
- Jaw and screw-type pullers
- Scraper
- Valve spring compressor
- Ring groove cleaner
- Piston ring expander and compressor
- Ridge reamer
- Cylinder hone or glaze breaker
- Plastigage®
- Engine stand

The use of most of these tools is illustrated in this section. Many can be rented for a one-time use from a local parts jobber or tool supply house specializing in automotive work.

Occasionally, the use of special tools is called for. See the information on Special Tools and the Safety Notice in the front of this book before substituting another tool.

OVERHAUL TIPS

Aluminum has become extremely popular for use in engines, due to its low weight. Observe the following precautions when handling aluminum parts:
- Never hot tank aluminum parts (the caustic hot tank solution will eat the aluminum.
- Remove all aluminum parts (identification tag, etc.) from engine parts prior to the tanking.
- Always coat threads lightly with engine oil or anti-seize compounds before installation, to prevent seizure.
- Never overtighten bolts or spark plugs especially in aluminum threads.

When assembling the engine, any parts that will be exposed to frictional contact must be prelubed to provide lubrication at initial start-up. Any product specifically formulated for this purpose can be used, but engine oil is not recommended as a prelube in most cases.

When semi-permanent (locked, but removable) installation of bolts or nuts is desired, threads should be cleaned and coated with Loctite® or another similar, commercial non-hardening sealant.

CLEANING

▶ **See Figures 227, 228, 229, 230, and 231**

Before the engine and its components are inspected, they must be thoroughly cleaned. You will need to remove any engine varnish, oil sludge and/or carbon deposits from all of the components to insure an accurate inspection. A crack in the engine block or cylinder head can easily become overlooked if hidden by a layer of sludge or carbon.

Fig. 227 Thoroughly clean the gasket surfaces of the cylinder head as well as . . .

Fig. 228 . . . the engine block before reassembling the engine

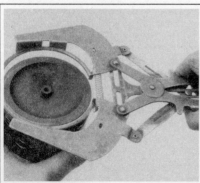
Fig. 229 Use a ring expander tool to remove the piston rings

Fig. 230 Clean the piston ring grooves using a ring groove cleaner tool, or . . .

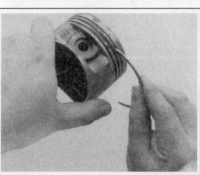
Fig. 231 . . . use a piece of an old ring to clean the grooves. Be careful, the ring can be quite sharp

Most of the cleaning process can be carried out with common hand tools and readily available solvents or solutions. Carbon deposits can be chipped away using a hammer and a hard wooden chisel. Old gasket material and varnish or sludge can usually be removed using a scraper and/or cleaning solvent. Extremely stubborn deposits may require the use of a power drill with a wire brush. If using a wire brush, use extreme care around any critical machined surfaces (such as the gasket surfaces, bearing saddles, cylinder bores, etc.). USE OF A WIRE BRUSH IS NOT RECOMMENDED ON ANY ALUMINUM COMPONENTS. Always follow any safety recommendations given by the manufacturer of the tool and/or solvent. You should always wear eye protection during any cleaning process involving scraping, chipping or spraying of solvents.

An alternative to the mess and hassle of cleaning the parts yourself is to drop them off at a local garage or machine shop. They will, more than likely, have the necessary equipment to properly clean all of the parts for a nominal fee.

❊❊❊ CAUTION

Always wear eye protection during any cleaning process involving scraping, chipping or spraying of solvents.

Remove any oil galley plugs, freeze plugs and/or pressed-in bearings and carefully wash and degrease all of the engine components including the fasteners and bolts. Small parts such as the valves, springs, etc., should be placed in a metal basket and allowed to soak. Use pipe cleaner type brushes, and clean all passageways in the components. Use a ring expander and remove the rings from the pistons. Clean the piston ring grooves with a special tool or a piece of broken ring. Scrape the carbon off of the top of the piston. You should never use a wire brush on the pistons. After preparing all of the piston assemblies in this manner, wash and degrease them again.

❊❊❊ WARNING

Use extreme care when cleaning around the cylinder head valve seats. A mistake or slip may cost you a new seat.

When cleaning the cylinder head, remove carbon from the combustion chamber with the valves installed. This will avoid damaging the valve seats.

REPAIRING DAMAGED THREADS

▶ **See Figures 232, 233, 234, 235 and 236**

Several methods of repairing damaged threads are available. Heli-Coil® (shown here), Keenserts® and Microdot® are among the most widely used. All involve basically the same principle—drilling out stripped threads, tapping the hole and installing a prewound insert—making welding, plugging and oversize fasteners unnecessary.

Two types of thread repair inserts are usually supplied: a standard type for most inch coarse, inch fine, metric course and metric fine thread sizes and a spark lug type to fit most spark plug port sizes. Consult the individual tool manufacturer's catalog to determine exact applications. Typical thread repair kits will contain a selection of prewound threaded inserts, a tap (corresponding to the outside diameter threads of the insert) and an installation tool. Spark plug inserts usually differ because they require a tap equipped with pilot threads and a combined reamer/tap section. Most manufacturers also supply blister-packed thread repair inserts separately in addition to a master kit containing a variety of taps and inserts plus installation tools.

Before attempting to repair a threaded hole, remove any snapped, broken or damaged bolts or studs. Penetrating oil can be used to free frozen threads. The offending item can usually be removed with locking pliers or using a screw/stud extractor. After the hole is clear, the thread can be repaired, as shown in the series of accompanying illustrations and in the kit manufacturer's instructions.

Engine Preparation

To properly rebuild an engine, you must first remove it from the vehicle, then disassemble and diagnose it. Ideally you should place your engine on an engine stand. This affords you the best access to the engine components. Follow the manufacturer's directions for using the stand with your particular engine. Remove the flywheel or flexplate before installing the engine to the stand.

Now that you have the engine on a stand, and assuming that you have drained the oil and coolant from the engine, it's time to strip it of all but the necessary components. Before you start disassembling the engine, you may want to take a moment to draw some pictures, or fabricate some labels or containers to mark the locations of various components and the bolts and/or studs which fasten them. Modern day engines use a lot of little brackets and clips which hold wiring harnesses and such, and these holders are often mounted on studs and/or bolts that can be easily mixed up. The manufacturer spent a lot of time and money designing your vehicle, and they wouldn't have wasted any of it by haphazardly placing brackets, clips or fasteners on the vehicle. If it's present when you disassemble it, put it back when you assemble, you will regret not remembering that little bracket which holds a wire harness out of the path of a rotating part.

You should begin by unbolting any accessories still attached to the engine, such as the water pump, power steering pump, alternator, etc. Then, unfasten any manifolds (intake or exhaust) which were not removed during the engine removal procedure. Finally,

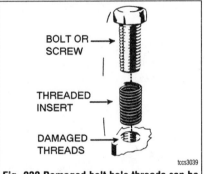

Fig. 232 Damaged bolt hole threads can be replaced with thread repair inserts

Fig. 233 Standard thread repair insert (left), and spark plug thread insert

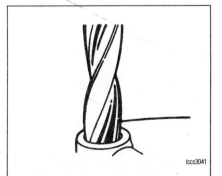

Fig. 234 Drill out the damaged threads with the specified size bit. Be sure to drill completely through the hole or to the bottom of a blind hole

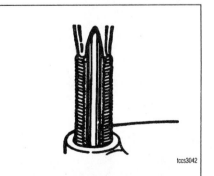

Fig. 235 Using the kit, tap the hole in order to receive the thread insert. Keep the tap well oiled and back it out frequently to avoid clogging the threads

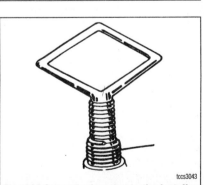

Fig. 236 Screw the insert onto the installer tool until the tang engages the slot. Thread the insert into the hole until it is $1/4$–$1/2$ turn below the top surface, then remove the tool and break off the tang using a punch

remove any covers remaining on the engine such as the rocker arm, front or timing cover and oil pan. Some front covers may require the vibration damper and/or crank pulley to be removed beforehand. The idea is to reduce the engine to the bare necessities (cylinder head(s), valve train, engine block, crankshaft, pistons and connecting rods), plus any other 'in block' components such as oil pumps, balance shafts and auxiliary shafts.

Finally, remove the cylinder head(s) from the engine block and carefully place on a bench. Disassembly instructions for each component follow later in this section.

Cylinder Head

There are two basic types of cylinder heads used on today's automobiles: the Overhead Valve (OHV) and the Overhead Camshaft (OHC). The latter can also be broken down into two subgroups: the Single Overhead Camshaft (SOHC) and the Dual Overhead Camshaft (DOHC). Generally, if there is only a single camshaft on a head, it is just referred to as an OHC head. Also, an engine with an OHV cylinder head is also known as a pushrod engine.

Most cylinder heads these days are made of an aluminum alloy due to its light weight, durability and heat transfer qualities. However, cast iron was the material of choice in the past, and is still used on many vehicles today. Whether made from aluminum or iron, all cylinder heads have valves and seats. Some use two valves per cylinder, while the more hi-tech engines will utilize a multi-valve configuration using 3, 4 and even 5 valves per cylinder. When the valve contacts the seat, it does so on precision machined surfaces, which seals the combustion chamber. All cylinder heads have a valve guide for each valve. The guide centers the valve to the seat and allows it to move up and down within it. The clearance between the valve and guide can be critical. Too much clearance and the engine may consume oil, lose vacuum and/or damage the seat. Too little, and the valve can stick in the guide causing the engine to run poorly if at all, and possibly causing severe damage. The last component all cylinder heads have are valve springs. The spring holds the valve against its seat. It also returns the valve to this position when the valve has been opened by the valve train or camshaft. The spring is fastened to the valve by a retainer and valve locks (sometimes called keepers). Aluminum heads will also have a valve spring shim to keep the spring from wearing away the aluminum.

An ideal method of rebuilding the cylinder head would involve replacing all of the valves, guides, seats, springs, etc. with new ones. However, depending on how the engine was maintained, often this is not necessary. A major cause of valve, guide and seat wear is an improperly tuned engine. An engine that is running too rich, will often wash the lubricating oil out of the guide with gasoline, causing it to wear rapidly. Conversely, an engine which is running too lean will place higher combustion temperatures on the valves and seats allowing them to wear or even burn. Springs fall victim to the driving habits of the individual. A driver who often runs the engine rpm to the redline will wear out or break the springs faster then one that stays well below it. Unfortunately, mileage takes it toll on all of the parts. Generally, the valves, guides, springs and seats in a cylinder head can be machined and re-used, saving you money. However, if a valve is burnt, it may be wise to replace all of the valves, since they were all operating in the

same environment. The same goes for any other component on the cylinder head. Think of it as an insurance policy against future problems related to that component.

Unfortunately, the only way to find out which components need replacing, is to disassemble and carefully check each piece. After the cylinder head(s) are disassembled, thoroughly clean all of the components.

DISASSEMBLY

▶ **See Figures 237 and 238**

Whether it is a single or dual overhead camshaft cylinder head, the disassembly procedure is relatively

Fig. 237 Exploded view of a valve, seal, spring, retainer and locks from an OHC cylinder head

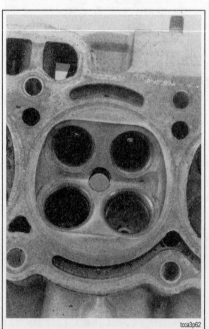

Fig. 238 Example of a multi-valve cylinder head. Note how it has 2 intake and 2 exhaust valve ports

unchanged. One aspect to pay attention to is careful labeling of the parts on the dual camshaft cylinder head. There will be an intake camshaft and followers as well as an exhaust camshaft and followers and they must be labeled as such. In some cases, the components are identical and could easily be installed incorrectly. DO NOT MIX THEM UP! Determining which is which is very simple; the intake camshaft and components are on the same side of the head as was the intake manifold. Conversely, the exhaust camshaft and components are on the same side of the head as was the exhaust manifold.

Cup Type Camshaft Followers

▶ **See Figures 239, 240, and 241**

Most cylinder heads with cup type camshaft followers will have the valve spring, retainer and locks recessed within the follower's bore. You will need a C-clamp style valve spring compressor tool, an OHC spring removal tool (or equivalent) and a small magnet to disassemble the head.

1. If not already removed, remove the camshaft(s) and/or followers. Mark their positions for assembly.
2. Position the cylinder head to allow use of a C-clamp style valve spring compressor tool.

➡**It is preferred to position the cylinder head gasket surface facing you with the valve springs facing the opposite direction and the head laying horizontal.**

3. With the OHC spring removal adapter tool positioned inside of the follower bore, compress the valve spring using the C-clamp style valve spring compressor.

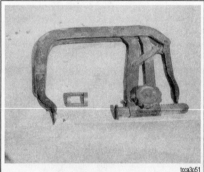

Fig. 239 C-clamp type spring compressor and an OHC spring removal tool (center) for cup type followers

Fig. 240 Most cup type follower cylinder heads retain the camshaft using bolt-on bearing caps

Fig. 241 Position the OHC spring tool in the follower bore, then compress the spring with a C-clamp type tool

4. Remove the valve locks. A small magnetic tool or screwdriver will aid in removal.

5. Release the compressor tool and remove the spring assembly.

6. Withdraw the valve from the cylinder head.

7. If equipped, remove the valve seal.

➡Special valve seal removal tools are available. Regular or needlenose type pliers, if used with care, will work just as well. If using ordinary pliers, be sure not to damage the follower bore. The follower and its bore are machined to close tolerances and any damage to the bore will effect this relationship.

8. If equipped, remove the valve spring shim. A small magnetic tool or screwdriver will aid in removal.

9. Repeat Steps 3 through 8 until all of the valves have been removed.

Rocker Arm Type Camshaft Followers

♦ **See Figures 242 thru 250**

Most cylinder heads with rocker arm-type camshaft followers are easily disassembled using a standard valve spring compressor. However, certain models may not have enough open space around the spring for the standard tool and may require you to use a C-clamp style compressor tool instead.

1. If not already removed, remove the rocker arms and/or shafts and the camshaft. If applicable, also remove the hydraulic lash adjusters. Mark their positions for assembly.

2. Position the cylinder head to allow access to the valve spring.

3. Use a valve spring compressor tool to relieve the spring tension from the retainer.

➡Due to engine varnish, the retainer may stick to the valve locks. A gentle tap with a hammer may help to break it loose.

4. Remove the valve locks from the valve tip and/or retainer. A small magnet may help in removing the small locks.

5. Lift the valve spring, tool and all, off of the valve stem.

6. If equipped, remove the valve seal. If the seal is difficult to remove with the valve in place, try removing the valve first, then the seal. Follow the steps below for valve removal.

7. Position the head to allow access for withdrawing the valve.

➡Cylinder heads that have seen a lot of miles and/or abuse may have mushroomed the valve lock grove and/or tip, causing difficulty in removal of the valve. If this has happened, use a metal file to carefully remove the high spots around the lock grooves and/or tip. Only file it enough to allow removal.

8. Remove the valve from the cylinder head.

9. If equipped, remove the valve spring shim. A small magnetic tool or screwdriver will aid in removal.

10. Repeat Steps 3 though 9 until all of the valves have been removed.

INSPECTION

Now that all of the cylinder head components are clean, it's time to inspect them for wear and/or dam-

Fig. 242 Example of the shaft mounted rocker arms on some OHC heads

Fig. 243 Another example of the rocker arm type OHC head. This model uses a follower under the camshaft

Fig. 244 Before the camshaft can be removed, all of the followers must first be removed . . .

Fig. 245 . . . then the camshaft can be removed by sliding it out (shown), or unbolting a bearing cap (not shown)

Fig. 246 Compress the valve spring . . .

Fig. 247 . . . then remove the valve locks from the valve stem and spring retainer

Fig. 248 Remove the valve spring and retainer from the cylinder head

Fig. 249 Remove the valve seal from the guide. Some gentle prying or pliers may help to remove stubborn ones

Fig. 250 All aluminum and some cast iron heads will have these valve spring shims. Remove all of them as well

age. To accurately inspect them, you will need some specialized tools:

- A 0–1 in. micrometer for the valves
- A dial indicator or inside diameter gauge for the valve guides
- A spring pressure test gauge

If you do not have access to the proper tools, you may want to bring the components to a shop that does.

Valves

▶ **See Figures 251 and 252**

The first thing to inspect are the valve heads. Look closely at the head, margin and face for any cracks, excessive wear or burning. The margin is the best place to look for burning. It should have a squared edge with an even width all around the diameter. When a valve burns, the margin will look melted and the edges rounded. Also inspect the valve head for any signs of tulipping. This will show as a lifting of the edges or dishing in the center of the head and will usually not occur to all of the valves. All of the heads should look the same, any that seem dished more than others are probably bad. Next, inspect the valve lock grooves and valve tips. Check for any burrs around the lock grooves, especially if you had to file them to remove the valve. Valve tips should appear flat, although slight rounding with high mileage engines is normal. Slightly worn valve tips will need to be machined flat. Last, measure the valve stem diameter with the micrometer. Measure the area that rides within the guide, especially towards the tip where most of the wear occurs. Take several measurements along its length and compare them to each other. Wear should be even along the length with little to no taper. If no minimum diameter is given in the specifications, then the stem should not read more than 0.001 in. (0.025mm) below the unworn area of the valve stem. Any valves that fail these inspections should be replaced.

Springs, Retainers and Valve Locks

▶ **See Figures 253 and 254**

The first thing to check is the most obvious, broken springs. Next check the free length and squareness of each spring. If applicable, insure to distinguish between intake and exhaust springs. Use a ruler and/or carpenter's square to measure the length. A carpenter's square should be used to check the springs for squareness. If a spring pressure test gauge is available, check each springs rating and compare to the specifications chart. Check the readings against the specifications given. Any springs that fail these inspections should be replaced.

The spring retainers rarely need replacing, however they should still be checked as a precaution. Inspect the spring mating surface and the valve lock retention area for any signs of excessive wear. Also check for any signs of cracking. Replace any retainers that are questionable.

Valve locks should be inspected for excessive wear on the outside contact area as well as on the inner notched surface. Any locks which appear worn or broken and its respective valve should be replaced.

Cylinder Head

There are several things to check on the cylinder head: valve guides, seats, cylinder head surface flatness, cracks and physical damage.

VALVE GUIDES

▶ **See Figure 255**

Now that you know the valves are good, you can use them to check the guides, although a new valve, if available, is preferred. Before you measure anything, look at the guides carefully and inspect them for any cracks, chips or breakage. Also if the guide is a removable style (as in most aluminum heads), check them for any looseness or evidence of movement. All of the guides should appear to be at the same height from the spring seat. If any seem lower (or higher) from another, the guide has moved. Mount a dial indicator onto the spring side of the cylinder head. Lightly oil the valve stem and insert it

Fig. 251 Valve stems may be rolled on a flat surface to check for bends

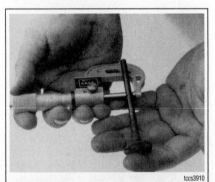

Fig. 252 Use a micrometer to check the valve stem diameter

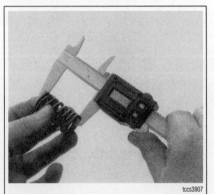

Fig. 253 Use a caliper to check the valve spring free-length

Fig. 254 Check the valve spring for squareness on a flat surface; a carpenter's square can be used

Fig. 255 A dial gauge may be used to check valve stem-to-guide clearance; read the gauge while moving the valve stem

into the cylinder head. Position the dial indicator against the valve stem near the tip and zero the gauge. Grasp the valve stem and wiggle towards and away from the dial indicator and observe the readings. Mount the dial indicator 90 degrees from the initial point and zero the gauge and again take a reading. Compare the two readings for a out of round condition. Check the readings against the specifications given. An Inside Diameter (I.D.) gauge designed for valve guides will give you an accurate valve guide bore measurement. If the I.D. gauge is used, compare the readings with the specifications given. Any guides that fail these inspections should be replaced or machined.

VALVE SEATS

A visual inspection of the valve seats should show a slightly worn and pitted surface where the valve face contacts the seat. Inspect the seat carefully for severe pitting or cracks. Also, a seat that is badly worn will be recessed into the cylinder head. A severely worn or recessed seat may need to be replaced. All cracked seats must be replaced. A seat concentricity gauge, if available, should be used to check the seat run-out. If run-out exceeds specifications the seat must be machined (if no specification is given use 0.002 in. or 0.051mm).

CYLINDER HEAD SURFACE FLATNESS

▶ **See Figures 256 and 257**

After you have cleaned the gasket surface of the cylinder head of any old gasket material, check the head for flatness.

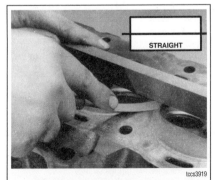

Fig. 256 Check the head for flatness across the center of the head surface using a straightedge and feeler gauge

Place a straightedge across the gasket surface. Using feeler gauges, determine the clearance at the center of the straightedge and across the cylinder head at several points. Check along the centerline and diagonally on the head surface. If the warpage exceeds 0.003 in. (0.076mm) within a 6.0 in. (15.2cm) span, or 0.006 in. (0.152mm) over the total length of the head, the cylinder head must be resurfaced. After resurfacing the heads of a V-type engine, the intake manifold flange surface should be checked, and if necessary, milled proportionally to allow for the change in its mounting position.

CRACKS AND PHYSICAL DAMAGE

Generally, cracks are limited to the combustion chamber, however, it is not uncommon for the head to crack in a spark plug hole, port, outside of the head or in the valve spring/rocker arm area. The first area to inspect is always the hottest: the exhaust seat/port area.

A visual inspection should be performed, but just because you don't see a crack does not mean it is not there. Some more reliable methods for inspecting for cracks include Magnaflux®, a magnetic process or Zyglo®, a dye penetrant. Magnaflux® is used only on ferrous metal (cast iron) heads. Zyglo® uses a spray on fluorescent mixture along with a black light to reveal the cracks. It is strongly recommended to have your cylinder head checked professionally for cracks, especially if the engine was known to have overheated and/or leaked or consumed coolant. Contact a local shop for availability and pricing of these services.

Physical damage is usually very evident. For example, a broken mounting ear from dropping the head or a bent or broken stud and/or bolt. All of these defects should be fixed or, if unrepairable, the head should be replaced.

Camshaft and Followers

Inspect the camshaft(s) and followers as described earlier in this section.

REFINISHING & REPAIRING

Many of the procedures given for refinishing and repairing the cylinder head components must be performed by a machine shop. Certain steps, if the inspected part is not worn, can be performed yourself inexpensively. However, you spent a lot of time and effort so far, why risk trying to save a couple bucks if you might have to do it all over again?

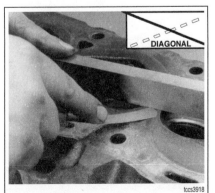

Fig. 257 Checks should also be made along both diagonals of the head surface

Valves

Any valves that were not replaced should be refaced and the tips ground flat. Unless you have access to a valve grinding machine, this should be done by a machine shop. If the valves are in extremely good condition, as well as the valve seats and guides, they may be lapped in without performing machine work.

It is a recommended practice to lap the valves even after machine work has been performed and/or new valves have been purchased. This insures a positive seal between the valve and seat.

LAPPING THE VALVES

➡**Before lapping the valves to the seats, read the rest of the cylinder head section to insure that any related parts are in acceptable enough condition to continue.**

➡**Before any valve seat machining and/or lapping can be performed, the guides must be within factory recommended specifications.**

1. Invert the cylinder head.
2. Lightly lubricate the valve stems and insert them into the cylinder head in their numbered order.
3. Raise the valve from the seat and apply a small amount of fine lapping compound to the seat.
4. Moisten the suction head of a hand-lapping tool and attach it to the head of the valve.
5. Rotate the tool between the palms of both hands, changing the position of the valve on the valve seat and lifting the tool often to prevent grooving.
6. Lap the valve until a smooth, polished circle is evident on the valve and seat.
7. Remove the tool and the valve. Wipe away all traces of the grinding compound and store the valve to maintain its lapped location.

✳✳ WARNING

Do not get the valves out of order after they have been lapped. They must be put back with the same valve seat with which they were lapped.

Springs, Retainers and Valve Locks

There is no repair or refinishing possible with the springs, retainers and valve locks. If they are found to be worn or defective, they must be replaced with new (or known good) parts.

Cylinder Head

Most refinishing procedures dealing with the cylinder head must be performed by a machine shop. Read the sections below and review your inspection data to determine whether or not machining is necessary.

VALVE GUIDE

➡**If any machining or replacements are made to the valve guides, the seats must be machined.**

Unless the valve guides need machining or replacing, the only service to perform is to thoroughly clean them of any dirt or oil residue.

There are only two types of valve guides used on automobile engines: the replaceable-type (all aluminum heads) and the cast-in integral-type (most cast iron heads). There are four recommended methods for repairing worn guides.

- Knurling
- Inserts
- Reaming oversize
- Replacing

Knurling is a process in which metal is displaced and raised, thereby reducing clearance, giving a true center, and providing oil control. It is the least expensive way of repairing the valve guides. However, it is not necessarily the best, and in some cases, a knurled valve guide will not stand up for more than a short time. It requires a special knurlizer and precision reaming tools to obtain proper clearances. It would not be cost effective to purchase these tools, unless you plan on rebuilding several of the same cylinder head.

Installing a guide insert involves machining the guide to accept a bronze insert. One style is the coil-type which is installed into a threaded guide. Another is the thin-walled insert where the guide is reamed oversize to accept a split-sleeve insert. After the insert is installed, a special tool is then run through the guide to expand the insert, locking it to the guide. The insert is then reamed to the standard size for proper valve clearance.

Reaming for oversize valves restores normal clearances and provides a true valve seat. Most cast-in type guides can be reamed to accept an valve with an oversize stem. The cost factor for this can become quite high as you will need to purchase the reamer and new, oversize stem valves for all guides which were reamed. Oversizes are generally 0.003 to 0.030 in. (0.076 to 0.762mm), with 0.015 in. (0.381mm) being the most common.

To replace cast-in type valve guides, they must be drilled out, then reamed to accept replacement guides. This must be done on a fixture which will allow centering and leveling off of the original valve seat or guide, otherwise a serious guide-to-seat misalignment may occur making it impossible to properly machine the seat.

Replaceable-type guides are pressed into the cylinder head. A hammer and a stepped drift or punch may be used to install and remove the guides. Before removing the guides, measure the protrusion on the spring side of the head and record it for installation. Use the stepped drift to hammer out the old guide from the combustion chamber side of the head. When installing, determine whether or not the guide also seals a water jacket in the head, and if it does, use the recommended sealing agent. If there is no water jacket, grease the valve guide and its bore. Use the stepped drift, and hammer the new guide into the cylinder head from the spring side of the cylinder head. A stack of washers the same thickness as the measured protrusion may help the installation process.

VALVE SEATS

➡Before any valve seat machining can be performed, the guides must be within factory recommended specifications.

➡If any machining or replacements were made to the valve guides, the seats must be

machined.

If the seats are in good condition, the valves can be lapped to the seats, and the cylinder head assembled. See the valves section for instructions on lapping.

If the valve seats are worn, cracked or damaged, they must be serviced by a machine shop. The valve seat must be perfectly centered to the valve guide, which requires very accurate machining.

CYLINDER HEAD SURFACE

If the cylinder head is warped, it must be machined flat. If the warpage is extremely severe, the head may need to be replaced. In some instances, it may be possible to straighten a warped head enough to allow machining. In either case, contact a professional machine shop for service.

➡Any OHC cylinder head that shows excessive warpage should have the camshaft bearing journals align bored after the cylinder head has been resurfaced.

⁂ WARNING

Failure to align bore the camshaft bearing journals could result in severe engine damage including but not limited to: valve and piston damage, connecting rod damage, camshaft and/or crankshaft breakage.

CRACKS AND PHYSICAL DAMAGE

Certain cracks can be repaired in both cast iron and aluminum heads. For cast iron, a tapered threaded insert is installed along the length of the crack. Aluminum can also use the tapered inserts, however welding is the preferred method. Some physical damage can be repaired through brazing or welding. Contact a machine shop to get expert advice for your particular dilemma.

ASSEMBLY

♦ **See Figure 258**

The first step for any assembly job is to have a clean area in which to work. Next, thoroughly clean all of the parts and components that are to be assembled. Finally, place all of the components onto a suitable work space and, if necessary, arrange the parts to their respective positions.

tcca3p64

Fig. 258 Once assembled, check the valve clearance and correct as needed

Cup Type Camshaft Followers

To install the springs, retainers and valve locks on heads which have these components recessed into the camshaft follower's bore, you will need a small screwdriver-type tool, some clean white grease and a lot of patience. You will also need the C-clamp style spring compressor and the OHC tool used to disassemble the head.

1. Lightly lubricate the valve stems and insert all of the valves into the cylinder head. If possible, maintain their original locations.
2. If equipped, install any valve spring shims which were removed.
3. If equipped, install the new valve seals, keeping the following in mind:
   - If the valve seal presses over the guide, lightly lubricate the outer guide surfaces.
   - If the seal is an O-ring type, it is installed just after compressing the spring but before the valve locks.
4. Place the valve spring and retainer over the stem.
5. Position the spring compressor and the OHC tool, then compress the spring.
6. Using a small screwdriver as a spatula, fill the valve stem side of the lock with white grease. Use the excess grease on the screwdriver to fasten the lock to the driver.
7. Carefully install the valve lock, which is stuck to the end of the screwdriver, to the valve stem then press on it with the screwdriver until the grease squeezes out. The valve lock should now be stuck to the stem.
8. Repeat Steps 6 and 7 for the remaining valve lock.
9. Relieve the spring pressure slowly and insure that neither valve lock becomes dislodged by the retainer.
10. Remove the spring compressor tool.
11. Repeat Steps 2 through 10 until all of the springs have been installed.
12. Install the followers, camshaft(s) and any other components that were removed for disassembly.

Rocker Arm Type Camshaft Followers

1. Lightly lubricate the valve stems and insert all of the valves into the cylinder head. If possible, maintain their original locations.
2. If equipped, install any valve spring shims which were removed.
3. If equipped, install the new valve seals, keeping the following in mind:
   - If the valve seal presses over the guide, lightly lubricate the outer guide surfaces.
   - If the seal is an O-ring type, it is installed just after compressing the spring but before the valve locks.
4. Place the valve spring and retainer over the stem.
5. Position the spring compressor tool and compress the spring.
6. Assemble the valve locks to the stem.
7. Relieve the spring pressure slowly and insure that neither valve lock becomes dislodged by the retainer.
8. Remove the spring compressor tool.
9. Repeat Steps 2 through 8 until all of the springs have been installed.

10. Install the camshaft(s), rockers, shafts and any other components that were removed for disassembly.

Engine Block

GENERAL INFORMATION

A thorough overhaul or rebuild of an engine block would include replacing the pistons, rings, bearings, timing belt/chain assembly and oil pump. For OHV engines also include a new camshaft and lifters. The block would then have the cylinders bored and honed oversize (or if using removable cylinder sleeves, new sleeves installed) and the crankshaft would be cut undersize to provide new wearing surfaces and perfect clearances. However, your particular engine may not have everything worn out. What if only the piston rings have worn out and the clearances on everything else are still within factory specifications? Well, you could just replace the rings and put it back together, but this would be a very rare example. Chances are, if one component in your engine is worn, other components are sure to follow, and soon. At the very least, you should always replace the rings, bearings and oil pump. This is what is commonly called a "freshen up".

Cylinder Ridge Removal

Because the top piston ring does not travel to the very top of the cylinder, a ridge is built up between the end of the travel and the top of the cylinder bore.

Pushing the piston and connecting rod assembly past the ridge can be difficult, and damage to the piston ring lands could occur. If the ridge is not removed before installing a new piston or not removed at all, piston ring breakage and piston damage may occur.

➡ It is always recommended that you remove any cylinder ridges before removing the piston and connecting rod assemblies. If you know that new pistons are going to be installed and the engine block will be bored oversize, you may be able to forego this step. However, some ridges may actually prevent the assemblies from being removed, necessitating its removal.

There are several different types of ridge reamers on the market, none of which are inexpensive. Unless a great deal of engine rebuilding is anticipated, borrow or rent a reamer.

1. Turn the crankshaft until the piston is at the bottom of its travel.
2. Cover the head of the piston with a rag.
3. Follow the tool manufacturers instructions and cut away the ridge, exercising extreme care to avoid cutting too deeply.
4. Remove the ridge reamer, the rag and as many of the cuttings as possible. Continue until all of the cylinder ridges have been removed.

DISASSEMBLY

▸ **See Figures 259 and 260**

The engine disassembly instructions following assume that you have the engine mounted on an engine stand. If not, it is easiest to disassemble the engine on a bench or the floor with it resting on the bell

Fig. 259 Place rubber hose over the connecting rod studs to protect the crankshaft and cylinder bores from damage

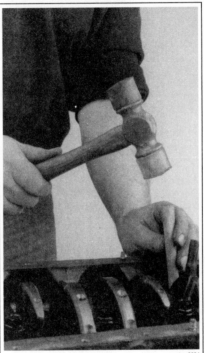

Fig. 260 Carefully tap the piston out of the bore using a wooden dowel

housing or transmission mounting surface. You must be able to access the connecting rod fasteners and turn the crankshaft during disassembly. Also, all engine covers (timing, front, side, oil pan, whatever) should have already been removed. Engines which are seized or locked up may not be able to be completely disassembled, and a core (salvage yard) engine should be purchased.

If not done during the cylinder head removal, remove the timing chain/belt and/or gear/sprocket assembly. Remove the oil pick-up and pump assembly and, if necessary, the pump drive. If equipped, remove any balance or auxiliary shafts. If necessary, remove the cylinder ridge from the top of the bore. See the cylinder ridge removal procedure earlier in this section.

Rotate the engine over so that the crankshaft is exposed. Use a number punch or scribe and mark each connecting rod with its respective cylinder number. The cylinder closest to the front of the engine is al-

ways number 1. However, depending on the engine placement, the front of the engine could either be the flywheel or damper/pulley end. Generally the front of the engine faces the front of the vehicle. Use a number punch or scribe and also mark the main bearing caps from front to rear with the front most cap being number 1 (if there are five caps, mark them 1 through 5, front to rear).

✳✳ WARNING

Take special care when pushing the connecting rod up from the crankshaft because the sharp threads of the rod bolts/studs will score the crankshaft journal. Insure that special plastic caps are installed over them, or cut two pieces of rubber hose to do the same.

Again, rotate the engine, this time to position the number one cylinder bore (head surface) up. Turn the crankshaft until the number one piston is at the bottom of its travel, this should allow the maximum access to its connecting rod. Remove the number one connecting rods fasteners and cap and place two lengths of rubber hose over the rod bolts/studs to protect the crankshaft from damage. Using a sturdy wooden dowel and a hammer, push the connecting rod up about 1 in. (25mm) from the crankshaft and remove the upper bearing insert. Continue pushing or tapping the connecting rod up until the piston rings are out of the cylinder bore. Remove the piston and rod by hand, put the upper half of the bearing insert back into the rod, install the cap with its bearing insert installed, and hand-tighten the cap fasteners. If the parts are kept in order in this manner, they will not get lost and you will be able to tell which bearings came form what cylinder if any problems are discovered and diagnosis is necessary. Remove all the other piston assemblies in the same manner. On V-style engines, remove all of the pistons from one bank, then reposition the engine with the other cylinder bank head surface up, and remove that banks piston assemblies.

The only remaining component in the engine block should now be the crankshaft. Loosen the main bearing caps evenly until the fasteners can be turned by hand, then remove them and the caps. Remove the crankshaft from the engine block. Thoroughly clean all of the components.

INSPECTION

Now that the engine block and all of its components are clean, it's time to inspect them for wear and/or damage. To accurately inspect them, you will need some specialized tools:

• Two or three separate micrometers to measure the pistons and crankshaft journals
• A dial indicator
• Telescoping gauges for the cylinder bores
• A rod alignment fixture to check for bent connecting rods

If you do not have access to the proper tools, you may want to bring the components to a shop that does.

Generally, you shouldn't expect cracks in the engine block or its components unless it was known to leak, consume or mix engine fluids, it was severely overheated, or there was evidence of bad bearings and/or crankshaft damage. A visual inspection should be performed on all of the components, but just because you don't see a crack does not mean it is not there. Some more reliable methods for inspecting for cracks include Magnaflux®, a magnetic process or Zyglo®, a dye penetrant. Magnaflux® is used only on ferrous metal (cast iron). Zyglo® uses a spray on fluorescent mixture along with a black light to reveal the cracks. It is strongly recommended to have your engine block checked professionally for cracks, especially if the engine was known to have overheated and/or leaked or consumed coolant. Contact a local shop for availability and pricing of these services.

Engine Block

ENGINE BLOCK BEARING ALIGNMENT

Remove the main bearing caps and, if still installed, the main bearing inserts. Inspect all of the main bearing saddles and caps for damage, burrs or high spots. If damage is found, and it is caused from a spun main bearing, the block will need to be align-bored or, if severe enough, replacement. Any burrs or high spots should be carefully removed with a metal file.

Place a straightedge on the bearing saddles, in the engine block, along the centerline of the crankshaft. If any clearance exists between the straightedge and the saddles, the block must be align-bored.

Align-boring consists of machining the main bearing saddles and caps by means of a flycutter that runs through the bearing saddles.

DECK FLATNESS

The top of the engine block where the cylinder head mounts is called the deck. Insure that the deck surface is clean of dirt, carbon deposits and old gasket material. Place a straightedge across the surface of the deck along its centerline and, using feeler gauges, check the clearance along several points. Repeat the checking procedure with the straightedge placed along both diagonals of the deck surface. If the reading exceeds 0.003 in. (0.076mm) within a 6.0 in. (15.2cm) span, or 0.006 in. (0.152mm) over the total length of the deck, it must be machined.

CYLINDER BORES

▶ See Figure 261

The cylinder bores house the pistons and are slightly larger than the pistons themselves. A common piston-to-bore clearance is 0.0015–0.0025 in.

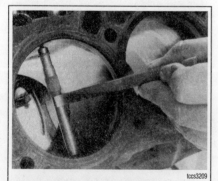

Fig. 261 Use a telescoping gauge to measure the cylinder bore diameter—take several readings within the same bore

(0.0381mm–0.0635mm). Inspect and measure the cylinder bores. The bore should be checked for out-of-roundness, taper and size. The results of this inspection will determine whether the cylinder can be used in its existing size and condition, or a rebore to the next oversize is required (or in the case of removable sleeves, have replacements installed).

The amount of cylinder wall wear is always greater at the top of the cylinder than at the bottom. This wear is known as taper. Any cylinder that has a taper of 0.0012 in. (0.305mm) or more, must be rebored. Measurements are taken at a number of positions in each cylinder: at the top, middle and bottom and at two points at each position; that is, at a point 90 degrees from the crankshaft centerline, as well as a point parallel to the crankshaft centerline. The measurements are made with either a special dial indicator or a telescopic gauge and micrometer. If the necessary precision tools to check the bore are not available, take the block to a machine shop and have them mike it. Also if you don't have the tools to check the cylinder bores, chances are you will not have the necessary devices to check the pistons, connecting rods and crankshaft. Take these components with you and save yourself an extra trip.

For our procedures, we will use a telescopic gauge and a micrometer. You will need one of each, with a measuring range which covers your cylinder bore size.

1. Position the telescopic gauge in the cylinder bore, loosen the gauges lock and allow it to expand.

➡ **Your first two readings will be at the top of the cylinder bore, then proceed to the middle and finally the bottom, making a total of six measurements.**

2. Hold the gauge square in the bore, 90 degrees from the crankshaft centerline, and gently tighten the lock. Tilt the gauge back to remove it from the bore.
3. Measure the gauge with the micrometer and record the reading.
4. Again, hold the gauge square in the bore, this time parallel to the crankshaft centerline, and gently tighten the lock. Again, you will tilt the gauge back to remove it from the bore.
5. Measure the gauge with the micrometer and record this reading. The difference between these two readings is the out-of-round measurement of the cylinder.
6. Repeat steps 1 through 5, each time going to the next lower position, until you reach the bottom of the cylinder. Then go to the next cylinder, and continue until all of the cylinders have been measured.

The difference between these measurements will tell you all about the wear in your cylinders. The measurements which were taken 90 degrees from the crankshaft centerline will always reflect the most wear. That is because at this position is where the engine power presses the piston against the cylinder bore the hardest. This is known as thrust wear. Take your top, 90 degree measurement and compare it to your bottom, 90 degree measurement. The difference between them is the taper. When you measure your pistons, you will compare these readings to your piston sizes and determine piston-to-wall clearance.

Crankshaft

Inspect the crankshaft for visible signs of wear or damage. All of the journals should be perfectly round and smooth. Slight scores are normal for a used

crankshaft, but you should hardly feel them with your fingernail. When measuring the crankshaft with a micrometer, you will take readings at the front and rear of each journal, then turn the micrometer 90 degrees and take two more readings, front and rear. The difference between the front-to-rear readings is the journal taper and the first-to-90 degree reading is the out-of-round measurement. Generally, there should be no taper or out-of-roundness found, however, up to 0.0005 in. (0.0127mm) for either can be overlooked. Also, the readings should fall within the factory specifications for journal diameters.

If the crankshaft journals fall within specifications, it is recommended that it be polished before being returned to service. Polishing the crankshaft insures that any minor burrs or high spots are smoothed, thereby reducing the chance of scoring the new bearings.

Pistons and Connecting Rods

PISTONS

▶ See Figure 262

The piston should be visually inspected for any signs of cracking or burning (caused by hot spots or detonation), and scuffing or excessive wear on the skirts. The wrist pin attaches the piston to the connecting rod. The piston should move freely on the wrist pin, both sliding and pivoting. Grasp the connecting rod securely, or mount it in a vise, and try to rock the piston back and forth along the centerline of the wrist pin. There should not be any excessive play evident between the piston and the pin. If there are C-clips retaining the pin in the piston then you have wrist pin bushings in the rods. There should not be any excessive play between the wrist pin and the rod bushing. Normal clearance for the wrist pin is approx. 0.001–0.002 in. (0.025mm–0.051mm).

Use a micrometer and measure the diameter of the piston, perpendicular to the wrist pin, on the skirt. Compare the reading to its original cylinder measurement obtained earlier. The difference between the two readings is the piston-to-wall clearance. If the clearance is within specifications, the piston may be used as is. If the piston is out of specification, but the bore is not, you will need a new piston. If both are out of specification, you will need the cylinder rebored and oversize pistons installed. Generally if two or more pistons/bores are out of specification, it is best to rebore the entire block and purchase a complete set of oversize pistons.

Fig. 262 Measure the piston's outer diameter, perpendicular to the wrist pin, with a micrometer

CONNECTING ROD

You should have the connecting rod checked for straightness at a machine shop. If the connecting rod is bent, it will unevenly wear the bearing and piston, as well as place greater stress on these components. Any bent or twisted connecting rods must be replaced. If the rods are straight and the wrist pin clearance is within specifications, then only the bearing end of the rod need be checked. Place the connecting rod into a vice, with the bearing inserts in place, install the cap to the rod and torque the fasteners to specifications. Use a telescoping gauge and carefully measure the inside diameter of the bearings. Compare this reading to the rods original crankshaft journal diameter measurement. The difference is the oil clearance. If the oil clearance is not within specifications, install new bearings in the rod and take another measurement. If the clearance is still out of specifications, and the crankshaft is not, the rod will need to be reconditioned by a machine shop.

➥You can also use Plastigage® to check the bearing clearances. The assembling section has complete instructions on its use.

Camshaft

Inspect the camshaft and lifters/followers as described earlier in this section.

Bearings

All of the engine bearings should be visually inspected for wear and/or damage. The bearing should look evenly worn all around with no deep scores or pits. If the bearing is severely worn, scored, pitted or heat blued, then the bearing, and the components that use it, should be brought to a machine shop for inspection. Full-circle bearings (used on most camshafts, auxiliary shafts, balance shafts, etc.) require specialized tools for removal and installation, and should be brought to a machine shop for service.

Oil Pump

➥The oil pump is responsible for providing constant lubrication to the whole engine and so it is recommended that a new oil pump be installed when rebuilding the engine.

Completely disassemble the oil pump and thoroughly clean all of the components. Inspect the oil pump gears and housing for wear and/or damage. Insure that the pressure relief valve operates properly and there is no binding or sticking due to varnish or debris. If all of the parts are in proper working condition, lubricate the gears and relief valve, and assemble the pump.

REFINISHING

▶ See Figure 263

Almost all engine block refinishing must be performed by a machine shop. If the cylinders are not to be rebored, then the cylinder glaze can be removed with a ball hone. When removing cylinder glaze with a ball hone, use a light or penetrating type oil to lubricate the hone. Do not allow the hone to run dry as this may cause excessive scoring of the cylinder bores and wear on the hone. If new pistons are required, they will need to be installed to the connecting rods. This should be performed by a machine

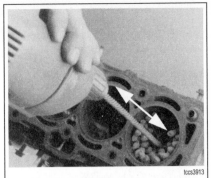

Fig. 263 Use a ball type cylinder hone to remove any glaze and provide a new surface for seating the piston rings

shop as the pistons must be installed in the correct relationship to the rod or engine damage can occur.

Pistons and Connecting Rods

▶ See Figure 264

Only pistons with the wrist pin retained by C-clips are serviceable by the home-mechanic. Press fit pistons require special presses and/or heaters to remove/install the connecting rod and should only be performed by a machine shop.

All pistons will have a mark indicating the direction to the front of the engine and the must be installed into the engine in that manner. Usually it is a notch or arrow on the top of the piston, or it may be the letter F cast or stamped into the piston.

ASSEMBLY

Before you begin assembling the engine, first give yourself a clean, dirt free work area. Next, clean every engine component again. The key to a good assembly is cleanliness.

Mount the engine block into the engine stand and wash it one last time using water and detergent (dishwashing detergent works well). While washing it, scrub the cylinder bores with a soft bristle brush and thoroughly clean all of the oil passages. Completely dry the engine and spray the entire assembly down with an anti-rust solution such as WD-40® or similar product. Take a clean lint-free rag and wipe up any excess anti-rust solution from the bores, bearing saddles, etc. Repeat the final cleaning process on the

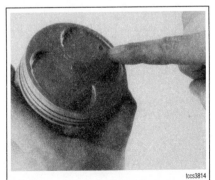

Fig. 264 Most pistons are marked to indicate positioning in the engine (usually a mark means the side facing the front)

crankshaft. Replace any freeze or oil galley plugs which were removed during disassembly.

Crankshaft

▶ See Figures 265, 266, 267, and 268

1. Remove the main bearing inserts from the block and bearing caps.

2. If the crankshaft main bearing journals have been refinished to a definite undersize, install the correct undersize bearing. Be sure that the bearing inserts and bearing bores are clean. Foreign material under inserts will distort bearing and cause failure.

3. Place the upper main bearing inserts in bores with tang in slot.

➥The oil holes in the bearing inserts must be aligned with the oil holes in the cylinder block.

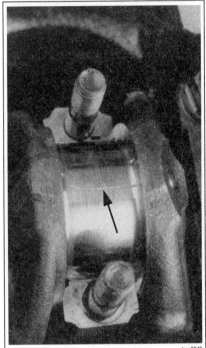

Fig. 265 Apply a strip of gauging material to the bearing journal, then install and torque the cap

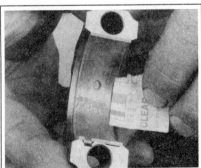

Fig. 266 After the cap is removed again, use the scale supplied with the gauging material to check the clearance

Fig. 267 A dial gauge may be used to check crankshaft end-play

Fig. 268 Carefully pry the crankshaft back and forth while reading the dial gauge for end-play

4. Install the lower main bearing inserts in bearing caps.

5. Clean the mating surfaces of block and rear main bearing cap.

6. Carefully lower the crankshaft into place. Be careful not to damage bearing surfaces.

7. Check the clearance of each main bearing by using the following procedure:

a. Place a piece of Plastigage® or its equivalent, on bearing surface across full width of bearing cap and about $\frac{1}{4}$ in. off center.

b. Install cap and tighten bolts to specifications. Do not turn crankshaft while Plastigage® is in place.

c. Remove the cap. Using the supplied Plastigage® scale, check width of Plastigage® at widest point to get maximum clearance. Difference between readings is taper of journal.

d. If clearance exceeds specified limits, try a 0.001 in. or 0.002 in. undersize bearing in combination with the standard bearing. Bearing clearance must be within specified limits. If standard and 0.002 in. undersize bearing does not bring clearance within desired limits, refinish crankshaft journal, then install undersize bearings.

8. Install the rear main seal.

9. After the bearings have been fitted, apply a light coat of engine oil to the journals and bearings. Install the rear main bearing cap. Install all bearing caps except the thrust bearing cap. Be sure that main bearing caps are installed in original locations. Tighten the bearing cap bolts to specifications.

10. Install the thrust bearing cap with bolts finger-tight.

11. Pry the crankshaft forward against the thrust surface of upper half of bearing.

12. Hold the crankshaft forward and pry the thrust bearing cap to the rear. This aligns the thrust surfaces of both halves of the bearing.

13. Retain the forward pressure on the crankshaft. Tighten the cap bolts to specifications.

14. Measure the crankshaft end-play as follows:

a. Mount a dial gauge to the engine block and position the tip of the gauge to read from the crankshaft end.

b. Carefully pry the crankshaft toward the rear of the engine and hold it there while you zero the gauge.

c. Carefully pry the crankshaft toward the front of the engine and read the gauge.

d. Confirm that the reading is within specifications. If not, install a new thrust bearing and repeat the procedure. If the reading is still out of specifications with a new bearing, have a machine shop inspect the thrust surfaces of the crankshaft, and if possible, repair it.

15. Rotate the crankshaft so as to position the first rod journal to the bottom of its stroke.

Pistons and Connecting Rods

♦ See Figures 269, 270, 271, and 272

1. Before installing the piston/connecting rod assembly, oil the pistons, piston rings and the cylinder walls with light engine oil. Install connecting rod bolt protectors or rubber hose onto the connecting rod bolts/studs. Also perform the following:

a. Select the proper ring set for the size cylinder bore.

b. Position the ring in the bore in which it is going to be used.

c. Push the ring down into the bore area where normal ring wear is not encountered.

d. Use the head of the piston to position the ring in the bore so that the ring is square with the cylinder wall. Use caution to avoid damage to the ring or cylinder bore.

e. Measure the gap between the ends of the ring with a feeler gauge. Ring gap in a worn cylinder is normally greater than specification. If the ring gap is greater than the specified limits, try an oversize ring set.

f. Check the ring side clearance of the compression rings with a feeler gauge inserted between the ring and its lower land according to specification. The gauge should slide freely around the entire ring circumference without binding. Any wear that occurs will form a step at

the inner portion of the lower land. If the lower lands have high steps, the piston should be replaced.

2. Unless new pistons are installed, be sure to install the pistons in the cylinders from which they were removed. The numbers on the connecting rod and bearing cap must be on the same side when installed in the cylinder bore. If a connecting rod is ever transposed from one engine or cylinder to another, new bearings should be fitted and the connecting rod should be numbered to correspond with the new cylinder number. The notch on the piston head goes toward the front of the engine.

3. Install all of the rod bearing inserts into the rods and caps.

4. Install the rings to the pistons. Install the oil control ring first, then the second compression ring and finally the top compression ring. Use a piston ring expander tool to aid in installation and to help reduce the chance of breakage.

5. Make sure the ring gaps are properly spaced around the circumference of the piston. Fit a piston ring compressor around the piston and slide the piston and connecting rod assembly down into the cylinder bore, pushing it in with the wooden hammer handle. Push the piston down until it is only slightly below the top of the cylinder bore. Guide the connecting rod onto the crankshaft bearing journal carefully, to avoid damaging the crankshaft.

6. Check the bearing clearance of all the rod bearings, fitting them to the crankshaft bearing journals. Follow the procedure in the crankshaft installation above.

7. After the bearings have been fitted, apply a light coating of assembly oil to the journals and bearings.

8. Turn the crankshaft until the appropriate bearing journal is at the bottom of its stroke, then push the piston assembly all the way down until the connecting rod bearing seats on the crankshaft journal. Be careful not to allow the bearing cap screws to strike the crankshaft bearing journals and damage them.

9. After the piston and connecting rod assemblies have been installed, check the connecting rod side clearance on each crankshaft journal.

10. Prime and install the oil pump and the oil pump intake tube.

11. Install the auxiliary/balance shaft(s)/assembly(ies).

Cylinder Head(S)

1. Install the cylinder head(s) using new gaskets.

2. Install the timing sprockets/gears and the belt/chain assemblies.

Engine Covers and Components

Install the timing cover(s) and oil pan. Refer to your notes and drawings made prior to disassembly and install all of the components that were removed. Install the engine into the vehicle.

Fig. 269 Checking the piston ring-to-ring groove side clearance using the ring and a feeler gauge

Fig. 272 Install the piston and rod assembly into the block using a ring compressor and the handle of a hammer

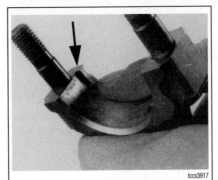

Fig. 270 The notch on the side of the bearing cap matches the tang on the bearing insert

Engine Start-up and Break-in

STARTING THE ENGINE

Now that the engine is installed and every wire and hose is properly connected, go back and double check that all coolant and vacuum hoses are connected. Check that your oil drain plug is installed and properly tightened. If not already done, install a new oil filter onto the engine. Fill the crankcase with the proper amount and grade of engine oil. Fill the cooling system with a 50/50 mixture of coolant/water.

1. Connect the vehicle battery.
2. Start the engine. Keep your eye on your oil pressure indicator; if it does not indicate oil pressure within 10 seconds of starting, turn the vehicle off.

✳✳ WARNING

Damage to the engine can result if it is allowed to run with no oil pressure. Check the engine oil level to make sure that it is full. Check for any leaks and if found, repair the leaks before continuing. If there is still no indication of oil pressure, you may need to prime the system.

3. Confirm that there are no fluid leaks (oil or other).

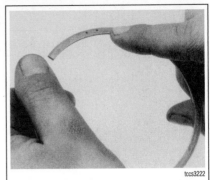

Fig. 271 Most rings are marked to show which side of the ring should face up when installed to the piston

4. Allow the engine to reach normal operating temperature (the upper radiator hose will be hot to the touch).
5. At this point you can perform any necessary checks or adjustments, such as checking the ignition timing.
6. Install any remaining components or body panels which were removed.

BREAKING IT IN

Make the first miles on the new engine, easy ones. Vary the speed but do not accelerate hard. Most importantly, do not lug the engine, and avoid sustained high speeds until at least 100 miles. Check the engine oil and coolant levels frequently. Expect the engine to use a little oil until the rings seat. Change the oil and filter at 500 miles, 1500 miles, then every 3000 miles past that.

KEEP IT MAINTAINED

Now that you have just gone through all of that hard work, keep yourself from doing it all over again by thoroughly maintaining it. Not that you may not have maintained it before, heck you could have had one to two hundred thousand miles on it before doing this. However, you may have bought the vehicle used, and the previous owner did not keep up on maintenance. Which is why you just went through all of that hard work. See?

1.5L ENGINE MECHANICAL SPECIFICATIONS

Description			English Specifications	Metric Specifications
General Information				
Engine type			4 Cylinder In-Line Overhead Camshaft	
Displacement			89.6 cubic in.	1.5L
Bore			2.972 in.	75.5mm
Stroke			3.228 in.	82mm
Compression ratio			9.2:1	
Firing order			1-3-4-2	
Cylinder Head				
Overall height			4.209-4.217 in.	106.9-107.1mm
Flatness (maximum)			0.002 in.	0.05mm
Camshaft bearing-to-camshaft clearance			0.0016-0.0031 in.	0.04-0.08mm
Camshaft				
Camshaft height	Intake	Standard	1.5256 in.	38.75mm
		Limit	1.5059 in.	38.25mm
	Exhaust	Standard	1.5394 in.	39.1mm
		Limit	1.5197 in.	38.6mm
Journal outside diameter			1.8110 in.	46mm
Bearing oil clearance		Standard	0.0024-0.0039 in.	0.06-0.10mm
		Limit	0.0055 in.	0.14mm
Rocker arms				
Inside diameter			0.744 in.	18.9mm
Arm-to-shaft clearance		Standard	0.0004-0.0016 in.	0.01-0.04mm
		Limit	0.004 in.	0.1mm
Rocker arm shaft				
Outside diameter			0.744 in.	18.9mm
Valves				
Valve length	Intake		3.9665 in.	100.75mm
	Exhaust		3.9783 in.	101.05mm
Stem outside diameter	Intake		0.2585-0.2591 in.	6.565-6.580mm
	Exhaust		0.2571-0.2579 in.	6.530-6.550mm
Face angle (all)			45-45.5°	
Head thickness (margin)	Intake	Standard	0.039 in.	1.0mm
		Limit	0.020 in.	0.5mm
	Exhaust	Standard	0.059 in.	1.5mm
		Limit	0.039 in.	1.0mm
Stem-to-guide clearance	Intake	Standard	0.0008-0.0020 in.	0.02-0.05mm
		Limit	0.0039 in.	0.10mm
	Exhaust	Standard	0.0020-0.0035 in.	0.05-0.09mm
		Limit	0.0059 in.	0.15mm
Valve clearance	Hot engine	Intake	0.0059 in.	0.15mm
		Exhaust	0.0098 in.	0.25mm
	Cold engine	Intake	0.0028 in.	0.07mm
		Exhaust	0.0067 in.	0.17mm

9315c01

1.5L ENGINE MECHANICAL SPECIFICATIONS

Description			English Specifications	Metric Specifications
Valve guide				
Length	Intake		1.732 in.	44.0mm
	Exhaust		1.949 in.	49.5mm
Service sizes			0.002, 0.010, 0.020 in.	0.05, 0.25, 0.50mm
Valve seat				
Seat contact width			0.035-0.051 in.	0.9-1.3mm
Seat angle (all)			44-44.5°	
Valve spring				
Free length	Intake	Standard	1.815 in.	46.1mm
		Limit	1.776 in.	45.1mm
	Exhaust	Standard	1.843 in.	46.8mm
		Limit	1.803 in.	45.8mm
Load	Intake		51 ft. lbs.	230Nm
	Exhaust		64 ft. lbs.	290Nm
Cylinder Block				
Bore	Diameter		2.9724-2.9736 in.	75.50-75.53mm
	Out-of-round (max.)		0.008 in.	0.02mm
	Taper (max.)		0.008 in.	0.02mm
Overall height		Standard	10.075-10.083 in.	255.9-256.1mm
		Limit	10.073 in.	254.82mm
Gasket surface flatness (max.)			0.004 in.	0.1mm
Piston				
Outside diameter			2.9713-2.9724 in.	75.47-75.50mm
Piston-to-cylinder clearance			0.0008-0.0016 in.	0.02-0.04mm
Ring groove width	No. 1		0.0598-0.0606 in.	1.52-1.54mm
	No. 2		0.0594-0.0602 in.	1.51-1.53mm
	Oil Control		0.1581-0.1593 in.	4.015-4.045mm
Service sizes			0.002, 0.010, 0.020 in.	0.05, 0.25, 0.50mm
Piston Rings				
Side clearance	No. 1	Standard	0.0012-0.0028 in.	0.03-0.07mm
		Limit	0.0047 in.	0.12mm
	No. 2	Standard	0.0008-0.0024 in.	0.02-0.06mm
		Limit	0.0047 in.	0.12mm
End gap	No. 1	Standard	0.0079-0.0157 in.	0.20-0.40mm
		Limit	0.031 in.	0.8mm
	No. 2	Standard	0.0079-0.0138 in.	0.20-0.35mm
		Limit	0.031 in.	0.8mm
	Oil	Standard	0.0079-0.0276 in.	0.20-0.70mm
		Limit	0.039 in.	1.0mm
Connecting rod				
Bend (max.)			0.0020 in.	0.05mm
Twist (max.)			0.0039 in.	0.10mm
Rod big end side clearance		Standard	0.0039-0.0098 in.	0.10-0.25mm
		Limit	0.016 in.	0.4mm

9315c02

1.5L ENGINE MECHANICAL SPECIFICATIONS

Description	English Specifications	Metric Specifications
Connecting rod (cont'd)		
Piston pin press-in load	1,100-3,300 ft. lbs.	5,000-15,000Nm
Connecting rod bearing oil clearance		
Standard	0.0008-0.0024 in.	0.02-0.06mm
Limit	0.0059 in.	0.15mm
Crankshaft		
Main bearing oil clearance		
Standard	0.0008-0.0028 in.	0.02-0.07mm
Limit	0.0059 in.	0.15mm
Pin outside diameter	1.65 in.	42mm
Journal outside diameter	1.89 in.	48mm
Out-of-round (max.)	0.0006 in.	0.015mm
Crankshaft end-play		
Standard	0.002-0.0071 in.	0.05-0.18mm
Limit	0.0098 in.	0.25mm
Flywheel		
Run-out (max.)	0.0051 in.	0.13mm
Oil Pump		
Tip clearance		
Standard	0.0024-0.0071 in.	0.06-0.18mm
Limit	0.0138 in.	0.35mm
Side clearance		
Standard	0.0016-0.0039 in.	0.04-0.10mm
Limit	0.0079 in.	0.20mm
Body clearance		
Standard	0.0039-0.0071 in.	0.10-0.18mm
Limit	0.0138 in.	0.35mm
Relief spring		
Free length	1.835 in.	46.6mm
Load (@ 1.579 in. (40.1mm)	13 ft. lbs.	61Nm

1.6L ENGINE MECHANICAL SPECIFICATIONS

Description	English Specifications	Metric Specifications
General Information		
Engine type	4 Cylinder In-Line Double Overhead Camshaft	
Displacement	97.3 cubic in.	1.6L
Bore	3.240 in.	82.3mm
Stroke	2.953 in.	75mm
Compression ratio	9.2:1	
Firing order	1-3-4-2	
Cylinder Head		
Overall height	5.193-5.201 in.	131.9-132.1mm
Flatness (maximum)	0.002 in.	0.05mm
Camshaft bearing-to-camshaft clearance	0.0016-0.0031 in.	0.04-0.08mm
Camshaft		
Camshaft height		
Intake		
Standard	1.3858 in.	35.20mm
Limit	1.3661 in.	34.70mm
Exhaust		
Standard	1.3743 in.	34.907mm
Limit	1.3546 in.	34.407mm
Journal outside diameter	1.02 in.	26mm
Bearing oil clearance	0.0020-0.0035 in.	0.05-0.09mm
End-play	0.004-0.008 in.	0.1-0.2mm

1.6L ENGINE MECHANICAL SPECIFICATIONS

Description	English Specifications	Metric Specifications
Valves		
Valve length		
Intake	4.311 in.	109.50mm
Exhaust	4.319 in.	109.70mm
Stem outside diameter		
Intake	0.2585-0.2586 in.	6.565-6.568mm
Exhaust	0.2571-0.2579 in.	6.530-6.550mm
Face angle (all)	45-45.5°	
Head thickness (margin)		
Intake		
Standard	0.039 in.	1.0mm
Limit	0.028 in.	0.7mm
Exhaust		
Standard	0.059 in.	1.5mm
Limit	0.039 in.	1.0mm
Stem-to-guide clearance		
Intake		
Standard	0.0008-0.0020 in.	0.02-0.05mm
Limit	0.0039 in.	0.10mm
Exhaust		
Standard	0.0020-0.0035 in.	0.05-0.09mm
Limit	0.0059 in.	0.15mm
Valve guide		
Length		
Intake	1.791 in.	45.5mm
Exhaust	1.988 in.	50.5mm
Service sizes	0.002, 0.010, 0.020 in.	0.05, 0.25, 0.50mm
Valve seat		
Seat contact width	0.035-0.051 in.	0.9-1.3mm
Seat angle (all)	44-44.5°	
Valve spring		
Free length		
Standard	1.902 in.	48.3mm
Limit	1.862 in.	47.3mm
Load	66 ft. lbs.	300Nm
Out of squareness		
Standard		less than 1.5°
Limit		4.0°
Cylinder Block		
Bore		
Diameter	3.2402-3.2413 in.	82.30-82.33mm
Out-of-round (max.)	0.004 in.	0.01mm
Taper (max.)	0.004 in.	0.01mm
Gasket surface flatness (max.)	0.0039 in.	0.1mm
Piston		
Outside diameter	3.2390-3.2402 in.	82.27-82.30mm
Piston-to-cylinder clearance	0.0008-0.0016 in.	0.02-0.04mm
Ring groove width		
No. 1	0.0480-0.0488 in.	1.22-1.24mm
No. 2	0.0598-0.0606 in.	1.52-1.54mm
Oil Control	0.1185-0.1193 in.	3.01-3.03mm
Service sizes	0.010, 0.020, 0.030, 0.039 in.	0.25, 0.50, 0.75, 1.0mm
Piston Rings		
Side clearance		
No. 1		
Standard	0.0012-0.0028 in.	0.03-0.07mm
Limit	0.0047 in.	0.12mm
No. 2		
Standard	0.0012-0.0028 in.	0.03-0.07mm
Limit	0.0047 in.	0.12mm

1.6L ENGINE MECHANICAL SPECIFICATIONS

Description	English Specifications	Metric Specifications
Piston Rings (cont'd)		
End gap		
No. 1		
Standard	0.0098-0.0157 in.	0.25-0.40mm
Limit	0.031 in.	0.8mm
No. 2		
Standard	0.0138-0.0197 in.	0.35-0.50mm
Limit	0.039 in.	1.0mm
Oil		
Standard	0.0079-0.0276 in.	0.20-0.70mm
Limit	0.039 in.	1.0mm
Service sizes	0.010, 0.020, 0.030, 0.039 in.	0.25, 0.50, 0.75, 1.0mm
Connecting rod		
Bend (max.)	0.0020 in.	0.05mm
Twist (max.)	0.0039 in.	0.10mm
Rod big end side clearance		
Standard	0.0039-0.0098 in.	0.10-0.25mm
Limit	0.016 in.	0.4mm
Piston pin press-in load	1,653-3,858 ft. lbs.	7,500-17,500Nm
Connecting rod bearing oil clearance		
Standard	0.0008-0.0020 in.	0.02-0.05mm
Limit	0.004 in.	0.1mm
Crankshaft		
Main bearing oil clearance		
Standard	0.0008-0.0020 in.	0.02-0.05mm
Limit	0.004 in.	0.1mm
Pin outside diameter	1.77 in.	45mm
Journal outside diameter	2.24 in.	57mm
Out-of-round (max.)	0.0006 in.	0.015mm
Crankshaft end-play		
Standard	0.002-0.0071 in.	0.05-0.18mm
Limit	0.0098 in.	0.25mm
Flywheel		
Run-out (max.)	0.0051 in.	0.13mm
Oil Pump		
Tip clearance		
Drive gear		
Standard	0.0063-0.0083 in.	0.16-0.21mm
Limit	0.0098 in.	0.25mm
Driven gear		
Standard	0.0051-0.0071 in.	0.13-0.18mm
Limit	0.0098 in.	0.25mm
Side clearance		
Drive gear		
Standard	0.0031-0.0055 in.	0.08-0.14mm
Limit	0.0098 in.	0.25mm
Driven gear		
Standard	0.0024-0.0047 in.	0.06-0.12mm
Limit	0.0098 in.	0.25mm
Relief spring		
Free length	1.835 in.	46.6mm
Load (@1.579 in. (40.1mm))	13 ft. lbs.	61Nm

93153c05

1.8L ENGINE MECHANICAL SPECIFICATIONS

Description	English Specifications	Metric Specifications
General Information		
Engine type	4 Cylinder In-Line Overhead Camshaft	
Displacement	111.9 cubic in.	1.8L
Bore	3.19 in.	81mm
Stroke	3.50 in.	89mm
Compression ratio	9.5:1	
Firing order	1-3-4-2	
Cylinder Head		
Overall height	4.720-4.728 in.	119.9-120.1mm
Flatness (maximum)	0.008 in.	0.2mm
Camshaft		
Camshaft height		
Intake		
Standard	1.46 in.	37.11mm
Limit	1.44 in.	36.61mm
Exhaust		
Standard	1.46 in.	37.15mm
Limit	1.44 in.	36.65mm
Valves		
Valve length		
Intake		
Standard	4.337 in.	110.15mm
Limit	4.317 in.	109.65mm
Exhaust		
Standard	4.476 in.	113.70mm
Limit	4.457 in.	113.25mm
Stem outside diameter		
Intake	0.2340 in.	6.0mm
Exhaust	0.2340 in.	6.0mm
Face angle (all)	45-45.5°	
Head thickness (margin)		
Intake		
Standard	0.039 in.	1.0mm
Limit	0.020 in.	0.5mm
Exhaust		
Standard	0.051 in.	1.3mm
Limit	0.031 in.	0.8mm
Stem-to-guide clearance		
Intake		
Standard	0.0008-0.0020 in.	0.02-0.05mm
Limit	0.0039 in.	0.10mm
Exhaust		
Standard	0.0020-0.0035 in.	0.05-0.09mm
Limit	0.0059 in.	0.15mm
Valve guide		
Projection	0.551 in.	14.0mm
Inside diameter	0.234 in.	6.0mm
Valve seat		
Seat contact width	0.035-0.051 in.	0.9-1.3mm
Seat angle (all)	44-44.5°	
Valve spring		
Free length		
Intake		
Standard	2.00 in.	50.9mm
Limit	1.96 in.	49.9mm
Exhaust		
Standard	2.00 in.	50.9mm
Limit	1.96 in.	49.9mm
Load @ 1.74 in. (44.2mm)		
Intake	59 ft. lbs.	216Nm
Exhaust	59 ft. lbs.	216Nm

93153c06

1.8L ENGINE MECHANICAL SPECIFICATIONS

Description	English Specifications	Metric Specifications
Cylinder Block		
Bore		
Diameter	3.19 in.	81.0mm
Out-of-round (max.)	0.0004 in.	0.01mm
Taper(max.)	0.0004 in.	0.01mm
Overall height	10.374 in.	263.5mm
Gasket surface flatness (max.)	0.004 in.	0.1mm
Piston		
Outside diameter	3.19 in.	81.0mm
Piston pin outside diameter	0.75 in.	19.0mm
Piston pin press-in load	1,100-3,300 ft. lbs.	5,000-15,000Nm
Piston-to-cylinder clearance	0.0008-0.0016 in.	0.02-0.04mm
Piston Rings		
Side clearance		
No. 1		
Standard	0.0012-0.0028 in.	0.03-0.07mm
Limit	0.0039 in.	0.1mm
No. 2		
Standard	0.0008-0.0024 in.	0.02-0.06mm
Limit	0.0039 in.	0.1mm
End gap		
No. 1		
Standard	0.0098-0.0157 in.	0.25-0.40mm
Limit	0.031 in.	0.8mm
No. 2		
Standard	0.0157-0.0217 in.	0.40-0.55mm
Limit	0.031 in.	0.8mm
Oil		
Standard	0.0078-0.0236 in.	0.20-0.60mm
Limit	0.039 in.	1.0mm
Connecting rod		
Rod big end side clearance		
Standard	0.0039-0.0098 in.	0.10-0.25mm
Limit	0.016 in.	0.4mm
Crankshaft pin oil clearance		
Standard	0.0008-0.0020 in.	0.02-0.08mm
Limit	0.004 in.	0.1mm
Crankshaft		
Crankshaft journal outside diameter	1.97 in.	50mm
Pin outside diameter	1.77 in.	45mm
Journal oil clearance		
Standard	0.0008-0.0016 in.	0.02-0.04mm
Limit	0.004 in.	0.1mm
Out-of-round (max.)	0.0006 in.	0.015mm
Crankshaft end-play		
Standard	0.002-0.0098 in.	0.05-0.25mm
Limit	0.004 in.	0.1mm
Oil Pump		
Tip clearance		
Standard	0.0024-0.0071 in.	0.06-0.18mm
Limit	0.0138 in.	0.35mm
Side clearance		
Standard	0.0016-0.0039 in.	0.04-0.10mm
Limit	0.0079 in.	0.20mm

93153c07

1.8L ENGINE MECHANICAL SPECIFICATIONS

Description	English Specifications	Metric Specifications
Oil Pump (cont'd)		
Body clearance		
Standard	0.0039-0.0071 in.	0.10-0.18mm
Limit	0.0138 in.	0.35mm

2.0L SOHC ENGINE MECHANICAL SPECIFICATIONS

Description	English Specifications	Metric Specifications
General Information		
Engine type	4 Cylinder In-Line Overhead Camshaft	
Displacement	121.9 cubic in.	2.0L
Bore	3.35 in.	85mm
Stroke	3.46 in.	88mm
Compression ratio	8.5:1	
Firing order	1-3-4-2	
Cylinder Head		
Overall height	3.539-3.547 in.	89.9-90.1mm
Flatness (maximum)	0.008 in.	0.2mm
Camshaft		
Camshaft height		
Indentification mark D		
Intake		
Standard	1.67 in.	42.4mm
Limit	1.65 in.	41.9mm
Exhaust		
Standard	1.67 in.	42.4mm
Limit	1.65 in.	41.9mm
Indentification mark AR		
Intake		
Standard	1.75 in.	44.53mm
Limit	1.73 in.	44.03mm
Exhaust		
Standard	1.75 in.	44.53mm
Limit	1.73 in.	44.03mm
Camshaft journal outside diameter	1.34 in.	33.95mm
Valves		
Stem outside diameter		
Intake	0.315 in.	8.0mm
Exhaust	0.311 in.	7.9mm
Face angle (all)	45-45.5°	
Head thickness (margin)		
Intake		
Standard	0.047 in.	1.2mm
Limit	0.020 in.	0.5mm
Exhaust		
Standard	0.079 in.	2.0mm
Limit	0.031 in.	0.8mm
Stem-to-guide clearance		
Intake		
Standard	0.0008-0.0024 in.	0.03-0.06mm
Limit	0.0039 in.	0.10mm
Exhaust		
Standard	0.0020-0.0035 in.	0.05-0.09mm
Limit	0.0059 in.	0.15mm
Valve guide		
Inside diameter	0.315 in.	8.0mm
Outside diameter	0.516 in.	13.1mm
Valve seat		
Seat contact width	0.035-0.051 in.	0.9-1.3mm
Seat angle (all)	44-44.5°	

93153c08

2.0L DOHC (NON-TURBO) ENGINE MECHANICAL SPECIFICATIONS

Description	English Specifications	Metric Specifications
General Information		
Engine type	4 Cylinder In-Line Dual Overhead Camshaft	
Displacement	121.9 cubic in.	2.0L
Bore	3.35 in.	85mm
Stroke	3.46 in.	88mm
Compression ratio	9.8:1	
Firing order	1-3-4-2	
Cylinder Head		
Overall height	5.193-5.201 in.	131.9-132.1mm
Flatness (maximum)	0.008 in.	0.2mm
Camshaft		
Camshaft height		
Indentification mark A, D		
Intake		
Standard	1.4 in.	35.49mm
Limit	1.38 in.	34.99mm
Indentification mark B, C, E, F		
Intake		
Standard	1.39 in.	35.20mm
Limit	1.37 in.	34.70mm
Indentification mark A		
Exhaust		
Standard	1.39 in.	35.20mm
Limit	1.37 in.	34.70mm
Indentification mark C		
Exhaust		
Standard	1.4 in.	35.49mm
Limit	1.38 in.	34.99mm
Indentification mark E, F		
Exhaust		
Standard	1.37 in.	34.91mm
Limit	1.35 in.	34.41mm
Camshaft journal outside diameter	1.02 in.	25.96mm
Valves		
Stem outside diameter		
Intake	0.260 in.	6.6mm
Exhaust	0.256 in.	6.5mm
Face angle (all)	45-45.5°	
Head thickness (margin)		
Intake		
Standard	0.039 in.	1.0mm
Limit	0.020 in.	0.5mm
Exhaust		
Standard	0.059 in.	1.5mm
Limit	0.031 in.	0.8mm
Stem-to-guide clearance		
Intake		
Standard	0.0008-0.0020 in.	0.02-0.05mm
Limit	0.0039 in.	0.10mm
Exhaust		
Standard	0.0020-0.0035 in.	0.05-0.09mm
Limit	0.0059 in.	0.15mm
Valve guide		
Inside diameter	0.260 in.	6.6mm
Outside diameter	0.476 in.	12.1mm
Valve seat		
Seat contact width	0.035-0.051 in.	0.9-1.3mm
Seat angle (all)	44-44.5°	
Valve spring		
Free length		
Standard	1.90 in.	48.3mm

93153c10

2.0L SOHC ENGINE MECHANICAL SPECIFICATIONS

Description	English Specifications	Metric Specifications
Valve spring		
Free length		
Standard	1.96 in.	49.8mm
Limit	1.98 in.	49.9mm
Squareness		
Standard	2°	
Limit	4°	
Cylinder Block		
Inside diameter	3.35 in.	85mm
Out-of-round (max.)	0.008 in.	0.02mm
Taper (max.)	0.008 in.	0.02mm
Overall height	11.413-11.421 in.	289.9-290.1mm
Gasket surface flatness (max.)	0.002 in.	0.05mm
Piston		
Outside diameter	3.346 in.	84.99mm
Piston-to-cylinder clearance	0.004-0.0012 in.	0.01-0.03mm
Piston Rings		
Side clearance		
No. 1		
Standard	0.0012-0.0028 in.	0.03-0.07mm
Limit	0.004 in.	0.1mm
No. 2		
Standard	0.0008-0.0024 in.	0.02-0.06mm
Limit	0.004 in.	0.1mm
End gap		
No. 1		
Standard	0.0098-0.0157 in.	0.25-0.40mm
Limit	0.031 in.	0.8mm
No. 2		
Standard	0.0079-0.0138 in.	0.20-0.35mm
Limit	0.031 in.	0.8mm
Oil		
Standard	0.0079-0.0276 in.	0.20-0.70mm
Limit	0.039 in.	1.0mm
Connecting rod		
Rod big end side clearance		
Standard	0.0039-0.0098 in.	0.10-0.25mm
Limit	0.016 in.	0.4mm
Piston pin outside diameter	0.83 in.	21mm
Piston pin press-in load	1,653-3,858 ft. lbs.	7,500-17,500Nm
Crankshaft pin oil clearance		
Standard	0.0008-0.0020 in.	0.02-0.05mm
Limit	0.004 in.	0.1mm
Crankshaft		
Main bearing oil clearance		
Standard	0.0008-0.0020 in.	0.02-0.05mm
Limit	0.004 in.	0.1mm
Pin outside diameter	1.77 in.	45mm
Journal outside diameter	2.24 in.	57mm
Out-of-round (max.)	0.0006 in.	0.015mm
Crankshaft end-play		
Standard	0.002-0.0071 in.	0.05-0.18mm
Limit	0.0098 in.	0.25mm
Flywheel		
Run-out (max.)	0.0051 in.	0.13mm
Oil Pump		
Side clearance		
Drive gear	0.0031-0.0055 in.	0.08-0.14mm
Driven gear	0.0024-0.0047 in.	0.06-0.12mm

93153c09

2.0L DOHC (TURBO) ENGINE MECHANICAL SPECIFICATIONS

Description	English Specifications	Metric Specifications
General Information		
Engine type	4 Cylinder In-Line Dual Overhead Camshaft	2.0L
Displacement	121.9 cubic in.	
Bore	3.35 in.	85mm
Stroke	3.46 in.	88mm
Compression ratio	7.8:1	
Firing order	1-3-4-2	
Cylinder Head		
Overall height	5.193-5.201 in.	131.9-132.1mm
Flatness (maximum)	0.008 in.	0.2mm
Camshaft		
Camshaft height		
Indentification mark A, D		
Intake		
Standard	1.4 in.	35.49mm
Limit	1.38 in.	34.99mm
Indentification mark B, C, E, F		
Intake		
Standard	1.39 in.	35.20mm
Limit	1.37 in.	34.70mm
Indentification mark A		
Exhaust		
Standard	1.39 in.	35.20mm
Limit	1.37 in.	34.70mm
Indentification mark C		
Exhaust		
Standard	1.4 in.	35.49mm
Limit	1.38 in.	34.99mm
Indentification mark E, F		
Exhaust		
Standard	1.37 in.	34.91mm
Limit	1.35 in.	34.41mm
Camshaft journal outside diameter	1.02 in.	25.96mm
Valves		
Stem outside diameter		
Intake	0.260 in.	6.6mm
Exhaust	0.256 in.	6.5mm
Face angle (all)	45-45.5°	
Head thickness (margin)		
Intake		
Standard	0.039 in.	1.0mm
Limit	0.020 in.	0.5mm
Exhaust		
Standard	0.059 in.	1.5mm
Limit	0.031 in.	0.8mm
Stem-to-guide clearance		
Intake		
Standard	0.0008-0.0020 in.	0.02-0.05mm
Limit	0.0039 in.	0.10mm
Exhaust		
Standard	0.0020-0.0035 in.	0.05-0.09mm
Limit	0.0059 in.	0.15mm
Valve guide		
Inside diameter	0.260 in.	6.6mm
Outside diameter	0.476 in.	12.1mm
Valve seat		
Seat contact width	0.035-0.051 in.	0.9-1.3mm
Seat angle (all)	44-44.5°	

93153c12

2.0L DOHC (NON-TURBO) ENGINE MECHANICAL SPECIFICATIONS

Description	English Specifications	Metric Specifications
Valve spring (cont'd)		
Limit	1.98 in.	49.9mm
Squareness		
Standard		2°
Limit		4°
Cylinder Block		
Inside diameter	3.35 in.	85mm
Out-of-round (max.)	0.008 in.	0.02mm
Taper (max.)	0.008 in.	0.02mm
Overall height	11.413-11.421 in.	289.9-290.1mm
Gasket surface flatness (max.)	0.002 in.	0.05mm
Piston		
Outside diameter	3.346 in.	84.99mm
Piston-to-cylinder clearance	0.008-0.0016 in.	0.02-0.04mm
Piston Rings		
Side clearance		
No. 1		
Standard	0.0012-0.0028 in.	0.03-0.07mm
Limit	0.004 in.	0.1mm
No. 2		
Standard	0.0012-0.0028 in.	0.03-0.07mm
Limit	0.004 in.	0.1mm
End gap		
No. 1		
Standard	0.0098-0.0157 in.	0.25-0.40mm
Limit	0.031 in.	0.8mm
No. 2		
Standard	0.0177-0.0236 in.	0.45-0.60mm
Limit	0.031 in.	0.8mm
Oil		
Standard	0.0079-0.0276 in.	0.20-0.70mm
Limit	0.039 in.	1.0mm
Connecting rod		
Rod big end side clearance		
Standard	0.0039-0.0098 in.	0.10-0.25mm
Limit	0.016 in.	0.4mm
Piston pin outside diameter	0.83 in.	21mm
Piston pin press-in load	1,653-3,858 ft. lbs.	7,500-17,500Nm
Crankshaft pin oil clearance		
Standard	0.0008-0.0020 in.	0.02-0.05mm
Limit	0.004 in.	0.1mm
Crankshaft		
Main bearing oil clearance		
Standard	0.0008-0.0020 in.	0.02-0.05mm
Limit	0.004 in.	0.1mm
Pin outside diameter	1.77 in.	45mm
Journal outside diameter	2.24 in.	57mm
Out-of-round (max.)	0.0006 in.	0.015mm
Crankshaft end-play		
Standard	0.002-0.0071 in.	0.05-0.18mm
Limit	0.0098 in.	0.25mm
Flywheel		
Run-out (max.)	0.0051 in.	0.13mm
Oil Pump		
Side clearance		
Drive gear	0.0031-0.0055 in.	0.08-0.14mm
Driven gear	0.0024-0.0047 in.	0.06-0.12mm

93153c11

2.4L SOHC ENGINE MECHANICAL SPECIFICATIONS

Description	English Specifications	Metric Specifications
General Information		
Engine type	4 Cylinder In-Line Overhead Camshaft	
Displacement	143.4 cubic in.	2.4L
Bore	3.41 in.	86.5mm
Stroke	3.94 in.	100mm
Compression ratio	8.5:1	
Firing order	1-3-4-2	
Cylinder Head		
Overall height	3.539-3.547 in.	89.9-90.1mm
Flatness (maximum)	0.008 in.	0.2mm
Camshaft		
Camshaft height		
Indentification mark D		
Intake		
Standard	1.67 in.	42.4mm
Limit	1.65 in.	41.9mm
Exhaust		
Standard	1.67 in.	42.4mm
Limit	1.65 in.	41.9mm
Indentification mark AR		
Intake		
Standard	1.75 in.	44.53mm
Limit	1.73 in.	44.03mm
Exhaust		
Standard	1.75 in.	44.53mm
Limit	1.73 in.	44.03mm
Camshaft journal outside diameter	1.34 in.	33.95mm
Valves		
Stem outside diameter		
Intake	0.315 in.	8.0mm
Exhaust	0.311 in.	7.9mm
Face angle (all)	45-45.5°	
Head thickness (margin)		
Intake		
Standard	0.047 in.	1.2mm
Limit	0.020 in.	0.5mm
Exhaust		
Standard	0.079 in.	2.0mm
Limit	0.031 in.	0.8mm
Stem-to-guide clearance		
Intake		
Standard	0.0008-0.0024 in.	0.03-0.06mm
Limit	0.0039 in.	0.10mm
Exhaust		
Standard	0.0020-0.0035 in.	0.05-0.09mm
Limit	0.0059 in.	0.15mm
Valve guide		
Inside diameter	0.315 in.	8.0mm
Outside diameter	0.516 in.	13.1mm
Valve seat		
Seat contact width	0.035-0.051 in.	0.9-1.3mm
Seat angle (all)	44-44.5°	
Valve spring		
Free length		
Standard	1.96 in.	49.8mm
Limit	1.98 in.	49.9mm
Squareness		
Standard	2°	
Limit	4°	

93153c14

2.0L DOHC (TURBO) ENGINE MECHANICAL SPECIFICATIONS

Description	English Specifications	Metric Specifications
Valve spring		
Free length		
Standard	1.90 in.	48.3mm
Limit	1.98 in.	49.9mm
Squareness		
Standard	2°	
Limit	4°	
Cylinder Block		
Inside diameter	3.35 in.	85mm
Out-of-round (max.)	0.008 in.	0.02mm
Taper (max.)	0.008 in.	0.02mm
Overall height	11.413-11.421 in.	289.9-290.1mm
Gasket surface flatness (max.)	0.002 in.	0.05mm
Piston		
Outside diameter	3.334 in.	84.98mm
Piston-to-cylinder clearance	0.0012-0.0020 in.	0.03-0.05mm
Piston Rings		
Side clearance		
No. 1		
Standard	0.0012-0.0028 in.	0.03-0.07mm
Limit	0.004 in.	0.1mm
No. 2		
Standard	0.0012-0.0028 in.	0.03-0.07mm
Limit	0.004 in.	0.1mm
End gap		
No. 1		
Standard	0.0098-0.0157 in.	0.25-0.40mm
Limit	0.031 in.	0.8mm
No. 2		
Standard	0.0177-0.0236 in.	0.45-0.60mm
Limit	0.031 in.	0.8mm
Oil		
Standard	0.0079-0.0276 in.	0.20-0.70mm
Limit	0.039 in.	1.0mm
Connecting rod		
Rod big end side clearance		
Standard	0.0039-0.0098 in.	0.10-0.25mm
Limit	0.016 in.	0.4mm
Piston pin outside diameter	0.83 in.	21mm
Piston pin press-in load	1,653-3,858 ft. lbs.	7,500-17,500Nm
Crankshaft pin oil clearance		
Standard	0.0008-0.0020 in.	0.02-0.05mm
Limit	0.004 in.	0.1mm
Crankshaft		
Main bearing oil clearance		
Standard	0.0008-0.0020 in.	0.02-0.05mm
Limit	0.004 in.	0.1mm
Pin outside diameter	1.77 in.	45mm
Journal outside diameter	2.24 in.	57mm
Out-of-round (max.)	0.0006 in.	0.015mm
Crankshaft end-play		
Standard	0.002-0.0071 in.	0.05-0.18mm
Limit	0.0098 in.	0.25mm
Flywheel		
Run-out (max.)	0.0051 in.	0.13mm
Oil Pump		
Side clearance		
Drive gear	0.0031-0.0055 in.	0.08-0.14mm
Driven gear	0.0024-0.0047 in.	0.06-0.12mm

93153c13

2.4L DOHC ENGINE MECHANICAL SPECIFICATIONS

Description	English Specifications	Metric Specifications
General Information (cont'd)		
Bore	3.41 in.	86.5mm
Stroke	3.94 in.	100mm
Compression ratio	8.5:1	
Firing order	1-3-4-2	
General Information		
Engine type	4 Cylinder In-Line Dual Overhead Camshaft 2.0L	
Displacement	121.9 cubic in.	
Bore	3.35 in.	85mm
Stroke	3.46 in.	88mm
Compression ratio	9.8:1	
Firing order	1-3-4-2	
Cylinder Head		
Overall height	5.193-5.201 in.	131.9-132.1mm
Flatness (maximum)	0.008 in.	0.2mm
Camshaft		
Camshaft height		
Indentification mark A, D		
Intake		
Standard	1.4 in.	35.49mm
Limit	1.38 in.	34.99mm
Indentification mark B, C, E, F		
Intake		
Standard	1.39 in.	35.20mm
Limit	1.37 in.	34.70mm
Indentification mark A		
Exhaust		
Standard	1.39 in.	35.20mm
Limit	1.37 in.	34.70mm
Indentification mark C		
Exhaust		
Standard	1.4 in.	35.49mm
Limit	1.38 in.	34.99mm
Indentification mark E, F		
Exhaust		
Standard	1.37 in.	34.91mm
Limit	1.35 in.	34.41mm
Camshaft journal outside diameter	1.02 in.	25.96mm
Valves		
Stem outside diameter		
Intake	0.260 in.	6.6mm
Exhaust	0.256 in.	6.5mm
Face angle (all)	45-45.5°	
Head thickness (margin)		
Intake		
Standard	0.039 in.	1.0mm
Limit	0.020 in.	0.5mm
Exhaust		
Standard	0.059 in.	1.5mm
Limit	0.031 in.	0.8mm
Stem-to-guide clearance		
Intake		
Standard	0.0008-0.0020 in.	0.02-0.05mm
Limit	0.0039 in.	0.10mm
Exhaust		
Standard	0.0020-0.0035 in.	0.05-0.09mm
Limit	0.0059 in.	0.15mm
Valve guide		
Inside diameter	0.260 in.	6.6mm
Outside diameter	0.476 in.	12.1mm

93153c16

2.4L SOHC ENGINE MECHANICAL SPECIFICATIONS

Description	English Specifications	Metric Specifications
Cylinder Block		
Inside diameter	3.35 in.	85mm
Out-of-round (max.)	0.008 in.	0.02mm
Taper (max.)	0.008 in.	0.02mm
Overall height	11.413-11.421 in.	289.9-290.1mm
Gasket surface flatness (max.)	0.002 in.	0.05mm
Piston		
Outside diameter	3.346 in.	84.99mm
Piston-to-cylinder clearance	0.004-0.0012 in.	0.01-0.03mm
Piston Rings		
Side clearance		
No. 1		
Standard	0.0012-0.0028 in.	0.03-0.07mm
Limit	0.004 in.	0.1mm
No. 2		
Standard	0.0008-0.0024 in.	0.02-0.06mm
Limit	0.004 in.	0.1mm
End gap		
No. 1		
Standard	0.0098-0.0157 in.	0.25-0.40mm
Limit	0.031 in.	0.8mm
No. 2		
Standard	0.0079-0.0138 in.	0.20-0.35mm
Limit	0.031 in.	0.8mm
Oil		
Standard	0.0079-0.0276 in.	0.20-0.70mm
Limit	0.039 in.	1.0mm
Connecting rod		
Rod big end side clearance		
Standard	0.0039-0.0098 in.	0.10-0.25mm
Limit	0.016 in.	0.4mm
Piston pin outside diameter	0.83 in.	21mm
Piston pin press-in load	1,653-3,858 ft. lbs.	7,500-17,500Nm
Crankshaft pin oil clearance		
Standard	0.0008-0.0020 in.	0.02-0.05mm
Limit	0.004 in.	0.1mm
Crankshaft		
Main bearing oil clearance		
Standard	0.0008-0.0020 in.	0.02-0.05mm
Limit	0.004 in.	0.1mm
Pin outside diameter	1.77 in.	45mm
Journal outside diameter	2.24 in.	57mm
Out-of-round (max.)	0.0006 in.	0.015mm
Crankshaft end-play		
Standard	0.002-0.0071 in.	0.05-0.18mm
Limit	0.0098 in.	0.25mm
Flywheel		
Run-out (max.)	0.0051 in.	0.13mm
Oil Pump		
Side clearance		
Drive gear	0.0031-0.0055 in.	0.08-0.14mm
Driven gear	0.0024-0.0047 in.	0.06-0.12mm

2.4L DOHC ENGINE MECHANICAL SPECIFICATIONS

Description	English Specifications	Metric Specifications
General Information		
Engine type	4 Cylinder In-Line Dual Overhead Camshaft	2.4L
Displacement	143.4 cubic in.	

93153c15

2.4L DOHC ENGINE MECHANICAL SPECIFICATIONS

Description	English Specifications	Metric Specifications
Oil Pump		
Side clearance		
Drive gear	0.0031–0.0055 in.	0.08–0.14mm
Driven gear	0.0024–0.0047 in.	0.06–0.12mm

3.0L SOHC ENGINE MECHANICAL SPECIFICATIONS

Description	English Specifications	Metric Specifications
General Information		
Engine type	6 Cylinder 60° Single Overhead Camshaft	
Displacement	181.4 cubic in.	3.0L
Bore	3.59 in.	91.1mm
Stroke	2.99 in.	76mm
Compression ratio	10.0:1	
Firing order	1-2-3-4-5-6	
Cylinder Head		
Overall height	3.31 in.	84mm
Flatness (maximum)	0.008 in.	0.2mm
Camshaft		
Camshaft height		
Standard	1.62 in.	41.25mm
Limit	1.60 in.	40.75mm
Camshaft journal outside diameter	1.34 in.	33.95mm
Valves		
Stem outside diameter		
Intake	0.315 in.	8.0mm
Exhaust	0.311 in.	7.9mm
Face angle (all)	45-45.5°	
Head thickness (margin)		
Intake		
Standard	0.047 in.	1.2mm
Limit	0.028 in.	0.7mm
Exhaust		
Standard	0.079 in.	2.0mm
Limit	0.059 in.	1.5mm
Stem-to-guide clearance		
Intake		
Standard	0.0012-0.0024 in.	0.03-0.06mm
Limit	0.0039 in.	0.10mm
Exhaust		
Standard	0.0020-0.0035 in.	0.05-0.09mm
Limit	0.0059 in.	0.15mm
Valve guide		
Inside diameter	0.315 in.	8.0mm
Outside diameter	0.516 in.	13.1mm
Valve seat		
Seat contact width	0.035-0.051 in.	0.9-1.3mm
Seat angle (all)	44-44.5°	
Valve spring		
Free length		
Standard	1.96 in.	49.8mm
Limit	1.92 in.	48.8mm
Load (installed height) lbs. (Nm) at in. (mm)	72.5 lbs. @1.591 in.	329 Nm @ 40.4mm
Squareness		
Standard	2°	
Limit	4°	
Cylinder Block		
Inside diameter	3.59 in.	91.1mm
Out-of-round (max.)	0.008 in.	0.02mm

93153c18

2.4L DOHC ENGINE MECHANICAL SPECIFICATIONS

Description	English Specifications	Metric Specifications
Valve seat		
Seat contact width	0.035-0.051 in.	0.9-1.3mm
Seat angle (all)	44-44.5°	
Valve spring		
Free length		
Standard	1.90 in.	48.3mm
Limit	1.98 in.	49.9mm
Squareness		
Standard	2°	
Limit	4°	
Cylinder Block		
Inside diameter	3.35 in.	85mm
Out-of-round (max.)	0.008 in.	0.02mm
Taper (max.)	0.008 in.	0.02mm
Overall height	11.413-11.421 in.	289.9-290.1mm
Gasket surface flatness (max.)	0.002 in.	0.05mm
Piston		
Outside diameter	3.346 in.	84.99mm
Piston-to-cylinder clearance	0.009-0.0016 in.	0.02-0.04mm
Piston Rings		
Side clearance		
No. 1		
Standard	0.0012-0.0028 in.	0.03-0.07mm
Limit	0.004 in.	0.1mm
No. 2		
Standard	0.0012-0.0028 in.	0.03-0.07mm
Limit	0.004 in.	0.1mm
End gap		
No. 1		
Standard	0.0098-0.0157 in.	0.25-0.40mm
Limit	0.031 in.	0.8mm
No. 2		
Standard	0.0177-0.0236 in.	0.45-0.60mm
Limit	0.031 in.	0.8mm
Oil		
Standard	0.0079-0.0276 in.	0.20-0.70mm
Limit	0.039 in.	1.0mm
Connecting rod		
Rod big end side clearance		
Standard	0.0039-0.0098 in.	0.10-0.25mm
Limit	0.016 in.	0.4mm
Piston pin outside diameter	0.83 in.	21mm
Piston pin press-in load	1,653-3,858 ft. lbs.	7,500-17,500Nm
Crankshaft pin oil clearance		
Standard	0.0008-0.0020 in.	0.02-0.05mm
Limit	0.004 in.	0.1mm
Crankshaft		
Main bearing oil clearance		
Standard	0.0008-0.0020 in.	0.02-0.05mm
Limit	0.004 in.	0.1mm
Pin outside diameter	1.77 in.	45mm
Journal outside diameter	2.24 in.	57mm
Out-of-round (max.)	0.0006 in.	0.015mm
Crankshaft end-play		
Standard	0.002-0.0071 in.	0.05-0.18mm
Limit	0.0098 in.	0.25mm
Flywheel		
Run-out (max.)	0.0051 in.	0.13mm

93153c17

3.0L SOHC ENGINE MECHANICAL SPECIFICATIONS

Description	English Specifications	Metric Specifications
Cylinder Block (cont'd)		
Taper (max.)	0.008 in.	0.02mm
Overall height	8.28-8.29 in.	210.4-210.6mm
Gasket surface flatness (max.)	0.0039 in.	0.1mm
Piston		
Outside diameter	3.58 in.	91.1mm
Piston-to-cylinder clearance	0.008-0.0020 in.	0.02-0.04mm
Piston Rings		
Side clearance		
No. 1		
Standard	0.0012-0.0028 in.	0.03-0.07mm
Limit	0.004 in.	0.1mm
No. 2		
Standard	0.0008-0.0024 in.	0.02-0.06mm
Limit	0.004 in.	0.1mm
End gap		
No. 1		
Standard	0.0118-0.0177 in.	0.30-0.40mm
Limit	0.031 in.	0.8mm
No. 2		
Standard	0.0177-0.0236 in.	0.45-0.60mm
Limit	0.031 in.	0.8mm
Oil		
Standard	0.0079-0.0236 in.	0.20-0.60mm
Limit	0.039 in.	1.0mm
Connecting rod		
Rod big end side clearance		
Standard	0.0039-0.0098 in.	0.10-0.25mm
Limit	0.016 in.	0.4mm
Piston pin outside diameter	0.87 in.	22mm
Piston pin press-in load	1,652-3,867 ft. lbs.	7,350-17,200Nm
Crankshaft pin oil clearance		
Standard	0.0008-0.0020 in.	0.02-0.05mm
Limit	0.004 in.	0.1mm
Crankshaft		
Main bearing oil clearance		
Standard	0.0008-0.0020 in.	0.02-0.05mm
Limit	0.004 in.	0.1mm
Pin outside diameter	1.97 in.	50mm
Journal outside diameter	2.36 in.	60mm
Out-of-round (max.)	0.0006 in.	0.015mm
Crankshaft end-play		
Standard	0.002-0.0098 in.	0.05-0.25mm
Limit	0.012 in.	0.3mm
Oil Pump		
Tip clearance	0.0024-0.0071 in.	0.06-0.18mm
Side clearance	0.0016-0.0039 in.	0.04-0.10mm
Body clearance		
Standard	0.0039-0.0071 in.	0.10-0.18mm
Limit	0.0138 in.	0.35mm

3.0L DOHC ENGINE MECHANICAL SPECIFICATIONS

Description	English Specifications	Metric Specifications
General Information		
Engine type	6 Cylinder 60° Dual Overhead Camshaft	
Displacement	181.4 cubic in.	3.0L
Bore	3.59 in.	91.1mm
Stroke	2.99 in.	76mm

93153c19

3.0L DOHC ENGINE MECHANICAL SPECIFICATIONS

Description	English Specifications	Metric Specifications
General Information (cont'd)		
Compression ratio	10.0:1	
Firing order	1-2-3-4-5-6	
Cylinder Head		
Overall height	5.20 in.	132mm
Flatness (maximum)	0.008 in.	0.2mm
Camshaft		
Camshaft height		
Standard	1.37 in.	34.91mm
Limit	1.37 in.	34.91mm
Camshaft journal outside diameter	1.02 in.	25.96mm
Valves		
Stem outside diameter		
Intake	0.260 in.	6.0mm
Exhaust	0.256 in.	6.5mm
Face angle (all)	45-45.5°	
Head thickness (margin)		
Intake		
Standard	0.039 in.	1.0mm
Limit	0.019 in.	0.5mm
Exhaust		
Standard	0.059 in.	1.5mm
Limit	0.039 in.	1.0mm
Stem-to-guide clearance		
Intake		
Standard	0.0008-0.0020 in.	0.02-0.05mm
Limit	0.0039 in.	0.10mm
Exhaust		
Standard	0.0020-0.0035 in.	0.05-0.09mm
Limit	0.0059 in.	0.15mm
Valve guide		
Inside diameter	0.260 in.	6.6mm
Outside diameter	0.476 in.	12.1mm
Valve seat		
Seat contact width	0.035-0.051 in.	0.9-1.3mm
Seat angle (all)	44-44.5°	
Valve spring		
Free length		
Standard	1.78 in.	45.2mm
Limit	1.74 in.	44.2mm
Load (installed height) lbs. (Nm) at in. (mm)	52.9 lbs. @1.492 in.	240 Nm @37.9mm
Squareness		
Standard	2°	
Limit	4°	
Cylinder Block		
Inside diameter	3.66 in.	93mm
Out-of-round (max.)	0.008 in.	0.02mm
Taper (max.)	0.008 in.	0.02mm
Overall height	8.97-8.98 in.	227.9-228.1mm
Gasket surface flatness (max.)	0.0039 in.	0.1mm
Piston		
Outside diameter	3.66 in.	93mm
Piston-to-cylinder clearance	0.008-0.0020 in.	0.02-0.04mm
Piston Rings		
Side clearance		
No. 1		
Standard	0.0012-0.0028 in.	0.03-0.07mm
Limit	0.004 in.	0.1mm
No. 2		
Standard	0.0008-0.0024 in.	0.02-0.06mm
Limit	0.004 in.	0.1mm

93153c20

3.0L DOHC ENGINE MECHANICAL SPECIFICATIONS

Description	English Specifications	Metric Specifications
Piston Rings (cont'd)		
End gap		
No. 1		
Standard	0.0118-0.0177 in.	0.30-0.40mm
Limit	0.031 in.	0.8mm
No. 2		
Standard	0.0177-0.0236 in.	0.45-0.60mm
Limit	0.031 in.	0.8mm
Oil		
Standard	0.0039-0.0137 in.	0.10-0.35mm
Limit	0.039 in.	1.0mm
Connecting rod		
Rod big end side clearance		
Standard	0.0039-0.0098 in.	0.10-0.25mm
Limit	0.016 in.	0.4mm
Piston pin outside diameter	0.87 in.	22mm
Piston pin press-in load	1,652-3,867 ft. lbs.	7,350-17,200Nm
Crankshaft pin oil clearance		
Standard	0.0012-0.0020 in.	0.03-0.05mm
Limit	0.004 in.	0.1mm
Crankshaft		
Main bearing oil clearance		
Standard	0.0008-0.0020 in.	0.02-0.05mm
Limit	0.004 in.	0.1mm
Pin outside diameter	2.17 in.	55mm
Journal outside diameter	2.52 in.	64mm
Out-of-round (max.)	0.0006 in.	0.015mm
Crankshaft end-play		
Standard	0.002-0.0098 in.	0.05-0.25mm
Limit	0.012 in.	0.3mm
Oil Pump		
Tip clearance	0.0024-0.0071 in.	0.06-0.18mm
Side clearance	0.0016-0.0039 in.	0.04-0.10mm
Body clearance		
Standard	0.0039-0.0071 in.	0.10-0.18mm
Limit	0.0138 in.	0.35mm

3.5L SOHC ENGINE MECHANICAL SPECIFICATIONS

Description	English Specifications	Metric Specifications
General Information		
Engine type	6 Cylinder 60° Single Overhead Camshaft	
Displacement	213.5 cubic in.	3.5L
Bore	3.65 in.	93mm
Stroke	3.37 in.	85.8mm
Compression ratio	9.0:1	
Firing order	1-2-3-4-5-6	
Cylinder Head		
Overall height	4.72 in.	120mm
Flatness (maximum)	0.008 in.	0.2mm
Camshaft		
Camshaft height		
Intake		
Standard	1.48 in.	37.58mm
Limit	1.46 in.	37.08mm
Exhaust		
Standard	1.45 in.	36.95mm
Limit	1.44 in.	36.45mm
Camshaft journal outside diameter	1.77 in.	44.95mm

9315z21

3.5L SOHC ENGINE MECHANICAL SPECIFICATIONS

Description	English Specifications	Metric Specifications
Valves		
Stem outside diameter		
Intake	0.236 in.	6.0mm
Exhaust	0.236 in.	6.0mm
Face angle (all)	45-45.5°	
Head thickness (margin)		
Intake		
Standard	0.0039 in.	0.10mm
Limit	0.019 in.	0.5mm
Exhaust		
Standard	0.047 in.	1.2mm
Limit	0.028 in.	0.7mm
Stem-to-guide clearance		
Intake		
Standard	0.0008-0.0020 in.	0.02-0.05mm
Limit	0.0039 in.	0.10mm
Exhaust		
Standard	0.0016-0.0028 in.	0.04-0.07mm
Limit	0.0059 in.	0.15mm
Valve guide		
Inside diameter	0.315 in.	6.0mm
Outside diameter	0.433 in.	11.0mm
Valve seat		
Seat contact width	0.035-0.051 in.	0.9-1.3mm
Seat angle (all)	44-44.5°	
Valve spring		
Free length		
Standard	2.01 in.	51mm
Limit	1.97 in.	50mm
Squareness		
Standard	2°	
Limit	4°	
Cylinder Block		
Inside diameter	3.65 in.	93mm
Out-of-round (max.)	0.008 in.	0.02mm
Taper (max.)	0.008 in.	0.02mm
Overall height	8.28-8.29 in.	210.4-210.6mm
Gasket surface flatness (max.)	0.002 in.	0.05mm
Piston		
Outside diameter	3.65 in.	93mm
Piston-to-cylinder clearance	0.004-0.0012 in.	0.01-0.03mm
Piston Rings		
Side clearance		
No. 1		
Standard	0.0012-0.0028 in.	0.03-0.07mm
Limit	0.004 in.	0.1mm
No. 2		
Standard	0.0008-0.0024 in.	0.02-0.06mm
Limit	0.004 in.	0.1mm
End gap		
No. 1		
Standard	0.0118-0.0177 in.	0.30-0.45mm
Limit	0.031 in.	0.8mm
No. 2		
Standard	0.0177-0.0236 in.	0.45-0.60mm
Limit	0.031 in.	0.8mm
Oil		
Standard	0.0079-0.0236 in.	0.20-0.60mm
Limit	0.039 in.	1.0mm

9315z22

3.5L SOHC ENGINE MECHANICAL SPECIFICATIONS

Description	English Specifications	Metric Specifications
Connecting rod		
Rod big end side clearance		
Standard	0.0039-0.0098 in.	0.10-0.25mm
Limit	0.016 in.	0.4mm
Piston pin outside diameter	0.87 in.	22mm
Piston pin press-in load	Finger pressure	
Crankshaft pin oil clearance		
Standard	0.0008-0.0020 in.	0.02-0.05mm
Limit	0.004 in.	0.1mm
Crankshaft		
Main bearing oil clearance		
Standard	0.0008-0.0020 in.	0.02-0.05mm
Limit	0.004 in.	0.1mm
Pin outside diameter	1.97 in.	50mm
Journal outside diameter	2.36 in.	60mm
Out-of-round (max.)	0.0006 in.	0.015mm
Crankshaft end-play		
Standard	0.002-0.0098 in.	0.05-0.25mm
Limit	0.012 in.	0.3mm
Oil pump		
Tip clearance	0.0024-0.0071 in.	0.06-0.18mm
Side clearance	0.0016-0.0039 in.	0.04-0.10mm
Body clearance		
Standard	0.0039-0.0071 in.	0.10-0.18mm
Limit	0.0138 in.	0.35mm

93153c23

TORQUE SPECIFICATIONS

Components	English	Metric
Camshaft		
Camshaft sprocket bolt		
1.5L engine	51 ft. lbs.	70 Nm
1.6L, 1.8L, and 2.0L (SOHC and DOHC) engines	65 ft. lbs.	90 Nm
2.4L engine	58-72 ft. lbs.	80-100 Nm
3.0L (SOHC and DOHC) engine	65 ft. lbs.	90 Nm
Bearing cap retaining bolts		
2.0L SOHC engine	15 ft. lbs.	20 Nm
1.6L and 2.0L DOHC engines	21-25 ft. lbs.	29-35 Nm
2.4L engine	15 ft. lbs.	20 Nm
3.0L (SOHC and DOHC) engine	①	
3.5L engine	23 ft. lbs.	31 Nm
Crankshaft damper/pulley		
Pulley bolts		
1.5L engine	10 ft. lbs.	14 Nm
1.6L and 2.0L (SOHC and DOHC)engines	14-22 ft. lbs.	20-30 Nm
2.4L engine	18 ft. lbs.	25 Nm
Center retaining bolt		
1.5L engine	51-72 ft. lbs.	70-100 Nm
1.8L and 3.5L engines	134 ft. lbs.	185 Nm
3.0L (SOHC and DOHC) engine	108-116 ft. lbs.	150-160 Nm
Cylinder head		
Cylinder head bolts (all engines)	①	
Exhaust manifold retaing bolts/nuts		
1.5L engine	13 ft. lbs.	18 Nm
1.6L and 2.0L DOHC engines	18-22 ft. lbs.	25-30 Nm
1.8L engine	22 ft. lbs.	30 Nm
2.0L SOHC engine	11-14 ft. lbs.	15-19 Nm
2.4L engine	18-21 ft. lbs.	25-29 Nm
3.0L SOHC engine	21 ft. lbs.	29 Nm
3.0L DOHC engine	14 ft. lbs.	19 Nm
3.5L engine	21 ft. lbs.	29 Nm
Flywheel/driveplate retaining bolts		
1.5L engine	98 ft. lbs.	135 Nm
1.6L, 2.0L (SOHC and DOHC), and 2.4L engines	94-101 ft. lbs.	130-140 Nm
1.8L engine	72 ft. lbs.	100 Nm
3.0L SOHC, 3.0L DOHC, and 3.5L engines	53-56 ft. lbs.	72-76 Nm
Intake manifold retaining bolts		
1.5L engine	13 ft. lbs.	18 Nm
1.6L and 2.0L DOHC engines	11-14 ft. lbs.	15-19 Nm
1.8L engine	14 ft. lbs.	20 Nm
2.0L SOHC engine		
Plenum bolts	11-14 ft. lbs.	15-19 Nm
Manifold bolts	11-14 ft. lbs.	15-19 Nm
2.4L engine	18 ft. lbs.	25 Nm
1994 models		
Bolts	15 ft. lbs.	20 Nm
Nuts	26 ft. lbs.	35 Nm
1995-00 models		
Bolts	15 ft. lbs.	20 Nm
Nuts	15 ft. lbs.	20 Nm
3.0L SOHC, 3.0L DOHC, and 3.5L engines	①	

93153c24

TORQUE SPECIFICATIONS

Components	English	Metric
Oil pan retaining bolts		
1.5L engine	60 inch lbs.	7 Nm
1.6L and 2.0L DOHC engines	4-6 ft. lbs.	6-8 Nm
1.8L engine	60 inch lbs.	7 Nm
2.0L SOHC engine	4-6 ft. lbs.	6-8 Nm
2.4L engine	6 ft. lbs.	8 Nm
3.0L SOHC engine	48 inch lbs.	6 Nm
3.0L DOHC engine	48 inch lbs.	6 Nm
3.5L engine		
Upper oil pan	4 ft. lbs.	6 Nm
Lower oil pan	7-9 ft. lbs.	10-12 Nm
Oil Pump		
1.5L and 1.8L engines		
Pump cover	84 inch lbs.	10 Nm
Relief valve	33 ft. lbs.	45 Nm
Pump screen	14 ft. lbs.	19 Nm
1.6L, 2.0L (SOHC and DOHC), and 2.4L engines		
Oil filter bracket	14 ft. lbs.	19 Nm
Pump cover	17 ft. lbs.	24 Nm
Pump drive gear retaining bolt	27 ft. lbs.	37 Nm
Plug cap	17 ft. lbs.	24 Nm
3.0L (SOHC and DOHC) engine		
Baffle plate retaining bolts	8 ft. lbs.	11 Nm
Pump case retaining bolts	10 ft. lbs.	14 Nm
Pump cover retaining bolts	7 ft. lbs.	10 Nm
3.5L engine		
Baffle plate retaining bolts	7 ft. lbs.	10 Nm
Pump case retaining bolts	10 ft. lbs.	14 Nm
Pick-up retaining bolts	13 ft. lbs.	18 Nm
Rotor cover	7 ft. lbs.	10 Nm
Rocker arm (valve) cover retaining bolts		
1.5L engine	12-18 inch lbs.	1-2 Nm
1.6L, 1.8L, 2.0L DOHC, and 2.4L engines	24-36 inch lbs.	2-3 Nm
2.0L SOHC engine	48-60 inch lbs.	4-5 Nm
3.0L SOHC engine	7 ft. lbs.	9 Nm
3.0L DOHC engine	42-54 inch lbs.	4-5 Nm
3.5L engine	30 inch lbs.	3 Nm
Rocker arms and pushrods		
Rocker arm retaining bolts		
1.5L, 1.8L and 2.4L engines	23 ft. lbs.	32 Nm
1.6L and 2.0L DOHC engines	21-25 ft. lbs.	29-35 Nm
3.5L engine	18 ft. lbs.	25 Nm
Thermostat		
1.8L engine	16 ft. lbs.	22 Nm
1.5L, 1.6L, 2.0L DOHC, and 1990-92 2.0L SOHC engines	12-17 ft. lbs.	17-20 Nm
1993 2.0L SOHC engine	7-10 ft. lbs.	10-15 Nm
2.4L engine	10 ft. lbs.	13 Nm
3.0L SOHC, 3.0L DOHC, and 3.5L engines	12-14 ft. lbs.	17-20 Nm

93153c25

TORQUE SPECIFICATIONS

Components	English	Metric
Timing belts		
1.5L engine		
Pivot bolt	18 ft. lbs.	25 Nm
1.8L engine		
1990-94 models	14-20 ft. lbs.	20-27 Nm
1995-00 models	17 ft. lbs.	24 Nm
2.0L DOHC turbo engine		
Balance shaft tensioner pulley bolt	14 ft. lbs.	19 Nm
Timing belt tensioner pulley bolt	35 ft. lbs.	48 Nm
2.4L engine		
Balance shaft tensioner pulley bolt	15 ft. lbs.	20 Nm
Timing belt tensioner pulley bolt	35 ft. lbs.	48 Nm
3.0L SOHC engine		
Tensioner lock bolt	21 ft. lbs.	29 Nm
3.0L DOHC engine		
1992-94 models		
Tensioner lock bolt	7 ft. lbs.	10 Nm
1995-96 models		
Tensioner retaining bolts	17 ft. lbs.	24 Nm
3.5L engine	18 ft. lbs.	25 Nm
Tensioner pulley fixed bolt	35 ft. lbs.	48 Nm
Water pump		
Pump retaining bolts		
1.5L and 1.8L engines	17 ft. lbs.	24 Nm
1.6L and 2.0L (SOHC and DOHC) engines	9-11 ft. lbs.	12-15 Nm
2.4L engine		
Bolts marked with <4>	10 ft. lbs.	14 Nm
Bolts marked with <7>	18 ft. lbs.	24 Nm
3.0L SOHC, 3.0L DOHC, and 3.5L engines	17 ft. lbs.	24 Nm

① Refer to the procedure

93153c26

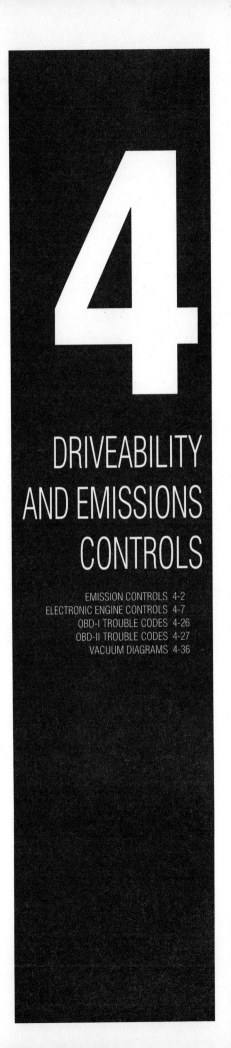

4

DRIVEABILITY AND EMISSIONS CONTROLS

EMISSION CONTROLS

Crankcase Ventilation System

OPERATION

▶ **See Figures 1, 2, and 3**

All engines are equipped with the Positive Crankcase Ventilation (PCV) system. The PCV system vents crankcase gases into the engine air intake where they are burned with the fuel and air mixture. The PCV system keeps pollutants from being released into the atmosphere. It also helps to keep the engine oil clean, by ridding the crankcase of moisture and corrosive fumes. The PCV system consists of the PCV valve, the nipple in the air intake and the connecting hoses.

Incorrect operation of the PCV system can cause multiple driveability symptoms.

A plugged valve or hose may cause:
- Rough idle
- Stalling or slow idle speed
- Oil leaks

- Sludge in engine

A leaking valve or hose would cause:
- Rough idle
- Stalling
- High idle speed

COMPONENT TESTING

▶ **See Figures 4 and 5**

1. Disconnect the ventilation hose from the PCV valve. Remove the PCV valve from the engine. Once removed, reconnect the ventilation hose to the valve.
2. Start the engine and allow to idle. Place a finger over open end of the PCV valve. Make sure intake manifold vacuum is felt on finger.
3. If vacuum is not felt, the PCV valve may be restricted.
4. Turn the engine **OFF** and remove the PCV valve from the hose.
5. Insert a thin stick into the threaded end of the PCV valve. Push on the inner plunger and inspect for movement.
6. If plunger inside the PCV valve is not free to move back and forth, the valve is clogged and will require replacement.

➡ **It is possible to clean the valve using the appropriate solvent, but replacement is recommended.**

REMOVAL & INSTALLATION

For PCV valve removal and installation, please refer to Section 1 of this manual.

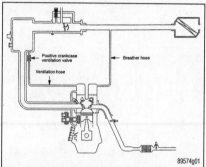

Fig. 1 Typical PCV system airflow

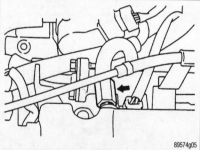

Fig. 2 The PCV valve can be found either threaded to the valve cover, . . .

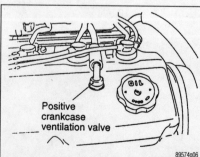

Fig. 3 . . . or mounted in a grommet on the valve cover

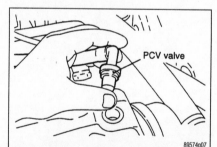

Fig. 4 With the engine idling, check the end of the PCV valve to see if vacuum is present

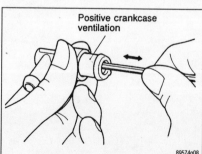

Fig. 5 Inspect the PCV valve for inner plunger movement. If the plunger is bound or sticking, replace the valve

Evaporative Emission Controls

OPERATION

▶ **See Figures 6 and 7**

Changes in atmospheric temperature cause fuel tanks to breathe, that is, the air within the tank expands and contracts with outside temperature changes. If an unsealed system was used, when the temperature rises, air would escape through the tank vent tube or the vent in the tank cap. The air which escapes contains gasoline vapors.

The Evaporative Emission Control System provides a sealed fuel system with the capability to store and condense fuel vapors. When the fuel evaporates in the fuel tank, the vapor passes through the EVAP emission valve, through vent hoses or tubes to a carbon filled evaporative canister. When the engine is operating the vapors are drawn into the intake manifold and burned during combustion.

A sealed, maintenance free evaporative canister is used. The canister is filled with granules of an activated carbon mixture. Fuel vapors entering the canister are absorbed by the charcoal granules. A vent cap is located on the top of the canister to provide fresh air to the canister when it is being purged. The vent cap opens to provide fresh air into the canister, which circulates through the charcoal, releasing trapped vapors and carrying them to the engine to be burned.

Fuel tank pressure vents fuel vapors into the canister. They are held in the canister until they can be drawn into the intake manifold. The canister purge valve allows the canister to be purged at a pre-determined time and engine operating conditions.

Vacuum to the canister is controlled by the canister purge valve. The valve is operated by the PCM. The PCM regulates the valve by switching the ground circuit on and off based on engine operating conditions. When energized, the valve prevents vacuum from reaching the canister. When not energized the valve allows vacuum to purge the vapors from the canister.

During warm up and for a specified time after hot starts, the PCM energizes (grounds) the valve preventing vacuum from reaching the canister. When the engine temperature reaches the operating level of about 120°F (49°C), the PCM removes the ground from the valve allowing vacuum to flow through the canister and purges vapors through the throttle body. During certain idle conditions, the purge valve may be grounded to control fuel mixture calibrations.

The fuel tank is sealed with a pressure-vacuum relief filler cap. The relief valve in the cap is a safety feature, preventing excessive pressure or vacuum in the fuel tank. If the cap is malfunctioning, and needs to be replaced, ensure that the replacement is the identical cap to ensure correct system operation.

OBD-II EVAP System Monitor

Some models have added system components due to the EVAP system monitor incorporated in the OBD-II engine control system. A pressure sensor is mounted on the fuel tank which measures pressure inside the tank, and a purge flow sensor measures the flow of the gases from the canister into the engine.

The PCM can store trouble codes for EVAP system performance, a list of the codes is provided later

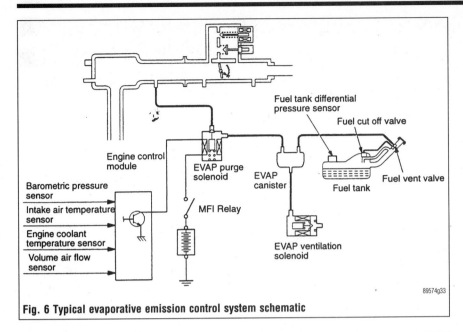

Fig. 6 Typical evaporative emission control system schematic

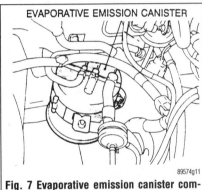

Fig. 7 Evaporative emission canister commonly used on most models

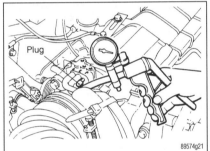

Fig. 8 To test the purge control operation, connect the vacuum hose from the throttle body to a vacuum pump

in this section. Normal testing procedures can be used, see EVAP System Component Testing in this Section.

COMPONENT TESTING

Purge Control System Check

1990–93 VEHICLES EXCEPT 1990–92 2.0L DOHC TURBO

▶ See Figure 8

1. Disconnect the red striped vacuum hose from the throttle body and connect it to a hand held vacuum pump.
2. Plug the open nipple on the throttle body.
3. Using the hand pump, apply vacuum while the engine is idling. Check that vacuum is maintained or released as outlined below:
    a. With the engine coolant at 140°F (60°C) or less—14.8 in. Hg of vacuum is maintained.
    b. With the coolant at 158°F (70°C) or higher—14.8 in. Hg of vacuum is maintained.
4. With the engine coolant at 158°F (70°C) or higher, run the engine at 3000 rpm within 3 minutes of starting vehicle. Try to apply vacuum using the hand held pump. Vacuum should leak.
5. With the engine coolant at 158°F (70°C) or higher, run the engine at 3000 rpm after 3 minutes

have elapsed after starting vehicle. Apply 14.8 in. Hg of vacuum. The vacuum should be maintained momentarily, after which it should leak.

➡ **The vacuum will leak continuously if the altitude is 7,200 ft. or higher, or the intake air temperature is 122°F (50°C) or higher.**

6. If the test results differ from the desired results, the purge control system is not operating properly.

1990–92 2.0L DOHC TURBO ENGINES

1. Disconnect the purge air hose from the intake hose and plug the air intake hose.
2. Connect a hand vacuum pump to the purge air hose.
3. Under various engine conditions, inspect the system operation:
    a. Allow the engine to cool to a temperature of 140°F (60°C) or below.
    b. Start the engine and run at idle.
    c. Using the hand pump, apply 14.8 in. Hg of vacuum. In this condition, the vacuum should be maintained.
    d. Raise the engine speed to 3000 rpm.
    e. Using the hand pump, apply 14.8 in. Hg of vacuum. In this condition, the vacuum should be maintained.
4. Run the engine until the coolant temperature reaches 158°F (70°C). Inspect system operations as follows:

a. Using the hand pump, apply 14.8 in. Hg of vacuum with the engine at idle. In this condition, vacuum should be maintained.
    b. Increase the engine speed to 3000 rpm within 3 minutes of starting the engine. Try applying vacuum. The vacuum should leak.
    c. After 3 minutes have elapsed after starting engine, raise the engine speed to 3000 rpm. Apply 14.8 in. Hg of vacuum. Vacuum should be maintained momentarily, after which it will leak.

➡ **The vacuum will leak continuously if the altitude is 7200 ft. or higher or the air temperature is 122°F (50°C) or higher.**

5. If the results of either test differs from specifications, the system is not functioning properly and will require further diagnosis.

1994–00 VEHICLES

▶ See Figure 9

➡ **This test requires the use of a special purge flow indicator tool, MB991700, or equivalent.**

1. Disconnect the purge hose from the EVAP canister, then connect Purge Flow Indicator MB991700, or equivalent between the canister and the purge hose.
2. The engine should be warmed up to operating temperature, 170–203°F. (80–95°C), with all lights, fans and accessories off. The transaxle should be in Park for automatics or Neutral for manuals.
3. Run the engine at idle for at least 3–4 minutes.
4. Check the purge flow volume when the brake is depressed suddenly a few times. The reading should be 2.5 SCFH (20cm/sec.)
5. If the volume is less than the standard value, check it again with the vacuum hose disconnected from the canister. If the purge flow volume is less than the standard, check for blockages in the vacuum port and vacuum hose, and also inspect the evaporative emission purge solenoid and purge control valve.

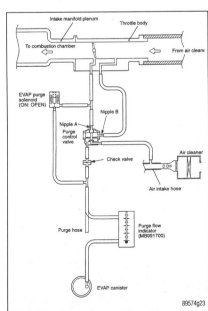

Fig. 9 Purge control system check—2.4L engine

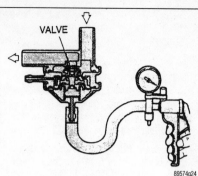

Fig. 10 Attach a hand vacuum pump to the nipple on the purge control valve

6. If the purge flow volume is at the standard value, replace the EVAP canister.

Purge Control Valve

1990–93 2.0L TURBO ENGINE

▶ See Figure 10

1. The purge control valve is located to the right side of the battery. Remove the purge control valve from the engine compartment.
2. Connect a hand vacuum pump to the vacuum nipple of the purge control valve.
3. Apply 15.7 in. Hg of vacuum and check air tightness. Blow in air lightly from the evaporative emission canister side nipple and check conditions as follows:
   • If there is no vacuum applied to the valve—air will not pass.
   • When 8.0 in. Hg of vacuum is applied to the valve—air will pass through.
4. Connect a hand vacuum pump to the positive pressure nipple of the purge control valve.
5. Apply a vacuum of 15.7 in. Hg and check for air tightness. The valve should be air tight.
6. If the results differ from the desired outcomes, replace the purge control valve.

Evaporative Emission Purge Solenoid

1990–93 VEHICLES EXCEPT 1990–92 2.0L DOHC TURBO

▶ See Figures 11, 12, and 13

1. Label and disconnect the 2 vacuum hoses from the purge control solenoid valve.
2. Detach the electrical harness connector from the solenoid.
3. Connect a hand vacuum pump to the nipple which the red striped vacuum hose was connected.
4. Check air tightness by applying a vacuum with voltage applied directly from the battery to the evaporative emission purge solenoid and without applying voltage. The desired results are as follows:
   • With battery voltage applied—vacuum should leak
   • With battery voltage not applied—vacuum should be maintained
5. Measure the resistance across the terminals of the solenoid. The desired reading is 36–44 ohms when at 68°F (20°C).
6. If any of the test results differ from the desired outcomes, replace the purge control solenoid.

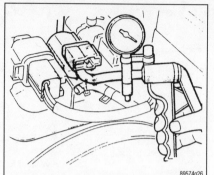

Fig. 11 Use a hand-held vacuum gauge to check for air-tightness—1990–93 2.0L non-turbo and 1993 2.0L turbo engines

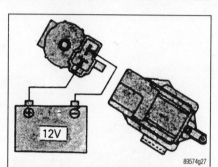

Fig. 12 Battery voltage applied to the terminals of the evaporative emission purge solenoid

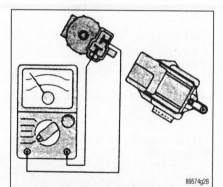

Fig. 13 Measuring the resistance between the terminals of the evaporative emission purge solenoid

1990–92 2.0L DOHC TURBO ENGINE

1. Label and disconnect the 2 vacuum hoses from the purge control solenoid valve.
2. Detach the electrical harness connector from the solenoid.
3. Connect a hand vacuum pump to the nipple which the red striped vacuum hose was connected.
4. Check air tightness by applying a vacuum with voltage applied directly from the battery to the evaporative emission purge solenoid and without applying voltage. With battery voltage applied, vacuum should be maintained. Without voltage, vacuum should leak.
5. Measure the resistance across the terminals of the solenoid. The desired reading is 36–44 ohms when at 68°F (20°C).
6. If any of the test results differ from the specifications, replace the emission purge control solenoid.

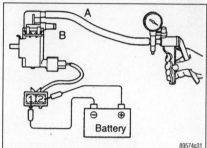

Fig. 14 Test connections for the evaporative purge solenoid—2.4L engine

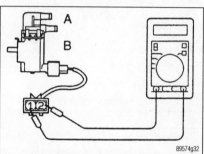

Fig. 15 Measure the resistance across the terminal of the solenoid valve—2.4L engine shown, others similar

1994–00 VEHICLES

▶ See Figures 14 and 15

1. Tag and disconnect the vacuum hoses from the solenoid valve.
2. Detach the harness connector.
3. Attach a hand-held vacuum pump to the nipple (A) of the solenoid valve, as shown in the accompanying figures.
4. Check air tightness by applying a vacuum with voltage applied directly from the battery to the evaporative emission purge solenoid and without applying voltage. The desired results are as follows:
   • With battery voltage applied—vacuum should be maintained
   • With battery voltage not applied—vacuum should leak
5. Measure the resistance across the terminals of the solenoid. The standard values are as follows:
   a. 25–44 ohms when at 68°F (20°C).
6. If any of the test results differ from the specifications, replace the emission purge control solenoid.

REMOVAL & INSTALLATION

EVAP Canister

▶ See Figure 16

1. Disconnect the negative battery cable.
2. If necessary, raise and safely support the vehicle, remove the front passenger side wheel, then remove the splash shield.
3. Tag and disconnect all necessary vacuum lines.
4. Unfasten and retaining bolts and/or straps, then remove the canister from the vehicle
5. Installation is the reverse of the removal procedure.

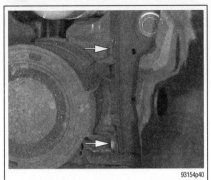

Fig. 16 Remove the canister retaining bolts and remove the canister

Solenoid Valves

▶ **See Figures 17 and 18**

1. Disconnect the negative battery cable.
2. Label and remove the vacuum and electrical harness connections from the purge control solenoid.
3. Remove the solenoid and mounting bracket from the engine compartment.
4. Installation is the reverse of the removal procedure.

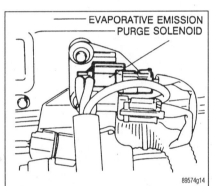

Fig. 17 Evaporative emission purge solenoid location– 2.0L DOHC engine

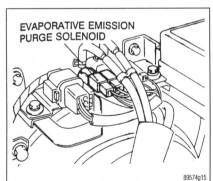

Fig. 18 Location of the evaporative emission purge solenoid—1990–93 2.0L DOHC turbo engine

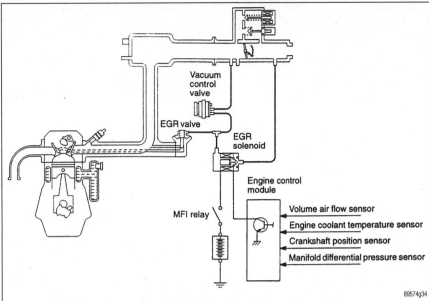

Fig. 19 Typical EGR system schematic—2.4L engine shown, others similar

Exhaust Gas Recirculation System

OPERATION

▶ **See Figure 19**

The Exhaust Gas Recirculation (EGR) system is designed to reintroduce exhaust gas into the combustion chambers, thereby lowering combustion temperatures and reducing the formation of Oxides of Nitrogen (NO_x).

The amount of exhaust gas that is reintroduced into the combustion cycle is determined by several factors, such as: engine speed, engine vacuum, exhaust system backpressure, coolant temperature, throttle position. All EGR valves are vacuum operated. The EGR vacuum diagram for your particular vehicle is displayed on the Vehicle Emission Control Information (VECI) label.

COMPONENT TESTING

EGR Valve

▶ **See Figure 20**

1. Remove the EGR valve from the vehicle. Check for sticking of plunger caused by excess carbon deposits. If such a condition exists, clean with appropriate solvent so the valve seats correctly.

2. Connect a vacuum pump to the valve and apply 20 in. Hg (67 kPa) of vacuum.
3. Check for air tightness. If the valve has 2 vacuum ports; pick one and plug the other. The vacuum must be retained.
4. For 1990–93 vehicles, blow air from 1 passage of the EGR to check condition as follows:
    a. With 1.8 in. Hg (6 kPa) of vacuum or less applied to the valve, air should not pass through the valve.
    b. With 8.5 in. Hg (28.7 kPa) of vacuum or more applied to the valve, air should pass through the valve.
5. For 1994–00 vehicles, apply vacuum (specified below) and check the passage of air by blowing through either side of the EGR passages, as follows:
    a. With 1.6 in. Hg or less of vacuum applied to the valve, air should blow out of the opposite passage.
    b. With 8.7 in. Hg or more of vacuum applies to the valve, air should not blow out of the opposite passage.
6. If the results are not as described, replace the EGR valve.

EGR Temperature Sensor

▶ **See Figure 21**

The EGR temperature sensor is used on California vehicles only. The EGR temperature sensor detects

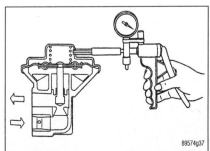

Fig. 20 Use a vacuum pump to test the EGR

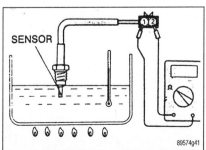

Fig. 21 Put the EGR temperature sensor in a container of water, then measure resistance as the water temperature is increased

the temperature of the gas passing through the EGR control valve. It converts the detected temperature into an electrical voltage signal which is sent the vehicle's Powertrain Control Module (PCM). If the circuit of the EGR temperature sensor is broken, the warning light will come on.

1. Remove the EGR temperature sensor from the engine.

2. Place the EGR sensor into water. While increasing the temperature of the water, measure the sensor resistance. Compare the values to following specifications:

    a. 122°F (50°C)—60–83 kohms resistance
    b. 212°F (100°C)—11–14 kohms resistance

3. If the resistance obtained varies significantly from specifications, replace the sensor.

Thermal Vacuum Valve

▶ See Figure 22

1. Label and disconnect the vacuum hose at the thermo valve.

2. Connect a hand held vacuum pump to the vacuum hose on the thermo valve.

3. Apply vacuum and check the air passage through the thermo valve. Compare results to the following specifications:

    a. Engine coolant temperature of 122°F (50°C) or less—vacuum leaks
    b. Engine coolant temperature of 176°F (80°C) or more—vacuum is maintained

4. If the results differ from the desired specifications, replace the valve.

EGR Port Vacuum Check

▶ See Figure 23

1. Disconnect the vacuum hose from the throttle body EGR vacuum nipple. Connect a hand-held vacuum pump to the nipple.

2. Start the engine, then slowly raise the speed and compare with the following specifications.

    a. For 1990–93 vehicles, check to be sure the vacuum raised proportionally with the rise in engine speed.
    b. For 1994–00 vehicles, the vacuum reading on the pump should remain constant.

EGR Solenoid

1990–93 VEHICLES

▶ See Figures 24 and 25

1. Label and disconnect the yellow and green striped vacuum hose from the EGR solenoid.

2. Detach the electrical harness connector.

3. Connect a hand vacuum pump to the nipple to which the green-striped vacuum hose was connected.

4. Apply vacuum and check for air-tightness when voltage is applied and discontinued. When voltage is applied, the vacuum should be maintained. When voltage is discontinued, vacuum should leak.

5. Measure the resistance between the terminals of the solenoid valve. The resistance should be 36–44 ohms at 68°F (20°C).

6. If the test results differ from the specifications, replace the EGR solenoid.

1994–00 VEHICLES

▶ See Figure 26

➡Before disconnecting the vacuum hoses, tag them to assure proper connection during installation

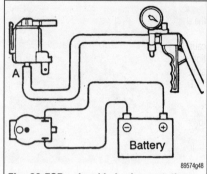

Fig. 26 EGR solenoid check connections—2.4L engine

1. Tag and disconnect the vacuum hose (2.0L turbo engine: yellow stripe, white and green stripe, 2.4L engine: yellow stripe and white stripe) from the solenoid valve.

2. Detach the harness connector.

3. Connect a hand-held vacuum pump to the A nipple.

4. Check air tightness by applying vacuum with voltage applied directly from the battery to the EGR control solenoid valve and without applying voltage.

5. For the 2.4L engines, compare with the following:

    a. With battery voltage not applied, vacuum should be maintained.
    b. With battery voltage applied, vacuum should leak.

6. Using an ohmmeter, measure the resistance between the solenoid valve terminals. The resistance should fall between 36–44 ohms when the engine temperature is 68°F (20°C).

REMOVAL & INSTALLATION

EGR Valve

▶ See Figure 27

1. Disconnect the negative battery cable.

2. Remove the air cleaner and intake hoses as required.

3. If necessary, detach the EGR temperature sensor connector.

4. Tag and disconnect the vacuum hose from the EGR valve.

5. Remove the mounting bolts and the EGR valve from the engine.

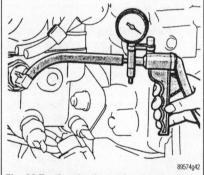

Fig. 22 Testing the thermal vacuum valve—2.0L engine (Federal) shown, others similar

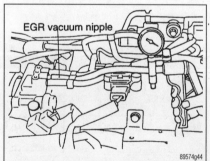

Fig. 23 Location of the throttle body EGR valve vacuum nipple—2.4L engine shown

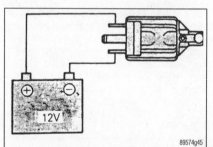

Fig. 24 Apply voltage to the EGR solenoid using jumper wires and check for air-tightness using a vacuum pump

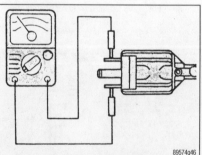

Fig. 25 Measure the resistance between the terminals of the EGR solenoid

Fig. 27 The EGR valve is retained to the intake manifold with two bolts—2.4L engine

6. Clean the mating surfaces on the valve and the engine. Make sure to remove all gasket material.

7. Inspect the valve for a sticking plunger, caused by excess carbon deposits. If such a condition exists, clean with appropriate solvent so valve seats correctly.

To install:

8. Install EGR valve with a new gasket in place.

9. Install the mounting bolts and tighten as follows:

- 1.5L, 1.6L, and 1.8L engines—7–10 ft. lbs. (10—15 Nm)
- 2.0L engines—10–15 ft. lbs. (15—22 Nm)
- 2.4L and 3.5L engines—16 ft. lbs. (22 Nm)
- 3.0L engines—8 ft. lbs. (11 Nm)

10. Connect the vacuum hose to the EGR valve.

11. If detached, attach the EGR temperature sensor.

12. Install the air cleaner and air intake hoses as required.

13. Connect the negative battery cable.

EGR Temperature Sensor

1. Disconnect the negative battery cable.

2. Detach the electrical connector from the sensor.

3. Remove the sensor from the engine.

To install:

4. Install the sensor to the engine and tighten to 8 ft. lbs. (12 Nm).

5. Attach the electrical connector to the sensor.

6. Connect the negative battery cable.

Thermal Vacuum Valve

1. Disconnect the negative battery cable.

2. Detach the vacuum line from the thermo valve.

3. Using a wrench, remove the valve from the engine.

➡When removing or installing the valve, do not allow wrenches or other tool to contact the resin part of the valve. Damage to the valve may occur.

4. Inspect the vacuum hose for cracks and replace as required.

To install:

5. Apply sealant to the threads of the thermo valve and install into the engine.

6. Tighten the valve to 15–30 ft. lbs. (20–40 Nm). When installing the valve, do not allow the wrench to come in contact with the resin part of the valve.

7. Attach the vacuum hose to the valve.

8. Connect the negative battery cable.

EGR Solenoid

▶ **See Figures 28, 29, 30, 31, and 32**

1. Disconnect the negative battery cable.

2. Label and disconnect the vacuum hoses from the EGR solenoid.

3. Disconnect the electrical harness from the solenoid.

4. Remove the solenoid from the mounting bracket and replace as required.

To install:

5. Install the solenoid to the mounting bracket and secure in position.

6. Attach the electrical connector.

7. Connect the vacuum hoses to the solenoid making sure they are installed in their original location.

8. Connect the negative battery cable.

Fig. 28 Location of the EGR solenoid—2.4L Galant shown

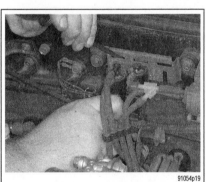

Fig. 29 Release the retaining tab and remove the solenoid from the retaining bracket

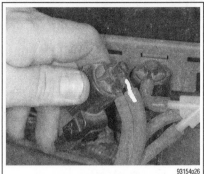

Fig. 30 Matchmark the hoses on the solenoid . . .

Fig. 31 . . . then disconnect the hoses from the solenoid

Fig. 32 Detach the electrical connector and remove the solenoid from the vehicle

ELECTRONIC ENGINE CONTROLS

Engine Control Unit/Powertrain Control Module (ECU/PCM)

OPERATION

The Engine Control Unit/Powertrain Control Module (ECU/PCM) performs many functions on your vehicle. The module accepts information from various engine sensors and computes the required fuel flow rate necessary to maintain the correct amount of air/fuel ratio throughout the entire engine operational range.

Based on the information that is received and programmed into the PCM's memory, the PCM generates output signals to control relays, actuators and solenoids. The PCM also sends out a command to the fuel injectors that meters the appropriate quantity of fuel. The module automatically senses and compensates for any changes in altitude when driving your vehicle.

REMOVAL & INSTALLATION

✷✷ WARNING

A grounded wrist strap should be used to prevent static discharge to the PCM. Static discharge can easily destroy the electronic components inside the PCM.

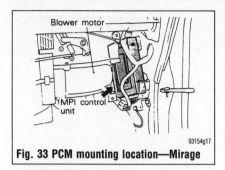

Fig. 33 PCM mounting location—Mirage

Mirage and 1999–00 Galant

♦ See Figure 33

➡ **The Powertrain Control Module (PCM) is located above the passenger side kickpanel.**

1. Disconnect the negative battery cable.
2. Remove the glove box, right side kickpanel and lower panel assemblies.
3. Unplug the connectors and remove fasteners. Remove the PCM.
4. Installation is the reverse of the removal procedure.

1994–98 Galant

♦ See Figure 34

1. Disconnect negative battery cable.
2. Remove both center console side panels.
3. Unplug the wiring connector and remove the mounting hardware. Slide the PCM out the side.
4. Installation is the reverse of the removal procedure.

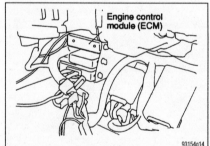

Fig. 34 PCM mounting location—1994–98 Galant

Diamante and 1990–93 Galant

♦ See Figures 35 and 36

➡ **The Powertrain Control Module (PCM) is located behind the glove box assembly.**

1. If equipped, disarm the air bag system.
2. Remove the passenger side lower instrument panel and shower duct.
3. Remove the glove box striker, glove box, glove box outer casing and the screw below the assembly.
4. Unplug wiring connector and remove mounting hardware. Slide out the PCM.

To install:

5. Install the PCM with the mounting hardware.
6. Attach the wire connector.
7. Install the glove box striker, the glove box, glove box casing and the screw below the assembly.

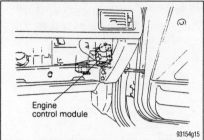

Fig. 35 PCM mounting location—1990–93 Galant

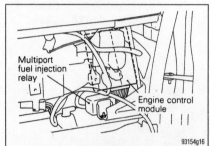

Fig. 36 PCM mounting location—Diamante

8. Install the passenger side lower instrument panel and the shower duct.
9. Reconnect the negative battery cable.

Oxygen Sensor

OPERATION

The Oxygen (O2) sensor is a device which produces an electrical voltage when exposed to the oxygen present in the exhaust gases. The sensor is mounted in the exhaust system, usually in the manifold or a boss located on the down pipe before the catalyst. The oxygen sensors used on some models are electrically heated internally for faster switching when the engine is started cold. The oxygen sensor produces a voltage within 0 and 1 volt. When there is a large amount of oxygen present (lean mixture), the sensor produces a low voltage (less than 0.4v). When there is a lesser amount present (rich mixture) it produces a higher voltage (0.6–1.0v). The stoichiometric or correct fuel to air ratio will read between 0.4 and 0.6v. By monitoring the oxygen content and converting it to electrical voltage, the sensor acts as a rich-lean switch. The voltage is transmitted to the PCM.

Some models have two sensors, one before the catalyst and one after. This is done for a catalyst efficiency monitor that is a part of the OBD-II engine controls. The one before the catalyst measures the exhaust emissions right out of the engine, and sends the signal to the PCM about the state of the mixture as previously talked about. The second sensor reports the difference in the emissions after the exhaust gases have gone through the catalyst. This sensor reports to the PCM the amount of emissions reduction the catalyst is performing.

The oxygen sensor will not work until a predetermined temperature is reached, until this time the PCM is running in what as known as OPEN LOOP operation. OPEN LOOP means that the PCM has not yet begun to correct the air-to-fuel ratio by reading

the oxygen sensor. After the engine comes to operating temperature, the PCM will monitor the oxygen sensor and correct the air/fuel ratio from the sensor's readings. This is what is known as CLOSED LOOP operation.

A Heated Oxygen Sensor (HO2S) has a heating element that keeps the sensor at proper operating temperature during all operating modes. Maintaining correct sensor temperature at all times allows the system to enter into CLOSED LOOP operation sooner.

In CLOSED LOOP operation, the PCM monitors the sensor input (along with other inputs) and adjusts the injector pulse width accordingly. During OPEN LOOP operation, the PCM ignores the sensor input and adjusts the injector pulse to a preprogrammed value based on other inputs.

TESTING

♦ See Figure 37

Fig. 37 The HO2S can be monitored with an appropriate and Data-stream capable scan tool

> ※※ **WARNING**
>
> **Do not pierce the wires when testing this sensor; this can lead to wiring harness damage. Backprobe the connector to properly read the voltage of the HO2S.**

1. Disconnect the HO2S.
2. Measure the resistance between PWR and GND terminals of the sensor. Resistance should be approximately 6 ohms at 68°F (20°C). If resistance is not within specification, the sensor's heater element is faulty.
3. With the HO2S connected and engine running, measure the voltage with a Digital Volt-Ohmmeter (DVOM) between terminals **HO2S** and **SIG RTN** (GND) of the oxygen sensor connector. Voltage should fluctuate between 0.01–1.0 volts. If voltage fluctuation is slow or voltage is not within specification, the sensor may be faulty.

REMOVAL & INSTALLATION

♦ See Figures 38, 39, 40, 41, and 42

1. Disconnect the negative battery cable.
2. Raise and support the vehicle safely.

Fig. 38 Detach the connector from the oxygen sensor

Fig. 39 A special socket is available to remove the oxygen sensor. The socket contains a slot that the wire slides out of

Fig. 40 Use the tool to loosen the sensor . . .

Fig. 41 . . . then remove the sensor from the exhaust manifold/pipe

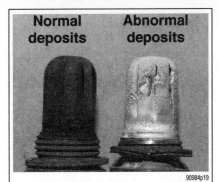

Fig. 42 Inspect the oxygen sensor tip for abnormal deposits

3. Label and disconnect the HO2S from the engine control wiring harness.

➡**Lubricate the sensor with penetrating oil prior to removal.**

4. Remove the sensor using an oxygen sensor wrench or another suitable tool.

To install:

5. Install the sensor in the mounting boss and tighten to 27–33 ft. lbs. (37–45 Nm).

6. Connect the engine control wiring harness to the sensor.

7. Lower the vehicle.

8. Connect the negative battery cable.

Idle Air Control Motor

OPERATION

The Idle Air Control (IAC) motor is a DC stepper motor controlled by the PCM. The IAC contains a built-in position sensor which detects the amount of opening of the motor. The position sensor outputs a pulse signal that the PCM receives and uses to adjust the motor to properly maintain the correct idle speed of the engine.

TESTING

▶ **See Figure 43**

Place a stethoscope (a long screwdriver works also, just place the screwdriver on the IAC and place your ear on or near the handle) on the IAC motor. Have an assistant turn the key **ON** with the engine **OFF**, and listen to the IAC motor. Several clicks should be heard as the stepper motor moves. If the clicks are heard, the driver in the PCM and the circuit are OK.

If the driver and circuits test OK, detach the connector from IAC motor. Using an ohmmeter, probe the connector on the IAC motor, NOT THE WIRING HARNESS> between pins **2** and **1**, and pins **2** and **3**. Resistance should measure between 28–33 ohms. If the resistance values are different replace the IAC motor. If the tests between pins **1**, **2**, and **3** are within specification, check the resistance between pins **5** and **4**, and pins **5** and **6**. Resistance should measure between 28–33 ohms. If the resistance values are different replace the IAC motor.

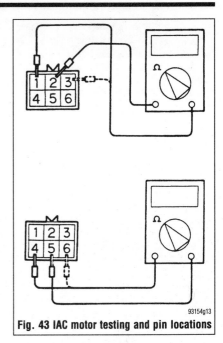

Fig. 43 IAC motor testing and pin locations

REMOVAL & INSTALLATION

▶ **See Figure 44**

1. Disconnect the negative battery cable.

2. Remove the air cleaner intake hose.

3. Remove any necessary hoses from the IAC motor.

4. Detach the electrical connectors from the IAC motor.

5. Remove the retaining bolts and remove the IAC from the throttle body.

6. The installation is the reverse of removal. Replace the IAC gasket.

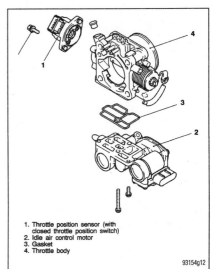

1. Throttle position sensor (with closed throttle position switch)
2. Idle air control motor
3. Gasket
4. Throttle body

Fig. 44 The IAC motor is usually mounted on the throttle body

Engine Coolant Temperature SENSOR

OPERATION

The Engine Coolant Temperature (ECT) sensor resistance changes in response to engine coolant temperature. The sensor resistance decreases as the coolant temperature increases, and increases as the coolant temperature decreases. This provides a reference signal to the PCM, which indicates engine coolant temperature. The signal sent to the PCM by the ECT sensor helps the PCM to determine spark advance, EGR flow rate, air/fuel ratio, and engine temperature. The ECT is a two wire sensor, a 5-volt reference signal is sent to the sensor and the signal return is based upon the change in the measured resistance due to temperature.

TESTING

▶ See Figures 45, 46, 47, and 48

1. Drain the engine coolant to a level below the intake manifold.
2. Disconnect the sensor wiring harness and remove the coolant temperature sensor from the engine.
3. Place the temperature sensing portion of the sensor into a pan of hot water. Use a thermometer to monitor the water temperature.
4. Measure the resistance across the sensor terminals while the sensor is in the water. Compare obtained reading to specifications:

Fig. 45 Unplug the ECT sensor electrical connector

Fig. 46 Test the resistance of the ECT sensor across the two sensor pins

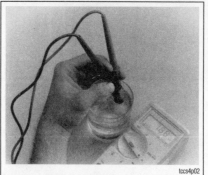

Fig. 47 Another method of testing the ECT is to submerge it in cold or hot water and check resistance

Fig. 48 The ECT can be monitored with an appropriate and Data-stream capable scan tool

    a. Water temperature of 32°F (0°C)—5.1–6.5 kilo-ohms present
    b. Water temperature of 68°F (20°C)— 2.1–2.7 kilo-ohms present
    c. Water temperature of 104°F (40°C)— 0.9–1.3 kilo-ohms present
    d. Water temperature of 176°F (80°C)— 0.26–0.36 kilo-ohms present
5. If the resistance differs greatly from standard value, replace the sensor.

REMOVAL & INSTALLATION

▶ See Figures 49, 50, 51, and 52

1. Disconnect the negative battery cable.

Fig. 49 Unplug the ECT sensor electrical connector

Fig. 50 Use a deep socket and an extension to reach the ECT sensor . . .

Fig. 51 . . . then remove the ECT sensor from the thermostat housing

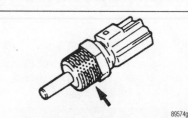

Fig. 52 Before installation, coat the threads of the sensor with a suitable sealant

2. Drain the engine coolant to a level below the intake manifold.
3. Unplug the sensor wiring harness.
4. Unthread and remove the sensor from the engine.
To install:
5. Coat the threads of the sensor with a suitable sealant and thread into the housing.
6. Tighten the sensor to 22 ft. lbs. (30 Nm).
7. Refill the cooling system to the proper level.
8. Attach the electrical connector to the sensor securely.
9. Connect the negative battery cable.

Intake Air Temperature Sensor

OPERATION

▶ See Figure 53

The Intake Air Temperature (IAT) sensor determines the air temperature entering the intake mani-

Fig. 53 The IAT sensor tip is visible when looking into the MAF sensor

fold. Resistance changes in response to the ambient air temperature. The sensor has a negative temperature coefficient. As the temperature of the sensor rises the resistance across the sensor decreases. This provides a signal to the PCM indicating the temperature of the incoming air charge. This sensor helps the PCM to determine spark timing and air/fuel ratio. Information from this sensor is added to the pressure sensor information to calculate the air mass being sent to the cylinders. The IAT receives a 5-volt reference signal and the signal return is based upon the change in the measured resistance due to temperature.

TESTING

▶ **See Figures 54, 55, 56, 57, and 58**

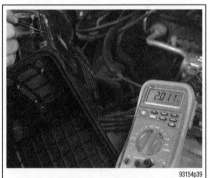

Fig. 54 Testing the resistance of the IAT sensor across the two sensor pins

Fig. 55 The IAT sensor can be monitored with an appropriate and Data-stream capable scan tool

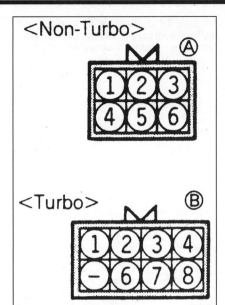

Fig. 56 IAT sensor terminal identification— 1990–93 Galant

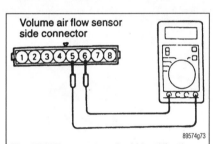

Fig. 57 IAT sensor terminal identification— 2.4L engines

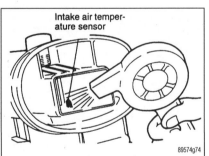

Fig. 58 Measure the intake air temperature sensor resistance while heating it with a hair drier

1. Detach the air flow sensor electrical connector.
2. Measure the resistance between terminals No. 4 and No. 6 of the electrical connector, except on the 2.0L DOHC turbo engine.
3. If equipped with the 2.0L DOHC turbo engine, measure the resistance between terminals No. 6 and No. 8 of the sensor electric connector.
4. Compare test readings to the following specifications:
   a. Sensor temperature of 32°F (0°C)— 5.3–6.7 kilo-ohms

   b. Sensor temperature of 68°F (20°C)— 2.3–3.0 kilo-ohms
   c. Sensor temperature of 176°F (80°C)— 0.30–0.42 kilo-ohms
5. Measure the sensor resistance while heating the sensor area with a hair dryer. As the temperature of the sensor increases, sensor resistance should become smaller.
6. If the measured resistance deviates from the standard value or the resistance remains unchanged, replace the air flow sensor assembly.

REMOVAL & INSTALLATION

The IAT sensor is part of the Mass Air Flow (MAF) sensor. The IAT sensor cannot be replaced separately. Refer to MAF sensor removal and installation in this section.

Mass Air Flow Sensor

OPERATION

The Mass Air Flow (MAF) sensor directly measures the mass of air being drawn into the engine. The sensor output is used to calculate injector pulse width. The MAF sensor is what is referred to as a "hot-wire sensor". The sensor uses a thin platinum wire filament, wound on a ceramic bobbin and coated with glass, that is heated to 417°F (200°C) above the ambient air temperature and subjected to the intake airflow stream. A "cold-wire" is used inside the MAF sensor to determine the ambient air temperature.

Battery voltage, a reference signal, and a ground signal from the PCM are supplied to the MAF sensor. The sensor returns a signal proportionate to the current flow required to keep the "hot-wire" at the required temperature. The increased airflow across the "hot-wire" acts as a cooling fan, lowering the resistance and requiring more current to maintain the temperature of the wire. The increased current is measured by the voltage in the circuit, as current increases, voltage increases. As the airflow increases the signal return voltage of a normally operating MAF sensor will increase.

TESTING

1. Using a multimeter, check for voltage by back-probing the MAF sensor connector.
2. With the ignition key **ON**, and the engine **OFF**, verify that there is at least 10.5 volts between the BATT and GND terminals of the MAF sensor connector. If voltage is not within specification, check power and ground circuits and repair as necessary.
3. With the ignition key **ON**, and the engine **ON**, verify that there is at least 4.5 volts between the SIG and GND terminals of the MAF sensor connector. If voltage is not within specification, check power and ground circuits and repair as necessary.
4. With the ignition key **ON**, and the engine **ON**, check voltage between GND and SIG RTN terminals. Voltage should be approximately 0.34–1.96 volts. If voltage is not within specification, the sensor may be faulty.

REMOVAL & INSTALLATION

▶ **See Figures 59 thru 67**

1. Disconnect the negative battery cable.
2. Release the retaining clips from the air cleaner housing.
3. Loosen the clamp on the air outlet tube at the throttle body.
4. Remove the breather hose and detach the connector from the MAF sensor.
5. Remove the air outlet tube and upper housing from the lower housing.
6. Loosen the hose clamp and slide the outlet hose off of the MAF sensor.
7. Remove the four sensor-to-air cleaner housing retaining nuts.
8. Remove the sensor from the air cleaner upper housing.

➡**Handle the sensor assembly carefully, protecting it from impact, extremes of temperature and/or exposure to shop chemicals.**

9. Installation is the reverse of the removal procedure.

Manifold Absolute Pressure Sensor

OPERATION

The most important information for measuring engine fuel requirements comes from the Manifold Absolute Pressure (MAP) sensor. Using the pressure and temperature data, the PCM calculates the intake air mass. It is connected to the engine intake manifold and takes readings of the absolute pressure.

Atmospheric pressure is measured both when the engine is started and when driving fully loaded, then the pressure sensor information is adjusted accordingly.

TESTING

1. Using a multimeter, check for voltage by back-probing the MAP sensor connector.
2. With the key **ON**, and the engine **OFF**, verify that there is at least 4.8 volts between the SIG and GND terminals of the MAP sensor connector. If voltage is not within specification, check power and ground circuits and repair as necessary.
3. With the key **ON**, and the engine **ON**, check the voltage between GND and SIG RTN terminals. Voltage should be approximately between 0.8 and 2.4 volts. If voltage is not within specification, the sensor may be faulty.

Fig. 59 Release the retaining clips from the air cleaner housing

Fig. 60 Unplug the MAF sensor connector

Fig. 61 Detach the breather hose from the air inlet tube

Fig. 62 Loosen the clamp on the air outlet tube at the throttle body . . .

Fig. 63 . . . then remove the air outlet tube and upper housing from the lower housing

Fig. 64 Loosen the hose clamp retaining screw . . .

Fig. 65 . . . then slide the outlet hose off of the MAF sensor

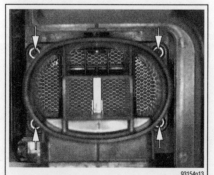
Fig. 66 Remove the four sensor-to-air cleaner housing retaining nuts . . .

Fig. 67 . . . then remove the MAF sensor from the air cleaner cover

4. If the voltage check in step 3 was **OK**, then check the voltage between GND and SIG RTN terminals and suddenly depress the accelerator, the voltage should rise and stay at 2.4 volts. If the voltage does not stay at 2.4 volts, replace the MAP sensor.

REMOVAL & INSTALLATION

▶ **See Figures 68, 69, and 70**

1. Disconnect the negative battery cable.
2. Detach the connector for the MAP sensor.
3. Remove the sensor mounting screws.
4. Lift the sensor up and remove it from the intake manifold.
5. The installation is the reverse of removal.

Fig. 68 Detach the electrical connector from the MAP sensor

Fig. 69 Remove the two MAP sensor retaining bolts . . .

Fig. 70 . . . then remove the sensor from the intake manifold. Inspect the tip of the sensor and replace if damaged or plugged

Throttle Position Sensor

OPERATION

The Throttle Position (TP) sensor is a potentiometer that provides a signal to the PCM that is directly proportional to the throttle plate position. The TP sensor is mounted on the side of the throttle body and is connected to the throttle plate shaft. The TP sensor monitors throttle plate movement and position, and transmits an appropriate electrical signal to the PCM. These signals are used by the PCM to adjust the air/fuel mixture, spark timing and EGR operation according to engine load at idle, part throttle, or full throttle. The TP sensor is not adjustable.

The TP sensor receives a 5 volt reference signal and a ground circuit from the PCM. A return signal circuit is connected to a wiper that runs on a resistor internally on the sensor. The further the throttle is opened, the wiper moves along the resistor, at wide open throttle, the wiper essentially creates a loop between the reference signal and the signal return returning the full or nearly full 5 volt signal back to the PCM. At idle, the signal return should be approximately 0.9 volts.

TESTING

▶ **See Figures 71, 72, 73, and 74**

1. With the engine **OFF** and the ignition **ON**, check the voltage at the signal return circuit of the TP sensor by carefully backprobing the connector using a DVOM.

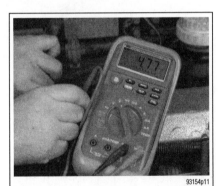

Fig. 71 Testing the SIG circuit to the TP sensor

Fig. 72 Testing the SIG RTN circuit of the TP sensor

Fig. 73 Testing the operation of the potentiometer inside the TP sensor while slowly opening the throttle

Fig. 74 The TP sensor can be monitored with an appropriate and Data-stream capable scan tool

2. Voltage should be between 0.2 and 1.4 volts at idle.
3. Slowly move the throttle pulley to the Wide Open Throttle (WOT) position and watch the voltage on the DVOM. The voltage should slowly rise to slightly less than 4.8 volts at WOT.
4. If no voltage is present, check the wiring harness for supply voltage (5.0 volts) and ground (0.3 volts or less), by referring to your corresponding wiring guide. If supply voltage and ground are present, but no output voltage from TP, replace the TP sensor. If supply voltage and ground do not meet specifications, make necessary repairs to the harness or PCM.

REMOVAL & INSTALLATION

▶ **See Figures 75 and 76**

1. Disconnect the negative battery cable.
2. Disconnect the wiring harness from the TP sensor.
3. Remove the two sensor mounting screws, then pull the TP sensor off of the throttle shaft:
   To install:
4. Carefully slide the rotary tangs on the sensor into position over the throttle shaft, then rotate the sensor clockwise to the installed position.

Fig. 75 Unplug the TP sensor connector

93154p06

Fig. 76 The TP sensor is secured with two retaining bolts

93154p23

✳✳ CAUTION

Failure to install the TP sensor in this manner may result in sensor damage or high idle speeds.

➡ The TP sensor is not adjustable.

5. Install and tighten the sensor mounting screws.
6. Connect the wiring harness to the sensor.
7. Connect the negative battery cable.

Camshaft Position Sensor

OPERATION

The computer control module uses the Camshaft Position (CMP) sensor to determine the position of the No. 1 piston during its power stroke. This signal is used by the computer control module to calculate fuel injection mode of operation.

If the cam signal is lost while the engine is running, the fuel injection system will shift to a calculated fuel injected mode based on the last fuel injection pulse, and the engine will continue to run.

TESTING

This sensor produces an A/C voltage signal based on information gathered while the engine is running. Testing the CMP sensor requires several special tools that are very expensive to purchase. Due to this fact, we at Chilton have determined testing this sen-

sor to be beyond the scope of the do-it-yourself mechanic. The sensor can be monitored with an appropriate scan tool using a data display or other data stream information. Follow the instructions included with the scan tool for information on accessing the data.

REMOVAL & INSTALLATION

1.6L, 2.0L DOHC and 1997–00 1.8L Engines

1. Disconnect the negative battery cable.
2. Detach the electrical throttle body stay.
3. Remove the sensor retaining screws.
4. Remove the sensor assembly from the engine.

To install:

5. Install the sensor in the opening in the engine and tighten the sensor retaining screws.
6. Install the throttle body stay.
7. Attach the electrical connector to the sensor.
8. Connect the negative battery cable.

1.5L, 2.4L, 3.0L SOHC, 3.5L, and 1993–96 1.8L Engines

▶ See Figure 77

The camshaft position sensor on these engines is located in the distributor. Refer to the distributor removal and installation procedure in Section 2.

3.0L DOHC Engine

▶ See Figure 78

1. Disconnect the negative battery cable.
2. Remove the timing belt, as outlined in Section 3 of this manual.
3. Unplug the sensor connector.
4. Unfasten the retaining bolts, then remove the sensor from the vehicle.
5. Installation is the reverse of the removal procedure.

Crankshaft Position Sensor/Crank Angle Sensor

OPERATION

The Crankshaft Position (CKP) sensor (also referred to as the crank angle sensor) senses the crank angle (piston position) of each cylinder and converts

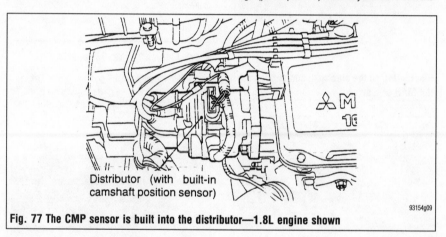

Distributor (with built-in camshaft position sensor)

93154g09

Fig. 77 The CMP sensor is built into the distributor—1.8L engine shown

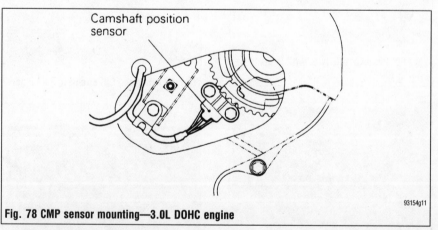

Camshaft position sensor

93154g11

Fig. 78 CMP sensor mounting—3.0L DOHC engine

it into a pulse signal. The PCM receives this signal and then computes the engine speed ad controls the fuel injector timing and ignition timing based on this input.

TESTING

This sensor produces a pulse signal based on information gathered while the engine is running. Testing the CKP sensor requires several special tools that are very expensive to purchase. Due to this fact, we at Chilton have determined testing this sensor to be beyond the scope of the do-it-yourself mechanic. The sensor can be monitored with an appropriate scan tool using a data display or other data stream information. Follow the instructions included with the scan tool for information on accessing the data.

REMOVAL & INSTALLATION

2.0L SOHC and 1990–96 1.5L Engines

▶ See Figure 79

The CKP sensor on these engines is located in the distributor. Refer to the distributor removal and installation procedure in Section 2.

1.6L and 2.0L DOHC Engines

▶ See Figure 80

1. Disconnect the negative battery cable.
2. Detach the electrical throttle body stay.
3. Remove the sensor retaining screws.
4. Remove the sensor assembly from the engine.
To install:
5. Install the sensor in the opening in the engine and tighten the sensor retaining screws.
6. Install the throttle body stay.
7. Attach the electrical connector to the sensor.
8. Connect the negative battery cable.

1.8L, 2.4L, 3.0L (SOHC and DOHC), 3.5L, and 1997–00 1.5L Engines

▶ See Figures 81 and 82

1. Disconnect the negative battery cable.
2. Remove the timing belt, as outlined in Section 3 of this manual.
3. Unplug the sensor connector.
4. Unfasten the retaining bolts, then remove the sensor from the vehicle.
5. Installation is the reverse of the removal procedure.

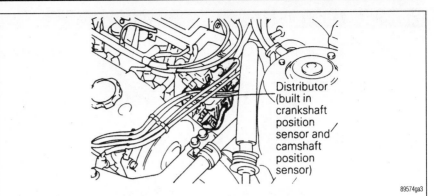

Fig. 79 On the 1.5L engine the crankshaft and camshaft position sensors are built into the distributor

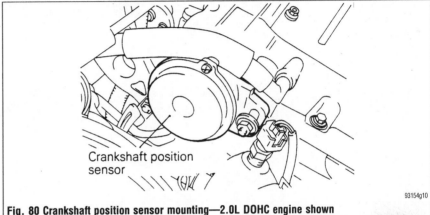

Fig. 80 Crankshaft position sensor mounting—2.0L DOHC engine shown

Fig. 81 Remove the two CKP sensor retaining bolts—2.4L engine shown, others similar

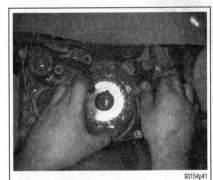

Fig. 82 Remove the sensor and slide the reluctor wheel off of the crankshaft—2.4L engine shown, others similar

COMPONENT LOCATIONS

EMISSIONS AND ELECTRONIC CONTROL COMPONENT LOCATIONS—1.8L ENGINE

1. Mass Air Flow (MAF) sensor w/integrated Intake Air Temperature (IAT) sensor
2. Engine Coolant Temperature (ECT) sensor
3. Camshaft Position (CMP) sensor
4. Exhaust Gas Recirculation (EGR) valve
5. Idle Air Control (IAC) valve (located on underside of throttle body)
6. Throttle Position (TP) sensor
7. Manifold Absolute Pressure (MAP) sensor
8. Evaporative emissions purge solenoid
9. Positive Crankcase Ventilation (PCV) valve
10. EGR control solenoid

EMISSIONS AND ELECTRONIC CONTROL COMPONENT LOCATIONS—2.4L ENGINE

1. Crankshaft Position (CKP) sensor
2. Positive Crankcase Ventilation (PCV) valve
3. Manifold Absolute Pressure (MAP) sensor
4. Exhaust Gas Recirculation (EGR) solenoid
5. Throttle Position (TP) sensor
6. Exhaust Gas Recirculation (EGR) valve (located on underside of throttle body)
7. Evaporative emissions purge solenoid
8. Mass Air Flow (MAF) sensor w/integrated Intake Air Temperature (IAT) sensor
9. Idle Air Control (IAC) valve (located on underside of throttle body)
10. Camshaft Position (CMP) sensor (located inside distributor)
11. Engine Coolant Temperature (ECT) sensor
12. EVAP canister (located under fender)

Name	Symbol	Name	Symbol
Air conditioning compressor clutch relay	N	Heated oxygen sensor (Rear)	V
Air conditioning switch	S	Idle air control motor	F
Check engine/Malfunction indicator lamp	Q	Ignition timing adjustment connector	D
Crankshaft position sensor	M	Injector	O
Data link connector	P	Intake air temperature sensor	K
Distributor (with built-in camshaft position sensor, ignition coil and ignition power transistor)	B	Manifold absolute pressure sensor	H
		Multiport fuel injection (MFI) relay	T
EGR solenoid	J	Park/Neutral position switch	A
Engine control module	U	Power steering pressure switch	L
Engine coolant temperature sensor	C	Throttle position sensor (with built-in closed throttle position switch)	G
Evaporative emission purge solenoid	I		
Fuel pump check terminal	E	Vehicle speed sensor (reed switch)	R
Heated oxygen sensor (Front)	W	–	–

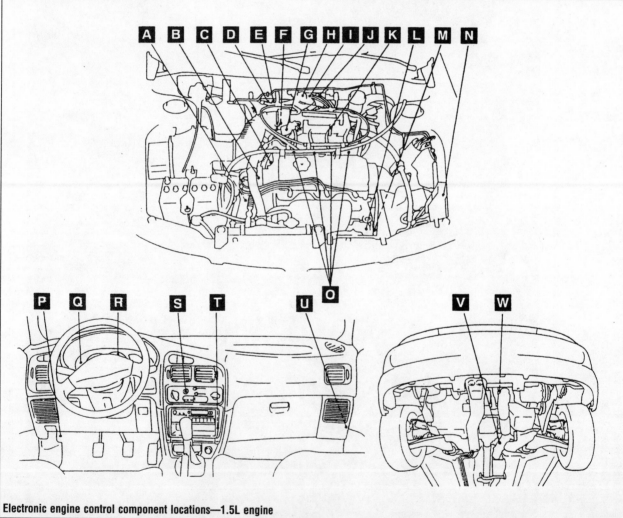

Electronic engine control component locations—1.5L engine

93154g01

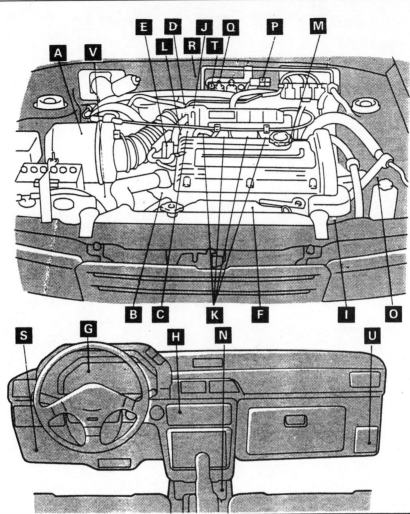

Name	Symbol	Name	Symbol
Air conditioner relay	O	Ignition coil (power transistor)	M
Air conditioner switch	H	Ignition timing adjustment terminal	R
Air flow sensor (incorporating intake air temperature sensor and barometric pressure sensor)	A	Inhibitor switch <A/T>	V
Crank angle sensor and top dead center sensor	E	Injector	K
EGR control solenoid valve <California>	Q	MPI control relay	N
EGR temperature sensor <California>	J	Oxygen sensor	F
Engine control unit	U	Power steering oil pressure switch	I
Engine coolant temperature sensor	B	Purge control solenoid valve	P
Fuel pump check terminal	T	Self-diagnosis terminal	S
Idle position switch	D	Throttle position sensor	C
Idle speed control servo (stepper motor)	L	Vehicle speed sensor (reed switch)	G

Electronic engine control component locations—1.6L engine

93154g02

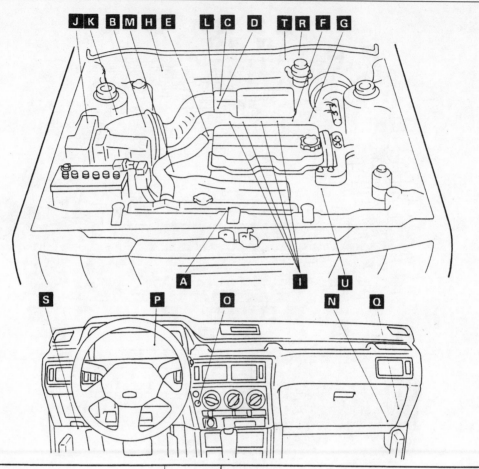

Name	Symbol	Name	Symbol
Air conditioning compressor clutch relay	J	Ignition coil (ignition power transistor)	F
Air conditioning switch	O	Ignition timing adjustment terminal	R
Crankshaft position sensor and camshaft position sensor	G	Injector	I
Data link connector	S	Multiport fuel injection relay	N
EGR solenoid <California>	K	Oxygen sensor	A
EGR temperature sensor <California>	L	Park/neutral position switch <A/T>	M
Engine control module	Q	Power steering pressure switch	U
Engine coolant temperature sensor	E	Throttle position sensor	D
Evaporative emission purge solenoid	H	Vehicle speed sensor (reed switch)	P
Fuel pump check terminal	T	Volume air flow sensor (incorporating intake air temperature sensor and barometric pressure sensor)	B
Idle speed control motor (closed throttle position switch, idle speed control motor position sensor)	C		

Electronic engine control component locations—2.0L SOHC engine

93154g03

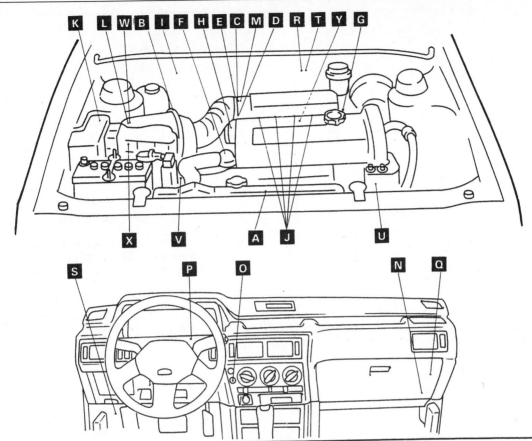

Name	Symbol	Name	Symbol
Air conditioning compressor clutch relay	K	Idle air control motor (stepper motor)	C
Air conditioning switch	O	Ignition coil (ignition power transistor)	G
Closed throttle position switch (fixed SAS)	E	Ignition timing adjustment terminal	R
Crankshaft position sensor and camshaft position sensor	H	Injector	J
Data link connector	S	Knock sensor	Y
Engine control module	Q	Multiport fuel injection relay	N
Engine coolant temperature sensor	F	Park/neutral position switch <A/T>	V
EGR solenoid	L	Power steering pressure switch	U
EGR temperature sensor	M	Throttle position sensor	D
Evaporative emission purge solenoid	I	Turbocharger waste gate solenoid	X
Fuel pressure solenoid	W	Vehicle speed sensor (reed switch)	P
Fuel pump check terminal	T	Volume air flow sensor (incorporating intake air temperature sensor and barometric pressure sensor)	B
Heated oxygen sensor	A		

NOTE
The "Name" column is arranged in alphabetical order.

Electronic engine control component locations—2.0L DOHC engine

93154g04

Name	Symbol	Name	Symbol
Air conditioning compressor clutch relay	P	Ignition timing adjusting terminal	H
Air conditioning switch	S	Idle air control motor (stepper motor)	B
Camshaft position sensor and crankshaft position sensor	L	Injector	N
Check engine/malfunction indicator lamp	R	Knock sensor	I
Diagnostic output terminal and diagnostic test mode control terminal	U	Multiport fuel injector (MFI) relay	T
		Park/neutral position switch	Q
EGR solenoid <For California and for Federal from 1995 models>	F	Power steering pressure switch	M
EGR temperature sensor <For California and for Federal from 1995 models>	E	Throttle position sensor (with built-in closed throttle switch)	D
Engine control module	T		
Engine coolant temperature sensor	O	Variable induction control motor (DC motor) (with built-in induction control valve position sensor)	J
Evaporative emission purge solenoid	C	Vehicle speed sensor (reed switch)	R
Heated oxygen sensor	G	Volume air flow sensor (with built-in intake air temperature sensor and barometric pressure sensor)	A
Ignition coil (ignition power transistor)	K		

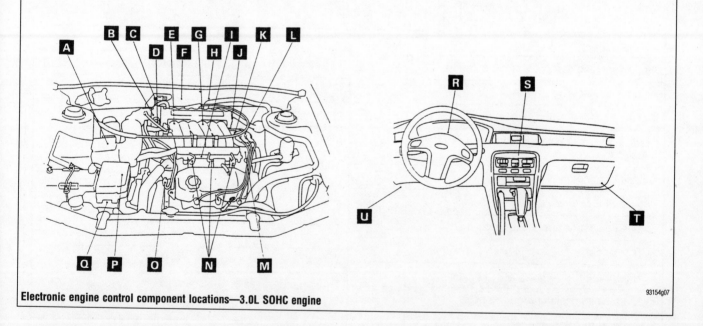

Electronic engine control component locations—3.0L SOHC engine

93154g07

Name	Symbol	Name	Symbol
Accelerator pedal position sensor (with built-in closed throttle position switch) <Vehicles with TCL>	C	Ignition coil (ignition power transistor)	Q
Air conditioning compressor clutch relay	R	Ignition timing adjusting terminal	H
		Injector	N
Air conditioning switch	U	Knock sensor	I
Camshaft position sensor	M	Multiport fuel injection (MFI) relay	V
Check engine/malfunction indicator lamp	T	Park/neutral position switch	S
Crankshaft position sensor	P	Power steering pressure switch	L
Diagnostic output terminal and diagnostic test mode control terminal	W	Throttle position sensor <Vehicles with TCL>	E
EGR solenoid <California>	G	Throttle position sensor (with built-in closed throttle position switch) <Except for vehicles with TCL>	E
EGR temperature sensor <California>	F		
Engine control module	V	Traction control vacuum solenoid and traction control ventilation solenoid <Vehicles with TCL>	D
Engine coolant temperature sensor	O	Variable induction control motor (DC motor) (with built-in induction control valve position sensor)	K
Evaporative emission purge solenoid	D	Vehicle speed sensor (reed switch)	T
Heated oxygen sensor	J	Volume air flow sensor (with built-in intake air temperature sensor and barometric pressure sensor)	A
Idle air control motor (stepper motor)	B		

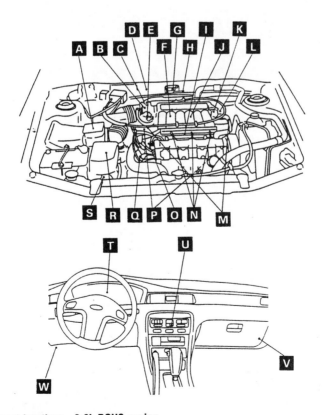

Electronic engine control component locations—3.0L DOHC engine

93154g08

Name	Symbol	Name	Symbol
Air conditioning compressor clutch relay	L	Heated oxygen sensor (Rear)	C
Air conditioner switch	T	Idle air control motor	H
Camshaft position sensor	I	Ignition coil (Ignition power transistor)	R
Check engine/malfunction indicator lamp	S	Injector	N
Crankshaft position sensor	M	Manifold differential pressure sensor	F
Data link connector	U	Multiport fuel injection (MFI) relay/Fuel pump relay	V
EGR solenoid	E	Park/Neutral position switch	Q
Engine control module	W	Power steering pressure switch	A
Engine coolant temperature sensor	O	Throttle position sensor (with built-in closed throttle position switch)	G
Evaporative emission purge solenoid	D	Vehicle speed sensor	P
Fuel pump check terminal	J	Volume air flow sensor (with built-in intake air temperature sensor and barometric pressure sensor)	K
Heated oxygen sensor (Front)	B		

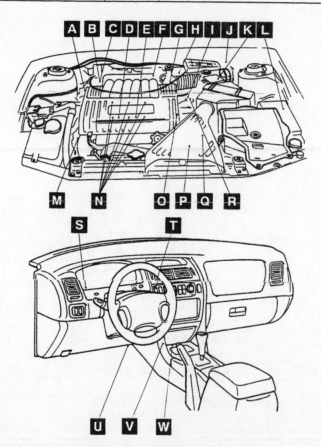

Electronic engine control component locations—3.5L engine

93154g05

NAME	SYMBOL	NAME	SYMBOL
Air conditioning compressor clutch relay	K	Knock sensor	D
Crankshaft position sensor	A	Left bank heated oxygen sensor (front) <California>	N
Data link connector	T	Left bank heated oxygen sensor (rear) <California>	M
Distributor (built-in camshaft position sensor and ignition coil)	J	Manifold differential pressure sensor	F
EGR solenoid	B	Multiport fuel injection (MFI) relay/fuel pump relay	K
Engine coolant temperature sensor	Q	Park/neutral position switch	R
Evaporative emission purge solenoid	B	Powertrain control module	U
Evaporative emission ventilation solenoid	Y	Power steering pressure switch	L
Fan controller	O	Right bank heated oxygen sensor (front) <California>	C
Fuel tank differential pressure sensor	V	Right bank heated oxygen sensor (rear) <California>	E
Heated oxygen sensor (front) <Federal>	W	Throttle position sensor	H
Heated oxygen sensor (rear) <Federal>	X	Vehicle speed sensor	P
Idle air control motor	I	Volume air flow sensor (with built-in intake air temperature sensor and barometric pressure sensor)	S
Injector	G		

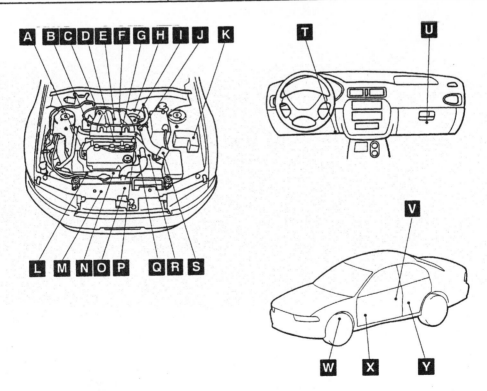

93154g06

Electronic engine control component locations—1999–00 Galant with the 3.0L SOHC engine

OBD-I TROUBLE CODES

General Information

The Powertrain Control Module (PCM) monitors the signals of input and output sensors, some all the time and others at certain times and processes each signal. When the PCM notices that an irregularity has continued for a specified time or longer from when the irregular signal was initially monitored, the PCM judges that a malfunction has occurred and will memorize the malfunction code. The code is then stored in the memory of the PCM and is accessible through the data link (diagnostic connector) with the use of an electronic scan tool or a voltmeter.

CHECK ENGINE/MALFUNCTION INDICATOR LIGHT

Among the on-board diagnostic items, a check engine/malfunction indicator light comes on to notify the driver of a emission control component irregularity. If the irregularity detected returns to normal or the PCM judges that the component has returned to normal, the check engine/malfunction indicator light will be turned off. Moreover, if the ignition is turned **OFF** and then the engine is restarted, the check engine/malfunction indicator light will not be turned on until a malfunction is detected.

The check engine/malfunction indicator light will come on immediately after the ignition switch is turned **ON**. The light should stay lit for 5 seconds and then will go off. This indicates that the check engine/malfunction indicator lamp is operating normally. This does not signify a problem with the system.

➡**The check engine/malfunction indicator lamp will come on when the terminal for the ignition timing adjustment is shorted to ground. Therefore, it is not abnormal that the light comes on even when the terminal for ignition timing is shorted at time of ignition timing adjustment.**

To test the light, perform the following:
1. Turn the ignition switch **ON**. Inspect the check engine/malfunction indicator lamp for illumination.
2. The light should be lit for 5 seconds and then should go out.
3. If the lamp does not illuminate, check for open circuit in the harness, blown fuse or blown bulb.

SERVICE PRECAUTIONS

• Before attaching or detaching the PCM harness connectors, make sure the ignition switch is **OFF** and the negative battery cable is disconnected to avoid the possibility of damage to the PCM.
• When performing PCM input/output signal diagnosis, remove the pin terminal retainer from the connectors to make it easier to insert tester probes into the connector.
• When attaching or detaching pin connectors from the PCM, take care not to bend or break any pin terminals. Check that there are no bends or breaks on PCM pin terminals before attempting any connections.
• Before replacing any PCM, perform the PCM input/output signal diagnosis to make sure the PCM is functioning properly.

• When measuring supply voltage of PCM-controlled components with a circuit tester, separate 1 tester probe from another. If the 2 tester probes accidentally make contact with each other during measurement, a short circuit will result and damage the PCM.

Reading Codes

▶ **See Figures 83 and 84**

Remember that the diagnostic trouble code identification refers only to the circuit, not necessarily to a specific component. For example, fault code 14 may indicate an error in the throttle position sensor circuit; it does not necessarily mean the TPS sensor has failed. Testing of all related wiring, connectors and the sensor itself may be required to locate the problem.

The PCM memory is capable of storing multiple codes. During diagnosis the codes will be transmitted in numerical order from lowest to highest, regardless of the order of occurrence. If multiple codes are stored, always begin diagnostic work with the lowest numbered code.

Make a note of the following:
1. When battery voltage is low, no detection of failure is possible. Be sure to check the battery voltage and other conditions before starting the test.
2. Diagnostic items are erased if the battery or the engine controller connection is detached. Do not dis-

connect either of these components until the diagnostic material present in the PCM has been read completely.
3. Be sure to attach and detach the scan tool to the data link connector with the ignition key **OFF**. If the scan tool in connected or disconnected with the ignition key **ON**, diagnostic trouble codes may be falsely stored and the engine warning light may be illuminated.

WITH A SCAN TOOL

▶ **See Figures 85 and 86**

The procedure listed below is to be used only as a guide, when using Mitsubishi's MUT-II, or equivalent scan tool. For specific operating instructions, follow the directions supplied with the particular scan tool being used.

1. Remove the underdash cover, if equipped. Attach the scan tool to the data link connector, located on the left underside of the instrument panel.
2. Using the scan tool, read and record the on-board diagnostic output.
3. Diagnose and repair the faulty components as required.
4. Turn the ignition switch **OFF** and then turn it **ON**.
5. Erase the diagnostic trouble code.
6. Recheck the diagnostic trouble code and make sure that the normal code is output.

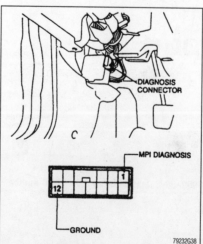

Fig. 83 Diagnosis terminal connector location—Galant

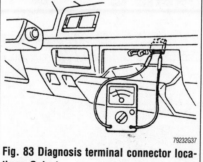

Fig. 84 Diagnostic connector location—Mirage

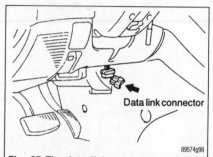

Fig. 85 The data link connector is located on the left under side of the instrument panel

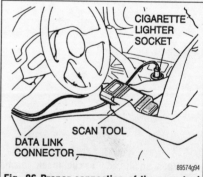

Fig. 86 Proper connection of the scan tool to read codes on OBD-I vehicles

WITHOUT A SCAN TOOL

♦ **See Figure 87.**

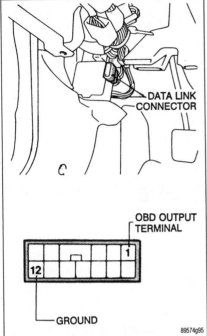

DATA LINK CONNECTOR

OBD OUTPUT TERMINAL

GROUND

89574g95

Fig. 87 Location of the On-Board Diagnostic (OBD) output and ground terminal locations on the data link connector

1. Remove the under dash cover, if equipped.
2. Attach an analog voltmeter between the on-board diagnostic output terminal of the data link connector and the ground terminal.
3. Turn the ignition switch **ON**.
4. Read the on-board diagnostic output pattern from the voltmeter and record.
5. Diagnose and repair the faulty components as required.
6. Erase the trouble code.
7. Turn the ignition switch **ON**, and read the diagnostic trouble codes, checking that a normal code is output.

Clearing Codes

➡**To erase diagnostic trouble codes with a scan tool, follow the directions given by the tools manufacturer.**

1. Turn the ignition switch **OFF**.
2. Disconnect the negative battery cable from the battery for 1 minute or more, then reattach it.
3. Turn **ON** the ignition switch and read the diagnostic trouble codes checking that a normal code is output.

Diagnostic Trouble Codes

Code 11 Oxygen sensor
Code 12 Air flow sensor
Code 13 Intake Air Temperature Sensor
Code 14 Throttle Position Sensor (TPS)
Code 15 SC Motor Position Sensor (MPS)

Code 21 Engine Coolant Temperature Sensor
Code 22 Crank angle sensor
Code 23 No. 1 cylinder TDC (camshaft position) Sensor
Code 24 Vehicle speed sensor
Code 25 Barometric pressure sensor
Code 31 Knock sensor (KS)
Code 32 Manifold pressure sensor
Code 36 Ignition timing adjustment signal
Code 39 Oxygen sensor (rear - turbocharged)
Code 41 Injector
Code 42 Fuel pump
Code 43 EGR-California
Code 44 Ignition Coil; power transistor unit (No. 1 and No. 4 cylinders) on 3.0L
Code 52 Ignition Coil; power transistor unit (No. 2 and No. 5 cylinders) on 3.0L
Code 53 Ignition Coil; power transistor unit (No. 3 and No. 6 cylinders) on 3.0L
Code 55 AC valve position sensor
Code 59 Heated oxygen sensor
Code 61 Transaxle control unit cable (automatic transmission)
Code 62 Warm-up control valve position sensor (non-turbo)

OBD-II TROUBLE CODES

General Information

The Powertrain Control Module (PCM) is given responsibility for the operation of the emission control devices, cooling fans, ignition and advance and in some cases, automatic transaxle functions. Because the PCM oversees both the ignition timing and the fuel injection operation, a precise air/fuel ratio will be maintained under all operating conditions. The PCM is a microprocessor, or small computer, which receives electrical inputs from several sensors, switches and relays on and around the engine.

Based on combinations of these inputs, the PCM controls outputs to various devices concerned with engine operation and emissions. The control module relies on the signals to form a correct picture of current vehicle operation. If any of the input signals is incorrect, the PCM reacts to whatever picture is painted for it. For example, if the coolant temperature sensor is inaccurate and reads too low, the PCM may see a picture of the engine never warming up. Consequently, the engine settings will be maintained as if the engine were cold. Because so many inputs can affect one output, correct diagnostic procedures are essential on these systems.

One part of the PCM is devoted to monitoring both input and output functions within the system. This ability forms the core of the self-diagnostic system. If a problem is detected within a circuit, the control module will recognize the fault, assign it a Diagnostic Trouble Code (DTC), and store the code in memory. The stored code(s) may be retrieved during diagnosis.

While the OBD-II system is capable of recognizing many internal faults, certain faults will not be recognized. Because the control module sees only electrical signals, it cannot sense or react to mechanical or vacuum faults affecting engine operation. Some of these faults may affect another component which will set a code. For example, the PCM monitors the output signal to the fuel injectors, but cannot detect a partially clogged injector. As long as the output driver responds correctly, the computer will read the system as functioning correctly. However, the improper flow of fuel may result in a lean mixture. This would, in turn, be detected by the oxygen sensor and noticed as a constantly lean signal by the PCM. Once the signal falls outside the pre-programmed limits, the control module would notice the fault and set a trouble code.

Additionally, the OBD-II system employs adaptive fuel logic. This process is used to compensate for normal wear and variability within the fuel system. Once the engine enters steady-state operation, the control module watches the oxygen sensor signal for a bias or tendency to run slightly rich or lean. If such a bias is detected, the adaptive logic corrects the fuel delivery to bring the air/fuel mixture towards a centered or 14.7:1 ratio. This compensating shift is stored in a non-volatile memory which is retained by battery power even with the ignition switched **OFF**. The correction factor is then available the next time the vehicle is operated.

Reading Codes

WITH A SCAN TOOL

♦ **See Figures 88, 89, 90, and 91**

The Diagnostic Link Connector (DLC), under the left-hand side of the instrument panel, must be located to retrieve any DTC's.

Reading the control module memory is on of the first steps in OBD II system diagnostics. This step should be initially performed to determine the general nature of the fault. Subsequent readings will determine if the fault has been cleared.

Reading codes can be performed by any of the methods below:
• Read the control module memory with the Generic Scan Tool (GST)
• Read the control module memory with the vehicle manufacturer's specific tester

To read the fault codes, connect the scan tool or tester according to the manufacturer's instructions. Follow the manufacturer's specified procedure for reading the codes.

WITHOUT A SCAN TOOL

♦ **See Figure 92**

The Diagnostic Link Connector (DLC), under the left-hand side of the instrument panel, must be located to retrieve any DTC's.

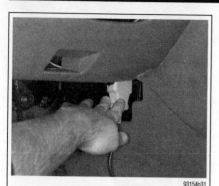

Fig. 88 Plug the scan tool into the DLC under the driver's side of the instrument panel

Fig. 89 Follow the directions on the scan tool screen to retrieve the DTC's

Fig. 90 In this case, we would choose 1-Trouble Codes to retrieve the DTC's

Fig. 91 The PCM in this vehicle contains no DTC's

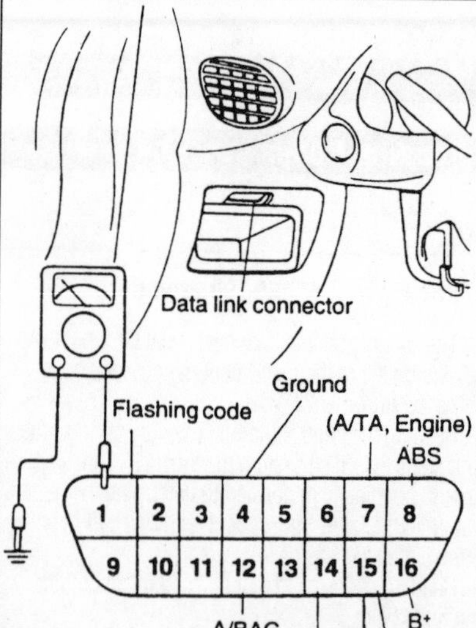

Fig. 92 For OBD II code retrieval without using a scan tool on Mitsubishi models, connect the DVOM and jumper wire as shown

In 1996, all Mitsubishi switched from an arbitrary code listing and format, to the federally regulated On Board Diagnostics 2nd Generation (OBD II) code system. Normally, OBD II equipped vehicles do not have the option of allowing the person servicing the vehicle to flash the codes out with a voltmeter; usually a scan tool is necessary to retrieve OBD II codes. Mitsubishi, however, does provide this option.

The Federal government decided that it was time to create a standard for vehicle diagnostic systems codes for ease of servicing and to insure that certain of the vehicle's systems were being monitored for emissions purposes. Since OBD II codes are standardized (they all contain one letter and four numbers), they are easy to decipher.

The OBD II system in the Mitsubishi models is designed so that it will flash the DTC's out on a voltmeter (even though a scan tool is better). However, the first two characters of the code are not used. This is because the transaxle is a part of the powertrain, so all transaxle related codes will begin with a P. Also, since there are no overlapping numbers between SAE and Mitsubishi codes, the second digit is also not necessary.

The system flashes the codes out in a series of flashes in three groups, each group corresponding to one of the three last digits of the OBD II code. Therefore, Code P0753 would be flashed out in seven flashes, followed by five flashes, then by three flashes. Each group of flashes is separated by a brief pause. All of the flashes are of the same duration, with the only exception being zero. Zero is represented by a long flash. Therefore, seven flashes, one long flash, two flashes would indicate a P0702 code (shorted TP sensor circuit).

To retrieve the codes, perform the following:
1. Perform the preliminary inspection, located earlier in this section. This is very important, since a loose or disconnected wire, or corroded connector terminals can cause a whole slew of unrelated DTC's to be stored by the computer; you will waste a lot of time performing a diagnostic "goose chase."
2. Grab some paper and a pencil or pen to write down the DTC's when they are flashed out.

3. Locate the Diagnostic Link Connector (DLC), which is usually under the left-hand side of the instrument panel.
4. Start the engine and drive the vehicle until the transaxle goes into the failsafe mode.
5. Park the vehicle, but do not turn the ignition **OFF**. Allow it to idle.
6. Attach a voltmeter (analog or digital) to the test terminals on the Diagnostic Link Connector (DLC). The negative lead should be attached to terminal 4 and the positive lead to terminal 1.
7. Observe the voltmeter and count the flashes (or arm sweeps if using an analog voltmeter); note the applicable codes.
8. After all of the DTC(s) have been retrieved, fix the applicable problems, clear the codes, drive the vehicle, and perform the retrieval procedure again to ensure that all of the codes are gone.

Clearing Codes

WITH A SCAN TOOL

Control module reset procedures are a very important part of OBD II System diagnostics.

This step should be done at the end of any fault code repair and at the end of any driveability repair.

Clearing codes can be performed by any of the methods below:
• Clear the control module memory with the Generic Scan Tool (GST)
• Clear the control module memory with the vehicle manufacturer's specific tester

➡**The MIL will may also be de-activated for some codes if the vehicle completes three consecutive trips without a fault detected with vehicle conditions similar to those present during the fault.**

WITHOUT A SCAN TOOL

If there are still codes present, either the codes were not properly cleared (Are the codes identical to those flashed out previously?), or the underlying problem is still there (Are only some of the codes the same as previously?).

Diagnostic Trouble Codes

SCAN TOOL CODES

P0000 No Failures
P0100 Mass or Volume Air Flow Circuit Malfunction
P0101 Mass or Volume Air Flow Circuit Range/Performance Problem
P0102 Mass or Volume Air Flow Circuit Low Input
P0103 Mass or Volume Air Flow Circuit High Input
P0104 Mass or Volume Air Flow Circuit Intermittent
P0105 Manifold Absolute Pressure/Barometric Pressure Circuit Malfunction
P0106 Manifold Absolute Pressure/Barometric Pressure Circuit Range/Performance Problem
P0107 Manifold Absolute Pressure/Barometric Pressure Circuit Low Input

P0108 Manifold Absolute Pressure/Barometric Pressure Circuit High Input

P0109 Manifold Absolute Pressure/Barometric Pressure Circuit Intermittent

P0110 Intake Air Temperature Circuit Malfunction

P0111 Intake Air Temperature Circuit Range/Performance Problem

P0112 Intake Air Temperature Circuit Low Input

P0113 Intake Air Temperature Circuit High Input

P0114 Intake Air Temperature Circuit Intermittent

P0115 Engine Coolant Temperature Circuit Malfunction

P0116 Engine Coolant Temperature Circuit Range/Performance Problem

P0117 Engine Coolant Temperature Circuit Low Input

P0118 Engine Coolant Temperature Circuit High Input

P0119 Engine Coolant Temperature Circuit Intermittent

P0120 Throttle Position Sensor/Switch "A" Circuit Malfunction

P0121 Throttle Position Sensor/Switch "A" Circuit Range/Performance Problem

P0122 Throttle Position Sensor/Switch "A" Circuit Low Input

P0123 Throttle Position Sensor/Switch "A" Circuit High Input

P0124 Throttle Position Sensor/Switch "A" Circuit Intermittent

P0125 Insufficient Coolant Temperature For Closed Loop Fuel Control

P0126 Insufficient Coolant Temperature For Stable Operation

P0130 02 Circuit Malfunction (Bank no. 1 Sensor no. 1)

P0131 02 Sensor Circuit Low Voltage (Bank no. 1 Sensor no. 1)

P0132 02 Sensor Circuit High Voltage (Bank no. 1 Sensor no. 1)

P0133 02 Sensor Circuit Slow Response (Bank no. 1 Sensor no. 1)

P0134 02 Sensor Circuit No Activity Detected (Bank no. 1 Sensor no. 1)

P0135 02 Sensor Heater Circuit Malfunction (Bank no. 1 Sensor no. 1)

P0136 02 Sensor Circuit Malfunction (Bank no. 1 Sensor no. 2)

P0137 02 Sensor Circuit Low Voltage (Bank no. 1 Sensor no. 2)

P0138 02 Sensor Circuit High Voltage (Bank no. 1 Sensor no. 2)

P0139 02 Sensor Circuit Slow Response (Bank no. 1 Sensor no. 2)

P0140 02 Sensor Circuit No Activity Detected (Bank no. 1 Sensor no. 2)

P0141 02 Sensor Heater Circuit Malfunction (Bank no. 1 Sensor no. 2)

P0142 02 Sensor Circuit Malfunction (Bank no. 1 Sensor no. 3)

P0143 02 Sensor Circuit Low Voltage (Bank no. 1 Sensor no. 3)

P0144 02 Sensor Circuit High Voltage (Bank no. 1 Sensor no. 3)

P0145 02 Sensor Circuit Slow Response (Bank no. 1 Sensor no. 3)

P0146 02 Sensor Circuit No Activity Detected (Bank no. 1 Sensor no. 3)

P0147 02 Sensor Heater Circuit Malfunction (Bank no. 1 Sensor no. 3)

P0150 02 Sensor Circuit Malfunction (Bank no. 2 Sensor no. 1)

P0151 02 Sensor Circuit Low Voltage (Bank no. 2 Sensor no. 1)

P0152 02 Sensor Circuit High Voltage (Bank no. 2 Sensor no. 1)

P0153 02 Sensor Circuit Slow Response (Bank no. 2 Sensor no. 1)

P0154 02 Sensor Circuit No Activity Detected (Bank no. 2 Sensor no. 1)

P0155 02 Sensor Heater Circuit Malfunction (Bank no. 2 Sensor no. 1)

P0156 02 Sensor Circuit Malfunction (Bank no. 2 Sensor no. 2)

P0157 02 Sensor Circuit Low Voltage (Bank no. 2 Sensor no. 2)

P0158 02 Sensor Circuit High Voltage (Bank no. 2 Sensor no. 2)

P0159 02 Sensor Circuit Slow Response (Bank no. 2 Sensor no. 2)

P0160 02 Sensor Circuit No Activity Detected (Bank no. 2 Sensor no. 2)

P0161 02 Sensor Heater Circuit Malfunction (Bank no. 2 Sensor no. 2)

P0162 02 Sensor Circuit Malfunction (Bank no. 2 Sensor no. 3)

P0163 02 Sensor Circuit Low Voltage (Bank no. 2 Sensor no. 3)

P0164 02 Sensor Circuit High Voltage (Bank no. 2 Sensor no. 3)

P0165 02 Sensor Circuit Slow Response (Bank no. 2 Sensor no. 3)

P0166 02 Sensor Circuit No Activity Detected (Bank no. 2 Sensor no. 3)

P0167 02 Sensor Heater Circuit Malfunction (Bank no. 2 Sensor no. 3)

P0170 Fuel Trim Malfunction (Bank no. 1)

P0171 System Too Lean (Bank no. 1)

P0172 System Too Rich (Bank no. 1)

P0173 Fuel Trim Malfunction (Bank no. 2)

P0174 System Too Lean (Bank no. 2)

P0175 System Too Rich (Bank no. 2)

P0176 Fuel Composition Sensor Circuit Malfunction

P0177 Fuel Composition Sensor Circuit Range/Performance

P0178 Fuel Composition Sensor Circuit Low Input

P0179 Fuel Composition Sensor Circuit High Input

P0180 Fuel Temperature Sensor "A" Circuit Malfunction

P0181 Fuel Temperature Sensor "A" Circuit Range/Performance

P0182 Fuel Temperature Sensor "A" Circuit Low Input

P0183 Fuel Temperature Sensor "A" Circuit High Input

P0184 Fuel Temperature Sensor "A" Circuit Intermittent

P0185 Fuel Temperature Sensor "B" Circuit Malfunction

P0186 Fuel Temperature Sensor "B" Circuit Range/Performance

P0187 Fuel Temperature Sensor "B" Circuit Low Input

P0188 Fuel Temperature Sensor "B" Circuit High Input

P0189 Fuel Temperature Sensor "B" Circuit Intermittent

P0190 Fuel Rail Pressure Sensor Circuit Malfunction

P0191 Fuel Rail Pressure Sensor Circuit Range/Performance

P0192 Fuel Rail Pressure Sensor Circuit Low Input

P0193 Fuel Rail Pressure Sensor Circuit High Input

P0194 Fuel Rail Pressure Sensor Circuit Intermittent

P0195 Engine Oil Temperature Sensor Malfunction

P0196 Engine Oil Temperature Sensor Range/Performance

P0197 Engine Oil Temperature Sensor Low

P0198 Engine Oil Temperature Sensor High

P0199 Engine Oil Temperature Sensor Intermittent

P0200 Injector Circuit Malfunction

P0201 Injector Circuit Malfunction—Cylinder no. 1

P0202 Injector Circuit Malfunction—Cylinder no. 2

P0203 Injector Circuit Malfunction—Cylinder no. 3

P0204 Injector Circuit Malfunction—Cylinder no. 4

P0205 Injector Circuit Malfunction—Cylinder no. 5

P0206 Injector Circuit Malfunction—Cylinder no. 6

P0214 Cold Start Injector no. 2 Malfunction

P0215 Engine Shutoff Solenoid Malfunction

P0216 Injection Timing Control Circuit Malfunction

P0217 Engine Over Temperature Condition

P0218 Transmission Over Temperature Condition

P0219 Engine Over Speed Condition

P0220 Throttle Position Sensor/Switch "B" Circuit Malfunction

P0221 Throttle Position Sensor/Switch "B" Circuit Range/Performance Problem

P0222 Throttle Position Sensor/Switch "B" Circuit Low Input

P0223 Throttle Position Sensor/Switch "B" Circuit High Input

P0224 Throttle Position Sensor/Switch "B" Circuit Intermittent

P0225 Throttle Position Sensor/Switch "C" Circuit Malfunction

P0226 Throttle Position Sensor/Switch "C" Circuit Range/Performance Problem

P0227 Throttle Position Sensor/Switch "C" Circuit Low Input

P0228 Throttle Position Sensor/Switch "C" Circuit High Input

P0229 Throttle Position Sensor/Switch "C" Circuit Intermittent

P0230 Fuel Pump Primary Circuit Malfunction

P0231 Fuel Pump Secondary Circuit Low

P0232 Fuel Pump Secondary Circuit High

P0233 Fuel Pump Secondary Circuit Intermittent

P0261 Cylinder no. 1 Injector Circuit Low

P0262 Cylinder no. 1 Injector Circuit High

P0263 Cylinder no. 1 Contribution/Balance Fault

P0264 Cylinder no. 2 Injector Circuit Low

P0265 Cylinder no. 2 Injector Circuit High

P0266 Cylinder no. 2 Contribution/Balance Fault

P0267 Cylinder no. 3 Injector Circuit Low

P0268 Cylinder no. 3 Injector Circuit High

P0269 Cylinder no. 3 Contribution/Balance Fault

P0270 Cylinder no. 4 Injector Circuit Low

P0271 Cylinder no. 4 Injector Circuit High

P0272 Cylinder no. 4 Contribution/Balance Fault

P0273 Cylinder no. 5 Injector Circuit Low

P0274 Cylinder no. 5 Injector Circuit High

P0275 Cylinder no. 5 Contribution/Balance Fault
P0276 Cylinder no. 6 Injector Circuit Low
P0277 Cylinder no. 6 Injector Circuit High
P0278 Cylinder no. 6 Contribution/Balance Fault
P0300 Random/Multiple Cylinder Misfire Detected
P0301 Cylinder no. 1—Misfire Detected
P0302 Cylinder no. 2—Misfire Detected
P0303 Cylinder no. 3—Misfire Detected
P0304 Cylinder no. 4—Misfire Detected
P0305 Cylinder no. 5—Misfire Detected
P0306 Cylinder no. 6—Misfire Detected
P0320 Ignition/Distributor Engine Speed Input Circuit Malfunction
P0321 Ignition/Distributor Engine Speed Input Circuit Range/Performance
P0322 Ignition/Distributor Engine Speed Input Circuit No Signal
P0323 Ignition/Distributor Engine Speed Input Circuit Intermittent
P0325 Knock Sensor no. 1—Circuit Malfunction (Bank no. 1 or Single Sensor)
P0326 Knock Sensor no. 1—Circuit Range/Performance (Bank no. 1 or Single Sensor)
P0327 Knock Sensor no. 1—Circuit Low Input (Bank no. 1 or Single Sensor)
P0328 Knock Sensor no. 1—Circuit High Input (Bank no. 1 or Single Sensor)
P0329 Knock Sensor no. 1—Circuit Input Intermittent (Bank no. 1 or Single Sensor)
P0330 Knock Sensor no. 2—Circuit Malfunction (Bank no. 2)
P0331 Knock Sensor no. 2—Circuit Range/Performance (Bank no. 2)
P0332 Knock Sensor no. 2—Circuit Low Input (Bank no. 2)
P0333 Knock Sensor no. 2—Circuit High Input (Bank no. 2)
P0334 Knock Sensor no. 2—Circuit Input Intermittent (Bank no. 2)
P0335 Crankshaft Position Sensor "A" Circuit Malfunction
P0336 Crankshaft Position Sensor "A" Circuit Range/Performance
P0337 Crankshaft Position Sensor "A" Circuit Low Input
P0338 Crankshaft Position Sensor "A" Circuit High Input
P0339 Crankshaft Position Sensor "A" Circuit Intermittent
P0340 Camshaft Position Sensor Circuit Malfunction
P0341 Camshaft Position Sensor Circuit Range/Performance
P0342 Camshaft Position Sensor Circuit Low Input
P0343 Camshaft Position Sensor Circuit High Input
P0344 Camshaft Position Sensor Circuit Intermittent
P0350 Ignition Coil Primary/Secondary Circuit Malfunction
P0351 Ignition Coil "A" Primary/Secondary Circuit Malfunction
P0352 Ignition Coil "B" Primary/Secondary Circuit Malfunction
P0353 Ignition Coil "C" Primary/Secondary Circuit Malfunction
P0354 Ignition Coil "D" Primary/Secondary Circuit Malfunction
P0355 Ignition Coil "E" Primary/Secondary Circuit Malfunction

P0356 Ignition Coil "F" Primary/Secondary Circuit Malfunction
P0357 Ignition Coil "G" Primary/Secondary Circuit Malfunction
P0358 Ignition Coil "H" Primary/Secondary Circuit Malfunction
P0359 Ignition Coil "I" Primary/Secondary Circuit Malfunction
P0360 Ignition Coil "J" Primary/Secondary Circuit Malfunction
P0361 Ignition Coil "K" Primary/Secondary Circuit Malfunction
P0362 Ignition Coil "L" Primary/Secondary Circuit Malfunction
P0370 Timing Reference High Resolution Signal "A" Malfunction
P0371 Timing Reference High Resolution Signal "A" Too Many Pulses
P0372 Timing Reference High Resolution Signal "A" Too Few Pulses
P0373 Timing Reference High Resolution Signal "A" Intermittent/Erratic Pulses
P0374 Timing Reference High Resolution Signal "A" No Pulses
P0375 Timing Reference High Resolution Signal "B" Malfunction
P0376 Timing Reference High Resolution Signal "B" Too Many Pulses
P0377 Timing Reference High Resolution Signal "B" Too Few Pulses
P0378 Timing Reference High Resolution Signal "B" Intermittent/Erratic Pulses
P0379 Timing Reference High Resolution Signal "B" No Pulses
P0385 Crankshaft Position Sensor "B" Circuit Malfunction
P0386 Crankshaft Position Sensor "B" Circuit Range/Performance
P0387 Crankshaft Position Sensor "B" Circuit Low Input
P0388 Crankshaft Position Sensor "B" Circuit High Input
P0389 Crankshaft Position Sensor "B" Circuit Intermittent
P0400 Exhaust Gas Recirculation Flow Malfunction
P0401 Exhaust Gas Recirculation Flow Insufficient Detected
P0402 Exhaust Gas Recirculation Flow Excessive Detected
P0403 Exhaust Gas Recirculation Circuit Malfunction
P0404 Exhaust Gas Recirculation Circuit Range/Performance
P0405 Exhaust Gas Recirculation Sensor "A" Circuit Low
P0406 Exhaust Gas Recirculation Sensor "A" Circuit High
P0407 Exhaust Gas Recirculation Sensor "B" Circuit Low
P0408 Exhaust Gas Recirculation Sensor "B" Circuit High
P0410 Secondary Air Injection System Malfunction
P0411 Secondary Air Injection System Incorrect Flow Detected
P0412 Secondary Air Injection System Switching Valve "A" Circuit Malfunction
P0413 Secondary Air Injection System Switching Valve "A" Circuit Open
P0414 Secondary Air Injection System Switching Valve "A" Circuit Shorted

P0415 Secondary Air Injection System Switching Valve "B" Circuit Malfunction
P0416 Secondary Air Injection System Switching Valve "B" Circuit Open
P0417 Secondary Air Injection System Switching Valve "B" Circuit Shorted
P0418 Secondary Air Injection System Relay "A" Circuit Malfunction
P0419 Secondary Air Injection System Relay "B" Circuit Malfunction
P0420 Catalyst System Efficiency Below Threshold (Bank no. 1)
P0421 Warm Up Catalyst Efficiency Below Threshold (Bank no. 1)
P0422 Main Catalyst Efficiency Below Threshold (Bank no. 1)
P0423 Heated Catalyst Efficiency Below Threshold (Bank no. 1)
P0424 Heated Catalyst Temperature Below Threshold (Bank no. 1)
P0430 Catalyst System Efficiency Below Threshold (Bank no. 2)
P0431 Warm Up Catalyst Efficiency Below Threshold (Bank no. 2)
P0432 Main Catalyst Efficiency Below Threshold (Bank no. 2)
P0433 Heated Catalyst Efficiency Below Threshold (Bank no. 2)
P0434 Heated Catalyst Temperature Below Threshold (Bank no. 2)
P0440 Evaporative Emission Control System Malfunction
P0441 Evaporative Emission Control System Incorrect Purge Flow
P0442 Evaporative Emission Control System Leak Detected (Small Leak)
P0443 Evaporative Emission Control System Purge Control Valve Circuit Malfunction
P0444 Evaporative Emission Control System Purge Control Valve Circuit Open
P0445 Evaporative Emission Control System Purge Control Valve Circuit Shorted
P0446 Evaporative Emission Control System Vent Control Circuit   Malfunction
P0447 Evaporative Emission Control System Vent Control Circuit Open
P0448 Evaporative Emission Control System Vent Control Circuit Shorted
P0449 Evaporative Emission Control System Vent Valve/Solenoid Circuit Malfunction
P0450 Evaporative Emission Control System Pressure Sensor Malfunction
P0451 Evaporative Emission Control System Pressure Sensor Range/Performance
P0452 Evaporative Emission Control System Pressure Sensor Low Input
P0453 Evaporative Emission Control System Pressure Sensor High Input
P0454 Evaporative Emission Control System Pressure Sensor Intermittent
P0455 Evaporative Emission Control System Leak Detected (Gross Leak)
P0460 Fuel Level Sensor Circuit Malfunction
P0461 Fuel Level Sensor Circuit Range/Performance
P0462 Fuel Level Sensor Circuit Low Input
P0463 Fuel Level Sensor Circuit High Input
P0464 Fuel Level Sensor Circuit Intermittent
P0465 Purge Flow Sensor Circuit Malfunction
P0466 Purge Flow Sensor Circuit Range/Performance
P0467 Purge Flow Sensor Circuit Low Input

P0468 Purge Flow Sensor Circuit High Input
P0469 Purge Flow Sensor Circuit Intermittent
P0470 Exhaust Pressure Sensor Malfunction
P0471 Exhaust Pressure Sensor Range/Performance
P0472 Exhaust Pressure Sensor Low
P0473 Exhaust Pressure Sensor High
P0474 Exhaust Pressure Sensor Intermittent
P0475 Exhaust Pressure Control Valve Malfunction
P0476 Exhaust Pressure Control Valve Range/Performance
P0477 Exhaust Pressure Control Valve Low
P0478 Exhaust Pressure Control Valve High
P0479 Exhaust Pressure Control Valve Intermittent
P0480 Cooling Fan no. 1 Control Circuit Malfunction
P0481 Cooling Fan no. 2 Control Circuit Malfunction
P0482 Cooling Fan no. 3 Control Circuit Malfunction
P0483 Cooling Fan Rationality Check Malfunction
P0484 Cooling Fan Circuit Over Current
P0485 Cooling Fan Power/Ground Circuit Malfunction
P0500 Vehicle Speed Sensor Malfunction
P0501 Vehicle Speed Sensor Range/Performance
P0502 Vehicle Speed Sensor Circuit Low Input
P0503 Vehicle Speed Sensor Intermittent/Erratic/High
P0505 Idle Control System Malfunction
P0506 Idle Control System RPM Lower Than Expected
P0507 Idle Control System RPM Higher Than Expected
P0510 Closed Throttle Position Switch Malfunction
P0520 Engine Oil Pressure Sensor/Switch Circuit Malfunction
P0521 Engine Oil Pressure Sensor/Switch Range/Performance
P0522 Engine Oil Pressure Sensor/Switch Low Voltage
P0523 Engine Oil Pressure Sensor/Switch High Voltage
P0530 A/C Refrigerant Pressure Sensor Circuit Malfunction
P0531 A/C Refrigerant Pressure Sensor Circuit Range/Performance
P0532 A/C Refrigerant Pressure Sensor Circuit Low Input
P0533 A/C Refrigerant Pressure Sensor Circuit High Input
P0534 A/C Refrigerant Charge Loss
P0550 Power Steering Pressure Sensor Circuit Malfunction
P0551 Power Steering Pressure Sensor Circuit Range/Performance
P0552 Power Steering Pressure Sensor Circuit Low Input
P0553 Power Steering Pressure Sensor Circuit High Input
P0554 Power Steering Pressure Sensor Circuit Intermittent
P0560 System Voltage Malfunction
P0561 System Voltage Unstable
P0562 System Voltage Low
P0563 System Voltage High
P0565 Cruise Control On Signal Malfunction
P0566 Cruise Control Off Signal Malfunction

P0567 Cruise Control Resume Signal Malfunction
P0568 Cruise Control Set Signal Malfunction
P0569 Cruise Control Coast Signal Malfunction
P0570 Cruise Control Accel Signal Malfunction
P0571 Cruise Control/Brake Switch "A" Circuit Malfunction
P0572 Cruise Control/Brake Switch "A" Circuit Low
P0573 Cruise Control/Brake Switch "A" Circuit High
P0574 Through P0580 Reserved for Cruise Codes
P0600 Serial Communication Link Malfunction
P0601 Internal Control Module Memory Check Sum Error
P0602 Control Module Programming Error
P0603 Internal Control Module Keep Alive Memory (KAM) Error
P0604 Internal Control Module Random Access Memory (RAM) Error
P0605 Internal Control Module Read Only Memory (ROM) Error
P0606 PCM Processor Fault
P0608 Control Module VSS Output "A" Malfunction
P0609 Control Module VSS Output "B" Malfunction
P0620 Generator Control Circuit Malfunction
P0621 Generator Lamp "L" Control Circuit Malfunction
P0622 Generator Field "F" Control Circuit Malfunction
P0650 Malfunction Indicator Lamp (MIL) Control Circuit Malfunction
P0654 Engine RPM Output Circuit Malfunction
P0655 Engine Hot Lamp Output Control Circuit Malfunction
P0656 Fuel Level Output Circuit Malfunction
P0700 Transmission Control System Malfunction
P0701 Transmission Control System Range/Performance
P0702 Transmission Control System Electrical
P0703 Torque Converter/Brake Switch "B" Circuit Malfunction
P0704 Clutch Switch Input Circuit Malfunction
P0705 Transmission Range Sensor Circuit Malfunction (PRNDL Input)
P0706 Transmission Range Sensor Circuit Range/Performance
P0707 Transmission Range Sensor Circuit Low Input
P0708 Transmission Range Sensor Circuit High Input
P0709 Transmission Range Sensor Circuit Intermittent
P0710 Transmission Fluid Temperature Sensor Circuit Malfunction
P0711 Transmission Fluid Temperature Sensor Circuit Range/Performance
P0712 Transmission Fluid Temperature Sensor Circuit Low Input
P0713 Transmission Fluid Temperature Sensor Circuit High Input
P0714 Transmission Fluid Temperature Sensor Circuit Intermittent
P0715 Input/Turbine Speed Sensor Circuit Malfunction
P0716 Input/Turbine Speed Sensor Circuit Range/Performance
P0717 Input/Turbine Speed Sensor Circuit No Signal

P0718 Input/Turbine Speed Sensor Circuit Intermittent
P0719 Torque Converter/Brake Switch "B" Circuit Low
P0720 Output Speed Sensor Circuit Malfunction
P0721 Output Speed Sensor Circuit Range/Performance
P0722 Output Speed Sensor Circuit No Signal
P0723 Output Speed Sensor Circuit Intermittent
P0724 Torque Converter/Brake Switch "B" Circuit High
P0725 Engine Speed Input Circuit Malfunction
P0726 Engine Speed Input Circuit Range/Performance
P0727 Engine Speed Input Circuit No Signal
P0728 Engine Speed Input Circuit Intermittent
P0730 Incorrect Gear Ratio
P0731 Gear no. 1 Incorrect Ratio
P0732 Gear no. 2 Incorrect Ratio
P0733 Gear no. 3 Incorrect Ratio
P0734 Gear no. 4 Incorrect Ratio
P0735 Gear no. 5 Incorrect Ratio
P0736 Reverse Incorrect Ratio
P0740 Torque Converter Clutch Circuit Malfunction
P0741 Torque Converter Clutch Circuit Performance or Stuck Off
P0742 Torque Converter Clutch Circuit Stuck On
P0743 Torque Converter Clutch Circuit Electrical
P0744 Torque Converter Clutch Circuit Intermittent
P0745 Pressure Control Solenoid Malfunction
P0746 Pressure Control Solenoid Performance or Stuck Off
P0747 Pressure Control Solenoid Stuck On
P0748 Pressure Control Solenoid Electrical
P0749 Pressure Control Solenoid Intermittent
P0750 Shift Solenoid "A" Malfunction
P0751 Shift Solenoid "A" Performance or Stuck Off
P0752 Shift Solenoid "A" Stuck On
P0753 Shift Solenoid "A" Electrical
P0754 Shift Solenoid "A" Intermittent
P0755 Shift Solenoid "B" Malfunction
P0756 Shift Solenoid "B" Performance or Stuck Off
P0757 Shift Solenoid "B" Stuck On
P0758 Shift Solenoid "B" Electrical
P0759 Shift Solenoid "B" Intermittent
P0760 Shift Solenoid "C" Malfunction
P0761 Shift Solenoid "C" Performance Or Stuck Off
P0762 Shift Solenoid "C" Stuck On
P0763 Shift Solenoid "C" Electrical
P0764 Shift Solenoid "C" Intermittent
P0765 Shift Solenoid "D" Malfunction
P0766 Shift Solenoid "D" Performance Or Stuck Off
P0767 Shift Solenoid "D" Stuck On
P0768 Shift Solenoid "D" Electrical
P0769 Shift Solenoid "D" Intermittent
P0770 Shift Solenoid "E" Malfunction
P0771 Shift Solenoid "E" Performance Or Stuck Off
P0772 Shift Solenoid "E" Stuck On
P0773 Shift Solenoid "E" Electrical
P0774 Shift Solenoid "E" Intermittent
P0780 Shift Malfunction
P0781 1–2 Shift Malfunction
P0782 2–3 Shift Malfunction
P0783 3–4 Shift Malfunction
P0784 4–5 Shift Malfunction

P0785 Shift/Timing Solenoid Malfunction
P0786 Shift/Timing Solenoid Range/Performance
P0787 Shift/Timing Solenoid Low
P0788 Shift/Timing Solenoid High
P0789 Shift/Timing Solenoid Intermittent
P0790 Normal/Performance Switch Circuit Malfunction
P0801 Reverse Inhibit Control Circuit Malfunction
P0803 1–4 Upshift (Skip Shift) Solenoid Control Circuit Malfunction
P0804 1–4 Upshift (Skip Shift) Lamp Control Circuit Malfunction
P1100 Induction Control Motor Position Sensor Fault
P1101 Traction Control Vacuum Solenoid Circuit Fault
P1102 Traction Control Ventilation Solenoid Circuit Fault
P1105 Fuel Pressure Solenoid Circuit Fault

P1294 Target Idle Speed Not Reached
P1295 No 5-Volt Supply To TP Sensor
P1296 No 5-Volt Supply To MAP Sensor
P1297 No Change In MAP From Start To Run
P1300 Ignition Timing Adjustment Circuit
P1390 Timing Belt Skipped One Tooth Or More
P1391 Intermittent Loss Of CMP Or CKP Sensor Signals
P1400 Manifold Differential Pressure Sensor Fault
P1443 EVAP Purge Control Solenoid "2" Circuit Fault
P1486 EVAP Leak Monitor Pinched Hose Detected
P1487 High Speed Radiator Fan Control Relay Circuit Fault
P1490 Low Speed Fan Control Relay Fault
P1492 Battery Temperature Sensor High Voltage
P1494 EVAP Ventilation Switch Or Mechanical Fault

P1495 EVAP Ventilation Solenoid Circuit Fault
P1496 5-Volt Supply Output Too Low
P1500 Generator FR Terminal Circuit Fault
P1600 PCM-TCM Serial Communication Link Circuit Fault
P1696 PCM Failure- EEPROM Write Denied
P1715 No CCD Messages From TCM
P1750 TCM Pulse Generator Circuit Fault
P1791 Pressure Control, Shift Control, TCC Solenoid Fault
P1899 PCM ECT Level Signal to TCM Circuit Fault
P1989 High Speed Condenser Fan Control Relay Fault

FLASH OUT CODE LIST

▶ **See Figures 93, 94, 95, and 96**

Code	Output pattern (for voltmeter)	Cause	Remedy
P1702	 A5AT005E	Shorted throttle position sensor circuit	o Check the throttle position sensor connector o check the throttle position sensor itself o Check the closed throttle position switch o Check the throttle position sensor wiring harness o Check the wiring between ECM and throttle position sensor
P1701	 A5AT005F	Open throttle position sensor circuit	
P1704	 A5AT005H	Throttle position sensor malfunction Improperly adjusted throttle position sensor	
P0712	 A5AT005I	Open fluid temperature sensor circuit	o Fluid temperature sensor connector inspection o Fluid temperature sensor inspection o Fluid temperature sensor wiring harness inspection
P0713	 A5AT005J	Shorted fluid temperature sensor circuit	
P1709	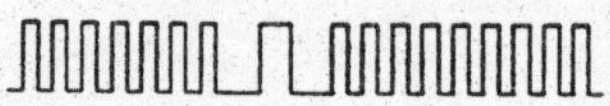 A5AT005K	Open kickdown servo switch circuit Shorted kickdown servo switch circuit	o Check the kickdown servo switch connector o Check the kickdown servo switch o Check the kickdown servo switch wiring harness

Fig. 93 Mitsubishi flash out DTC's, 1 of 4—Type 4 (OBD II) Codes

89446g27

Code	Output pattern (for voltmeter)	Cause	Remedy
P0727	 A5AT005L	Open ignition pulse pickup cable circuit	o Check the ignition pulse signal line o Check the wiring between ECM and ignisiton system
P1714	 A5AT005M	Short-circuited or improperly adjusted closed throttle position switch	o Check the closed throttle position switch connector o Check the closed throttle position switch itself o Adjust the closed throttle position switch o Check the closed throttle position switch wiring harness
P0717	 A5AT005N	Open-circuited pulse generator A	o Check the pulse generator A and pulse generator B o Check the vehicle speed reed switch (for chattering) o Check the pulse generator A and B wiring harness
P0722	 A5AT005O	Open-circuited pulse generator B	
P0707	 A5AT005Z	No input signal	o Check the transaxle range switch o Check the transaxle range wiring harness o Check the manual control cable
P0708	 A5ATA05A	More than two input signals	
P0752	 A5AT005P	Open shift control solenoid vave A circuit	o Check the solenoid valve connector o Check the shift control solenoid valve A o Check the shift control solenoid valve A wiring harness
P0753	 A5AT005Q	Shorted shift control solenoid valve A circuit	
P0757	 A5AT005R	Open shift control solenoid valve B circuit	o Check the shift control solenoid valve connector o Check the shift control solenoid valve B wiring harness o Check the shift control solenoid valve B
P0758	 A5AT005S	Short shift control solenoid valve B circuit	
P0747	 A5AT005T	Open pressure control solenoid valve circuit	o Check the pressure control solenoid valve o Check the pressure control solenoid valve wiring harness
P0748	 A5AT005U	Shorted pressure control solenoid valve circuit	

89446g28

Fig. 94 Mitsubishi flash out DTC's, 2 of 4—Type 4 (OBD II) Codes

Code	Output pattern (for voltmeter)	Cause	Remedy
P0743	 A5AT005V	Open circuit in damper clutch control solenoid valve Short circuit in damper clutch control solenoid valve Defect in the damper clutch system	o Inspection of solenoid valve connector o Individual inspection of damper clutch control solenoid valve o Check the damper clutch control solenoid valve wiring harness o Chck the TCM o Inspection of damper clutch hydraulic system
P0742	 A5AT005W		
P0740	 A5AT005X		
P1744	 A5AT005Y		
P0731	 A5ATA05B	Shifting to first gear does not match the engine speed	o Check the pulse generator A and pulse generator B connector o Check the pulse generator A and puls generator B o Check the one way clutch or rear clutch o Check the pulse generator wiring harness o Kickdown brake slippage
P0732	 A5ATA05C	Shifting to second gear does not match the engine speed	
P0733	 A5ATA05D	Shifting to third gear does not match the engine speed	o Check the rear clutch or control system o Check the pulse generator A and pulse generator B connector o Check the pulse generator A and pulse generator B o Check the pulse generator wiring harness o Check the rear clutch slippage or control system o Check the front clutch slippage or control system
P0734	 A5ATA05E	Shifting to fourth gear does not match the engine speed	o Check the pulse generator A and B connector o Check the pulse generator A and B o Kickdown brake slippage o Check the end clutch or control system o Check the pulse generator wiring harness
-		Normal	

Fig. 95 Mitsubishi flash out DTC's, 3 of 4—Type 4 (OBD II) Codes

89446g29

FAIL-SAFE ITEM

Code No.	Output code — Output pattern (for voltmeter)	Description	Fail-safe	Note (relation to diagnostic trouble code)
P0717	 A5AT005N	Open-circuited pulse generator A	Locked in third (D) or second (2,L)	When code No.0717 is generated fourth time
P0722	 A5AT005O	Open-circuited pulse generator B	Locked in third (D) or second (2,L)	When code No.0722 is generated fourth time
P0752	 A5AT005P	Open-circuited or shorted shift control solenoid valve A	Lock in third	When code No.0752 or 0753 is generated fourth time
P0753	 A5AT005Q			
P0757	 A5AT005R	Open-circuited or shorted shift control solenoid valve B	Lock in third gear	When code No.0757 or 0758 is generated fourth time
P0758	 A5AT005S			
P0747	 A5AT005T	Open-circuited or shorted pressure control solenoid valve	Locked in third (D) or second (2,L)	When code No.0747 or 0748 is generated fourth time
P0748	 A5AT005U			
P0731	 A5ATA05B	Gear shifting does not match the engine speed	Locked in third (D) or second (2,L)	When either code No.0731, 0732, 0733 or 0734 is generated fourth time
P0732	 A5ATA05C			
P0733	 A5ATA05D			
P0734	 A5ATA05E			

89446g30

Fig. 96 Mitsubishi flash out DTC's, 4 of 4—Type 4 (OBD II) Codes

VACUUM DIAGRAMS

Following are vacuum diagrams for most of the engine and emissions package combinations covered by this manual. Because vacuum circuits will vary based on various engine and vehicle options, always refer first to the vehicle emission control information label, if present. Should the label be missing, or should vehicle be equipped with a different engine from the vehicle's original equipment, refer to the diagrams below for the same or similar configuration.

If you wish to obtain a replacement emissions label, most manufacturers make the labels available for purchase. The labels can usually be ordered from a local dealer.

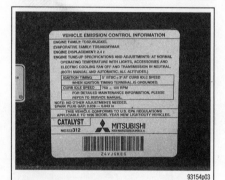

The Emission Control Label contains information about the vehicle's emissions systems, along with other pertinent service information

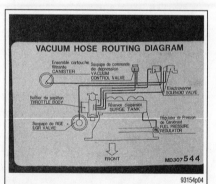

A vacuum diagram is typically affixed to a label in the engine compartment

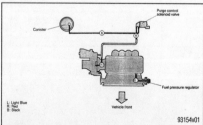

Emission control system vacuum hose routing—1990–92 1.5L engine, Federal emissions

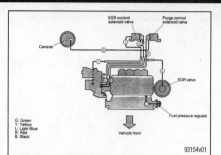

Emission control system vacuum hose routing—1990–92 1.5L engine, California emissions

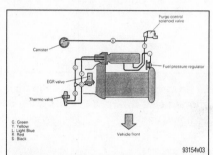

Emission control system vacuum hose routing—1990–92 1.6L engine, Federal emissions

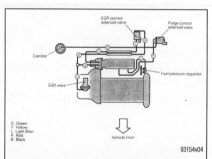

Emission control system vacuum hose routing—1990–92 1.6L engine, California emissions

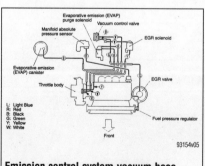

Emission control system vacuum hose routing—1993 1.5L engine, California emissions

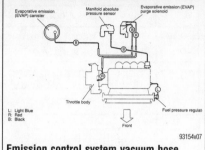

Emission control system vacuum hose routing—1993 1.5L engine, Federal emissions

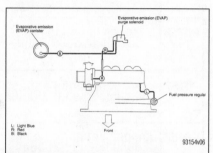

Emission control system vacuum hose routing—1993 1.8L engine, Federal emissions

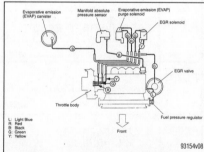

Emission control system vacuum hose routing—1994–96 1.5L engine, California and Federal emissions

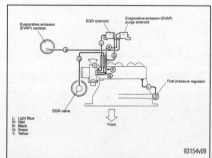

Emission control system vacuum hose routing—1994–96 1.8L engine, Federal emissions; 1994 California emissions

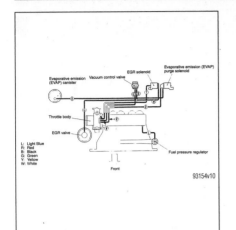

Emission control system vacuum hose routing—1995–96 1.8L engine, California emissions

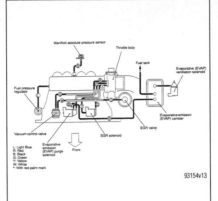

Emission control system vacuum hose routing—1998 1.5L engine, California and Federal emissions

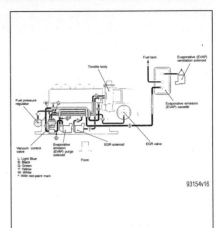

Emission control system vacuum hose routing—1999–00 1.8L engine, California and Federal emissions

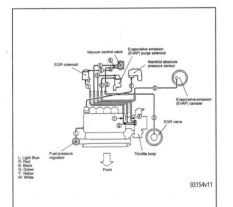

Emission control system vacuum hose routing—1997 1.5L engine, California and Federal emissions

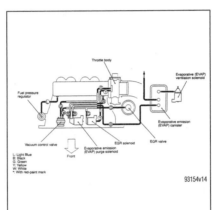

Emission control system vacuum hose routing—1998 1.8L engine, California and Federal emissions

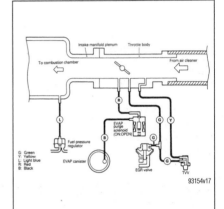

Emission control system vacuum hose routing—1990–93 2.0L SOHC engine, Federal emissions

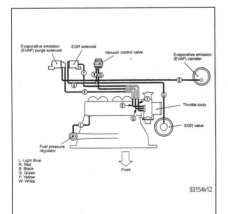

Emission control system vacuum hose routing—1997 1.8L engine, California and Federal emissions

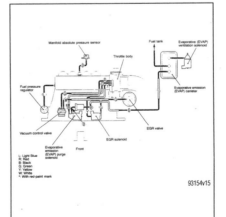

Emission control system vacuum hose routing—1999–00 1.5L engine, California and Federal emissions

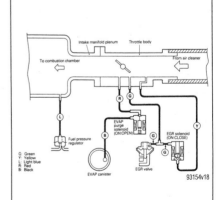

Emission control system vacuum hose routing—1990–93 2.0L SOHC engine, California emissions

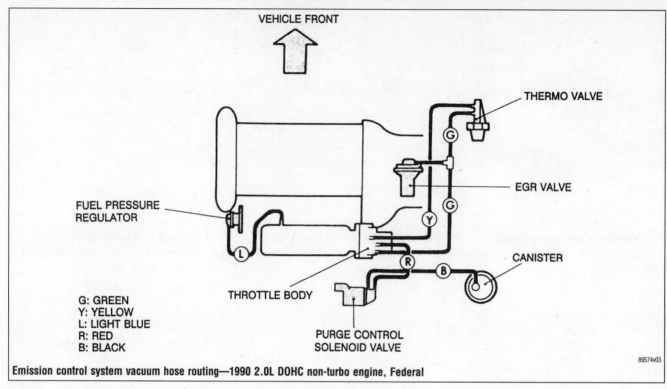

Emission control system vacuum hose routing—1990 2.0L DOHC non-turbo engine, Federal

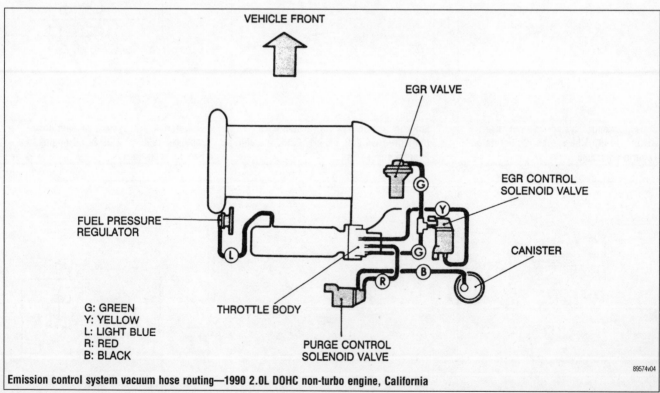

Emission control system vacuum hose routing—1990 2.0L DOHC non-turbo engine, California

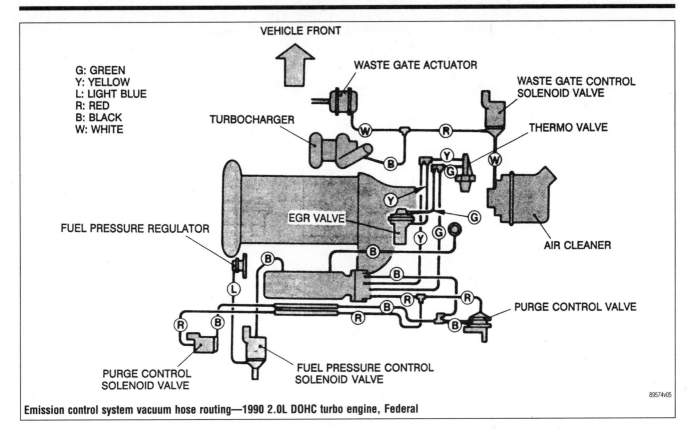

Emission control system vacuum hose routing—1990 2.0L DOHC turbo engine, Federal

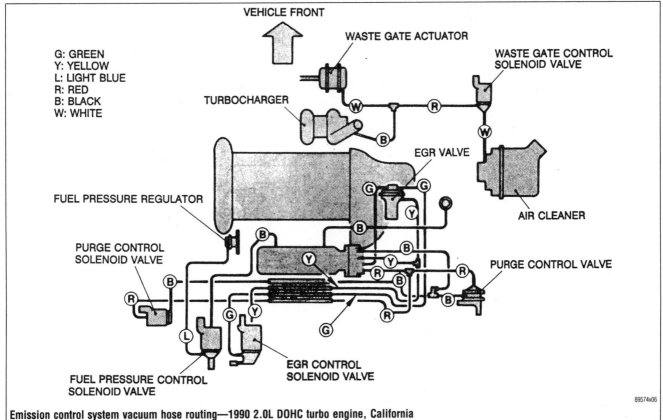

Emission control system vacuum hose routing—1990 2.0L DOHC turbo engine, California

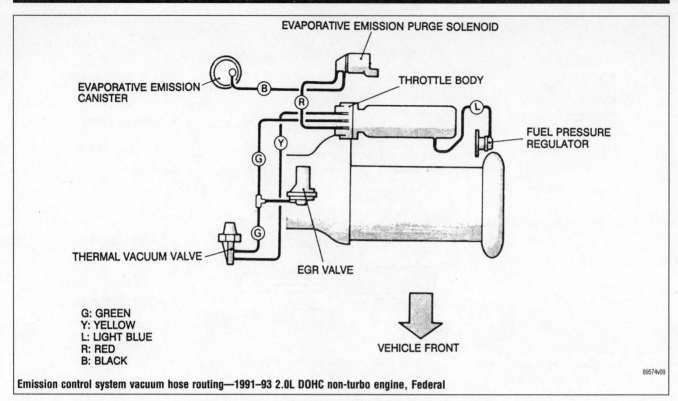

EVAPORATIVE EMISSION PURGE SOLENOID

THROTTLE BODY

EVAPORATIVE EMISSION CANISTER

FUEL PRESSURE REGULATOR

THERMAL VACUUM VALVE

EGR VALVE

G: GREEN
Y: YELLOW
L: LIGHT BLUE
R: RED
B: BLACK

VEHICLE FRONT

89574v09

Emission control system vacuum hose routing—1991–93 2.0L DOHC non-turbo engine, Federal

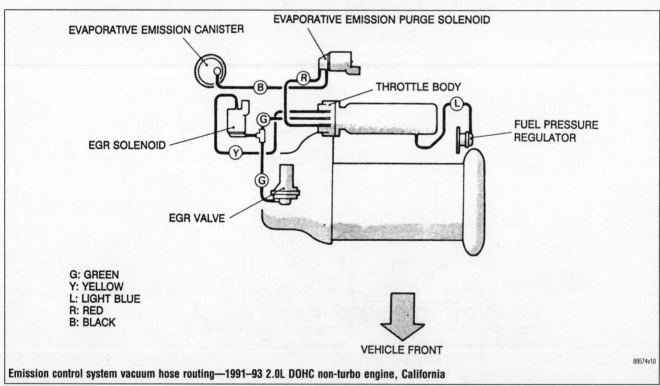

EVAPORATIVE EMISSION CANISTER

EVAPORATIVE EMISSION PURGE SOLENOID

THROTTLE BODY

FUEL PRESSURE REGULATOR

EGR SOLENOID

EGR VALVE

G: GREEN
Y: YELLOW
L: LIGHT BLUE
R: RED
B: BLACK

VEHICLE FRONT

89574v10

Emission control system vacuum hose routing—1991–93 2.0L DOHC non-turbo engine, California

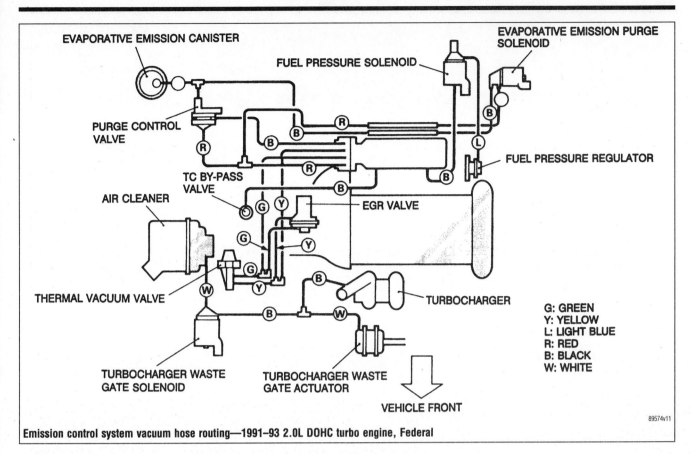

Emission control system vacuum hose routing—1991–93 2.0L DOHC turbo engine, Federal

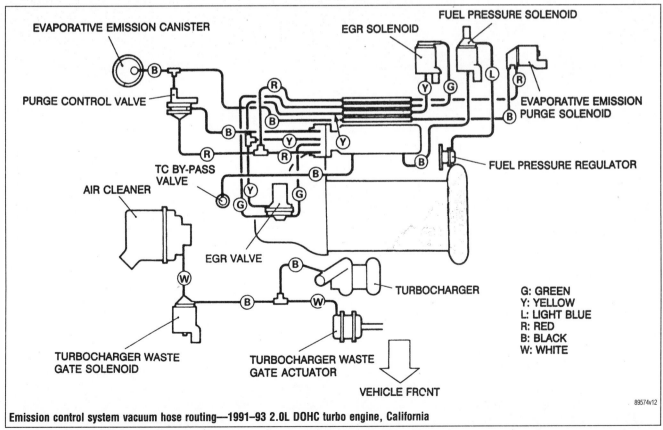

Emission control system vacuum hose routing—1991–93 2.0L DOHC turbo engine, California

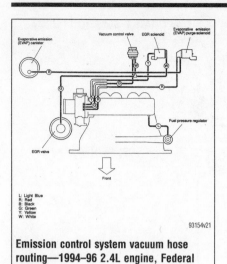

93154v21

Emission control system vacuum hose routing—1994–96 2.4L engine, Federal emissions

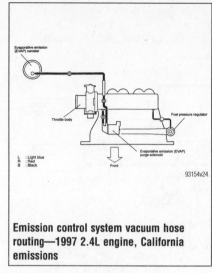

93154v24.

Emission control system vacuum hose routing—1997 2.4L engine, California emissions

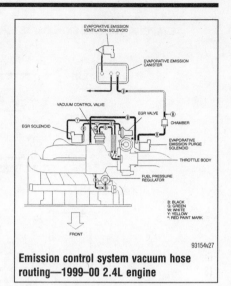

93154v27

Emission control system vacuum hose routing—1999–00 2.4L engine

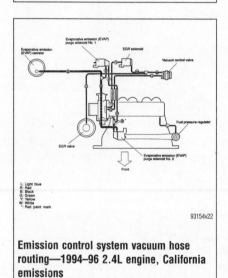

93154v22

Emission control system vacuum hose routing—1994–96 2.4L engine, California emissions

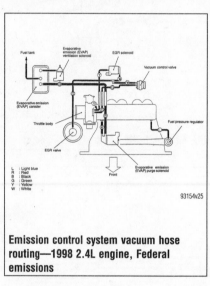

93154v25

Emission control system vacuum hose routing—1998 2.4L engine, Federal emissions

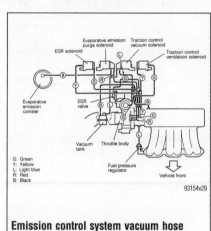

93154v29

Emission control system vacuum hose routing—1992 3.0L engines (SOHC and DOHC) w/traction control, California emissions

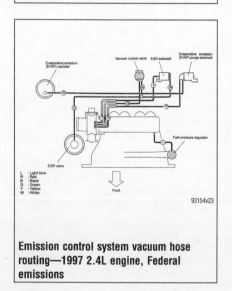

93154v23

Emission control system vacuum hose routing—1997 2.4L engine, Federal emissions

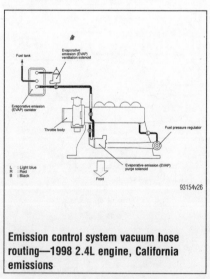

93154v26

Emission control system vacuum hose routing—1998 2.4L engine, California emissions

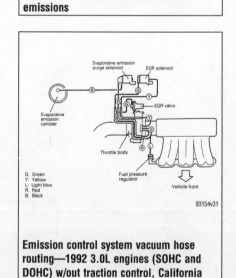

93154v31

Emission control system vacuum hose routing—1992 3.0L engines (SOHC and DOHC) w/out traction control, California emissions

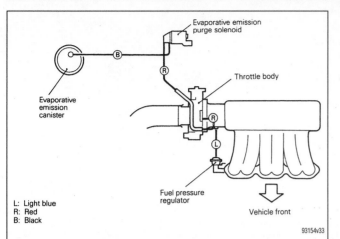

L: Light blue
R: Red
B: Black

93154v33

Emission control system vacuum hose routing—1992 3.0L engines (SOHC and DOHC) w/out traction control, Federal emissions

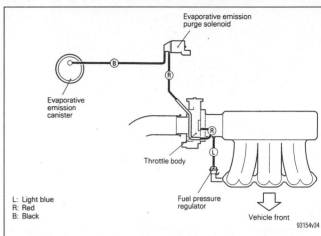

L: Light blue
R: Red
B: Black

93154v34

Emission control system vacuum hose routing—1993–94 3.0L engines (SOHC and DOHC) w/out traction control, Federal emissions

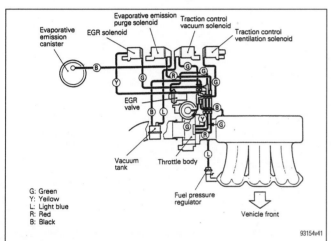

G: Green
Y: Yellow
L: Light blue
R: Red
B: Black

93154v41

Emission control system vacuum hose routing—1995–96 3.0L engines (SOHC and DOHC) w/traction control, Federal emissions

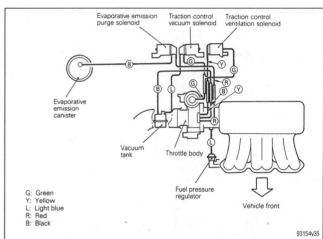

G: Green
Y: Yellow
L: Light blue
R: Red
B: Black

93154v35

Emission control system vacuum hose routing—1992 3.0L engines (SOHC and DOHC) w/traction control, Federal emissions

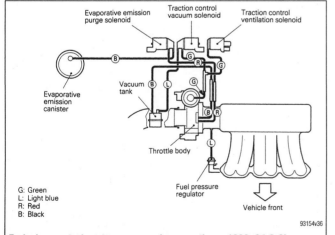

G: Green
L: Light blue
R: Red
B: Black

93154v36

Emission control system vacuum hose routing—1993–94 3.0L engines (SOHC and DOHC) w/traction control, Federal emissions

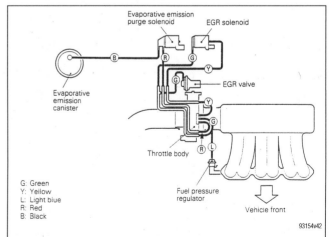

G: Green
Y: Yellow
L: Light blue
R: Red
B: Black

93154v42

Emission control system vacuum hose routing—1995–96 3.0L engines (SOHC and DOHC) w/out traction control, Federal emissions

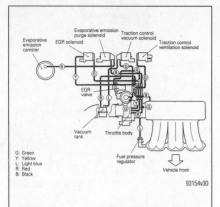

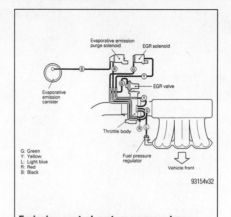

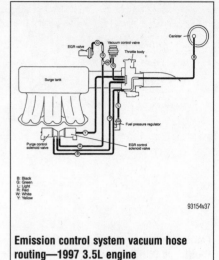

Emission control system vacuum hose routing—1993–96 3.0L engines (SOHC and DOHC) w/traction control, California emissions

Emission control system vacuum hose routing—1993–96 3.0L engines (SOHC and DOHC) w/out traction control, California emissions

Emission control system vacuum hose routing—1997 3.5L engine

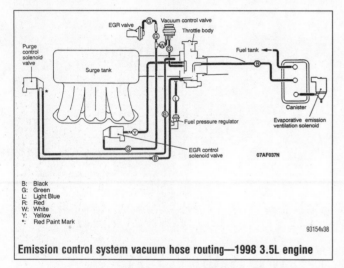

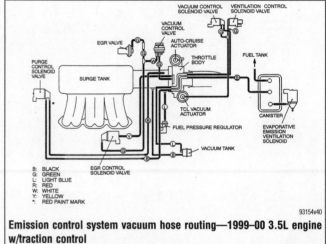

Emission control system vacuum hose routing—1998 3.5L engine

Emission control system vacuum hose routing—1999–00 3.5L engine w/traction control

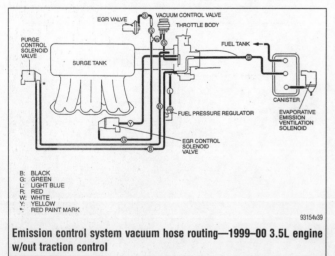

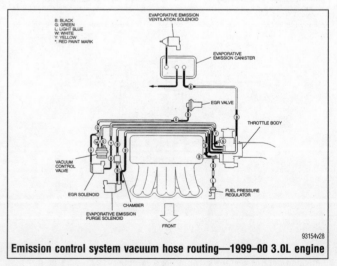

Emission control system vacuum hose routing—1999–00 3.5L engine w/out traction control

Emission control system vacuum hose routing—1999–00 3.0L engine

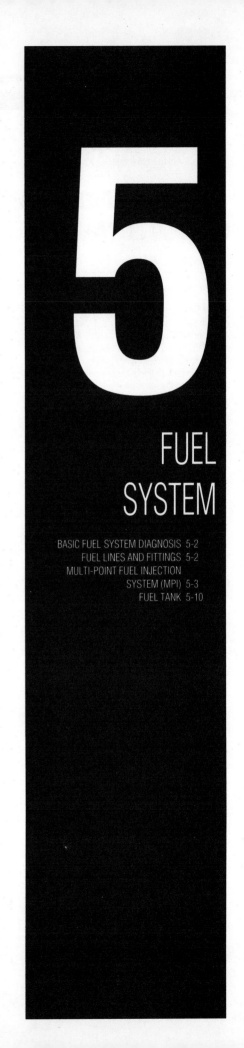

5

FUEL
SYSTEM

BASIC FUEL SYSTEM DIAGNOSIS

When there is a problem starting or driving a vehicle, two of the most important checks involve the ignition and the fuel systems. The questions most mechanics attempt to answer first, "is there spark?" and "is there fuel?" will often lead to solving most basic problems. For ignition system diagnosis and testing, please refer to the information on engine electrical components and ignition systems found earlier in this manual. If the ignition system checks out (there is spark), then you must determine if the fuel system is operating properly (is there fuel?).

FUEL LINES AND FITTINGS

Fuel Line Fittings

REMOVAL & INSTALLATION

▸ **See Figures 1 thru 7**

The fuel lines used on all models covered by this manual are quite straight forward. Typically the fittings are either rubber hoses connecting to steel lines with clamps, or steel lines connecting to steel lines using retaining bolts or flare fittings. Several fittings are unique such as the banjo-bolt fitting on the fuel feed line from the fuel filter.

✳✳ CAUTION

Observe all applicable safety precautions when working around fuel. Whenever servicing the fuel system, always work in a well ventilated area. Do not allow fuel spray or vapors to come in contact with a spark or open flame. Keep a dry chemical fire extinguisher near the work area. Always keep fuel in a container specifically designed for fuel storage; also, always properly seal fuel containers to avoid the possibility of fire or explosion.

Fig. 5 . . . then remove the fuel feed line from the fuel injector rail

Fig. 1 This photo of the fuel pump lines is an example of the type of fittings found on most models. The return line utilizes a rubber hose and a hose clamp, while the feed line utilizes a flare fitting

Fig. 3 . . . then disconnect the hose from the pressure regulator

Fig. 6 The fitting on the top of the fuel filter utilizes a banjo-bolt type fitting. Remove the bolt from the filter feed line on the top of the filter

Fig. 2 This fitting on the fuel pressure regulator utilizes a rubber hose and a hose clamp. Remove the hose clamp . . .

Fig. 4 The fuel feed line-to-fuel rail fitting is held by retaining bolts. Unfasten the bolts . . .

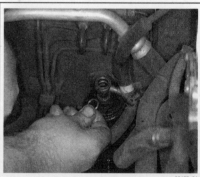

Fig. 7 On the banjo-bolt type fitting, it is crucial that the copper washers are replaced every time the fitting is removed

MULTI-POINT FUEL INJECTION SYSTEM (MPI)

General Information

The Multi-Point Injection (MPI) system is electronically controlled by the Engine Control Module (ECM), based on data from various sensors. The ECM controls the fuel flow, idle speed and ignition timing.

Fuel is supplied to the injectors by an electric in-tank fuel pump and is distributed to the respective injectors via the main fuel pipe. The fuel pressure applied to the injector is constant and higher than the pressure in the intake manifold. The pressure is controlled by the fuel pressure regulator. The excess fuel is returned to the fuel tank through the fuel return pipe.

When an electric current flows in the injector, the injector valve is fully opened to supply fuel. Since the fuel pressure is constant, the amount of the fuel injected from the injector into the manifold is increased or decreased in proportion to the time the electric current flows. Based on ECU signals, the injectors inject fuel to the cylinder manifold ports in firing order.

The flow rate of the air drawn through the air cleaner is measured by the air flow sensor. The air enters the air intake plenum or manifold through the throttle body. In the intake manifold, the air is mixed with the fuel from the injectors and is drawn into the cylinder. The air flow rate is controlled according to the degree of the throttle valve and the servo motor openings. The system is monitored through a number of sensors which feed information on engine conditions and requirements to the ECM. The ECM calculates the injection time and rate according to the signals from the sensors.

Fuel System Service Precautions

Safety is the most important factor when performing not only fuel system maintenance but any type of maintenance. Failure to conduct maintenance and repairs in a safe manner may result in serious personal injury or death. Maintenance and testing of the vehicle's fuel system components can be accomplished safely and effectively by adhering to the following rules and guidelines.

• To avoid the possibility of fire and personal injury, always disconnect the negative battery cable unless the repair or test procedure requires that battery voltage be applied.

• Always relieve the fuel system pressure prior to disconnecting any fuel system component (injector, fuel rail, pressure regulator, etc.), fitting or fuel line connection. Exercise extreme caution whenever relieving fuel system pressure to avoid exposing skin, face and eyes to fuel spray. Please be advised that fuel under pressure may penetrate the skin or any part of the body that it contacts.

• Always place a shop towel or cloth around the fitting or connection prior to loosening to absorb any excess fuel due to spillage. Ensure that all fuel spillage (should it occur) is quickly removed from engine surfaces. Ensure that all fuel soaked cloths or towels are deposited into a suitable waste container.

• Always keep a dry chemical (Class B) fire extinguisher near the work area.

• Do not allow fuel spray or fuel vapors to come into contact with a spark or open flame.

• Always use a backup wrench when loosening and tightening fuel line connection fittings. This will prevent unnecessary stress and torsion to fuel line piping. Always follow the proper torque specifications.

• Always replace worn fuel fitting O-rings with new. Do not substitute fuel hose or equivalent, where fuel pipe is installed.

Relieving Fuel System Pressure

✳✳ CAUTION

Fuel injection systems remain under pressure after the engine has been turned OFF. Properly relieve fuel pressure before disconnecting any fuel lines. Failure to do so may result in fire or personal injury.

1. Turn the ignition to the **OFF** position.
2. Loosen the fuel filler cap to release fuel tank pressure.

✳✳ CAUTION

Observe all applicable safety precautions when working around fuel. Whenever servicing the fuel system, always work in a well ventilated area. Do not allow fuel spray or vapors to come in contact with a spark or open flame. Keep a dry chemical fire extinguisher near the work area. Always keep fuel in a container specifically designed for fuel storage; also, always properly seal fuel containers to avoid the possibility of fire or explosion.

3. For the Mirage, Diamante, and 1994–00 Galant, remove the rear seat cushion, then remove the service cover and detach the fuel pump harness connector.
4. For the 1990–93 FWD Galant, detach the fuel pump harness connector located in the area of the fuel tank. It may be necessary to raise the vehicle to access the connector.
5. For the 1990–93 AWD Galant, remove the carpet from the trunk, locate the fuel tank wiring at the pump access cover, then detach the wiring.
6. Start the vehicle and allow it to run until it stalls from lack of fuel. Turn the key to the **OFF** position.
7. Disconnect the negative battery cable, then attach the fuel pump connector. Install the access cover, cushion or carpet as necessary.
8. Wrap shop towels around the fitting that is being disconnected to absorb residual fuel in the lines.
9. Place shop towels into proper safety container.

Throttle Body

REMOVAL & INSTALLATION

◆ See Figures 8 thru 16

1. Properly relieve the fuel system pressure as outlined earlier in this section.
2. Drain the engine cooling system into a suitable container.
3. Matchmark the location of the adjuster bolt on the accelerator cable mounting flange. This will assure that the cable is installed in its original location. Remove the throttle cable adjusting bolt and disconnect the cable from the lever on the throttle body. Position cable aside.

Fig. 8 Detach the connector for the throttle position (TP) sensor

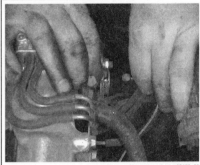
Fig. 9 Remove the accelerator cable end from the throttle lever

Fig. 10 Remove the hose shown here from the throttle body

Fig. 11 The throttle body is retained by four bolts—2.4L engine

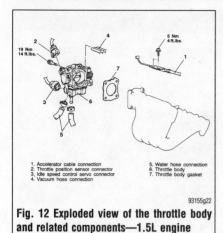

Fig. 12 Exploded view of the throttle body and related components—1.5L engine

1. Accelerator cable connection
2. Throttle position sensor connector
3. Idle speed control servo connector
4. Vacuum hose connection
5. Water hose connection
6. Throttle body
7. Throttle body gasket

93155g22

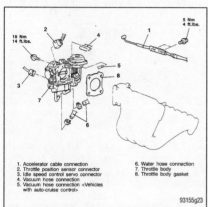

Fig. 13 Exploded view of the throttle body and related components—1.8L engine

1. Accelerator cable connection
2. Throttle position sensor connector
3. Idle speed control servo connector
4. Vacuum hose connection
5. Vacuum hose connection <Vehicles with auto-cruise control>
6. Water hose connection
7. Throttle body
8. Throttle body gasket

93155g23

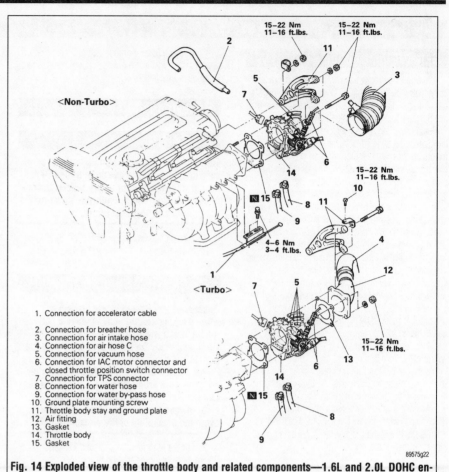

<Non-Turbo>

<Turbo>

1. Connection for accelerator cable
2. Connection for breather hose
3. Connection for air intake hose
4. Connection for air hose C
5. Connection for vacuum hose
6. Connection for IAC motor connector and closed throttle position switch connector
7. Connection for TPS connector
8. Connection for water hose
9. Connection for water by-pass hose
10. Ground plate mounting screw
11. Throttle body stay and ground plate
12. Air fitting
13. Gasket
14. Throttle body
15. Gasket

89575g22

Fig. 14 Exploded view of the throttle body and related components—1.6L and 2.0L DOHC engine

Fig. 15 Exploded view of the throttle body and related components—3.0L SOHC engine, DOHC similar

1. ACCELERATOR CABLE CONNECTION
2. THROTTLE POSITION SENSOR CONNECTOR
3. IDLE AIR CONTROL MOTOR CONNECTOR
4. VACUUM HOSE CONNECTION
5. WATER HOSE CONNECTION
6. VACUUM PIPE ASSEMBLY
7. THROTTLE BODY
8. THROTTLE BODY GASKET

93155g24

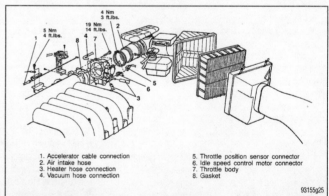

Fig. 16 Exploded view of the throttle body and related components—3.5L engine

1. Accelerator cable connection
2. Air intake hose
3. Heater hose connection
4. Vacuum hose connection
5. Throttle position sensor connector
6. Idle speed control motor connector
7. Throttle body
8. Gasket

93155g25

4. Remove the connection for the breather hose and the air intake hose from the throttle body and position aside.

5. Tag and disconnect the necessary vacuum hoses.

6. Label and detach the electrical connectors at the throttle body, as necessary.

7. Disconnect the water and water by-pass hoses at the base of the throttle body.

8. If equipped, unfasten the ground plate mounting screws, then remove the throttle body stay and ground plate from the engine.

9. Remove the air fitting and gasket.

10. Unfasten the throttle body mounting bolts, then remove the throttle body from the engine. Remove and discard the gasket.

To install:

11. Clean all old gasket material from the both throttle body mounting surfaces. Install new gasket onto the intake manifold plenum mounting surface.

➡**Poor idling quality and poor performance may be experienced if the gasket is installed incorrectly.**

12. Install the throttle body to the intake manifold plenum and tighten the mounting bolts.

13. Install the air fitting, if equipped, making sure new gasket is in place.

14. If equipped, install the throttle body stay and ground plate. Secure with retainers tightened to 11–16 ft. lbs. (15–22 Nm).

15. Install the ground plate mounting screw.

16. Connect the water hoses to the throttle body. Install new hose clamps if required.

17. Attach the electrical and vacuum connectors to the throttle body, as tagged during removal.

18. Connect the accelerator cable to the throttle body and install the adjusting bolt in original position. Check adjustment of cable.

19. Install the air intake and breather hoses.

20. If removed, install the battery and connect the positive cable.

21. Connect the negative battery cable. Refill the cooling system.

Fuel Rail and Injector(s)

REMOVAL & INSTALLATION

1.5L, 1.8L, And 2.0L SOHC Engines

▶ See Figures 17, 18, and 19

1. Relieve the fuel system pressure as described in this section.

2. Disconnect the PCV hose from the valve cover. Also disconnect the breather hose at the opposite end of the valve cover.

3. Remove the bolts holding the high pressure fuel line to the fuel rail and disconnect the line. Be prepared to contain fuel spillage; plug the line to keep out dirt and debris.

✳✳ CAUTION

Observe all applicable safety precautions when working around fuel. Whenever servicing the fuel system, always work in a well ventilated area. Do not allow fuel spray or vapors to come in contact with a spark or open flame. Keep a dry chemical fire extinguisher near the work area. Always keep fuel in a container specifically designed for fuel storage; also, always properly seal fuel containers to avoid the possibility of fire or explosion.

4. Remove the vacuum hose from the fuel pressure regulator.

5. Disconnect the fuel return hose from the pressure regulator.

6. Label and detach the electrical connectors from each injector.

7. Remove the bolt(s) holding the fuel rail to the manifold. Carefully lift the rail up and remove it with the injectors attached. Take great care not to drop an injector. Place the rail and injectors in a safe location on the workbench; protect the tips of the injectors from dirt and/or impact.

8. Remove and discard the injector insulators from the intake manifold. The insulators are not reusable.

9. Remove the injectors from the fuel rail by pulling gently in a straight outward motion. Make certain the grommet and O-ring come off with the injector.

To install:

10. Install a new insulator in each injector port in the manifold.

11. Remove the old grommet and O-ring from each injector. Install a new grommet and O-ring; coat the O-ring lightly with clean, thin oil.

12. If the fuel pressure regulator was removed, replace the O-ring with a new one and coat it lightly with clean, thin oil. Insert the regulator straight into the rail, then check that it can be rotated freely. If it does not rotate smoothly, remove it and inspect the O-ring for deformation or jamming. When properly installed, align the mounting holes and tighten the retaining bolts to 7 ft. lbs. (9 Nm). This procedure must be followed even if the fuel rail was not removed.

13. Install the injector into the fuel rail, constantly turning the injector left and right during installation.

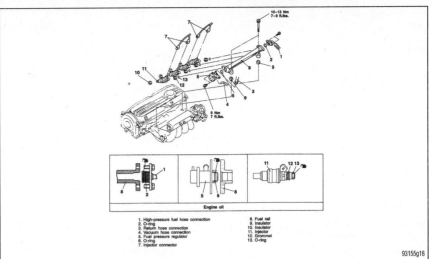

Fig. 17 Exploded view of the fuel injectors and related components—1.5L engine

1. High-pressure fuel hose connection
2. O-ring
3. Return hose connection
4. Vacuum hose connection
5. Fuel pressure regulator
6. O-ring
7. Injector connector
8. Fuel rail
9. Insulator
10. Insulator
11. Injector
12. Grommet
13. O-ring

93155g18

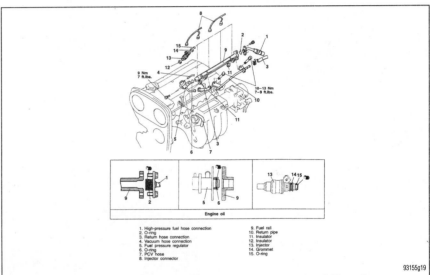

Fig. 18 Exploded view of the fuel injectors and related components—1.8L engine

1. High-pressure fuel hose connection
2. O-ring
3. Return hose connection
4. Vacuum hose connection
5. Fuel pressure regulator
6. O-ring
7. PCV hose
8. Injector connector
9. Fuel rail
10. Return pipe
11. Insulator
12. Insulator
13. Injector
14. Grommet
15. O-ring

93155g19

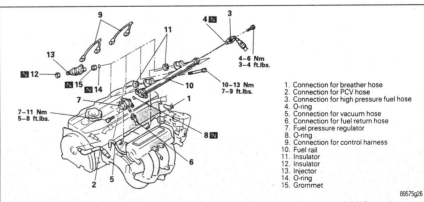

Fig. 19 Exploded view of the fuel injectors and related components—2.0L SOHC engine

1. Connection for breather hose
2. Connection for PCV hose
3. Connection for high pressure fuel hose
4. O-ring
5. Connection for vacuum hose
6. Connection for fuel return hose
7. Fuel pressure regulator
8. O-ring
9. Connection for control harness
10. Fuel rail
11. Insulator
12. Insulator
13. Injector
14. O-ring
15. Grommet

89575g26

When fully installed, the injector should still turn freely in the rail. If it does not, remove the injector and inspect the O-ring for deformation or damage.

14. Install the delivery pipe and injectors to the engine. Make certain that each injector fits correctly into its port and that the rubber insulators for the fuel rail mounts are in position.

15. Install the fuel rail retaining bolts and tighten them to 9 ft. lbs. (12 Nm).

16. Connect the wiring harnesses to the appropriate injector.

17. Connect the fuel return hose to the pressure regulator, then connect the vacuum hose.

18. Replace the O-ring on the high pressure fuel line, coat the O-ring lightly with clean, thin oil and

install the line to the fuel rail. Tighten the mounting bolts.

19. Attach the PCV hose and the breather hose if they were disconnected.

20. Connect the negative battery cable. Pressurize the fuel system and inspect all connections for leaks.

1.6L and 2.0L DOHC Engines

▶ See Figure 20

1. Relieve the fuel system pressure as described in this section.

2. Disconnect the negative battery cable.

3. Wrap the connection with a shop towel and disconnect the high pressure fuel line at the fuel rail.

⁘ CAUTION

Observe all applicable safety precautions when working around fuel. Whenever servicing the fuel system, always work in a well ventilated area. Do not allow fuel spray or vapors to come in contact with a spark or open flame. Keep a dry chemical fire extinguisher near the work area. Always keep fuel in a container specifically designed for fuel storage; also, always properly seal fuel containers to avoid the possibility of fire or explosion.

4. Disconnect the fuel return hose and remove the O-ring.

5. Disconnect the vacuum hose from the fuel pressure regulator.

6. Disconnect the PCV hose. On 2.0L engine, remove the center cover.

7. Label and detach the electrical connectors from each injector.

8. Remove the injector rail retaining bolts. Make sure the rubber mounting bushings do not get lost.

9. Lift the rail assembly up and away from the engine.

10. Remove the injectors from the rail by pulling gently. Discard the lower insulator. Check the resistance through the injector. The specification for 2.0L turbocharged engine is 2–3 ohms at 70°F (20°C). The specification for the others is 13–15 ohms at 70°F (20°C).

To install:

11. Install a new grommet and O-ring to the injector. Coat the O-ring with light oil.

12. Install the injector to the fuel rail.

13. Replace the seats in the intake manifold. Install the fuel rail and injectors to the manifold. Make sure the rubber bushings are in place before tightening the mounting bolts.

14. Tighten the retaining bolts to 72 inch lbs. (11 Nm).

15. Attach the connectors to the injectors and install the center cover. Connect the PCV hose.

16. Connect the fuel pressure regulator vacuum hose.

17. Connect the fuel return hose.

18. Replace the O-ring, lightly lubricate it and connect the high pressure fuel line.

19. Connect the negative battery cable and check the entire system for proper operation and leaks.

2.4L Engine

▶ See Figures 21 thru 30

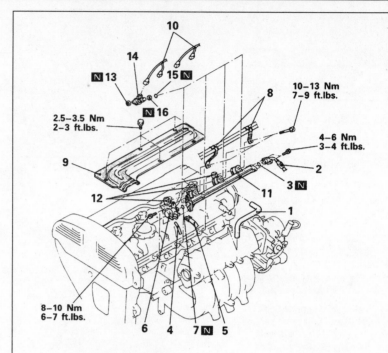

1. Connection for PCV hose
2. Connection for high pressure fuel hose
3. O-ring
4. Connection for vacuum hose
5. Connection for fuel return hose
6. Fuel pressure regulator
7. O-ring
8. Accelerator cable clamp
9. Center cover
10. Connection for control harness
11. Fuel rail
12. Insulator
13. Insulator
14. Injector
15. O-ring
16. Grommet

Fig. 20 Exploded view of the fuel injectors and related components —1.6L and 2.0L DOHC engines

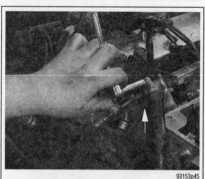

Fig. 21 Remove the fuel feed line-to-fuel rail retaining fitting bolts . . .

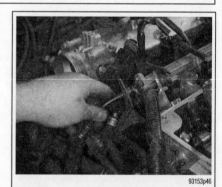

Fig. 22 . . . then remove the fuel feed line from the fuel injector rail

Fig. 23 Remove the hose clamp on the fuel return line . . .

Fig. 24 . . . then disconnect the hose from the pressure regulator

Fig. 25 Remove the vacuum hose from the pressure regulator

Fig. 26 Detach the connectors from all of the fuel injectors

Fig. 27 Remove the two fuel rail retaining bolts . . .

Fig. 28 . . . then lift the rail and the injectors from the intake manifold

Fig. 29 Remove the fuel injectors from the rail by gently rocking them loose

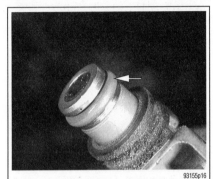

Fig. 30 Always replace the O-rings on the injectors before reinstalling them

1. Relieve the fuel system pressure as described in this section.
2. Label and disconnect the spark plug wires. Position the wires aside.
3. Disconnect the PCV hose from the valve cover.
4. Remove the bolts holding the high pressure fuel line to the fuel rail, then disconnect the line. Be prepared to contain fuel spillage; plug the line to keep out dirt and debris.

❊❊ CAUTION

Observe all applicable safety precautions when working around fuel. Whenever servicing the fuel system, always work in a well ventilated area. Do not allow fuel spray or vapors to come in contact with a spark or open flame. Keep a dry chemical fire extinguisher near the work area. Always keep fuel in a container specifically designed for fuel storage; also, always properly seal fuel containers to avoid the possibility of fire or explosion.

5. Remove the vacuum hose from the fuel pressure regulator.
6. Disconnect the fuel return hose from the pressure regulator.
7. Label and detach the electrical connectors from each injector.
8. Remove the bolt(s) holding the fuel rail to the manifold. Carefully lift the rail up and remove it with the injectors attached. Take great care not to drop an injector. Place the rail and injectors in a safe location

on the workbench; protect the tips of the injectors from dirt and/or impact.
9. Remove and discard the injector insulators from the intake manifold. The insulators are not reusable.
10. Remove the injectors from the fuel rail by pulling gently in a straight outward motion. Make certain the grommet and O-ring come off with the injector.

To install:

11. Install a new insulator in each injector port in the manifold.
12. Remove the old grommet and O-ring from each injector. Install a new grommet and O-ring; coat the O-ring lightly with clean, thin oil.
13. If the fuel pressure regulator was removed, replace the O-ring with a new one and coat it lightly with clean, thin oil. Insert the regulator straight into the rail, then check that it can be rotated freely. If it does not rotate smoothly, remove it and inspect the O-ring for deformation or jamming. When properly installed, align the mounting holes and tighten the retaining bolts to 7 ft. lbs. (9 Nm). This procedure must be followed even if the fuel rail was not removed.
14. Install the injector into the fuel rail, constantly turning the injector left and right during installation. When fully installed, the injector should still turn freely in the rail. If it does not, remove the injector and inspect the O-ring for deformation or damage.
15. Install the delivery pipe and injectors to the engine. Make certain that each injector fits correctly into its port and that the rubber insulators for the fuel rail mounts are in position.
16. Install the fuel rail retaining bolts and tighten them to 9 ft. lbs. (12 Nm).
17. Connect the wiring harnesses to the appropriate injector.

18. Connect the fuel return hose to the pressure regulator, then connect the vacuum hose.
19. Replace the O-ring on the high pressure fuel line, coat the O-ring lightly with clean, thin oil and install the line to the fuel rail. Tighten the mounting bolts to 4 ft. lbs. (6 Nm).
20. Connect the PCV hose and spark plug wires.
21. Connect the negative battery cable. Pressurize the fuel system and inspect all connections for leaks.

3.0L and 3.5L Engines

▶ See Figures 31 and 32

1. Relieve the fuel system pressure.
2. Disconnect the negative battery cable.

❊❊ CAUTION

Work MUST NOT be started until at least 90 seconds after the ignition switch is turned to the LOCK position and the negative battery cable is disconnected from the battery. This will allow time for the air bag system backup power supply to deplete its stored energy, preventing accidental air bag deployment which could result in unnecessary air bag system repairs and/or personal injury.

3. Drain the cooling system.
4. Disconnect all components from the air intake plenum and remove the plenum from the intake manifold. Refer to Section 3.
5. Wrap the connection with a shop towel and disconnect the high pressure fuel line at the fuel rail.

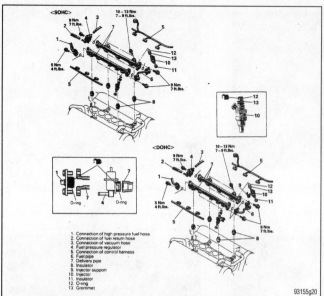

Fig. 31 Exploded view of the fuel injectors and related components—3.0L engines

1. Connection of high pressure fuel hose
2. Connection of fuel return hose
3. Connection of vacuum hose
4. Fuel pressure regulator
5. Connection of control harness
6. Fuel pipe
7. Delivery pipe
8. Insulator
9. Injector support
10. Injector
11. Insulator
12. O-ring
13. Grommet

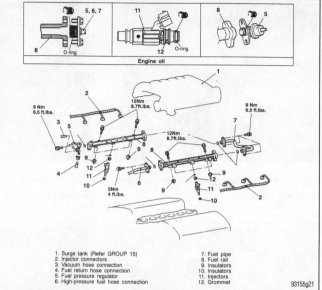

Fig. 32 Exploded view of the fuel injectors and related components—3.5L engine

1. Surge tank (Refer GROUP 15)
2. Injector connectors
3. Vacuum hose connection
4. Fuel return hose connection
5. Fuel pressure regulator
6. High-pressure fuel hose connection
7. Fuel pipe
8. Fuel rail
9. Insulators
10. Insulators
11. Injectors
12. Grommet

6. Disconnect the fuel return hose and remove the O-ring.

7. Disconnect the vacuum hose from the fuel pressure regulator.

8. Detach the electrical connectors from each injector.

9. Remove the fuel pipe connecting the fuel rails. Remove the injector rail retaining bolts. Make sure the rubber mounting bushings do not get lost.

10. Lift the rail assemblies up and away from the engine.

11. Remove the injectors from the rail by pulling gently. Discard the lower insulator.

To install:

➡Some of the vehicles may have a clip that secures the injector to the fuel rail. Be sure to remove or install the injector clip where necessary.

12. Install a new grommet and O-ring to the injector. Coat the O-ring with light oil.

13. Install the injector to the fuel rail.

14. Replace the seats in the intake manifold. Install the fuel rails and injectors to the manifold. Make sure the rubber bushings are in place before tightening the mounting bolts.

15. Tighten the retaining bolts to 7–9 ft. lbs. (10–13 Nm). Install the fuel pipe with new gasket.

16. Attach the electrical connectors to the injectors.

17. Connect the fuel return hose.

18. Replace the O-ring, lightly lubricate it and connect the high pressure fuel line.

19. Using new gaskets, install the intake plenum and all related items. Refer to Section 3.

20. Fill the cooling system.

21. Connect the negative battery cable and check the entire system for proper operation and leaks.

TESTING

The easiest way to test the operation of the fuel injectors is to listen for a clicking sound coming from the injectors while the engine is running. This is accomplished using a mechanic's stethoscope, or a long screwdriver. Place the end of the stethoscope or the screwdriver (tip end, not handle) onto the body of the injector. Place the ear pieces of the stethoscope in your ears, or if using a screwdriver, place your ear on top of the handle. An audible clicking noise should be heard; this is the solenoid operating. If the injector makes this noise, the injector driver circuit and computer are operating as designed. Continue testing all the injectors this way.

All Injectors Clicking

If all the injectors are clicking, but you have determined that the fuel system is the cause of your driveability problem, continue diagnostics. Make sure that you have checked fuel pump pressure as outlined earlier in this section. An easy way to determine a weak or unproductive cylinder is a cylinder drop test. This is accomplished by removing one spark plug wire at a time, and seeing which cylinder causes the least difference in the idle. The one that causes the least change is the weak cylinder.

If the injectors were all clicking and the ignition system is functioning properly, remove the injector of the suspect cylinder and bench test it. This is accomplished by checking for a spray pattern from the injector itself. Install a fuel supply line to the injector (or rail if the injector is left attached to the rail) and momentarily apply 12 volts DC and a ground to the injector itself; a visible fuel spray should appear. If no spray is achieved, replace the injector and check the running condition of the engine.

One or More Injectors Are Not Clicking

▶ **See Figures 33, 34, 35, and 36**

If one or more injectors are found to be not operating, testing the injector driver circuit and computer can be accomplished using a "noid" light. First, with the engine not running and the ignition key in the **OFF** position, remove the connector from the injector you plan to test, then plug the "noid" light tool into the injector connector. Start the engine and the "noid" light should flash, signaling that the injector driver circuit is working. If the "noid" light flashes, but the injector does not click when plugged in, test the injector's resistance. Resistance should be between:

- All non-turbo engines: 13–16 ohms at 68°F (20°C)
- Turbocharged engines: 2–3 ohms at 68 °F (20°C)

If the "noid" light does not flash, the injector driver circuit is faulty. Disconnect the negative battery cable. Unplug the "noid" light from the injector connector and also unplug the PCM. Check the harness between the appropriate pins on the harness side of the PCM connector and the injector connector. Resistance should be less than 5.0 ohms; if not, repair the circuit. If resistance is within specifications, the injector driver inside the PCM is faulty and replacement of the PCM will be necessary.

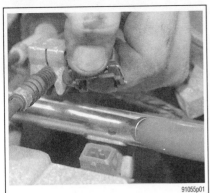

Fig. 33 Unplug the fuel injector connector

Fig. 34 Probe the two terminals of a fuel injector to check it's resistance

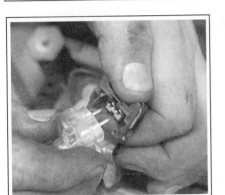

Fig. 35 Plug the correct "noid" light directly into the injector harness connector

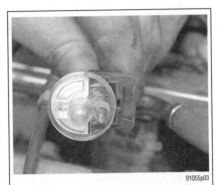

Fig. 36 If the correct "noid" light flashes while the engine is running, the injector driver circuit inside the PCM is working

Fig. 37 Remove the hose clamp on the fuel return line . . .

Fig. 38 . . . then disconnect the hose from the pressure regulator

Fig. 39 Remove the vacuum hose from the pressure regulator

Fig. 40 Remove the regulator-to-fuel rail retaining bolts, then remove the pressure regulator from the fuel rail

Fig. 41 Always replace the O-ring on the pressure regulator before reinstalling it

Fuel Pressure Regulator

REMOVAL & INSTALLATION

▶ **See Figures 37, 38, 39, 40, and 41**

1. Properly relieve the fuel system pressure as outlined earlier in this section.
2. Remove the vacuum hose from the fuel pressure regulator.
3. Disconnect the fuel return hose from the pressure regulator.

✳✳ CAUTION

Observe all applicable safety precautions when working around fuel. Whenever servicing the fuel system, always work in a well ventilated area. Do not allow fuel spray or vapors to come in contact with a spark or open flame. Keep a dry chemical fire extinguisher near the work area. Always keep fuel in a container specifically designed for fuel storage; also, always properly seal fuel containers to avoid the possibility of fire or explosion.

4. Remove the fuel regulator retainer bolts or remove the retaining snapring, then remove the fuel regulator from the fuel rail.
   To install:
5. Replace the O-ring on fuel pressure regulator with a new one and coat it lightly with clean, thin oil.
6. Insert the regulator straight into the rail, then check that it can be rotated freely.

➡ **If it does not rotate smoothly, remove it and inspect the O-ring for deformation or damage.**

7. When properly installed, align the mounting holes. If equipped, install and tighten the retaining bolts to 8 ft. lbs. (11 Nm). If equipped, install the regulator retaining snapring.
8. Connect the fuel return hose to the pressure regulator.
9. Install the vacuum hose to the fuel pressure regulator.
10. Connect the negative battery cable and pressurize the fuel system. Inspect for leaks.

Pressure Relief Valve

REMOVAL & INSTALLATION

▶ **See Figures 42 and 43**

1. Raise and safely support the vehicle securely on jackstands.
2. Remove the hoses and remove the pressure relief valve.
3. The installation is the reverse of removal.

➡ **Always install the pressure relief valve with the arrow pointing toward the EVAP canister side, not the fuel tank**

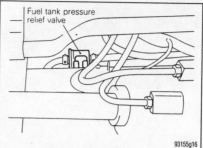

Fig. 42 Pressure relief valve location—Diamante shown, others similar

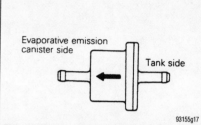

Fig. 43 Always install the pressure relief valve with the arrow pointing toward the EVAP canister side, not the fuel tank

FUEL TANK

Tank Assembly

REMOVAL & INSTALLATION

▶ **See Figures 44 thru 58**

1. Properly relieve the fuel system pressure using proper procedures.
2. Disconnect the negative battery cable.
3. Raise the vehicle and support safely.
4. Drain the fuel from the fuel tank into an approved container.

✳✳ CAUTION

Observe all applicable safety precautions when working around fuel. Whenever servicing the fuel system, always work in a well ventilated area. Do not allow fuel spray or vapors to come in contact with a spark or open flame. Keep a dry chemical fire extinguisher near the work area. Always keep fuel in a container specifically designed for fuel storage; also, always properly seal fuel containers to avoid the possibility of fire or explosion.

5. On Diamante models:
   a. Remove the left rear wheel well liner.
   b. Disconnect the center exhaust system from the main muffler. Disconnect the rear exhaust hangers, lower the exhaust and secure aside.
   c. On models equipped with 4-wheel steering, remove the mounting bolts and lower the rear steering gear.
6. Disconnect the return hose, high pressure hose and vapor hoses from the fuel pump.
7. Detach the electrical connectors at the pump/sending unit.
8. Disconnect the filler and vent hoses.
9. Place a suitable jack under the center of the fuel tank and apply a slight upward pressure. Remove the fuel tank strap retaining nuts.
10. Lower the tank slightly and detach any remaining electrical or hose connectors at the fuel tank.
11. Remove the fuel tank from the vehicle.

To install:

12. If replacing the tank, transfer any necessary components to the new tank including any heat shields, hoses, valves, and the fuel pump.
13. Install the fuel tank onto the jack. Raise the tank in position under the vehicle. Leave enough clearance to attach the electrical and hose connections to the top of the fuel pump.
14. Attach all connections to the top of the tank.
15. Raise the tank completely and position the retainer straps around the fuel tank. Install new fuel tank self-locking nuts and tighten the nuts.
16. Connect the return hose and high pressure hoses.
17. Install the vapor hose and the filler hose. Install the filler hose retainer screws to the fender, if removed.
18. On Diamante models:
   a. If equipped with 4-wheel steering, install the power cylinder unit and tighten the mounting bolts to 31 ft. lbs. (43 Nm).
   b. Connect the exhaust pipe and secure the rear hangers.
   c. Install the left rear wheel well liner, if removed.
19. Lower the vehicle and pour the drained fuel into the gas tank.
20. Connect the negative battery cable. Check the fuel pump for proper pressure and inspect the entire system for leaks.

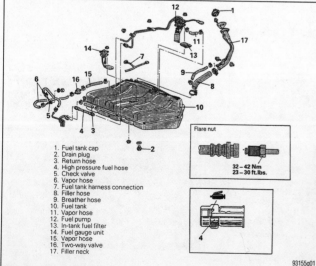

1. Fuel tank cap
2. Drain plug
3. Return hose
4. High pressure fuel hose
5. Check valve
6. Vapor hose
7. Fuel tank harness connection
8. Filler hose
9. Breather hose
10. Fuel tank
11. Vapor hose
12. Fuel pump
13. In-tank fuel filter
14. Fuel gauge unit
15. Vapor hose
16. Two-way valve
17. Filler neck

Flare nut
32 – 42 Nm
23 – 30 ft.lbs.

Fig. 44 Fuel tank and related components exploded view—1990–92 Mirage

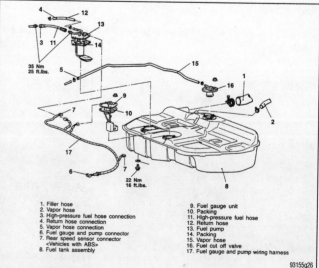

35 Nm
25 ft.lbs.

22 Nm
16 ft.lbs.

1. Filler hose
2. Vapor hose
3. High-pressure fuel hose connection
4. Return hose connection
5. Vapor hose connection
6. Fuel gauge and pump connector
7. Rear speed sensor connector
   <Vehicles with ABS>
8. Fuel tank assembly
9. Fuel gauge unit
10. Packing
11. High-pressure fuel hose
12. Return hose
13. Fuel pump
14. Packing
15. Vapor hose
16. Fuel cut off valve
17. Fuel gauge and pump wiring harness

Fig. 45 Fuel tank and related components exploded view—1993–96 Mirage

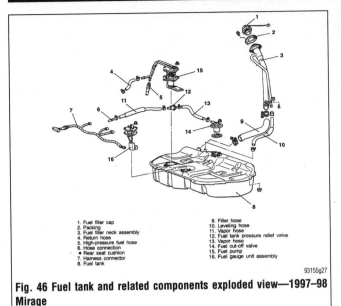

Fig. 46 Fuel tank and related components exploded view—1997–98 Mirage

1. Fuel filler cap
2. Packing
3. Fuel filler neck assembly
4. Return hose
5. High-pressure fuel hose
6. Hose connection
7. Rear seat cushion
7. Harness connector
8. Fuel tank
9. Filler hose
10. Leveling hose
11. Vapor hose
12. Fuel tank pressure relief valve
13. Vapor hose
14. Fuel cut-off valve
15. Fuel pump
16. Fuel gauge unit assembly

93155g27

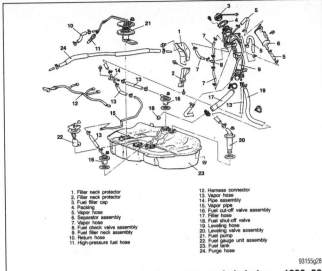

Fig. 47 Fuel tank and related components exploded view—1999–00 Mirage

1. Filler neck protector
2. Filler neck protector
3. Fuel filler cap
4. Packing
5. Separator assembly
6. Vapor hose
7. Vapor hose
8. Fuel check valve assembly
9. Fuel filler neck assembly
10. Return hose
11. High-pressure fuel hose
12. Harness connector
13. Vapor hose
14. Pipe assembly
15. Vapor pipe
16. Fuel cut-off valve assembly
17. Filler hose
18. Fuel shut-off valve
19. Leveling hose
20. Leveling valve assembly
21. Fuel pump
22. Fuel gauge unit assembly
23. Fuel tank
24. Purge hose

93155g28

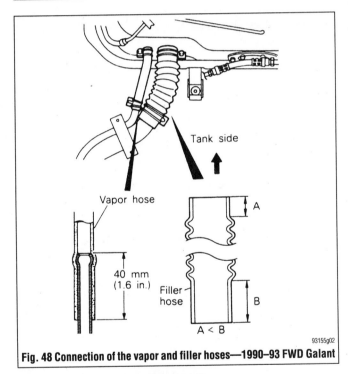

Fig. 48 Connection of the vapor and filler hoses—1990–93 FWD Galant

93155g02

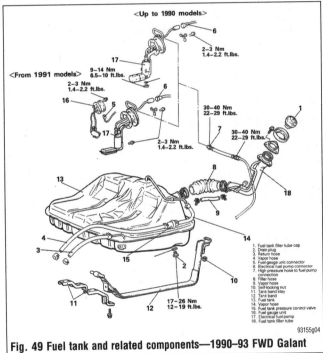

Fig. 49 Fuel tank and related components—1990–93 FWD Galant

1. Fuel tank filler tube cap
2. Drain plug
3. Return hose
4. Vapor hose
5. Fuel gauge unit connector
6. Electrical fuel pump connector
7. High pressure hose to fuel pump connection
8. Filler hose
9. Vapor hose
10. Self-locking nut
11. Tank band stay
12. Tank band
13. Fuel tank
14. Vapor hose
15. Fuel tank pressure control valve
16. Fuel gauge unit
17. Electrical fuel pump
18. Fuel tank filler tube

93155g04

Electric Fuel Pump

REMOVAL & INSTALLATION

✳✳ CAUTION

Fuel injection systems remain under pressure after the engine has been turned OFF. Properly relieve fuel pressure before disconnecting any fuel lines. Failure to do so may result in fire or personal injury.

➡ **Cover all fuel hose connections with a shop towel, prior to disconnecting, to prevent splash of fuel that could be caused by residual pressure remaining in the fuel line.**

1990–92 Mirage

♦ See Figure 44

1. Properly relieve the fuel system pressure using proper procedures. Disconnect the negative battery cable.
2. Raise the vehicle and support safely.
3. Drain the fuel from the fuel tank into an approved container.

✳✳ CAUTION

Observe all applicable safety precautions when working around fuel. Whenever servicing the fuel system, always work in a well ventilated area. Do not allow fuel spray or vapors to come in contact with a spark or open flame. Keep a dry chemical fire extin-

guisher near the work area. Always keep fuel in a container specifically designed for fuel storage; also, always properly seal fuel containers to avoid the possibility of fire or explosion.

4. Lower the tank slightly and detach any remaining electrical or hose connectors at the fuel tank.
5. Remove the fuel tank from the vehicle as described in this section.
6. Remove the five nuts securing the fuel pump to the fuel tank and remove the pump assembly.

To install:

7. Install fuel pump into fuel tank, with new packing gasket, and tighten mounting nuts.
8. Install the fuel tank into the vehicle. Refer to the procedure in this section.

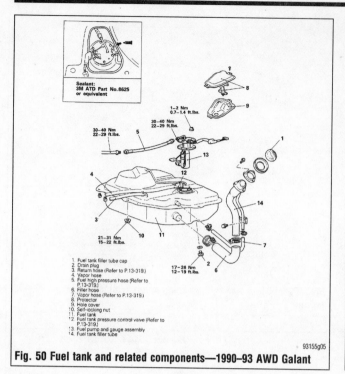

Sealant:
3M ATD Part No. 8625
or equivalent

30–40 Nm
22–29 ft.lbs.

30–40 Nm
22–29 ft.lbs.

1–2 Nm
0.7–1.4 ft.lbs.

21–31 Nm
15–22 ft.lbs.

17–26 Nm
12–19 ft.lbs.

1. Fuel tank filler tube cap
2. Drain plug
3. Return hose (Refer to P.13-319.)
4. Vapor hose
5. Fuel high pressure hose (Refer to P.13-319.)
6. Filler hose
7. Vapor hose (Refer to P.13-319.)
8. Protector
9. Hole cover
10. Self-locking nut
11. Fuel tank
12. Fuel tank pressure control valve (Refer to P.13-319.)
13. Fuel pump and gauge assembly
14. Fuel tank filler tube

93155g05

Fig. 50 Fuel tank and related components—1990–93 AWD Galant

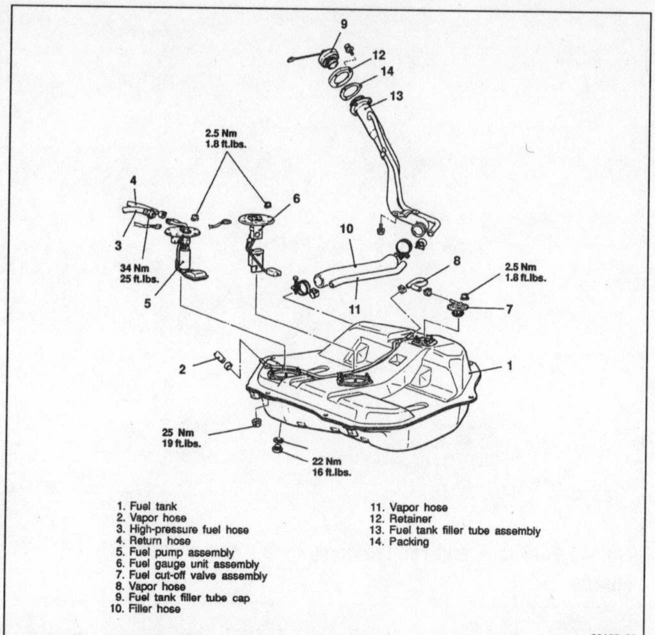

2.5 Nm
1.8 ft.lbs.

34 Nm
25 ft.lbs.

25 Nm
19 ft.lbs.

22 Nm
16 ft.lbs.

2.5 Nm
1.8 ft.lbs.

1. Fuel tank
2. Vapor hose
3. High-pressure fuel hose
4. Return hose
5. Fuel pump assembly
6. Fuel gauge unit assembly
7. Fuel cut-off valve assembly
8. Vapor hose
9. Fuel tank filler tube cap
10. Filler hose
11. Vapor hose
12. Retainer
13. Fuel tank filler tube assembly
14. Packing

93155g29

Fig. 51 Fuel tank and related components—1994–96 Galant except California emissions

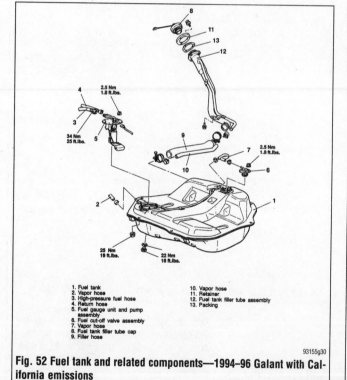

2.5 Nm
1.8 ft.lbs.

34 Nm
25 ft.lbs.

2.5 Nm
1.8 ft.lbs.

25 Nm
19 ft.lbs.

22 Nm
16 ft.lbs.

1. Fuel tank
2. Vapor hose
3. High-pressure fuel hose
4. Return hose
5. Fuel gauge unit and pump assembly
6. Fuel cut-off valve assembly
7. Vapor hose
8. Fuel tank filler tube cap
9. Filler hose
10. Vapor hose
11. Retainer
12. Fuel tank filler tube assembly
13. Packing

93155g30

Fig. 52 Fuel tank and related components—1994–96 Galant with California emissions

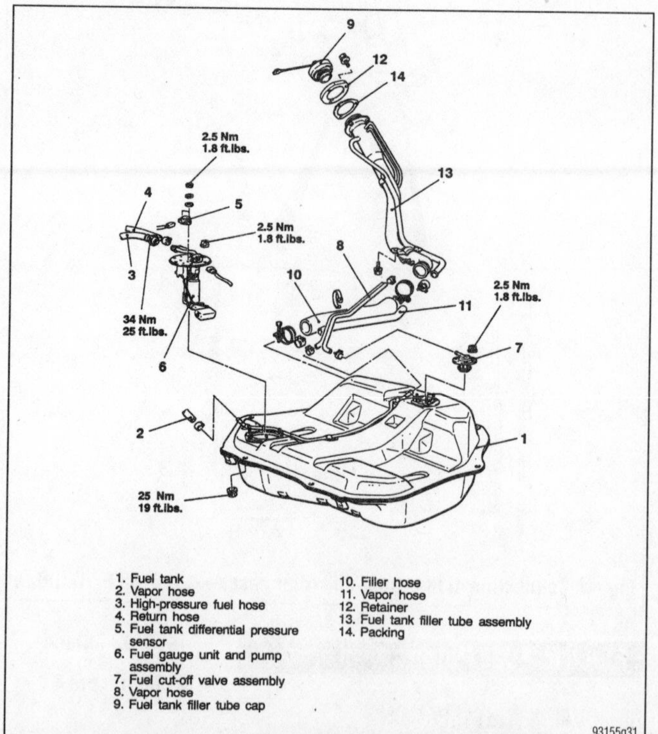

2.5 Nm
1.8 ft.lbs.

2.5 Nm
1.8 ft.lbs.

34 Nm
25 ft.lbs.

2.5 Nm
1.8 ft.lbs.

25 Nm
19 ft.lbs.

1. Fuel tank
2. Vapor hose
3. High-pressure fuel hose
4. Return hose
5. Fuel tank differential pressure sensor
6. Fuel gauge unit and pump assembly
7. Fuel cut-off valve assembly
8. Vapor hose
9. Fuel tank filler tube cap
10. Filler hose
11. Vapor hose
12. Retainer
13. Fuel tank filler tube assembly
14. Packing

93155g31

Fig. 53 Fuel tank and related components—1997–98 Galant

9. Lower the vehicle and pour the drained fuel into the gas tank.

10. Connect the negative battery cable.

11. Check the fuel pump for proper pressure and inspect the entire system for leaks.

1990–93 Galant

FRONT WHEEL DRIVE (FWD)

▶ See Figures 59, 60, and 61

1. Relieve the fuel system pressure using proper procedure.

2. Disconnect negative battery cable.

3. Raise and safely support the vehicle.

4. Drain the fuel from the fuel tank into an approved gasoline container.

※ CAUTION

Observe all applicable safety precautions when working around fuel. Whenever servicing the fuel system, always work in a well ventilated area. Do not allow fuel spray or vapors to come in contact with a spark or open flame. Keep a dry chemical fire extinguisher near the work area. Always keep fuel in a container specifically designed for fuel storage; also, always properly seal fuel containers to avoid the possibility of fire or explosion.

5. Remove the electrical connectors at the fuel pump. Make sure there is enough slack in the electri-

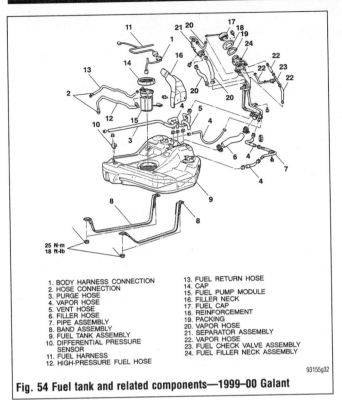

1. BODY HARNESS CONNECTION
2. HOSE CONNECTION
3. PURGE HOSE
4. VAPOR HOSE
5. VENT HOSE
6. FILLER HOSE
7. PIPE ASSEMBLY
8. BAND ASSEMBLY
9. FUEL TANK ASSEMBLY
10. DIFFERENTIAL PRESSURE SENSOR
11. FUEL HARNESS
12. HIGH-PRESSURE FUEL HOSE
13. FUEL RETURN HOSE
14. CAP
15. FUEL PUMP MODULE
16. FILLER NECK
17. FUEL CAP
18. REINFORCEMENT
19. PACKING
20. VAPOR HOSE
21. SEPARATOR ASSEMBLY
22. VAPOR HOSE
23. FUEL CHECK VALVE ASSEMBLY
24. FUEL FILLER NECK ASSEMBLY

93155g32

Fig. 54 Fuel tank and related components—1999–00 Galant

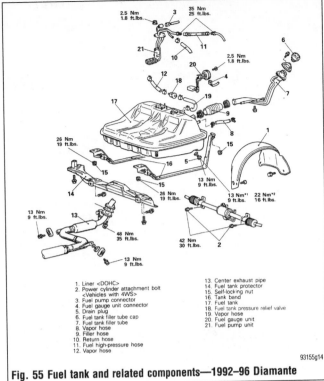

1. Liner <DOHC>
2. Power cylinder attachment bolt <Vehicles with 4WS>
3. Fuel pump connector
4. Fuel gauge unit connector
5. Drain plug
6. Fuel tank filler tube cap
7. Fuel tank filler tube
8. Vapor hose
9. Filler hose
10. Return hose
11. Fuel high-pressure hose
12. Vapor hose
13. Center exhaust pipe
14. Fuel tank protector
15. Self-locking nut
16. Tank band
17. Fuel tank
18. Fuel tank pressure relief valve
19. Vapor hose
20. Fuel gauge unit
21. Fuel pump unit

93155g14

Fig. 55 Fuel tank and related components—1992–96 Diamante

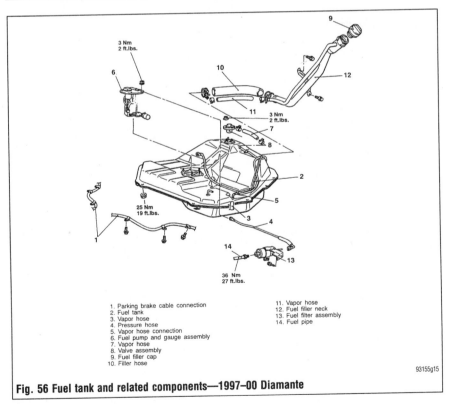

1. Parking brake cable connection
2. Fuel tank
3. Vapor hose
4. Pressure hose
5. Vapor hose connection
6. Fuel pump and gauge assembly
7. Vapor hose
8. Valve assembly
9. Fuel filler cap
10. Filler hose
11. Vapor hose
12. Fuel filler neck
13. Fuel filter assembly
14. Fuel pipe

93155g15

Fig. 56 Fuel tank and related components—1997–00 Diamante

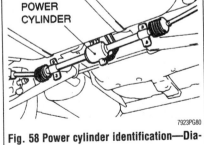

7923PG79

Fig. 57 Proper method of supporting rear exhaust system—Diamante 3.0L engine

POWER CYLINDER

7923PG80

Fig. 58 Power cylinder identification—Diamante 3.0L engine

cal harness of the fuel gauge unit to allow for the fuel tank to be lowered slightly. If not, label and disconnect the electrical harness at the fuel gauge unit.

6. Detach the high pressure fuel line connector at the pump.

7. Loosen self-locking nuts on tank support straps to the end of the stud bolts.

8. Remove the right side lateral rod attaching bolt and disconnect the arm from the right body cou-

pling. Lower the lateral rod and suspend from the axle beam using wire.

9. Remove the six retaining bolts and gasket from the base of the tank.

10. Remove the fuel pump assembly.

To install:

➡ **If the packing material is damaged or deformed, replace it with new packing.**

11. Align the 3 projections on packing with the holes on the fuel pump and the nipples on the pump facing the same direction as before removal.

12. Install the holding bolt through the bottom of the tank. Make sure the gasket on the bolt is replaced and is not pinched during installation. Torque to 10 ft. lbs. (14 Nm).

Fig. 59 Loosen self-locking nuts on tank support straps to the end of the stud bolts —1990–93 FWD Galant

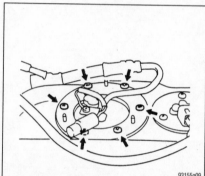

Fig. 60 Remove the six retaining bolts and gasket from the base of the tank—1990–93 FWD Galant

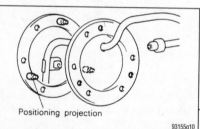

Fig. 61 Align the 3 projections on packing with the holes on the fuel pump and the nipples on the pump facing the same direction as before removal—1990–93 FWD Galant

13. Install the right side lateral rod and attaching bolt into the right body coupling. Tighten loosely only, at this time.

14. Tighten the self-locking nuts on the tank support straps until the tank is fully seated. Torque the nuts to 22 ft. lbs. (31 Nm).

15. Install the high pressure fuel hose connector and tighten to 29 ft. lbs. (40 Nm).

16. Install the electrical connectors onto the fuel pump and gauge unit assemblies.

17. Lower the vehicle so the suspension supports the weight of the vehicle. Tighten the lateral rod attaching bolt to 58–72 ft. lbs. (80–100 Nm).

18. Refill the fuel tank with fuel drained during this procedure.

19. Connect the negative battery cable and check the entire system for proper operation and leaks.

ALL WHEEL DRIVE (AWD)

▶ **See Figures 62, 63, and 64**

1. Relieve the fuel system pressure using proper procedure.

2. Disconnect negative battery cable.

3. The fuel pump is located in the fuel tank. Remove the access cover located in the rear floor pan.

4. Partially drain the fuel tank into an approved gasoline container.

✳✳ CAUTION

Observe all applicable safety precautions when working around fuel. Whenever servicing the fuel system, always work in a well ventilated area. Do not allow fuel spray or vapors to come in contact with a spark or open flame. Keep a dry chemical fire extinguisher near the work area. Always keep fuel in a container specifically designed for fuel

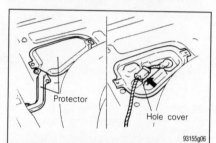

Fig. 62 The fuel pump is located in the fuel tank. Remove the access cover located in the rear floor pan —1990–93 AWD Galant

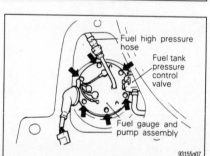

Fig. 63 Remove the six pump retaining bolts and remove the fuel pump and gauge assembly from the tank—1990–93 AWD Galant

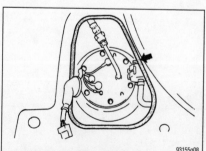

Fig. 64 Install 3M ATD Part No. 8625 or equivalent, to the rear floor pan and install the access cover into place —1990–93 AWD Galant

storage; also, always properly seal fuel containers to avoid the possibility of fire or explosion.

5. Remove the electrical connector from the fuel pump.

6. Remove the overfill limiter (two-way valve), as required.

7. Remove the high pressure fuel hose connector.

8. Remove the six pump retaining bolts and remove the fuel pump and gauge assembly from the tank. Note positioning of pump prior to removal from tank.

To install:

➡**If the packing material is damaged or deformed, replace it with new packing.**

9. Align the 3 projections on the packing with the holes on the fuel pump and the nipples on the pump facing the same direction as before removal. Install the retainers and tighten to 2 ft. lbs. (3 Nm).

10. Install the high pressure hose connection and tighten to 29 ft. lbs. (40 Nm).

11. Install the overfill limiter (two-way valve) and the electrical connector to the fuel pump.

12. Fill the fuel tank with the gasoline removed during this procedure.

13. Reconnect the negative battery cable and check the entire system for leaks.

14. Install 3M ATD Part No. 8625 or equivalent, to the rear floor pan and install the access cover into place.

Diamante, 1993–00 Mirage, and 1994–98 Galant

▶ **See Figures 65 thru 72**

1. Properly relieve the fuel system pressure.

2. Disconnect the negative battery cable.

3. Remove the rear seat cushion, by pulling the seat stopper outward and lifting the lower cushion upward.

4. Remove the access cover.

5. Disconnect the fuel pump wiring.

6. Disconnect the return hose and the high pressure fuel hose.

7. Remove the pump mounting nuts and remove the pump assembly.

✳✳ CAUTION

Observe all applicable safety precautions when working around fuel. Whenever servicing the fuel system, always work in a well ventilated area. Do not allow fuel spray or vapors to come in contact with a spark or open flame. Keep a dry chemical fire extinguisher near the work area. Always keep fuel in a container specifically designed for fuel storage; also, always properly seal fuel containers to avoid the possibility of fire or explosion.

To install:

➡**If the packing material is damaged or deformed, replace it with new packing.**

8. Install the packing to the fuel tank.

9. Install the fuel pump assembly to the tank and tighten the retaining nuts to 22 inch lbs. (2.5 Nm).

Fig. 65 After the seat cushion is removed, the access cover for the fuel pump is visible

Fig. 66 Remove the four access cover retaining screws . . .

Fig. 67 . . . then lift the cover from the floor-pan

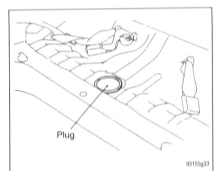

Fig. 68 On Mirage models there is a plug rather than an access cover

Fig. 69 Detach the electrical connector from the fuel pump

Return line   Feed line

Fig. 70 Remove the return and feed lines from the fuel pump

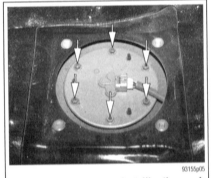

Fig. 71 The fuel pump, just like the sending unit (shown here), is held by six retaining nuts; remove them and lift the pump out of the fuel tank

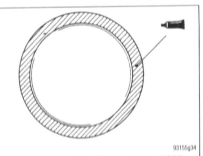

Fig. 72 Install 3M ATD Part No. 8625 or equivalent, to the rear floor pan and install the access cover or plug into place

➡ Tilt the float to the left of the vehicle, when installing the pump assembly.

10. Connect the high pressure hose, return hose and the fuel tank wiring.
11. Connect the negative battery cable.
12. Check the fuel pump for proper pressure and inspect the entire system for leaks.
13. Apply sealant to the access cover and install the cover.
14. Install the rear seat cushion.

1999–00 Galant

♦ See Figures 65 thru 75

1. Properly relieve the fuel system pressure.
2. Disconnect the negative battery cable.
3. Remove the rear seat cushion, by pulling the seat stopper outward and lifting the lower cushion upward.
4. Remove the access cover.
5. Disconnect the fuel pump wiring.

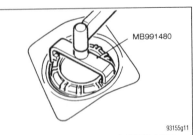

MB991480

Fig. 73 Using special tool MB991480 or equivalent, remove the fuel pump retaining cap and remove the pump assembly — 1999–00 Galant

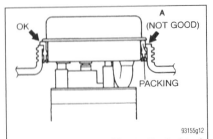

OK   A (NOT GOOD)   PACKING

Fig. 74 Install the packing to the fuel tank —1999–00 Galant

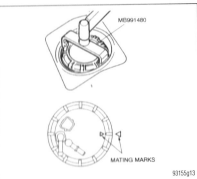

MB991480

MATING MARKS

Fig. 75 Install the fuel pump assembly to the tank and align the mating marks on the pump and the floorpan —1999–00 Galant

6. Disconnect the return hose and the high pressure fuel hose.

7. Using special tool MB991480 or equivalent, remove the fuel pump retaining cap and remove the pump assembly.

✳✳ CAUTION

Observe all applicable safety precautions when working around fuel. Whenever servicing the fuel system, always work in a well ventilated area. Do not allow fuel spray or vapors to come in contact with a spark or open flame. Keep a dry chemical fire extinguisher near the work area. Always keep fuel in a container specifically designed for fuel storage; also, always properly seal fuel containers to avoid the possibility of fire or explosion.

To install:

➡**If the packing material is damaged or deformed, replace it with new packing.**

8. Install the packing to the fuel tank.

9. Install the fuel pump assembly to the tank and align the mating marks on the pump and the floorpan.

10. Tighten the fuel pump retaining cap using tool MB991480 or equivalent.

11. Connect the high pressure hose, return hose and the fuel tank wiring.

12. Connect the negative battery cable.

13. Check the fuel pump for proper pressure and inspect the entire system for leaks.

14. Apply sealant to the access cover and install the cover.

15. Install the rear seat cushion.

TESTING

1. Relieve fuel system pressure.
2. Disconnect the battery negative cable.
3. Disconnect the fuel high pressure hose at the delivery pipe side.

✳✳ CAUTION

Observe all applicable safety precautions when working around fuel. Whenever servicing the fuel system, always work in a well ventilated area. Do not allow fuel spray or vapors to come in contact with a spark or open flame. Keep a dry chemical fire extinguisher near the work area. Always keep fuel in a container specifically designed for fuel storage; also, always properly seal fuel containers to avoid the possibility of fire or explosion.

4. Connect a fuel pressure gauge to tools MD998709 and MD998742 or exact equivalent, with appropriate adapters, seals and/or gaskets to prevent leaks during the test. Install the gauge and adapter between the delivery pipe and high pressure hose. Install carefully to prevent leaks.

5. Connect the negative battery cable.

6. Apply battery voltage to the terminal for fuel pump activation (located in the engine compartment) to run the fuel pump, and check for leaks.

7. Start the engine and run at curb idle speed.

8. Measure the fuel pressure and compare to the specifications listed in the chart in Section 1.

9. Locate and disconnect the vacuum hose running to the fuel pressure regulator. Plug the end of the hose and record the fuel pressure again. The fuel pressure should have increased approximately 10 psi.

10. Reconnect the vacuum hose the fuel pressure regulator. After the fuel pressure stabilizes, race the engine 2–3 times and check that the fuel pressure does not fall when the engine is running at idle.

11. Check to be sure there is fuel pressure in the return hose by gently pressing the fuel return hose with fingers while racing the engine. There will be no fuel pressure in the return hose when the volume of fuel flow is low.

12. If fuel pressure is too low, check for a clogged fuel filter, a defective fuel pressure regulator or a defective fuel pump, any of which will require replacement.

13. If fuel pressure is too high, the fuel pressure regulator is defective and will have to be replaced or the fuel return is bent or clogged. If the fuel pressure reading does not change when the vacuum hose is disconnected, the hose is clogged or the valve is stuck in the fuel pressure regulator and it will have to be replaced.

14. Stop the engine and check for changes in the fuel pressure gauge. It should not drop. If the gauge reading does drop, watch the rate of drop. If fuel pressure drops slowly, the likely cause is a leaking injector which will require replacement. If the fuel pressure drops immediately after the engine is stopped, the check valve in the fuel pump isn't closing and the fuel pump will have to be replaced.

15. Relieve fuel system pressure.

16. Disconnect the high pressure hose and remove the fuel pressure gauge from the delivery pipe.

17. Install a new O-ring in the groove of the high pressure hose. Connect the hose to the delivery pipe and tighten the screws. After installation, apply battery voltage to the terminal for fuel pump activation to run the fuel pump. Check for leaks.

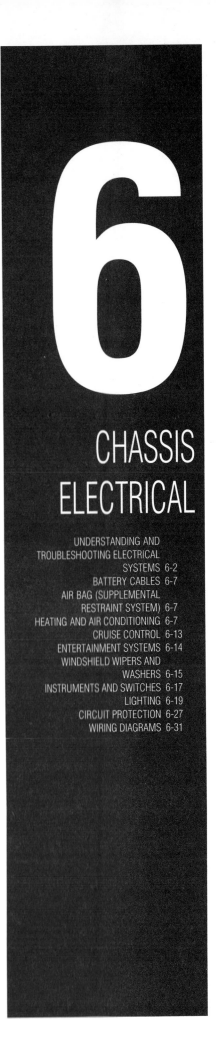

6

CHASSIS
ELECTRICAL

UNDERSTANDING AND TROUBLESHOOTING ELECTRICAL SYSTEMS

Basic Electrical Theory

♦ See Figure 1

For any 12 volt, negative ground, electrical system to operate, the electricity must travel in a complete circuit. This simply means that current (power) from the positive (+) terminal of the battery must eventually return to the negative (-) terminal of the battery. Along the way, this current will travel through wires, fuses, switches and components. If, for any reason, the flow of current through the circuit is interrupted, the component fed by that circuit will cease to function properly.

Perhaps the easiest way to visualize a circuit is to think of connecting a light bulb (with two wires attached to it) to the battery—one wire attached to the negative (-) terminal of the battery and the other wire to the positive (+) terminal. With the two wires touching the battery terminals, the circuit would be complete and the light bulb would illuminate. Electricity would follow a path from the battery to the bulb and back to the battery. It's easy to see that with longer wires on our light bulb, it could be mounted anywhere. Further, one wire could be fitted with a switch so that the light could be turned on and off.

The normal automotive circuit differs from this simple example in two ways. First, instead of having a return wire from the bulb to the battery, the current travels through the frame of the vehicle. Since the negative (-) battery cable is attached to the frame (made of electrically conductive metal), the frame of the vehicle can serve as a ground wire to complete the circuit. Secondly, most automotive circuits contain multiple components which receive power from a single circuit. This lessens the amount of wire needed to power components on the vehicle.

HOW DOES ELECTRICITY WORK: THE WATER ANALOGY

Electricity is the flow of electrons—the subatomic particles that constitute the outer shell of an atom. Electrons spin in an orbit around the center core of

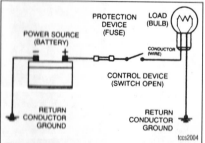

Fig. 1 This example illustrates a simple circuit. When the switch is closed, power from the positive (+) battery terminal flows through the fuse and the switch, and then to the light bulb. The light illuminates and the circuit is completed through the ground wire back to the negative (-) battery terminal. In reality, the two ground points shown in the illustration are attached to the metal frame of the vehicle, which completes the circuit back to the battery

an atom. The center core is comprised of protons (positive charge) and neutrons (neutral charge). Electrons have a negative charge and balance out the positive charge of the protons. When an outside force causes the number of electrons to unbalance the charge of the protons, the electrons will split off the atom and look for another atom to balance out. If this imbalance is kept up, electrons will continue to move and an electrical flow will exist.

Many people have been taught electrical theory using an analogy with water. In a comparison with water flowing through a pipe, the electrons would be the water and the wire is the pipe.

The flow of electricity can be measured much like the flow of water through a pipe. The unit of measurement used is amperes, frequently abbreviated as amps (a). You can compare amperage to the volume of water flowing through a pipe. When connected to a circuit, an ammeter will measure the actual amount of current flowing through the circuit. When relatively few electrons flow through a circuit, the amperage is low. When many electrons flow, the amperage is high.

Water pressure is measured in units such as pounds per square inch (psi); The electrical pressure is measured in units called volts (v). When a voltmeter is connected to a circuit, it is measuring the electrical pressure.

The actual flow of electricity depends not only on voltage and amperage, but also on the resistance of the circuit. The higher the resistance, the higher the force necessary to push the current through the circuit. The standard unit for measuring resistance is an ohm. Resistance in a circuit varies depending on the amount and type of components used in the circuit. The main factors which determine resistance are:

• Material—some materials have more resistance than others. Those with high resistance are said to be insulators. Rubber materials (or rubber-like plastics) are some of the most common insulators used in vehicles as they have a very high resistance to electricity. Very low resistance materials are said to be conductors. Copper wire is among the best conductors. Silver is actually a superior conductor to copper and is used in some relay contacts, but its high cost prohibits its use as common wiring. Most automotive wiring is made of copper.

• Size—the larger the wire size being used, the less resistance the wire will have. This is why components which use large amounts of electricity usually have large wires supplying current to them.

• Length—for a given thickness of wire, the longer the wire, the greater the resistance. The shorter the wire, the less the resistance. When determining the proper wire for a circuit, both size and length must be considered to design a circuit that can handle the current needs of the component.

• Temperature—with many materials, the higher the temperature, the greater the resistance (positive temperature coefficient). Some materials exhibit the opposite trait of lower resistance with higher temperatures (negative temperature coefficient). These principles are used in many of the sensors on the engine.

OHM'S LAW

There is a direct relationship between current, voltage and resistance. The relationship between cur-

rent, voltage and resistance can be summed up by a statement known as Ohm's law.

Voltage (E) is equal to amperage (I) times resistance (R): $E = I \times R$

Other forms of the formula are $R = E/I$ and $I = E/R$

In each of these formulas, E is the voltage in volts, I is the current in amps and R is the resistance in ohms. The basic point to remember is that as the resistance of a circuit goes up, the amount of current that flows in the circuit will go down, if voltage remains the same.

The amount of work that the electricity can perform is expressed as power. The unit of power is the watt (w). The relationship between power, voltage and current is expressed as:

Power (w) is equal to amperage (I) times voltage (E): $W = I \times E$

This is only true for direct current (DC) circuits; The alternating current formula is a tad different, but since the electrical circuits in most vehicles are DC type, we need not get into AC circuit theory.

Electrical Components

POWER SOURCE

Power is supplied to the vehicle by two devices: The battery and the alternator. The battery supplies electrical power during starting or during periods when the current demand of the vehicle's electrical system exceeds the output capacity of the alternator. The alternator supplies electrical current when the engine is running. Just not does the alternator supply the current needs of the vehicle, but it recharges the battery.

The Battery

In most modern vehicles, the battery is a lead/acid electrochemical device consisting of six 2 volt subsections (cells) connected in series, so that the unit is capable of producing approximately 12 volts of electrical pressure. Each subsection consists of a series of positive and negative plates held a short distance apart in a solution of sulfuric acid and water.

The two types of plates are of dissimilar metals. This sets up a chemical reaction, and it is this reaction which produces current flow from the battery when its positive and negative terminals are connected to an electrical load. The power removed from the battery is replaced by the alternator, restoring the battery to its original chemical state.

The Alternator

On some vehicles there isn't an alternator, but a generator. The difference is that an alternator supplies alternating current which is then changed to direct current for use on the vehicle, while a generator produces direct current. Alternators tend to be more efficient and that is why they are used.

Alternators and generators are devices that consist of coils of wires wound together making big electromagnets. One group of coils spins within another set and the interaction of the magnetic fields causes a current to flow. This current is then drawn off the coils and fed into the vehicles electrical system.

GROUND

Two types of grounds are used in automotive electric circuits. Direct ground components are grounded to the frame through their mounting points. All other components use some sort of ground wire which is attached to the frame or chassis of the vehicle. The electrical current runs through the chassis of the vehicle and returns to the battery through the ground (-) cable; if you look, you'll see that the battery ground cable connects between the battery and the frame or chassis of the vehicle.

➡ **It should be noted that a good percentage of electrical problems can be traced to bad grounds.**

PROTECTIVE DEVICES

▶ **See Figure 2**

It is possible for large surges of current to pass through the electrical system of your vehicle. If this surge of current were to reach the load in the circuit, the surge could burn it out or severely damage it. It can also overload the wiring, causing the harness to get hot and melt the insulation. To prevent this, fuses, circuit breakers and/or fusible links are connected into the supply wires of the electrical system. These items are nothing more than a built-in weak spot in the system. When an abnormal amount of current flows through the system, these protective devices work as follows to protect the circuit:

• Fuse—when an excessive electrical current passes through a fuse, the fuse "blows" (the conductor melts) and opens the circuit, preventing the passage of current.

• Circuit Breaker—a circuit breaker is basically a self-repairing fuse. It will open the circuit in the same fashion as a fuse, but when the surge subsides, the circuit breaker can be reset and does not need replacement.

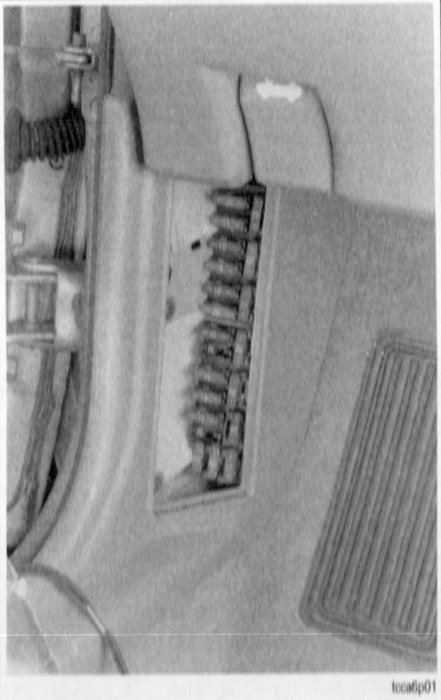

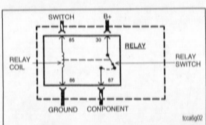

Fig. 2 Most vehicles use one or more fuse panels. This one is located on the driver's side kick panel

• Fusible Link—a fusible link (fuse link or main link) is a short length of special, high temperature insulated wire that acts as a fuse. When an excessive electrical current passes through a fusible link, the thin gauge wire inside the link melts, creating an intentional open to protect the circuit. To repair the circuit, the link must be replaced. Some newer type fusible links are housed in plug-in modules, which are simply replaced like a fuse, while older type fusible links must be cut and spliced if they melt. Since this link is very early in the electrical path, it's the first place to look if nothing on the vehicle works, yet the battery seems to be charged and is properly connected.

✳✳ CAUTION

Always replace fuses, circuit breakers and fusible links with identically rated components. Under no circumstances should a component of higher or lower amperage rating be substituted.

SWITCHES & RELAYS

▶ **See Figures 3 and 4**

Switches are used in electrical circuits to control the passage of current. The most common use is to

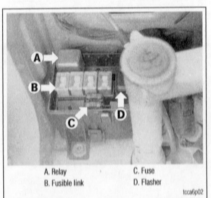

A. Relay   C. Fuse
B. Fusible link   D. Flasher

Fig. 3 The underhood fuse and relay panel usually contains fuses, relays, flashers and fusible links

SWITCH   B+

RELAY
COIL   RELAY
                                 SWITCH

GROUND   COMPONENT

Fig. 4 Relays are composed of a coil and a switch. These two components are linked together so that when one operates, the other operates at the same time. The large wires in the circuit are connected from the battery to one side of the relay switch (B+) and from the opposite side of the relay switch to the load (component). Smaller wires are connected from the relay coil to the control switch for the circuit and from the opposite side of the relay coil to ground

open and close circuits between the battery and the various electric devices in the system. Switches are rated according to the amount of amperage they can handle. If a sufficient amperage rated switch is not used in a circuit, the switch could overload and cause damage.

Some electrical components which require a large amount of current to operate use a special switch called a relay. Since these circuits carry a large amount of current, the thickness of the wire in the circuit is also greater. If this large wire were connected from the load to the control switch, the switch would have to carry the high amperage load and the fairing or instrument panel would be twice as large to accommodate the increased size of the wiring harness. To prevent these problems, a relay is used.

Relays are composed of a coil and a set of contacts. When the coil has a current passed though it, a magnetic field is formed and this field causes the contacts to move together, completing the circuit. Most relays are normally open, preventing current from passing through the circuit, but they can take any electrical form depending on the job they are intended to do. Relays can be considered "remote control switches." They allow a smaller current to operate devices that require higher amperages. When a small current operates the coil, a larger current is allowed to pass by the contacts. Some common circuits which may use relays are the horn, headlights, starter, electric fuel pump and other high draw circuits.

LOAD

Every electrical circuit must include a "load" (something to use the electricity coming from the source). Without this load, the battery would attempt to deliver its entire power supply from one pole to another. This is called a "short circuit." All this electricity would take a short cut to ground and cause a great amount of damage to other components in the circuit by developing a tremendous amount of heat. This condition could develop sufficient heat to melt the insulation on all the surrounding wires and reduce a multiple wire cable to a lump of plastic and copper.

WIRING & HARNESSES

The average vehicle contains meters and meters of wiring, with hundreds of individual connections. To protect the many wires from damage and to keep them from becoming a confusing tangle, they are organized into bundles, enclosed in plastic or taped together and called wiring harnesses. Different harnesses serve different parts of the vehicle. Individual wires are color coded to help trace them through a harness where sections are hidden from view.

Automotive wiring or circuit conductors can be either single strand wire, multi-strand wire or printed circuitry. Single strand wire has a solid metal core and is usually used inside such components as alternators, motors, relays and other devices. Multi-strand wire has a core made of many small strands of wire twisted together into a single conductor. Most of the wiring in an automotive electrical system is made up of multi-strand wire, either as a single conductor or grouped together in a harness. All wiring is color coded on the insulator, either as a solid color or as a colored wire with an identification stripe. A printed circuit is a thin film of copper or other conductor that is printed on an insulator backing. Occasionally, a printed circuit is sandwiched between two sheets of plastic for more protection and flexibility. A complete printed circuit, consisting of conductors, insulating material and connectors for lamps or other components is called a printed circuit board. Printed circuitry is used in place of individual wires or harnesses in places where space is limited, such as behind instrument panels.

Since automotive electrical systems are very sensitive to changes in resistance, the selection of properly sized wires is critical when systems are repaired. A loose or corroded connection or a replacement wire that is too small for the circuit will add extra resistance and an additional voltage drop to the circuit.

The wire gauge number is an expression of the cross-section area of the conductor. Vehicles from countries that use the metric system will typically describe the wire size as its cross-sectional area in square millimeters. In this method, the larger the wire, the greater the number. Another common system for expressing wire size is the American Wire Gauge (AWG) system. As gauge number increases, area decreases and the wire becomes smaller. An 18 gauge wire is smaller than a 4 gauge wire. A wire with a higher gauge number will carry less current than a wire with a lower gauge number. Gauge wire size refers to the size of the strands of the conductor, not the size of the complete wire with insulator. It is possible, therefore, to have two wires of the same gauge with different diameters because one may have thicker insulation than the other.

It is essential to understand how a circuit works before trying to figure out why it doesn't. An electrical schematic shows the electrical current paths when a circuit is operating properly. Schematics break the entire electrical system down into individual circuits. In a schematic, usually no attempt is made to represent wiring and components as they physically appear on the vehicle; switches and other components are shown as simply as possible. Face views of harness connectors show the cavity or terminal locations in all multi-pin connectors to help locate test points.

CONNECTORS

▶ **See Figures 5 and 6**

Three types of connectors are commonly used in automotive applications—weatherproof, molded and hard shell.

• Weatherproof—these connectors are most commonly used where the connector is exposed to the elements. Terminals are protected against moisture and dirt by sealing rings which provide a weathertight seal. All repairs require the use of a special terminal and the tool required to service it. Unlike standard blade type terminals, these weatherproof terminals cannot be straightened once they are bent. Make certain that the connectors are properly seated and all of the sealing rings are in place when connecting leads.

• Molded—these connectors require complete replacement of the connector if found to be defective. This means splicing a new connector assembly into the harness. All splices should be soldered to insure proper contact. Use care when probing the connections or replacing terminals in them, as it is possible to create a short circuit between opposite terminals. If this happens to the wrong terminal pair, it is possible to damage certain components. Always use jumper wires between connectors for circuit checking and NEVER probe through weatherproof seals.

• Hard Shell—unlike molded connectors, the terminal contacts in hard-shell connectors can be replaced. Replacement usually involves the use of a special terminal removal tool that depresses the locking tangs (barbs) on the connector terminal and allows the connector to be removed from the rear of the shell. The connector shell should be replaced if it shows any evidence of burning, melting, cracks, or breaks. Replace individual terminals that are burnt, corroded, distorted or loose.

Test Equipment

Pinpointing the exact cause of trouble in an electrical circuit is most times accomplished by the use of special test equipment. The following describes different types of commonly used test equipment and briefly explains how to use them in diagnosis. In addition to the information covered below, the tool manufacturer's instructions booklet (provided with the tester) should be read and clearly understood before attempting any test procedures.

JUMPER WIRES

✳✳ CAUTION

Never use jumper wires made from a thinner gauge wire than the circuit being tested. If

the jumper wire is of too small a gauge, it may overheat and possibly melt. Never use jumpers to bypass high resistance loads in a circuit. Bypassing resistances, in effect, creates a short circuit. This may, in turn, cause damage and fire. Jumper wires should only be used to bypass lengths of wire or to simulate switches.

Jumper wires are simple, yet extremely valuable, pieces of test equipment. They are basically test wires which are used to bypass sections of a circuit. Although jumper wires can be purchased, they are usually fabricated from lengths of standard automotive wire and whatever type of connector (alligator clip, spade connector or pin connector) that is required for the particular application being tested. In cramped, hard-to-reach areas, it is advisable to have insulated boots over the jumper wire terminals in order to prevent accidental grounding. It is also advisable to include a standard automotive fuse in any jumper wire. This is commonly referred to as a "fused jumper". By inserting an in-line fuse holder between a set of test leads, a fused jumper wire can be used for bypassing open circuits. Use a 5 amp fuse to provide protection against voltage spikes.

Jumper wires are used primarily to locate open electrical circuits, on either the ground (-) side of the circuit or on the power (+) side. If an electrical component fails to operate, connect the jumper wire between the component and a good ground. If the component operates only with the jumper installed, the ground circuit is open. If the ground circuit is good, but the component does not operate, the circuit between the power feed and component may be open. By moving the jumper wire successively back from the component toward the power source, you can isolate the area of the circuit where the open is located. When the component stops functioning, or the power is cut off, the open is in the segment of wire between the jumper and the point previously tested.

You can sometimes connect the jumper wire directly from the battery to the "hot" terminal of the component, but first make sure the component uses 12 volts in operation. Some electrical components, such as fuel injectors or sensors, are designed to operate on about 4 to 5 volts, and running 12 volts directly to these components will cause damage.

TEST LIGHTS

▶ **See Figure 7**

The test light is used to check circuits and components while electrical current is flowing through

Fig. 5 Hard shell (left) and weatherproof (right) connectors have replaceable terminals

Fig. 6 Weatherproof connectors are most commonly used in the engine compartment or where the connector is exposed to the elements

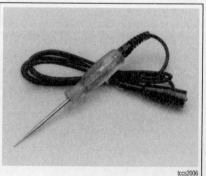

Fig. 7 A 12 volt test light is used to detect the presence of voltage in a circuit

them. It is used for voltage and ground tests. To use a 12 volt test light, connect the ground clip to a good ground and probe wherever necessary with the pick. The test light will illuminate when voltage is detected. This does not necessarily mean that 12 volts (or any particular amount of voltage) is present; it only means that some voltage is present. It is advisable before using the test light to touch its ground clip and probe across the battery posts or terminals to make sure the light is operating properly.

Do not use a test light to probe electronic ignition, spark plug or coil wires. Never use a pick-type test light to probe wiring on computer controlled systems unless specifically instructed to do so. Any wire insulation that is pierced by the test light probe should be taped and sealed with silicone after testing.

Like the jumper wire, the 12 volt test light is used to isolate opens in circuits. But, whereas the jumper wire is used to bypass the open to operate the load, the 12 volt test light is used to locate the presence of voltage in a circuit. If the test light illuminates, there is power up to that point in the circuit; if the test light does not illuminate, there is an open circuit (no power). Move the test light in successive steps back toward the power source until the light in the handle illuminates. The open is between the probe and a point which was previously probed.

The self-powered test light is similar in design to the 12 volt test light, but contains a 1.5 volt penlight battery in the handle. It is most often used in place of a multimeter to check for open or short circuits when power is isolated from the circuit (continuity test).

The battery in a self-powered test light does not provide much current. A weak battery may not provide enough power to illuminate the test light even when a complete circuit is made (especially if there is high resistance in the circuit). Always make sure that the test battery is strong. To check the battery, briefly touch the ground clip to the probe; if the light glows brightly, the battery is strong enough for testing.

➡**A self-powered test light should not be used on any computer controlled system or component. The small amount of electricity transmitted by the test light is enough to damage many electronic automotive components.**

MULTIMETERS

Multimeters are an extremely useful tool for troubleshooting electrical problems. They can be purchased in either analog or digital form and have a price range to suit any budget. A multimeter is a voltmeter, ammeter and ohmmeter (along with other features) combined into one instrument. It is often used when testing solid state circuits because of its high input impedance (usually 10 megaohms or more). A brief description of the multimeter main test functions follows:

• Voltmeter—the voltmeter is used to measure voltage at any point in a circuit, or to measure the voltage drop across any part of a circuit. Voltmeters usually have various scales and a selector switch to allow the reading of different voltage ranges. The

voltmeter has a positive and a negative lead. To avoid damage to the meter, always connect the negative lead to the negative (-) side of the circuit (to ground or nearest the ground side of the circuit) and connect the positive lead to the positive (+) side of the circuit (to the power source or the nearest power source). Note that the negative voltmeter lead will always be black and that the positive voltmeter will always be some color other than black (usually red).

• Ohmmeter—the ohmmeter is designed to read resistance (measured in ohms) in a circuit or component. Most ohmmeters will have a selector switch which permits the measurement of different ranges of resistance (usually the selector switch allows the multiplication of the meter reading by 10, 100, 1,000 and 10,000). Some ohmmeters are "auto-ranging" which means the meter itself will determine which scale to use. Since the meters are powered by an internal battery, the ohmmeter can be used like a self-powered test light. When the ohmmeter is connected, current from the ohmmeter flows through the circuit or component being tested. Since the ohmmeter's internal resistance and voltage are known values, the amount of current flow through the meter depends on the resistance of the circuit or component being tested. The ohmmeter can also be used to perform a continuity test for suspected open circuits. In using the meter for making continuity checks, do not be concerned with the actual resistance readings. Zero resistance, or any ohm reading, indicates continuity in the circuit. Infinite resistance indicates an opening in the circuit. A high resistance reading where there should be none indicates a problem in the circuit. Checks for short circuits are made in the same manner as checks for open circuits, except that the circuit must be isolated from both power and normal ground. Infinite resistance indicates no continuity, while zero resistance indicates a dead short.

Never use an ohmmeter to check the resistance of a component or wire while there is voltage applied to the circuit.

• Ammeter—an ammeter measures the amount of current flowing through a circuit in units called amperes or amps. At normal operating voltage, most circuits have a characteristic amount of amperes, called "current draw" which can be measured using an ammeter. By referring to a specified current draw rating, then measuring the amperes and comparing the two values, one can determine what is happening within the circuit to aid in diagnosis. An open circuit, for example, will not allow any current to flow, so the ammeter reading will be zero. A damaged component or circuit will have an increased current draw, so the reading will be high. The ammeter is always connected in series with the circuit being tested. All of the current that normally flows through the circuit must also flow through the ammeter; if there is any other path for the current to follow, the ammeter reading will not be accurate. The ammeter itself has very little resistance to current flow and, therefore, will not affect the circuit, but it will measure current draw only when the circuit is closed and electricity is flowing. Excessive current draw can blow fuses and drain the battery, while a reduced current draw can cause motors to run slowly, lights to dim and other components to not operate properly.

Troubleshooting Electrical Systems

When diagnosing a specific problem, organized troubleshooting is a must. The complexity of a modern automotive vehicle demands that you approach any problem in a logical, organized manner. There are certain troubleshooting techniques, however, which are standard:

• Establish when the problem occurs. Does the problem appear only under certain conditions? Were there any noises, odors or other unusual symptoms? Isolate the problem area. To do this, make some simple tests and observations, then eliminate the systems that are working properly. Check for obvious problems, such as broken wires and loose or dirty connections. Always check the obvious before assuming something complicated is the cause.

• Test for problems systematically to determine the cause once the problem area is isolated. Are all the components functioning properly? Is there power going to electrical switches and motors? Performing careful, systematic checks will often turn up most causes on the first inspection, without wasting time checking components that have little or no relationship to the problem.

• Test all repairs after the work is done to make sure that the problem is fixed. Some causes can be traced to more than one component, so a careful verification of repair work is important in order to pick up additional malfunctions that may cause a problem to reappear or a different problem to arise. A blown fuse, for example, is a simple problem that may require more than another fuse to repair. If you don't look for a problem that caused a fuse to blow, a shorted wire (for example) may go undetected.

Experience has shown that most problems tend to be the result of a fairly simple and obvious cause, such as loose or corroded connectors, bad grounds or damaged wire insulation which causes a short. This makes careful visual inspection of components during testing essential to quick and accurate troubleshooting.

Testing

OPEN CIRCUITS

◆ See Figure 8

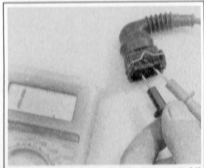

tcca6p10

Fig. 8 The infinite reading on this multimeter indicates that the circuit is open

This test already assumes the existence of an open in the circuit and it is used to help locate the open portion.

1. Isolate the circuit from power and ground.
2. Connect the self-powered test light or ohmmeter ground clip to the ground side of the circuit and probe sections of the circuit sequentially.
3. If the light is out or there is infinite resistance, the open is between the probe and the circuit ground.
4. If the light is on or the meter shows continuity, the open is between the probe and the end of the circuit toward the power source.

SHORT CIRCUITS

➡️**Never use a self-powered test light to perform checks for opens or shorts when power is applied to the circuit under test. The test light can be damaged by outside power.**

1. Isolate the circuit from power and ground.
2. Connect the self-powered test light or ohmmeter ground clip to a good ground and probe any easy-to-reach point in the circuit.
3. If the light comes on or there is continuity, there is a short somewhere in the circuit.
4. To isolate the short, probe a test point at either end of the isolated circuit (the light should be on or the meter should indicate continuity).
5. Leave the test light probe engaged and sequentially open connectors or switches, remove parts, etc. until the light goes out or continuity is broken.
6. When the light goes out, the short is between the last two circuit components which were opened.

VOLTAGE

This test determines voltage available from the battery and should be the first step in any electrical troubleshooting procedure after visual inspection. Many electrical problems, especially on computer controlled systems, can be caused by a low state of charge in the battery. Excessive corrosion at the battery cable terminals can cause poor contact that will prevent proper charging and full battery current flow.

1. Set the voltmeter selector switch to the 20V position.
2. Connect the multimeter negative lead to the battery's negative (-) post or terminal and the positive lead to the battery's positive (+) post or terminal.
3. Turn the ignition switch **ON** to provide a load.
4. A well charged battery should register over 12 volts. If the meter reads below 11.5 volts, the battery power may be insufficient to operate the electrical system properly.

VOLTAGE DROP

▸ **See Figure 9**

When current flows through a load, the voltage beyond the load drops. This voltage drop is due to the resistance created by the load and also by small resistances created by corrosion at the connectors and damaged insulation on the wires. The maximum allowable voltage drop under load is critical, especially

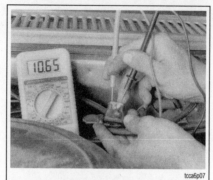

Fig. 9 This voltage drop test revealed high resistance (low voltage) in the circuit

if there is more than one load in the circuit, since all voltage drops are cumulative.

1. Set the voltmeter selector switch to the 20 volt position.
2. Connect the multimeter negative lead to a good ground.
3. Operate the circuit and check the voltage prior to the first component (load).
4. There should be little or no voltage drop in the circuit prior to the first component. If a voltage drop exists, the wire or connectors in the circuit are suspect.
5. While operating the first component in the circuit, probe the ground side of the component with the positive meter lead and observe the voltage readings. A small voltage drop should be noticed. This voltage drop is caused by the resistance of the component.
6. Repeat the test for each component (load) down the circuit.
7. If a large voltage drop is noticed, the preceding component, wire or connector is suspect.

RESISTANCE

▸ **See Figures 10 and 11**

❋ WARNING

Never use an ohmmeter with power applied to the circuit. The ohmmeter is designed to operate on its own power supply. The normal 12 volt electrical system voltage could damage the meter!

1. Isolate the circuit from the vehicle's power source.
2. Ensure that the ignition key is **OFF** when disconnecting any components or the battery.
3. Where necessary, also isolate at least one side of the circuit to be checked, in order to avoid reading parallel resistances. Parallel circuit resistances will always give a lower reading than the actual resistance of either of the branches.
4. Connect the meter leads to both sides of the circuit (wire or component) and read the actual measured ohms on the meter scale. Make sure the selector switch is set to the proper ohm scale for the circuit being tested, to avoid misreading the ohmmeter test value.

Fig. 10 Checking the resistance of a coolant temperature sensor with an ohmmeter. Reading is 1.04 kilohms

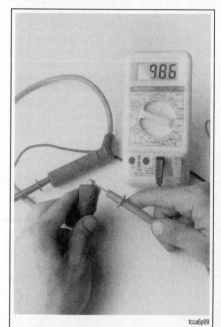

Fig. 11 Spark plug wires can be checked for excessive resistance using an ohmmeter

Wire and Connector Repair

Almost anyone can replace damaged wires, as long as the proper tools and parts are available. Wire and terminals are available to fit almost any need. Even the specialized weatherproof, molded and hard shell connectors are now available from aftermarket suppliers.

Be sure the ends of all the wires are fitted with the proper terminal hardware and connectors. Wrapping a wire around a stud is never a permanent solution and will only cause trouble later. Replace wires one at a time to avoid confusion. Always route wires exactly the same as the factory.

➡️**If connector repair is necessary, only attempt it if you have the proper tools. Weatherproof and hard shell connectors require special tools to release the pins inside the connector. Attempting to repair these connectors with conventional hand tools will damage them.**

BATTERY CABLES

Disconnecting the Cables

When working on any electrical component on the vehicle, it is always a good idea to disconnect the negative (-) battery cable. This will prevent potential damage to many sensitive electrical components such as the Powertrain Control Module (PCM), radio, alternator, etc.

→Any time you disengage the battery cables, it is recommended that you disconnect the negative (-) battery cable first. This will prevent your accidentally grounding the positive (+) terminal to the body of the vehicle when disconnecting it, thereby preventing damage to the above mentioned components.

Before you disconnect the cable(s), first turn the ignition to the OFF position. This will prevent a draw on the battery which could cause arcing (electricity trying to ground itself to the body of a vehicle, just like a spark plug jumping the gap) and, of course,

damaging some components such as the alternator diodes.

When the battery cable(s) are reconnected (negative cable last), be sure to check that your lights, windshield wipers and other electrically operated safety components are all working correctly. If your vehicle contains an Electronically Tuned Radio (ETR), don't forget to also reset your radio stations. Ditto for the clock.

AIR BAG (SUPPLEMENTAL RESTRAINT SYSTEM)

General Information

SERVICE PRECAUTIONS

♦ See Figures 12, 13, and 14

Fig. 12 To prevent personal injury, ALWAYS carry a live air bag facing away from you in case of accidental deployment

Fig. 13 To prevent personal injury, ALWAYS place a live airbag with the cover facing up in case of accidental deployment

Fig. 14 Be sure to observe any precaution labels on the vehicle regarding the air bag system

✵✵ CAUTION

Some vehicles are equipped with an air bag system, also known as the Supplemental Inflatable Restraint (SIR) or Supplemental Restraint System (SRS). The system must be disabled before performing service on or around system components, steering column, instrument panel components, wiring and sensors. Failure to follow safety and disabling procedures could result in accidental air bag deployment, possible personal injury and unnecessary system repairs.

Several precautions must be observed when handling the inflator module to avoid accidental deployment and possible personal injury.
• Never carry the inflator module by the wires or connector on the underside of the module.
• When carrying a live inflator module, hold securely with both hands, and ensure that the bag and trim cover are pointed away.
• Place the inflator module on a bench or other surface with the bag and trim cover facing up.

• With the inflator module on the bench, never place anything on or close to the module which may be thrown in the event of an accidental deployment.

DISARMING

♦ See Figure 15

1. Before servicing the vehicle, refer to the precautions in the beginning of this section.
2. Position the front wheels in the straight-ahead position and place the key in the LOCK position. Remove the key from the ignition lock cylinder.
3. Disconnect the negative battery cable and insulate the cable end with high-quality electrical tape or similar non-conductive wrapping.
4. Wait at least one minute before working on the vehicle. The air bag system is designed to retain enough voltage to deploy the air bag for a short period of time after the battery has been disconnected.

REARMING

1. Connect the negative battery cable, turn the ignition switch to the ON position and check the SRS warning light for proper operation.

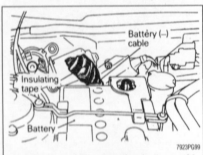

Fig. 15 Insulate the negative battery cable to prevent accidental deployment of the air bag

HEATING AND AIR CONDITIONING

Blower Motor

REMOVAL & INSTALLATION

Mirage

♦ See Figures 16, 17, and 18

1. Disconnect the negative battery cable.
2. Remove the right side instrument panel undercover panel.
3. Remove the glove box panel and frame.
4. Detach the blower motor electrical connection.
5. Disconnect and remove the resistor.
6. Disconnect the blower motor ventilation tube.

7. Remove the blower motor mounting bolts, remove the blower motor.
To install:
8. Position the blower motor and install the mounting bolts.
9. Attach the blower motor electrical connection.
10. Connect the blower motor ventilation tube.

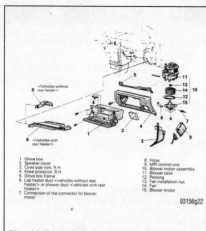

1. Glove box
2. Speaker cover
3. Cowl side trim, R.H.
4. Knee protector, R.H.
5. Glove box frame
6. Lap heater duct <vehicles without rear heater> or shower duct <vehicles with rear heater>
7. Connection of the connector for blower motor
8. Hose
9. MFI control unit
10. Blower motor assembly
11. Blower case
12. Packing
13. Fan installation nut
14. Fan
15. Blower motor

93156g22

Fig. 16 Exploded view of the blower motor and related components—1990–92 Mirage

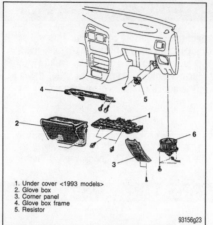

1. Under cover <1993 models>
2. Glove box
3. Corner panel
4. Glove box frame
5. Resistor

93156g23

Fig. 17 Exploded view of the blower motor and related components—1993–96 Mirage

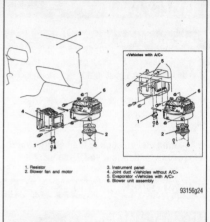

1. Resistor
2. Blower fan and motor
3. Instrument panel
4. Joint duct <Vehicles without A/C>
5. Evaporator <Vehicles with A/C>
6. Blower unit assembly

93156g24

Fig. 18 Exploded view of the blower motor and related components—1997–00 Mirage

11. Install the resistor and the glove box assembly.

12. Install the right side instrument panel undercover panel.

13. Connect the negative battery cable.

1990–93 Galant

▶ See Figure 19

1. Disconnect the negative battery cable.
2. Remove the glove box stopper.
3. Swing the glove box door open all the way and remove the bottom retaining screws. Remove the glovebox.

4. Remove the dash undercover. Note that some of the screws and retainers are concealed behind small covers which must be removed.

5. Remove the heater duct for the passenger's feet.

6. Carefully detach the 10-pin connector running to the back of the glove box frame. Disconnect the single wire (glove box switch) running to the back of the glove box frame.

7. Remove the four bolts holding the glove box frame and remove the frame.

8. Disconnect the small air hose running from the fan motor to the fan housing.

9. Detach the electrical connector from the fan motor.

10. Remove the three small bolts holding the motor to the housing, then remove the motor and fan.

To install:

11. Check the inside of the case carefully; any debris can snag the fan and cause noise or poor airflow.

12. Inspect the gasket (packing) under the motor and replace it if cracked or damaged. Reinstall the fan and motor to the case and install the retaining bolts.

13. Attach the air hose and electrical connector.

14. Install the glove box frame and connect both the 10-pin and single pin connectors properly.

15. Install the heater duct

16. Install the undercover, taking care to insure it is in place and all the fasteners are secure.

17. Install the glove box and its stopper.

18. Connect the negative battery cable.

1994–00 Galant

▶ See Figures 20 and 21

1. Disconnect the negative battery cable.
2. Remove the three instrument panel undercover mounting screws and remove the cover.
3. If equipped with A/C, unplug and remove the compressor module.
4. Detach the electrical connector from the fan motor.
5. Remove the three small bolts holding the motor to the housing and remove the motor and fan.

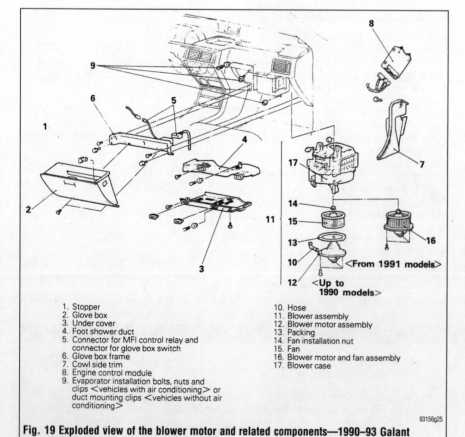

1. Stopper
2. Glove box
3. Under cover
4. Foot shower duct
5. Connector for MFI control relay and connector for glove box switch
6. Glove box frame
7. Cowl side trim
8. Engine control module
9. Evaporator installation bolts, nuts and clips <vehicles with air conditioning> or duct mounting clips <vehicles without air conditioning>
10. Hose
11. Blower assembly
12. Blower motor assembly
13. Packing
14. Fan installation nut
15. Fan
16. Blower motor and fan assembly
17. Blower case

<From 1991 models>
<Up to 1990 models>

93156g25

Fig. 19 Exploded view of the blower motor and related components—1990–93 Galant

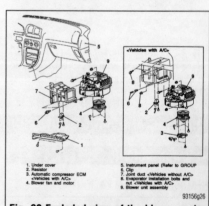

1. Under cover
2. Resistor
3. Automatic compressor ECM <Vehicles with A/C>
4. Blower fan and motor
5. Instrument panel (Refer to GROUP)
6. Clip
7. Joint duct <Vehicles without A/C>
8. Evaporator installation bolts and nut <Vehicles with A/C>
9. Blower unit assembly

93156g26

Fig. 20 Exploded view of the blower motor and related components—1994–98 Galant

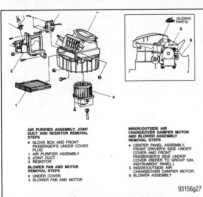

Fig. 21 Exploded view of the blower motor and related components—1999–00 Galant

To install:

6. Check the inside of the case carefully; any debris can snag the fan and cause noise or poor airflow.

7. Install the blower motor, in the blower case and secure with the three mounting bolts.

8. Attach the blower motor electrical connector.

9. Install the compressor module, if removed.

10. Install the undercover, taking care to insure it is in place and all the fasteners are secure.

11. Connect the negative battery cable.

Diamante

♦ **See Figures 22 and 23**

1. Disarm the air bag, as outlined earlier in this section.

❄❄ CAUTION

Wait at least 1 minute before working on the vehicle. The air bag system is designed to retain enough voltage to deploy the air bag for a short period of time even after the battery has been disconnected.

2. Remove the passenger side lower instrument panel and shower duct.

3. Remove the glove box striker, glove box, glove box outer casing and the screw below the assembly.

4. Remove the evaporator case mounting bolt and nut.

5. Remove the inside/outside air changeover damper motor assembly.

6. Remove the PCM, mounting bracket and MFI control relay.

7. Remove the instrument panel passengers side lower bracket.

8. Remove the molded hose from the blower assembly.

9. Remove the blower motor assembly.

10. Remove the fan retaining nut and fan in order to replace the motor.

To install:

11. Check that the blower motor shaft is not bent and that the packing is in good condition. Clean all parts of dust, etc.

12. Assemble the motor and fan. Install the blower motor then attach the connector.

13. Install the molded hose. Install the duct or undercover.

14. Install the evaporator case mounting bolt and nut.

15. Install the instrument panel passengers side lower bracket.

16. Install the PCM, mounting bracket and MFI control relay.

17. Install the inside/outside air changeover damper motor assembly.

18. Install the screw below the glove box assembly, and the entire glove box unit.

19. Install the lower instrument panel and shower duct.

20. Connect the negative battery cable and check the entire climate control system for proper operation.

Heater Core

REMOVAL & INSTALLATION

Diamante

♦ **See Figures 24 and 25**

1. Disarm the air bag. Refer to the procedure earlier in this section.

2. Drain the cooling system and disconnect the heater hoses from the core tubes. Plug the hoses.

3. Remove the passenger side undercover.

4. Remove the right side foot shower duct.

5. To remove the console, remove the ashtray and remove the revealed screw. Then remove the 4 screws from the sides of the assembly and remove.

6. Remove the decorative plugs from the driver's knee protector. Remove the revealed screws, the knee protector assembly and the protector support bracket.

7. Remove the steering column covers.

8. Remove the glove box striker, glove box, glove box outer casing and the screw below the assembly.

9. Remove the radio bezel and the stereo entertainment system.

10. Remove the climate control system control head.

11. Remove the cup holder.

12. Remove the speakers from the top of the instrument panel.

13. Remove the instrument cluster bezel and the instrument cluster.

14. To remove the speedometer cable adapter from the instrument panel, first disconnect the speedometer cable from the transaxle. Then unlock the adapter from the instrument panel, pull the speedometer cable slightly inwards, and remove the adapter.

15. Detach all steering column connectors, remove the column mounting bolts, and allow the steering column to rest on the front seat. Be very

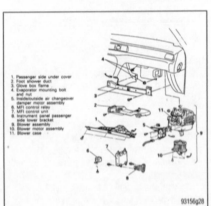

Fig. 22 Exploded view of the blower motor and related components—1992–96 Diamante

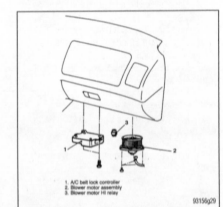

Fig. 23 Exploded view of the blower motor and related components—1997–00 Diamante

Fig. 24 Heater core and related components exploded view—1992–96 Diamante

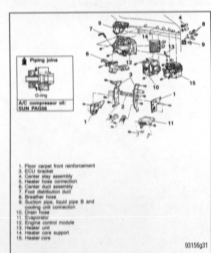

Fig. 25 Heater core and related components exploded view—1997–00 Diamante

careful not to allow anything to come in contact with the air bag unit.

16. Remove the glove box lamp assembly.

17. Remove the remaining instrument panel mounting screws and remove the instrument panel from the vehicle.

18. Remove the left side foot shower ductwork, lap cooler duct and center duct.

19. Remove the front and center reinforcements and center stay assembly.

20. Remove the air distribution duct assembly.

21. Detach all connectors from heater-box-mounted items.

22. Remove the heater box mounting screws and nut, then remove the unit from the vehicle.

23. Disassemble on a workbench. Remove the heater core from the heater case.

To install:

24. Thoroughly clean and dry the inside of the case and install the heater core and all related parts.

25. Install the heater unit to the vehicle and install the mounting screws and nut. Be sure the evaporator case and heater case are fitted together properly. Attach all connectors to heater-box-mounted items.

26. Install the air distribution duct assembly. Install the front and center reinforcements and center stay assembly.

27. Install the center duct, lap cooler duct and left side foot shower duct.

28. Install the instrument panel and mounting screws.

29. Install the glove box lamp assembly.

30. Secure the steering column and attach all steering column connectors.

31. Install the speedometer cable adapter to the instrument panel.

32. Install the instrument cluster and the instrument cluster bezel.

33. Install the speakers to the top of the instrument panel.

34. Install the cup holder.

35. Install the climate control system control head.

36. Install the stereo entertainment system and bezel.

37. Install the screw below the glove box assembly, and the entire glove box unit.

38. Install the steering column covers.

39. Install the knee protector support bracket, the protector and the decorative plugs.

40. Install the console and the ashtray.

41. Install the right side foot shower duct.

42. Install the passenger side undercover.

43. Connect the heater hoses to the core tubes.

44. Fill the cooling system.

45. Connect the negative battery cable and check the entire climate control system for proper operation and leaks.

Galant

▶ **See Figures 26, 27, and 28**

1. Disconnect the negative battery cable.

2. Disarm the air bag. Refer to the procedure earlier in this section.

3. With the engine cold, set the temperature control lever to the FULL HOT position. Drain the engine coolant.

4. Disconnect the coolant hoses running to the heater pipes at the firewall.

5. Remove the center console.

6. Remove the heater cover.

7. Remove the steering wheel.

8. Remove the small steering column panel.

9. Remove the undercover.

10. Remove the upper and lower steering column covers and detach the wiring connectors.

11. Remove the instrument cluster hood.

12. Remove the mounting screws for the instrument cluster.

13. Pull the cluster out and disconnect the speedometer adapter behind the cluster. Remove the cluster.

14. Remove the floor console and the underframe.

15. Disconnect and remove the air duct, lap heater duct, side defroster duct and the vertical defroster duct.

16. Remove the glove box.

17. Remove the ashtray and its mount. Disconnect the light wiring before removing.

18. Remove the heater control faceplate.

19. Remove the heater control panel and disconnect its harness.

20. Remove the right side undercover from the instrument panel and remove the underframe.

21. On the left side of the instrument panel, remove the fuse box cover and unbolt the fusebox from the instrument panel.

22. Remove the front pillar (windshield pillar trim) from each pillar.

23. Remove the kick panel trim from each side.

24. Loosen the defroster garnish, disconnect the photo sensor wiring and remove the garnish and defroster grille.

25. Remove the grille for the center air outlet.

26. Remove the bolts holding the steering column bracket to the instrument panel.

27. Remove the center reinforcement bracket.

28. On the left side, remove the retaining nuts holding the instrument panel underframe to the body.

29. On the right side, remove the underframe retaining bolts. Note that the bolts are different; the flanged bolt must be correctly reinstalled.

30. Remove the remaining nuts and bolts holding the instrument panel. As the instrument panel comes loose, label and disconnect the wiring harnesses. Carefully remove the instrument panel.

31. If equipped with automatic climate control, remove the power control unit on the lower front of the heater unit.

32. Remove the duct joint between the heater unit and evaporator case (with air conditioning) or blower assembly (heater only).

33. Carefully separate the vacuum hose harness at the connector.

34. Remove the heater unit from the vehicle.

35. To remove the heater core, first remove the cover from the water valve. Disconnect the links and remove the vacuum actuator.

36. Remove the clamps and slide the heater core out of the case. Remove the water valve after the core is removed.

37. With the case removed, the heater core may be changed after the water valve is removed. Remove the plastic cover, remove the clamps and hose and remove the water valve.

To install:

38. Thoroughly clean and dry the inside of the case. Install the core and the water valve, using new hose or clamps.

39. Install the vacuum actuator and the connecting link. Put the cover on the water valve.

40. Install the heater unit and tighten the mounting bolts.

41. Carefully attach the vacuum hose connector to the vacuum harness. Make certain the hoses mate firmly and securely.

42. Install the heater cover, then install the center console.

43. Install the duct joint between heater and evaporator or blower.

44. Install the power control unit and carefully connect the links and rods.

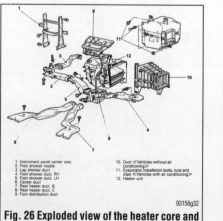

1. Instrument panel center stay
2. Foot shower nozzle
3. Lap shower duct
4. Foot shower duct, RH
5. Foot shower duct, LH
6. Center duct
7. Rear heater duct, B
8. Rear heater duct, C
9. Foot distribution duct
10. Duct <Vehicles without air conditioning>
11. Evaporator installation bolts, nuts and clips <Vehicles with air conditioning>
12. Heater unit

93156g32

Fig. 26 Exploded view of the heater core and related components—1990–93 Galant

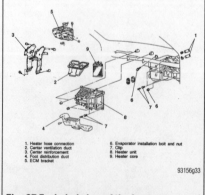

1. Heater hose connection
2. Center ventilation duct
3. Center reinforcement
4. Foot distribution duct
5. ECM bracket
6. Evaporator installation bolt and nut
7. Clip
8. Heater unit
9. Heater core

93156g33

Fig. 27 Exploded view of the heater core and related components—1994–98 Galant

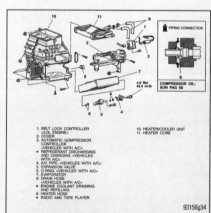

1. BELT LOCK CONTROLLER <3.0L ENGINE>
2. COVER
3. AUTOMATIC COMPRESSOR CONTROLLER <VEHICLES WITH A/C>
4. A/C PIPE <VEHICLES WITH A/C>
5. EXPANSION VALVE <VEHICLES WITH A/C>
6. O-RING <VEHICLES WITH A/C>
7. EVAPORATOR <VEHICLES WITH A/C>
8. DRAIN HOSE <VEHICLES WITH A/C>
9. HEATER HOSE
10. HEATER/COOLER UNIT
11. HEATER CORE

REFRIGERANT DISCHARGING AND CHARGING <VEHICLES WITH A/C>
ENGINE COOLANT DRAINING AND REFILLING
RADIO AND TAPE PLAYER

PIPING CONNECTION

4.9 Nm
43.4 in-lb

COMPRESSOR OIL
SUN PAG S6

93156g34

Fig. 28 Exploded view of the heater core and related components—1999–00 Galant

45. Install the heater hoses under the hood.
46. Install the instrument panel by reversing its removal procedure.
47. Install the center console.
48. Install the upper and lower steering column covers.
49. Install the center panel undercover.
50. Install the small column panel.
51. Install the steering wheel.
52. Fill the cooling system.
53. Connect the negative battery cable and check the entire climate control system for proper operation and leaks.

Mirage

♦ See Figures 29, 30, and 31

1. Disconnect the negative battery cable.
2. Drain the cooling system and disconnect the heater hoses.
3. Remove the front seats by removing the covers over the anchor bolts, the underseat tray, the seat belt guide ring, the seat mounting nuts and bolts and disconnect the seat belt switch wiring harness from under the seat. Then lift out the seats.
4. Remove the floor console by first taking out the coin holder and the console box tray. Remove the remote control mirror switch or cover. All of these items require only a plastic trim tool to carefully pry them out.
5. Remove the rear half of the console.
6. Remove the shift lever knob on manual transmission vehicles.
7. Remove the front console box assembly.
8. A number of the instrument panel pieces may be retained by pin type fasteners. They may be removed using the following procedure:

   a. Press down on the center pin with a suitable blunt pointed tool. Press down a little more than $\frac{1}{16}$ in. (2mm) to release the clip. Pull the clip outward to remove it.

   b. Do not push the pin inward more than necessary because it may damage the grommet or the pin may fall in if pushed in too far. Once the clips are removed, use a plastic trim stick to pry the piece loose.

9. Remove both lower cowl trim panels (kick panels).
10. Remove the ashtray.
11. Remove the center panel around the radio.
12. Remove the sunglass pocket at the upper left side of panel and the side panel into which it mounts.
13. Remove the driver's side knee protector and the hood release handle.
14. Remove the steering column top and bottom covers.
15. Remove the radio.
16. Remove the glove box striker and box assembly.
17. Remove the instrument panel lower cover, 2 small pieces in the center, by pulling forward.
18. Remove the heater control assembly screw.
19. Remove the instrument cluster bezel and pull out the gauge assembly.
20. Remove the speedometer adapter by disconnecting the speedometer cable at the transaxle pulling the cable sightly towards the vehicle interior and giving a slight twist on the adapter to release it.
21. Insert a small flat-tipped tool to open the tab on the gauge cluster connector. Remove the harness connectors.

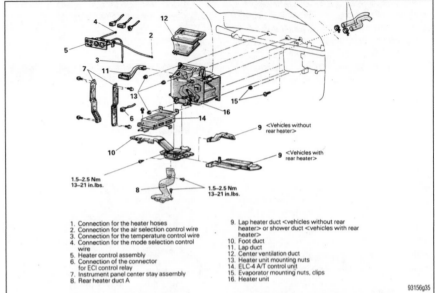

1. Connection for the heater hoses
2. Connection for the air selection control wire
3. Connection for the temperature control wire
4. Connection for the mode selection control wire
5. Heater control assembly
6. Connection of the connector for ECI control relay
7. Instrument panel center stay assembly
8. Rear heater duct A
9. Lap heater duct <vehicles without rear heater> or shower duct <vehicles with rear heater>
10. Foot duct
11. Lap duct
12. Center ventilation duct
13. Heater unit mounting nuts
14. ELC-4 A/T control unit
15. Evaporator mounting nuts, clips
16. Heater unit

1.5–2.5 Nm
13–21 in.lbs.

1.5–2.5 Nm
13–21 in.lbs.

93156g35

Fig. 29 Exploded view of the heater core and related components—1990–92 Mirage

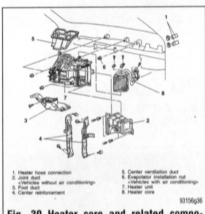

1. Heater hose connection
2. Joint duct <Vehicles without air conditioning>
3. Foot duct
4. Center reinforcement
5. Center ventilation duct
6. Evapolator installation nut <Vehicles with air conditioning>
7. Heater unit
8. Heater core

93156g36

Fig. 30 Heater core and related components—1993–96 Mirage

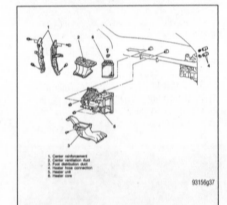

1. Center reinforcement
2. Center ventilation duct
3. Foot distribution duct
4. Heater hose connection
5. Heater unit
6. Heater core

93156g37

Fig. 31 Exploded view of the heater core and related components—1997–00 Mirage

22. Remove, by prying with a plastic trim tool, the right side speaker cover and the speaker, the upper side defroster grilles and the clock or plug to gain access to some of the instrument panel mounting bolts.
23. Lower the steering column by removing the bolt and nut.
24. Remove the instrument panel bolts and the instrument panel.
25. Disconnect the air selection, temperature and mode selection control cables from the heater box and remove the heater control assembly.
26. Remove the connector for the MFI control relay.
27. Remove both stamped steel instrument panel supports.
28. Remove the heater ductwork.
29. Remove the heater box mounting nuts.
30. Remove the automatic transmission ELC control box.
31. Remove the evaporator mounting nuts and clips.
32. With the evaporator pulled toward the vehicle interior, remove the heater unit. Be careful not to damage the heater tubes or to spill coolant.
33. Remove the cover plate around the heater tubes and the core fastener clips. Pull the heater core

from the heater box, being careful not to damage the fins or tank ends.

To install:

34. Thoroughly clean and dry the inside of the case. Install the heater core to the heater box. Install the clips and cover.
35. Install the evaporator and the automatic transmission ELC box.
36. Install the heater box and connect the duct work.
37. Connect all wires and control cables.
38. Install the instrument panel assembly and the console by reversing their removal procedures.
39. Install the seats.
40. Refill the cooling system.
41. Connect the negative battery cable and check the entire climate control system for proper operation. Check the system for leaks.

Air Conditioning Components

REMOVAL & INSTALLATION

Repair or service of air conditioning components is not covered by this manual, because of the risk of personal injury or death, and because of the legal ramifications of servicing these components without the proper EPA certification and experience. Cost, personal injury or death, environmental damage, and legal considerations (such as the fact that it is a federal crime to vent refrigerant into the atmosphere), dictate that the A/C components on your vehicle should be serviced only by a Motor Vehicle Air Conditioning (MVAC) trained, and EPA certified automotive technician.

➡️If your vehicle's A/C system uses R-12 refrigerant and is in need of recharging, the A/C system can be converted over to R-134a refrigerant (less environmentally harmful and expensive). Refer to Section 1 for additional information on R-12 to R-134a conversions, and for additional considerations dealing with your vehicle's A/C system.

Control Cables

ADJUSTMENT

1. Disconnect the negative battery cable. Remove the glove box, if necessary.
2. Move the mode selection lever to the DEFROST position. Move the mode selection damper lever FULLY INWARD and connect the cable to the lever. Adjust as required.
3. Move the temperature control lever to its HOTTEST position. Move the blend air damper lever FULLY DOWNWARD and connect the cable to the lever. Adjust as required.

4. Move the air selection control lever to the RECIRC position. Move the air selection damper FULLY INWARD and connect the cable to the lever. Adjust as required.

Control Panel

REMOVAL & INSTALLATION

◆ **See Figures 32 thru 45**

1. Disconnect the negative battery cable.
2. Unfasten the retaining clips and remove the center trim panel.
3. Remove the radio/tape and/or CD player assembly.
4. Remove the control assembly as follows:
   a. Remove the retaining screw(s).
   b. Press the lever pin to disconnect the air outlet changeover damper cable.

➡️The boss and clamp are needed for the assembly line during factory installation, however they are not necessary for service procedures.

   c. Snap the boss and clamp with a pair of nippers, to remove the heater control assembly from the vehicle.
To install:
5. Install the control panel, as follows:
   a. Set the temperature control knob on the panel to MAX HOT.
   b. Set the air mix damper lever at the upper part of the heater unit to the MAX HOT position, then attach the cable to the lever pin.

   c. Push the outer cable in the direction of the arrow so that there is no looseness, then secure with the clip.
   d. Set the knob for the air outlet changeover on the control to the DEF position.
   e. Set the air outlet changeover damper lever of the heater unit to the DEF position, then attach the cable to the lever pin.
   f. Push the outer cable in the direction of the arrow so there is no looseness, then secure it with the clip.
   g. Set the lever for the inside/outside air changeover on the heater control assembly to the air recirculation position.
   h. Set the inside/outside air changeover damper lever of the blower unit to the air recirculation position (with the inside/outside air changeover damper lever touched to the stopper of the blower case), then attach the cable to the lever pin.
   i. Push the outer cable in the direction of the arrow so that there is no looseness, then secure it with the clip.
   j. Properly position the control assembly and secure with the retaining screw(s).
6. Install the stopper.
7. Connect the negative battery cable and check the climate control system for proper operation before installing the remaining components.
8. Install the radio/tape and/or CD player assembly.
9. Install the center trim panel, making sure the clips are engaged properly.
10. Connect the negative battery cable.

Fig. 32 Using a suitable prytool, release the shifter trim plate retaining tabs . . .

Fig. 33 . . . then remove the shifter trim plate (automatic transaxles only)—1994–98 Galant shown

Fig. 34 Remove the two center trim panel retaining screws . . .

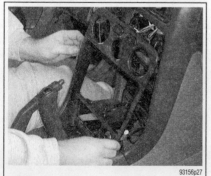

Fig. 35 . . . then remove the center trim panel from the vehicle

Fig. 36 Remove the radio retaining screws (two per side) . . .

Fig. 37 . . . then slide the radio chassis and bracket out of the instrument panel

Fig. 38 Pull the radio far enough out to access the electrical connectors . . .

Fig. 39 . . . then detach the connectors from the rear of the radio

Fig. 40 Finally, detach the antenna cable and remove the radio from the vehicle

Fig. 41 Remove the heater control panel retaining screws

Fig. 42 Remove the control cable from the selector knob

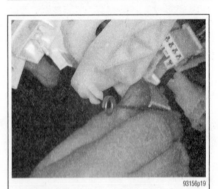

Fig. 43 Remove the control cable from the blend door

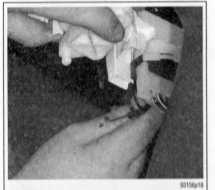

Fig. 44 Remove the cable retaining clips from the back of the control panel

Fig. 45 Detach the electrical connectors for the control panel, then remove the panel from the instrument panel

CRUISE CONTROL

Cruise control is a speed control system that maintains a desired vehicle speed under normal driving conditions. However, steep grades up or down may cause variations in the selected speeds. The electronic cruise control system has the capability to cruise, coast, resume speed, accelerate, "tap-up" and "tap-down".

The main parts of the cruise control system are the functional control switches, speed control assembly,

actuator, intermediate link, auto-cruise control module assembly, speed sensor, and the release switches.

Depending upon the year and/or model of your vehicle, the cruise control system is either vacuum or electronically controlled. The cruise control module assembly contains a low speed limit which will prevent system engagement below 25 mph (40 km/h). The module is controlled by the functional switches

located on a lever on the steering column or steering wheel and on the instrument panel.

The release switches are mounted on the brake/clutch/accelerator pedal bracket. When the brake or clutch pedal is depressed, the cruise control system is electrically disengaged and the throttle is returned to the idle position.

CRUISE CONTROL TROUBLESHOOTING

Problem	Possible Cause
Will not hold proper speed	Incorrect cable adjustment Binding throttle linkage Leaking vacuum servo diaphragm Leaking vacuum tank Faulty vacuum or vent valve Faulty stepper motor Faulty transducer Faulty speed sensor Faulty cruise control module
Cruise intermittently cuts out	Clutch or brake switch adjustment too tight Short or open in the cruise control circuit Faulty transducer Faulty cruise control module
Vehicle surges	Kinked speedometer cable or casing Binding throttle linkage Faulty speed sensor Faulty cruise control module
Cruise control inoperative	Blown fuse Short or open in the cruise control circuit Faulty brake or clutch switch Leaking vacuum circuit Faulty cruise control switch Faulty stepper motor Faulty transducer Faulty speed sensor Faulty cruise control module

Note: Use this chart as a guide. Not all systems will use the components listed.

tcca6c01

ENTERTAINMENT SYSTEMS

Radio Receiver/Amplifier/Tape Player/CD Player

REMOVAL & INSTALLATION

♦ **See Figures 32 thru 40, 46 and 47**

1. Disconnect battery negative cable.

➡**If equipped with an air bag, be sure to disarm it before entering the vehicle.**

2. Remove the panel from around the radio. On some models the panel is retained with screws. On others, use a plastic trim tool to pry the lower part of the radio panel loose.

3. Remove the radio/tape/CD player mounting bracket retaining screws.

4. Slide the radio chassis out of the instrument panel and disconnect the radio wiring harness and antenna cable.

➡**Depending on the speaker installation, it may save time at installation to identify and tag all wires before they are disconnected.**

5. Remove the mounting brackets from the radio.
To install:

6. The installation is the reverse of the removal procedure. Make all electrical and antenna connections before fastening the radio assembly in place.

7. Test all functions of the entertainment system prior to final installation. If all are satisfactory, install the unit and center panel.

8. Connect the negative battery cable and recheck the entire system for proper operation.

CD Changer

1. Disconnect the negative battery cable.
2. Open the trunk lid.
3. Remove any necessary trim to access the CD changer.
4. Remove the CD-changer-to-bracket retaining screws.
5. Lift the changer from the bracket and detach the electrical connectors.
6. Remove the changer from the vehicle.
To install:
7. The installation is the reverse of removal.

Speakers

REMOVAL & INSTALLATION

Front (Instrument Panel Mounted) Speaker

♦ **See Figure 48**

1. Disconnect the negative battery cable.
2. Remove the front speaker garnish.
3. Remove the retainers, detach the harness connector and remove the front speaker.

✳✳ WARNING

Handle the speaker carefully to avoid damaging the cone during removal and installation.

4. Installation is the reverse of the removal procedure

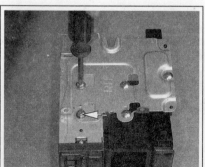

Fig. 46 Remove the radio-to-bracket retaining screws . . .

93156p24

Fig. 47 . . . then separate the radio chassis from the bracket assembly

93156p22

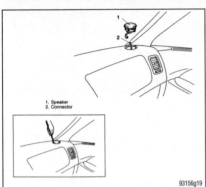

Fig. 48 Typical front (instrument panel mounted) speaker mounting

Door Mounted Tweeters

▶ **See Figure 49**

1. Disconnect the negative battery cable.
2. Remove the delta cover (triangular shaped cover behind the side mirror and above the door panel.
3. Remove the speaker retaining screws.
4. Lift the speaker out of the cavity.
5. Detach the electrical and remove the speaker.
6. The installation is the reverse of removal.

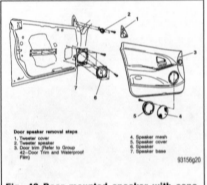

Fig. 49 Door mounted speaker with separate tweeter

Door Speakers

▶ **See Figures 50, 51, and 52**

1. Disconnect the negative battery cable.
2. Remove the door trim panel. Refer to the procedure in Section 10.
3. Remove the mounting screws, detach the harness connector and remove the front speaker.

❈❈ WARNING

Handle the speaker carefully to avoid damaging the cone during removal and installation.

Fig. 50 Remove the four speaker retaining screws

Fig. 52 . . . then detach the connector from the back of the speaker

4. Installation is the reverse of the removal procedure

Rear Deck Speakers

▶ **See Figure 53**

1. Disconnect the negative battery cable.
2. Remove the speaker cover.
3. Remove the speaker retaining screws.
4. Lift the speaker out of the cavity.
5. Detach the electrical and remove the speaker.
6. The installation is the reverse of removal.

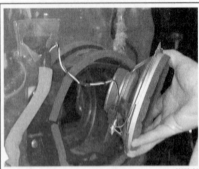

Fig. 51 Lift the speaker from the door cavity . . .

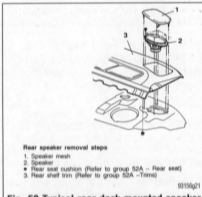

Fig. 53 Typical rear deck mounted speaker

WINDSHIELD WIPERS AND WASHERS

Windshield Wiper Blade and Arm

REMOVAL & INSTALLATION

▶ **See Figures 54 and 55**

➡ This procedure also applies to rear wiper arms on the Diamante Wagon and Mirage Hatchbacks.

1. Disconnect the negative battery cable.
2. Remove the windshield wiper arms by removing the cap, unscrewing the cap nuts then lifting the arms from the linkage posts.

Fig. 54 Remove the wiper arm retaining nut cap, then loosen the windshield wiper arm retaining nut

Fig. 55 Remove the wiper arm by lifting it from the linking posts

To install:

3. Install the wiper blade and arm assemblies. Tighten the retaining nuts to 7–12 ft. lbs. (10–16 Nm).

4. Note that the driver's side wiper arm should be marked **D** or **Dr** and the passenger's side wiper arm should be marked **A** or **As**. The identification marks should be located at the base of the arm, near the pivot. Install the arms so the blades are 1 inch from the garnish molding when parked.

5. Connect the negative battery cable and check the wiper system for proper operation.

Windshield Wiper Motor

REMOVAL & INSTALLATION

1990–92 Mirage

FRONT

1. Disconnect the negative battery cable.
2. Remove the windshield wiper arms by unscrewing the cap nuts and lifting the arms from the linkage posts.
3. Remove the front deck garnish panel.
4. Remove both windshield holders.
5. Remove the clips that hold the deck cover. If they are the pin type, they may be removed using the following procedure:

a. Remove the clip by pressing down on the center pin with a suitable blunt pointed tool. Press down a little more than $1/16$ in. (2mm). This releases the clip. Pull the clip outward to remove it.

b. Do not push the pin inward more than necessary because it may damage the grommet, or if pushed too far, the pin may fall in. Once the clips are removed, use a plastic trim stick to pry the deck cover loose.

6. On Mirage, remove the air intake screen.
7. Loosen the wiper motor assembly mounting bolts and remove the windshield wiper motor. Disconnect the linkage from the motor assembly. If necessary, remove the linkage from the vehicle.

➡The installation angle of the crank arm and motor has been factory set, do not remove them unless it is necessary to do so. If arm must be removed, remove them only after marking their mounting positions.

To install:

8. Install the windshield wiper motor and connect the linkage. Connect the electrical harness to the motor.

9. When installing the trim and garnish pieces and reusing pin type clips, use the following procedure:

a. With the pin pulled out, insert the trim clip into the hole in the trim.

b. Push the pin inward until the pin's head is flush with the grommet.

c. Check that the trim is secure.

10. Install the wiper arms and tighten nuts to 17 ft. lbs. (24 Nm).

11. Connect the negative battery cable and check the wiper system for proper operation.

REAR

1. Disconnect the negative battery cable.

2. Remove the rear wiper arm by removing the cap nut cover, unscrewing the cap nut and lifting the arm from the linkage post.

3. Remove the large interior trim panel. Use a plastic trim stick to unhook the trim clips of the liftgate trim. There will be a row of metal liftgate clips across the top. There will be 2 rows of trim clips that retain the rest of the panel.

4. Disconnect the electrical harness at the wiper motor. Remove the rear wiper assembly. Do not loosen the grommet for the wiper post.

To install:

5. Install the motor and grommet. Mount the grommet so the arrow on the grommet is pointing downward.

6. Install the wiper arm.

7. Connect the negative battery cable and check rear wiper system for proper operation.

8. If operation is satisfactory, fit the tabs on the upper part of the liftgate trim into the liftgate clips and secure the liftgate trim.

1993–00 Mirage

1. Disconnect the negative battery cable.
2. Remove the windshield wiper arms by unscrewing the cap nuts and lifting the arms from the linkage posts.
3. Remove the front deck garnish panel.
4. Remove both windshield holders.
5. Remove the clips that hold the deck cover. If they are the pin type, they may be removed using the following procedure:

a. Remove the clip by pressing down on the center pin with a suitable blunt pointed tool. Press down a little more than $1/16$ in. (2mm). This releases the clip. Pull the clip outward to remove it.

b. Do not push the pin inward more than necessary because it may damage the grommet or if pushed too far, the pin may fall in. Once the clips are removed, use a plastic trim stick to pry the deck cover loose.

6. Remove the air intake screen.
7. Loosen the wiper motor assembly mounting bolts and remove the windshield wiper motor. Disconnect the linkage from the motor assembly. If necessary, remove the linkage from the vehicle.

➡The installation angle of the crank arm and motor has been factory set. Do not remove unless necessary. If arm must be removed, remove only after marking mounting positions.

To install:

8. Install the windshield wiper motor and connect the linkage. Connect the electrical harness to the motor.

9. When installing the trim and garnish pieces and reusing pin type clips, use the following procedure:

a. With the pin pulled out, insert the trim clip into the hole in the trim.

b. Push the pin inward until the pin's head is flush with the grommet.

c. Check that the trim is secure.

10. Install the wiper arms and tighten the nuts.

11. Connect the negative battery cable and check the wiper system for proper operation.

1990–93 Galant

1. Disconnect the negative battery cable.

2. Remove the windshield wiper arms by unscrewing the cap nuts and lifting the arms from the linkage posts.

3. Remove the front garnish panel.
4. Remove the air inlet trim pieces.
5. Remove the hole cover.
6. Remove the wiper motor by loosening the mounting bolts, removing the motor assembly, then disconnecting the linkage.

➡The installation angle of the crank arm and motor has been factory set; do not remove them unless it is necessary to do so. If they must be removed, remove them only after marking their mounting positions.

To install:

7. Install the windshield wiper motor and connect the linkage.

8. Reinstall all trim pieces.

9. Reinstall the wiper blades. Note that the driver's side wiper arm should be marked **D** or **Dr** and the passenger's side wiper arm should be marked **A** or **As**. The identification marks should be located at the base of the arm, near the pivot. Install the arms so the blades are 1 inch from the garnish molding when parked.

10. Connect the negative battery cable and check the wiper system for proper operation.

Diamante and 1994–00 Galant

FRONT

▶ **See Figures 56, 57, 58, and 59**

1. Disconnect the negative battery cable.

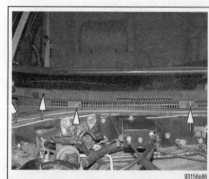

Fig. 56 Remove the retaining clips from the front garnish panel

Fig. 57 Lift the panel up and remove it from the vehicle

Fig. 58 Detach the connector and remove the three wiper motor retaining bolts

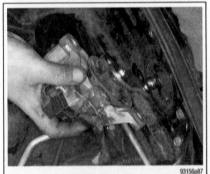

Fig. 59 Pull the motor from the firewall and detach the linkage

2. Matchmark the wiper arms to the shaft and mark the arms to the proper side for reinstallation purposes.

3. Remove the windshield wiper arms by unscrewing the cap nuts and lifting the arms from the linkage posts.
4. Remove the front deck garnish assembly.
5. Remove the air inlet cover.
6. Disconnect the electrical harness plug from the wiper motor.
7. Remove the access hole cover.
8. Remove the wiper motor mounting bolts.
9. Detach the motor crank arm from the wiper linkage and remove the motor.

➡**The installation angle of the crank arm and motor has been factory set. Do not remove them unless necessary. If they must be removed, remove them only after marking their mounting positions.**

To install:
10. Install the windshield wiper motor and connect the linkage.
11. Attach the electrical harness plug.
12. Install the access hole cover.
13. Install the air inlet cover.
14. Install the front deck garnish assembly.
15. Reinstall the wiper arm and tighten the mounting nuts to 14 ft. lbs. (19 Nm). Install the arms so the blades are parallel to the garnish molding when parked.
16. Connect the negative battery cable and check the wiper system for proper operation.

REAR

1. Disconnect the negative battery cable.
2. Remove the liftgate lower trim.
3. Lift the small cover, remove the retaining nut and remove the wiper arm.
4. Remove the mounting bolts and remove the wiper motor.

To install:
5. Install the motor and install the retaining bolts.
6. Install the wiper arm so that the arm is 3.35 inches (85mm) between the measurement points, when parked. Secure the wiper arm with the retaining nut.

➡**Before proceeding, connect the battery and check the operation of the motor. If satisfactory, disconnect the cable and complete the installation.**

7. Install the interior trim piece.
8. Connect the negative battery cable and recheck the system for proper operation.

Windshield Washer Pump

REMOVAL & INSTALLATION

Front and Rear

1. Disconnect the negative battery cable.
2. Remove the windshield washer fluid reservoir.
3. Drain any washer fluid in the reservoir into an appropriate container.
4. Remove the pump from the reservoir by either removing the retaining hardware or twisting gently until it is free from the reservoir.

To install:
5. Inspect the pump seal on the reservoir, replace if necessary.
6. Install the pump into place until seated on the seal.
7. Install the windshield washer fluid reservoir.
8. Refill the washer fluid reservoir.
9. Connect the negative battery cable.

INSTRUMENTS AND SWITCHES

Instrument Cluster

REMOVAL & INSTALLATION

Mirage

1. Disconnect the negative battery cable. Remove the center trim panel.
2. Remove the knee protector. If pin type clips are used, they may be removed using the following procedure:
   a. Press down on the center pin with a suitable blunt pointed tool. Press down a little more than $1/16$ in. (2mm). This releases the clip. Pull the clip outward to remove it.
   b. Do not push the pin inward more than necessary because it may damage the grommet or the pin may fall in, if pushed in too far. Once the clips are removed, use a plastic trim stick if necessary to pry the knee protector loose.
3. Remove the instrument cluster bezel.
4. Remove the instrument cluster. Disassemble and remove gauges or the speedometer as required.

➡**If the speedometer cable adapter requires service, disconnect the cable at the transaxle end. Pull the cable slightly toward the vehi-**
cle interior, release the lock by turning the adapter to the right or left and remove the adapter.

5. The installation is the reverse of the removal procedure. Use care not to damage the printed circuit board or any gauge components.
6. Connect the negative battery cable and check all cluster-related items for proper operation.

Galant

♦ **See Figures 60 thru 66**

1. Disconnect negative battery cable.
2. Remove the 2 retainer screws from the lower surface of the meter hood.
3. Remove the retainer screws from the underside top portion of the meter hood.
4. Carefully remove the meter hood from the face of the combination meter.
5. Remove the 4 retainer screws and the combination meter assembly with the bezel attached. Remove the front bezel and remove gauges or the speedometer as required.

➡**If the speedometer cable adapter requires service, disconnect the cable at the transaxle end. Pull the cable slightly toward the vehi-**
cle interior, release the lock by turning the adapter to the right or left and remove the adapter.

6. The installation is the reverse of the removal procedure. Use care not to damage the printed circuit board or any gauge components.
7. Connect the negative battery cable and check all cluster-related items for proper operation.

Fig. 60 Remove the retainer screws from the underside top portion of the meter hood

Fig. 61 . . . then remove the hood from the instrument panel

Fig. 62 Remove the retaining screws from the driver's side . . .

Fig. 63 . . . and also from the passenger side of the instrument cluster

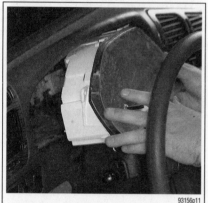

Fig. 64 Grasp the instrument cluster and carefully pull it out of the instrument panel

Fig. 65 On some models, the instrument cluster requires no connections to be detached; the cluster has sockets on the back . . .

Fig. 66 . . . these sockets engage connectors solidly mounted behind the cluster

Diamante

1. Disconnect the negative battery cable.

➡**If equipped with an air bag, be sure to disarm it before entering the vehicle.**

2. Remove the hood lock release handle and switches from the knee protector below the steering column. Then remove the exposed retaining screws and remove the knee protector.

3. Remove the upper and the lower steering column covers.

4. Remove the instrument cluster bezel.

5. Remove the instrument cluster. Disassemble and remove gauges or the speedometer as required.

➡**If the speedometer cable adapter must be serviced, disconnect the cable at the transaxle end. Pull the cable slightly toward the vehicle interior, release the lock by turning the adapter to the right or left and remove the adapter.**

6. The installation is the reverse of the removal procedure. Use care not to damage the printed circuit board or any gauge components.

7. Connect the negative battery cable and check all cluster-related items for proper operation.

Gauges

REMOVAL & INSTALLATION

▸ See Figures 67, 68, 69, and 70

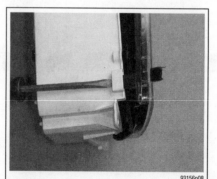

Fig. 67 Release the cluster lens retaining tabs . . .

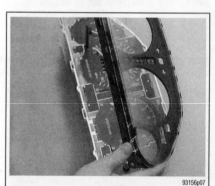

Fig. 68 . . . then remove the instrument cluster lens and cover assembly

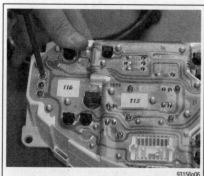

Fig. 69 Remove the gauge retaining screws . . .

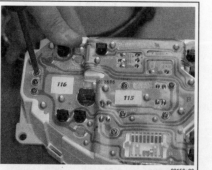

Fig. 70 . . . then carefully lift the gauges from the instrument cluster to remove them

1. Disconnect the negative battery cable.
2. Remove the instrument cluster, as outlined earlier in this section.
3. Remove the retaining screws for the instrument cluster lens and cover assembly. Remove the cover and lens.
4. Remove the retaining screws for the gauge or warning lamp to be replaced, then remove the gauge or warning lamp.

To install:
5. Place the gauge or warning lamp into place and tighten the retaining screws.
6. Install the instrument cluster lens and cover assembly.
7. Install the instrument cluster.
8. Connect the negative battery cable.

Windshield Wiper Switch

REMOVAL & INSTALLATION

➡ **The headlights, turn signals, dimmer switch, horn switch, windshield wiper/washer, intermittent wiper switch and on some models, the cruise control function**

Fig. 71 Using a suitable tool, carefully pry the retaining clips from either side of the switch trim plate . . .

---

are all built into 1 multi-function combination switch that is mounted on the steering column. Refer to Section 8 for procedures regarding the combination switch.

Rear Window Wiper Switch

REMOVAL & INSTALLATION

1. Disconnect the negative battery cable.
2. Using a suitable prytool, disengage the switch retaining tabs.
3. Gently pull the switch from the instrument panel.
4. Detach the electrical connector and remove the switch.
5. The installation is the reverse of removal.

Dimmer Switch

REMOVAL & INSTALLATION

▶ **See Figures 71, 72, and 73**

Fig. 72 . . . then carefully pull the switch and trim plate out of the instrument panel

---

1. Disconnect the negative battery cable.
2. Using a small screwdriver or other suitable tool, carefully pry the retaining clips from either side of the switch trim plate.
3. Carefully pull the switch and trim plate out of the instrument panel.
4. Detach the electrical connectors and remove the switch.
5. The installation is the reverse of removal.

Headlight Switch

REMOVAL & INSTALLATION

➡ **On all models the headlights, turn signals, and on some models, the cruise control function are all built into 1 multi-function combination switch that is mounted on the steering column. Refer to Section 8 for procedures regarding the combination switch.**

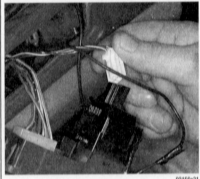

Fig. 73 Detach the electrical connectors and remove the switch

---

LIGHTING

Headlights

REMOVAL & INSTALLATION

Sealed Beam Headlights

1. Raise the headlights using the pop-up switch.
2. Disconnect the negative battery cable.
3. Unfasten the retaining screws, then remove the upper and the lower headlight bezels.
4. Remove the headlight retaining ring screws, and the headlight retaining ring.
5. Pull the headlight partially out, detach the connector, then remove headlight assembly from the vehicle.

To install:
6. Attach the headlight electrical connector.
7. Properly position the headlight and the retaining ring, then install the retaining screws.
8. Install the headlight bezels and secure with the retaining screws.

---

9. Connect the negative battery cable.

Composite Headlights

▶ **See Figures 74, 75, 76, 77, and 78**

✳✳ CAUTION

Halogen bulbs contain gas under pressure. Handling the bulb incorrectly could cause it to shatter into flying glass fragments. Do NOT leave the light switch ON. Always allow the bulb to cool before removal. Handle the bulb only by the base; avoid touching the glass itself. Whenever handling a halogen bulb, ALWAYS follow these precautions:

• Turn the headlight switch OFF and allow the bulb to cool before changing it. Leave the switch OFF until the change is complete.
• ALWAYS wear eye protection when changing a halogen bulb.

• Handle the bulb only by its base. Avoid touching the glass.
• DO NOT drop or scratch the bulb.
• Keep dirt and moisture away from the bulb.
• Place the used bulb in the new bulb's carton and dispose of it properly.

1. Open the vehicle's hood and secure it in an upright position.
2. Disconnect the negative battery cable.
3. Remove the socket cover by pulling it straight off, or turning it clockwise then pulling it off.
4. Carefully twist the bulb and socket counterclockwise, then pull the assembly from the headlight housing.
5. Holding the base of the bulb, detach it from the connector harness.

To install:
6. Holding the base of the bulb, install it securely in the connector.
7. Install the connector and bulb assembly in the housing and twist to lock into position.
8. Install the sealing cover by pushing it on

Fig. 74 Twist and pull on the cover to unlock it in order to access the headlight bulb and socket assembly

Fig. 75 Turn the inner head light bulb and socket . . .

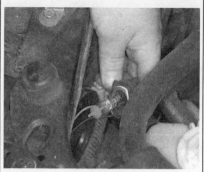

Fig. 76 . . . then carefully pull it from the headlight housing assembly

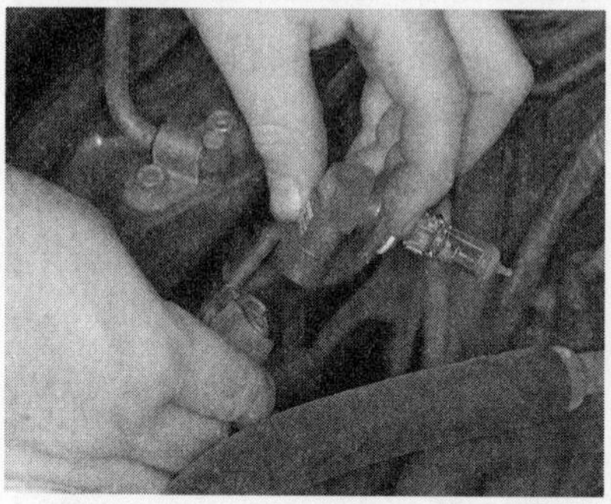

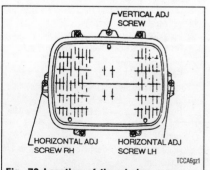

Fig. 77 Unplug the bulb from the socket, being careful not to touch the glass portion of the bulb

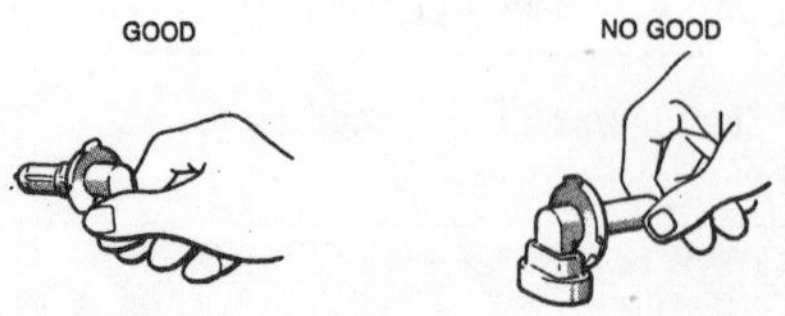

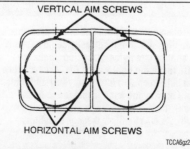

Fig. 78 NEVER hold the halogen bulb by the glass, ALWAYS hold it with the base

and/or turning it counterclockwise. Make sure the cover is installed securely or the lens will be out of focus, or water may get into the light unit.

9. Disconnect the negative battery cable and check the headlight operation.

AIMING THE HEADLIGHTS

▶ **See Figures 79, 80, 81, 82, and 83**

The headlights must be properly aimed to provide the best, safest road illumination. The lights should be checked for proper aim and adjusted as necessary. Certain state and local authorities have requirements for headlight aiming; these should be checked before adjustment is made.

✳✳ CAUTION

About once a year, when the headlights are replaced or any time front end work is performed on your vehicle, the headlight should be accurately aimed by a reputable repair shop using the proper equipment. Headlights not properly aimed can make it virtually impossible to see and may blind other drivers on the road, possibly causing an accident. Note that the following procedure is a temporary fix, until you can take your vehicle to a repair shop for a proper adjustment.

Headlight adjustment may be temporarily made using a wall, as described below, or on the rear of another vehicle. When adjusted, the lights should not glare in oncoming car or truck windshields, nor should they illuminate the passenger compartment of vehicles driving in front of you. These adjustments are rough and should always be fine-tuned by a repair shop which is equipped with headlight aiming tools. Improper adjustments may be both dangerous and illegal.

For most of the vehicles covered by this manual, horizontal and vertical aiming of each sealed beam unit is provided by two adjusting screws which move the retaining ring and adjusting plate against the tension of a coil spring. There is no adjustment for focus; this is done during headlight manufacturing.

➡**Because the composite headlight assembly is bolted into position, no adjustment should be necessary or possible. Some applications, however, may be bolted to an adjuster plate or may be retained by adjusting screws. If so, follow this procedure when adjusting the lights, BUT always have the adjustment checked by a reputable shop.**

Before removing the headlight bulb or disturbing the headlamp in any way, note the current settings in order to ease headlight adjustment upon reassembly. If the high or low beam setting of the old lamp still works, this can be done using the wall of a garage or a building:

1. Park the vehicle on a level surface, with the fuel tank about 1/2 full and with the vehicle empty of all extra cargo (unless normally carried). The vehicle should be facing a wall which is no less than 6 feet (1.8m) high and 12 feet (3.7m) wide. The front of the vehicle should be about 25 feet from the wall.

2. If aiming is to be performed outdoors, it is advisable to wait until dusk in order to properly see the

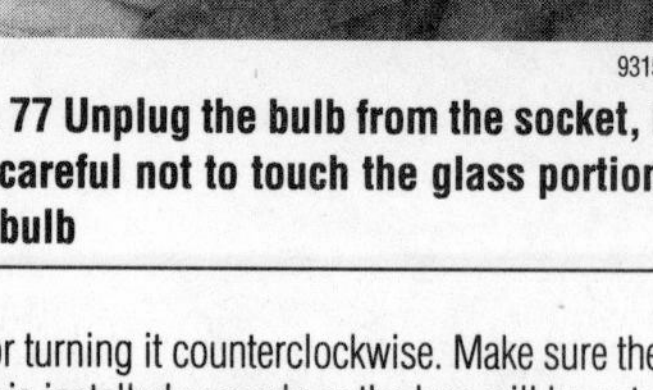

Fig. 79 Location of the aiming screws on most vehicles with sealed beam headlights

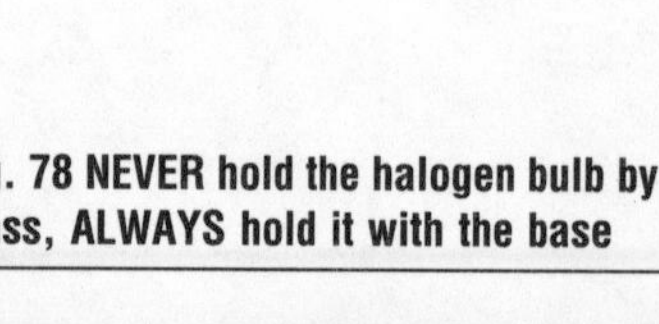

Fig. 80 Dual headlight adjustment screw locations—one side shown here (other side should be mirror image)

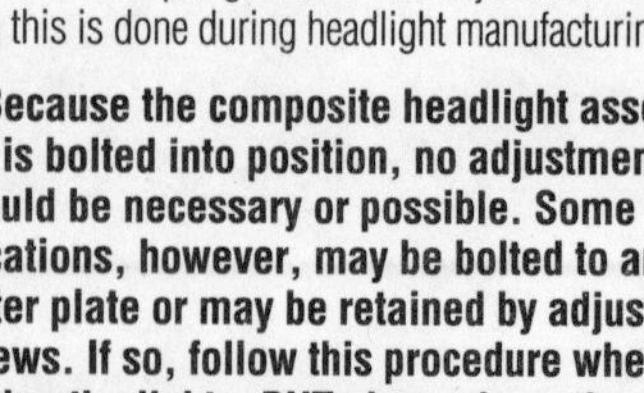

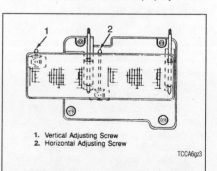

1. Vertical Adjusting Screw
2. Horizontal Adjusting Screw

Fig. 81 Example of headlight adjustment screw location for composite headlamps

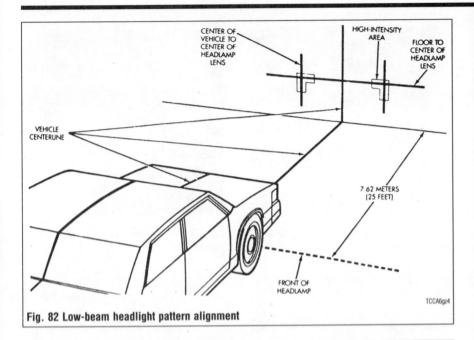

Fig. 82 Low-beam headlight pattern alignment

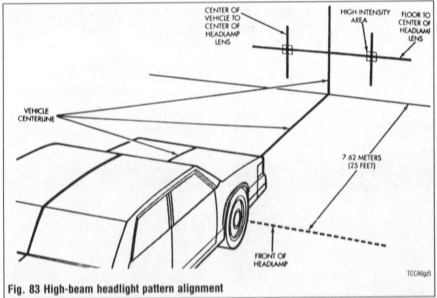

Fig. 83 High-beam headlight pattern alignment

Fig. 84 On 1994–98 Galant models, remove the power steering reservoir mounting bolts, and position the reservoir to the side

Fig. 85 Remove the washer fluid reservoir retaining screws . . .

Fig. 86 . . . then move the reservoir out of the way to access the parking and side marker lamp bulbs on 1994–98 Galant models

headlight beams on the wall. If done in a garage, darken the area around the wall as much as possible by closing shades or hanging cloth over the windows.

3. Turn the headlights **ON** and mark the wall at the center of each light's low beam, then switch on the brights and mark the center of each light's high beam. A short length of masking tape which is visible from the front of the vehicle may be used. Although marking all four positions is advisable, marking one position from each light should be sufficient.

4. If neither beam on one side is working, and if another like-sized vehicle is available, park the second one in the exact spot where the vehicle was and mark the beams using the same-side light. Then switch the vehicles so the one to be aimed is back in the original spot. It must be parked no closer to or farther away from the wall than the second vehicle.

5. Perform any necessary repairs, but make sure the vehicle is not moved, or is returned to the exact spot from which the lights were marked. Turn the

headlights **ON** and adjust the beams to match the marks on the wall.

6. Have the headlight adjustment checked as soon as possible by a reputable repair shop.

Signal and Marker Lights

REMOVAL & INSTALLATION

Parking And Side Marker Lights

◆ See Figures 84, 85, 86, 87, 88, and 89

1. Disconnect the negative battery cable.
2. Remove any necessary components to access the bulbs.
3. Rotate the bulb sockets and rotate them counterclockwise to remove them.
4. Grasp the bulb and remove it from the socket by pulling it straight out.

5. The installation is the reverse of removal.

Front Turn Signal

◆ See Figures 90, 91, 92, and 93

1. Disconnect the negative battery cable.
2. Remove the two retaining screws from the lens.
3. Remove the lens from the front fascia.
4. Grasp the bulb socket and rotate it counterclockwise to remove it from the lamp.
5. Pull the bulb out to remove it from the socket.
6. Installation is the reverse of removal.

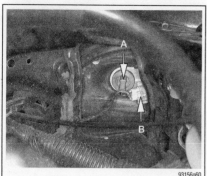

Fig. 87 After the washer fluid reservoir is removed, the parking lamp bulb (B) and the side marker lamp (A) are accessible on 1994–98 Galant models

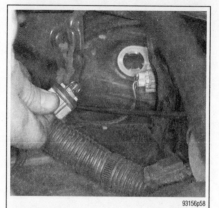

Fig. 88 Twist the bulb socket to release it from the lens

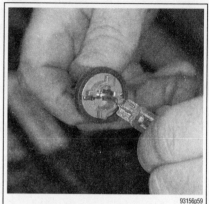

Fig. 89 Pull the bulb assembly out of the socket to remove

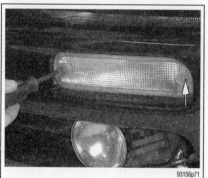

Fig. 90 Remove the turn signal lens retaining screw . . .

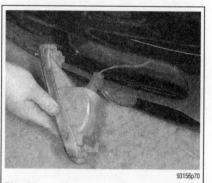

Fig. 91 . . . then remove the lens from the front fascia

Fig. 92 Twist the bulb socket to release it from the lens

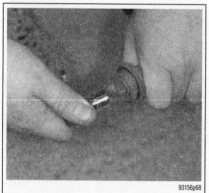

Fig. 93 Pull the bulb assembly out of the socket to remove

Fig. 94 The back-up lamp socket assembly is located on the underside of the trunk lid. Detach the electrical connector . . .

Fig. 95 . . . then unfasten the trim panel retaining screws for access to the bulb(s)

Rear Turn Signal, Brake and Tail Lights

▶ See Figures 94, 95, 96, and 97

1. Disconnect the negative battery cable.
2. Open the trunk lid, hatch, or tailgate and remove the retainers, then remove the inner trim panel in order to get to the rear lamp assembly.
3. Turn the necessary bulb and socket assembly to unlock it from the housing, then pull it from the housing.
4. Depress and twist the bulb $1/8$ turn counter-clockwise. Pull the bulb from the socket and replace with a new one of the same type.
5. Installation is the reverse of the removal procedure.

Fig. 96 Twist the bulb socket to release it from the lens

Fig. 97 Depress and turn the bulb assembly, then pull it out of the socket to remove

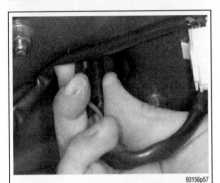

Fig. 98 The back-up lamp socket assembly is located on the underside of the trunk lid

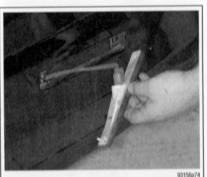

Fig. 99 Twist the bulb socket to release the locking tabs from the lens

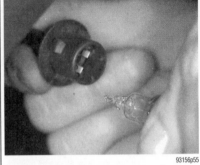

Fig. 100 Pull the bulb assembly straight out of the socket to remove it

Back-up Light

♦ See Figures 98, 99, and 100

1. Disconnect the negative battery cable.
2. Open the trunk lid.
3. If equipped, remove the trim on the underside of the trunk lid.
4. Turn the socket counterclockwise ¼ of a turn to release it from the lens.
5. Pull the bulb out to remove it from the socket.
6. The installation is the reverse of removal.
7. Connect the negative battery cable.
8. Verify the operation of the lamp.

Side Marker Light

♦ See Figures 101, 102, 103, and 104

1. Remove the two retaining screws from the lens.
2. Remove the lens from the rear fascia.
3. Grasp the bulb socket and rotate it counterclockwise to remove it from the lamp.
4. Pull the bulb out to remove it from the socket.
5. Installation is the reverse of removal.

High-mount Brake Light

1994–98 GALANT

♦ See Figures 105, 106, 107, 108, and 109

1. Disconnect the negative battery cable.

➡ The lamp assembly is accessible from the trunk underneath the package shelf.

2. Open the trunk lid and detach the electrical connector from the lamp assembly.
3. Remove the retaining screw holding the lamp assembly.
4. Lower the lamp assembly from the lamp lens.
5. Rotate the bulb clockwise while pushing it gently inward to remove it from the socket.
6. The installation is the reverse of removal.

1990–96 MIRAGE, 1990–93 GALANT, AND 1992–96 DIAMANTE

1. Disconnect the negative battery cable.
2. On the Mirage and Galant, remove the square retainer clips or bolts from the high-mount brake light cover and remove the cover.
3. On the Diamante, press gently inward on the sides of the light cover and remove it from the lamp.

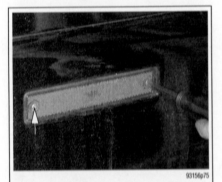

Fig. 101 Remove the side marker light retaining screw . . .

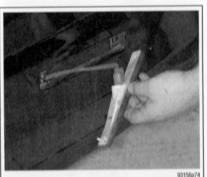

Fig. 102 . . . then pull the lens away from the rear fascia

Fig. 103 Twist the bulb socket to release it from the lens

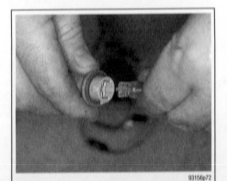

Fig. 104 Pull the bulb assembly straight out of the socket to remove

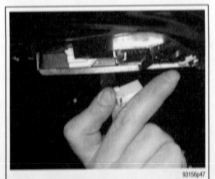

Fig. 105 Detach the high-mount brake light electrical connector

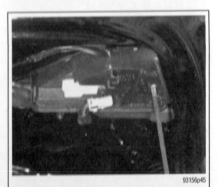

Fig. 106 Remove the lamp retaining screws . . .

Fig. 107 . . . then lower the lamp assembly for access to the bulbs

Fig. 108 Rotate the bulb assembly. . .

Fig. 109 . . . then pull it from the socket

4. Rotate the bulb clockwise while pushing it gently inward to remove it from the socket.

5. The installation is the reverse of removal.

1997–00 MIRAGE, 1999–00 GALANT, AND 1997–00 DIAMANTE

1. Disconnect the negative battery cable.

➡ The bulb socket is accessible from the trunk underneath the package shelf.

2. Open the trunk lid and detach the electrical connector from the bulb socket.

3. Rotate the socket counterclockwise and remove it from the lamp assembly.

4. Rotate the bulb clockwise while pushing it gently inward to remove it from the socket.

5. The installation is the reverse of removal.

License Plate Lights

▶ See Figures 110, 111, and 112

1. Disconnect the negative battery cable.

2. Remove the two retaining screws for the lamp lens.

3. Lower the lens from the trunk lid.

4. Grasp the bulb and remove it from the terminals on the lens.

To install:

5. Place the bulb into place on the lens and lightly press into the terminals on the lens.

6. Place the lens into position on the trunk lid and tighten the two retaining screws.

7. Connect the negative battery cable.

8. Verify the operation of the lamp.

Dome/ Passenger Area Lamps

▶ See Figures 113, 114, and 115

1. Using a small prytool, carefully remove the cover lens from the lamp assembly.

2. Remove the bulb from its retaining clip contacts. If the bulb has tapered ends, gently depress the spring clip/metal contact and disengage the light bulb, then pull it free of the two metal contacts.

To install:

3. Before installing the light bulb into the metal contacts, ensure that all electrical conducting surfaces are free of corrosion or dirt.

4. Position the bulb between the two metal contacts. If the contacts have small holes, be sure that the tapered ends of the bulb are situated in them.

Fig. 110 Remove the two lamp lens retaining screws . . .

Fig. 111 . . . then lower the lens to access the bulb

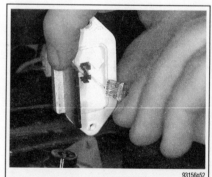

Fig. 112 Remove the bulb by pulling it from the terminals on the lens

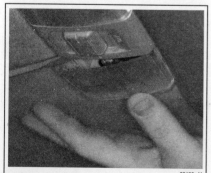

Fig. 113 Using a suitable tool, carefully pry the lamp lens loose . . .

Fig. 114 . . . then remove the lens from the dome lamp assembly

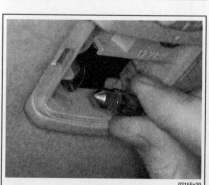

Fig. 115 Pull the bulb straight out to remove it

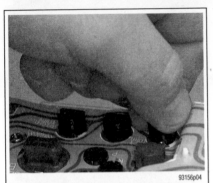

Fig. 116 With the cluster removed, turn the socket counterclockwise . . .

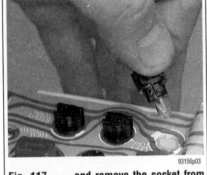

Fig. 117 . . . and remove the socket from the instrument cluster

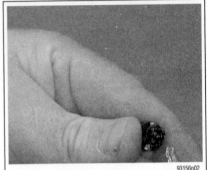

Fig. 118 Pull the bulb straight out to remove it

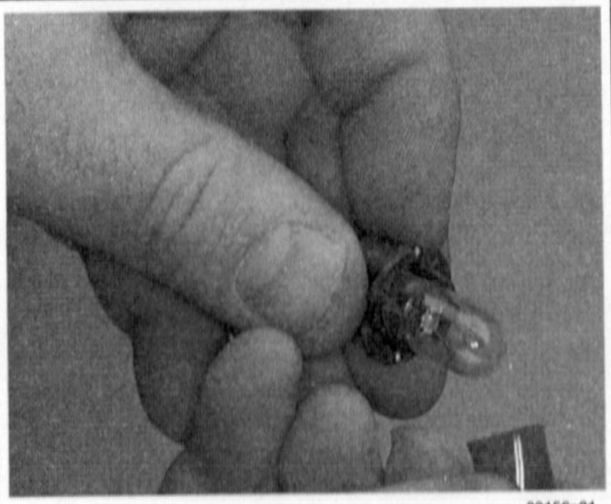

Fig. 119 On some of the bulbs, it is necessary to transfer the colored bulb cover to the new bulb

5. To ensure that the replacement bulb functions properly, activate the applicable switch to illuminate the bulb which was just replaced. If the replacement light bulb does not illuminate, either it is faulty or there is a problem in the bulb circuit or switch. Correct as necessary.

6. Install the cover lens until its retaining tabs are properly engaged.

Instrument Cluster Light bulbs

♦ See Figures 116, 117, 118, and 119

1. Disconnect the negative battery cable.
2. Remove the instrument cluster as outlined in this section.
3. Turn the desired bulb socket counterclockwise to remove it from the cluster.
4. Grasp the bulb and pull it straight out to remove it from the socket.

To install:

5. If necessary, transfer the colored bulb cover to the new bulb.
6. Place a new bulb into the socket and lightly press it into place.
7. Place the socket into the cluster and turn the socket clockwise to engage it into the cluster.
8. Install the instrument cluster.
9. Connect the negative battery cable.

Light bulb application chart—1990–92 Mirage

Bulb Chart – Outside

Specification	Wattage	SAE trade No.
Headlights	Outboard 55W	9006
	Inboard 65W	9005
Front turn-signal lights	27W	1156
Position lights	5W	–
Front side-marker lights	3cp	168
High-mounted stoplights	21cp	–
Stop and taillights	32/2cp	2057
Rear turn-signal lights	32cp	1156
Rear side-marker lights	3cp	168
Backup lights	27W	1156
Licence plate lights		
Sedan	3cp	168
Hatchback	10W	–

Bulb Chart – Inside

Specification	Wattage	SAE Trade No.
Dome light	10W	–
Luggage compartment light	5W	–
Heater control panel light	1.4W	74
Cigarette lighter illumination light	1.4W	74
Shift indicator light (automatic transaxle)	1.4W	74
Overdrive indicator light (automatic transaxle)	1.4W	74

Light bulb application chart—1993–96 Mirage

Description	Wattage	SAE Trade No.
1 · Headlights	65/45W	9004
2 · Front turn-signal light/ Parking and front side-marker light	32/3cp	1157
3 · High-mounted stop light	21cp	921
4 · Stop and tail light	32/2cp	2057
5 · Stop and tail light	32/2cp	2057
6 · License plate light	3cp	168
7 · Back up light	32cp	1156
8 · Rear turn-signal light	32cp	1156
9 · Rear side-marker light	3cp	168

Inside

Description	Wattage	SAE Trade No.
Dome light	10w	·
Luggage compartment light	5w	·
Cigarette lighter illumination light	1.4W	74
Shift indicator light (automatic transaxle)	3.4W	158

Light bulb application chart—1997–00 Mirage

Outside

Description	Wattage	SAE Trade No.
1 · Headlights (inside)	65W	9005
2 · Headlights (outside)	55W	9006
3 · Position light	3cp	168
4 · Front side-marker light	3cp	168
5 · Front turn signal light	27W	1156NA
6 · Front fog light	55W	–
7 · High-mounted stop light (on rear shelf)	21cp	921
8 · Stop and tail light	32/2cp	2057
9 · Stop and tail light	32/2cp	2057
10 · License plate light	3cp	168
11 · Back up light	45cp	3497
12 · Rear turn signal light	45cp	3497
13 · Rear side-marker light	3cp	168

Inside

Description	Wattage	SAE Trade No.
Dome light	8W	—
Dome light (for sunroof)	7.5W	—
Reading light	7.5W	—
Trunk light	5W	—
Vanity mirror light	1.4W	—
Ashtray light	1.4W	74
Cigarette lighter illumination light	1.4W	74

Light bulb application chart—1990–93 Galant

Outside

Description		Wattage	SAE Trade No.
1 - Headlights		60/55W	HB2
2 - Front turn signal and position and front side-marker lights	2-door models	27/8W	—
	4-door models	32/3cp	1157
3 - Front fog light		55W	H3
4 - Rear turn signal light		32cp	1156
5 - Stop and tail light		32/2cp	2057
6 - Back up light		32cp	1156
7 - Rear side-marker light		3cp	168
8 - High-mounted stop light (On rear shelf)		21W	—
9 - License plate light		3cp	168

Inside

Description		Wattage	SAE Trade No.
Dome light		8W	—
Reading light	Car with sunroof	8W	—
	Except for car with sunroof	7.5W	—
Trunk light		5W	—

93156g03

Light bulb application chart—1994–98 Galant

Outside

Description	Wattage	SAE Trade No.
1 - Headlights	60/55W	HB2
2 - Front turn signal and position light (Side marker light)	27/8W	1157
3 - Front fog light	37 5W	893
4 - Back up light	32cp	1156
5 - Rear turn signal light and tail light (Side marker light)	32/2cp	2057
6 - High-mounted stop light (on rear shelf)	21cp	921
7 - License plate light	3cp	168
8 - Stop and tail light	32/2cp	2057

Inside

Description	Wattage	SAE Trade No.
Dome light	8W	—
Trunk light	5W	—

93156g06

Light bulb application chart—1999–00 Galant

Light Bulbs – Outside

Description	Wattage	SAE Trade No.
Headlight (outside)	55W	9006
Headlight (inside)	65W	9005
Front turn-signal lights	27/8W	1157NA
Front side-marker lights	2cp	194
Parking lights	3cp	168
Stop and taillights	32/2cp	2057
Rear turn-signal lights	32cp	1156
Backup lights	32cp	1156
Rear side-marker lights	3cp	168
High-mounted stoplights (On rear shelf)	21cp	—
License plate lights	3cp	168

Light Bulbs – Inside

Description	Wattage	SAE Trade No.
Reading lights	8W	—
Reading lights (for sunroof)	8W	—
Dome lights	8W	—
Dome lights (for sunroof)	10W	—
Door lights	5W	—
Luggage compartment light	5W	—
Glove compartment light	1.4W	—
Vanity mirror light	1.4W	—
Heater control panel light	1.4W	—
Cigarette lighter illumination light	1.4W	—
Ashtray light	1.4W	—
Shift indicator light (automatic transaxle)	1.4W	—
Overdrive indicator light (automatic transaxle)	1.4W	—

93156g04

Light bulb application chart—1992–96 Diamante

Outside

Description	Wattage	SAE trade No.
1 – Headlight (inside)	65W	9005
2 – Headlight (outside)	55W	9006
3 – Parking and front side marker light	3cp	168
4 – Front turn-signal light	24cp	1156NA
5 – High-mounted stop light	21cp	921
6 – Back up light	21cp	921
7 – Stop/tail light	32/2cp	2057
8 – Rear side-marker light	3cp	168
9 – License plate light	3cp	168
10 – Rear turn-signal light	32cp	1156

Inside

Description	Wattage	SAE trade No.
Reading light	7.5W	–
Dome light	10W	–
Door light	5W	–
Luggage compartment light	5W	–
Rear personal light	7.5W	–
Glove compartment light	3.4W	158
Vanity mirror light	1.4W	74
Air conditioner control panel light	1.4W	74
Cigarette lighter illumination light	1.4W	74
Ashtray light	1.4W	74
Overdrive indicator light	1.4W	74

93156g07

Light bulb application chart—1997–00 Diamante

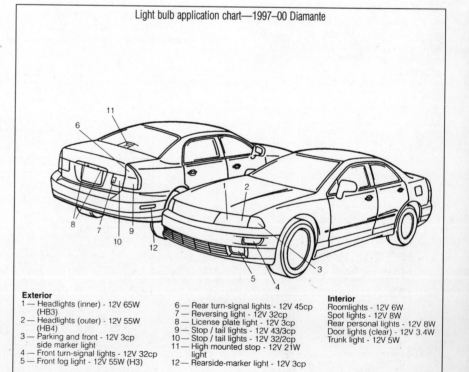

Exterior
1 — Headlights (inner) - 12V 65W (HB3)
2 — Headlights (outer) - 12V 55W (HB4)
3 — Parking and front 12V 3cp side marker light
4 — Front turn-signal lights - 12V 32cp
5 — Front fog light - 12V 55W (H3)
6 — Rear turn-signal lights - 12V 45cp
7 — Reversing light - 12V 32cp
8 — License plate light - 12V 3cp
9 — Stop / tail lights - 12V 43/3cp
10 — Stop / tail lights - 12V 32/2cp
11 — High mounted stop - 12V 21W light
12 — Rearside-marker light - 12V 3cp

Interior
Roomlights - 12V 6W
Spot lights - 12V 8W
Rear personal lights - 12V 8W
Door lights (clear) - 12V 3.4W
Trunk light - 12V 5W

93156g08

CIRCUIT PROTECTION

Fuses

REPLACEMENT

▶ See Figures 120 thru 127

Fuses are located either in the engine compartment or passenger compartment fuse and relay panels. If a fuse blows, at least one, but possibly several components/circuits will not function properly.

1. Remove the fuse box cover.
2. Inspect the fuses to determine which is faulty.
3. Grasp the fuse and remove it from the fuse box.
4. Inspect the box terminals and clean if corroded. If any terminals are damaged, replace the terminals.
5. Plug in a new fuse of the same amperage rating.

6. Check for proper operation of the affected component or circuit.

Fusible Links

A number of fusible links are used on these vehicles to protect wiring and electrical components. There is a collection of fusible links located near the battery. These are referred to as the main fuse links. A second group of links are located in the box with the dedicated fuses. If replacement of a fuse link is required, use the exact same link as removed.

When a fusible link blows it is very important to find out why. They are placed in the electrical system for protection against dead shorts to ground, which can be caused by electrical component failure or various wiring failures.

Fig. 120 The engine compartment fuse box is typically located adjacent to the battery

Fig. 121 Grasp the engine compartment fuse box cover and pull it straight up to remove it

Fig. 122 The engine compartment fuse box contains a combination of fuses, maxi-fuses, relays, and diodes. Most can be removed by simply pulling upward

Fig. 123 The interior fuse box is located under the driver's side of the instrument panel

Fig. 124 Grasp the interior fuse box cover, depress the retaining tabs and lift up to remove

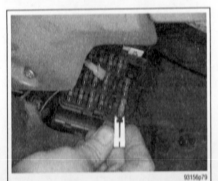
Fig. 125 Typically a fuse removal tool is located in the fuse box to aid in removing the fuses

Fig. 126 Grasp the fuse with the removal tool and pull it straight out to remove it

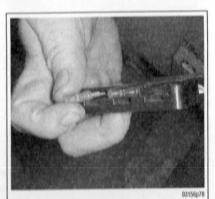
Fig. 127 There are usually spare fuses located in the interior fuse box cover

⚙ CAUTION

Do not just replace the fusible link to correct a problem!

When replacing all fusible links, they are to be replaced with the same type of prefabricated link available from your vehicle manufacturer.

Circuit Breakers

RESETTING AND/OR REPLACEMENT

Circuit breakers are located inside the fuse panel. They are automatically reset when the problem corrects itself, is repaired, or the circuit cools down to allow operation again.

Flashers

REPLACEMENT

The turn signal and hazard flasher unit is located in the interior fuse panel located under the driver's left side knee protector. They are replaced by simply pulling them straight out. Note that the prongs are arranged in such a way that the flasher must be properly oriented before attempting to install it. Turn the flasher until the orientation of the prongs is correct and simply push it firmly in until the prongs are fully engaged.

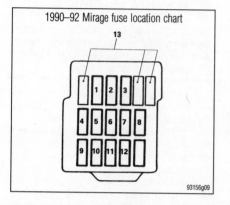

1990–92 Mirage fuse location chart

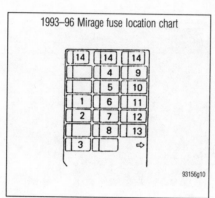

1993–96 Mirage fuse location chart

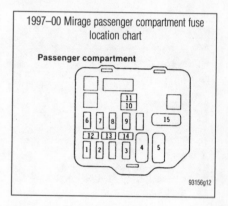

1997–00 Mirage passenger compartment fuse location chart

1997–00 Mirage engine compartment fuse location chart

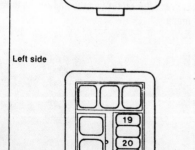

Engine compartment

NO	Symbol	Electrical system	Capacity
1	STOP	Stop lights	15A
2	⚠	Hazard warning flashers	10A
3	⚡D	Fog lights	15A
4	≡○≡	Tail lights	10A
5	≡○≡	Tail lights	10A
6	✿	Air conditioning	10A
7	≡D	Headlight upper beam	10A
8	⌐	Horn	10A
9	♫	Radio	10A
10	☰	Dome light	10A
11	⌒	Engine control	20A
12	⊞	Power window control	30A
13	⊗	Radiator fan motor	30A
14	≡D	Headlights	40A
15	⌐	Ignition switch	30A

NO	Symbol	Electrical system	Capacity
16	⊟	Fuse(+B)	60A
17	✿	Air conditioning	25A
18	⊟	Alternator	100A
19	✿	Air conditioning	10A
20	✻	Condensor fan motor	20A

Some fuses may not be installed on your vehicle, depending on the vehicle model or specifications.

Identification of fuse

10A	Red
15A	Light blue
20A	Yellow
30A	Green

1990–93 Galant fuse location chart

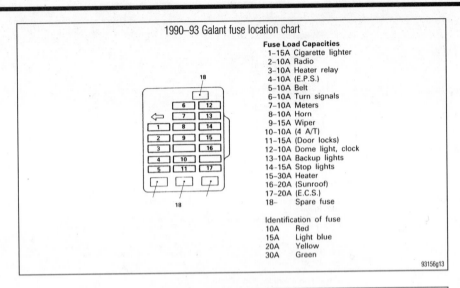

Fuse Load Capacities
1–15A Cigarette lighter
2–10A Radio
3–10A Heater relay
4–10A (E.P.S.)
5–10A Belt
6–10A Turn signals
7–10A Meters
8–10A Horn
9–15A Wiper
10–10A (4 A/T)
11–15A (Door locks)
12–10A Dome light, clock
13–10A Backup lights
14–15A Stop lights
15–30A Heater
16–20A (Sunroof)
17–20A (E.C.S.)
18– Spare fuse

Identification of fuse
10A   Red
15A   Light blue
20A   Yellow
30A   Green

93156g13

1994–98 Galant fuse location chart

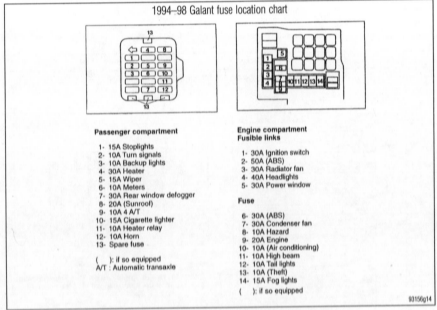

Passenger compartment

1- 15A Stoplights
2- 10A Turn signals
3- 10A Backup lights
4- 30A Heater
5- 15A Wiper
6- 10A Meters
7- 30A Rear window defogger
8- 20A (Sunroof)
9- 10A 4 A/T
10- 15A Cigarette lighter
11- 10A Heater relay
12- 10A Horn
13- Spare fuse

(   ): if so equipped
A/T : Automatic transaxle

Engine compartment
Fusible links

1- 30A Ignition switch
2- 50A (ABS)
3- 30A Radiator fan
4- 40A Headlights
5- 30A Power window

Fuse

6- 30A (ABS)
7- 30A Condenser fan
8- 10A Hazard
9- 20A Engine
10- 10A (Air conditioning)
11- 10A High beam
12- 10A Tail lights
13- 10A (Theft)
14- 15A Fog lights
(   ): if so equipped

93156g14

1999–00 Galant fuse location chart

Passenger compartment

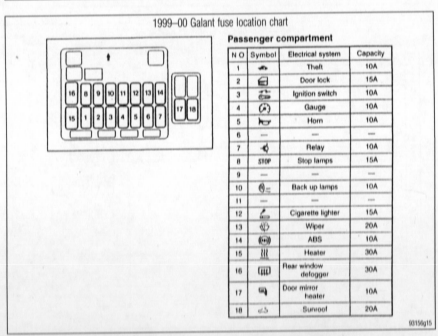

N O	Symbol	Electrical system	Capacity
1		Theft	10A
2		Door lock	15A
3		Ignition switch	10A
4		Gauge	10A
5		Horn	10A
6	—	—	—
7		Relay	10A
8	STOP	Stop lamps	15A
9	—	—	—
10		Back up lamps	10A
11	—	—	—
12		Cigarette lighter	15A
13		Wiper	20A
14		ABS	10A
15		Heater	30A
16		Rear window defogger	30A
17		Door mirror heater	10A
18		Sunroof	20A

93156g15

1992–96 Diamante fuse location chart

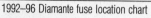
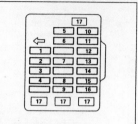

Fuse load capacities

1 – 15A Cigarette lighter
2 – 10A Radio
3 – 10A Heater relay, (Power window relay)
4 – 10A (E.P.S)
5 – 10A Turn signals, SRS
6 – 10A Meters, SRS
7 – 15A Wiper
8 – 10A (4 A/T)
9 – 15A Steering handle lock, (Door locks)
10 – 10A Dome light, Clock
11 – 10A Backup lights
12 – 20A Stoplights
13 – 30A Heater
14 – 20A (Sunroof)

15 – 20A Horn
16 – 20A (E.C.S.)
17 – Spare fuse

( ) indicates optional equipment
E.P.S.: Electronic Control Power Steering
E.C.S.: Electronic Control Suspension
SRS: Supplement Restraint System
A/T: Automatic Transaxle

93156g16

1997–00 Diamante passenger compartment fuse location chart

No.	Symbol	Electrical System	Capacity
1			
2	🚗	Trunk lid opener	15A
3		Ignition switch	10A
4		Instrument cluster	10A
5		Antiglare mirror	10A
6		SWS	10A
7		Demister, heater relay	10A
8	STOP	Stop lights	15A
9	⇦⇨	Turn-signal lights (SRS)	10A
10		Reversing lights	10A
11	♫	Radio	10A
12		Cigarette lighter	15A
13		Wiper/Washer	20A
14		Sunroof	10A
15	‖‖	Heater	30A
16	⊞	Demister	30A
17		Spare fuse	30A
18		Spare fuse	10A
19		Spare fuse	15A
20		Spare fuse	20A

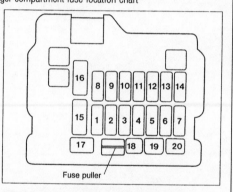

Fuse puller

NOTE: Spare fuses are contained in the fuse housing. Always use a fuse of the same capacity for replacement.

93156g17

1997–00 Diamante engine compartment fuse location chart

Engine Compartment —

No.	Symbol	Electrical System	Capacity
1	⫶O⫶	Tail lights (left)	10A
2	⫶O⫶	Tail lights (right)	10A
3	⫶D	Headlights (lower beam-left)	15A
4	⫶D	Headlights (lower beam-right)	15A
5	⫶D	Headlights (upper beam-left)	10A
6	⫶D	Headlights (upper beam-right)	10A
7	⫶D	Fog lamps	15A
8	✱	Condenser fan	20A
9	♫	Audio	20A
10	♫	Audio	10A
11		Room light	15A
12	⫯	ECU	10A
13	⚠	Hazard warning flashers	10A
14		—	—
15	♛	Engine control	20A
16		Alternator	10A
17	✿	A/C compressor	10A
18		—	—
19		Ignition switch	30A
20		Power windows	40A
21		Radiator fan	40A
22	(ABS)	ABS brakes	60A
23		Main fuse	120A
24		Fuse (+B)	60A

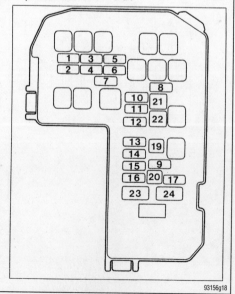

93156g18

INDEX OF WIRING DIAGRAMS

INDEX OF WIRING DIAGRAMS

INDEX OF WIRING DIAGRAMS

INDEX OF WIRING DIAGRAMS

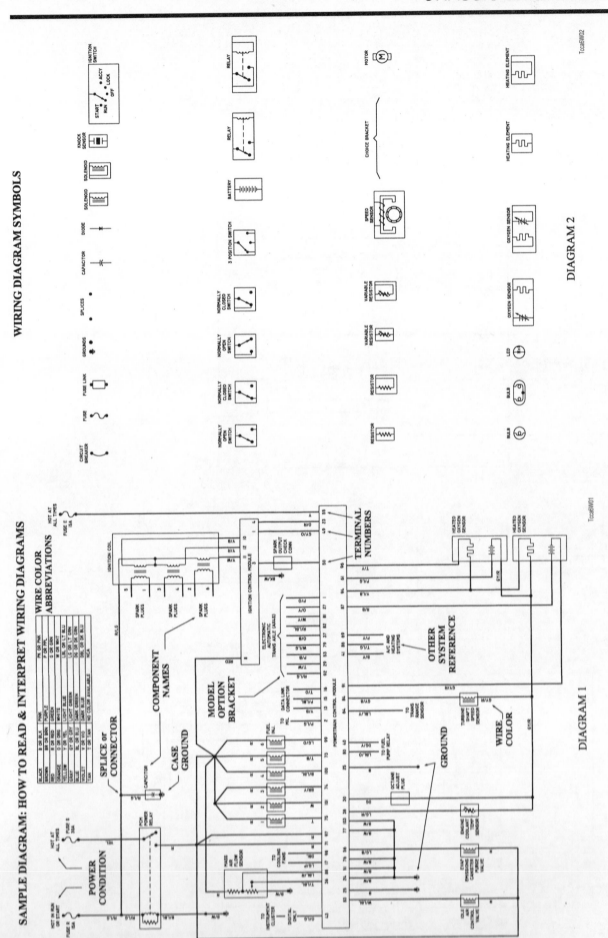

WIRING DIAGRAM SYMBOLS

DIAGRAM 2

SAMPLE DIAGRAM: HOW TO READ & INTERPRET WIRING DIAGRAMS

DIAGRAM 1

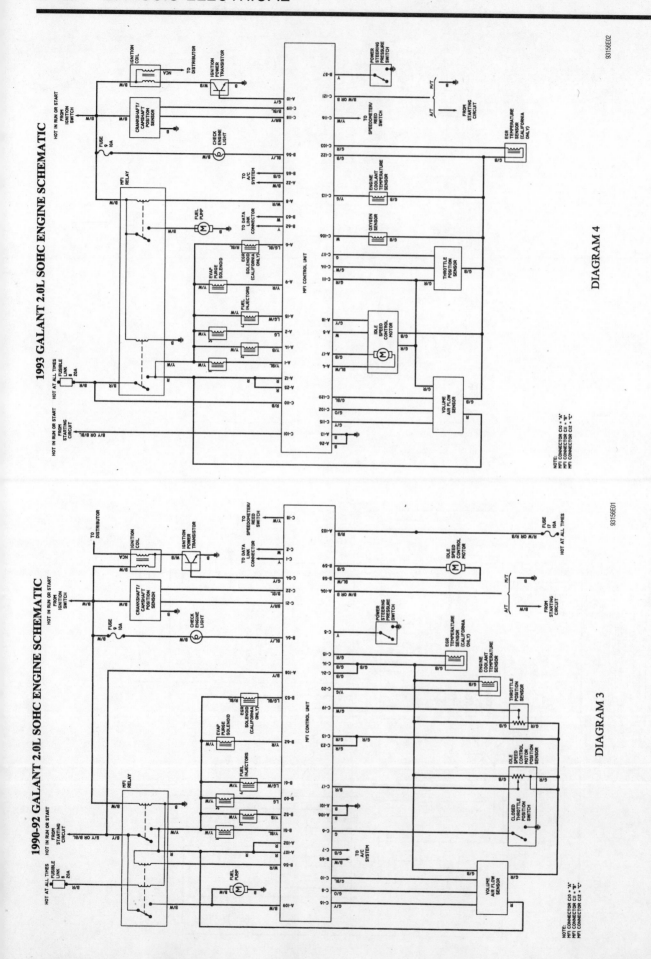

1993 GALANT 2.0L SOHC ENGINE SCHEMATIC

DIAGRAM 4

1990-92 GALANT 2.0L SOHC ENGINE SCHEMATIC

DIAGRAM 3

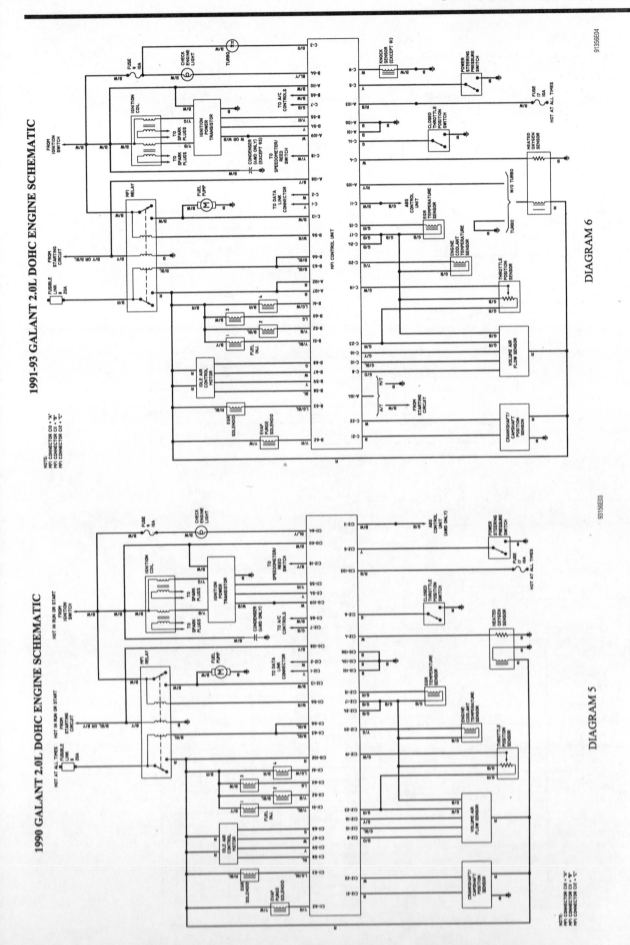

DIAGRAM 6

1991-93 GALANT 2.0L DOHC ENGINE SCHEMATIC

DIAGRAM 5

1990 GALANT 2.0L DOHC ENGINE SCHEMATIC

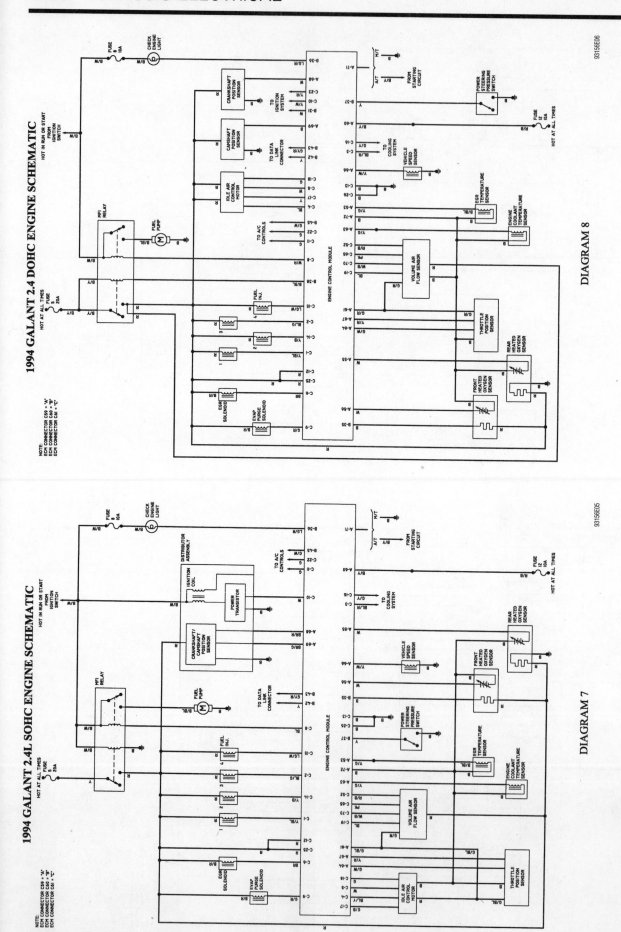

1994 GALANT 2.4 DOHC ENGINE SCHEMATIC

DIAGRAM 8

1994 GALANT 2.4L SOHC ENGINE SCHEMATIC

DIAGRAM 7

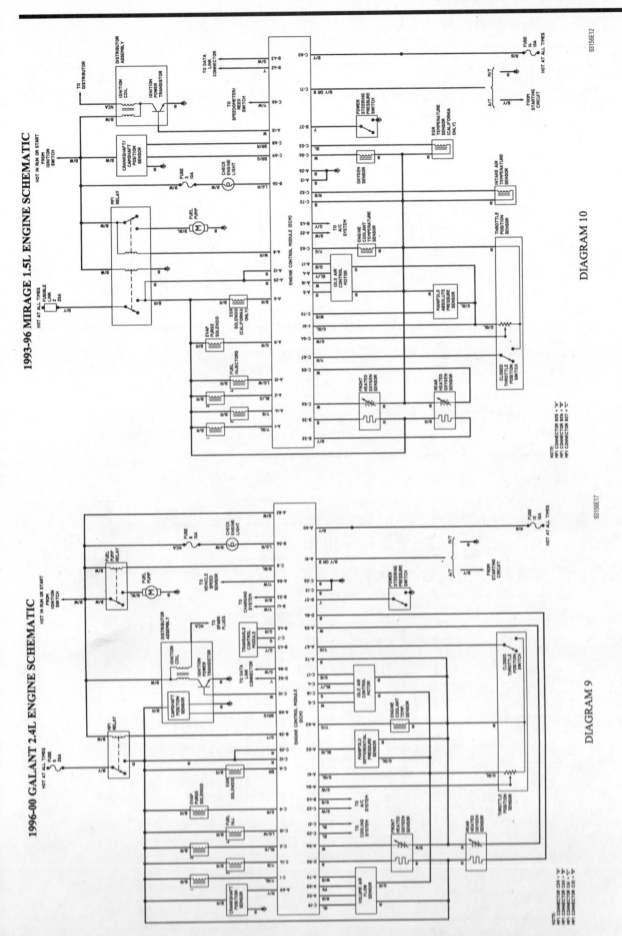

1993-96 MIRAGE 1.5L ENGINE SCHEMATIC

DIAGRAM 10

1996-00 GALANT 2.4L ENGINE SCHEMATIC

DIAGRAM 9

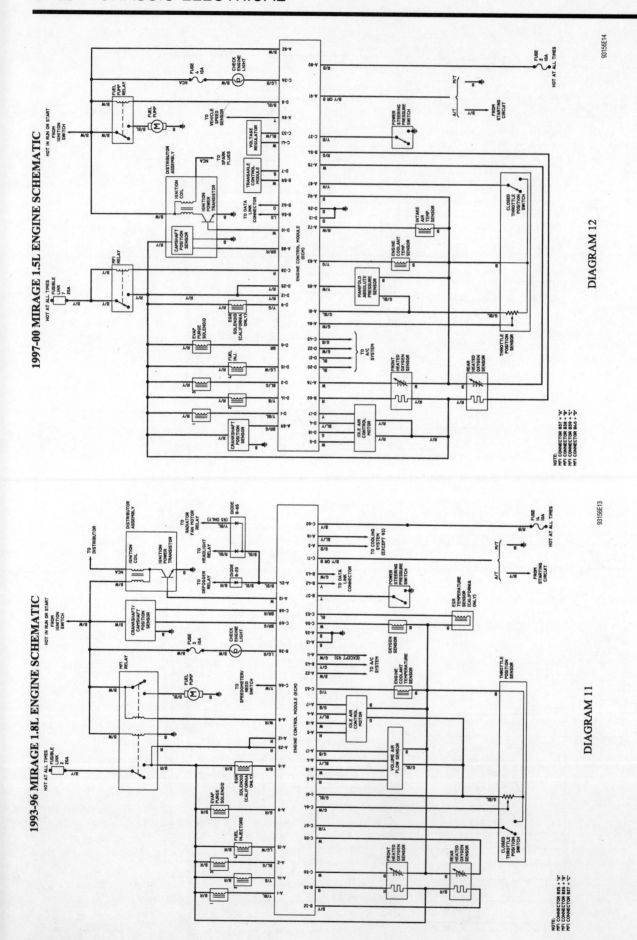

1997-00 MIRAGE 1.5L ENGINE SCHEMATIC

DIAGRAM 12

1993-96 MIRAGE 1.8L ENGINE SCHEMATIC

DIAGRAM 11

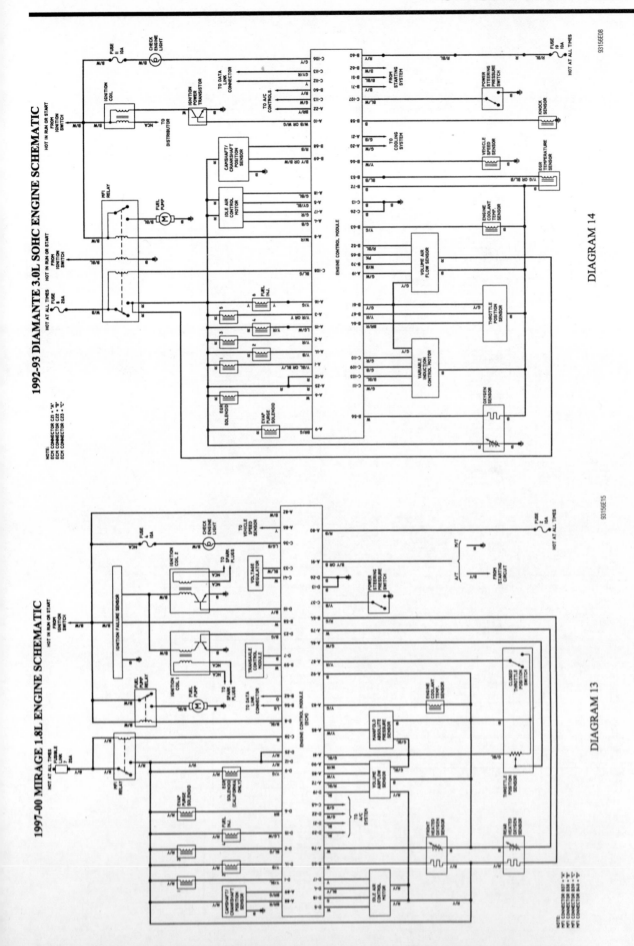

1992-93 DIAMANTE 3.0L SOHC ENGINE SCHEMATIC

DIAGRAM 14

1997-00 MIRAGE 1.8L ENGINE SCHEMATIC

DIAGRAM 13

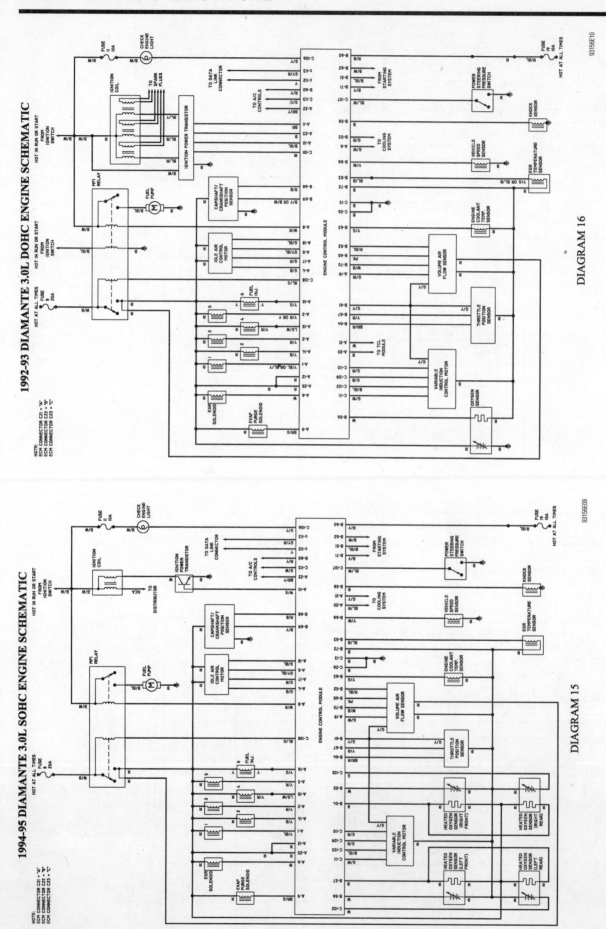

1992-93 DIAMANTE 3.0L DOHC ENGINE SCHEMATIC

DIAGRAM 16

1994-95 DIAMANTE 3.0L SOHC ENGINE SCHEMATIC

DIAGRAM 15

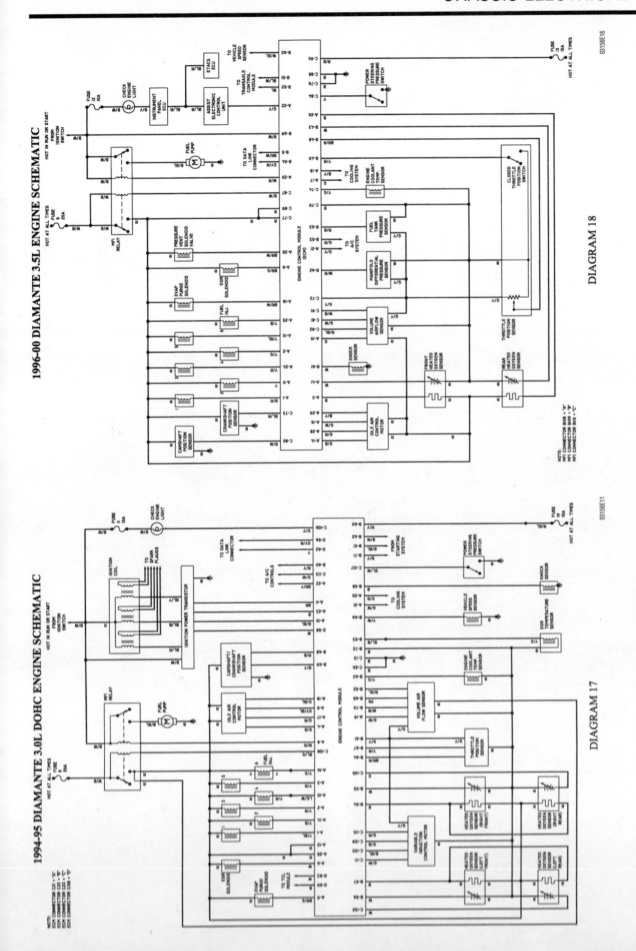

1996-00 DIAMANTE 3.5L ENGINE SCHEMATIC

DIAGRAM 18

1994-95 DIAMANTE 3.0L DOHC ENGINE SCHEMATIC

DIAGRAM 17

1990-93 GALANT CHASSIS SCHEMATIC

DIAGRAM 20

93156802

1990-95 GALANT/MIRAGE CHASSIS SCHEMATIC

DIAGRAM 19

93156801

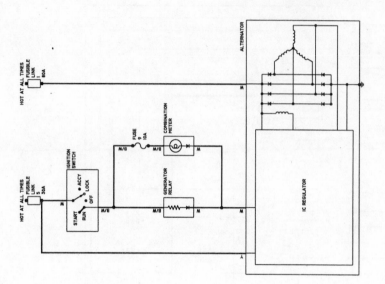

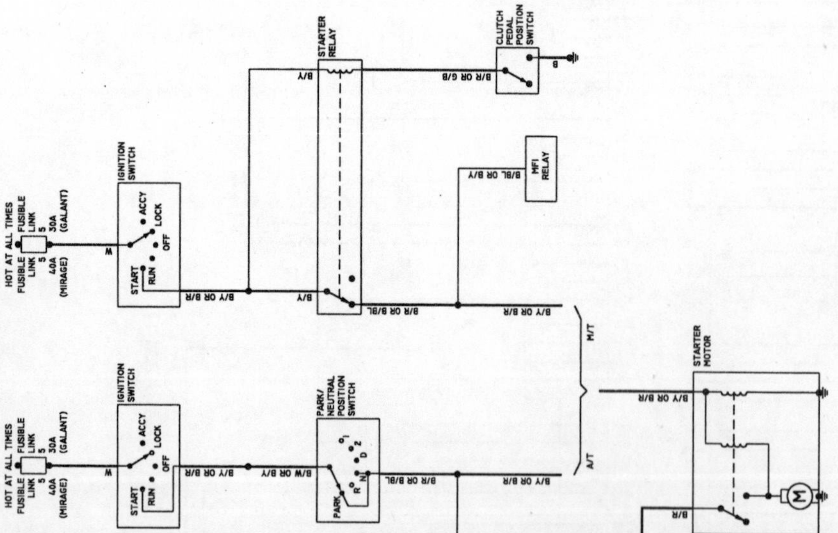

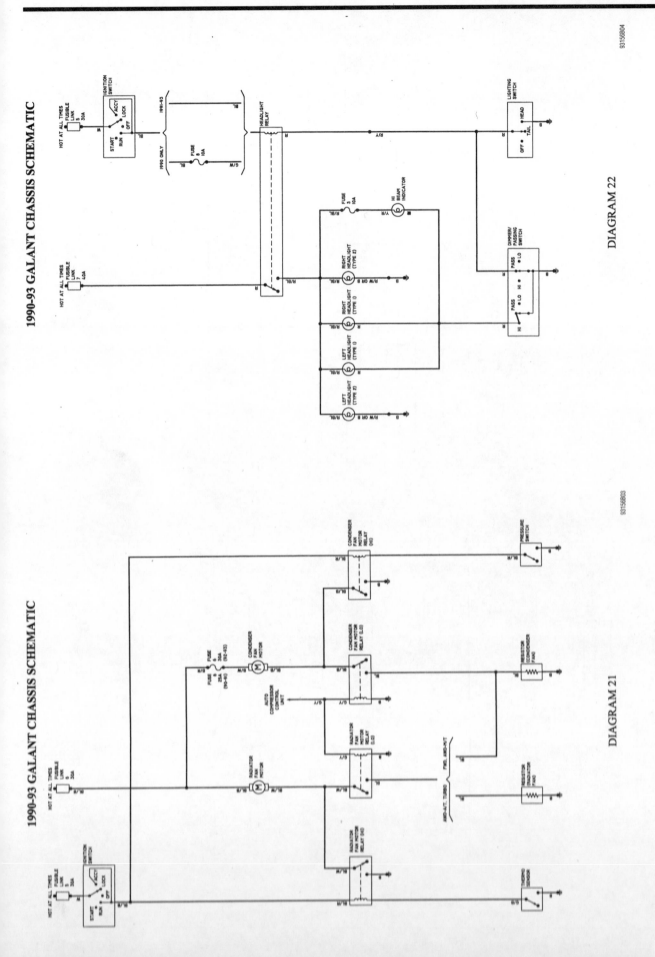

DIAGRAM 22

DIAGRAM 21

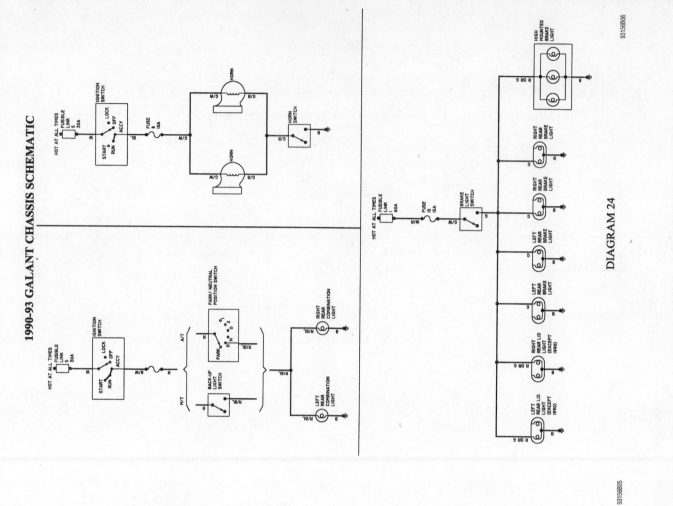

1990-93 GALANT CHASSIS SCHEMATIC

DIAGRAM 24

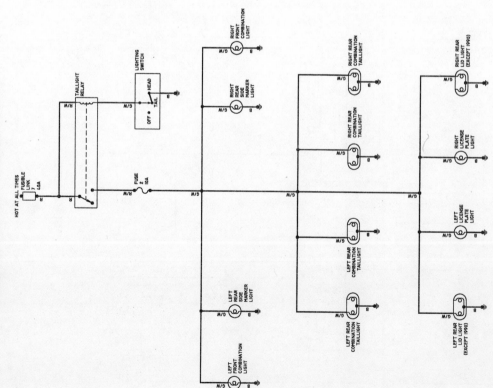

1990-93 GALANT CHASSIS SCHEMATIC

DIAGRAM 23

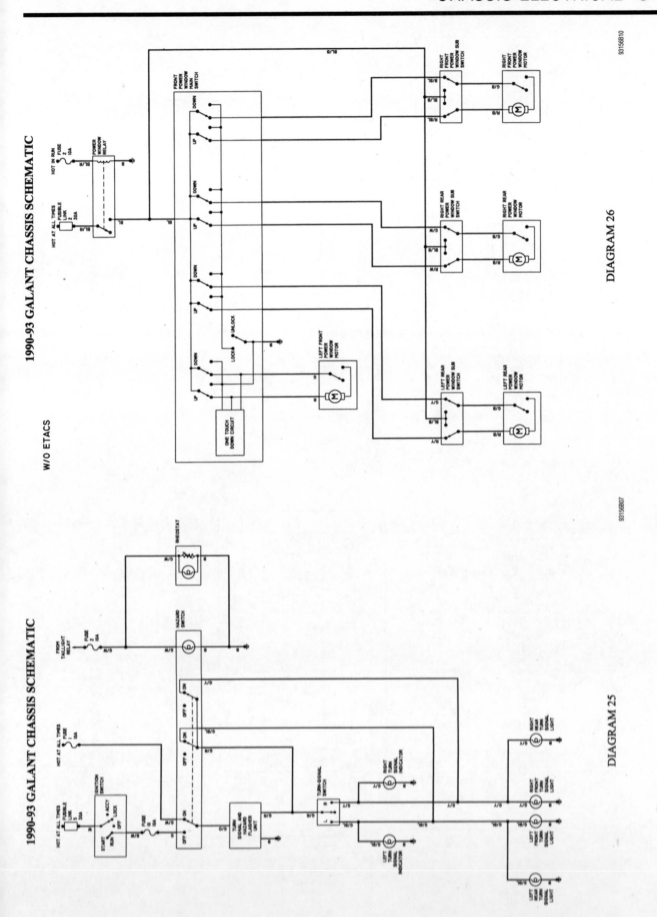

1990-93 GALANT CHASSIS SCHEMATIC

W/O ETACS

DIAGRAM 26

1990-93 GALANT CHASSIS SCHEMATIC

DIAGRAM 25

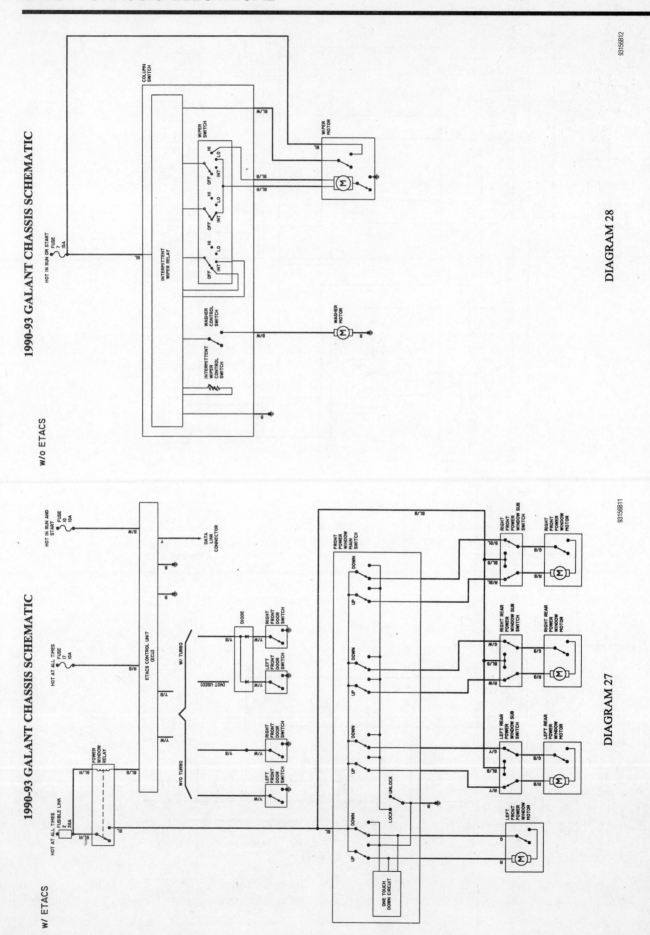

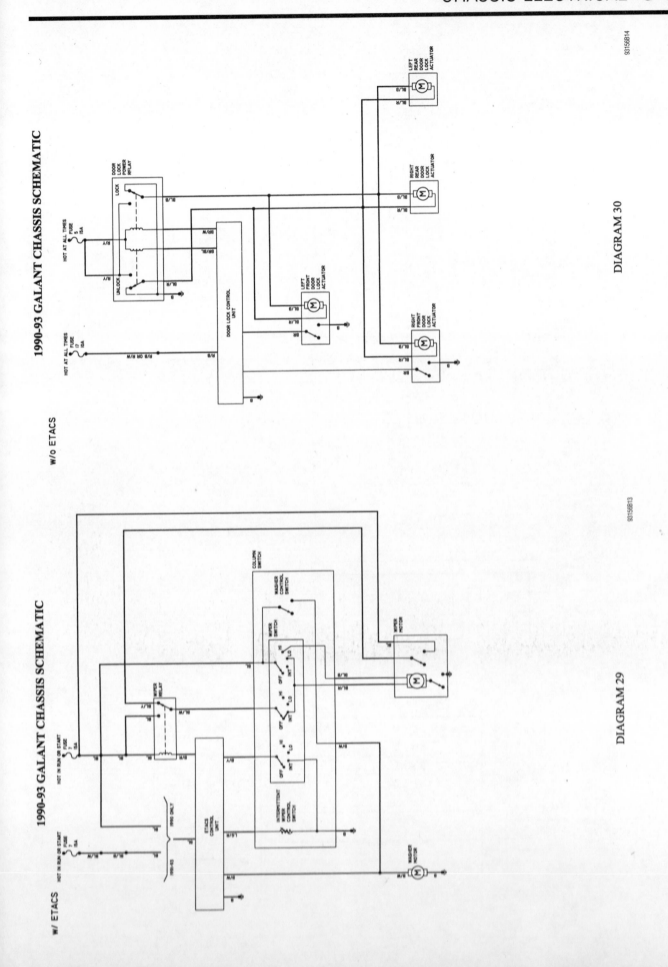

1990-93 GALANT CHASSIS SCHEMATIC

w/o ETACS

DIAGRAM 30

1990-93 GALANT CHASSIS SCHEMATIC

w/ ETACS

DIAGRAM 29

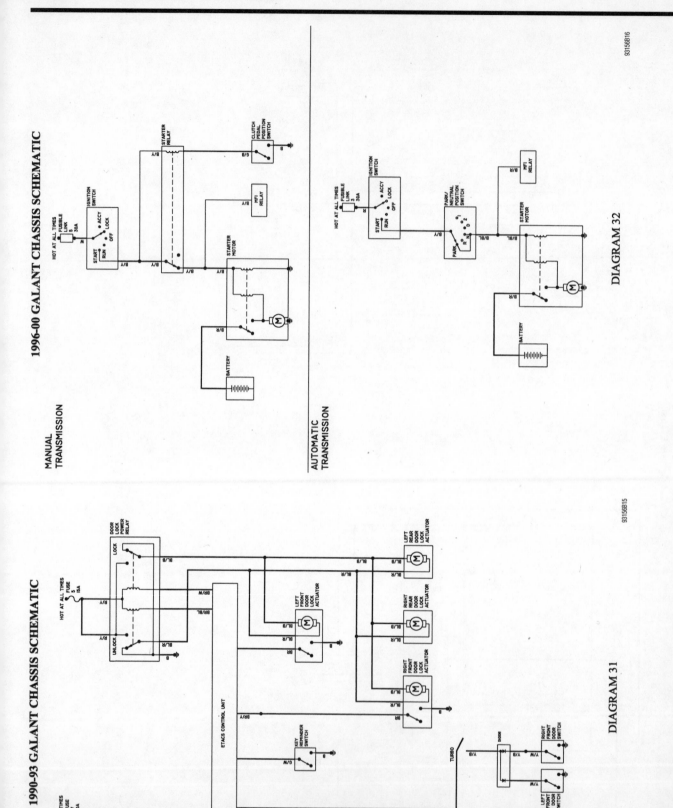

1996-00 GALANT CHASSIS SCHEMATIC

MANUAL TRANSMISSION

AUTOMATIC TRANSMISSION

DIAGRAM 32

1990-93 GALANT CHASSIS SCHEMATIC

w/ ETACS

DIAGRAM 31

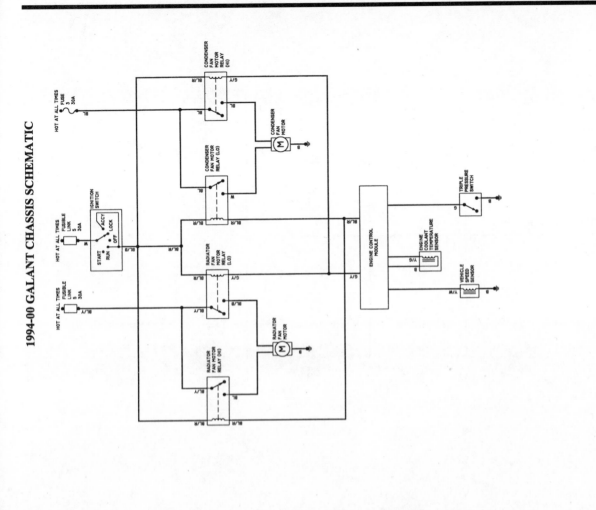

1994-00 GALANT CHASSIS SCHEMATIC

DIAGRAM 34

DIAGRAM 33

1994-00 GALANT CHASSIS SCHEMATIC

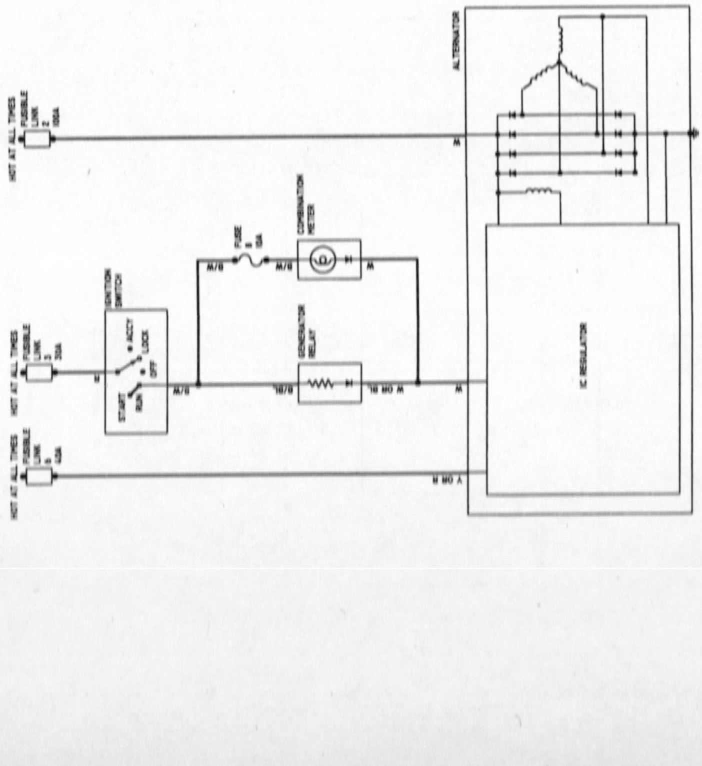

1994-00 GALANT CHASSIS SCHEMATIC

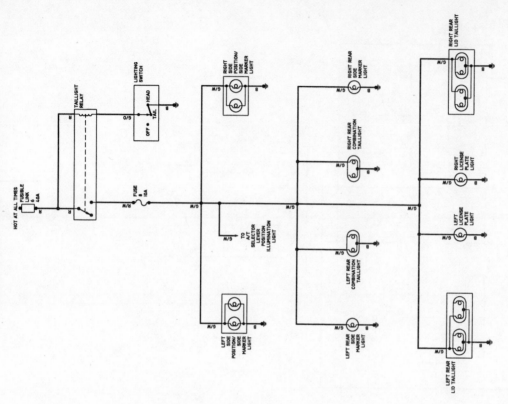

DIAGRAM 36

1994-00 GALANT CHASSIS SCHEMATIC

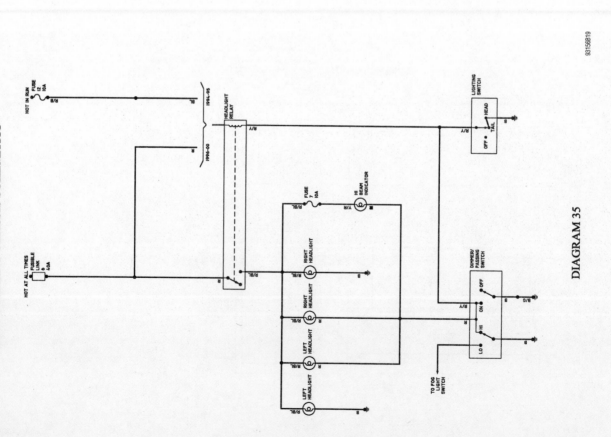

DIAGRAM 35

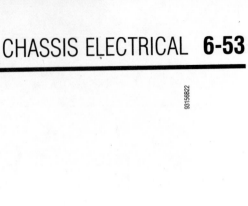

1994-00 GALANT CHASSIS SCHEMATIC

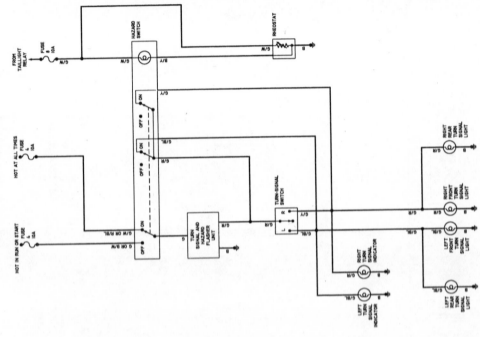

DIAGRAM 38

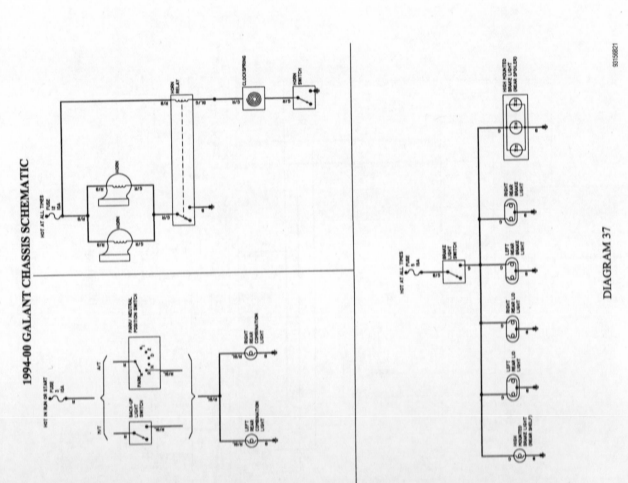

1994-00 GALANT CHASSIS SCHEMATIC

DIAGRAM 37

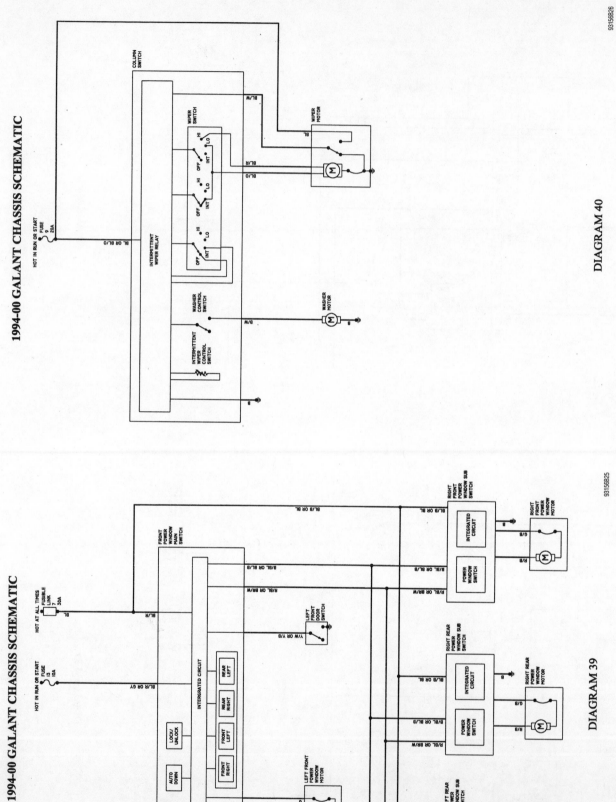

1994-00 GALANT CHASSIS SCHEMATIC

DIAGRAM 40

1994-00 GALANT CHASSIS SCHEMATIC

DIAGRAM 39

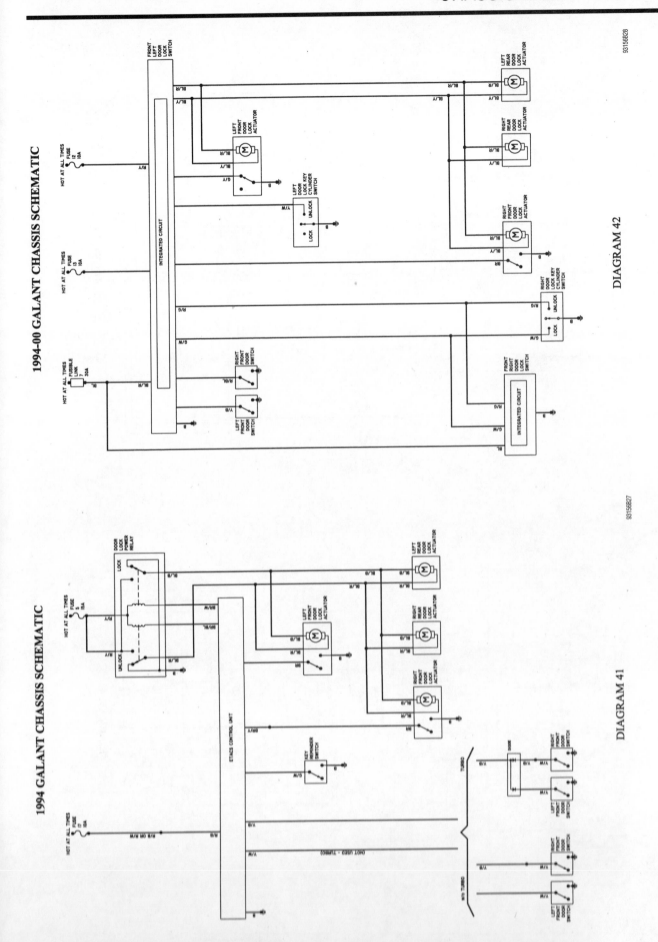

1994-00 GALANT CHASSIS SCHEMATIC

DIAGRAM 42

1994 GALANT CHASSIS SCHEMATIC

DIAGRAM 41

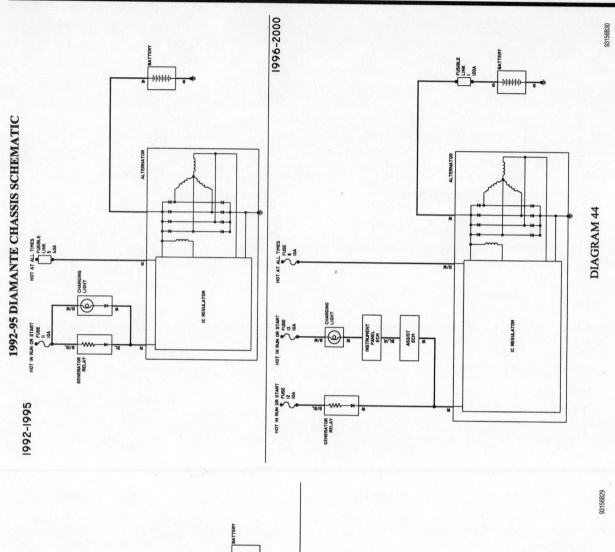

1992-1995

1992-95 DIAMANTE CHASSIS SCHEMATIC

1996-2000

DIAGRAM 44

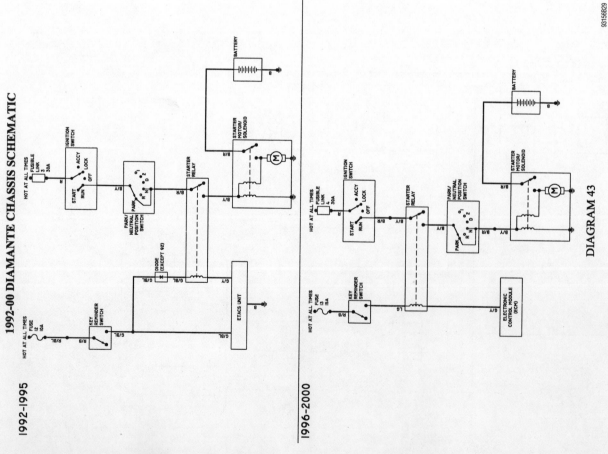

1992-1995

1992-00 DIAMANTE CHASSIS SCHEMATIC

1996-2000

DIAGRAM 43

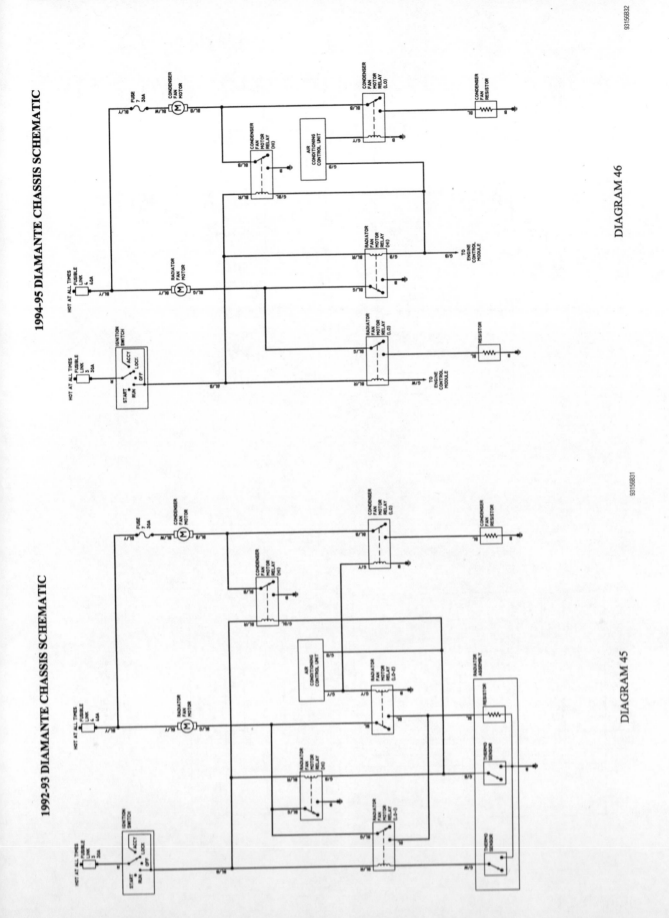

1994-95 DIAMANTE CHASSIS SCHEMATIC

DIAGRAM 46

1992-93 DIAMANTE CHASSIS SCHEMATIC

DIAGRAM 45

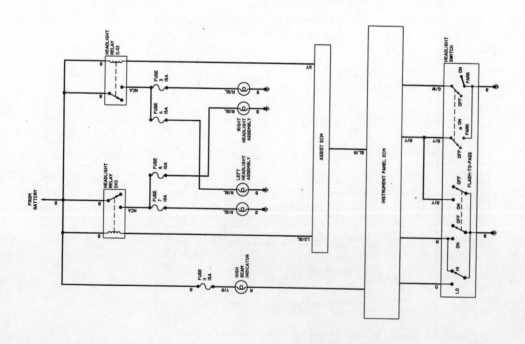

1992-95 DIAMANTE CHASSIS SCHEMATIC

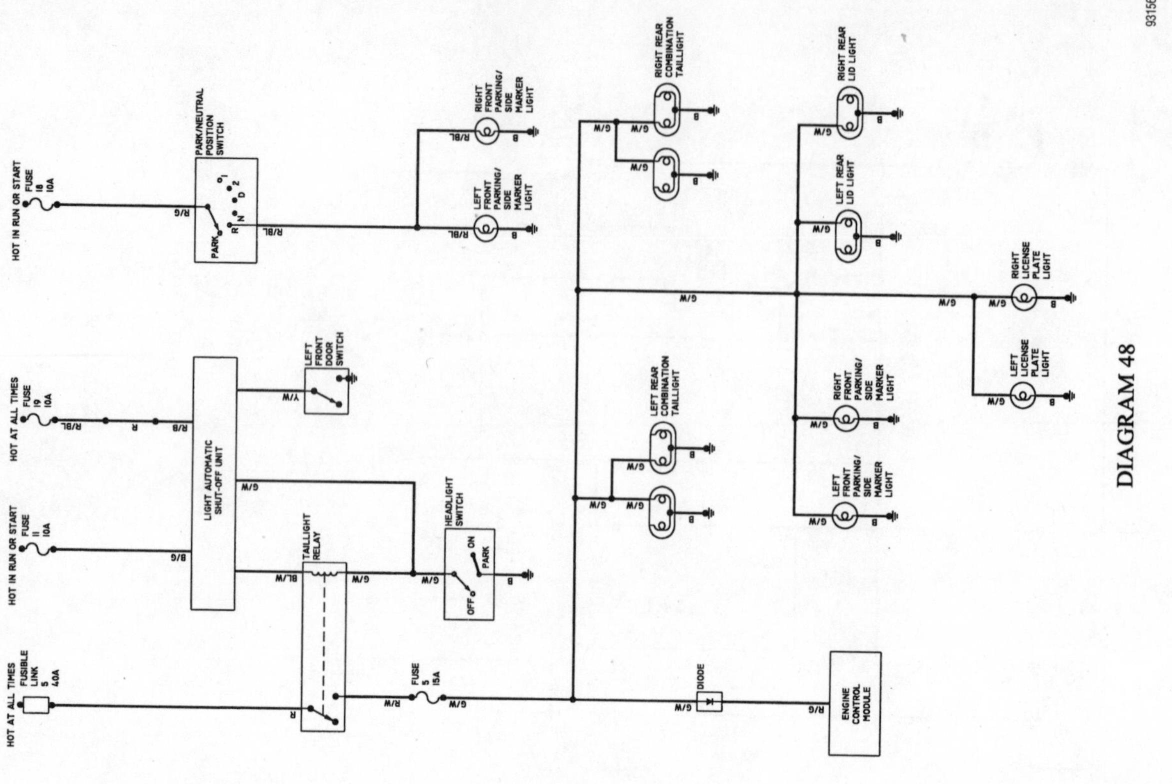

DIAGRAM 48

1992-95 DIAMANTE CHASSIS SCHEMATIC

DIAGRAM 47

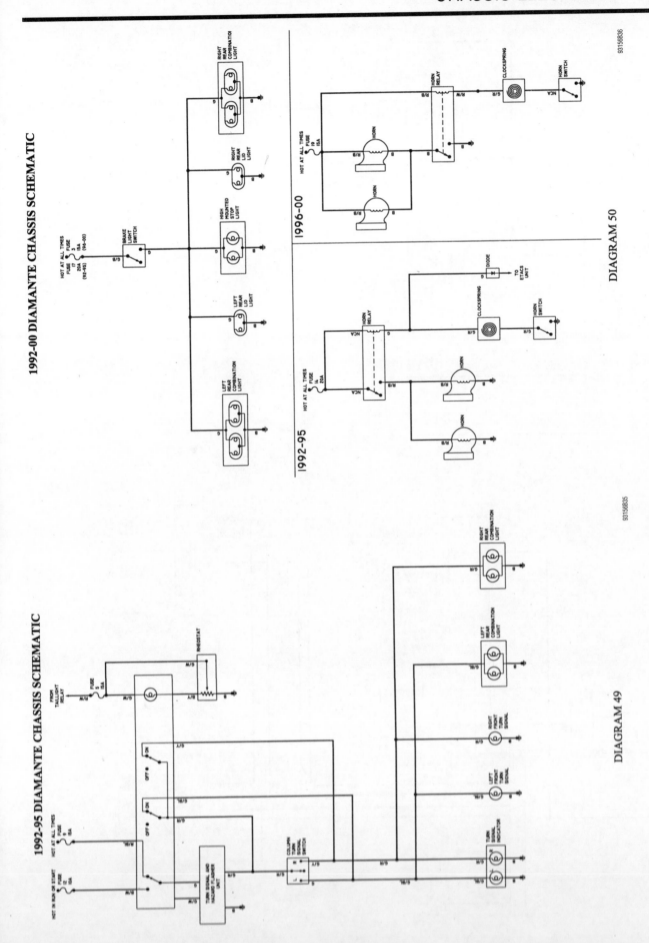

1992-00 DIAMANTE CHASSIS SCHEMATIC

1996-00

1992-95

DIAGRAM 50

1992-95 DIAMANTE CHASSIS SCHEMATIC

DIAGRAM 49

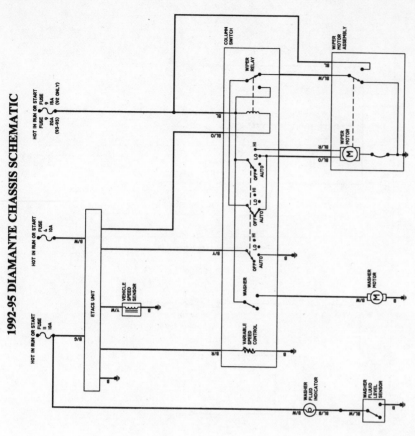

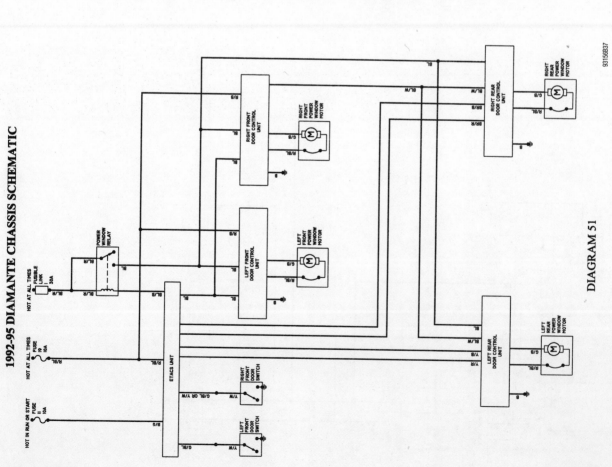

1992-95 DIAMANTE CHASSIS SCHEMATIC

DIAGRAM 52

1992-95 DIAMANTE CHASSIS SCHEMATIC

DIAGRAM 51

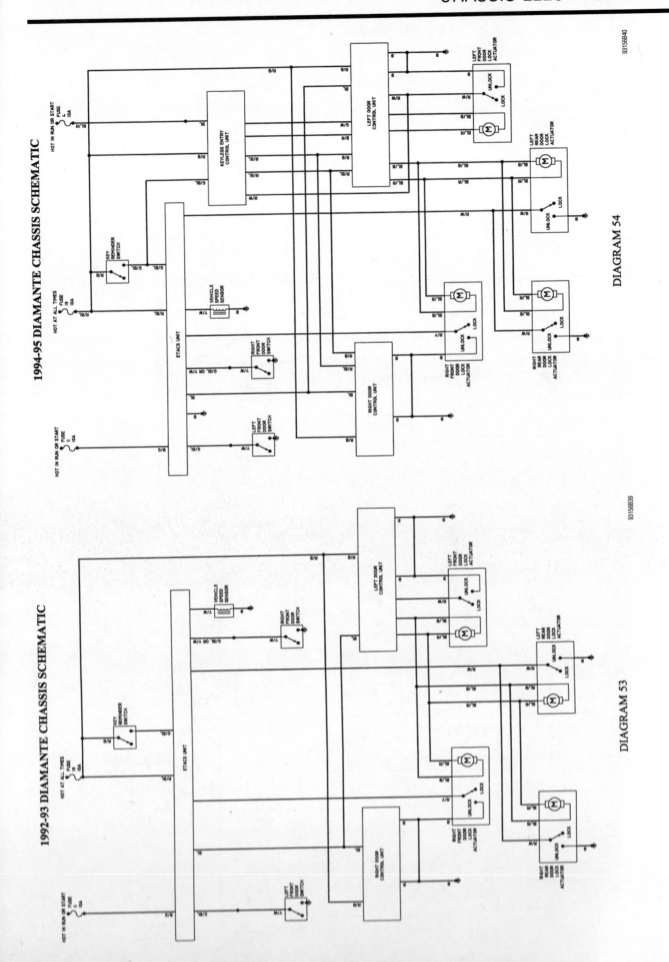

1994-95 DIAMANTE CHASSIS SCHEMATIC

DIAGRAM 54

1992-93 DIAMANTE CHASSIS SCHEMATIC

DIAGRAM 53

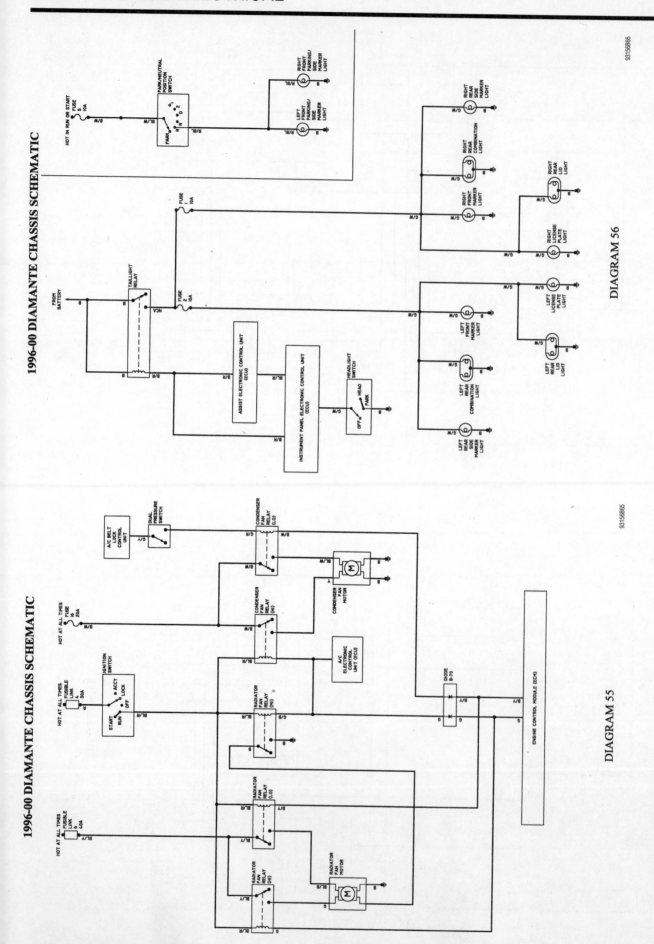

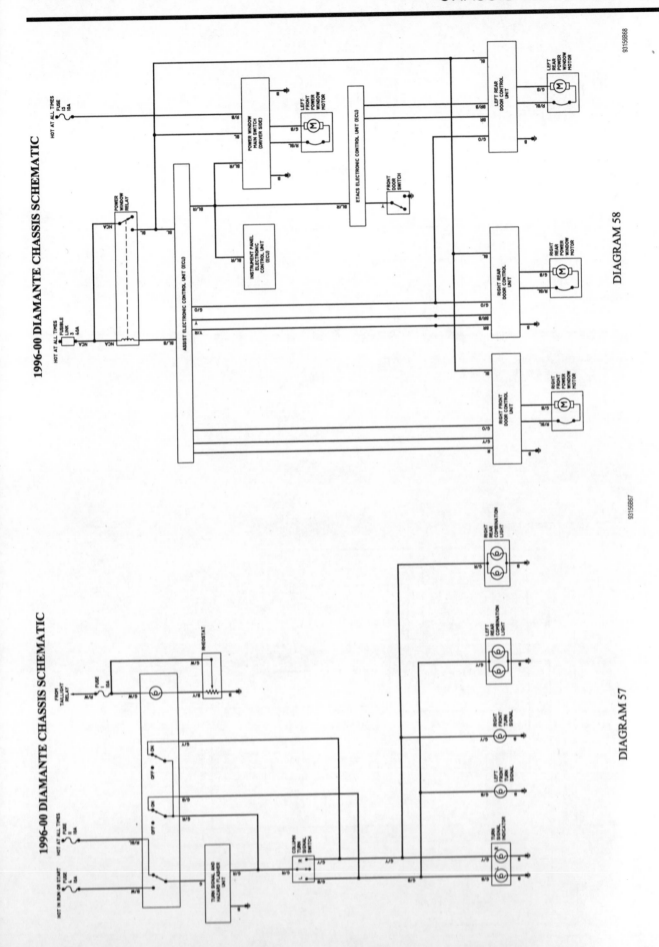

1996-00 DIAMANTE CHASSIS SCHEMATIC

DIAGRAM 58

1996-00 DIAMANTE CHASSIS SCHEMATIC

DIAGRAM 57

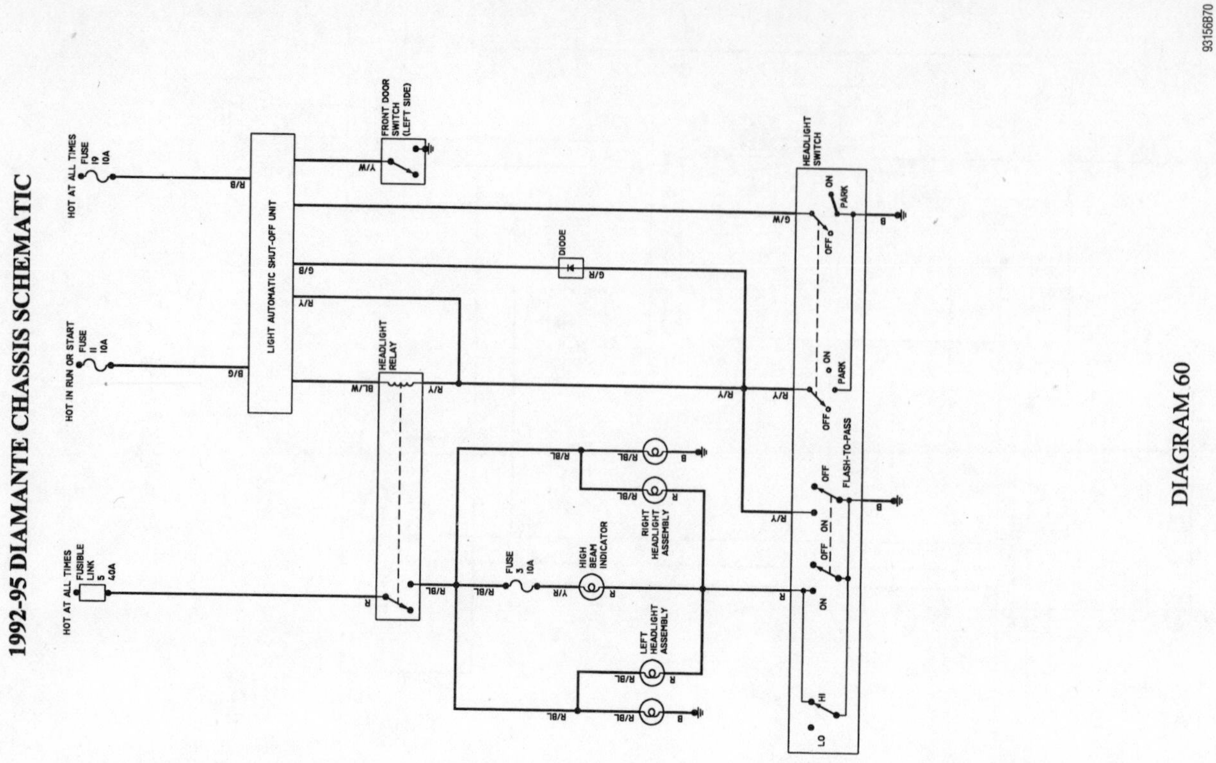

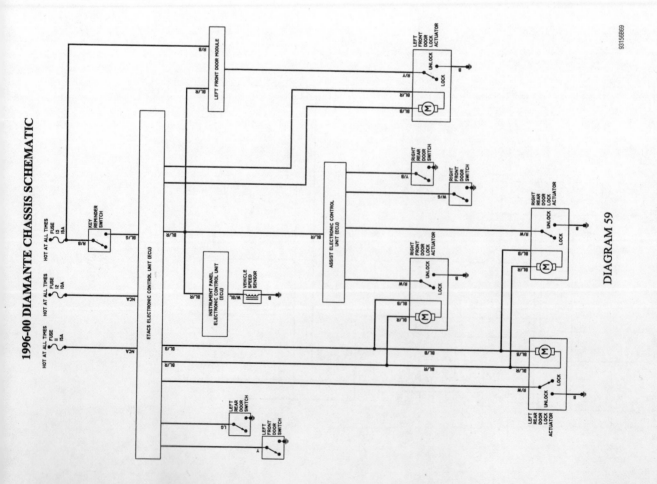

1992-95 DIAMANTE CHASSIS SCHEMATIC
HOT AT ALL TIMES FUSE 19 10A
HOT IN RUN OR START FUSE 11 10A
HOT AT ALL TIMES FUSIBLE LINK 5 40A
LIGHT AUTOMATIC SHUT-OFF UNIT
FRONT DOOR SWITCH (LEFT SIDE)
HEADLIGHT RELAY
DIODE
FUSE 3 10A
HIGH BEAM INDICATOR
RIGHT HEADLIGHT ASSEMBLY
LEFT HEADLIGHT ASSEMBLY
HEADLIGHT SWITCH
FLASH-TO-PASS
DIAGRAM 60
93156B70

1996-00 DIAMANTE CHASSIS SCHEMATIC
HOT AT ALL TIMES FUSE 11 15A
HOT AT ALL TIMES FUSE 12 10A
HOT AT ALL TIMES FUSE 15 15A
KEY REMINDER SWITCH
ETACS ELECTRONIC CONTROL UNIT (ECU)
INSTRUMENT PANEL ELECTRONIC CONTROL UNIT (ECU)
VEHICLE SPEED SENSOR
LEFT FRONT DOOR MODULE
ASSIST ELECTRONIC CONTROL UNIT (ECU)
LEFT FRONT DOOR LOCK ACTUATOR
RIGHT REAR DOOR SWITCH
RIGHT FRONT DOOR SWITCH
RIGHT REAR DOOR LOCK ACTUATOR
RIGHT FRONT DOOR LOCK ACTUATOR
LEFT REAR DOOR LOCK ACTUATOR
LEFT REAR DOOR SWITCH
LEFT FRONT DOOR SWITCH
DIAGRAM 59
93156B69

1993-96 MIRAGE CHASSIS SCHEMATIC

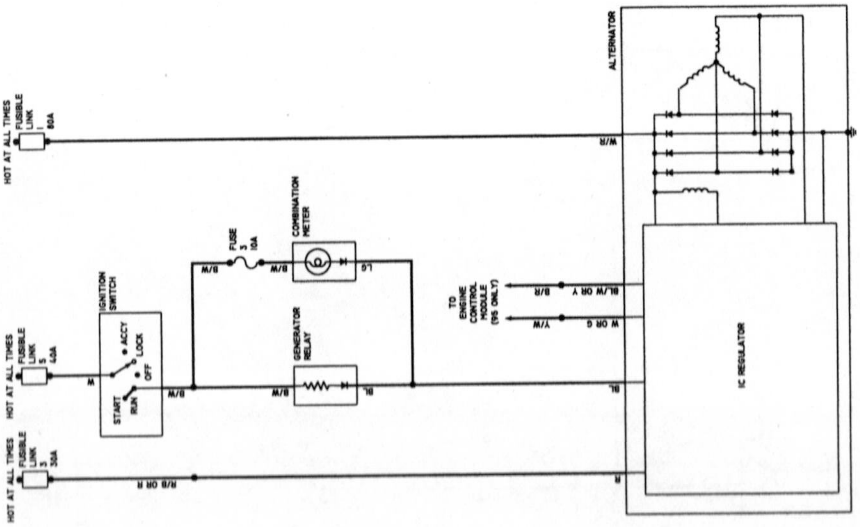

DIAGRAM 62

1996-00 DIAMANTE CHASSIS SCHEMATIC

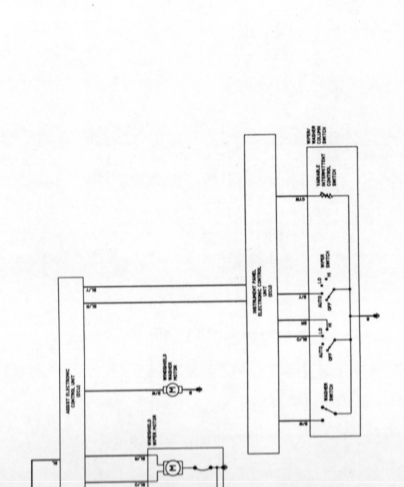

DIAGRAM 61

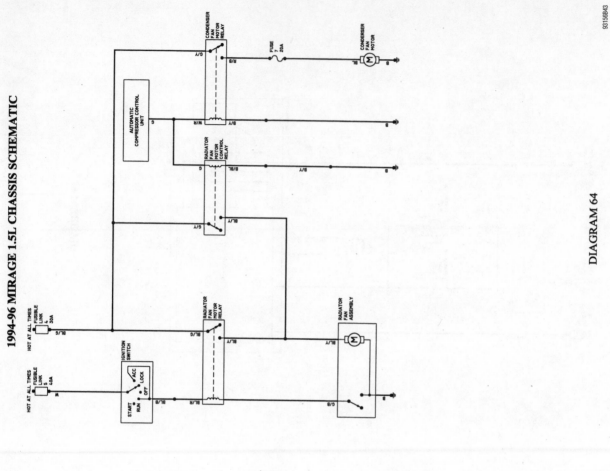

1994-96 MIRAGE 1.5L CHASSIS SCHEMATIC

DIAGRAM 64

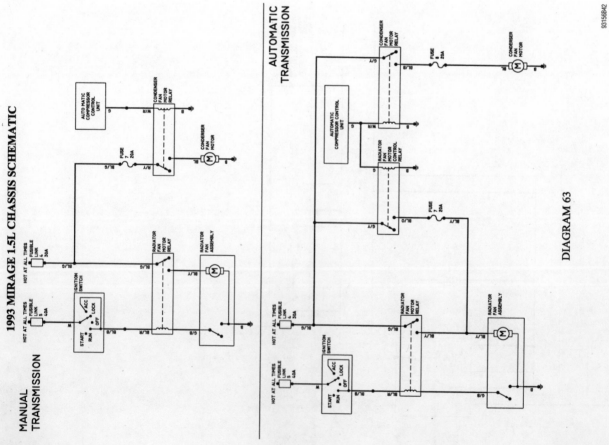

1993 MIRAGE 1.5L CHASSIS SCHEMATIC

MANUAL TRANSMISSION

AUTOMATIC TRANSMISSION

DIAGRAM 63

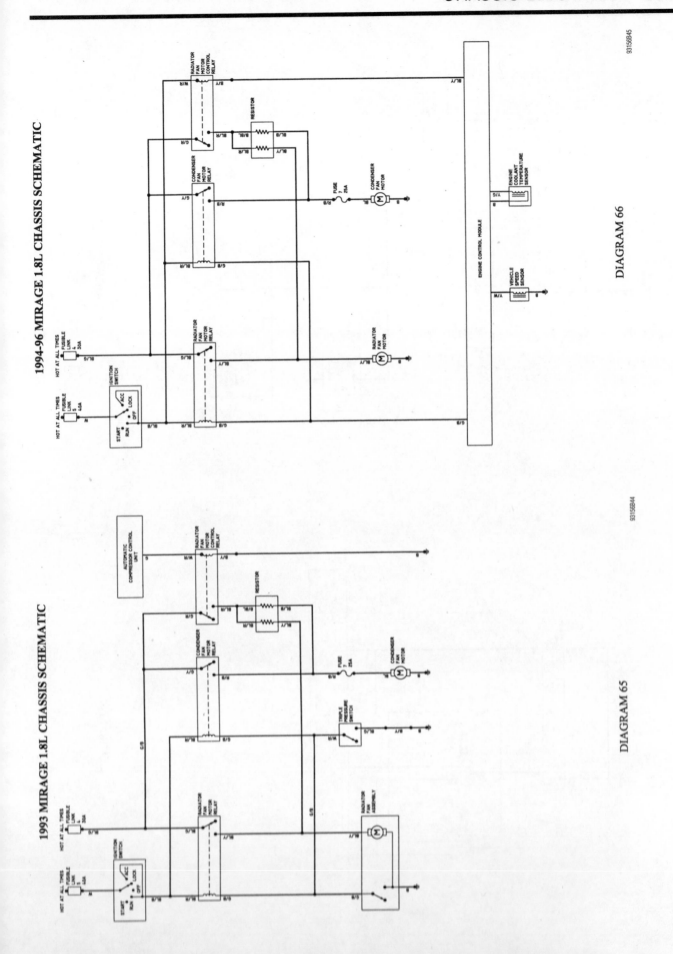

1994-96 MIRAGE 1.8L CHASSIS SCHEMATIC

DIAGRAM 66

1993 MIRAGE 1.8L CHASSIS SCHEMATIC

DIAGRAM 65

1993-96 MIRAGE CHASSIS SCHEMATIC

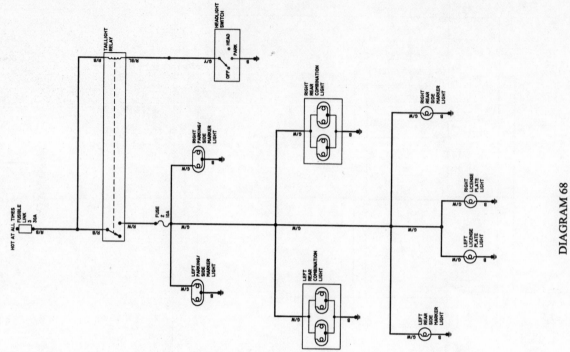

DIAGRAM 68

1993-96 MIRAGE CHASSIS SCHEMATIC

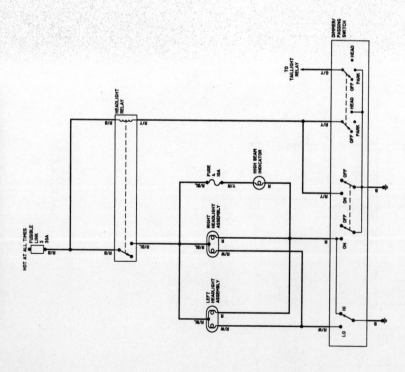

DIAGRAM 67

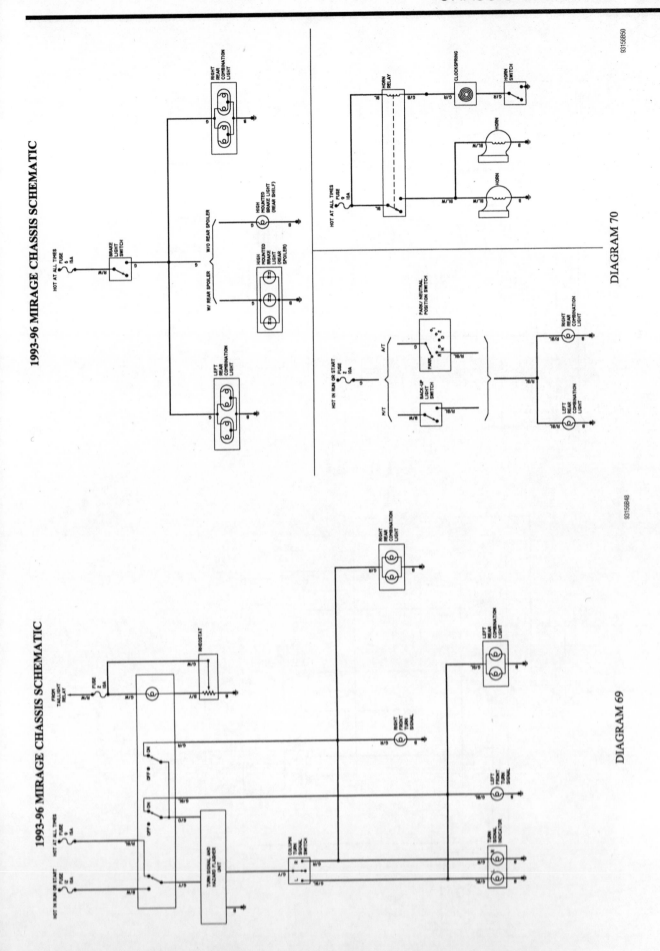

1993-96 MIRAGE CHASSIS SCHEMATIC

DIAGRAM 70

1993-96 MIRAGE CHASSIS SCHEMATIC

DIAGRAM 69

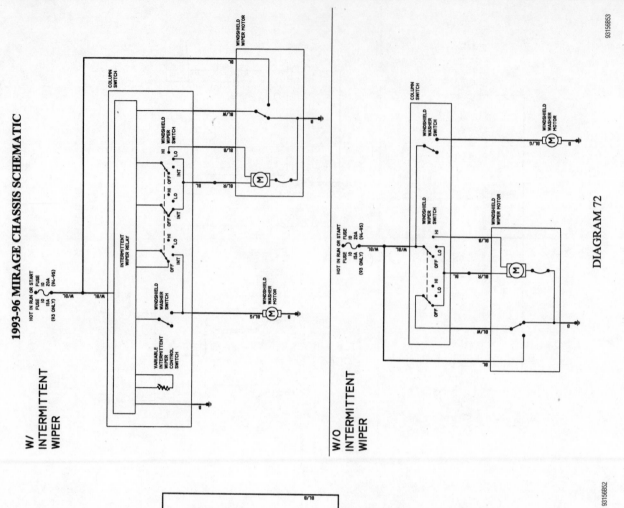

1993-96 MIRAGE CHASSIS SCHEMATIC

W/ INTERMITTENT WIPER

W/O INTERMITTENT WIPER

DIAGRAM 72

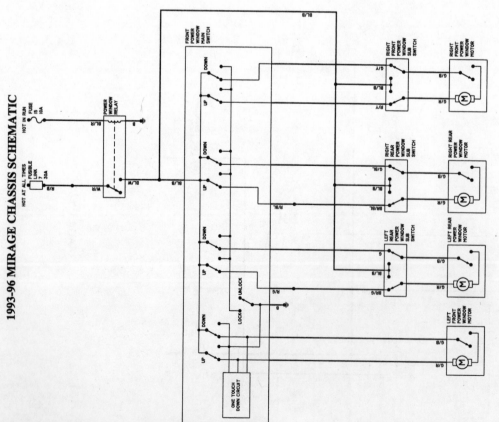

1993-96 MIRAGE CHASSIS SCHEMATIC

DIAGRAM 71

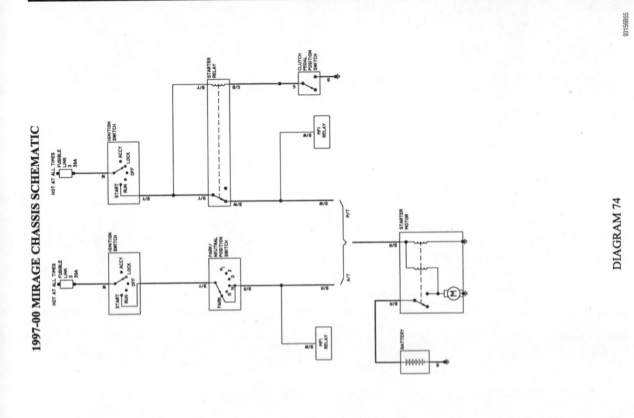

1997-00 MIRAGE CHASSIS SCHEMATIC

DIAGRAM 74

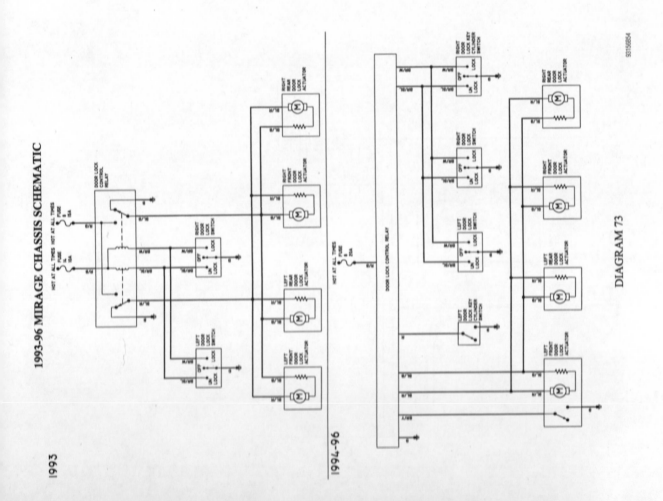

1993-96 MIRAGE CHASSIS SCHEMATIC

DIAGRAM 73

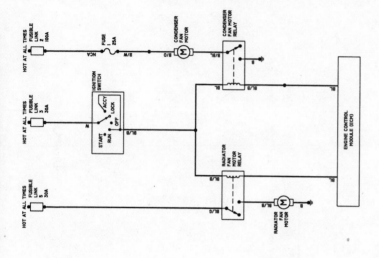

1997-00 MIRAGE CHASSIS SCHEMATIC

DIAGRAM 76

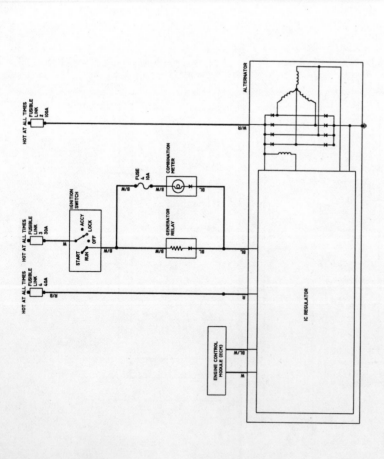

1997-00 MIRAGE CHASSIS SCHEMATIC

DIAGRAM 75

1997-00 MIRAGE CHASSIS SCHEMATIC

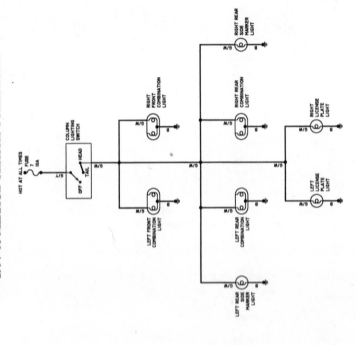

DIAGRAM 78

1997-00 MIRAGE CHASSIS SCHEMATIC

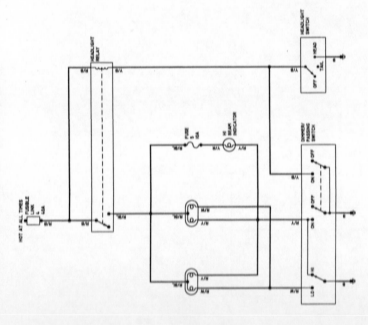

DIAGRAM 77

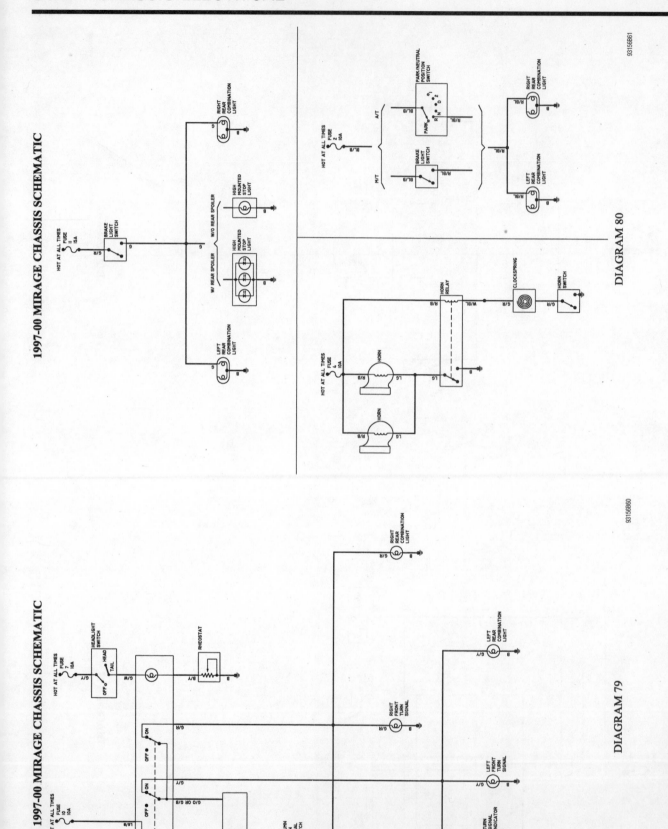

1997-00 MIRAGE CHASSIS SCHEMATIC

DIAGRAM 80

1997-00 MIRAGE CHASSIS SCHEMATIC

DIAGRAM 79

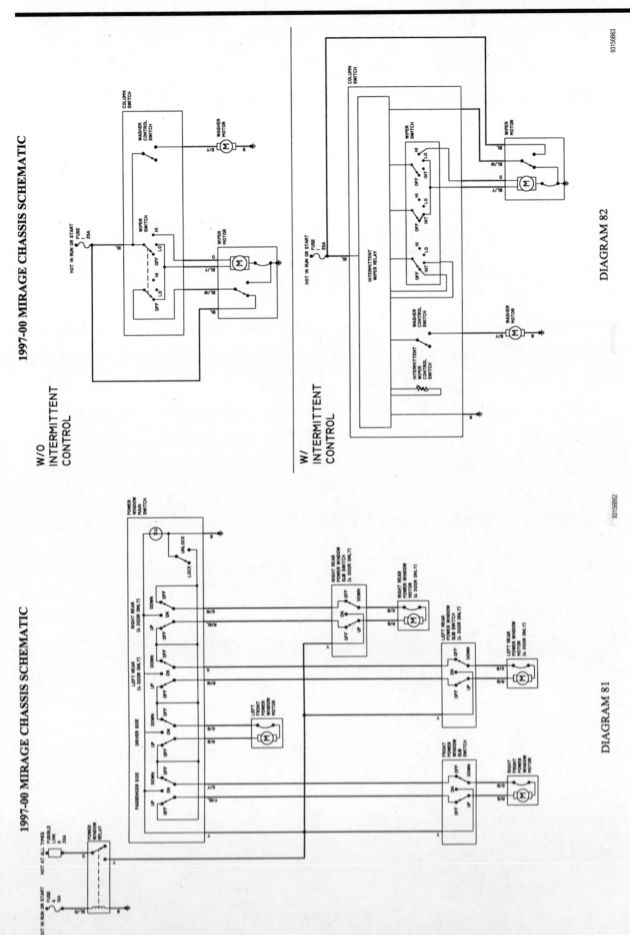

1997-00 MIRAGE CHASSIS SCHEMATIC

W/O INTERMITTENT CONTROL

W/ INTERMITTENT CONTROL

DIAGRAM 82

1997-00 MIRAGE CHASSIS SCHEMATIC

DIAGRAM 81

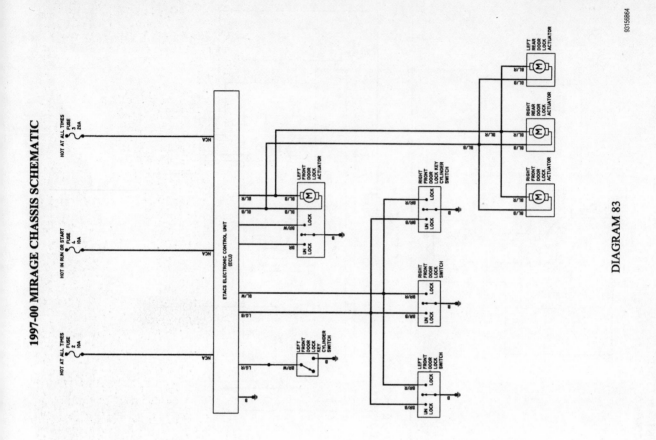

1997-00 MIRAGE CHASSIS SCHEMATIC

DIAGRAM 83

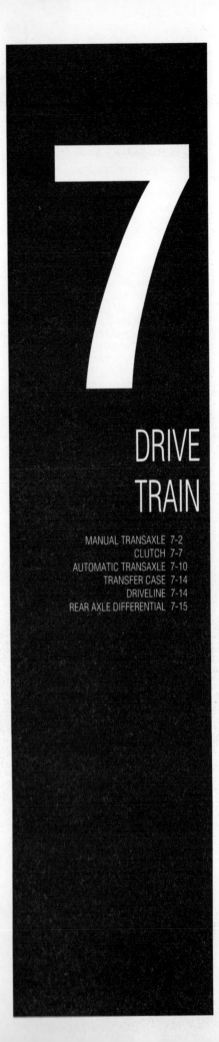

7

DRIVE
TRAIN

MANUAL TRANSAXLE

Understanding the Manual Transaxle

Because of the way an internal combustion engine breathes, it can produce torque, or twisting force, only within a narrow speed range. Most modern, overhead valve pushrod engines must turn at about 2500 rpm to produce their peak torque. By 4500 rpm they are producing so little torque that continued increases in engine speed produce no power increases. The torque peak on overhead camshaft engines is generally much higher, but much narrower.

The manual transaxle and clutch are employed to vary the relationship between engine speed and the speed of the wheels so that adequate engine power can be produced under all circumstances. The clutch allows engine torque to be applied to the transaxle input shaft gradually, due to mechanical slippage. Consequently, the vehicle may be started smoothly from a full stop. The transaxle changes the ratio between the rotating speeds of the engine and the wheels by the use of gears. The gear ratios allow full engine power to be applied to the wheels during acceleration at low speeds and at highway/passing speeds.

In a front wheel drive transaxle, power is usually transmitted from the input shaft to a mainshaft or output shaft located slightly beneath and to the side of the input shaft. The gears of the mainshaft mesh with gears on the input shaft, allowing power to be carried from one to the other. All forward gears are in constant mesh and are free from rotating with the shaft unless the synchronizer and clutch is engaged. Shifting from one gear to the next causes one of the gears to be freed from rotating with the shaft and locks another to it. Gears are locked and unlocked by internal dog clutches which slide between the center of the gear and the shaft. The forward gears employ synchronizers; friction members which smoothly bring gear and shaft to the same speed before the toothed dog clutches are engaged.

Adjustments

SHIFT LINKAGE

1. Disconnect the shift linkage from the transaxle.
2. On the transaxle, put select lever in **N** and move the shift lever in **4th** gear. Depress the clutch, if necessary, to shift.
3. Move the shift lever in the vehicle to the **4th** gear position until it contacts the stop.
4. Turn the adjuster turnbuckle so the shift cable eye aligns with the eye in the gear shift lever. When installing the cable eye, make sure the flange side of the plastic bushing at the shift cable end is on the cotter pin side.
5. The cables should be adjusted so the clearance between the shift lever and the 2 stoppers are equal when the shift lever is moved to 3rd and 4th gear. Move the shift lever to each position and check that the shifting is smooth.

Back-Up Light Switch

REMOVAL & INSTALLATION

1. Disconnect the negative battery cable.

2. Remove any components necessary to access the back-up light switch.
3. Unplug the back-up light switch connector.
4. Remove the switch from the case using the appropriate size socket and drive tool.

To install:

5. Install the switch and tighten it to 22–25 ft. lbs. (30–35 Nm).
6. Attach the back-up light switch connector.
7. Install any components removed to access the back-up light switch.
8. Connect the negative battery cable.

Manual Transaxle Assembly

REMOVAL & INSTALLATION

Mirage

➡ If the vehicle is going to be rolled while the halfshafts are out of the vehicle, obtain 2 outer CV-joints or proper equivalent tools and install to the hubs. If the vehicle is rolled without the proper torque applied to the front wheel bearings, the bearings will no longer be usable.

➡ The suspension components should not be tightened until the vehicles weight is resting on the ground.

1. Remove the battery and battery tray.
2. Remove the air cleaner assembly and vacuum hoses.
3. Note the locations and disconnect the shifter cables.
4. If equipped with 1.6L engine, remove the tension rod.
5. Detach the backup lamp switch connector, speedometer cable connection and remove the starter motor.
6. Raise the vehicle and support safely.
7. Remove the front wheels and the inner wheel panels.
8. Remove the undercover and splash pan.
9. Drain the transaxle oil into a suitable container.
10. Support the engine and remove the crossmember.
11. Remove the upper transaxle mounting bolt and bracket.
12. Disconnect the stabilizer bar, tie rod ends and the lower ball joint connections.
13. Remove the clutch release cylinder and clutch oil line bracket. Do not disconnect the fluid lines and secure the slave cylinder with wire.
14. Disconnect the clutch cable, if equipped with cable controlled clutch system.
15. Remove the halfshafts by inserting a prybar between the transaxle case and the driveshaft and prying the shaft from the transaxle. Do not pull on the driveshaft. Doing so damages the inboard joint. Do not insert the prybar so far the oil seal in the case is damaged.

➡ It is not necessary to disconnect the halfshafts from the steering knuckle. Remove the shaft with the hub and knuckle as an assembly. Tie the shafts aside. Note the circle clip on the end of the inboard shafts should not be reused.

16. Remove the bellhousing lower cover.
17. Remove the transaxle to engine bolts and lower the transaxle from the vehicle.

To install:

➡ When installing the transaxle, be sure to align the splines of the transaxle with the clutch disc.

18. Install the transaxle to the engine and install the mounting bolts. Tighten the bolts to 31–40 ft. lbs. (43–55 Nm) on 1990–92 models and 35 ft. lbs. (48 Nm) on 1993–00 models.
19. Install the bellhousing cover.

➡ When installing the halfshafts, use new circlips on the axle ends. Care must be taken to ensure that the oil seal lip of the transaxle is not damaged by the serrated part of the driveshaft.

20. Install and fully seat the halfshafts into the transaxle.
21. Install the slave cylinder.
22. Connect the ball joints, tie rod ends and the stabilizer bar connections.
23. Install the upper transaxle mounting bracket and bolt.
24. Install the crossmember.
25. Install the undercover.
26. Install the upper transaxle-to-engine mounting bolts. Tighten the bolts to 31–40 ft. lbs. (43–55 Nm) on 1990–92 models and 35 ft. lbs. (48 Nm) on 1993–00 models.
27. Install the starter motor.
28. Connect the backup light switch connector and speedometer cable.
29. Connect and adjust the shifter cables.
30. Install the air cleaner assembly.
31. Install the front wheels.
32. Make sure the vehicle is level when refilling the transaxle. Use Hypoid gear oil or equivalent, GL-4 or higher.
33. Connect the negative battery cable and check the transaxle for proper operation. Make sure the reverse lights operate when in reverse.

Galant

1990–93 MODELS

➡ If the vehicle is going to be rolled on its wheels while the halfshafts are out of the vehicle, obtain two outer CV-joints or proper equivalent tools and install to the hubs. If the vehicle is rolled without the proper torque applied to the front wheel bearings, the bearings will no longer be usable.

1. Remove the battery and the air intake hoses.
2. If equipped with Active-ECS, unplug the compressor wiring.
3. Remove the auto-cruise actuator and underhood bracket, located on the passenger side inner fender well.
4. Drain the transaxle and transfer case fluid, if equipped, into a suitable waste container.
5. Remove the retainer bolt and pull the speedometer cable from the transaxle assembly.
6. Remove the cotter pin securing the select and shift cables and remove the cable ends from the transaxle.

7. Remove the connection for the clutch release cylinder and without disconnecting the hydraulic line, and secure it aside.

8. Disconnect the backup light switch harness and position aside.

9. Detach the starter electrical connections, if necessary, remove the starter motor and position aside.

10. Remove the transaxle mount bracket.

11. Remove the upper transaxle mounting bolts.

12. Raise the vehicle and support safely on jackstands.

13. Remove the undercover and the front wheels.

14. Remove the cotter pin and disconnect the tie rod end from the steering knuckle.

15. Remove the self-locking nut from the halfshafts.

16. Disconnect the lower arm ball joint from the steering knuckle.

17. Remove the halfshafts from the transaxle.

18. On AWD models, disconnect the front exhaust pipe.

19. On AWD models, remove the transfer case by removing the attaching bolts, moving the transfer case to the left and lowering the front side. Remove it from the rear driveshaft. Be careful of the oil seal. Do not allow the driveshaft to hang; once the front is removed from the transfer, tie it up. Cover the transfer case openings to keep out dirt.

20. Remove the cover from the transaxle bellhousing.

21. On AWD models, remove the crossmember and the triangular gusset.

22. Remove the transaxle lower coupling bolt. It is just above the halfshaft opening on FWD or transfer case opening on AWD.

23. Support the weight of the engine from above (chain hoist). Support the transaxle using a transmission jack and remove the remaining lower mounting bolts.

24. On turbocharged vehicle, be careful not to damage the lower radiator hose with the transaxle housing during removal. Wrap tape on both the lower hose and the transaxle housing to prevent damage. Move the transaxle assembly to the right and carefully lower it from the vehicle.

To install:

25. Install the transaxle to the engine and install the mounting bolts. Tighten the bolts to 35 ft. lbs. (48 Nm). Install the transaxle lower coupling bolt.

26. Install the underpan, crossmember and the triangular gusset.

27. Install the transfer case on AWD models and connect the exhaust pipe.

28. Install the halfshafts, using new circlips on the axle ends. Try to keep the inboard joint straight in relation to the axle. Be careful not to damage the oil seal lip of the transaxle with the serrated part of the halfshaft.

29. Connect the tie rod and ball joint to the steering knuckle.

30. Install the transaxle mount bracket.

31. Install wheels and lower vehicle. Retorque axle shaft nuts to 145–188 ft. lbs. (200–260 Nm).

32. Install the starter motor.

33. Connect the backup light switch and the speedometer cable.

34. Install the clutch release cylinder.

35. Connect the select and shift cables and install new cotter pins.

36. Install the air intake hose.

37. Install the auto-cruise actuator and bracket.

38. Install the battery.

39. If equipped with Active-ECS, connect the air compressor.

40. Make sure the vehicle is level when refilling the transaxle. Use Hypoid gear oil or equivalent, GL-4 or higher.

41. Check the transaxle and transfer case for proper operation. Make sure the reverse lights come on when in reverse.

1994–00 MODELS

1. Disconnect the negative battery cable and wait at least 90 seconds before performing any work.

2. Remove the air cleaner and intake hoses.

3. Drain the transaxle into a suitable waste container.

4. Remove the cotter pins and clips securing the select and shift cables and remove the cable ends from the transaxle.

5. If equipped with Active-ECS, disconnect the air compressor.

6. Disconnect the backup light switch harness and position aside.

7. Disconnect the speedometer electrical connector, from the transaxle assembly.

8. Remove the starter motor and position aside.

9. Using special tool MZ203827 or equivalent, support the engine assembly.

10. Remove the rear roll stopper mounting bracket.

11. Remove the transaxle mount bracket.

12. Remove the upper transaxle mounting bolts.

13. Raise and safely support the vehicle.

14. Remove the front wheel assemblies.

15. Remove the right hand undercover.

16. Remove the cotter pin and disconnect the tie rod end, from the steering knuckle.

17. Disconnect the stabilizer bar link, from the damper fork.

18. Disconnect the damper fork, from the lateral lower control arm.

19. Disconnect the later lower arm, and the compression arm, lower ball joints, from the steering knuckle.

20. Pry the halfshafts from the transaxle, and secure aside.

21. Remove the connection for the clutch release cylinder and without disconnecting the hydraulic line, secure aside.

22. Remove the cover from the transaxle bellhousing.

23. Remove the engine front roll stopper through-bolt.

24. Remove the crossmember and the triangular right hand stay.

25. Support the transaxle, using a transmission jack, and remove the transaxle lower coupling bolt.

➡ The coupling bolt threads from the engine side, into the transaxle, and is located just above the halfshaft opening.

26. Slide the transaxle rearward and carefully lower it from the vehicle.

To install:

27. Install the transaxle to the engine. Install the mounting bolts and tighten to 35 ft. lbs. (48 Nm). Install the transaxle lower coupling bolt and tighten to 22–25 ft. lbs. (30–34 Nm).

28. Install the cover to the transaxle bellhousing and tighten the mounting bolts to 7 ft. lbs. (9 Nm).

29. Install the crossmember and tighten the front mounting bolts to 65 ft. lbs. (88 Nm) and the rear

bolt to 54 ft. lbs. (73 Nm). Install the front engine roll stopper through-bolt and hand-tighten. Once the full weight of the engine is on the mounts, tighten the bolt to 42 ft. lbs. (57 Nm).

30. Install the triangular stay bracket and tighten the mounting bolts to 65 ft. lbs. (88 Nm).

31. Connect the clutch release cylinder.

32. Install the halfshafts, using new circlips on the axle ends.

✳✳ WARNING

When installing the axleshaft, keep the inboard joint straight in relation to the axle, so not to damage the oil seal lip of the transaxle, with the serrated part of the halfshaft.

33. Connect the tie rod and ball joints to the steering knuckle. Tighten the ball joint self-locking nuts to 48 ft. lbs. (65 Nm). Tighten the tie rod end nut to 21 ft. lbs. (28 Nm) and secure with a new cotter pin.

34. Connect the damper fork to the lower control arm and tighten the through-bolt to 65 ft. lbs. (88 Nm).

35. Connect the stabilizer link to the damper fork, and tighten the self-locking nut to 29 ft. lbs. (39 Nm).

36. Install the underpan.

37. Install wheels and lower vehicle.

38. Install the transaxle mount bracket to the transaxle, and tighten the mounting nuts to 32 ft. lbs. (43 Nm).

39. Install the rear roll stopper mounting bracket.

40. Remove the engine support. Tighten the transaxle mount through-bolt to 51 ft. lbs. (69 Nm) and tighten the front engine roll stopper through-bolt.

41. Install the upper transaxle mounting bolts and tighten to 35 ft. lbs. (48 Nm).

42. Install the starter motor.

43. Attach the backup light switch and the speedometer connector.

44. Connect the select and shift cables and install new cotter pins.

45. Install the air cleaner and the air intake hose.

46. Connect the negative battery cable.

47. Make sure the vehicle is level, and refill the transaxle.

48. Check the transaxle for proper operation. Make sure the reverse lights come on when in reverse.

Halfshafts

REMOVAL & INSTALLATION

♦ See Figures 1 thru 13

93157p03

Fig. 1 Remove the cotter pin from the axle shaft . . .

Fig. 2 . . . then loosen the axle nut while the vehicle is still on the ground

Fig. 3 Use a suitable wrench to loosen . . .

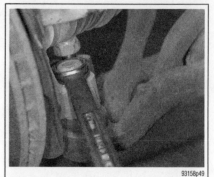

Fig. 4 . . . the nuts from the lower ball joint-to-steering knuckle junctions

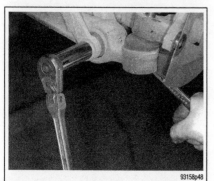

Fig. 5 Remove the lower coil-over shock lower mounting bolt and nut from the control arm

Fig. 6 Use a suitable prytool to separate . . .

Fig. 7 . . . the lower ball joints from the steering knuckle

Fig. 8 Use a suitable prytool to release the inner CV-joint retaining ring from the transaxle by gently prying outward

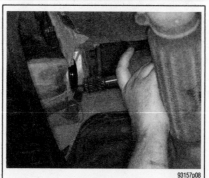

Fig. 9 Remove the inner joint from the transaxle until the spline completely clears the transaxle

Fig. 10 Using a suitable punch and hammer, gently tap the halfshaft out of the steering knuckle . . .

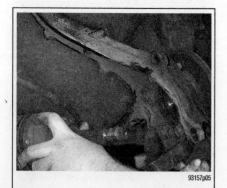

Fig. 11 . . . then slide the halfshaft out of the knuckle

Fig. 12 Remove the halfshaft from the vehicle

Fig. 13 Always replace the circlip on the inner joint before installing the shaft into the transaxle

1. While the vehicle is still on the ground, remove the cotter pin, and loosen the axle nut.

2. Raise the vehicle and support it safely.

3. If equipped with ABS, remove the front wheel speed sensor.

4. If equipped with Active Electronic Control Suspension (Active-ECS), perform the following:

   a. Loosen the nut that secures the air line to the to the top of the strut and discard the O-ring.

   b. Remove the bolts that secure the actuator to the top of the strut and remove the component. Disconnect the wiring harness.

5. Disconnect the lower ball joint and the tie rod end from the steering knuckle.

6. Remove the axle nut and the washer.

7. If removing the left side axle with an inner shaft, remove the center support bearing bracket bolts and washers. Then, remove the halfshaft by setting up a puller on the outside wheel hub and pushing the halfshaft from the front hub. Tap the shaft union at the joint case with a plastic hammer to remove the halfshaft and inner shaft from the transaxle.

8. If removing right side axle shafts without an inner shaft, remove the halfshaft by setting up a puller on the outside wheel hub and pushing the halfshaft from the front hub. After pressing the outer shaft, insert a prybar between the transaxle case and the halfshaft and pry the shaft from the transaxle.

➠Do not pull on the shaft; doing so damages the inboard joint.

To install:

9. Replace the circlips on the ends of the halfshafts.

10. Insert the halfshaft into the transaxle. Be sure it is fully seated.

11. Pull the strut assembly out and install the other end to the hub.

12. Install the center bearing bracket bolts and tighten to 33 ft. lbs. (45 Nm).

13. Install the washer on the axle shaft so the chamfered edge faces outward. Install the axle nut, but do not tighten it fully at this time.

14. Connect the ball joint to the steering knuckle. Torque the new retaining nut to 43–52 ft. lbs. (60–72 Nm) and secure with a new cotter pin.

15. Connect the tie rod end to the steering knuckle. Torque the retaining nut to 21 ft. lbs. (29 Nm) and secure with a new cotter pin.

16. If equipped with ABS, install the front wheel speed sensor.

17. If equipped with Active-ECS, perform the following:

   a. Install the air line with a new O-ring.

   b. Install the actuator to the top of the strut. Connect the wiring harness.

18. Install the wheel and lower the vehicle to the floor.

19. Tighten the axle nut to 145–188 ft. lbs. (200–260 Nm) and secure with a new cotter pin.

CV-JOINTS OVERHAUL

▸ **See Figures 14 thru 27**

These vehicles use several different types of joints. Engine size, transaxle type, whether the joint is an inboard or outboard joint, even which side of the vehicle is being serviced could make a difference in joint type. Be sure to properly identify the joint before attempting joint or boot replacement. Look for identification numbers at the large end of the boots and/or on the end of the metal retainer bands.

The 3 types of joints used are the Birfield Joint, (B.J.), the Tripod Joint (T.J.) and the Double Offset Joint (D.O.J.).

➠Do not disassemble a Birfield joint. Service with a new joint or clean and repack using a new boot kit.

The distance between the large and small boot bands is important and should be checked prior to and after boot service. This is so the boot will not be installed either too loose or too tight, which could cause early wear and cracking, allowing the grease to get out and water and dirt in, leading to early joint failure.

➠The driveshaft joints use special grease; do not add any grease other than that supplied with the kit.

Double Offset Joint

The Double Offset Joint (D.O.J.) is bigger than other joints and, in these applications, is normally used as an inboard joint.

1. Remove the halfshaft from the vehicle.

2. Side cutter pliers can be used to cut the metal retaining bands. Remove the boot from the joint outer race.

Fig. 14 Check the CV-boot for wear

Fig. 15 Removing the outer band from the CV-boot

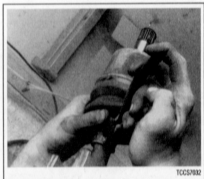
Fig. 16 Removing the inner band from the CV-boot

Fig. 17 Removing the CV-boot from the joint housing

Fig. 18 Clean the CV-joint housing prior to removing boot

Fig. 19 Removing the CV-joint housing assembly

Fig. 20 Removing the CV-joint

Fig. 21 Inspecting the CV-joint housing

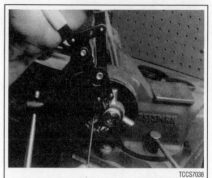

Fig. 22 Removing the CV-joint outer snapring

Fig. 23 Checking the CV-joint snapring for wear

Fig. 24 CV-joint snapring (typical)

Fig. 25 Removing the CV-joint assembly

Fig. 26 Removing the CV-joint inner snapring

Fig. 27 Installing the CV-joint assembly (typical)

3. Locate and remove the large circlip at the base of the joint. Remove the outer race (the body of the joint).

4. Remove the small snapring and take off the inner race, cage and balls as an assembly. Clean the inner race, cage and balls without disassembling.

5. If the boot is to be reused, wipe the grease from the splines and wrap the splines in vinyl tape before sliding the boot from the shaft.

6. Remove the inner (D.O.J.) boot from the shaft. If the outer (B.J.) boot is to be replaced, remove the boot retainer rings and slide the boot down and off of the shaft at this time.

To install:

7. Be sure to tape the shaft splines before installing the boots. Fill the inside of the boot with the specified grease. Often the grease supplied in the replacement parts kit is meant to be divided in half, with half being used to lubricate the joint and half being used inside the boot.

8. Install the cage onto the halfshaft so the small diameter side of the cage is installed first. With a brass drift pin, tap lightly and evenly around the inner race to install the race until it comes into contact with the rib of the shaft. Apply the specified grease to the inner race and cage and fit them together. Insert the balls into the cage.

9. Install the outer race (the body of the joint) after filling with the specified grease. The outer race should be filled with this grease.

10. Tighten the boot bands securely. Make sure the distance between the boot bands is correct.

11. Install the halfshaft to the vehicle.

Except Double Offset Joint

1. Disconnect the negative battery cable. Remove the halfshaft.

2. Use side cutter pliers to remove the metal retaining bands from the boot(s) that will be removed. Slide the boot from the T.J. case.

3. Remove the snapring and the tripod joint spider assembly from the halfshaft. Do not disassemble the spider and use care in handling.

4. If the boot is be reused, wrap vinyl tape around the spline part of the shaft so the boot(s) will not be damaged when removed. Remove the dynamic damper, if used, and the boots from the shaft.

To install:

5. Double check that the correct replacement parts are being installed. Wrap vinyl tape around the splines to protect the boot and install the boots and damper, if used, in the correct order.

6. Install the joint spider assembly to the shaft and install the snapring.

7. Fill the inside of the boot with the specified grease. Often the grease supplied in the replacement parts kit is meant to be divided in half, with half being used to lubricate the joint and half being used inside the boot. Keep grease off the rubber part of the dynamic damper (if used).

8. Secure the boot bands with the halfshaft in a horizontal position. Make sure distance between boot bands is correct.

9. Install the halfshaft to the vehicle and reconnect the negative battery cable.

CLUTCH

Understanding the Clutch

** CAUTION

The clutch driven disc may contain asbestos, which has been determined to be a cancer causing agent. Never clean clutch surfaces with compressed air! Avoid inhaling any dust from any clutch surface! When cleaning clutch surfaces, use a commercially available brake cleaning fluid.

The purpose of the clutch is to disconnect and connect engine power at the transaxle. A vehicle at rest requires a lot of engine torque to get all that weight moving. An internal combustion engine does not develop a high starting torque (unlike steam engines) so it must be allowed to operate without any load until it builds up enough torque to move the vehicle. Torque increases with engine rpm. The clutch allows the engine to build up torque by physically disconnecting the engine from the transaxle, relieving the engine of any load or resistance.

The transfer of engine power to the transaxle (the load) must be smooth and gradual; if it weren't, drive line components would wear out or break quickly. This gradual power transfer is made possible by gradually releasing the clutch pedal. The clutch disc and pressure plate are the connecting link between the engine and transaxle. When the clutch pedal is released, the disc and plate contact each other (the clutch is engaged) physically joining the engine and transaxle. When the pedal is pushed inward, the disc and plate separate (the clutch is disengaged) disconnecting the engine from the transaxle.

Most clutches utilize a single plate, dry friction disc with a diaphragm-style spring pressure plate. The clutch disc has a splined hub which attaches the disc to the input shaft. The disc has friction material where it contacts the flywheel and pressure plate. Torsion springs on the disc help absorb engine torque pulses. The pressure plate applies pressure to the clutch disc, holding it tight against the surface of the flywheel. The clutch operating mechanism consists of a release bearing, fork and cylinder assembly.

The release fork and actuating linkage transfer pedal motion to the release bearing. In the engaged position (pedal released) the diaphragm spring holds the pressure plate against the clutch disc, so engine torque is transmitted to the input shaft. When the clutch pedal is depressed, the release bearing pushes the diaphragm spring center toward the flywheel. The diaphragm spring pivots the fulcrum, relieving the load on the pressure plate. Steel spring straps riveted to the clutch cover lift the pressure plate from the clutch disc, disengaging the engine drive from the transaxle and enabling the gears to be changed.

The clutch is operating properly if:

- It will stall the engine when released with the vehicle held stationary.
- The shift lever can be moved freely between 1st and reverse gears when the vehicle is stationary and the clutch disengaged.

Driven Disc and Pressure Plate

REMOVAL & INSTALLATION

Galant and Mirage

- **See Figures 28 thru 41**

** CAUTION

The clutch driven disc may contain asbestos, which has been determined to be a cancer causing agent. Never clean clutch surfaces with compressed air! Avoid inhaling any dust from any clutch surface! When cleaning clutch surfaces, use a commercially available brake cleaning fluid.

1. Disconnect the negative battery cable.
2. Raise and safely support the vehicle.
3. Remove the transaxle assembly from the vehicle. Refer to the procedure earlier in this section.
4. Remove the pressure plate attaching bolts, pressure plate and clutch disc. If the pressure plate is to be reused, loosen the bolts in a diagonal pattern, 1 or 2 turns at a time. This will prevent warping the clutch cover assembly.
5. Remove the return clip and the pressure plate release bearing. Do not use solvent to clean the bearing.
6. Inspect the clutch release fork and fulcrum for

TCCS7116

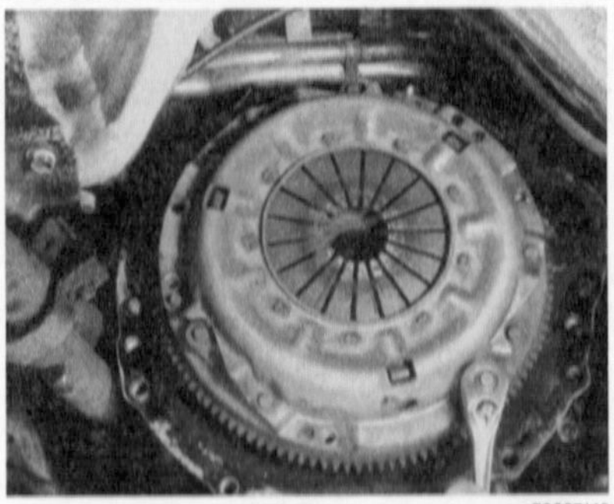

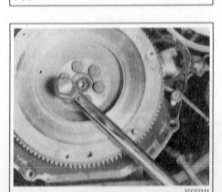

Fig. 28 Loosen and remove the clutch and pressure plate bolts evenly, a little at a time . . .

TCCS7118

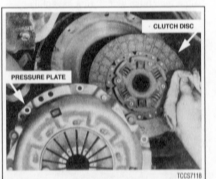

Fig. 29 . . . then carefully remove the clutch and pressure plate assembly from the flywheel

TCCS7125

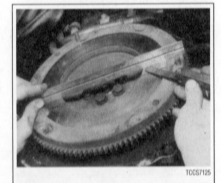

Fig. 30 Check across the flywheel surface, it should be flat

TCCS7121

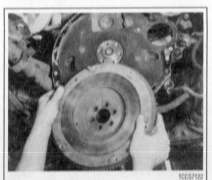

Fig. 31 If necessary, lock the flywheel in place and remove the retaining bolts . . .

TCCS7122

Fig. 32 . . . then remove the flywheel from the crankshaft in order replace it or have it machined

TCCS7123

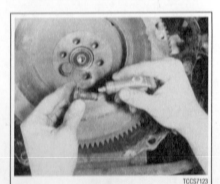

Fig. 33 Upon installation, it is usually a good idea to apply a threadlocking compound to the flywheel bolts

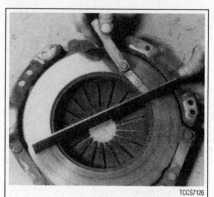

Fig. 34 Check the pressure plate for excessive wear

Fig. 35 Be sure that the flywheel surface is clean, before installing the clutch

Fig. 36 Typical clutch alignment tool, note how the splines match the transaxle's input shaft

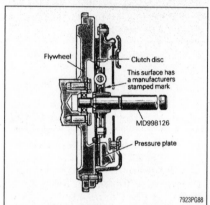

Fig. 37 Use the alignment dowel to center the disc on the flywheel—Mirage

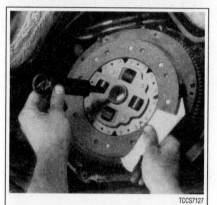

Fig. 38 Use the clutch alignment tool to align the clutch disc during assembly

Fig. 39 Pressure plate-to-flywheel bolt holes should align

Fig. 40 You may want to use a threadlocking compound on the clutch assembly bolts

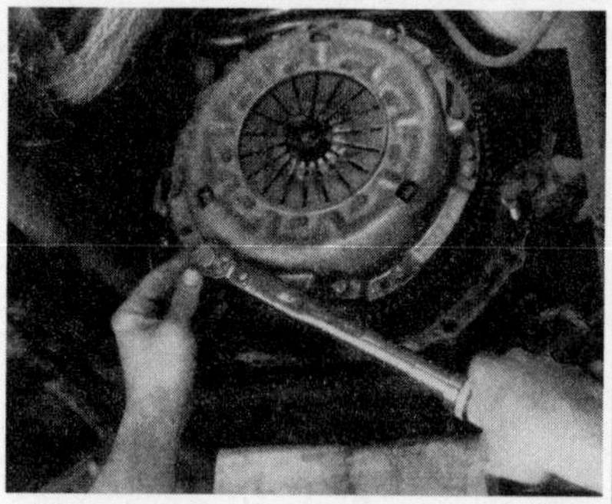

Fig. 41 Be sure to use a torque wrench to tighten all bolts

damage or wear. If necessary, remove the release fork and unthread the fulcrum from the transaxle.

7. Carefully inspect the condition of the clutch components and replace any worn or damaged parts.

To install:

8. Inspect the flywheel for heat damage or cracks. Resurface or replace the flywheel as required.

9. Install the fulcrum and tighten to 25 ft. lbs. (35 Nm).

10. Install the release fork.

11. Apply a coating of multi-purpose grease to the point of contact with the fulcrum and the point of contact with the release bearing.

12. Apply a coating of multi-purpose grease to

the end of the release cylinder pushrod and the pushrod hole in the release fork.

13. Apply multi-purpose grease to the clutch release bearing. Pack the bearing inner surface and the groove with grease. Do not apply grease to the resin portion of the bearing.

14. Place the bearing in position and install the return clip.

15. Using the proper alignment tool, install the clutch disc to the flywheel.

16. Install the pressure plate assembly.

17. Install the retainer bolts and tighten a little at a time, in a diagonal sequence. Tighten them to a final torque of 14 ft. lbs. (19 Nm) on 1994–98 Galant

models and 16 ft. lbs. (22 Nm) on all other models. Remove the aligning tool.

18. Install the transaxle assembly.

19. Check for proper clutch operation.

ADJUSTMENTS

Pedal Free Play

1. Measure the clutch pedal height from the face of the pedal pad to the firewall. The desired distances are as follows:

 a. Mirage—6.61–6.8 in. (168–171mm)
 b. Galant —6.93–7.17 in. (176–182mm)

2. Measure the clutch pedal clevis pin play at the face of the pedal pad. The standard values are as follows:

 a. Mirage—0.04–0.12 in. (1–3mm)
 b. Galant—0.04–0.12 in. (1–3mm)

3. If the clutch pedal height or clevis pin play are not within the standard values, adjust as follows:

 a. For vehicles without cruise control, turn and adjust the bolt so the pedal height is the standard value, then tighten the locknut.

 b. For vehicles with the auto-cruise control system, detach the clutch switch connector and turn the switch to obtain the standard clutch pedal height. Then, lock with the locknut.

 c. Turn the pushrod to adjust the clutch pedal clevis pin play to agree with the standard value and secure the pushrod with the locknut.

➡ When adjusting the clutch pedal height or the clutch pedal clevis pin play, be careful not to push the pushrod toward the master cylinder.

    d. Check that when the clutch pedal is depressed all the way, the interlock switch switches over from ON to OFF.

Clutch Cable

ADJUSTMENT

▶ See Figure 42

➡ The following adjustment is for the cable actuated clutch system on the Mirage. The Hydraulic systems on all other models are self-adjusting.

    1. Measure the clutch pedal height (measurement A). The specification is 6.38–6.50 in. (162–165mm).

➡ The clutch pedal height is not adjustable. If not within specifications, part replacement is required.

    2. Depress clutch pedal several times and check the pedal free-play (measurement B).
    3. If measurement is not 0.67–0.87 in. (17–22mm), adjustment is required.
    4. To adjust, turn the outer cable adjusting nut, located at the firewall, until free-play is within range.
    5. Depress the clutch pedal several times and recheck the measurement.

REMOVAL AND INSTALLATION

    1. Rotate the adjusting wheel counterclockwise to loosen the cable.
    2. Remove the cable retaining clamps.
    3. Remove the cotter pin from the clutch actuating arm at the transaxle and disconnect the cable.
    4. Disconnect the cable at the pedal and remove the cable from the vehicle.

➡ In order to prevent cable binding or abrasion, be sure to take note of the cable routing, so that it can be reinstalled in the same position.

To install:
    5. Route the cable and make the connection at the clutch pedal.
    6. Make the connection at the transaxle and secure the cable with the retaining clamp. Install a new cotter pin.
    7. Lubricate all pivot points.
    8. Adjust the cable to achieve proper free-play.

Clutch Master Cylinder

REMOVAL & INSTALLATION

    1. Disconnect the negative battery cable.
    2. Remove necessary underhood components in order to gain access to the clutch master cylinder.

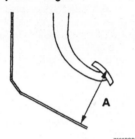

Fig. 42 Clutch pedal height (A) measurement—Mirage

    3. Place a suitable drain pan under the vehicle to catch the fluid once the line is disconnected, or place a rag or shop towel under the fluid line of the master cylinder.
    4. Loosen the line at the cylinder and allow the fluid to drain.

✳✳ WARNING

Clean, high quality brake fluid is essential to the safe and proper operation of the brake system. You should always buy the highest quality brake fluid that is available. If the brake fluid becomes contaminated, drain and flush the system, then refill the master cylinder with new fluid. Never reuse any brake fluid. Any brake fluid that is removed from the system should be discarded. Also, do not allow any brake fluid to come in contact with a painted surface; it will damage the paint.

    5. Remove the clevis pin retainer at the clutch pedal and remove the washer and clevis pin.
    6. Remove the 2 nuts and pull the cylinder from the firewall. A seal should be between the mounting flange and firewall. This seal should be replaced.
    7. The installation is the reverse of the removal procedure.
    8. Lubricate all pivot points with grease.
    9. Bleed the system at the slave cylinder using DOT 3 brake fluid and check the adjustment of the clutch pedal.

Clutch Slave Cylinder

REMOVAL & INSTALLATION

    1. Disconnect the negative battery cable.
    2. Remove necessary underhood components in order to gain access to the clutch release cylinder.
    3. Place a suitable drain pan under the vehicle, then remove the hydraulic line and allow the system to drain.

✳✳ WARNING

Clean, high quality brake fluid is essential to the safe and proper operation of the brake system. You should always buy the highest

quality brake fluid that is available. If the brake fluid becomes contaminated, drain and flush the system, then refill the master cylinder with new fluid. Never reuse any brake fluid. Any brake fluid that is removed from the system should be discarded. Also, do not allow any brake fluid to come in contact with a painted surface; it will damage the paint.

    4. Remove the bolts and pull the cylinder from the transaxle housing. On some 1.5L engines, instead of a pushrod bearing against the clutch arm, a clevis pin and yoke is used. Simply remove the circlip, pull out the clevis pin and remove the cylinder.
    5. The installation is the reverse of the removal procedure.
    6. Lubricate all pivot points with grease.
    7. Bleed the system using DOT 3 brake fluid.

HYDRAULIC SYSTEM BLEEDING

▶ See Figure 43

With Hydraulic Clutch

    1. Fill the reservoir with clean brake fluid meeting DOT 3 specifications.

✳✳ WARNING

Clean, high quality brake fluid is essential to the safe and proper operation of the brake system. You should always buy the highest quality brake fluid that is available. If the brake fluid becomes contaminated, drain and flush the system, then refill the master cylinder with new fluid. Never reuse any brake fluid. Any brake fluid that is removed from the system should be discarded. Also, do not allow any brake fluid to come in contact with a painted surface; it will damage the paint.

    2. Press the clutch pedal to the floor, then open the bleeder screw on the slave cylinder.
    3. Tighten the bleed screw and release the clutch pedal.
    4. Repeat the procedure until the fluid is free of air bubbles.

Fig. 43 Bleeding a typical clutch hydraulic system

AUTOMATIC TRANSAXLE

Understanding the Automatic Transaxle

The automatic transaxle allows engine torque and power to be transmitted to the front wheels within a narrow range of engine operating speeds. It will allow the engine to turn fast enough to produce plenty of power and torque at very low speeds, while keeping it at a sensible rpm at high vehicle speeds (and it does this job without driver assistance). The transaxle uses a light fluid as the medium for the transmission of power. This fluid also works in the operation of various hydraulic control circuits and as a lubricant. Because the transaxle fluid performs all of these functions, trouble within the unit can easily travel from one part to another. For this reason, and because of the complexity and unusual operating principles of the transaxle, a very sound understanding of the basic principles of operation will simplify troubleshooting.

Fluid Pan

REMOVAL & INSTALLATION

Pan removal, fluid and filter changes are covered in Section 1 of this manual.

Park/Neutral Position Switch

REMOVAL & INSTALLATION

1990–97 Mirage and 1990–93 Galant

▶ **See Figure 44**

1. Disconnect the negative battery cable.
2. Disconnect the selector cable from the lever.
3. Remove the two retaining screws and lift off the switch.

To install:

4. Mount and position new switch. Do not tighten the bolts until the switch is adjusted.
5. Connect selector cable and adjust switch.
6. After installation and adjustment make sure the engine only starts in the **P** and **N** selections. Also check that the reverse lights operate only in the **R** selection.

1994–00 Galant and 1998–00 Mirage

▶ **See Figure 44**

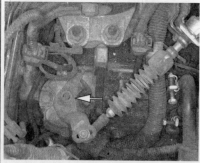

Fig. 44 Typically, the park/neutral position switch is located on the top of the transaxle

1. Disconnect the negative battery cable.
2. Remove the nut attaching the shift control cable from the transaxle manual shaft lever. Position the control cable out of the way.
3. Place the manual shaft lever in the Neutral position, remove the nut and the manual shaft lever.
4. Detach the park/neutral switch electrical connector.
5. Remove the park/neutral switch mounting bolts and remove the switch from the transaxle manual shaft.

To install:

6. Install the park/neutral switch to the transaxle manual shaft and install the switch mounting bolts. Do not tighten the mounting bolts until the switch is adjusted.
7. Install the manual shaft lever to the park/neutral switch with the nut. Make sure that the shaft lever is in the Neutral position.
8. Adjust the switch in the following manner: turn the switch body until the hole in the body of the switch aligns with the hole in the manual shaft lever. Insert a drill bit or equivalent into the holes. Tighten the switch mounting bolts to 8 ft. lbs. (11 Nm).
9. Attach the electrical connector.
10. Install the control cable to the manual shaft lever with the nut. Adjust the cable so that there is no slack in the cable and that the selector lever moves smoothly.
11. Reconnect the negative battery cable. Check for proper starting and proper reverse light operation.

Diamante

▶ **See Figure 44**

1. Disconnect the negative battery cable.

✳✳ CAUTION

Wait at least 90 seconds after the negative battery cable is disconnected to prevent possible deployment of the air bag.

2. Disconnect the selector cable from the lever.
3. Remove the two retaining screws and lift off the switch.

To install:

4. Install the lever, tighten the bolts only hand tight.
5. Rotate switch body so the manual control lever 0.20 inch (5mm) hole and the switch body 0.20 inch (5mm) holes are aligned.
6. Tighten the mounting bolts to 7–8 ft. lbs. (10–12 Nm).
7. Connect the selector cable to the lever.
8. Connect the negative battery cable.
9. After installation and adjustment make sure the engine only starts in the **P** and **N** selections. Also check that the reverse lights operate only in the **R** selection.

ADJUSTMENT

1990–97 Mirage and 1990–93 Galant

1. Disconnect the negative battery cable and locate the neutral safety switch on the top of the transaxle.

➡**Apply parking brake and chock wheels before placing transaxle into the N position**

2. At the transmission, loosen the shift cable adjustment nut. Inside the vehicle place the gearshift selector lever in **N**.
3. Place the manual shift control lever in **N**.
4. Loosen neutral safety switch mounting screws and rotate switch body so the manual control lever 0.20 in. (5mm) hole and the switch body 0.20 in. (5mm) holes are aligned.
5. Tighten switch body mounting bolts to 7–8 ft. lbs. (10–12 Nm).
6. At the shift cable adjusting nut, gently pull cable to remove any slack. Tighten locknut to 8 ft. lbs. (12 Nm).
7. Verify that the switch lever moves to positions corresponding to each position of the selector lever. Connect the negative battery terminal.
8. Make sure the engine only starts in the **P** and **N** positions. Also make sure the reverse lights operate only in **R** selection.

Automatic Transaxle Assembly

REMOVAL & INSTALLATION

Diamante

▶ **See Figures 45, 46, 47, and 48**

1. Properly disarm the SRS system (air bag). Refer to Section 6.
2. Raise and safely support the vehicle.
3. Remove the front wheels.
4. Remove the engine side cover and undercovers.
5. Drain the transaxle assembly into a suitable container.
6. If equipped, remove the front catalytic converter.
7. Remove the exhaust pipe, main muffler and catalytic converter.
8. Disconnect the tie rod end and ball joint from the steering knuckle.
9. Unbolt the support bearing for the left side halfshaft.
10. Remove the halfshafts by inserting a prybar between the transaxle case and the driveshaft and prying the shaft from the transaxle.
11. Remove the air cleaner assembly and adjoining duct work.
12. Detach the engine harness connection.
13. If the vehicle is equipped with Active Electronic Controlled Suspension (Active-ECS), remove the compressor assembly from the transaxle and suspend with wire. Do not allow the compressor to hang from the air hose.
14. If equipped, remove the roll stopper stay bracket.
15. Disconnect the speedometer cable from the transaxle.
16. Remove the clip that secures the shifter and disconnect the shifter control cable from the transaxle.
17. Disconnect and plug the oil cooler hoses from the transaxle.
18. Detach the following:

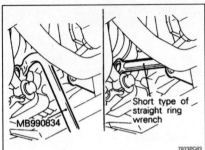

Fig. 45 Location of 4-wheel steering oil pump mounting bolts—Diamante with a F4A33 automatic transaxle

- Park/neutral switch electrical harness
- Kickdown servo switch
- Pulse generator
- Oil temperature sensor electrical harness
- Shift control solenoid valve harness.

19. Support the transaxle and remove the transaxle mounting bracket.

20. Remove the three upper transaxle-to-engine mounting bolts.

21. For vehicles with 4WS, remove the heat shield for the 4WS oil pump and remove the pump. Do not allow the pump to hang from the oil hoses.

22. For vehicles equipped with Active-ECS, disconnect the height sensor rod from the lower control arm.

23. Remove the bolt that secures the Heated Oxygen (HO$_2$S) sensor harness to the right side crossmember.

24. Remove the starter assembly.

25. Remove the mounting brackets for access to the bell housing cover.

26. Remove the bell housing/oil pan covers assembly.

27. Remove the bolts holding the flexplate to the torque converter.

28. Remove the lower transaxle to engine bolts and remove the transaxle assembly.

To install:

29. Install the transaxle assembly to the engine block, install the mounting bolts and tighten to 54 ft. lbs. (75 Nm).

30. Install the bolts that secure the torque converter to the driveplate. Tighten the bolts to 34–38 ft. lbs. (46–53 Nm).

31. Install the bell housing/oil pan covers.

32. Install the transaxle stay brackets that were removed for access to the bell housing cover.

33. Install the starter assembly and connect the wiring.

34. Install the bolt that secures the HO$_2$S sensor harness to the right side crossmember and tighten the bolt to 7–9 ft. lbs. (10–12 Nm).

35. For vehicles equipped with Active-ECS, connect the height sensor rod from the lower control arm. Check the height sensor rod for a length (A) of 10.59–10.63 in. (269–270mm).

36. If removed, install the 4WS oil pump and tighten the mounting bolts to 17 ft. lbs. (24 Nm).

37. If removed, install the 4WS oil pump heat shield and tighten the mounting bolts to 17 ft. lbs. (24 Nm).

38. Install the three upper transaxle-to-engine mounting bolts. Tighten the mounting bolts to 54 ft. lbs. (75 Nm).

➡ **One of the upper bolts has a grounding strap to secure under the bolt.**

39. Install and connect the transaxle mounting bracket. Tighten the mounting nut and bolts to 51 ft. lbs. (70 Nm).

40. Connect the shift control solenoid valve harness.

41. Connect the kickdown servo switch, pulse generator and oil temperature sensor electrical harness.

42. Connect the park/neutral switch electrical harness.

43. Using new hose clamps, install the oil cooler hoses to the transaxle.

44. Install shifter control cable to the transaxle and secure the cable with clip.

45. Connect the speedometer cable to the transaxle.

46. If removed, install the roll stopper stay bracket and tighten the one through nut and bolt to 36–43 ft. lbs. (50–60 Nm). Tighten the two mounting bolts to 16 ft. lbs. (22 Nm).

47. If removed, install the Active-ECS compressor assembly. Tighten the mounting bolts to 48 inch lbs. (5 Nm) and connect the electrical harness.

48. Attach the engine harness connection.

49. Install the air cleaner assembly and adjoining duct work.

50. Using new circlips, install the halfshafts and seat halfshafts into the transaxle. Install the bolt that secure the left side support bearing and tighten the bolts to 33 ft. lbs. (45 Nm).

51. Connect the ball joint and tie rod end to the steering knuckle. Using new nuts, tighten the ball joint castle nut to 43–52 ft. lbs. (60–72 Nm) and tighten the tie rod castle nut to 22 ft. lbs. (30 Nm). Install new cotter pins.

52. Using new gaskets, install the exhaust system.

53. If removed, install front catalytic converter.

54. Install the engine undercovers.

55. Connect the negative battery cable.

56. Fill the transaxle to the correct level.

57. Start the engine and check for leaks.

Galant

1990–1993 MODELS

1. On vehicles equipped with auto-cruise, remove the control actuator and bracket.

2. If equipped with an active ECS, disconnect the air compressor.

3. Drain the transaxle fluid into a suitable container.

4. Remove the air cleaner assembly, intercooler and air hose, as required.

5. Mark the shift cable. Remove the adjusting nut and disconnect the shift cable.

6. Tag and detach the electrical connectors for the solenoid, neutral safety switch (inhibitor switch), the pulse generator kickdown servo switch and oil temperature sensor.

7. Disconnect the speedometer cable and oil cooler lines.

8. Disconnect the wires to the starter motor and remove the starter.

9. Remove the upper transaxle to engine bolts.

10. Support the transaxle and remove the transaxle mounting bracket.

11. Raise the vehicle and support safely. Remove the sheet metal under guard.

12. Remove the tie rod ends and the ball joints from the steering knuckle.

13. Remove the halfshafts by inserting a prybar between the transaxle case and the driveshaft and prying the shaft from the transaxle. Do not pull on the driveshaft. Doing so damages the inboard joint. Use

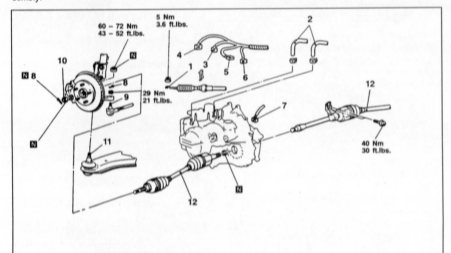

Removal steps
1. Transaxle control cable connection
2. Transaxle oil cooler hoses connection
3. PNP switch connector
4. A/T control solenoid valve connector
5. Input shaft speed sensor connector
6. Output shaft speed sensor connector
7. Vehicle speed sensor connector
8. Split pin
9. Connection of the tie rod end
10. Drive shaft nut
11. Connection for the lower arm ball joint
12. Drive shaft and inner shaft assembly (RH) and the drive shaft (LH)

Caution
Mounting locations marked by * should be provisionally tightened, and then fully tightened when the body is supporting the full weight of the engine.

Fig. 46 Transaxle removal (1 of 2)—Diamante with F4A51 transaxle

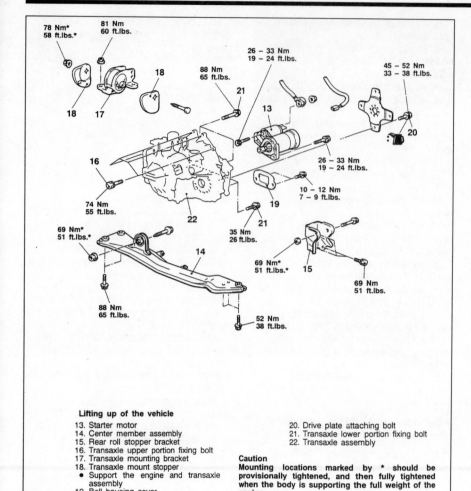

Lifting up of the vehicle
13. Starter motor
14. Center member assembly
15. Rear roll stopper bracket
16. Transaxle upper portion fixing bolt
17. Transaxle mounting bracket
18. Transaxle mount stopper
• Support the engine and transaxle assembly
19. Bell housing cover
20. Drive plate attaching bolt
21. Transaxle lower portion fixing bolt
22. Transaxle assembly

Caution
Mounting locations marked by * should be provisionally tightened, and then fully tightened when the body is supporting the full weight of the engine.

7923PG85

Fig. 47 Transaxle removal (2 of 2)—Diamante with F4A51 transaxle

the prybar. Do not insert the prybar so far the oil seal in the case is damaged. Tie the halfshafts aside.

14. On AWD vehicles, disconnect the exhaust pipe and remove the transfer case.

15. Remove the lower bellhousing cover and remove the special bolts holding the flexplate to the torque converter. To remove, turn the engine crankshaft with a box wrench and bring the bolts into a position appropriate for removal, one at a time. After removing the bolts, push the torque converter toward the transaxle so it doesn't stay on the engine allowing oil to pour out of the converter hub or cause damage to the converter.

16. Remove the lower transaxle to engine bolts and remove the transaxle assembly.

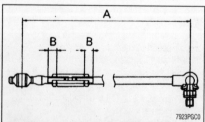

7923PGC0

Fig. 48 Height sensor rod adjustment—Diamante with a F4A33 automatic transaxle

To install:

17. After the torque converter has been mounted on the transaxle, install the transaxle assembly on the engine. Tighten the driveplate bolts to 34–38 ft. lbs. (46–53 Nm). Tighten the transaxle-to-engine bolts to 35 ft. lbs. (48 Nm). Install the bellhousing cover.

18. On AWD vehicles, install the transfer case and frame pieces. Connect the exhaust pipe using a new gasket.

19. Replace the circlips and install the halfshafts to the transaxle.

20. Install the tie rods and ball joint to the steering arm.

21. Install the transaxle mounting bracket.

22. Install the under guard.

23. Install the starter.

24. Connect the speedometer cable and oil cooler lines.

25. Connect the solenoid, neutral safety switch (inhibitor switch), the pulse generator kickdown servo switch and oil temperature sensor.

26. Install the shift control cable.

27. Install the air hose, intercooler and air cleaner assembly.

28. If equipped with an active ECS, connect the air compressor.

29. If equipped with auto-cruise, install the control actuator and bracket.

30. Refill with Dexron II, Mopar ATF Plus type 7176, Mitsubishi Plus ATF or equivalent, automatic transaxle fluid. If vehicle is AWD check and fill the transfer case.

31. Start the engine and allow to idle for 2 minutes. Apply parking brake and move selector through each gear position, ending in **N**. Recheck fluid level and add if necessary. Fluid level should be between the marks in the HOT range.

1994–00 MODELS

1. Disconnect the negative battery cable.

2. Remove the air cleaner and intake hoses.

3. Drain the transaxle into a suitable waste container.

4. Remove the nut securing the shifter lever to the transaxle. Remove the cable retaining clip and remove the cable from the transaxle.

5. Remove the shifter cable mounting bracket.

6. Tag and detach the electrical connectors for the speedometer, solenoid, neutral safety switch (inhibitor switch), the pulse generator, kickdown servo switch, and the oil temperature sensor.

7. Tag and disconnect the oil cooler lines at the transaxle.

8. Remove the bolt securing the fluid dipstick tube to the transaxle. Remove the dipstick and tube from the transaxle.

9. Remove the starter motor and position it aside.

10. Using special tool MZ203827 or equivalent, support the engine assembly.

11. Remove the rear roll stopper mounting bracket.

12. Remove the transaxle mount bracket.

13. Remove the upper transaxle mounting bolts.

14. Raise and safely support the vehicle.

15. Remove the front wheel assemblies.

16. Remove the right hand undercover.

17. Remove and discard the cotter pin, then disconnect the tie rod end from the steering knuckle.

18. Disconnect the stabilizer bar link from the damper fork.

19. Disconnect the damper fork from the lateral lower control arm.

20. Disconnect the lateral lower arm, and the compression arm lower ball joints from the steering knuckle.

21. Pry the halfshafts from the transaxle, and secure aside.

22. Remove the cover from the transaxle bellhousing.

23. Remove the engine front roll stopper through-bolt.

24. Remove the crossmember and the triangular right hand stay.

25. Remove the bolts holding the flexplate to the torque converter with a box wrench. Rotate the engine to bring the bolts into a position appropriate for removal, one at a time. After removing the bolts, push the torque converter toward the transaxle. This will prevent the converter from remaining intact with the engine, possibly damaging the converter.

26. Support the transaxle, using a transmission jack, and remove the transaxle lower coupling bolt.

➡**The coupling bolt threads from the engine side, into the transaxle, and is located just above the halfshaft opening.**

27. Slide the transaxle rearward and carefully lower it from the vehicle.

To install:

28. After the torque converter has been mounted on the transaxle, install the transaxle assembly to the engine. Install the mounting bolts and tighten to 35 ft. lbs. (48 Nm).

29. Install the transaxle lower coupling bolt and tighten to 21–25 ft. lbs. (29–34 Nm).

30. Connect the torque converter to the flexplate and tighten the bolts to 33–38 ft. lbs. (45–52 Nm).

31. Install the cover to the transaxle bellhousing and tighten the mounting bolts to 7 ft. lbs. (9 Nm).

32. Install the crossmember and tighten the front mounting bolts to 65 ft. lbs. (88 Nm) and the rear bolt to 54 ft. lbs. (73 Nm). Install the front engine roll stopper through-bolt and lightly tighten. Once the full weight of the engine is on the mounts, tighten the bolt to 42 ft. lbs. (57 Nm).

33. Install the triangular stay bracket and tighten the mounting bolts to 65 ft. lbs. (88 Nm).

34. Install the halfshafts, using new circlips on the axle ends.

❊❊ WARNING

When installing the axleshaft, keep the inboard joint straight in relation to the axle, so as not to damage the oil seal lip of the transaxle with the serrated part of the halfshaft.

35. Connect the tie rod and ball joints to the steering knuckle. Tighten the ball joint self-locking nuts to 48 ft. lbs. (65 Nm). Tighten the tie rod end nut to 21 ft. lbs. (28 Nm) and secure with a new cotter pin.

36. Connect the damper fork to the lower control arm and tighten the through-bolt to 65 ft. lbs. (88 Nm).

37. Connect the stabilizer link to the damper fork, and tighten the self-locking nut to 29 ft. lbs. (39 Nm).

38. Install the undercover.

39. Install the wheels and carefully lower the vehicle.

40. Install the transaxle mount bracket to the transaxle, and tighten the mounting nuts to 32 ft. lbs. (43 Nm).

41. Install the rear roll stopper mounting bracket.

42. Remove the engine support. Tighten the transaxle mount through-bolt to 51 ft. lbs. (69 Nm) and tighten the front engine roll stopper through-bolt.

43. Install the upper transaxle mounting bolts and tighten to 35 ft. lbs. (48 Nm).

44. Install the starter motor.

45. Install the dipstick tube and the dipstick.

46. Install the shifter cable mounting bracket.

47. Connect the shifter lever and tighten the retaining nut to 14 ft. lbs. (19 Nm).

48. Connect the oil cooler lines and secure with clamps.

49. Attach the electrical connectors for the speedometer, solenoid, neutral safety switch (inhibitor switch), the pulse generator, kickdown servo switch and oil temperature sensor.

50. Install the air cleaner and the air intake hose.

51. Connect the negative battery cable.

52. Make sure the vehicle is level, and refill the transaxle. Start the engine and allow to idle for 2 minutes. Apply parking brake and move selector through each gear position, ending in **N**. Recheck fluid level and add if necessary. Fluid level should be between the marks in the HOT range.

53. Check the transaxle for proper operation. Make sure the reverse lights come on when in reverse and the engine starts only in **P** or **N**.

Mirage

➡**If the vehicle is going to be rolled on its wheels while the halfshafts are out of the vehicle, obtain two outer CV-joints or proper equivalent tools and install to the hubs. If the vehicle is rolled without the proper torque applied to the front wheel bearings, the bearings will no longer be usable.**

1. Disconnect the negative battery cable then the positive battery cable.

2. Remove the battery and battery tray.

3. Remove the air hose and air cleaner assembly.

4. Raise the vehicle and support safely.

5. Remove the under guard pan.

6. Drain the transaxle oil into a suitable container.

7. If equipped with 1.6L engine, remove the tension rod.

8. Disconnect the control cable and cooler lines.

9. On 3-speed transaxles, disconnect the throttle control cable.

10. On 4-speed transaxles, perform the following:
   a. Detach the shift control solenoid valve connector.
   b. Disconnect the inhibitor switch and kickdown servo switch.
   c. Disconnect the pulse generator and oil temperature sensor.

11. Disconnect the speedometer cable and remove the starter.

12. Remove the transaxle mounting bolts and bracket.

13. Disconnect the stabilizer bar from the lower control arm.

14. Disconnect the steering tie rod end and the ball joint from the steering arm.

15. Remove the halfshafts at the inboard side from the transaxle. Tie the joint assembly aside.

➡**It is not necessary to disconnect the halfshafts from the wheel hubs.**

16. Support the engine and remove the center member.

17. Remove the bellhousing cover and remove the driveplate bolts.

18. Remove the transaxle assembly lower connecting bolt, located just over the halfshaft opening.

19. Properly support the transaxle assembly, then lower it, moving it to the right for clearance.

To install:

20. After the torque converter has been mounted on the transaxle, install the transaxle assembly on the engine. Install the mounting bolts and tighten to 31–40 ft. lbs. (43–55 Nm) on 1990–92 models and 35 ft. lbs. (48 Nm) on 1993–00 models.

21. Tighten the driveplate bolts to 33–38 ft. lbs. (46–53 Nm). Install the bellhousing cover.

22. Install the center member.

23. Replace the circlips and install the halfshafts to the transaxle.

24. Install the tie rods, ball joints and stabilizer links to the steering arm.

25. Install the transaxle mounting bracket and bolts.

26. Install the starter.

27. Connect the speedometer cable.

28. Connect the inhibitor switch, kickdown servo switch, the pulse generator and oil temperature sensor, if disconnected.

29. Connect the shift control solenoid valve connector.

30. Connect the control cables and oil cooler lines.

31. Install the tension rod, if removed.

32. Install the air cleaner assembly.

33. Install the battery tray and battery.

34. Connect the positive then the negative terminal.

35. Refill with Dexron® II, Mopar ATF Plus type 7176 or equivalent, automatic transaxle fluid.

36. Start the engine and allow to idle for two minutes. Apply parking brake and move selector through each gear position, ending in **N**. Recheck fluid level and add if necessary. Fluid level should be between the marks in the HOT range.

ADJUSTMENTS

Shifter Control Cable Adjustment

1. The shifter cable adjustment is done at the neutral safety switch (inhibitor switch). Locate the switch on the transaxle and note the alignment holes in the arm and the body of the switch. Place the selector lever in **N**. Place the manual lever of the transaxle in the neutral position.

2. Check alignment of the hole in the manual control lever to the hole in the inhibitor switch body. If the holes do not align, adjustment is required.

3. To adjust, loosen the nut on the cable end and pull the cable end by hand until the alignment holes match. Tighten the nut. Check that the transaxle shifts and conforms to the positions of the selector lever.

Throttle Valve Cable

The throttle valve adjustment applies only to the 1990–96 Mirage.

1. Place selector lever and manual control lever in **N** position.

2. Loosen adjusting nut. While lightly pulling on control cable tighten mounting nut to 7–10 ft. lbs. (10–14 Nm).

3. When adjustment is complete, be sure selector lever is still in the **N** position. Verify all functions correspond to the position indicated on the selector lever.

Halfshafts

The halfshaft removal and installation and overhaul are the same as a manual transaxle. Please refer to Manual Transaxle in this Section

TRANSFER CASE

The only model covered by this manual equipped with a transfer case is the 1990–93 AWD Galant.

Rear Output Shaft Seal

REMOVAL & INSTALLATION

♦ **See Figures 49 and 50**

1. Raise and support the vehicle safely.
2. Remove the propeller shaft from the transfer

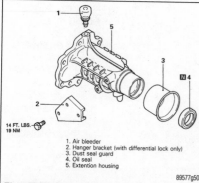

14 FT. LBS.
19 NM

1. Air bleeder
2. Hanger bracket (with differential lock only)
3. Dust seal guard
4. Oil seal
5. Extention housing

89577g50

Fig. 49 Exploded view of the transfer case extension housing and related components

assembly. Place a drain pan under the rear of the transfer assembly to catch any fluid that leaks out.

3. Using a flat-bladed prying tool, carefully remove the oil seal from the transfer dust seal guard.

To install:

4. Using proper size seal driver tool, install the seal into the dust seal guard and the transfer assembly.
5. Install the rear propeller shaft.
6. Carefully lower the vehicle and inspect the transfer assembly fluid level.

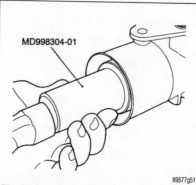

MD998304-01

89577g51

Fig. 50 Install the oil seal using the proper sized driver and a hammer

Transfer Case Assembly

REMOVAL & INSTALLATION

1. Disconnect the battery negative cable.
2. Raise the vehicle and support safely. Drain the transfer oil.
3. Disconnect the front exhaust pipe.
4. Unbolt the transfer case assembly and remove by sliding it off the rear driveshaft. Be careful not to damage the oil seal in the transfer case output housing. Do not let the rear driveshaft hang; suspend it from a frame piece. Cover the opening in the transaxle and transfer case to keep oil from dripping and to keep dirt out.
5. Lubricate the driveshaft sleeve yoke and oil seal lip on the transfer extension housing. Install the transfer case assembly to the transaxle. Use care when installing the rear driveshaft to the transfer case output shaft.
6. Tighten the transfer case to transaxle bolts to 40–43 ft. lbs. (55–60 Nm) with manual transaxle; 43–58 ft. lbs. (60–80 Nm) with automatic transaxle.
7. Install the exhaust pipe using a new gasket. Install removed bumper components.
8. Refill the transfer case and check oil levels in transaxle and transfer case.

DRIVELINE

The only model covered by this manual equipped with a driveshaft is the 1990–93 AWD Galant.

Driveshaft and U-Joints

REMOVAL & INSTALLATION

♦ **See Figures 51 and 52**

1. Disconnect the negative battery cable. Raise the vehicle and support safely.
2. The rear driveshaft is a 3-piece unit, with a front, center and rear propeller shaft. Remove the nuts and insulators from the center support bearing. Work carefully. There will be a number of spacers which will differ from vehicle to vehicle. Check the number of spacers and write down their locations for reference during reassembly.
3. Matchmark the rear differential companion flange and the rear driveshaft flange yoke. Remove the companion shaft bolts and remove the driveshaft, keeping it as straight as possible so as to ensure that the boot is not damaged or pinched. Use care to keep from damaging the oil seal in the output housing of the transfer case.

➡**Damage to the boot can be avoided and work will be easier if a piece of cloth or similar material is inserted in the boot.**

4. Do not lower the rear of the vehicle or oil will flow from the transfer case. Cover the opening to keep dirt out.

To install:

5. Position the driveshaft in the vehicle, making sure to align the matchmarks at the rear yoke.
6. Install the bolts at the rear differential flange and tighten to 22–25 ft. lbs. (30–35 Nm).

7. Install the center support bearing with all spacers in place. Tighten the retaining nuts to 22–25 ft. lbs. (30–35 Nm).
8. Check the fluid levels in the transfer case and rear differential case.

U-JOINT REPLACEMENT

1. Make mating marks on the yoke and the universal joint that is to be disassembled. Remove the snaprings from the yoke with snapring pliers.

2. Force out the bearing journals from the yoke using a large C-clamp. Install a collar on the fixed side of the C-clamp. Press the journal bearing into the collar by applying pressure with the C-clamp, on the opposite side.

3. Pull the journal bearing from the yoke.

➡**If the journal bearing is hard to remove, strike the yoke with a plastic hammer.**

4. Press the journal shaft using C-clamp or similar tool, to remove the remaining bearings.

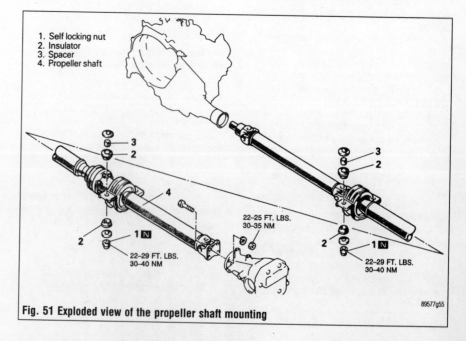

1. Self locking nut
2. Insulator
3. Spacer
4. Propeller shaft

22–25 FT. LBS.
30–35 NM

22–29 FT. LBS.
30–40 NM

22–29 FT. LBS.
30–40 NM

89577g55

Fig. 51 Exploded view of the propeller shaft mounting

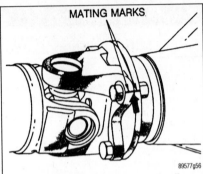

Fig. 52 Apply mating marks on the flange yoke and differential companion flange

5. Once all bearings are removed, remove the journal.

To install:

6. Apply multi-purpose grease to the shafts, grease sumps, dust seal lips and needle roller bearings of the replacement U-joint. Do not apply excessive grease. Otherwise, faulty fitting of bearing caps and errors in selection of snaprings may result.

7. Press fit the journal bearings to the yoke using a C-clamp as follows:

   a. Install a solid base onto the bottom of the C-clamp.

   b. Insert both bearings into the yoke. Hold and press fit them by tightening the C-clamp.

   c. Install snaprings of the same thickness onto both sides of each yoke.

   d. Press the bearing and journal into one

side, using a brass bar with diameter of 0.59 in. (15mm).

8. Measure the clearance between the snapring and the groove wall of the yoke with a feeler gauge. If the clearance exceeds 0.0008–0.0024 in. (0.02–0.06mm), the snap rings should be replaced.

DRIVESHAFT BALANCING

Driveshaft balancing is a process best left for a professional with the proper equipment. Makeshift methods using hose clamps or similar devices can work, but the process of correcting the imbalance in this manner is very tough and extremely time consuming.

Many machine shops can balance driveshafts; some parts stores and jobbers can also balance driveshafts using outside contractors.

Center Bearing

REMOVAL & INSTALLATION

1. Place mating marks on the companion flange and the Lobro joint assembly.

2. Remove the Lobro joint installation bolts. Separate the Lobro joint from the companion flange.

3. Place mating marks on the center yoke and center propeller shaft, and the companion flange and the rear propeller shaft.

4. Remove the self-locking nuts. Remove the center yoke and companion flange.

5. Place mating marks on the center bearing assembly front bracket and the center propeller shaft, and the center bearing assembly rear bracket and the rear propeller shaft. Remove the center bearing bracket.

➡**The mounting rubber can not be removed from the center bearing bracket.**

6. Pull out the front and rear center bearings with a commercially available puller.

To install:

7. Apply multi-purpose grease to the center bearing front and rear grease grooves and to the dust seal lip. Be sure to fit the bearing into the rubber mount groove on the center bearing bracket.

➡**Face the bearing dust seal to the side of the center bearing bracket mating mark.**

8. Assemble the center bearing to the center propeller shaft and rear propeller shaft. Face the side onto which the center bearing bracket mating marks is placed and the dust seal is installed toward the side of the center propeller shaft and rear propeller shaft.

9. Apply a thin and even coat of the grease, enclosed with the repair kit, to the rubber packing on the companion flange. Align the mating marks on the center propeller shaft and the companion flange, then press fit the center bearing with self-locking nuts.

10. Install the Lobro joint assembly installation bolts. Secure the companion flange and Lobro joint assembly with the installation bolts. Check for grease leakage from the Lobro joint boot and companion flange installation parts.

REAR AXLE DIFFERENTIAL

The only model covered by this manual equipped with a rear axle differential is the 1990–93 AWD Galant.

Rear Halfshaft and Seal

REMOVAL & INSTALLATION

◆ **See Figures 53 and 54**

1. Disconnect the negative battery cable. Raise the vehicle and support safely.

2. Remove the bolts that attach the rear halfshaft to the companion flange.

3. Use a prybar to pry the inner shaft out of the

differential case. Don't insert the prybar too far or the seal could be damaged.

4. Remove the rear driveshaft from the vehicle.

5. If necessary, carefully pry the oil seal from the rear differential using a flat tipped prying tool.

To install:

6. Install a new oil seal into the rear differential housing using proper size driver.

7. Replace the circlip and install the rear driveshaft to the differential case. Make sure it snaps in place.

8. Install the companion flange bolts and tighten to 40–47 ft. lbs. (55–65 Nm).

9. Check the fluid level in the rear differential.

Stub Axle Shaft, Bearing and Seal

REMOVAL & INSTALLATION

1. Disconnect the negative battery cable.

2. Raise and support the vehicle safely.

3. Remove the tire and wheel assembly from the vehicle.

4. If equipped with ABS, remove the rear wheel speed sensor.

➡**Be cautious to ensure that the tip of the pole piece on the rear speed sensor does not come in contact with other parts during removal. Sensor damage could occur.**

5. Remove the rear caliper and support assembly out of the way. Remove the brake disc.

6. Remove the driveshaft and companion flange installation bolts, nuts and washers. Move the end of shaft slightly to access the self-locking nut.

7. Using axle holding tool MB9b11-01 or equivalent, secure the rear axle shaft in position, then remove the self-locking nut.

8. Using puller and adapter MB9b11-01 and MB9b41-01 or equivalents, remove the rear axle shaft from the trailing arm.

9. If equipped with ABS, remove the rear rotor from the axle assembly using collar and press. The rotor is a press fit.

10. Remove the outer bearing and dust cover concurrently from the axle shaft using a press.

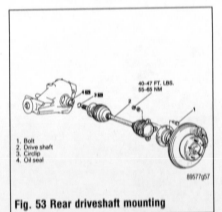

Fig. 53 Rear driveshaft mounting

1. Bolt
2. Drive shaft
3. Circlip
4. Oil seal

40–47 FT. LBS. 55–65 NM

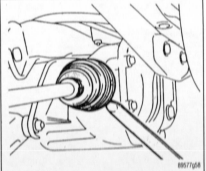

Fig. 54 Remove the driveshaft from the differential carrier with a prybar

11. Using puller, remove the oil seal and inner bearing from the trailing arm.

12. Inspect the companion flange and axle shaft for wear or damage. Inspect the dust cover for deformation or damage. Inspect the bearings for burning or declaration. Replace components as required.

To install:

13. Using the proper driver, press fit the inner bearing onto the trailing arm. Press fit the oil seal onto the trailing arm with the depression in the oil seal facing upward, and until it contacts the shoulder on the inner arm.

➡**When tapping the oil seal in, use a plastic hammer to lightly tap the top and circumference of the seal installation tool, press fitting gradually and evenly.**

14. Press fit the dust covers onto the axle until it contacts the axle shaft shoulder. Install the innermost cover so the depression is facing upward.

➡**When tapping the oil seal in, use a plastic hammer to lightly tap the top and circumference of the seal installation tool, press fitting gradually and evenly.**

15. Apply multi-purpose grease around the entire circumference of the inner side of the outer bearing seal lip. Press fit the outer bearing to the axle shaft so that the bearing seal lip surface is facing towards the axle shaft flange.

16. Press fit the rear rotor to the axle shaft with the rear rotor groove surface towards the axle shaft flange.

17. Install the rear axle shaft to the trailing arm temporarily. Install the companion flange to the rear axle shaft, then install a new self-locking nut.

18. While holding the rear axle shaft in position using holding fixture tool MB9g67-01 or equivalent, tighten a new self-locking nut to 159 ft. lbs. (220 Nm).

19. Install the drive shaft nuts, washers and bolts. Tighten to 40–47 ft. lbs. (55–65 Nm).

20. Install the rear brake disc, caliper assembly and parking brake.

21. Install the tire and wheel assembly and lower the vehicle. Check the parking brake stroke and adjust as required.

22. Before moving the vehicle, pump the brakes until a firm pedal is achieved.

Pinion Seal

REMOVAL & INSTALLATION

1. Raise the vehicle and support safely.

2. Matchmark the driveshaft and companion flange and remove the shaft. Don't let it hang from the transaxle. Tie it up to the underbody.

3. Hold the companion flange stationary and remove the large self-locking nut in the center of the companion flange.

4. Using a puller, remove the flange. Pry the old seal out.

To install:

5. Apply a thin coat of multi-purpose grease to the seal lip and the companion flange seal contacting surface. Install the new seal with an appropriate driver.

6. Install the companion flange. Install a new locknut and torque to 116–159 ft. lbs. (157–220 Nm). The rotation torque of the drive pinion should be about 4 inch lbs. for new or reused, oiled bearings.

7. Install the driveshaft.

Axle Housing Assembly

REMOVAL & INSTALLATION

1. Raise the vehicle and support safely.

2. Drain the differential gear oil and remove the center exhaust pipe.

3. Matchmark and remove the rear driveshaft.

4. Remove the rear halfshafts.

5. Remove the center exhaust pipe and muffler assembly, as required.

6. Remove or disconnect the 4 wheel steering oil pump.

7. The large mounting bolts that hold the differential carrier support plate to the underbody may use self-locking nuts. Before removing them, support the rear axle assembly in the middle with a transaxle jack. Remove the nuts, then remove the support plate(s) and the square dynamic damper from the rear of the carrier.

8. Lower the differential carrier and remove from the vehicle.

To install:

9. Raise the rear differential carrier into position and install support member bolts. Install new locknuts on all support bolts.

10. Install the 4 wheel steering oil pump.

11. Install new circlips on both rear driveshafts and install.

12. Install the propeller shaft.

13. Install the center exhaust pipe and muffler.

14. Lower the vehicle.

15. With the vehicle level, fill the rear differential.

TORQUE SPECIFICATIONS

Components	English	Metric
Automatic transaxle-to-engine mounting bolts		
Diamante models	54 ft. lbs.	75 Nm
1990-92 Mirage	31-40 ft. lbs.	43-55 Nm
1993-00 Mirage	35 ft. lbs.	48 Nm
1990-93 Galant	32-39 ft. lbs.	43-55 Nm
1994-00 Galant	35 ft. lbs.	48 Nm
Axle hub nuts	145-188 ft. lbs.	200-260 Nm
Back-up lamp switch	22-25 ft. lbs.	30-35 Nm
Clutch release fork fulcrum	25 ft. lbs.	35 Nm
Driveshaft-to-rear differential flange bolts	22-25 ft. lbs.	30-35 Nm
Driveshaft center bearing support bracket mounting nuts	22-25 ft. lbs.	30-35 Nm
Halfshaft center bearing support bracket	33 ft. lbs.	45 Nm
Manual transaxle-to-engine mounting bolts		
1990-92 Mirage	31-40 ft. lbs.	43-55 Nm
1993-00 Mirage	35 ft. lbs.	48 Nm
1990-93 Galant	32-39 ft. lbs.	43-55 Nm
1994-00 Galant	35 ft. lbs.	48 Nm
Manual transaxle lower coupling bolt	22-25 ft. lbs.	30-35 Nm
Manual transaxle mount retaining nuts	32 ft. lbs.	48 Nm
Manual transaxle mount through-bolt	51 ft. lbs.	69 Nm
Park/neutral safety switch retaining bolts		
1990-97 Mirage and 1990-93 Galant	7-8 ft. lbs.	10-12 Nm
1994-00 Galant and 1998-00 Mirage	8 ft. lbs.	11 Nm
Diamante models	7-8 ft. lbs.	10-12 Nm
Pinion nut	116-159 ft. lbs.	157-220 Nm
Pressure plate-to-flywheel bolts		
1994-98 Galant	14 ft. lbs.	19 Nm
All other models	16 ft. lbs.	22 Nm
Rear halfshaft-to-companion flange bolts	40-47 ft. lbs.	55-65 Nm
Stub axle shaft hub nut	159 ft. lbs.	220 Nm
Throttle valve cable mounting nut	7-10 ft. lbs.	10-14 Nm
Torque converter-to-driveplate bolts	34-38 ft. lbs.	46-53 Nm
Transfer case-to-transaxle mounting bolts		
Manual transaxle	40-43 ft. lbs.	55-60 Nm
Automatic transaxle	43-58 ft. lbs.	60-80 Nm

93157c01

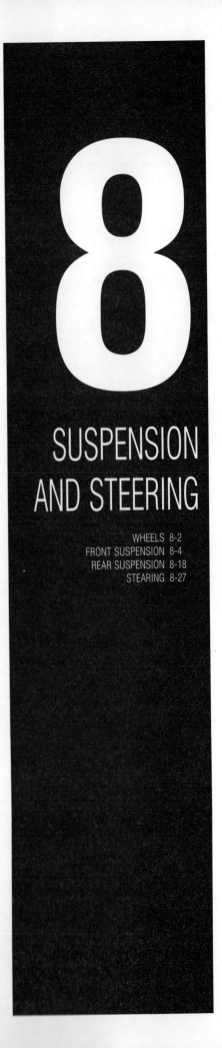

8

SUSPENSION AND STEERING

WHEELS

Wheel Assembly

REMOVAL & INSTALLATION

◆ **See Figures 1, 2, 3, and 4**

1. Park the vehicle on a level surface.
2. Remove the jack, tire iron and, if necessary, the spare tire from their storage compartments.
3. Check the owner's manual, or refer to Section 1 of this manual for the jacking points on your vehicle. Then, place the jack in the proper position.
4. If equipped with lug nut trim caps, remove them by either unscrewing or pulling them off the lug nuts, as appropriate. Consult the owner's manual, if necessary.
5. If equipped with a wheel cover or hub cap, insert the tapered end of the tire iron in the groove and pry off the cover.
6. Apply the parking brake and block the diagonally opposite wheel with a wheel chock or two.

➥Wheel chocks may be purchased at your local auto parts store, or a block of wood cut into wedges may be used. If possible, keep one or two of the chocks in your tire storage compartment, in case any of the tires has to be removed on the side of the road.

7. If equipped with an automatic transmission/transaxle, place the selector lever in P or Park; with a manual transmission/transaxle, place the shifter in Reverse.
8. With the tires still on the ground, use the tire iron/wrench to break the lug nuts loose.

➥If a nut is stuck, never use heat to loosen it or damage to the wheel and bearings may occur. If the nuts are seized, one or two heavy hammer blows directly on the end of the bolt usually loosens the rust. Be careful, as continued pounding will likely damage the brake drum or rotor.

9. Using the jack, raise the vehicle until the tire is clear of the ground. Support the vehicle safely using jackstands.
10. Remove the lug nuts, then remove the tire and wheel assembly.

To install:

11. Make sure the wheel and hub mating surfaces, as well as the wheel lug studs, are clean and free of all foreign material. Always remove rust from the wheel mounting surface and the brake rotor or drum. Failure to do so may cause the lug nuts to loosen in service.
12. Install the tire and wheel assembly and hand-tighten the lug nuts.

13. Using the tire wrench, tighten all the lug nuts, in a crisscross pattern, until they are snug.
14. Raise the vehicle and withdraw the jackstand, then lower the vehicle.
15. Using a torque wrench, tighten the lug nuts in a crisscross pattern to 65–80 ft. lbs. (90–110 Nm). Check your owner's manual or refer to Section 1 of this manual for the proper tightening sequence.

✳✳ WARNING

Do not overtighten the lug nuts, as this may cause the wheel studs to stretch or the brake disc (rotor) to warp.

16. If so equipped, install the wheel cover or hub cap. Make sure the valve stem protrudes through the proper opening before tapping the wheel cover into position.
17. If equipped, install the lug nut trim caps by pushing them or screwing them on, as applicable.
18. Remove the jack from under the vehicle, and place the jack and tire iron/wrench in their storage compartments. Remove the wheel chock(s).
19. If you have removed a flat or damaged tire, place it in the storage compartment of the vehicle and take it to your local repair station to have it fixed or replaced as soon as possible.

INSPECTION

Inspect the tires for lacerations, puncture marks, nails and other sharp objects. Repair or replace as necessary. Also check the tires for treadwear and air pressure as outlined in Section 1 of this manual.
Check the wheel assemblies for dents, cracks, rust and metal fatigue. Repair or replace as necessary.

Wheel Lug Studs

REMOVAL & INSTALLATION

With Disc Brakes

◆ **See Figures 5, 6, and 7**

Fig. 1 With the vehicle still on the ground, break the lug nuts loose

Fig. 3 Place the jackstands under the vehicle to support the vehicle's weight before attempting to remove the wheel(s)

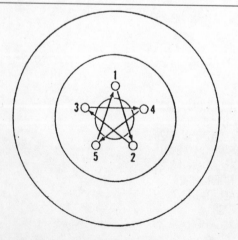

Fig. 2 After the lug nuts have been loosened, raise the vehicle using the jack until the tire is clear of the ground

Fig. 4 Typical wheel lug tightening sequence

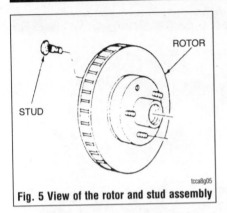

Fig. 5 View of the rotor and stud assembly

1. Raise and support the appropriate end of the vehicle safely using jackstands, then remove the wheel.

2. Remove the brake pads and caliper. Support the caliper aside using wire or a coat hanger. For details, please refer to Section 9 of this manual.

3. Remove the outer wheel bearing and lift off the rotor. For details on wheel bearing removal, installation and adjustment, please refer to Section 1 of this manual.

4. Properly support the rotor using press bars, then drive the stud out using an arbor press.

➡ **If a press is not available, CAREFULLY drive the old stud out using a blunt drift. MAKE SURE the rotor is properly and evenly supported or it may be damaged.**

To install:

5. Clean the stud hole with a wire brush and start the new stud with a hammer and drift pin. Do not use any lubricant or thread sealer.

6. Finish installing the stud with the press.

➡ **If a press is not available, start the lug stud through the bore in the hub, then position about 4 flat washers over the stud and thread the lug nut. Hold the hub/rotor while tightening the lug nut, and the stud should be drawn into position. MAKE SURE THE STUD IS FULLY SEATED, then remove the lug nut and washers.**

7. Install the rotor and adjust the wheel bearings.

8. Install the brake caliper and pads.

9. Install the wheel, then remove the jackstands and carefully lower the vehicle.

10. Tighten the lug nuts to the proper torque.

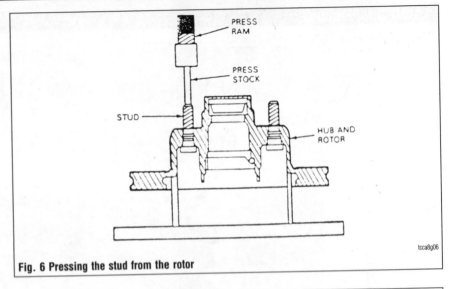

Fig. 6 Pressing the stud from the rotor

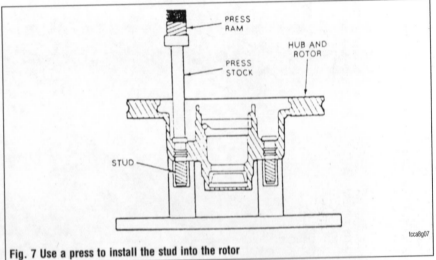

Fig. 7 Use a press to install the stud into the rotor

With Drum Brakes

◆ **See Figures 8, 9, and 10**

1. Raise the vehicle and safely support it with jackstands, then remove the wheel.

2. Remove the brake drum.

3. If necessary to provide clearance, remove the brake shoes, as outlined in Section 9 of this manual.

4. Using a large C-clamp and socket, press the stud from the axle flange.

5. Coat the serrated part of the stud with liquid soap and place it into the hole.

To install:

6. Position about 4 flat washers over the stud and thread the lug nut. Hold the flange while tightening the lug nut, and the stud should be drawn into position. MAKE SURE THE STUD IS FULLY SEATED, then remove the lug nut and washers.

7. If applicable, install the brake shoes.

8. Install the brake drum.

9. Install the wheel, then remove the jackstands and carefully lower the vehicle.

10. Tighten the lug nuts to the proper torque.

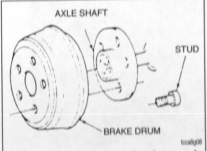

Fig. 8 Exploded view of the drum, axle flange and stud

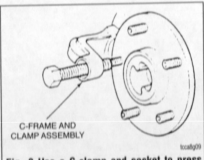

Fig. 9 Use a C-clamp and socket to press out the stud

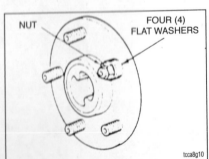

Fig. 10 Force the stud onto the axle flange using washers and a lug nut

FRONT SUSPENSION

1993–00 MIRAGE FRONT SUSPENSION COMPONENT LOCATIONS

1. Tie rod end
2. Lower ball joint
3. Lower control arm
4. Lower control arm mounts and bushings
5. Sway bar assembly
6. Sway bar link
7. Strut assembly
8. Hub and bearing assembly
9. Halfshaft assembly

93158p10

1994-98 GALANT FRONT SUSPENSION COMPONENT LOCATIONS

1. Shock and spring assembly
2. Steering knuckle assembly
3. Hub and bearing assembly
4. Lower ball joints
5. Compression lower control arm
6. Lateral lower control arm
7. Lower control arm mounts and bushings
8. Steering rack and pinion
9. Sway bar assembly
10. Halfshaft assembly
11. Upper ball joint
12. Upper control arm

1999–00 GALANT FRONT SUSPENSION COMPONENT LOCATIONS

1. Tie rod end
2. Lower ball joint
3. Lower control arm
4. Lower control arm mounts and bushings
5. Sway bar assembly
6. Strut assembly
7. Hub and bearing assembly
8. Halfshaft assembly

93156p07

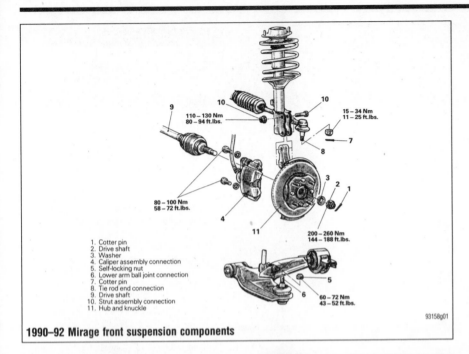

1. Cotter pin
2. Drive shaft
3. Washer
4. Caliper assembly connection
5. Self-locking nut
6. Lower arm ball joint connection
7. Cotter pin
8. Tie rod end connection
9. Drive shaft
10. Strut assembly connection
11. Hub and knuckle

93158g01

1990–92 Mirage front suspension components

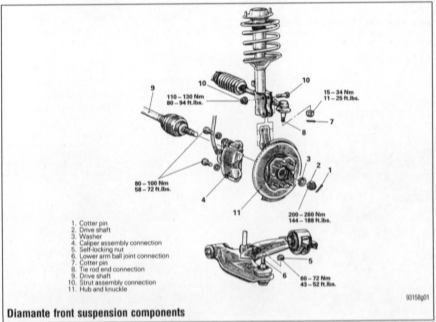

1. Cotter pin
2. Drive shaft
3. Washer
4. Caliper assembly connection
5. Self-locking nut
6. Lower arm ball joint connection
7. Cotter pin
8. Tie rod end connection
9. Drive shaft
10. Strut assembly connection
11. Hub and knuckle

93158g01

Diamante front suspension components

MacPherson Strut and Coil Spring

REMOVAL & INSTALLATION

Diamante, 1990–93 Galant, and 1999–00 Galant

1. Disconnect the negative battery cable.
2. Raise and safely support the vehicle.
3. Remove the brake hose and the tube bracket.

➡**Do not pry the brake hose and tube clamp away when removing it.**

4. If equipped with ABS, disconnect the front speed sensor mounting clamp from the strut.
5. Support the lower arm and remove the strut to knuckle bolts. Use a piece of wire to suspend the knuckle to keep the weight off the brake hose.
6. If equipped with Active Electronic Control Suspension (Active-ECS) perform the following:
   a. Loosen the nut that secures the air line to the to top of the strut and discard the O-ring.
   b. Remove the bolts that secure the actuator to the top of the strut and remove the component. Disconnect the wiring harness.

➡**Before removing the top bolts, make matchmarks on the body and the strut insulator for proper reassembly.**

7. Remove the strut upper nuts and remove the strut assembly from the vehicle.
To install:
8. Install the strut to the vehicle and tighten the upper mounting nuts to 33 ft. lbs. (45 Nm).
9. Align the strut to the knuckle and connect

with the mounting bolts. Tighten the mounting bolts to 70–76 ft. lbs. (90–105 Nm).
10. If equipped with Active-ECS, perform the following:
   a. Install the air line with a new O-ring.
   b. Install the actuator to the top of the strut. Connect the wiring harness.
11. Install the brake hose bracket and the ABS clamp, if equipped.
12. Install the wheel and tire assembly.
13. Have a front end alignment performed.

Mirage

◆ **See Figure 11**

1. Disconnect the negative battery cable.
2. Raise and safely support vehicle.
3. Remove the brake hose and tube bracket retainer bolt and bracket from the front strut. Do not pry the brake hose and tube clamp away when removing.
4. If equipped with ABS, disconnect the front speed sensor mounting clamp from the strut.
5. Support the lower arm using floor jack or equivalent. Remove the lower strut to knuckle bolts.

➡**Before removing the top bolts, make matchmarks on the body and the strut insulator for proper reassembly.**

6. Remove the strut upper mounting bolts.
7. Remove the strut assembly from the vehicle.
To install:
8. Install the strut to the vehicle and install the top mounting bolts. Tighten the mounting bolts to 29 ft. lbs. (40 Nm).
9. Position the strut on the knuckle and install the mounting bolts. While holding the head of the lower mounting bolt, tighten the nuts to 80–94 ft. lbs. (110–130 Nm).
10. Install the brake hose bracket and the ABS clamp, if equipped.
11. Install the wheel and tire assembly.
12. Have a front end alignment performed.

OVERHAUL

◆ **See Figures 12 thru 22**

1. Remove the strut assembly from the vehicle, as outlined earlier in this Section.
2. Mount the strut assembly into a suitable spring compressor.
3. Compress the strut approximately ¹/₂ its height after initial contact with the top cap.

❋❋❋ WARNING

Never bottom the spring or dampener rod!

4. Remove the center nut from the strut and remove the upper mounting bracket and bushings.
5. Remove the coil spring.
To install:
6. Install the compressed spring on the strut assembly.
7. Install the upper bushings and the mounting bracket. Install the nut and tighten it to 43 ft. lbs. (59 Nm).
8. Remove the strut from the spring compressor.
9. Install the strut into the vehicle.

44 Nm
32 ft.lbs.

N 4

5

2

25 Nm
18 ft.lbs.

1

3

108 – 127 Nm
80 – 94 ft.lbs. N

Removal steps
1. Brake hose clamp
2. Front speed sensor
   <Vehicles with ABS>
3. Bolts
4. Self-locking nut
5. Strut assembly

Caution
For vehicles with ABS, be careful when handling the pole piece at the tip of the speed sensor so as not to damage it by striking against other parts.

7923PGA6

Fig. 11 Front strut assembly and related parts—Mirage

REMOVAL & INSTALLATION

1994–98 Galant

♦ **See Figures 23 and 24**

1. Disconnect the negative battery cable.
2. Raise and safely support vehicle.
3. Remove the appropriate wheel assembly.
4. Disconnect the sway bar link from the damper fork.
5. Remove the damper fork lower through-bolt and upper pinch bolt. Remove the damper fork assembly.
6. Remove the shock absorber upper nuts and remove the shock and spring assembly from the vehicle.

To install:

7. Install the upper bracket assembly and position it so that the three bolts are in the correct position.
8. Install the upper bushing, washer, and locknut. Tighten the locknut to 18 ft. lbs.
9. Install the shock absorber and tighten the upper mounting nuts to 32 ft. lbs. (44 Nm).
10. Align the shock to the damper fork and install the damper fork. Tighten the lower through-bolt/nut to 65 ft. lbs. (88 Nm) and the upper pinch bolt to 76 ft. lbs. (103 Nm).
11. Connect the sway bar link to the damper fork and tighten the link nut to 29 ft. lbs. (39 Nm).
12. Install the wheel and tire assembly.
13. Have a front end alignment performed.

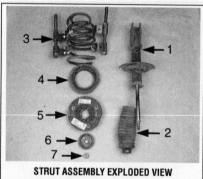

3
4
5
6
7
1
2

STRUT ASSEMBLY EXPLODED VIEW

1. Strut
2. Strut rod protective boot
3. Coil spring assembly
4. Spring seat upper washer
5. Upper strut mount and bearing
6. Top nut washer
7. Strut top nut

91148p36

91148p60

Fig. 12 Install a suitable strut spring compressor onto the strut spring

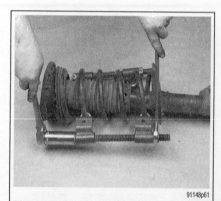

91148p61

Fig. 13 Tighten down the nuts on the top of the forcing screws on this type of spring compressor

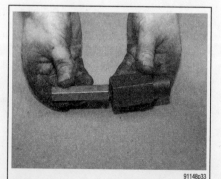

91148p33

Fig. 14 A special set of sockets is available to remove the nut from the top of the strut assembly

91148p32

Fig. 15 Place the larger socket over the nut . . .

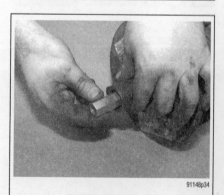

91148p34

Fig. 16 . . . then install the small socket over the strut rod

Fig. 17 Hold the small socket (strut rod) tight while loosening the larger socket (strut top nut) . . .

Fig. 18 . . . then remove the top nut from the strut . . .

Fig. 19 . . . and remove the washer underneath

Fig. 20 Remove the strut mount and bearing assembly

Fig. 21 Remove the upper spring seat washer

Fig. 22 Remove the coil spring assembly

Fig. 23 Remove the lower coil-over shock lower mounting bolt and nut from the control arm

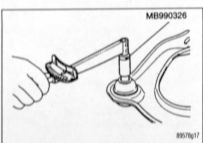

Fig. 24 Remove the three shock absorber-to-body retaining nuts, then remove the shock and spring from the vehicle

OVERHAUL

1. Remove the shock and spring assembly as outlined in this section.
2. Compress the coil spring with a special compression tool.
3. Remove the self-locking nut and washer. Remove the upper bushing, upper bracket assembly, the upper spring pad, and the collar.
4. Remove the other upper bushing, cup assembly, bump rubber, dust cover, and the coil spring. Carefully remove the coil spring compression tool.

To install:
5. Install the compressed coil spring to the shock

absorber assembly. Be sure to align the edge of coil spring to the stepped part of the spring seat. Install the dust cover, bump rubber, cup assembly, upper bushing, collar, and upper spring pad.
6. Install the shock and spring assembly as outlined in this section.

Upper Ball Joint

REMOVAL & INSTALLATION

The upper ball joint is an integral part of the upper control arm. If the ball joint becomes worn or damaged, the control arm must be replaced.

INSPECTION

♦ **See Figure 25**

1. Shake the ball joint stud a few times, then install the nut to the stud and use a preload socket (MB9c26 or equivalent) and an inch lb. torque wrench to measure the breakaway torque of the ball joint. The reading should be 3–22 inch lbs. (0.3–2.5 Nm).
2. If the measured value is higher than the standard, the upper control arm must be replaced.
3. If the value is lower than the standard, check that the ball joint turns smoothly without excessive plate. If so, the ball joint is OK.
4. Also, check the ball joint dust cover for cracks or other damage, if found, the upper control arm must be replaced.

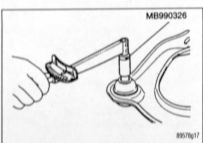

Fig. 25 Measure the torque of the ball joint to see if it needs to be replaced

Upper Control Arm

REMOVAL & INSTALLATION

Except 1994–98 Galant

These vehicles use a strut type front suspension. No upper control arm is used.

1994–98 Galant

◆ See Figures 26 thru 33

1. Raise and safely support the vehicle.
2. Remove the front wheel.
3. Disconnect the upper arm ball joint from the steering knuckle.
4. Remove the upper arm shaft mounting nuts from the body.
5. Remove the upper arm.

6. Remove the through-bolts that attach the upper arm to the shafts.
To install:
7. Assemble the upper arm to the shafts at the proper angle. Tighten the through-bolts and nuts to 41 ft. lbs. (57 Nm). The proper angle is 84–86°. After the arm and the shafts are connected at the right angle, measure dimensions A and B to insure correct assembly, and compare with the following specifications:
   - A O-ring: 11.8 in. (299.9mm)
   - B O-ring: 9.2 in. (234.0mm)
8. Install the control arm assembly to the body with new self-locking nuts. Tighten the self-locking nuts to 62 ft. lbs. (86 Nm).
9. Connect the upper arm ball joint to the steering knuckle with a new self-locking nut. Tighten the locking nut to 20 ft. lbs. (28 Nm).
10. Install the front wheel.
11. Lower the vehicle.
12. Have a front end alignment performed.

Lower Ball Joint

REMOVAL & INSTALLATION

The lower ball joint is an integral part of the lower control arm assembly, and can not be serviced separately. A worn or damaged ball joint requires replacement of lower control arm assembly.

INSPECTION

1. Raise and safely support the vehicles on jackstands. Allow the suspension to hang free.
2. Grasp the tire at the top and the bottom and move the top of the tire in and out.
3. Observe for any horizontal movement of the steering knuckle relative to the front lower control arm. If any movement is detected, replace the ball joint.
4. If the ball stud is disconnected from the steering knuckle and any looseness is detected, or if the ball stud can be twisted in its socket using finger pressure, replace the ball joint.

Lower Control Arm

REMOVAL & INSTALLATION

Diamante, 1990–93 Galant, and 1999–00 Galant

1. Disconnect the negative battery cable.
2. Raise the vehicle and support safely, allowing wheels and suspension to hang freely.
3. Remove the sway bar links from the lower control arm.
4. Disconnect the ball joint stud from the steering knuckle.
5. Remove the inner mounting frame through-bolt and nut.
6. Remove the rear mount bolts. Remove the clamp, if equipped.
7. Remove the rear rod bushing, if servicing.
To install:
8. Assemble the control arm and bushing.
9. Install the control arm to the vehicle and install the through-bolt. Replace the nut and snug temporarily.

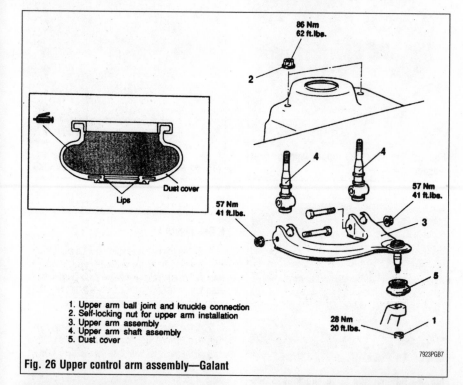

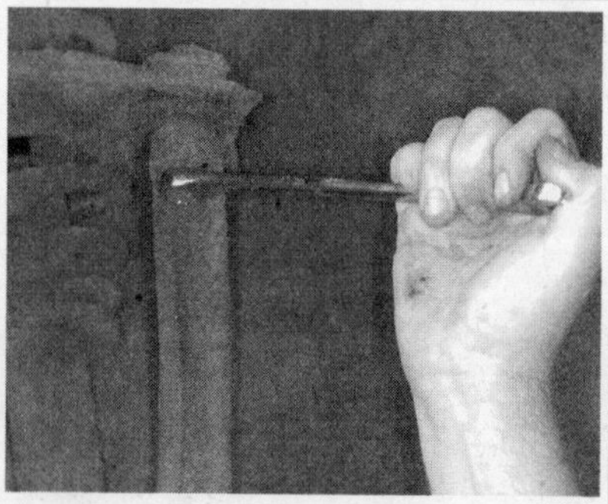

1. Upper arm ball joint and knuckle connection
2. Self-locking nut for upper arm installation
3. Upper arm assembly
4. Upper arm shaft assembly
5. Dust cover

7923PGB7

Fig. 26 Upper control arm assembly—Galant

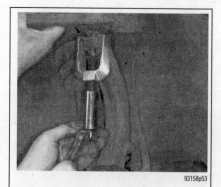

93158p56

Fig. 27 Remove the nut retaining the upper ball joint to the steering knuckle . . .

93158p53

Fig. 28 . . . then install a suitable puller like this to separate the connection

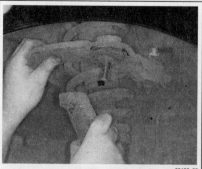

93158p52

Fig. 29 After the ball joint-to-steering knuckle connection is separated, remove the ball joint from the knuckle

Fig. 30 Remove the nuts retaining the upper control arm to the body . . .

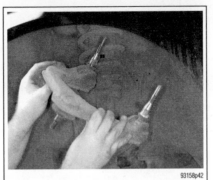

Fig. 31 . . . then remove the upper control arm from the vehicle

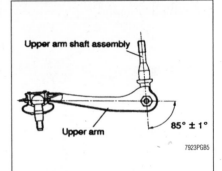

Fig. 32 Correct angle of control arm and shafts—Galant

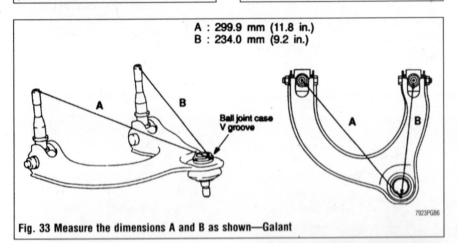

A : 299.9 mm (11.8 in.)
B : 234.0 mm (9.2 in.)

Ball joint case
V groove

Fig. 33 Measure the dimensions A and B as shown—Galant

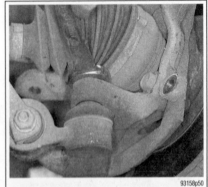

Fig. 34 Use a wrench to remove the retaining nuts from the . . .

10. Install the rear mount clamp, bolts and replacement nuts. Tighten the bolts to 72–87 ft. lbs. (100–120 Nm). Tighten the nuts to 29 ft. lbs. (40 Nm).

11. Connect the ball joint stud to the knuckle. Install a new nut and tighten to 43–52 ft. lbs. (60–72 Nm).

12. Install the sway bar and links.

13. Lower the vehicle to the floor for the final tightening of the frame mount through-bolt.

14. Once the full weight of the vehicle is on the floor, tighten the frame mount through-bolt nuts to 75–90 ft. lbs. (102–122 Nm).

15. Connect the negative battery cable.

16. Check the wheel alignment and adjust if necessary.

1994–98 Galant

♦ **See Figures 34 thru 40**

The lower lateral arm ball joint and the compression arm ball joint are integral components of the lateral arm and the compression arm respectively. If the ball joints are to be serviced, the arms must be replaced.

1. Raise and support the vehicle safely.

2. Disconnect both ball joint studs from the steering knuckle.

3. To remove the lower lateral arm, remove the crossmember brackets.

4. Remove the inner lateral arm mounting bolts and nut.

5. Remove the arm from the vehicle.

6. Remove the two bolts holding the compression arm.

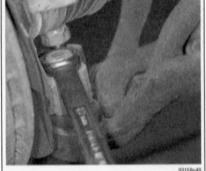

Fig. 35 . . . lower ball joint-to-steering knuckle junctions

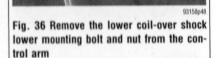

Fig. 36 Remove the lower coil-over shock lower mounting bolt and nut from the control arm

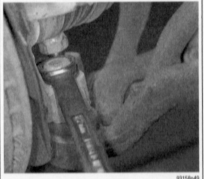

Fig. 37 Use a suitable prytool to separate . . .

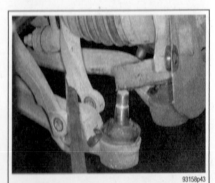

Fig. 38 . . . the lower ball joints from the steering knuckle

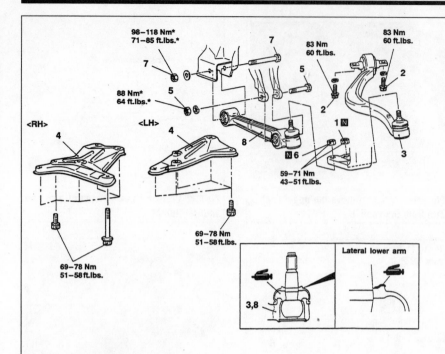

98–118 Nm*
71–85 ft.lbs.*

83 Nm
60 ft.lbs.

83 Nm
60 ft.lbs.

88 Nm*
64 ft.lbs.*

59–71 Nm
43–51 ft.lbs.

69–78 Nm
51–58 ft.lbs.

69–78 Nm
51–58 ft.lbs.

<RH> <LH>

Lateral lower arm

Compression lower arm assembly removal steps

1. Connection for compression lower arm ball joint and knuckle
2. Compression lower arm mounting bolt
3. Compression lower arm assembly

Lateral lower arm assembly removal steps

4. Stay
5. Shock absorber lower mounting bolt and nut
6. Connection for lateral lower arm ball joint and knuckle
7. Lateral lower arm mounting bolt and nut
8. Lateral lower arm assembly

Caution
*: Indicates parts which should be temporarily tightened, and then fully tightened with the vehicle on the ground in the unladen condition.

93158p62

Fig. 39 Remove the lower control arm-to-body mounting bolts, then remove the arm from the vehicle

7. Remove the compression arm.

To install:

8. Assemble the control arms and bushings.

9. Install the lateral control arm to the vehicle and install the inner mounting bolts. Install a new nut and snug temporarily.

10. Install the compression arm to the vehicle.

11. Connect the ball joint studs to the knuckle. Install new nuts and tighten to 43–51 ft. lbs. (59–71 Nm).

12. Lower the vehicle to the floor for the final tightening.

13. Once the full weight of the vehicle is on the suspension, tighten the lateral arm rear bolt to 71–85 ft. lbs. (98–118 Nm) and the front bolt to the damper fork to 64 ft. lbs. (88 Nm).

14. Tighten the bolts for the compression arm to 60 ft. lbs. (83 Nm).

15. Reinstall the crossmember brackets with their mounting bolts. Tighten the mounting bolts to 51–58 ft. lbs. (69–78 Nm).

16. Have a front end alignment performed.

Mirage

▶ See Figure 41

➡The suspension components should not be tightened until the vehicle's weight is resting on its wheels.

1. Raise the vehicle and support safely.

2. Remove the wheel and tire assembly.

3. Remove sway bar links or mounting nuts and bolts from lower control arm. Remove the joint cups and bushings.

4. Disconnect the ball joint stud from the steering knuckle.

5. Remove the inner lower arm mounting bolt and nut.

6. Remove the rear mount bolts from the retaining clamp. Remove the rear retainer clamp if equipped.

7. Remove the arm from the vehicle.

To install:

8. Install the control arm to the vehicle and install the inner mounting bolt. Install new nut and tighten to 78 ft. lbs. (108 Nm).

9. Install the rear mount clamp and bolts. Tighten the clamp mounting bolts to 65 ft. lbs. (90 Nm).

10. Connect the ball joint stud to the knuckle. Install a new nut and tighten to 43–52 ft. lbs. (60–72 Nm).

11. Install the sway bar and links.

12. Lower the vehicle to the floor for the final tightening of the inner frame mount bolt.

13. Install the wheel and tire assembly.

REMOVAL & INSTALLATION

Mirage

1. Disconnect the negative battery cable.

2. Raise and safely support vehicle.

3. Disassemble the links, remove the locknut, joint cup, bushing, and collar. Remove the sway bar link bolts.

4. It will be necessary to remove the center crossmember in order to remove the sway bar. The following steps are required to remove the crossmember:

   a. Remove the front exhaust pipe.

   b. Properly support the engine, remove the engine roll stopper bolts. Remove the four center member mounting bolts and remove the center member assembly.

   c. Remove both steering rack mounts.

   d. Disconnect the lower control arm from the crossmember.

   e. Support the crossmember, remove the mounting bolts and lower the crossmember for access.

5. Remove the sway bar mounts and remove the bar from the vehicle.

To install:

➡Note that the bar brackets are marked left and right.

6. Position the sway bar in the vehicle, then install the crossmember in the reverse order it was removed.

7. Install the sway bar mount brackets, and tighten the mounting bolts to 16 ft. lbs. (22 Nm).

8. Connect the sway bar links and tighten the bolts with rubber bushings, until the amount of bolt protrusion at the end of link mounting bolt is 0.87 inches (22mm).

9. Lower the vehicle and connect the negative battery cable.

1990–93 Galant

FWD VEHICLE

1. Disconnect the negative battery cable.

2. Raise and safely support vehicle.

3. Remove the front exhaust pipe and gasket from the manifold and using wire, tie it down and out of the way.

➡When relocating the front exhaust pipe, make sure the flexible joint is not bent more than a few degrees or damage to the pipe joint may occur.

4. Remove the center crossmember rear installation bolts.

5. Remove the sway bar link bolts. On the pillow-ball type, hold ball stud with a hex wrench and remove the self-locking nut with a box wrench.

6. Remove the sway bar bolts and mounts.

7. Remove the bar from the vehicle, as follows:

   a. Pull both ends of the sway bar toward the rear of the vehicle.

   b. Move the right sway bar end until the end clears the lower arm.

   c. Remove the sway bar out the right side of the vehicle.

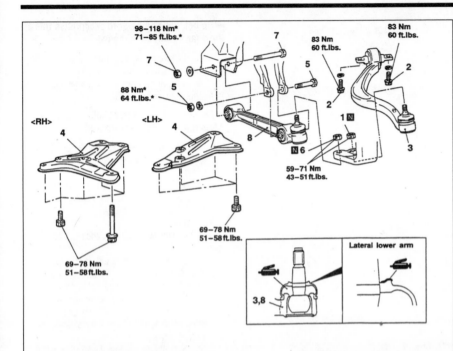

Compression lower arm assembly removal steps

1. Connection for compression lower arm ball joint and knuckle
2. Compression lower arm mounting bolt
3. Compression lower arm assembly

Lateral lower arm assembly removal steps

4. Stay
5. Shock absorber lower mounting bolt and nut
6. Connection for lateral lower arm ball joint and knuckle
7. Lateral lower arm mounting bolt and nut
8. Lateral lower arm assembly

Caution
*: Indicates parts which should be temporarily tightened, and then fully tightened with the vehicle on the ground in the unladen condition.

7923PG88

Fig. 40 Exploded view of the lower control arms—Galant

8. Inspect all bushings for wear and deterioration and replace as required.

9. Check the sway bar for damage, and replace as required.

To install:

10. Install the sway bar into the vehicle.

11. Install the sway bar brackets on the vehicle, following any side locating markings on the brackets. Temporarily tighten the sway bar bracket. Align the bushing end with the marked part of the sway bar and then fully tighten the sway bar bracket.

12. If equipped with the pillow-ball type mounting, install the sway bar links and link mounting nuts. Using a wrench, secure the ball studs at both ends of the sway bar link while tightening the mounting nuts. Tighten the nuts on the sway bar bolt so that the distance of bolt protrusion above the top of the nut is 0.63–0.70 in. (16–18mm).

13. Install the front exhaust pipe with new gasket in place. Tighten new self-locking nuts to 29 ft. lbs. (40 Nm).

14. Connect the negative battery cable.

AWD VEHICLE

1. Disconnect the negative battery cable.
2. Remove the front exhaust pipe.
3. Remove the center gusset and transfer assembly.
4. Using a wrench to secure the ball studs at both ends of the sway bar link, remove the sway bar link mounting nuts. Remove the sway bar link.

5. Remove the sway bar bracket installation bolt and the sway bar bracket and bushing.

6. Disconnect the sway bar coupling at the right lower control arm. Pull out the left side sway bar edge, pulling it out between the driveshaft and the lower arm. Pull out the right side bar below the lower arm.

To install:

7. Install the bar into the vehicle in the same manner as removal.

8. Temporarily tighten the sway bar bracket. Align the bushing end with the marked part of the sway bar and then fully tighten the stabilizer bar bracket.

9. Install and tighten the sway bar bracket bolt.

10. Install the sway bar links and link mounting nuts. Using a wrench, secure the ball studs at both ends of the sway bar link while tightening the mounting nuts. Tighten the nuts on the sway bar bolt so that the distance of bolt protrusion above the top of the nut is 0.63 to 0.70 in. (16 to 18mm).

11. Install the transfer assembly and gusset.

12. Install the left crossmember. Tighten the rear mounting bolts to 58 ft. lbs. (80 Nm) and the front mounting bolts to 72 ft. lbs. (100 Nm).

1994–00 Galant

♦ **See Figures 42, 43, and 44**

1. Disconnect the negative battery cable.
2. Raise and safely support the vehicle.

3. Disconnect the sway bar links by removing the self-locking nuts.

4. Remove the sway bar mounting brackets and bushings.

5. Remove the bar from the vehicle.

6. Inspect all components for wear or damage, and replace parts as needed.

To install:

7. Install the sway bar into the vehicle.

8. Loosely install the sway bar brackets on the vehicle.

9. Align the side locating markings on the sway bar, so that the marking on the bar, extends approximately 0.40 inches (10mm) from the inner edge of the mounting bracket, on both sides.

10. With the sway bar properly aligned, tighten the mounting bracket bolts to 28 ft. lbs. (39 Nm).

11. Connect the sway links to the damper fork and the sway bar. Tighten the locking nuts to 28 ft. lbs. (39 Nm).

12. Lower the vehicle and connect the negative battery cable.

Diamante

1. Disconnect the negative battery cable.
2. Raise the vehicle and support safely.
3. Remove the front exhaust pipe and engine undercover.
4. Remove the left and right frame members.
5. Remove the sway bar link.
6. Remove the sway bar brackets and remove the sway bar from the vehicle.

To install:

7. Note that the bar brackets are marked left and right. Lubricate all rubber parts and install the bushings, the sway bar and brackets.

8. Install the sway bar link.
9. Install the frame members.
10. Install the engine undercover and exhaust pipe.
11. Connect the negative battery cable.

Knuckle, Hub, and Bearing

REMOVAL & INSTALLATION

Diamante, Mirage, 1990–93 Galant, and 1999–00 Galant

♦ **See Figures 45, 46, and 47**

1. Disconnect the negative battery cable.

2. Raise the vehicle and support safely. Remove the halfshaft nut.

3. If equipped with ABS, remove the front wheel speed sensor.

4. If equipped with Active Electronic Control Suspension (Active-ECS), disconnect the height sensor from the lower control arm.

5. Remove the caliper assembly and brake pads. Suspend the caliper with a wire.

6. Using a suitable ball joint separator tool, disconnect the ball joint and tie rod end from the steering knuckle.

7. Remove the halfshaft from the hub.

8. Unbolt the lower end of the strut and remove the hub and steering knuckle assembly from the vehicle.

9. Remove the hub, bearings and races as follows:

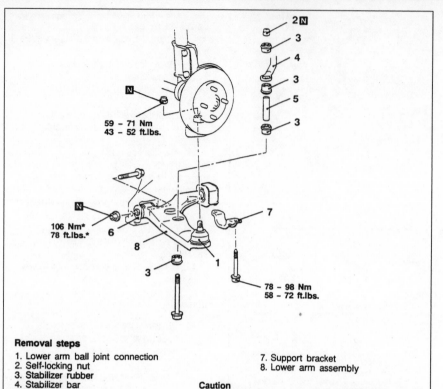

59 – 71 Nm
43 – 52 ft.lbs.

106 Nm*
78 ft.lbs.*

78 – 98 Nm
58 – 72 ft.lbs.

Removal steps

1. Lower arm ball joint connection
2. Self-locking nut
3. Stabilizer rubber
4. Stabilizer bar
5. Collar
6. Lower arm front bushing connection
7. Support bracket
8. Lower arm assembly

Caution

*: Indicates parts which should be temporarily tightened, and then fully tightened with the vehicle on the ground in the unladen condition.

7923PGB0

Fig. 41 Lower control arm assembly and related components—Mirage

➡ **Do not use a hammer to accomplish this or the bearing will be damaged.**

 a. Remove the oil seal from the axle side of the knuckle using a small prying tool.
 b. Remove the wheel bearing inner race from the front hub using a puller.

➡ **Be careful that the front hub does not fall when the inner race is removed.**

 c. Remove the snapring from the axle side of the knuckle. Remove the bearing from the knuckle using a puller.
 d. Once the bearing is removed, the bearing outer race can be removed by tapping out with a brass drift pin and a hammer.

To install:

10. Install the hub, bearings, and races as follows:

 a. Fill the wheel bearing with multipurpose grease. Apply a thin coating of multipurpose grease to the knuckle and bearing contact surfaces.
 b. Press the wheel bearing into the knuckle using an appropriate pressing tool. Once the bearing is installed, install the inner race using the proper driving tool.
 c. Drive the oil seal into the knuckle using the proper size driver. Drive seal into knuckle until it is flush with the knuckle end surface.
 d. Using pressing tool MB990998 or equivalent, mount the front hub assembly into the knuckle. Tighten the nut of the pressing tool to

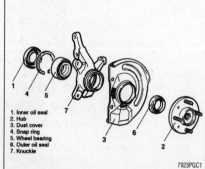

93158p60

Fig. 42 Remove the sway bar link self-locking nuts . . .

93158p59

Fig. 43 . . . then remove the sway bar links from the vehicle

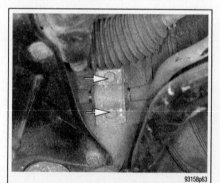

93158p63

Fig. 44 The sway bar mounting bracket and bushings are retained by 2 bolts

1. Inner oil seal
2. Hub
3. Dust cover
4. Snap ring
5. Wheel bearing
6. Outer oil seal
7. Knuckle

7923PGC1

Fig. 45 Front wheel bearing assembly exploded view—Mirage and Diamante

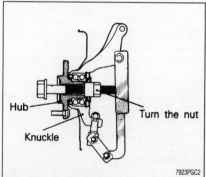

Hub

Knuckle

Turn the nut

7923PGC2

Fig. 46 Use of press tool for hub removal—Mirage and Diamante

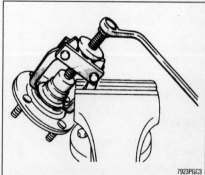

7923PGC3

Fig. 47 Removing inner race from hub—Mirage and Diamante

144–188 ft. lbs. (200–260 Nm). Rotate the hub to seat the bearing.

e. Mount the knuckle assembly in a vise. Check the hub assembly turning torque and end-play as follows:

• Using a torque wrench and socket MB990998 or equivalent, turn the hub in the knuckle assembly. Note the reading on the torque wrench and compare to the desired reading of 16 inch lbs. (1.8 Nm) or less. This is known as the breakaway torque.

• Check for roughness when turning the bearing.

• Mount a dial indicator on the hub so the pointer contacts the machined surface on the hub.

• Check the end-play.

• Compare the reading to the limit of 0.002 in. (0.05mm).

f. If the starting torque or the hub end-play are not within specifications while the nut is tightened to 144–188 ft. lbs. (200–260 Nm), the bearing, hub or knuckle have probably not been installed correctly. Repeat the disassembly and assembly procedure and recheck starting torque and end-play.

11. Install the hub and knuckle assembly onto the vehicle. Install the lower ball joint stud into the steer-ing knuckle and install a new nut. Tighten to 52 ft. lbs. (72 Nm).

12. Install the halfshaft into the hub/knuckle as-sembly.

13. Install the two front strut lower mounting bolts and tighten to 80–94 ft. lbs. (110–130 Nm) on Mirage or 65–76 ft. lbs. (90–105 Nm) on Diamante models.

14. Install the tie rod end and tighten the nut to 25 ft. lbs. (34 Nm) for Mirage and 21 ft. lbs. (29 Nm) on Diamante models

15. Install the brake disc and caliper assembly.

16. If equipped with Active-ECS, connect the height sensor and tighten the mounting bolt to 15 ft. lbs. (20 Nm).

17. Install the front speed sensor, if removed.

18. Install the washer and new locknut to the end of the halfshaft. Tighten the locknut snugly to 144–188 ft. lbs. (200–260 Nm).

19. Install the tire and wheel assembly onto the vehicle.

20. Lower the vehicle to the ground.

1994–98 Galant

♦ **See Figures 48 thru 58**

1. Raise the vehicle and support safely.
2. Remove the appropriate wheel assembly.

3. Remove the cotter pin, halfshaft nut and washer.

4. If equipped with ABS, remove the Vehicle Speed Sensor (VSS).

5. Remove the caliper and brake pads. Support the caliper out of the way using wire.

6. Remove the brake rotor from the hub assembly.

7. Disconnect the upper ball joint from the steering knuckle and pull the knuckle outward.

8. From the back of the knuckle, remove the four bolts securing the hub to the knuckle.

9. Remove the hub and bearing assembly from the knuckle.

➡ **The hub assembly is not serviceable and should not be disassembled.**

To install:

10. Install the hub to the steering knuckle and tighten the mounting bolts to 65 ft. lbs. (88 Nm).

11. Connect the upper ball joint to the steering knuckle and tighten the self-locking nut to 21 ft. lbs. (28 Nm).

12. Install the axle washer and nut. Tighten the nut to 145–188 ft. lbs. (200–260 Nm).

13. Position the rotor on the hub.

14. Install the caliper holder and the brake caliper.

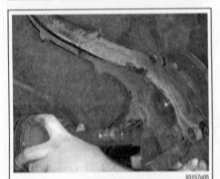

Fig. 48 Remove the cotter pin from the axle shaft . . .

Fig. 49 . . . then loosen the axle nut while the vehicle is still on the ground

Fig. 50 Using a suitable punch and hammer, gently tap the halfshaft out of the steering knuckle . . .

Fig. 51 . . . then slide the halfshaft out of the knuckle

Fig. 52 Remove the retaining clip, then remove the brake caliper hose from the steering knuckle

Fig. 53 Lift the knuckle up and remove it from the vehicle

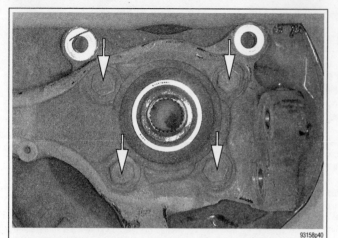

Fig. 54 To remove the hub and bearing assembly, unfasten the four retaining bolts . . .

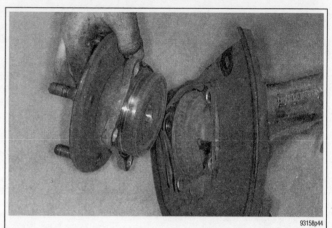

Fig. 55 . . . then remove the hub and bearing assembly from the knuckle

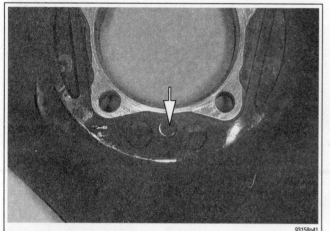

Fig. 56 If replacing the steering knuckle, you must remove the retaining bolt and transfer the brake dust shield . . .

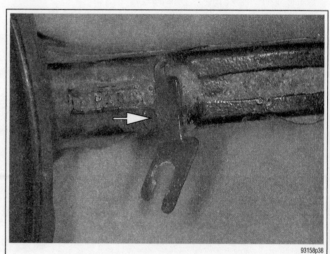

Fig. 57 . . . and the brake hose retaining clip to the new knuckle

15. If equipped with ABS, install the VSS.
16. Install the wheel assembly and lower the vehicle.

Wheel Alignment

If the tires are worn unevenly, if the vehicle is not stable on the highway or if the handling seems uneven in spirited driving, the wheel alignment should be checked. If an alignment problem is suspected, first check for improper tire inflation and other possible causes. These can be worn suspension or steering components, accident damage or even unmatched tires. If any worn or damaged components are found, they must be replaced before the wheels can be properly aligned. Wheel alignment requires very expensive equipment and involves minute adjustments which must be accurate; it should only be performed by a trained technician. Take your vehicle to a properly equipped shop.

Following is a description of the alignment angles which are adjustable on most vehicles and how they affect vehicle handling. Although these angles can apply to both the front and rear wheels, usually only the front suspension is adjustable.

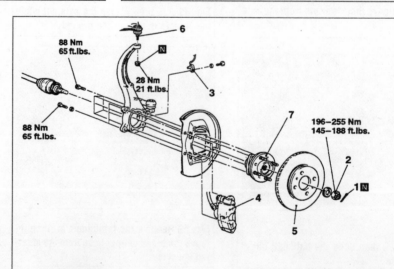

Removal steps

1. Cotter pin
2. Drive shaft nut
3. Front speed sensor <Vehicles with ABS>
4. Caliper assembly
5. Brake disc
6. Connection for upper arm
7. Front hub assembly

Caution
The front hub assembly should not be disassembled.

Fig. 58 Exploded view of the front hub removal—Galant

CASTER

▶ **See Figure 59**

Looking at a vehicle from the side, caster angle describes the steering axis rather than a wheel angle. The steering knuckle is attached to a control arm or strut at the top and a control arm at the bottom. The wheel pivots around the line between these points to steer the vehicle. When the upper point is tilted back, this is described as positive caster. Having a positive caster tends to make the wheels self-centering, increasing directional stability. Excessive positive caster makes the wheels hard to steer, while an uneven caster will cause a pull to one side. Overloading the vehicle or sagging rear springs will affect caster, as will raising the rear of the vehicle. If the rear of the vehicle is lower than normal, the caster becomes more positive.

CAMBER

▶ **See Figure 60**

Looking from the front of the vehicle, camber is the inward or outward tilt of the top of wheels. When the tops of the wheels are tilted in, this is negative camber; if they are tilted out, it is positive. In a turn, a slight amount of negative camber helps maximize contact of the tire with the road. However, too much negative camber compromises straight-line stability, increases bump steer and torque steer.

TOE

▶ **See Figure 61**

Looking down at the wheels from above the vehicle, toe angle is the distance between the front of the wheels, relative to the distance between the back of the wheels. If the wheels are closer at the front, they are said to be toed-in or to have negative toe. A small amount of negative toe enhances directional stability and provides a smoother ride on the highway.

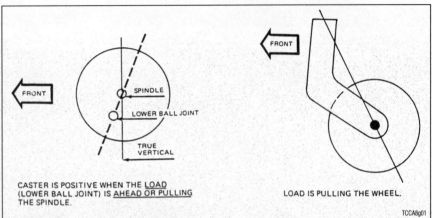

CASTER IS POSITIVE WHEN THE <u>LOAD</u> (LOWER BALL JOINT) IS <u>AHEAD OR PULLING</u> THE SPINDLE.

LOAD IS PULLING THE WHEEL.

TCCA8g01

Fig. 59 Caster affects straight-line stability. Caster wheels used on shopping carts, for example, employ positive caster

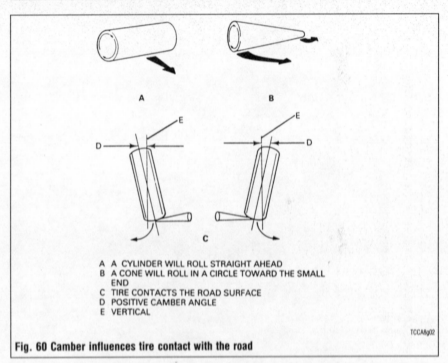

A A CYLINDER WILL ROLL STRAIGHT AHEAD
B A CONE WILL ROLL IN A CIRCLE TOWARD THE SMALL END
C TIRE CONTACTS THE ROAD SURFACE
D POSITIVE CAMBER ANGLE
E VERTICAL

TCCA8g02

Fig. 60 Camber influences tire contact with the road

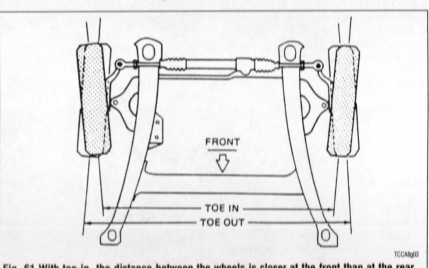

FRONT

TOE IN
TOE OUT

TCCA8g03

Fig. 61 With toe-in, the distance between the wheels is closer at the front than at the rear

REAR SUSPENSION

1993–00 MIRAGE REAR SUSPENSION COMPONENT LOCATIONS

1. Hub and bearing assembly
2. Lower control arm
3. Control link
4. Trailing arm
5. Strut assembly

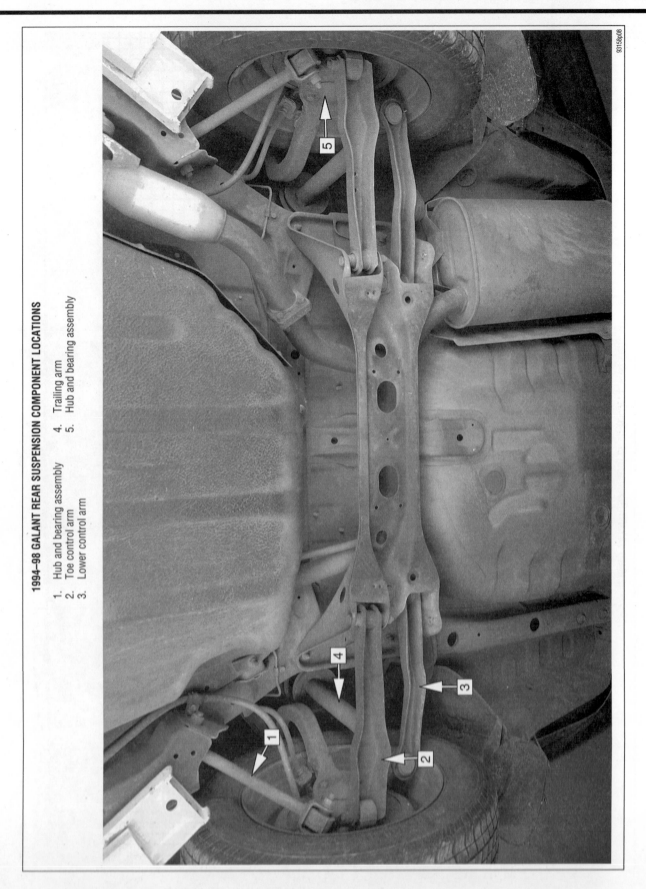

1994–98 GALANT REAR SUSPENSION COMPONENT LOCATIONS

1. Hub and bearing assembly
2. Toe control arm
3. Lower control arm
4. Trailing arm
5. Hub and bearing assembly

1999–00 GALANT REAR SUSPENSION COMPONENT LOCATIONS

1. Trailing arm
2. Hub and bearing assembly
3. Lower control arm
4. Strut assembly
5. Sway bar
6. Sway bar link
7. Steering knuckle
8. Toe control arm

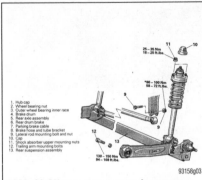

1990–92 Mirage rear suspension components

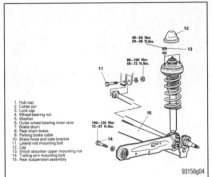

1990–93 Galant rear suspension components

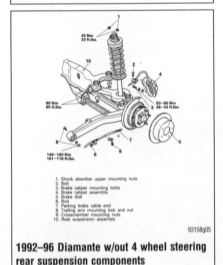

1992–96 Diamante w/out 4 wheel steering rear suspension components

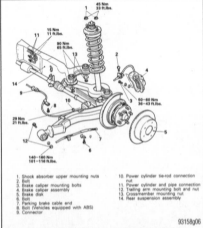

1992–96 Diamante with 4 wheel steering rear suspension components

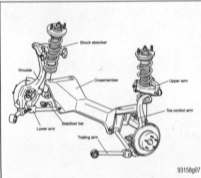

1997–00 Diamante rear suspension components

Strut And Coil Spring

REMOVAL & INSTALLATION

Diamante

1. Disconnect the negative battery cable.
2. Raise and properly support vehicle.
3. Remove both rear wheels.
4. Support the lower control arm with a jack.
5. Matchmark the positioning of the upper spring plate to the vehicle for reinstallation purposes.
6. If equipped with Active Electronic Control Suspension (Active-ECS), perform the following:
   a. Loosen the nut that secures the air line to

the to the top of the strut and discard the O-ring.
   b. Remove the bolts that secure the actuator to the top of the strut and remove the component. Disconnect the wiring harness.
7. Remove the shock absorber lower mounting bolt and remove the two nuts that secure the shock upper plate to the vehicle.
8. Lower the support jack and remove the shock from the vehicle.
To install:
9. Position the upper spring plate and install the strut. Use the support jack to assist with installation.
10. Tighten the upper strut mounting nuts to 33 ft. lbs. (45 Nm).
11. Tighten the lower strut mounting bolt to 71 ft. lbs. (98 Nm).
12. If equipped with Active-ECS perform the following:
   a. Using a new O-ring, tighten the nut that secures the air line to the to the top of the strut to 84 inch lbs. (9 Nm).
   b. Install the actuator to the top of the shock absorber and secure with mounting bolts. Connect the wiring harness.
13. Remove the support jack, install wheels and lower vehicle.
14. Connect the negative battery cable.

1990–93 Galant

FWD MODELS

➡The strut assembly is a load bearing component, therefore the vehicle chassis and

axle weight must be supported separately, requiring the use of two separate lifting devices.

1. Disconnect the negative battery cable.
2. Raise and support vehicle chassis.
3. Raise and support torsion axle and arm assembly slightly. Make sure the jack does not contact the lateral rod.

➡Always use a wooden block between the jack receptacle and the axle beam. Place the jack at the center of the axle beam.

4. Remove the trunk interior trim to gain access to the top mounting nuts.
5. If equipped with Active-ECS, perform the following steps:
   a. Label and disconnect the air tubes from the shock absorber.

➡Immediately plug or cap the lines with tape or similar product to prevent the entry of dirt into the system. Do NOT bend or crimp the air tubes. Plug or cover the air ports on the joint and actuator.

   b. Remove the O-ring and bushing.
   c. Remove the actuator assembly.
6. Remove the top cap and upper shock mounting nuts.
7. Remove the strut lower mounting bolt and remove the assembly from the vehicle.
To install:
8. Position the strut assembly so that the lower mounting bolt can be installed and lightly tightened.
9. Use the jack to raise or lower the axle assembly so that the top strut plate studs aligns through the body. Raise the jack to hold the strut assembly in position.
10. Install the top plate nuts on the studs. Tighten the upper shock mounting nuts to 29 ft. lbs. (40 Nm).
11. With the car on the ground, tighten the lower mounting bolt to 72 ft. lbs. (100 Nm).
12. If equipped with Active-ECS, assemble the actuator components in the following order:
   a. Install the adapter to the mounting bracket.
   b. Using new O-rings, connect the air line to the actuator. Tighten the locknuts to 6 ft. lbs. (9 Nm).
   c. Swab the air connectors with a solution of soapy water. Start the engine, cycle the suspension controls and observe the joints for any sign of air leaks.
13. Install top cap and interior trim.

AWD MODELS

1. Disconnect the negative battery cable.
2. Raise and support vehicle chassis.
3. Raise and support trailing arm assembly slightly.
4. Remove the trunk interior trim to gain access to the top mounting nuts.
5. Remove the top cap and upper shock mounting nuts.
6. Remove the brake tube bracket bolt.
7. Remove the shock lower mounting bolt and remove the assembly from the vehicle.
To install:
8. Position the strut assembly so that the lower mounting bolt can be installed and lightly tightened.
9. Use a jack to raise or lower the trailing arm, so that the top strut plate studs aligns through the

body. Raise the jack to hold the strut assembly in position.

10. Install the top plate nuts on the studs. Tighten the upper shock mounting nuts to 29 ft. lbs. (40 Nm).

11. With the car on the ground, tighten the lower mounting bolt to 65–80 ft. lbs. (90–110 Nm).

12. Connect the brake bracket and tighten the mounting bolt to 12 ft. lbs. (17 Nm).

13. Install the top cap and interior trim.

1994–00 Galant

♦ **See Figures 62, 63, and 64**

1. Raise and support the vehicle chassis.
2. Raise and support the lower control arm assembly slightly.
3. In order to gain access to the top mounting nuts, remove the rear seat as follows:

   a. While pulling the rear seat stopper outward, lift the lower cushion upward. Remove the lower cushion.

   b. Remove the seat back mounting bolts.

   c. Lift the seat back upward and remove the seat.

4. Remove the shock upper mounting nuts.
5. Remove the shock lower mounting bolt and remove the assembly from the vehicle.

To install:

6. Position the shock assembly so that the lower mounting bolt can be installed and lightly tightened.

7. Use a jack to raise or lower the lower control arm, so that the top shock plate studs align through the body. Raise the jack to hold the shock assembly in position.

8. Install the top plate nuts on the studs and tighten the mounting nuts to 32 ft. lbs. (44 Nm).

9. With the vehicle on the ground, tighten the lower mounting bolt to 71 ft. lbs. (98 Nm).

10. Install the rear seat back and cushion.

Mirage

1. Remove the trunk interior trim to gain access to the top mounting nuts.
2. Remove the top cap and upper shock mounting nuts.
3. Raise and support vehicle chassis.
4. Support the trailing arm assembly with a jack.
5. Matchmark the upper spring plate to the vehicle chassis for reassembly and remove the upper spring plate mounting nuts.
6. Remove the strut lower mounting bolt and remove the assembly from the vehicle.

To install:

7. Position the strut assembly so that the lower mounting bolt can be installed and lightly tightened.

8. Use a jack to raise or lower the axle assembly so that the top shock plate studs aligns through body. Raise the jack to hold the strut assembly in position.

9. Install the top plate nuts and tighten them to 20 ft. lbs. (27 Nm).

10. Lower the vehicle and tighten the lower mounting bolt to 65 ft. lbs. (90 Nm).

11. Install the top cap and interior trim.

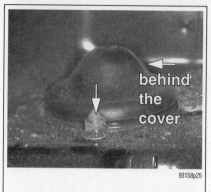

Fig. 62 Remove the two top mounting nuts

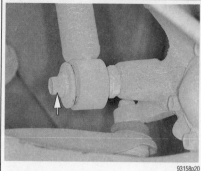

Fig. 63 Remove the shock lower mounting bolt

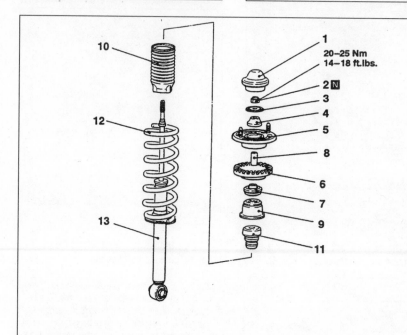

1. Cap	8. Collar
2. Self-locking nut	9. Cup
3. Washer	10. Dust cover
4. Upper bushing A	11. Bump rubber
5. Bracket	12. Coil spring
6. Spring pad	13. Shock absorber assembly
7. Upper bushing B	

Fig. 64 Exploded view of the rear shock absorber assembly—Galant and Mirage

OVERHAUL

Mirage and 1994–00 Galant

1. Remove the shock and spring assembly from the vehicle. Refer to the procedure above.
2. Use a coil spring compressor and compress the coil spring.
3. Remove the shock cap.
4. While holding the piston rod, remove the self-locking nut.
5. Remove the upper bracket assembly and spring pad.
6. Remove the collar, upper bushing, cup assembly, bump rubber and dust cover.
7. Remove the coil spring from the shock.

To install:

8. Align the end of the coil spring with the stepped part of the spring seat and install the compressed coil spring on the shock.

9. Install the dust cover, bump rubber, cup assembly, upper bushing, collar, upper spring pad and bracket assembly on the shock.

10. Install the upper bushing and washer on the piston rod.

11. Install a new self-locking nut on the piston rod. Temporarily tighten the nut.

12. Remove the spring compressor from the spring. Tighten the self-locking nut to 16 ft. lbs. (25 Nm).

13. Install the shock cap.

14. Install the shock and spring assembly into the vehicle. Refer to the procedure above.

Upper Control Arms

REMOVAL AND INSTALLATION

1990–93 Galant

1. Disconnect the negative battery cable.
2. Raise and safely support vehicle.
3. Remove the tire and wheel assembly.
4. Support the rear lower control arm.
5. Remove the brake line clamp bolt.
6. Remove the nut and separate the upper ball joint, using tool MB9f35 or equivalent, from the rear trailing arm/steering knuckle.

➡ **It is important to use proper method of joint separation when reusing joint. Damage can result from unapproved methods, resulting in possible joint failure.**

7. Matchmark the eccentric on the upper installation bolt and remove from the control arm.
8. Remove the upper arm from the vehicle.
   To install:
9. Install the arm to the vehicle and install the upper arm installation bolt. Align the matchmarks and tighten the nut snugly only.
10. Install the upper arm ball joint to the rear spindle assembly and install new nut. Tighten to 52 ft. lbs. (72 Nm).
11. Install the tire and wheel assembly.
12. Lower the vehicle until the suspension supports its weight.
13. Tighten the upper arm installation bolt to 116 ft. lbs. (160 Nm).
14. Check the rear wheel alignment.

1994–98 Galant

♦ **See Figures 65, 66, and 67**

1. Raise and safely support the vehicle.
2. Remove the wheel and tire assembly.
3. Remove the through-bolt securing the upper arm to the knuckle.
4. Remove the four bolts securing the upper arm to the body.
5. Remove the upper arm assembly.
6. Remove the through-bolts and nuts and remove the upper arm to body brackets.
   To install:
7. Install the upper arm to body brackets to the upper arm. Tighten the bolts and nuts to 41 ft. lbs. (57 Nm).
8. Install the upper arm to the vehicle and tighten the four bolts to 28 ft. lbs. (39 Nm).
9. Install the through-bolt securing the upper arm to the knuckle. Do not tighten the nut until the vehicle is on the floor at normal riding height.
10. Install the wheel and tire assembly.
11. Safely lower the vehicle to the floor and tighten the nut for the through-bolt to 71 ft. lbs. (98 Nm).
12. Check and adjust wheel alignment if necessary.

Diamante

1. Raise and properly support vehicle.
2. Remove appropriate wheel assembly.
3. Disconnect the sway bar and remove the strut assembly.

Fig. 65 Remove the through-bolt securing the upper arm to the knuckle

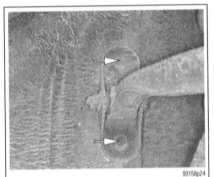

Fig. 66 Remove the bolts securing the upper arm to the body on the left and . . .

Fig. 67 . . . right side of the upper control arm

4. Support the trailing arm assembly and remove the self-locking nut connecting the control arm to the trailing arm.
5. Using a joint separation tool, disconnect the upper ball joint from the trailing arm.
6. Disconnect the control arm from the subframe and remove the assembly.
   To install:
7. Install the control arm to the subframe and lightly tighten the mounting bolt.
8. Connect the control arm to the trailing arm and tighten the self-locking nut to 54–61 ft. lbs. (75–89 Nm).
9. Install the strut assembly and connect the sway bar.
10. Install wheel and lower vehicle.
11. With full weight of vehicle on the ground, tighten the control arm to subframe bolt to 54–61 ft. lbs. (75–89 Nm).

12. Check rear wheel alignment and adjust if necessary.

Lower Control Arms

REMOVAL AND INSTALLATION

1990–93 Galant

1. Disconnect the negative battery cable.
2. Raise the vehicle and support safely.
3. Remove sway bar links or mounting nuts and bolts from lower control arm. Remove the joint cups and bushings, if equipped.
4. Disconnect the ball joint stud from the steering knuckle, using tool MB9f35 or equivalent.

➡ **It is important to use proper method when separating joints. Damage to joint could occur, resulting in possible failure.**

5. Remove the inner lower arm mounting bolts and nut.
6. Remove the rear mount bolts. Remove the rear retainer clamp if equipped.
7. Remove the arm from the vehicle.
8. Remove the rear rod bushing, if service is required.
   To install:
9. Assemble the control arm and bushing. Install the control arm to the vehicle and install the inner mounting bolts. Install new nut and snug temporarily.
10. Install the rear mount clamp, bolts and replacement nuts. Tighten the clamp mounting nuts to 34 ft. lbs. (47 Nm). Temporarily tighten the clamp mounting bolt. Once the weight of the vehicle is on the suspension, the bolt will be tightened to 72 ft. lbs. (100 Nm).
11. Connect the ball joint stud to the knuckle. Install a new nut and tighten to 43–52 ft. lbs. (60–72 Nm).
12. Install the sway bar and links.
13. Lower the vehicle to the floor for the final torquing of the inner frame mount bolt.
14. Once the full weight of the vehicle is on the suspension, tighten the inner lower arm mounting bolt nuts to 87 ft. lbs. (120 Nm). Tighten the inner clamp mounting bolt to 72 ft. lbs. (100 Nm).
15. Inspect all suspension bolts, making sure they all have been fully tightened.
16. Connect the negative battery cable.

1994–00 Galant

LOWER CONTROL ARM

♦ **See Figures 68 and 69**

1. Raise and support the vehicle safely.
2. Remove the appropriate wheel assembly.
3. If equipped with ABS, disconnect the speed sensor harness brackets from the lower control arm.
4. Disconnect the stabilizer bar link from the lower control arm.
5. Remove the through-bolt, connecting the knuckle assembly to the lower control arm.
6. Remove the mounting bolt connecting the lower control arm to the suspension crossmember.
7. Remove the lower control arm from the vehicle.

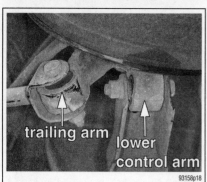

Fig. 68 Remove the through-bolt connecting the knuckle assembly to the lower control arm

Fig. 69 Remove the mounting bolt connecting the lower control arm to the suspension crossmember

To install:

➡**The control arm mounting bolts must not be fully tightened until the full weight of the vehicle is on the ground.**

8. Install the control arm to the suspension crossmember and temporarily tighten the mounting bolt.

9. Connect the knuckle to the lower control arm and lightly tighten the through-bolt.

10. Connect the stabilizer bar link to the control arm and tighten the nut to 28 ft. lbs. (39 Nm).

11. Install the wheels and lower the vehicle to the floor.

12. Once the full weight of the vehicle is on the suspension, tighten the lower arm mounting bolt nuts to 71 ft. lbs. (98 Nm).

13. Check rear wheel alignment and adjust if necessary.

TOE LOWER CONTROL ARM

♦ **See Figures 70 and 71**

The lower ball joint is integral with the lower toe control arm. They are removed and replaced as an assembly.

1. Raise and support the vehicle safely.
2. Remove the appropriate wheel assembly.
3. Matchmark the control arm adjusting bolt to aid in reassembly.
4. Using joint separator MB991113, disconnect the ball joint stud from the steering knuckle.
5. Remove the mounting bolts connecting the lower control arm to the suspension crossmember.

Fig. 70 Disconnect the ball joint stud from the steering knuckle

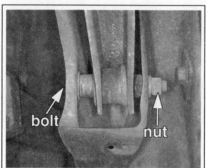

Fig. 71 Remove the mounting bolt connecting the toe lower control arm to the suspension crossmember

To install:

6. Connect the control arm to the suspension crossmember. Align the matchmarks on the adjustment bolt and lightly tighten the bolt.

7. Connect the ball joint stud to the knuckle and tighten the nut to 20 ft. lbs. (28 Nm).

8. Install the wheels and lower the vehicle to the floor.

9. With the full weight of the vehicle on the ground, tighten the control arm through-bolt to 50–56 ft. lbs. (69–78 Nm).

10. Check rear wheel alignment and adjust if necessary.

Diamante

1. Raise and properly support vehicle. Remove appropriate wheel assembly.

2. Matchmark the camber adjusting bolt to aid in reassembly.

3. On vehicles equipped with Active Suspension, disconnect the ECS height sensor rod from lower arm.

4. Support trailing arm assembly and remove the self-locking nut connecting the lower arm to the trailing arm.

5. Disconnect the lower arm at the rear subframe. Remove the arm assembly.

To install:

6. Connect the control arm to the rear crossmember. Align matchmarks and lightly tighten.

7. Connect the control arm to the trailing arm and tighten the self-locking nut to 54–61 ft. lbs. (75–89 Nm).

8. Connect the ECS height sensor rod to the lower arm, if equipped.

9. Install wheel and lower vehicle.

10. With the full weight of the vehicle on the ground, tighten the control arm to rear crossmember bolt to 54–61 ft. lbs. (75–89 Nm).

11. Check rear wheel alignment and adjust if necessary.

Trailing Arm

REMOVAL & INSTALLATION

1990–93 Galant

1. Raise and safely support the vehicle securely on jackstands.

2. Remove the wheel and tire assembly.

3. Remove the brake drum or rotor.

4. Remove the hub and bearing assembly.

5. Support the rear axle using a jack or other suitable device.

6. Remove the lower shock absorber-to-trailing arm connection.

7. Remove the trailing arm-to-axle connection.

8. Remove the trailing arm-to-body mounting through-bolt and remove the trailing arm.

To install:

9. Install the trailing arm and install the trailing arm-to-body mounting through-bolt. Tighten the bolt to 72–87 ft. lbs. (100–120 Nm).

10. Install the trailing arm-to-axle connection. Tighten the bolt to 72–87 ft. lbs. (100–120 Nm).

11. Install the lower shock absorber-to-trailing arm connection. Tighten the bolt to 58–72 ft. lbs. (80–100 Nm).

12. Remove the axle support device.

13. Install the hub and bearing assembly.

14. Install the brake drum or rotor.

15. Install the wheel and tire assembly.

16. Lower the vehicle.

1993–00 Mirage

1. Raise and safely support the vehicle securely on jackstands.

2. Remove the wheel and tire assembly.

3. Remove the brake drum or rotor.

4. Remove the hub and bearing assembly.

5. Support the rear axle using a jack or other suitable device.

6. Remove the lower control arm-to-trailing arm connection.

7. Remove the upper link-to-trailing arm connection.

8. Remove the trailing arm-to-body mounting through-bolt and remove the trailing arm.

To install:

9. Install the trailing arm and install the trailing arm-to-body mounting through-bolt. Tighten the bolt to 72–87 ft. lbs. (100–120 Nm).

10. Install the upper link-to-trailing arm connection. Tighten the bolt to 65 ft. lbs. (90 Nm).

11. Install the lower control arm-to-trailing arm connection. Tighten the bolt to 65 ft. lbs. (90 Nm).

12. Remove the axle support device.

13. Install the hub and bearing assembly.

14. Install the brake drum or rotor.

15. Install the wheel and tire assembly.

16. Lower the vehicle.

1994–00 Galant and 1997–00 Diamante

1. Raise and safely support the vehicle securely on jackstands.
2. Remove the wheel and tire assembly.
3. Support the rear axle using a jack or other suitable device.
4. Remove the trailing arm-to-knuckle connection.
5. Remove the trailing arm-to-body mounting through-bolt and remove the trailing arm.

To install:

6. Install the trailing arm and install the trailing arm-to-body mounting through-bolt. Tighten the bolt to 99–114 ft. lbs. (137–157 Nm).
7. Install the trailing arm-to-knuckle connection. Tighten the bolt to 85–99 ft. lbs. (118–137 Nm).
8. Remove the axle support device.
9. Install the wheel and tire assembly.
10. Lower the vehicle.

1992–96 Diamante

1. Raise and safely support the vehicle securely on jackstands.
2. Remove the wheel and tire assembly.
3. Remove the brake rotor.
4. Remove the hub and bearing assembly.
5. Support the rear axle using a jack or other suitable device.
6. Remove the lower shock absorber-to-trailing arm connection.
7. Remove the stabilizer bar link-to-trailing arm connection.
8. Remove the tie rod end-to-trailing arm connection.
9. Remove the lower control arm-to-trailing arm connection.
10. Remove the trailing arm-to-body mounting through-bolt and remove the trailing arm.

To install:

11. Install the trailing arm and install the trailing arm-to-body mounting through-bolt. Tighten the bolt to 101–116 ft. lbs. (140–160 Nm).
12. Install the trailing arm-to-lower control arm connection. Tighten the bolt to 101–116 ft. lbs. (140–160 Nm).
13. Install the tie rod end-to-trailing arm connection. Tighten the nut to 21 ft. lbs. (29 Nm).
14. Install the stabilizer bar link-to-trailing arm connection. Tighten the nut to 29 ft. lbs. (40 Nm).
15. Install the lower shock absorber-to-trailing arm connection. Tighten the bolt to 65 ft. lbs. (90 Nm).
16. Remove the axle support device.
17. Install the hub and bearing assembly.
18. Install the brake rotor.
19. Install the wheel and tire assembly.
20. Lower the vehicle.

Sway Bar

REMOVAL AND INSTALLATION

1990–93 Galant

1. Raise and support the vehicle safely.
2. Place a jack under the rear axle and suspension assembly.
3. Remove the self-locking nuts and crossmember bracket.

4. Remove the retainer bolts and the stabilizer bar brackets. Remove the bushing.
5. Hold the stabilizer bar with a wrench. Remove the self-locking nut.
6. Once the stabilizer bar nut is removed, remove the joint cups and stabilizer rubber bushing.
7. Hold the stabilizer link with a wrench and remove the self-locking nuts. Remove the stabilizer link.
8. Lower the jack supporting the rear axle slightly. Maintain a slight gap between the rear suspension and the body of the vehicle.
9. Remove the stabilizer bar.
10. Inspect the bar for damage, wear and deterioration and replace as required.

To install:

11. Install the stabilizer bar into the vehicle. Raise the rear axle and suspension into place.
12. Install the stabilizer link into the stabilizer bar and install a new self-locking nut. Tighten the nut to 33 ft. lbs. (45 Nm).
13. Install the joint cups and stabilizer rubber to the link. Install a new self-locking nut onto the link. While holding the stabilizer link ball studs with a wrench, tighten the self-locking nut so the protrusion of the stabilizer link is within 0.354–0.433 in. (9–11mm).
14. Install the center stabilizer bar bushings, brackets and bolts. Tighten the bolts to 10 ft. lbs. (14 Nm).
15. Install the parking brake cable and rear speed sensor installation bolt.
16. Install the crossmember bracket and tighten the bolt to 61 ft. lbs. (85 Nm). Tighten the crossmember bracket mounting nut to 94 ft. lbs. (130 Nm).
17. Install the rubber insulators and new self-locking nuts onto the crossmember brackets. Tighten the nuts to 80–94 ft. lbs. (110–130 Nm).
18. Lower the vehicle.

Diamante and 1994–98 Galant

♦ **See Figure 72**

1. Disconnect the negative battery cable.
2. Raise and safely support the vehicle.
3. Disconnect the stabilizer links by removing the self-locking nuts.
4. Remove the stabilizer bar mounting brackets and bushings.
5. Remove the bar from the vehicle.
6. Inspect all components for wear or damage, and replace parts as needed.

To install:

7. Install the stabilizer bar into the vehicle.

Fig. 72 Remove the self-locking nuts from the stabilizer bar link

8. Loosely install the stabilizer bar brackets on the vehicle.
9. Align the side locating markings on the stabilizer bar, so that the marking on the bar extends approximately 0.39 inches (10mm) from the outer edge of the mounting bracket, on both sides.
10. With the stabilizer bar properly aligned, tighten the mounting bracket bolts to 28 ft. lbs. (39 Nm).
11. Connect the stabilizer links to the damper fork and the stabilizer bar. Tighten the locking nuts to 28 ft. lbs. (38 Nm).
12. Lower the vehicle and connect the negative battery cable.

Hub & Bearings

ADJUSTMENT

Mirage

➡ **Never disassemble the rear hub bearing. The wheel bearing is serviced by replacement of the hub.**

1. Raise and safely support the vehicle.
2. Remove the rear wheel.
3. Remove the caliper and brake disc or brake drum.
4. Remove the dust cap and tighten the flange nut to 130 ft. lbs. (180 Nm).
5. Using a dial indicator, measure wheel bearing end-play. The maximum limit for end-play is 0.0020 inches (0.05mm).
6. Using a spring scale and a rope wrapped around the bolts, measure the rotary sliding resistance of the bearing/hub. The maximum limit for resistance is 4 lbs. (19 N).
7. If any of the readings exceed the specifications, replacement of the hub is required.
8. Install the dust cap.
9. Install the brake disc and caliper, or brake drum.
10. Install the rear wheel assembly and lower the vehicle to the floor.

1990–93 Galant

➡ **Vehicles equipped with rear disc brakes use a sealed hub and bearing assembly, which requires no adjustment. Drum brake models are adjusted using the following procedure.**

1. Raise the vehicle and support it safely.
2. Remove the wheel and tire assemblies.
3. If equipped with rear disc brakes, remove the caliper assembly.
4. Remove the grease cap and the hub nut.
5. Tighten the wheel bearing nut to 20 ft. lbs. (27 Nm) while rotating the drum/hub.
6. Back off the adjusting nut to remove the preload and then tighten it to 7 ft. lbs. (10 Nm).
7. Install the nut lock and a new cotter pin.
8. If brake caliper was removed, reinstall.
9. Install the wheel and lower the vehicle.

Diamante and 1994–00 Galant

Measure the wheel bearing end-play using a dial indicator. The end-play should be 0.002 inches (0.05mm) or less with the wheel bearing locknut torqued to specifications. The wheel bearings are sealed units and are not adjustable. If defective, replacement is the only option.

REMOVAL & INSTALLATION

Mirage

1990–92 MODELS

1. Raise the vehicle and support safely.
2. Remove the tire and wheel assembly.
3. If equipped with rear disc brakes, remove the caliper from the disc and remove the brake disc.
4. Remove the dust cap and bearing nut. Do not use an air gun to remove the nut.
5. Remove the outer wheel bearing.
6. Remove the drum and/or axle hub with the inner wheel bearing and the grease seal.
7. Remove the grease seal and remove the inner bearing.

To install:

8. Lubricate the inner bearing and install to the drum or hub.
9. Install a new grease seal.
10. To determine if the self-locking nut is reusable:
    a. Screw in the self-locking nut until about 0.07–0.11 in. (2–3mm) of thread is visible under the nut.
    b. Measure the torque required to turn the self-locking nut counterclockwise.
    c. The lowest allowable torque is 48 inch lbs. (6 Nm). If the measured torque is less than the specification, replace the nut.
11. Install the drum and/or hub to the vehicle.
12. Lubricate and install the outer wheel bearing to the spindle.
13. Tighten the self-locking nut to 108–145 ft. lbs. (150–200 Nm).
14. Set up a dial indicator and measure the endplay while moving the hub or drum in and out. If the endplay exceeds 0.008 in. (0.002mm), retorque the nut. If still beyond the limit, replace the bearings.
15. Install the grease cap and wheel assembly.

1993–00 MODELS

➡**Never disassemble the rear hub bearing. The wheel bearing is serviced by replacement of the hub.**

1. If equipped with ABS, remove the wheel speed sensor.
2. Raise and safely support the vehicle.
3. Remove the rear wheel.
4. Remove the caliper and brake disc or brake drum.
5. Remove the dust cap and flange nut.
6. Remove the rear hub assembly.

To install:

7. Install the rear hub assembly using a new flange nut. Tighten the flange nut to 130 ft. lbs. (180 Nm).
8. Install the dust cap.
9. Install the wheel speed sensor if removed. The air gap should be 0.012–0.035 in. (0.3–0.9mm).
10. Install the brake disc and caliper, or brake drum.
11. Install the rear wheel assembly and lower the vehicle to the floor.

1990–93 Galant

DRUM BRAKE VEHICLES

1. Raise the vehicle and support it safely.
2. Remove the wheel and tire assemblies.
3. Remove the grease cap and the hub nut.
4. Remove the brake drum. The outer bearing will fall out while the drum is coming off. Do not drop it. Remove the hub and rotor assembly.
5. Pry out and discard the oil seal.
6. Remove the inner bearing.

➡**Check the bearing races. If any scoring, heat checking or damage is noted, they should be replaced. When bearing or races need replacement, replace them as a set.**

7. If the bearings and races are to be replaced, drive out the race with a brass drift.

To install:

8. Before installing new races, coat them with wheel bearing grease. Drive into place with proper size driver. Make sure they are fully seated.
9. Thoroughly pack the bearings and lubricate the hubs with wheel bearing grease. Install the inner bearing and coat the lip and rim of the grease seal with grease. Drive the seal into place with a seal driver.
10. Install the drum assembly on the axle.
11. Lubricate and install the outer wheel bearing, washer and nut. To properly adjust the wheel bearing preload:
    a. Tighten the wheel bearing nut to 20 ft. lbs. (27 Nm) while rotating the drum.
    b. Back off the adjusting nut to remove the preload, then tighten it to 7 ft. lbs. (10 Nm).
    c. Install the nut lock and a new cotter pin.
12. Install the wheel and lower the vehicle.

DISC BRAKE VEHICLES

1. Raise the vehicle and support safely.
2. Remove the tire and wheel assembly.
3. Remove the bolt(s) holding the speed sensor bracket to the knuckle and remove the assembly from the vehicle.

✳✳ **WARNING**

The speed sensor has a pole piece projecting from it. This exposed tip must be protected from impact or scratches. Do not allow the pole piece to contact the toothed wheel during removal or installation.

4. Remove the caliper from the brake disc and suspend with a wire.
5. Remove the brake rotor.
6. Remove the grease cap, locking nut and tongued washer.
7. Remove the rear hub and bearing assembly.

➡**The rear hub assembly can not be disassembled. If bearing replacement is required, replace the assembly as a unit.**

8. If replacing the hub assembly, remove the two bolts securing the speed sensor ring to the hub.

To install:

9. Install the speed sensor to the hub and bearing assembly. Tighten the mounting bolts to 8 ft. lbs. (11 Nm).

10. Install the hub and bearing assembly to the axle shaft.
11. Install the tongued washer and a new locking nut. Tighten the locknut to 144–188 ft. lbs. (200–260 Nm). Once the locknut has been properly torqued, crimp the nut flange over the slot in the spindle, and install the grease cap.
12. Install the brake caliper and rotor.
13. Install the speed sensor and tighten the mounting bolt to 8 ft. lbs. (11 Nm).
14. Install the tire and wheel assembly.

✳✳ **WARNING**

Be sure to pump the brake pedal until it's firm, before moving vehicle.

1994–00 Galant

DRUM BRAKE VEHICLES

▶ **See Figure 73, 74, 75**

1. Raise the vehicle and support safely.
2. Remove the appropriate wheel assembly.
3. If equipped with ABS, remove the vehicle speed sensor.
4. Remove the brake drum from the hub assembly.
5. From the back of the knuckle, remove the four bolts securing the hub to the knuckle.
6. Remove the hub and bearing assembly from the knuckle.

➡**The hub assembly is not serviceable and should not be disassembled.**

7. If replacing the hub, use special socket MB991248 and a press to remove the wheel sensor rotor from the hub.

To install:

8. Press the wheel sensor rotor onto the hub.
9. Install the hub to the knuckle and tighten the mounting bolts to 54–65 ft. lbs. (74–88 Nm).
10. Install the brake drum on the hub.
11. If equipped with ABS, install the vehicle speed sensor.
12. Install the wheel assembly and lower the vehicle.

DISC BRAKE VEHICLES

1. Remove the cotter pin, halfshaft nut and washer.
2. Raise the vehicle and support safely.

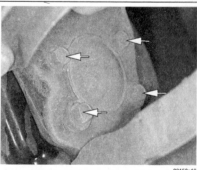

Fig. 73 The hub and bearing assembly is retained to the knuckle by four bolts

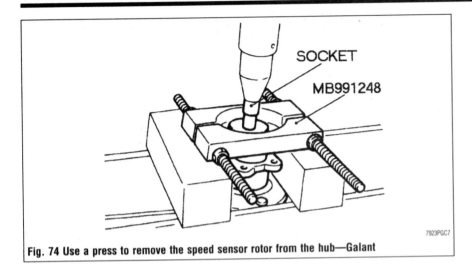

Fig. 74 Use a press to remove the speed sensor rotor from the hub—Galant

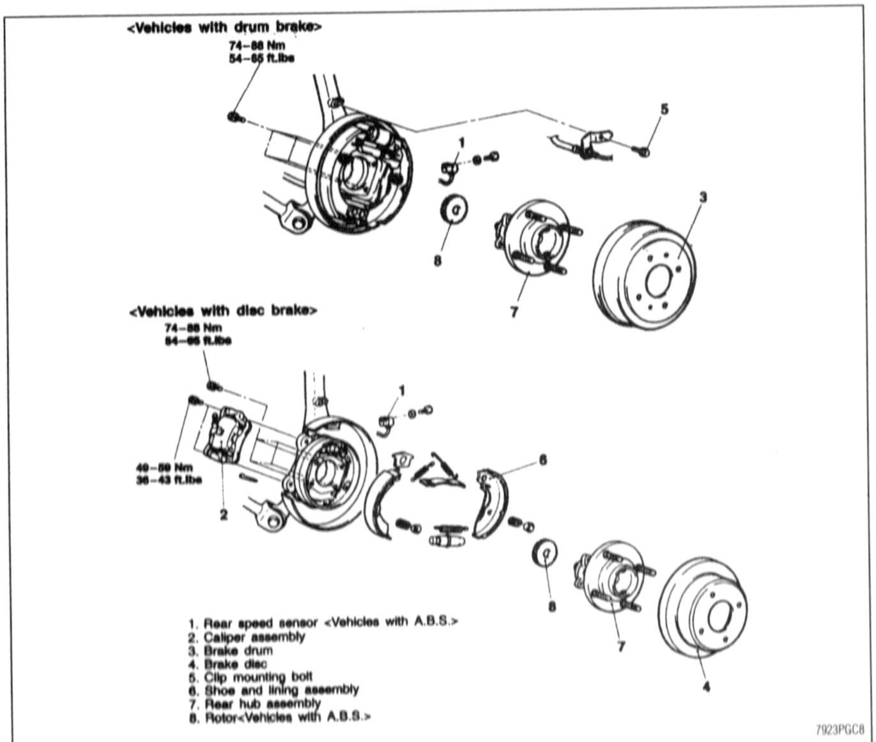

<Vehicles with drum brake>
74—88 Nm
54—65 ft.lbs

<Vehicles with disc brake>
74—88 Nm
54—65 ft.lbs

49—59 Nm
36—43 ft.lbs

1. Rear speed sensor <Vehicles with A.B.S.>
2. Caliper assembly
3. Brake drum
4. Brake disc
5. Clip mounting bolt
6. Shoe and lining assembly
7. Rear hub assembly
8. Rotor<Vehicles with A.B.S.>

Fig. 75 Exploded view of the rear hub/bearing assembly and related components—Galant

3. Remove the appropriate wheel assembly.

4. If equipped with ABS, remove the vehicle speed sensor.

5. Remove the caliper and brake pads. Support the caliper out of the way using wire.

6. Remove the brake rotor from the hub assembly.

7. Remove the parking brake shoes as follows:
   a. Remove the upper shoe to anchor springs.
   b. Remove the lower shoe to shoe spring.
   c. Remove the brake shoe hold-down springs.
   d. Disconnect the parking brake cable from the actuating lever.

8. From the back of the knuckle, remove the four bolts securing the hub to the knuckle.

9. Remove the hub and bearing assembly from the knuckle.

➡The hub assembly is not serviceable and should not be disassembled.

10. If replacing the hub, use special socket MB991248 and a press to remove the wheel sensor rotor from the hub.

To install:

11. Press the wheel sensor rotor onto the hub.

12. Install the hub to the knuckle and tighten the mounting bolts to 54–65 ft. lbs. (74–88 Nm).

13. Install the parking brake shoes.

14. Position the rotor on the hub. Install a couple of lug nuts and lightly tighten to hold rotor on hub.

15. Install the caliper holder and place brake pads in holder. Slide caliper over brake pads and install guide pins. Once caliper is secured, lug nuts can be removed.

16. If equipped with ABS, install the vehicle speed sensor.

17. Install the wheel assembly and lower the vehicle.

Diamante

➡The hub assembly is not repairable; if defective, replacement is the only option. If the hub is removed for any reason it must be replaced.

1. Raise and support vehicle safely.

2. Remove the both of the rear wheels.

3. Remove the caliper and the brake disc. Support the caliper with wire to prevent stress to the brake hose.

4. If equipped with ABS, remove the bolt holding the speed sensor to the trailing arm and remove the sensor.

➡The speed sensor has a pole piece projecting from it. This exposed tip must be protected from impact or scratches. Do not allow the pole piece to contact the toothed wheel during removal or installation.

5. Remove the grease cap, self-locking nut and tongued washer.

➡Do not use an air gun to remove the hub locknut.

6. Remove the rear hub assembly from the spindle.

7. Remove the bolts that secure the ABS sensor ring to the hub and remove the ring from the hub.

To install:

8. Secure the sensor ring to the hub assembly and tighten the mounting bolts.

9. Install the hub assembly, tongued washer and a new self-locking nut. Tighten the nut to 166 ft. lbs. (230 Nm), align with the indentation in the spindle, and crimp.

10. Using a rope around the hub bolts and a spring balance, measure the resistance necessary to rotate the hub. If the resistance exceeds 7 ft. lbs. (10 Nm), loosen and retighten the locknut. If the resistance still exceeds the specification, the hub must be replaced.

11. Using a dial indicator, measure the hub endplay. The endplay should be 0.002 inches (0.05mm) or less.

12. Install the brake rotor and caliper assembly.

13. Install the speed sensor to the knuckle.

➡Route the speed sensor cable correctly. Improper installation may cause cable damage and system failure. Use the white stripe on the outer insulation to keep the sensor harness properly positioned.

14. Use a brass or other non-magnetic feeler gauge to check the air gap between the tip of the pole piece and the toothed wheel. Correct gap is 0.008–0.028 in. (0.2–0.7mm). Tighten the sensor bracket nut with the sensor located so the gap is the same at several points on the toothed wheel. If the gap is incorrect, it is likely that the toothed wheel is worn or improperly installed.

15. Bleed the brake system and install the rear wheels.

STEERING

Steering Wheel

REMOVAL & INSTALLATION

1990–93 Mirage

1. Disconnect the negative battery cable.
2. Remove the horn pad from the steering wheel, by pulling the lower end of the pad upward. Detach horn button connector.
3. Remove steering wheel retaining nut.
4. Matchmark the steering wheel to the shaft.
5. Use a steering wheel puller to remove the steering wheel.

✳✳ WARNING

Do not hammer on steering wheel to remove it. The collapsible column mechanism may be damaged.

To install:

6. Line up the matchmarks and install the steering wheel to the shaft.
7. Tighten the steering wheel attaching nut to 29 ft. lbs. (40 Nm).
8. Reconnect the horn connector and install the horn pad.
9. Connect the negative battery cable.

1994–00 Mirage and Galant

▶ See Figures 76 thru 85

✳✳ CAUTION

If equipped with an air bag, be sure to disarm it before starting repairs on the vehicle. Failure to do so could result in severe personal injury and damage to vehicle.

1. Disarm the SRS system as outlined in Section 6.
2. Remove the covers and the air bag module mounting nut from behind the steering wheel.
3. To detach the connector of the clockspring from the air bag module, press the air bag's lock toward the module to spread the lock open. While holding lock in this position, use a small tipped prying tool to gently pry the connector from the module.
4. Remove the air bag module and store in a clean, dry place with the pad cover facing up.
5. Matchmark the steering wheel to the shaft.
6. Remove the steering wheel retaining nut and use a steering wheel puller to remove the wheel. Do not use a hammer, or the collapsible mechanism in the column could be damaged.

To install:

7. Confirm that the front wheels are in a straight-ahead position. Center the clockspring by aligning the NEUTRAL mark on the clockspring with the mating mark on the casing. Then, install the steering wheel and tighten the new retaining nut to 29 ft. lbs. (40 Nm).
8. Install the air bag module.
9. Connect the negative battery cable, turn the key to the ON position; the SRS warning light should illuminate for seven seconds and go out.

1990–93 Galant

1. Disconnect the negative battery cable.
2. Remove the horn pad from the steering wheel as follows:
   a. For 1990–91 models only, the horn pad is removed by pushing the pad upward, to release the pad from the retaining clips. Detach horn button connector and remove the pad.
   b. For 1992–93 models only, remove the screw from the bottom of the pad and push the pad upward, to release the pad from the retaining clips. Detach horn button connector and remove the pad.
3. Remove steering wheel retaining nut.
4. Matchmark the steering wheel to the shaft.
5. Use a steering wheel puller to remove the steering wheel.

Fig. 76 The air bag is retained by two screws located in access holes on the back of the wheel. Remove the covers to access the screws

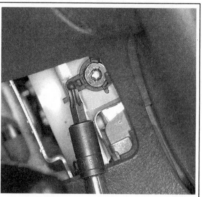

Fig. 77 The retaining screws usually require a Torx® drive tool to remove them

Fig. 78 After the air bag retaining screws are removed, grasp the airbag and carefully pull it from the steering wheel . . .

Fig. 79 . . . then detach the connector and remove the air bag module from the vehicle

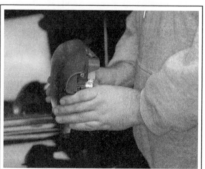

Fig. 80 To prevent personal injury, ALWAYS carry a live air bag facing away from you in case of accidental deployment

Fig. 81 To prevent personal injury, ALWAYS place a live airbag with the cover facing up in case of accidental deployment

Fig. 82 Remove the mounting bolt from the center of the steering wheel

Fig. 83 Install a suitable steering wheel puller . . .

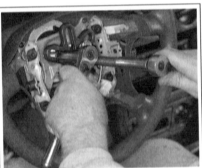

Fig. 84 . . . then tighten down on the puller until the wheel is sufficiently loose

Fig. 85 Lift the steering wheel straight off of the steering column and remove the wheel

⁕⁕ WARNING

Do not hammer on steering wheel to remove it. The collapsible column mechanism may be damaged.

To install:

6. Line up the matchmarks and install the steering wheel to the shaft.
7. Tighten the steering wheel attaching nut to 25–33 ft. lbs. (35–45 Nm).
8. Attach the horn connector and install the horn pad.
9. Connect the negative battery cable.

Diamante

⁕⁕ WARNING

Be sure to disarm the SRS (air bag) system, before starting repairs on the vehicle. Failure to do so could result in personal injury or death. DO NOT perform any work on the vehicle until after 90 seconds has passed. The air bag system is designed to retain enough short term voltage to make air bag deployment possible.

1. Disarm the SRS system as outlined in Section 6.
2. Remove the air bag module mounting nut from behind the steering wheel.
3. Matchmark the steering wheel.
4. Detach the connector of the clockspring from the air bag module, press the air bag's lock towards the module to spread the lock open. While holding lock in this position, use a small tipped prying tool to gently pry the connector from the module.
5. Store the air bag module in a clean, dry place with the pad cover facing up.
6. Remove the steering wheel retaining nut.
7. Matchmark the steering wheel to the shaft.
8. Use a steering wheel puller to remove the wheel.

⁕⁕ WARNING

Do not use a hammer or the collapsible mechanism in the column could be damaged.

To install:

9. Confirm that the front wheels are in a straight-ahead position. Center the clockspring by aligning the NEUTRAL mark on the clockspring with the mating mark on the casing.
10. Line up and install the steering wheel.
11. Tighten the retaining nut as follows:
   • On 1992–93 Diamante models, tighten the retaining nut to 29 ft. lbs. (40 Nm)
   • On 1994–00 Diamante models, tighten the retaining nut to 33 ft. lbs. (45 Nm)
12. Install the air bag module and tighten the retaining nuts to 48 inch lbs. (5 Nm).
13. Connect the negative battery cable and check the SRS warning light operation.

Combination Switch

REMOVAL AND INSTALLATION

⁕⁕ CAUTION

The air bag system (SRS or SIR) must be disarmed before removing the steering wheel. Failure to do so may cause accidental deployment, property damage or personal injury.

1. Disconnect the negative battery cable.
2. If equipped, disable the air bag system.
3. Remove the steering wheel as outlined earlier in this section.
4. For Diamante models, remove the hood lock release handle.
5. Remove the knee protector panel under the steering column, then the upper and lower column covers.
6. For Diamante models, remove the lap cooler and foot blower duct work as necessary. Carefully detach the combination switch connectors.
7. For Mirage models, detach all connectors, remove the wiring clip and remove the column switch assembly.
8. For Galant models, if equipped, remove the four screws retaining the cruise control slip ring to the switch.
9. For Galant models, remove the two retaining screws from the combination switch and remove the switch from the column.

To install:

10. Install the switch assembly and secure all harness connectors with clips if needed. Make sure the wires are not pinched or out of place.
11. Install the column covers and knee protector and all connectors.
12. If removed, install the foot blower duct work and lap cooler.
13. Confirm that the front wheels are in a straight-ahead position.
14. Install the steering wheel, as outlined earlier in this section.
15. Connect the negative battery cable, turn the key to the **ON** position, the SRS warning light should illuminate for seven seconds and go out. If the warning light is not functioning properly, refer to SRS system diagnosis.
16. Check all functions of the combination switch for proper operation.

Windshield Wiper Switch

REMOVAL & INSTALLATION

➡**On vehicles not covered here, the windshield wiper switch is incorporated into the combination switch and is not separately serviceable. Refer to the procedure above.**

Diamante

1. Disconnect the negative battery cable.
2. If equipped with an air bag, disarm as follows:
   a. Position the front wheels in the straight ahead position and place the key in the LOCK

position. Remove the key from the ignition lock cylinder.

b. Disconnect the negative battery cable and insulate the cable end with high-quality electrical tape or similar non-conductive wrapping.

c. Wait at least 1 minute before working on the vehicle. The air bag system is designed to retain enough voltage to deploy the air bag for a short period of time even after the battery has been disconnected.

3. Remove the steering wheel. as outlined earlier in this section.

4. Remove the hood lock release handle.

5. Remove the switches from the knee protector below the steering column, and remove the exposed retaining screws. Then remove the knee protector.

6. Remove the column covers.

7. Remove necessary duct work and detach the windshield wiper switch connectors.

8. Remove the retaining screws and remove the windshield wiper switch assembly from the steering column.

To install:

9. Install the wiper switch to the steering column and connect the connectors.

10. Install any removed duct work.

11. Install the column covers.

12. Install the knee protector and switches.

13. Install the hood release handle.

14. Confirm that the front wheels are in a straight ahead position. Install the steering wheel, as outlined earlier in this section.

15. Connect the negative battery cable and check the windshield wiper and washer for proper operation.

Ignition Lock Cylinder

REMOVAL & INSTALLATION

✴✴ CAUTION

The air bag system (SRS or SIR) must be disarmed before removing the steering wheel. Failure to do so may cause accidental deployment, property damage or personal injury.

1. If equipped, properly disarm the air bag system.

2. Disconnect the negative battery cable.

3. Remove the hood lock release lever from the lower panel.

4. Remove the lower instrument panel knee protector.

5. Remove the ductwork with the lower knee panel and remove the steering wheel assembly.

✴✴ WARNING

Use proper steering wheel puller equipment when removing the steering wheel. The use of a hammer for removal could damage the collapsible mechanism within the column.

6. Remove the lower and upper steering column covers.

7. For Diamante models, remove the lap cooler and foot shower duct work.

8. If necessary, remove the clip that holds the wiring harness against the steering column.

9. Detach all necessary connectors.

10. For Galant and Diamante models, remove the retaining screws, then remove the entire column switch/clockspring assembly from the left side of the steering column.

11. For Diamante models, remove the mounting screws from the ignition switch and pull the switch from the interlock cylinder.

12. Insert the key into the steering lock cylinder and turn to the **ACC** position.

13. With a small, pointed tool, push the lock pin of the steering lock cylinder inward and pull the lock cylinder out.

14. Remove the key reminder switch, if equipped.

To install:

15. For Mirage, install the lock cylinder in the lock cylinder bracket. Make sure the cylinder operates properly before breaking off the heads of the special bolts, if the bracket was replaced.

16. For Galant and Diamante models, install the lock cylinder into the interlock housing. Be sure the lock pin snaps into place. Install the ignition switch into the interlock housing. Align the keyway of the ignition switch with the lock cylinder and secure with the mounting screws.

17. For Galant and Diamante models, install the column switch/clockspring assembly to the and connect the harness.

18. Install the key reminder switch, if equipped.

19. Attach the harness connections and install the wiring clip.

20. If removed, install the lap cooler and foot shower duct work.

21. Install the steering column upper and lower covers.

22. If necessary, install the knee protector and the steering wheel.

23. Install the hood lock release lever.

24. Connect the negative battery cable, enable the air bag system, and check the ignition switch and lock for proper operation.

Ignition Switch

REMOVAL AND INSTALLATION

Mirage and Galant

1. Disconnect the negative battery cable. If equipped, disarm the air bag system.

2. Remove the hood lock release lever from the lower panel.

3. Remove the lower instrument panel knee protector.

4. Remove the ductwork with the lower knee panel and remove the steering wheel assembly.

➡**Use proper steering wheel puller equipment when removing the steering wheel. The use of a hammer for removal could damage the collapsible mechanism within the column.**

5. Remove the lower steering column cover.

6. Remove the upper steering column cover.

7. Remove the clip that holds the wiring harness against the steering column.

8. For Galant models, insert the key into the steering lock cylinder and turn to the **ACC** position.

9. For Galant models, using a small pointed tool, push the lock pin of the steering lock cylinder inward and pull the lock cylinder out.

10. For Galant models, remove the key reminder switch, if equipped.

11. Unplug the ignition switch harness connector. Remove the ignition switch mounting screws and pull the switch from the steering lock cylinder.

➡**Vehicles equipped with automatic transaxle have safety-lock systems and will have a key interlock cable installed in a slide lever on the side of the key cylinder. Carefully unhook the interlock cable from the lock cylinder while withdrawing the cylinder from the lock housing.**

To install:

➡**To remove the steering lock, use a hacksaw or equivalent to cut the special bolts through the bracket. The bracket and bolts must be replaced with new ones.**

12. With the ignition key removed, install the slide lever and the interlock cable to the steering lock cylinder. Apply grease to the interlock cable and install the cylinder into the lock housing. Check for normal operation of the interlock system.

13. Install the ignition switch into the rear of the lock cylinder housing. Be sure to align the keyway of the ignition switch with interlock cylinder.

14. Attach the harness connections and install the wiring clip.

15. Install the steering column upper and lower covers.

16. Install the knee protector.

17. Connect the negative battery cable, enable the air bag system (if equipped) and check the ignition switch and lock for proper operation.

Diamante

✴✴ CAUTION

Work MUST NOT be started until at least 90 seconds after the ignition switch is turned to the LOCK position and the negative battery cable is disconnected from the battery. This will allow time for the air bag system backup power supply to deplete its stored energy preventing accidental air bag deployment which could result in unnecessary air bag system repairs and/or personal injury.

1. Disconnect the negative battery cable.

2. Disarm the air bag system, as outlined in Section 6.

3. Remove the steering wheel, as outlined earlier in this section.

4. Remove the hood lock release handle.

5. Remove the switches from the knee protector below the steering column and remove the exposed retaining screws. Then remove the knee protector.

6. Remove the steering column upper and lower covers. Use care removing the covers to prevent breakage of alignment tabs.

7. Remove lap cooler and foot shower duct work. Detach the ignition switch harness connectors.

8. Remove mounting screws from the ignition switch and pull switch from interlock cylinder.

To install:

9. Install ignition switch into interlock housing. Align keyway of ignition switch with lock cylinder and secure with mounting screws.

10. Connect the ignition switch electrical harness plug.

11. Install lap cooler and foot shower duct work.

12. Install the upper and lower steering column covers.

13. Install the knee protector and switches.

14. Install the hood release handle.

15. Install the steering wheel, as outlined earlier in this section.

16. Connect the negative battery cable and check all functions of column-mounted switches and the ignition switch for proper operation.

Steering Linkage

REMOVAL & INSTALLATION

Tie Rod Ends

♦ **See Figures 86 thru 94**

1. Disconnect the negative battery cable.

2. Remove the wheel and tire assembly.

3. Remove the cotter pin and the castellated nut from the outer tie rod end. Discard the cotter pin.

4. Separate the outer tie rod end from the steering knuckle using an appropriate tie rod end remover.

5. Mark the outer tie rod jam nut on one side with a reference line for installation.

6. Hold the outer tie rod end with a wrench and loosen the tie rod end jam nut.

7. Back the tie rod end jam nut off ONE FULL TURN ONLY.

8. Remove the outer tie rod end from the inner tie rod spindle.

To install:

9. Clean the threads on the inner tie rod spindle (front wheel spindle connecting rod).

10. Thread the new outer tie rod end onto the inner tie rod until it bottoms on the jam nut.

11. Back the tie rod and jam nut out one full turn until the reference line is in the same position as before.

12. Place the outer tie rod end stud into the steering knuckle. Set the front wheels in a straight ahead position.

13. Connect the outer tie rod end to the steering knuckle and install the castle nut. Tighten the nut to 25 ft. lbs. (34 Nm) on Mirage models and 21 ft. lbs. (29 Nm) on the Galant and Diamante models.

14. Continue to tighten the castellated nut until a new cotter pin can be inserted through the hole in the stud. Install a new cotter pin.

15. If required, repeat the procedure for the opposite side.

16. Reinstall the wheel and tire assembly. Tighten the lug nuts to 65–80 ft. lbs. (90–110 Nm).

17. Reconnect the negative battery cable.

18. Tighten the tie rod end jam nut to 30 ft. lbs.

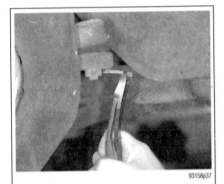

Fig. 86 Remove the cotter pin from the tie rod end . . .

Fig. 87 . . . then remove the retaining nut from the tie rod end

Fig. 88 A special puller is recommended for removing the tie rod end from the steering knuckle without damaging the tie rod end

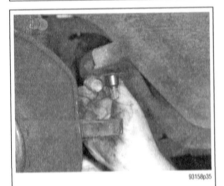

Fig. 89 Remove the tie rod end from the steering knuckle

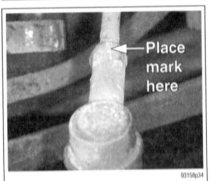

Fig. 90 Mark the outer tie rod jam nut on one side with a reference line for installation

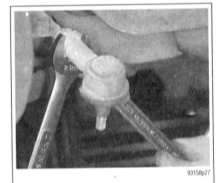

Fig. 91 Use two wrenches, one to hold the inner tie rod, and one to loosen the jam nut

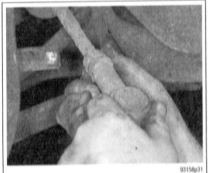

Fig. 92 Back the jam nut off ONE TURN ONLY . . .

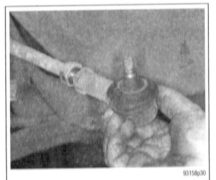

Fig. 93 . . . then unthread the tie rod end from the inner tie rod

Fig. 94 Remove the tie rod end from the vehicle

(42 Nm) on Mirage and 36–39 ft. lbs. (49–53 Nm) on Galant and Diamante models.

19. Have the front end alignment checked, and adjusted if necessary.

Inner Tie Rods

1. Raise the front of the vehicle and support it on jackstands.
2. Remove the wheel.
3. Remove the cotter pin and the outer tie rod ball joint stud nut. Note the position of the steering linkage.
4. Wire brush the threads on the tie rod shaft and lubricate with penetrating oil.
5. Using a suitable ball joint separator tool, remove the tie rod ball joint from the steering knuckle.
6. Loosen the locknut and remove the tie rod end from the tie rod. Count the number of complete turns it takes to completely remove it.
7. Remove the tie rod-to-steering gear locknut.
8. Remove the clamps that secure the flexible boot to the steering gear.
9. Slide the boot from the inner tie rod and remove the boot.
10. Bend the lock plate tabs from the inner tie rod end nut.

11. Loosen the inner tie rod end nut from the steering gear and remove the inner tie rod end.

To install:

12. Using a new lock plate, install the tie rod end and tighten the tie rod to 65 ft. lbs. (90 Nm).
13. Bend the tabs of the new lock plate to secure the inner tie rod end.
14. Slide the boot onto the steering gear and secure it with new clamps.
15. Install the outer tie rod end to the steering gear locknut.
16. Install the outer tie rod end, turning it in exactly as many turns as it was to remove the old one. Make sure it is correctly positioned in relationship to the steering linkage.
17. Connect the outer tie rod end to the steering knuckle and install the castle nut. Tighten the nut to 25 ft. lbs. (34 Nm.) on the Mirage and 21 ft. lbs. (29 Nm) on the Galant and Diamante models.
18. Install a new cotter pin to the castle nut.
19. Tighten the tie rod end locking nut to 30 ft. lbs. (42 Nm) on the Mirage and 36–39 ft. lbs. (49–53 Nm) on the Galant and Diamante models.
20. Install the wheel and tire assembly.
21. Lower the vehicle.
22. Have a front end alignment performed.

Manual Rack And Pinion Steering Gear

REMOVAL & INSTALLATION

Mirage

♦ See Figure 95

➡ Prior to removal of the steering rack, center the front wheels and remove the ignition key. Failure to do so may damage the SRS clockspring and render SRS system inoperative. Be sure to properly disarm the air bag system.

1. Disconnect the battery negative cable.
2. Raise the vehicle and support safely and remove the wheels.
3. Disconnect the Heated Oxygen (HO$_2$S) sensor and remove the front exhaust pipe.
4. Properly support the engine. Remove both roll stopper mounting bolts and the four center member installation bolts.
5. Remove the center member.

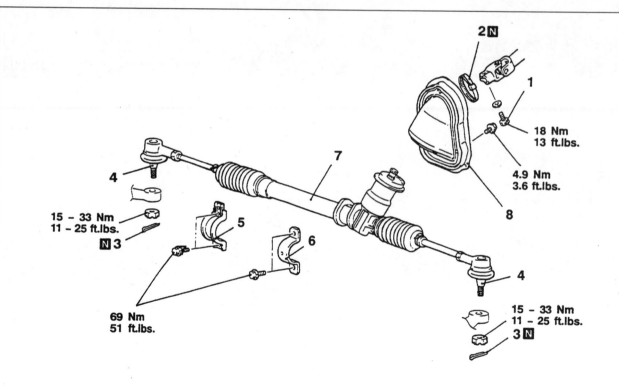

1. Steering shaft assembly and gear box connecting bolt
2. Band
3. Cotter pin
4. Tie-rod end and knuckle connection
5. Cylinder clamp
6. Gear housing clamp
7. Gear box assembly
8. Steering cover assembly

Fig. 95 Exploded view of the manual steering gear mounting—Mirage

7923PG00

➡️**Matchmark the pinion input shaft of the rack to the lower steering column joint for installation purposes.**

6. Remove the pinch bolt holding the lower steering column joint to the rack and pinion input shaft.

7. Remove the cotter pins and disconnect the tie rod ends from the steering knuckle.

8. Remove the rack and pinion steering assembly and its rubber mounts from the right side of the vehicle.

To install:

9. Align the matchmarks of the input shaft and install the rack to the vehicle.

10. Secure the rack using the retainer clamps and bolts. Tighten the bolts to 51 ft. lbs. (70 Nm).

11. Tighten the steering column pinch bolt to 13 ft. lbs. (18 Nm).

12. Install the center member.

13. Install the front exhaust pipe.

14. Connect the HO$_2$S sensor.

15. Connect the tie rod ends to the steering knuckles and tighten the castle nuts to 25 ft. lbs. (34 Nm). Install new cotter pins.

16. Install the wheels and connect the negative battery cable.

17. Have a front end alignment performed.

Power Rack And Pinion Steering Gear

REMOVAL & INSTALLATION

Diamante

FRONT

➡️**Prior to removal of the steering gear box, center the front wheels and remove the ignition key. Failure to do so may damage the SRS clock spring and render SRS system inoperative.**

1. Disconnect the negative battery cable.

2. Disconnect the front exhaust pipe.

3. If equipped with AWD, remove the transfer case assembly.

4. Remove the bolt holding the lower steering column joint to the rack and pinion input shaft.

5. Remove the cotter pins and disconnect the tie rod ends.

6. Remove the left and right frame members.

7. Remove the stabilizer bar bracket.

8. If equipped with four-wheel steering, disconnect the lines going to the rear pump.

9. Remove the rack and pinion steering assembly and its rubber mounts. Move the rack to the right to remove it from the crossmember.

To install:

10. Install the rack and mounting bolts. Tighten the bolts to 51 ft. lbs. (70 Nm). When installing the rubber rack mounts, align the projection of the mounting rubber with the indentation in the crossmember. Install the pinch bolt.

11. Connect the pressure and return lines to the rack and to the rear pump, if equipped.

12. Install the frame members and tighten the bolts to 43–51 ft. lbs. (60–70 Nm).

13. Connect the tie rods and install new cotter pins.

---

14. Install the transfer case and front exhaust pipe.

15. Refill the reservoir and bleed the system.

16. Have a front end alignment performed.

REAR

1. Disconnect the negative battery cable.

2. Raise the vehicle and support safely.

3. Drain the power steering fluid.

4. Remove the main muffler assembly.

5. Remove the rear shock absorber lower mounting bolts.

6. Using the proper equipment, support the weight of the rear differential. Remove the 2 small crossmember brackets.

7. Remove the large self-locking crossmember mounting nuts on the differential side.

8. Remove the oil line clamp bolts.

9. Remove the pressure tubes.

10. Hold the tie rod ends stationary and remove the tie rod end nuts. Remove the tie rod ends from the trailing arms.

11. Remove the mounting bolts and remove the rear steering gear.

To install:

12. Secure the unit to the crossmember. Move the power cylinder piston rod over its full stroke to determine its neutral position.

13. Align the tie rod ends with the holes in the trailing arms and install the nuts. Adjust the length of the tie rods with the nuts if necessary. The difference in length between the 2 tie rod ends should not exceed 0.04 in. (1mm). The nuts' torque specification is 42 ft. lbs. (58 Nm).

14. Replace the O-rings and install the pressure tubes. Clamp in place.

15. Install the large self-locking crossmember mounting nuts on the differential side. Tighten to 80–94 ft. lbs. (110–130 Nm).

16. Remove the support equipment.

17. Install the 2 small crossmember brackets.

18. Install the shock mounting bolts.

19. Install the muffler assembly.

20. Refill the reservoir and bleed the system.

21. Have a front end alignment performed.

Galant

1990–93 MODELS

1. Disconnect the negative battery cable.

2. Drain the power steering fluid.

3. Raise the vehicle and support safely.

4. Remove the bolt holding lower steering column joint to the rack and pinion input shaft.

5. Remove the transfer case, if equipped.

6. Remove the cotter pins and using the proper tools, separate the tie rod ends from the steering knuckle.

7. Locate the triangular brace near the stabilizer bar brackets on the crossmember and remove both the brace and the stabilizer bar bracket.

8. Support the center crossmember.

9. Remove the through-bolt from the round roll stopper and remove the rear bolts from the center crossmember.

10. Disconnect the front exhaust pipe, if equipped with FWD.

11. Disconnect the power steering fluid pressure pipe and return hose from the rack fittings. Plug the fittings to prevent excess fluid leakage.

---

12. Lower the crossmember slightly.

13. Remove the rack and pinion steering assembly and its rubber mounts. Move the rack to the right to remove from the crossmember. Tilt the assembly downward and remove from the left side of the vehicle. Use caution to avoid damaging the boots.

To install:

14. Install the rack and install the mounting bolts. Tighten the mounting bolts to 43–58 ft. lbs. (60–80 Nm). When installing the rubber rack mounts, align the projection of the mounting rubber with the indentation in the crossmember.

15. Connect the power steering fluid lines to the rack.

16. Connect the exhaust pipe, if removed.

17. Raise the crossmember into position. Install the center member mounting bolts and tighten to 72 ft. lbs. (100 Nm). Install the roll stopper bolt and new nut. Tighten nut to 47 ft. lbs. (65 Nm).

18. Install the stabilizer bar brackets and brace.

19. Connect the tie rod ends and tighten nuts to 25 ft. lbs. (34 Nm).

20. Install the transfer case, if removed. Check and fill fluid.

21. Refill the reservoir with power steering fluid and bleed the system.

22. Have a front end alignment performed.

1994–00 MODELS

◆ See Figure 96

⚠️ WARNING

Prior to removal of the steering gear box, center the front wheels and remove the ignition key. Failure to do so may damage the SRS clock spring and render SRS system inoperative.

1. Disconnect the negative battery cable.

2. Raise and properly support the vehicle.

3. Remove both front wheel assemblies.

4. Remove the bolt holding lower steering column joint to the rack and pinion input shaft.

5. Remove the stabilizer bar.

6. Remove the cotter pins, and using joint separator MB991113 or equivalent, disconnect the tie rod ends from the steering knuckle.

7. On vehicles equipped with Electronic Control Power steering (EPS), detach the wiring harness from the solenoid connector.

8. Locate the two triangular braces near the crossmember and remove both.

9. Support the center crossmember. Remove the through-bolt from the front round roll stopper and remove the bolts securing the center crossmember.

10. Remove the center crossmember.

11. Properly support the engine and remove the rear roll stopper through-bolt.

12. Disconnect the power steering fluid pressure pipe and return hose from the rack fittings. Plug the fittings to prevent excessive fluid leakage.

13. Remove the clamp bolts and the two bolts securing the rack assembly to the chassis.

14. Remove the rack and pinion steering assembly and its rubber mounts.

➡️**When removing the rack and pinion assembly, tilt the assembly to the vehicle side of the compression lower arm and remove from the left side of the vehicle.**

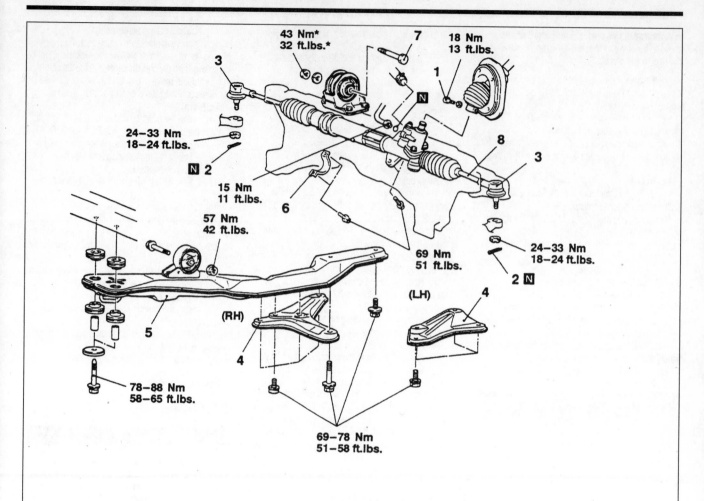

1. Joint assembly and gear box connecting bolt
2. Cotter pin
3. Connection for tie rod end and knuckle
4. Stay
5. Center member assembly
6. Clamp
7. Bolt

8. Gear box assembly

Caution
The fasteners marked * should be temporarily tightened before they are finally tightened once the total weight of the engine has been placed on the vehicle body.

Fig. 96 Exploded view of the power steering gear removal procedure—Galant

7923PGA4

To install:

15. Center the rack assembly and insert the pinion into the steering column shaft.

16. Install the rack and mounting bolts. Tighten the mounting bolts to 51 ft. lbs. (69 Nm).

17. Install the pinch bolt and tighten the bolt to 13 ft. lbs. (18 Nm).

18. Connect the power steering fluid lines to the rack and tighten the pressure hose fitting to 11 ft. lbs. (15 Nm). Secure the return hose with the clamp.

19. Raise the engine into position.

20. Install the rear roll stopper through-bolt and tighten to 32 ft. lbs. (43 Nm).

21. Raise the crossmember into position. Install the center member mounting bolts; tighten the front bolts to 58–65 ft. lbs. (78–88 Nm) and the rear bolt to 51–58 ft. lbs. (69–78 Nm).

22. Install the front roll stopper bolt and tighten the nut to 32 ft. lbs. (43 Nm).

23. Install the two triangular braces and tighten the mounting bolts to 50–56 ft. lbs. (69–78 Nm).

24. Install the stabilizer bar.

25. Connect the tie rod ends and tighten the nuts to 20 ft. lbs. (27 Nm).

26. On vehicles equipped with EPS, connect the wiring harness to the solenoid connector.

27. Install the wheel assemblies and lower the vehicle.

28. Refill the reservoir with power steering fluid and bleed the system.

29. Have a front end alignment performed.

Mirage

1990–92 MODELS

1. Disconnect the battery negative cable.
2. Raise the vehicle and support safely.
3. Remove the pinch bolt holding the lower steering column joint to the rack and pinion input shaft.

4. Remove the cotter pins and disconnect the tie rod ends from the steering knuckle.

5. Disconnect the power steering fluid pressure pipe and return hose from the rack fittings.

6. Remove the rack and pinion steering assembly and its rubber mounts.

To install:

7. Install the steering gear into the vehicle and secure using the retainer clamps and bolts.

8. Connect the power steering fluid lines to the rack fittings.

9. Install the stabilizer bar and rear transaxle bracket.

10. Connect the tie rod ends to the steering knuckles.

11. Connect the negative battery cable.

12. Refill the reservoir and bleed the system.

13. Have a front end alignment performed.

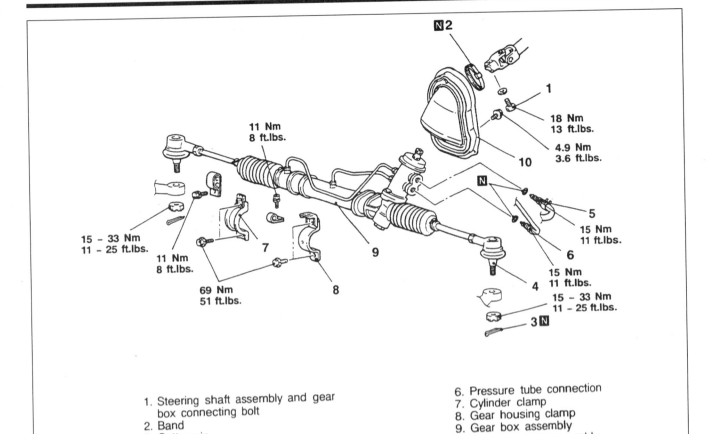

1. Steering shaft assembly and gear box connecting bolt
2. Band
3. Cotter pin
4. Tie-rod end and knuckle connection
5. Return tube connection
6. Pressure tube connection
7. Cylinder clamp
8. Gear housing clamp
9. Gear box assembly
10. Steering cover assembly

Fig. 97 Exploded view of the power steering gear assembly—Mirage

1993–00 MODELS

♦ See Figure 97

➡ **Prior to removal of the steering gear box, center the front wheels and remove the ignition key. Failure to do so may damage the SRS clockspring and render SRS system inoperative.**

1. Drain the power steering system.
2. Disconnect the battery negative cable. Raise the vehicle and support safely.
3. Disconnect the Heated Oxygen (HO₂S) sensor and remove the front exhaust pipe.
4. Properly support the engine.
5. Remove both roll stopper mounting bolts and the four center member installation bolts. Remove center member.
6. Remove the center member.

➡ **Matchmark the pinion input shaft of the rack to the lower steering column joint for installation purposes.**

7. Remove the pinch bolt holding the lower steering column joint to the rack and pinion input shaft.
8. Remove the cotter pins and disconnect the tie rod ends from the steering knuckle.
9. Disconnect the power steering fluid pressure pipe and return hose from the rack fittings.
10. Remove the rack and pinion steering assembly and its rubber mounts from the right side of the vehicle.

To install:
11. Align the matchmarks of the input shaft and install the rack to the vehicle.
12. Secure the rack using the retainer clamps and bolts. Tighten the bolts to 51 ft. lbs. (70 Nm).
13. Tighten the steering column pinch bolt to 13 ft. lbs. (18 Nm).
14. Using new O-rings, connect the power steering fluid lines to the rack fittings.
15. Install the center member.
16. Install the front exhaust pipe.
17. Connect the HO₂S sensor.
18. Connect the tie rod ends to the steering knuckles and tighten the castle nuts to 25 ft. lbs. (34 Nm). Install new cotter pins.
19. Install the wheels and connect the negative battery cable.
20. Refill the reservoir and bleed the system.
21. Have a front end alignment performed.

Power Steering Pump

REMOVAL AND INSTALLATION

Mirage

1. Drain the power steering system as follows:
   a. Disconnect the return hose at the reservoir and place into a suitable container.
   b. Disable the ignition system. While cranking the engine, turn the wheels several times, until system has been drained.

2. Disconnect the battery negative cable.
3. Remove the pressure switch connector from the side of the pump.
4. If the alternator is located under the oil pump, cover it with a shop towel to protect it from oil.
5. Disconnect the pressure line.
6. Remove the steering pump drive belt and the water pump pulley drive belt.
7. Remove the water pump pulley.
8. Remove the bolts that secure the oil pump, then remove the pump from its bracket.

To install:
9. Install the power steering pump and tighten the mounting bolts to specifications.
10. Install the water pump pulley and tighten the mounting bolts 14 ft. lbs. (19 Nm).
11. Install and adjust the drive belts.
12. Replace the O-rings and connect the pressure line. Connect the pressure line so the notch in the fitting aligns and contacts the pump's guide bracket. Tighten the nut that secures the pressure line to 13 ft. lbs. (18 Nm).
13. Connect the return line.
14. Attach the pressure switch connector.
15. Refill the reservoir and bleed the system.

1990–93 Galant

FRONT

1. Disconnect the battery negative cable.
2. Remove the pressure switch connector from the side of the pump.

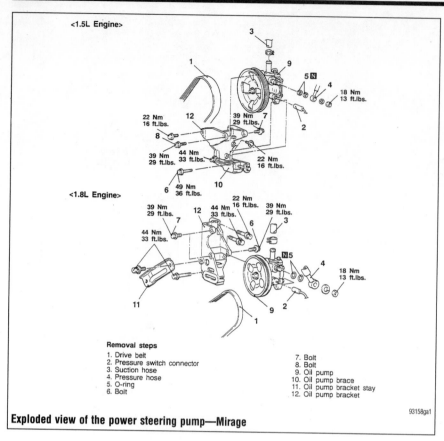

Removal steps
1. Drive belt
2. Pressure switch connector
3. Suction hose
4. Pressure hose
5. O-ring
6. Bolt
7. Bolt
8. Bolt
9. Oil pump
10. Oil pump brace
11. Oil pump bracket stay
12. Oil pump bracket

Exploded view of the power steering pump—Mirage

3. If the alternator is located under the oil pump, cover it with a shop towel to protect it from oil.

4. Disconnect the return fluid line.

5. Remove the reservoir cap and allow the return line to drain the fluid from the reservoir. If the fluid is contaminated, disconnect the ignition high tension cable and crank the engine several times to drain the fluid from the gearbox.

6. Disconnect the pressure line.

7. Remove the pump drive belt.

8. Remove the pump mounting bolts and remove the pump from the engine.

To install:

9. Install the pump, wrap the belt around the pulley and loosely tighten the mounting bolts.

10. Replace the O-rings and connect the pressure line. Connect the pressure line so the notch in the fitting aligns and contacts the pump's guide bracket.

11. Connect the return line. Attach the pressure switch connector.

12. Adjust the belt tension and tighten the adjusting bolts to 25–33 ft. lbs. (35–45 Nm).

13. Refill the reservoir and bleed the system.

REAR

1. Raise the vehicle and support safely.
2. Drain the differential gear oil.
3. Matchmark and remove the rear driveshaft.
4. Remove the rear halfshafts.
5. Remove the center exhaust pipe and muffler assembly, as required.

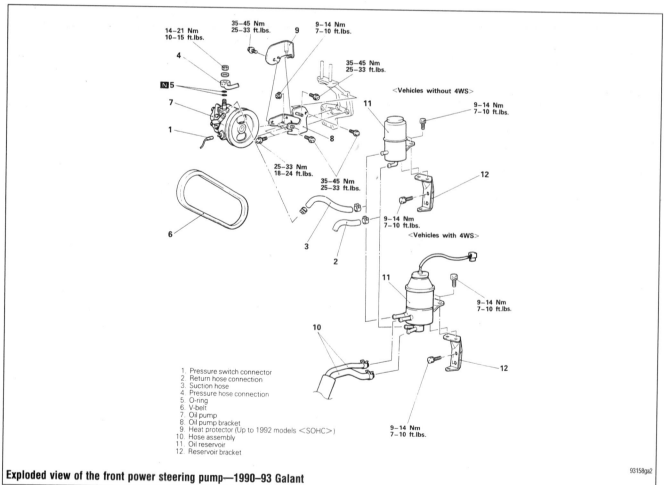

1. Pressure switch connector
2. Return hose connection
3. Suction hose
4. Pressure hose connection
5. O-ring
6. V-belt
7. Oil pump
8. Oil pump bracket
9. Heat protector (Up to 1992 models <SOHC>)
10. Hose assembly
11. Oil reservoir
12. Reservoir bracket

Exploded view of the front power steering pump—1990–93 Galant

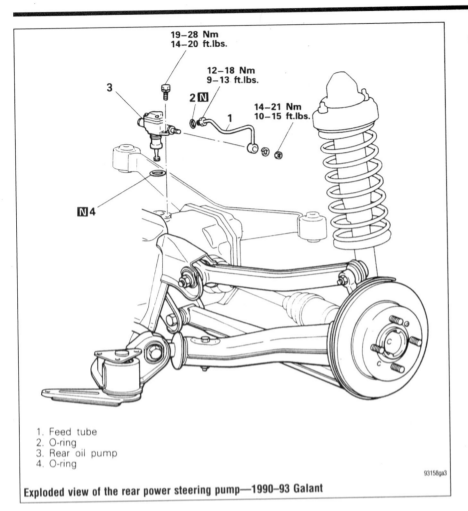

19–28 Nm
14–20 ft.lbs.

12–18 Nm
9–13 ft.lbs.

14–21 Nm
10–15 ft.lbs.

1. Feed tube
2. O-ring
3. Rear oil pump
4. O-ring

93158ga3

Exploded view of the rear power steering pump—1990–93 Galant

6. Disconnect the pressure and suction hoses from the fittings on the pump.

7. The large mounting bolts that hold the differential carrier support plate to the underbody may use self-locking nuts. Before removing them, support the rear axle assembly in the middle with a transaxle jack. Remove the nuts, then remove the support plate(s) and the square dynamic damper from the rear of the carrier.

8. Lower the differential carrier and remove from the vehicle.

9. Remove the pump retaining bolt and remove the pump from the rear differential assembly.

To install:

10. Install the pump and tighten the mounting bolt to 14–20 ft. lbs. (19–28 Nm).

11. Raise the rear differential carrier into position and install support member bolts. Replace all self-locking nuts. Tighten all mounting nuts and bolts as follows:

- Upper support plate to carrier bolts: 72–87 ft. lbs. (100–120 Nm)
- Support member/dynamic damper to carrier bolts: 58–72 ft. lbs. (80–100 Nm)
- Differential support member mounting bolt nuts: 80–94 ft. lbs. (110–130 Nm)

12. Connect the pressure and suction lines to the pump.

13. Install new circlips on both rear driveshafts and install.

14. Install the propeller shaft and tighten the mounting hardware to 22–25 ft. lbs. (30–35 Nm).

15. Install the center exhaust pipe and muffler.

16. Lower the vehicle. With the vehicle level, fill the rear differential.

17. Fill the power steering system and properly bleed.

1994–00 Galant

2.4L ENGINE

1. Disconnect the battery negative cable.

2. Loosen and remove the power steering pump drive belt.

3. Remove the pressure switch connector from the side of the pump.

➡**If the alternator is located under the oil pump, cover it with a shop towel to protect it from oil.**

4. Disconnect the return fluid line. Remove the reservoir cap and allow the return line to drain the fluid from the reservoir. If the fluid is contaminated, disconnect the ignition high tension cable and crank the engine several times to drain the fluid from the gearbox.

5. Disconnect the pressure line.

6. Unbolt and remove the pump from the mounting bracket.

To install:

7. Install the pump, wrap the belt around the pulley and lightly tighten the mounting bolts.

8. Replace the O-rings and connect the pressure line. Connect the pressure line so the notch in the fitting aligns and contacts the pump's guide bracket. Tighten the fitting to 13 ft. lbs. (18 Nm).

9. Connect the return line and secure with the clamp.

10. Attach the pressure switch connector.

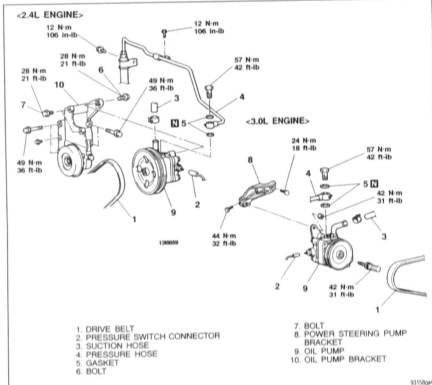

<2.4L ENGINE>

12 N·m
106 in-lb

12 N·m
106 in-lb

28 N·m
21 ft-lb

28 N·m
21 ft-lb

57 N·m
42 ft-lb

49 N·m
36 ft-lb

49 N·m
36 ft-lb

<3.0L ENGINE>

24 N·m
18 ft-lb

57 N·m
42 ft-lb

42 N·m
31 ft-lb

44 N·m
32 ft-lb

42 N·m
31 ft-lb

13I0059

1. DRIVE BELT
2. PRESSURE SWITCH CONNECTOR
3. SUCTION HOSE
4. PRESSURE HOSE
5. GASKET
6. BOLT
7. BOLT
8. POWER STEERING PUMP BRACKET
9. OIL PUMP
10. OIL PUMP BRACKET

93158ga4

Exploded view of the power steering pump—1994–00 Galant with 2.4L engine

11. Adjust the power steering belt for proper tension and tighten the adjusting bolts.

12. Reconnect the negative battery cable.

13. Refill the reservoir and bleed the system.

3.0L ENGINE

1. Disconnect the battery negative cable.

2. Disconnect the return fluid line. Remove the reservoir cap and allow the return line to drain the fluid from the reservoir. If the fluid is contaminated, disconnect the ignition high tension cable and crank the engine several times to drain the fluid from the gearbox.

3. Remove the power steering pump drive belt.

4. Remove the pressure switch connector from the side of the pump.

5. If the alternator is located under the oil pump, cover it with a shop towel to protect it from oil.

6. Disconnect the high pressure hose and the return hose from the pump.

7. Remove the pump drive belt and unbolt the pump from its bracket and remove the pump.

To install:

8. Install the pump, wrap the belt around the pulley and tighten the bolts that secure the pump to 17 ft. lbs. (24 Nm).

9. Replace the O-rings and connect the high pressure hose. Connect the pressure line so the notch in the fitting aligns and contacts the pump's guide bracket. Tighten the mounting nut with lockwasher to 17 ft. lbs. (24 Nm).

10. Using a new hose clamp, connect the return line.

11. Attach the pressure switch connector.

12. Adjust the belt tension and tighten the adjusting bolts.

13. Refill the reservoir and bleed the system.

Diamante

FRONT

1. Disconnect the battery negative cable.

2. Disconnect the return fluid line. Remove the reservoir cap and allow the return line to drain the fluid from the reservoir. If the fluid is contaminated, disconnect the ignition high tension cable and crank the engine several times to drain the fluid from the gearbox.

3. Remove the power steering pump drive belt.

4. Remove the pressure switch connector from the side of the pump.

5. If the alternator is located under the oil pump, cover it with a shop towel to protect it from oil.

6. Disconnect the high pressure hose and the return hose from the pump.

7. Remove the pump drive belt and unbolt the pump from its bracket and remove the pump.

To install:

8. Install the pump, wrap the belt around the pulley and tighten the bolts that secure the pump to 17 ft. lbs. (24 Nm).

9. Replace the O-rings and connect the high pressure hose. Connect the pressure line so the notch in the fitting aligns and contacts the pump's guide bracket. Tighten the mounting nut with lockwasher to 17 ft. lbs. (24 Nm).

10. Using a new hose clamp, connect the return line.

11. Attach the pressure switch connector.

12. Adjust the belt tension and tighten the adjusting bolts.

13. Refill the reservoir and bleed the system.

REAR

1. Disconnect the negative battery cable.

2. Drain the power steering fluid.

3. Remove the rear power steering pump heat protector, located on the engine side of the differential on the transaxle.

4. Disconnect the pressure line from the pump.

5. Disconnect the suction hose from the pump.

6. Remove the mounting bolts and remove the pump from the transaxle.

7. The installation is the reverse of the removal procedure. Tighten the mounting bolts to 17 ft. lbs. (24 Nm).

8. Refill the reservoir and bleed the system.

❋❋❋ CAUTION

Extreme caution should be taken when testing the rear steering pump. Ensure that the vehicle is supported safely and that all components are torqued to specification prior be testing.

SYSTEM BLEEDING

Front

1. Raise the vehicle and support safely.

2. Manually turn the pump pulley a few times.

3. Turn the steering wheel all the way to the left and to the right 5 or 6 times.

4. Disconnect the ignition high tension cable and, while operating the starter motor intermittently, turn the steering wheel all the way to the left and right 5–6 times for 15–20 seconds. During bleeding, make sure the fluid in the reservoir never falls below the lower position of the filter. If bleeding is attempted with the engine running, the air will be absorbed in the fluid. Bleed only while cranking.

5. Connect ignition high tension cable, start engine and allow to idle.

6. Turn the steering wheel left and right until there are no air bubbles in the reservoir. Confirm that the fluid is not milky and the level is up to the specified position on the gauge. Confirm that there is very little change in the fluid level when the steering wheel is turned. If the fluid level changes more than 0.2 in. (5mm), the air has not been completely bled. Repeat the process.

Rear

1. Bleed the front steering system.

2. Start the engine and let it idle.

3. Loosen the bleeder screw on the left side of the control valve and install special tool MB991230 to the bleeder.

4. Turn the steering wheel all the way to the left, then immediately turn it halfway back. Confirm that air has discharged with the fluid.

5. Repeat Step 4 two or three times as required, to remove all air from the rear system. Stop the engine.

6. Loosen the power cylinder (rear steering gear) bleeder screw about 1/8 turn and install the same special tool with the rotation prevention metal fixtures to prevent the bleeder from opening more.

7. Start the engine and run to 50 mph to circulate the fluid.

8. Maintain a speed of 20 mph and turn the steering wheel back and forth. Air should be discharged through the tube of the special tool and into the oil reservoir.

9. Repeat until all air is removed from the power cylinder.

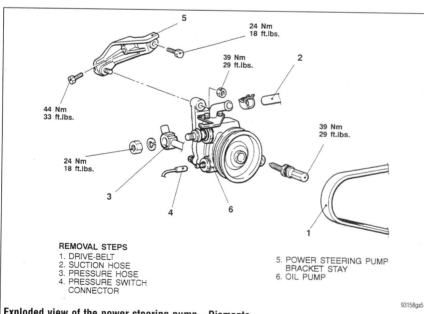

REMOVAL STEPS
1. DRIVE-BELT
2. SUCTION HOSE
3. PRESSURE HOSE
4. PRESSURE SWITCH CONNECTOR
5. POWER STEERING PUMP BRACKET STAY
6. OIL PUMP

93158ga5

Exploded view of the power steering pump—Diamante

TORQUE SPECIFICATIONS

Components	English	Metric
Air bag retaining screws	48 inch lbs.	5 Nm
Front Suspension		
Damper fork-to-lateral arm (1994-98 Galant)	64 ft. lbs.	88 Nm
Hub and bearing assembly-to-steering knuckle bolts	65 ft. lbs.	88 Nm
Lower ball joint-to-steering knuckle		
All	43-52 ft. lbs.	60-72 Nm
Lower control arm		
Diamante, 1990-93 Galant, and 1999-00 Galant		
Rear mount clamp retaining bolts	72-87 ft. lbs.	100-120 Nm
Rear mount clamp retaining nuts	29 ft. lbs.	40 Nm
Frame mount through bolt	75-90 ft. lbs.	102-122 Nm
1994-98 Galant		
Lateral arm rear bolt	71-85 ft. lbs.	98-118 Nm
Compression arm retaining bolt	60 ft. lbs.	83 Nm
Mirage		
Front mount	65 ft. lbs.	90 Nm
Rear mount	78 ft. lbs.	108 Nm
Shock absorber and coil spring-to-body nuts		
1994-98 Galant	32 ft. lbs.	44 Nm
Shock absorber and coil spring-to-damper fork through bolt		
1994-98 Galant	65 ft. lbs.	88 Nm
Shock absorber and coil spring-to-damper fork pinch bolt		
Mirage	76 ft. lbs.	103 Nm
Strut-to-body mounting bolts/nuts		
Diamante, 1990-93 Galant, and 1999-00 Galant	33 ft. lbs.	45 Nm
Mirage	29 ft. lbs.	40 Nm
Strut-to-steering knuckle mounting bolts		
Diamante, 1990-93 Galant, and 1999-00 Galant	70-76 ft. lbs.	90-105 Nm
Mirage	80-94 ft. lbs.	110-130 Nm
Sway bar mount retaining bolts		
1994-00 Galant	28 ft. lbs.	39 Nm
Diamante	32 ft. lbs.	44 Nm
Mirage	16 ft. lbs.	22 Nm
Sway bar links-to-damper fork (1994-98 Galant)	29 ft. lbs.	40 Nm
Tie-rod end-to-steering knuckle nuts		
Mirage	25 ft. lbs.	34 Nm
Galant and Diamante	21 ft. lbs.	29 Nm
Tie rod end jam nut		
Mirage	30 ft. lbs.	42 Nm
Galant and Diamante	36-39 ft. lbs.	49-53 Nm
Upper ball joint-to-steering knuckle nut (1994-98 galant)	20 ft. lbs.	28 Nm
Upper control arm-to-shaft through bolts (1994-98 Galant)	41 ft. lbs.	57 Nm
Upper control arm-to-body nuts (1994-98 Galant)	62 ft. lbs.	86 Nm
Wheel hub retaining nut	145-188 ft. lbs.	200-260 Nm
Manual rack and pinion		
Steering shaft upper pinch bolt	13 ft. lbs.	18 Nm
Rack retainer bolts	51 ft. lbs.	70 Nm
Power rack and pinion		
Front		
Inner tie rod-to-rack and pinion	65 ft. lbs.	88 Nm
Steering shaft upper pinch bolt		
Diamante	21 ft. lbs.	29 Nm
Except Diamante	13 ft. lbs.	18 Nm
Rack retainer bolts		
Diamante	51 ft. lbs.	70 Nm
1990-93 Galant	43-58 ft. lbs	60-80 Nm
1994-00 Galant	51 ft. lbs.	70 Nm
Mirage	51 ft. lbs.	70 Nm

TORQUE SPECIFICATIONS

Components	English	Metric
Rear		
Rack retainer bolts		
Diamante	51 ft. lbs.	70 Nm
Power steering pump		
Hose fittings	13 ft. lbs.	18 Nm
Front pump retaining bolts		
Mirage	14 ft. lbs.	19 Nm
1990-93 Galant	25-33 ft. lbs.	35-45 Nm
1994-00 Galant	17 ft. lbs.	24 Nm
Diamante	17 ft. lbs.	24 Nm
Rear pump retaining bolts		
1990-93 Galant	25-33 ft. lbs.	35-45 Nm
Diamante	17 ft. lbs.	24 Nm
Rear suspension		
Axle retaining nut		
1990-92 Mirage	108-145 ft. lbs.	150-200 Nm
1993-00 Mirage	130 ft. lbs.	180 Nm
1990-93 Galant w/drum brakes	20 ft. lbs.	27 Nm
1990-93 Disc brakes	145-188 ft. lbs.	200-260 Nm
Lower control arm		
Diamante		
Control arm-to-trailing arm nut	54-61 ft. lbs.	75-89 Nm
Control arm-to-crossmember	54-61 ft. lbs.	75-89 Nm
Galant		
Rear mount	72 ft. lbs.	100 Nm
Ball joint-to-knuckle	43-52 ft. lbs.	60-72 Nm
Strut		
Upper mounting nuts		
Diamante	33 ft. lbs.	45 Nm
1990-93 Galant	29 ft. lbs.	40 Nm
1994-00 Galant	32 ft. lbs.	44 Nm
Mirage	20 ft. lbs.	28 Nm
Lower strut mounting bolt		
All models	71 ft. lbs.	98 Nm
Sway bar mount retaining bolts		
Diamante and 1994-00 Galant	28 ft. lbs.	39 Nm
1990-93 Galant	33 ft. lbs.	45 Nm
Trailing arm-to-body through bolt		
1990-93 Galant	72-87 ft. lbs.	100-120 Nm
1993-00 Mirage	72-87 ft. lbs.	100-120 Nm
1994-00 Galant and 1997-00 Diamante	99-114 ft. lbs.	137-157 Nm
1992-96 Diamante	101-116 ft. lbs.	140-160 Nm
Upper ball joint retaining nut		
1990-93 Galant	52 ft. lbs.	72 Nm
1994-98 Galant	71 ft. lbs.	98 Nm
Upper control arm retaining bolts		
1990-93 Galant	116 ft. lbs.	160 Nm
1994-98 Galant	28 ft. lbs.	39 Nm
Diamante	54-61 ft. lbs.	75-89 Nm
Wheel hub mounting bolts	54-65 ft. lbs.	74-88 Nm
Steering wheel retaining nut		
1990-93 Galant	25-33 ft. lbs.	35-45 Nm
1994-00 Diamante	33 ft. lbs.	45 Nm
All other models	29 ft. lbs.	40 Nm
Wheel lug nuts	65-80 ft. lbs.	90-110 Nm

93158c02

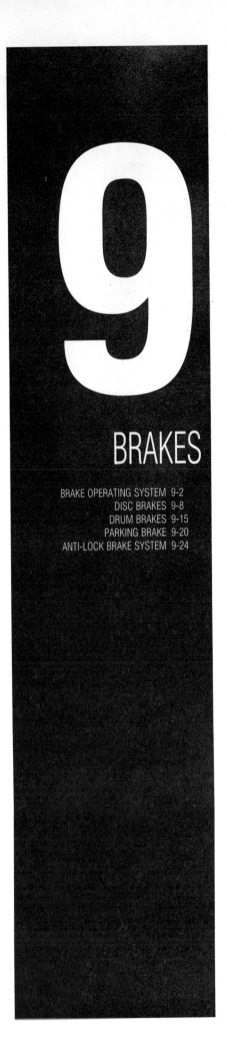

9

BRAKES

BRAKE OPERATING SYSTEM

Basic Operating Principles

Hydraulic systems are used to actuate the brakes of all modern automobiles. The system transports the power required to force the frictional surfaces of the braking system together from the pedal to the individual brake units at each wheel. A hydraulic system is used for two reasons.

First, fluid under pressure can be carried to all parts of an automobile by small pipes and flexible hoses without taking up a significant amount of room or posing routing problems.

Second, a great mechanical advantage can be given to the brake pedal end of the system, and the foot pressure required to actuate the brakes can be reduced by making the surface area of the master cylinder pistons smaller than that of any of the pistons in the wheel cylinders or calipers.

The master cylinder consists of a fluid reservoir along with a double cylinder and piston assembly. Double type master cylinders are designed to separate the front and rear braking systems hydraulically in case of a leak. The master cylinder converts mechanical motion from the pedal into hydraulic pressure within the lines. This pressure is translated back into mechanical motion at the wheels by either the wheel cylinder (drum brakes) or the caliper (disc brakes).

Steel lines carry the brake fluid to a point on the vehicle's frame near each of the vehicle's wheels. The fluid is then carried to the calipers and wheel cylinders by flexible tubes in order to allow for suspension and steering movements.

In drum brake systems, each wheel cylinder contains two pistons, one at either end, which push outward in opposite directions and force the brake shoe into contact with the drum.

In disc brake systems, the cylinders are part of the calipers. At least one cylinder in each caliper is used to force the brake pads against the disc.

All pistons employ some type of seal, usually made of rubber, to minimize fluid leakage. A rubber dust boot seals the outer end of the cylinder against dust and dirt. The boot fits around the outer end of the piston on disc brake calipers, and around the brake actuating rod on wheel cylinders.

The hydraulic system operates as follows: When at rest, the entire system, from the piston(s) in the master cylinder to those in the wheel cylinders or calipers, is full of brake fluid. Upon application of the brake pedal, fluid trapped in front of the master cylinder piston(s) is forced through the lines to the wheel cylinders. Here, it forces the pistons outward, in the case of drum brakes, and inward toward the disc, in the case of disc brakes. The motion of the pistons is opposed by return springs mounted outside the cylinders in drum brakes, and by spring seals, in disc brakes.

Upon release of the brake pedal, a spring located inside the master cylinder immediately returns the master cylinder pistons to the normal position. The pistons contain check valves and the master cylinder has compensating ports drilled in it. These are uncovered as the pistons reach their normal position. The piston check valves allow fluid to flow toward the wheel cylinders or calipers as the pistons withdraw. Then, as the return springs force the brake pads or shoes into the released position, the excess fluid reservoir through the compensating ports. It is during the time the pedal is in the released position that any fluid that has leaked out of the system will be replaced through the compensating ports.

Dual circuit master cylinders employ two pistons, located one behind the other, in the same cylinder. The primary piston is actuated directly by mechanical linkage from the brake pedal through the power booster. The secondary piston is actuated by fluid trapped between the two pistons. If a leak develops in front of the secondary piston, it moves forward until it bottoms against the front of the master cylinder, and the fluid trapped between the pistons will operate the rear brakes. If the rear brakes develop a leak, the primary piston will move forward until direct contact with the secondary piston takes place, and it will force the secondary piston to actuate the front brakes. In either case, the brake pedal moves farther when the brakes are applied, and less braking power is available.

All dual circuit systems use a switch to warn the driver when only half of the brake system is operational. This switch is usually located in a valve body which is mounted on the firewall or the frame below the master cylinder. A hydraulic piston receives pressure from both circuits, each circuit's pressure being applied to one end of the piston. When the pressures are in balance, the piston remains stationary. When one circuit has a leak, however, the greater pressure in that circuit during application of the brakes will push the piston to one side, closing the switch and activating the brake warning light.

In disc brake systems, this valve body also contains a metering valve and, in some cases, a proportioning valve. The metering valve keeps pressure from traveling to the disc brakes on the front wheels until the brake shoes on the rear wheels have contacted the drums, ensuring that the front brakes will never be used alone. The proportioning valve controls the pressure to the rear brakes to lessen the chance of rear wheel lock-up during very hard braking.

Warning lights may be tested by depressing the brake pedal and holding it while opening one of the wheel cylinder bleeder screws. If this does not cause the light to go on, substitute a new lamp, make continuity checks, and, finally, replace the switch as necessary.

The hydraulic system may be checked for leaks by applying pressure to the pedal gradually and steadily. If the pedal sinks very slowly to the floor, the system has a leak. This is not to be confused with a springy or spongy feel due to the compression of air within the lines. If the system leaks, there will be a gradual change in the position of the pedal with a constant pressure.

Check for leaks along all lines and at wheel cylinders. If no external leaks are apparent, the problem is inside the master cylinder.

DISC BRAKES

Instead of the traditional expanding brakes that press outward against a circular drum, disc brake systems utilize a disc (rotor) with brake pads positioned on either side of it. An easily-seen analogy is the hand brake arrangement on a bicycle. The pads squeeze onto the rim of the bike wheel, slowing its motion. Automobile disc brakes use the identical principle but apply the braking effort to a separate disc instead of the wheel.

The disc (rotor) is a casting, usually equipped with cooling fins between the two braking surfaces. This enables air to circulate between the braking surfaces making them less sensitive to heat buildup and more resistant to fade. Dirt and water do not drastically affect braking action since contaminants are thrown off by the centrifugal action of the rotor or scraped off the by the pads. Also, the equal clamping action of the two brake pads tends to ensure uniform, straight line stops. Disc brakes are inherently self-adjusting. There are three general types of disc brake:

1. A fixed caliper.
2. A floating caliper.
3. A sliding caliper.

The fixed caliper design uses two pistons mounted on either side of the rotor (in each side of the caliper). The caliper is mounted rigidly and does not move.

The sliding and floating designs are quite similar. In fact, these two types are often lumped together. In both designs, the pad on the inside of the rotor is moved into contact with the rotor by hydraulic force. The caliper, which is not held in a fixed position, moves slightly, bringing the outside pad into contact with the rotor. There are various methods of attaching floating calipers. Some pivot at the bottom or top, and some slide on mounting bolts. In any event, the end result is the same.

DRUM BRAKES

Drum brakes employ two brake shoes mounted on a stationary backing plate. These shoes are positioned inside a circular drum which rotates with the wheel assembly. The shoes are held in place by springs. This allows them to slide toward the drums (when they are applied) while keeping the linings and drums in alignment. The shoes are actuated by a wheel cylinder which is mounted at the top of the backing plate. When the brakes are applied, hydraulic pressure forces the wheel cylinder's actuating links outward. Since these links bear directly against the top of the brake shoes, the tops of the shoes are then forced against the inner side of the drum. This action forces the bottoms of the two shoes to contact the brake drum by rotating the entire assembly slightly (known as servo action). When pressure within the wheel cylinder is relaxed, return springs pull the shoes back away from the drum.

Most modern drum brakes are designed to self-adjust themselves during application when the vehicle is moving in reverse. This motion causes both shoes to rotate very slightly with the drum, rocking an adjusting lever, thereby causing rotation of the adjusting screw. Some drum brake systems are designed to self-adjust during application whenever the brakes are applied. This on-board adjustment system reduces the need for maintenance adjustments and keeps both the brake function and pedal feel satisfactory.

POWER BOOSTERS

Virtually all modern vehicles use a vacuum assisted power brake system to multiply the braking force and reduce pedal effort. Since vacuum is always available when the engine is operating, the system is simple and efficient. A vacuum diaphragm is located on the front of the master cylinder and assists the driver in applying the brakes, reducing both the effort and travel he must put into moving the brake pedal.

The vacuum diaphragm housing is normally connected to the intake manifold by a vacuum hose. A check valve is placed at the point where the hose enters the diaphragm housing, so that during periods of low manifold vacuum brakes assist will not be lost.

Depressing the brake pedal closes off the vacuum source and allows atmospheric pressure to enter on one side of the diaphragm. This causes the master cylinder pistons to move and apply the brakes. When the brake pedal is released, vacuum is applied to both sides of the diaphragm and springs return the diaphragm and master cylinder pistons to the released position.

If the vacuum supply fails, the brake pedal rod will contact the end of the master cylinder actuator rod and the system will apply the brakes without any power assistance. The driver will notice that much higher pedal effort is needed to stop the car and that the pedal feels harder than usual.

Vacuum Leak Test

1. Operate the engine at idle without touching the brake pedal for at least one minute.
2. Turn off the engine and wait one minute.
3. Test for the presence of assist vacuum by depressing the brake pedal and releasing it several times. If vacuum is present in the system, light application will produce less and less pedal travel. If there is no vacuum, air is leaking into the system.

System Operation Test

1. With the engine **OFF**, pump the brake pedal until the supply vacuum is entirely gone.
2. Put light, steady pressure on the brake pedal.
3. Start the engine and let it idle. If the system is operating correctly, the brake pedal should fall toward the floor if the constant pressure is maintained.

Power brake systems may be tested for hydraulic leaks just as ordinary systems are tested.

Brake Light Switch

REMOVAL & INSTALLATION

♦ See Figure 1

1. Disconnect the negative battery cable.
2. Detach the stop lamp switch electrical harness connector.
3. Loosen the locknut holding the switch to the bracket. Remove the locknut and the switch.

To install:
4. Install the new switch and install the locknut, tightening it just snug.
5. Reposition the brake light switch so that the distance between the outer case of the switch and the pedal is 0.02–0.04 in. (0.5–1.0mm). Note that the switch plunger must press against the pedal to keep the brake lights off. As the pedal moves away from the switch, the plunger extends and closes the switch, which turns on the stop lights.
6. Hold the switch in the correct position and tighten the locknut.
7. Connect the wiring to the switch.
8. Check the operation of the switch. Turn the ignition key to the ON position but do not start the en-

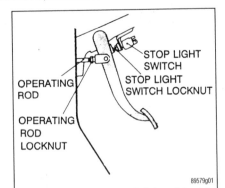

Fig. 1 The brake light switch is retained to the bracket with a locknut

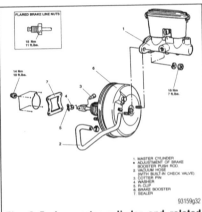

Fig. 2 Brake master cylinder and related components—Diamante

Fig. 6 Detach the fluid level sensor connector, then remove the master cylinder reservoir

gine. Have an assistant observe the brake lights at the rear of the vehicle while you push on the brake pedal. The lights should come on just as the brake pedal passes the point of free play.

9. Adjust the brake light switch as necessary. The small amount of free play in the pedal should not trigger the brake lights; if the switch is set incorrectly, the brake lights will flicker due to pedal vibration on road bumps.

Master Cylinder

REMOVAL & INSTALLATION

♦ See Figures 2 thru 10

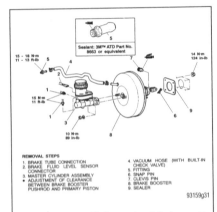

Fig. 3 Master cylinder and related components—1994–97 Galant

Fig.4 Unfasten the master cylinder reservoir mounting bracket bolts

Fig. 5 Unfasten the brake hose retaining clamps and disconnect the hose from the master cylinder

Fig. 7 Use a flare nut wrench to disconnect and plug the brake lines from the master cylinder

Fig. 8 Unfasten the master cylinder-to-power booster retaining nuts . . .

Fig. 9 . . . then remove the master cylinder assembly from the vehicle

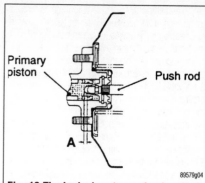

Fig. 10 The brake booster pushrod and primary piston clearance (A) must be adjusted

1. Disconnect the negative battery cable.
2. Remove the master cylinder reservoir cap, then use a clean turkey baster or equivalent to siphon out as much fluid as possible and place in a suitable container. Install the cap.

✳✳ CAUTION

Brake fluid contains polyglycol ethers and polyglycols. Avoid contact with the eyes and wash your hands thoroughly after handling brake fluid. If you do get brake fluid in your eyes, flush your eyes with clean, running water for 15 minutes. If eye irritation persists, or if you have taken brake fluid internally, IMMEDIATELY seek medical assistance.

3. Disconnect and plug the lines from the brake master cylinder reservoir.
4. Detach the fluid level sensor connector, unfasten the retainers, then remove the master cylinder reservoir.
5. For vehicles equipped with manual transaxle, remove the clutch master cylinder reservoir bracket.
6. Disconnect and plug the brake lines from the master cylinder.
7. Unfasten the master cylinder-to-power booster retaining nuts, then remove the master cylinder from the vehicle.

To install:
8. Adjust the clearance (A) between the brake booster pushrod and the primary piston as follows:
   a. Calculate the clearance A from the B, C and D measurements, as shown in the accompanying figure. A equals B minus C minus D.
   b. The clearance should be 0.256–0.335 in. (0.65–0.858mm). When brake booster negative pressure 9.7 psi (67 kPa) is applied, then clear-

ance value will become 0.004–0.012 in. (0.1–0.3mm).
9. Install the master cylinder to the brake booster, then install the retaining nuts. Tighten the nuts to 7 ft. lbs. (10 Nm).
10. Install the master cylinder reservoir, securing the retainers.
11. Attach the fluid level sensor connector, then unplug and connect the fluid lines to the reservoir.
12. The remainder of installation is the reverse of the removal procedure. Fill the reservoir with the proper type and amount of DOT 3 brake fluid from a fresh, sealed container.

✳✳ WARNING

Clean, high quality brake fluid is essential to the safe and proper operation of the brake system. You should always buy the highest quality brake fluid that is available. If the brake fluid becomes contaminated, drain and flush the system, then refill the master cylinder with new fluid. Never reuse any brake fluid. Any brake fluid that is removed from the system should be discarded. Also, do not allow any brake fluid to come in contact with a painted surface; it will damage the paint.

13. Bleed the brake system, as outlined later in this section.
14. Adjust the brake pedal, as outlined later in this section.

BRAKE PEDAL ADJUSTMENTS

Brake Pedal Height

▶ **See Figures 11, 12, and 13**

Measure the brake pedal height from the floor of the vehicle to the upper surface of the brake pedal. The distance should be 6.9–7.1 in (176–181mm). If the brake pedal height is incorrect, adjust as follows:
1. Detach the stop lamp switch connector.
2. Loosen the locknut on the base of the stop light switch and move the switch to a position where it does not contact the brake pedal.
3. Loosen the operating rod locknut. Adjust the height of the brake pedal by turning the operating rod using pliers. Once the desired pedal height is obtained, tighten the locknut on the operating rod.
4. Screw the stop light switch until the it contacts the brake pedal stopper. Turn switch in until the brake pedal just starts to move. At this point, return (loosen) the stoplight switch 1/2–1 turn and secure in this position by tightening the locknut. In this position, the distance between the lower stop light switch case and the brake pedal stop should be 0.02–0.04 in. (0.5–1.0mm).
5. Attach the electrical connector to the stop light switch.
6. Check to be sure that the stop lights are not illuminated with no pressure on the brake pedal.
7. Without starting the vehicle, depress the brake pedal. If the brake light switch is properly connected, the brake lights will illuminate.

Brake Pedal Free-Play

▶ **See Figure 14**

1. With the engine off, depress the brake pedal fully several times to evacuate the vacuum in the booster.
2. Once all the vacuum assist has been eliminated, press the brake pedal down by hand and con-

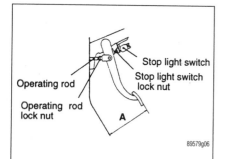

Fig. 11 Measure the brake pedal height at A and compare to specifications

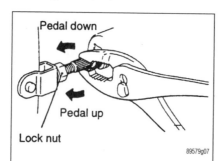

Fig. 12 Adjust the brake pedal height by increasing or decreasing the length of the operating rod

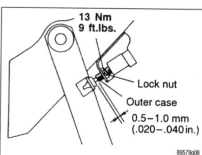

Fig. 13 Inspect the clearance between the stop light switch and the brake pedal stop and compare to specifications

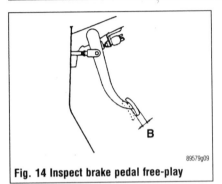

Fig. 14 Inspect brake pedal free-play

firm that the amount of movement before resistance is felt is within 0.1–0.3 in. (3–8mm).

3. If the free-play is less than desired, confirm that the brake light switch is in proper adjustment.

4. If there is excessive free-play, look for wear or play in the clevis pin and brake pedal arm. Replace worn parts as required and recheck brake pedal free-play.

Power Brake Booster

REMOVAL & INSTALLATION

♦ **See Figure 15**

1. Disconnect the negative battery cable.
2. Siphon the brake fluid from the master cylinder reservoir.

✳✳ CAUTION

Brake fluid contains polyglycol ethers and polyglycols. Avoid contact with the eyes and wash your hands thoroughly after handling brake fluid. If you do get brake fluid in your eyes, flush your eyes with clean, running water for 15 minutes. If eye irritation persists, or if you have taken brake fluid internally, IMMEDIATELY seek medical assistance.

3. Remove and relocate the air conditioning relay box and the solenoid valve located at the power brake unit.

4. Disconnect the vacuum hose from the booster by pulling it straight off. Prying off the vacuum hose could damage the check valve installed in the brake booster vacuum hose.

5. Detach the electrical harness connector from the brake level sensor.

6. Remove the nuts attaching the master cylinder to the booster and remove the master cylinder and position aside. If necessary, disconnect and plug the brake fluid lines at the master cylinder.

7. From inside the passenger compartment, remove the cotter pin and clevis pin that secures the booster pushrod to the brake pedal.

8. From inside the vehicle, remove the nuts that attach the booster to the dash panel. Remove the brake booster from the engine compartment.

To install:

9. Install the brake booster to the dash panel. From inside the vehicle, install the attaching nuts and tighten to 12 ft. lbs. (17 Nm).

10. Apply grease to the clevis pin and install with washers in place. Install new cotter pin and bend to secure in place.

11. Attach the vacuum hose to the booster fitting.

12. Install the master cylinder assembly to the mounting studs on the brake booster. Install the master cylinder mounting nuts and tighten to 9 ft. lbs. (12 Nm).

13. Reconnect the brake fluid reservoir to the master cylinder, if disconnected. Attach the electrical connector to the brake fluid level sensor.

14. Install the solenoid valve assembly and the relay box, if removed.

15. Connect the negative battery cable.

16. Add fluid to the brake fluid reservoir as required.

✳✳ WARNING

Clean, high quality brake fluid is essential to the safe and proper operation of the brake system. You should always buy the highest quality brake fluid that is available. If the brake fluid becomes contaminated, drain and flush the system, then refill the master cylinder with new fluid. Never reuse any brake fluid. Any brake fluid that is removed from the system should be discarded. Also, do not allow any brake fluid to come in contact with a painted surface; it will damage the paint.

17. Bleed the master cylinder. If after bleeding the master cylinder the brake pedal feels soft, bleed the brake system at all wheels.

18. Check the brake system for proper operation.

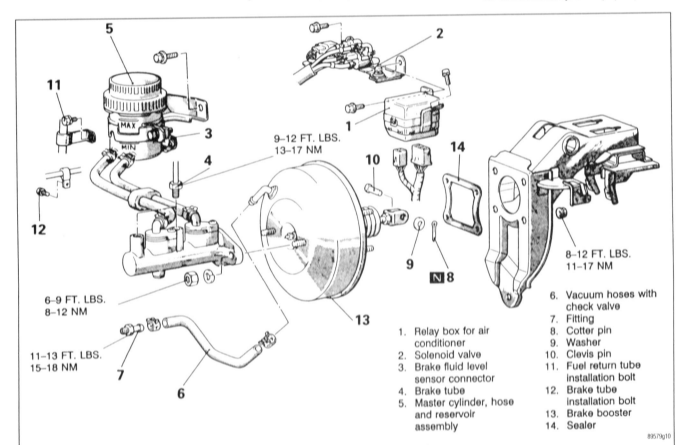

9–12 FT. LBS.
13–17 NM

6–9 FT. LBS.
8–12 NM

11–13 FT. LBS.
15–18 NM

8–12 FT. LBS.
11–17 NM

1. Relay box for air conditioner
2. Solenoid valve
3. Brake fluid level sensor connector
4. Brake tube
5. Master cylinder, hose and reservoir assembly
6. Vacuum hoses with check valve
7. Fitting
8. Cotter pin
9. Washer
10. Clevis pin
11. Fuel return tube installation bolt
12. Brake tube installation bolt
13. Brake booster
14. Sealer

Fig. 15 Exploded view of the power brake booster and related components—most models

Proportioning Valve

REMOVAL & INSTALLATION

▶ **See Figure 2**

1. Disconnect the negative battery cable.
2. Locate the proportioning valve, usually below the master cylinder.
3. Tag and disconnect the brake lines from the valve.

✳✳ CAUTION

Brake fluid contains polyglycol ethers and polyglycols. Avoid contact with the eyes and wash your hands thoroughly after handling brake fluid. If you do get brake fluid in your eyes, flush your eyes with clean, running water for 15 minutes. If eye irritation persists, or if you have taken brake fluid internally, IMMEDIATELY seek medical assistance.

4. Remove the proportioning valve from the engine compartment.

To install:

5. The installation is the reverse of the removal procedure. Bleed the brakes in the following order:
6. **Diamante**
   a. Right rear caliper
   b. Left front caliper
   c. Left rear caliper
   d. Right front caliper
7. **Mirage and Galant**
   a. Left rear wheel cylinder or caliper
   b. Right front cylinder
   c. Right rear wheel cylinder or caliper
   d. Left front caliper
8. Connect the negative battery cable and check the brakes for proper operation.

✳✳ WARNING

Clean, high quality brake fluid is essential to the safe and proper operation of the brake system. You should always buy the highest quality brake fluid that is available. If the brake fluid becomes contaminated, drain and flush the system, then refill the master cylinder with new fluid. Never reuse any brake fluid. Any brake fluid that is removed from the system should be discarded. Also, do not allow any brake fluid to come in contact with a painted surface; it will damage the paint.

Brake Hoses and Lines

Metal lines and rubber brake hoses should be checked frequently for leaks and external damage. Metal lines are particularly prone to crushing and kinking under the vehicle. Any such deformation can restrict the proper flow of fluid and therefore impair braking at the wheels. Rubber hoses should be checked for cracking or scraping; such damage can create a weak spot in the hose and it could fail under pressure.

Any time the lines are removed or disconnected, extreme cleanliness must be observed. Clean all joints and connections before disassembly (use a

stiff bristle brush and clean brake fluid); be sure to plug the lines and ports as soon as they are opened. New lines and hoses should be flushed clean with brake fluid before installation to remove any contamination.

REMOVAL & INSTALLATION

▶ **See Figures 16, 17, 18, and 19**

1. Disconnect the negative battery cable.
2. Raise and safely support the vehicle on jackstands.
3. Remove any wheel and tire assemblies necessary for access to the particular line you are removing.
4. Thoroughly clean the surrounding area at the joints to be disconnected.
5. Place a suitable catch pan under the joint to be disconnected.
6. Using two wrenches (one to hold the joint and one to turn the fitting), disconnect the hose or line to be replaced.
7. Disconnect the other end of the line or hose, moving the drain pan if necessary. Always use a back-up wrench to avoid damaging the fitting.
8. Disconnect any retaining clips or brackets holding the line and remove the line from the vehicle.

➡ **If the brake system is to remain open for more time than it takes to swap lines, tape or plug each remaining clip and port to keep contaminants out and fluid in.**

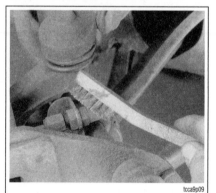

Fig. 16 Use a brush to clean the fittings of any debris

Fig. 18 Any gaskets/crush washers should be replaced with new ones during installation

To install:

9. Install the new line or hose, starting with the end farthest from the master cylinder. Connect the other end, then confirm that both fittings are correctly threaded and turn smoothly using finger pressure. Make sure the new line will not rub against any other part. Brake lines must be at least 1/2 in: (13mm) from the steering column and other moving parts. Any protective shielding or insulators must be reinstalled in the original location.

✳✳ WARNING

Make sure the hose is NOT kinked or touching any part of the frame or suspension after installation. These conditions may cause the hose to fail prematurely.

10. Using two wrenches as before, tighten each fitting.
11. Install any retaining clips or brackets on the lines.
12. If removed, install the wheel and tire assemblies, then carefully lower the vehicle to the ground.
13. Refill the brake master cylinder reservoir with clean, fresh brake fluid, meeting DOT 3 specifications. Properly bleed the brake system.

✳✳ WARNING

Clean, high quality brake fluid is essential to the safe and proper operation of the brake system. You should always buy the highest

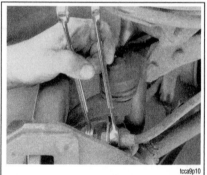

Fig. 17 Use two wrenches to loosen the fitting. If available, use flare nut type wrenches

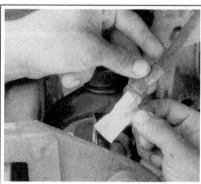

Fig.19 Tape or plug the line to prevent contamination

quality brake fluid that is available. If the brake fluid becomes contaminated, drain and flush the system, then refill the master cylinder with new fluid. Never reuse any brake fluid. Any brake fluid that is removed from the system should be discarded. Also, do not allow any brake fluid to come in contact with a painted surface; it will damage the paint.

14. Connect the negative battery cable.

Bleeding Brake System

▶ See Figures 20 thru 28

When any part of the hydraulic system has been disconnected for repair or replacement, air may get into the lines and cause spongy pedal action (because air can be compressed and brake fluid cannot). To correct this condition, it is necessary to bleed the hydraulic system so to be sure all air is purged.

When bleeding the brake system, bleed one brake cylinder at a time, beginning at the cylinder with the longest hydraulic line (farthest from the master cylinder) first. ALWAYS keep the master cylinder reservoir filled with brake fluid during the bleeding operation. Never use brake fluid that has been drained from the hydraulic system, no matter how clean it is.

The primary and secondary hydraulic brake systems are separate and are bled independently. During the bleeding operation, do not allow the reservoir to run dry. Keep the master cylinder reservoir filled with brake fluid.

1. Clean all dirt from around the master cylinder fill cap, remove the cap and fill the master cylinder with brake fluid until the level is within 1/4 in. (6mm) of the top edge of the reservoir.

Fig. 20 Remove the bleeder screw cap

Fig. 21 Install a hose and container to the bleeder screw

Fig. 22 Slowly crack open the bleeder screw while an assistant presses down the brake pedal

Fig. 23 The bleed screw for the rear brakes is located on the rear of the backing plate, just above the brake line

Fig. 24 Remove the protective rubber cap for the bleed screw

Fig. 25 Attach a hose connected to a bottle with a small amount of brake fluid in it to the bleed screw

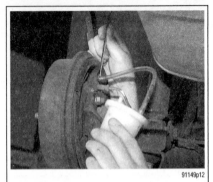

Fig. 26 Slowly open the bleed screw and have an assistant depress the brake pedal while observing the hose for bubbles

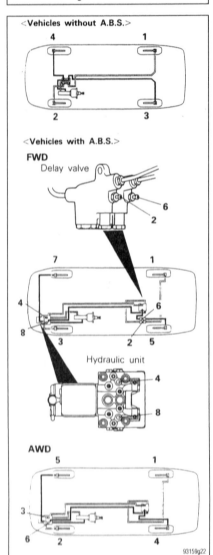

Fig. 27 Brake bleeding sequence—1993 Galant

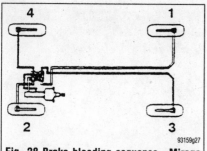

Fig. 28 Brake bleeding sequence—Mirage and Diamante

2. Clean the bleeder screws at all 4 wheels. The bleeder screws are located on the back of the brake backing plate (drum brakes) and on the top of the brake calipers (disc brakes).

3. Attach a length of rubber hose over the bleeder screw and place the other end of the hose in a glass jar, submerged in brake fluid.

4. Open the bleeder screw 1/2–3/4 turn. Have an assistant slowly depress the brake pedal.

✳✳ CAUTION

Brake fluid contains polyglycol ethers and polyglycols. Avoid contact with the eyes and wash your hands thoroughly after handling brake fluid. If you do get brake fluid in your eyes, flush your eyes with clean, running water for 15 minutes. If eye irritation persists, or if you have taken brake fluid internally, **IMMEDIATELY seek medical assistance.**

5. Close the bleeder screw and tell your assistant to allow the brake pedal to return slowly. Continue this process to purge all air from the system.

6. When bubbles cease to appear at the end of the bleeder hose, close the bleeder screw and remove the hose. Tighten the bleeder screw to the proper torque:

7. Check the master cylinder fluid level and add fluid accordingly. Do this after bleeding each wheel.

8. Repeat the bleeding operation at the remaining 3 wheels, ending with the one closet to the master cylinder.

9. Fill the master cylinder reservoir to the proper level.

DISC BRAKES

▶ **See Figures 29, 30, 31, and 32**

Brake Pads

REMOVAL & INSTALLATION

✳✳ CAUTION

Older brake pads or shoes may contain asbestos, which has been determined to be cancer causing agent. Never clean the brake surfaces with compressed air! Avoid inhaling any dust from any brake surface! When cleaning brake surfaces, use a commercially available brake cleaning fluid.

Mirage and 1990–93 Galant

FRONT

▶ **See Figure 33**

1. Remove some of the brake fluid from the master cylinder reservoir. The reservoir should be no more than half full. When the pistons are pressed into the calipers, excess fluid will flow up into the reservoir.

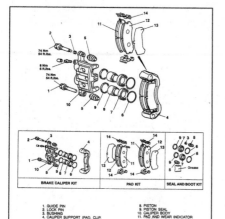

Fig. 29 Front dual piston caliper exploded view—Diamante

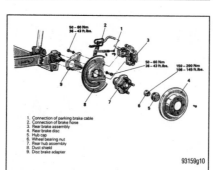

Fig. 30 Rear disc brake system component identification—1994–95 Galant

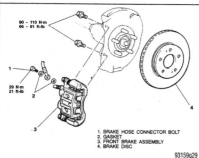

Fig. 31 Front brake system component identification—1996–00 Galant

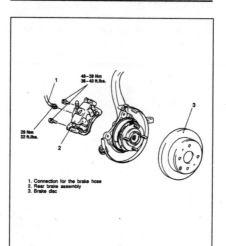

Fig. 32 Rear disc brake exploded view—1990–92 Mirage

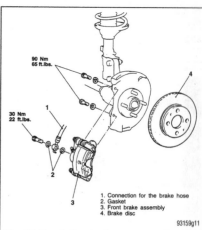

Fig. 33 Front disc brake components—Mirage

2. Raise the vehicle and support safely.

3. Remove the appropriate tire and wheel assemblies.

4. Remove the caliper guide and lock pins and lift the caliper assembly from the caliper support. Tie the caliper out of the way using wire. Do not allow the caliper to hang by the brake.line.

➡ **On some vehicles, the caliper can be flipped up by leaving the upper pin in place and using it as a pivot point.**

5. Remove the brake pads, spring clip and shims. Take note of positioning to aid installation.

6. Install two wheel lug nuts onto the studs and lightly tighten. This is done to hold the disc on the hub.

To install:

7. Use a large C-clamp to compress piston(s) back into caliper bore. On two piston calipers both pistons will have to be retracted together.

8. Lubricate slide points and install the brake pads, shims and spring clip onto the caliper support. Install the caliper over the brake pads.

➡ **Be careful that the piston boot does not become caught when lowering the caliper onto the support. Do not twist the brake hose during caliper installation.**

9. Lubricate and install the caliper guide and lock pins in their original positions. Tighten the caliper guide and locking pins.

10. Install the tire and wheel assemblies. Lower the vehicle.

➡ **Pump the brake pedal several times, until firm, before attempting to move the vehicle.**

11. Road test the vehicle and check brakes for proper operation.

REAR

◆ **See Figures 32 and 34**

1. Remove some of the brake fluid from the master cylinder reservoir. The reservoir should be no more than half full. When the pistons are depressed into the calipers, excess fluid will flow up into the reservoir.

2. Raise the vehicle and support safely.

3. Remove the appropriate tire and wheel assemblies.

4. Loosen the parking brake cable adjustment from inside the vehicle.

5. Disconnect the parking brake cable end installed to the rear brake caliper assembly.

6. Remove the caliper lower pin and swing the caliper assembly upwards. Tie the caliper out of the way using wire.

7. Remove the outer shim, brake pads and spring clips from the caliper support. Take note of positioning of each to aid in installation.

8. Install two of the wheel lug nuts onto the studs and lightly tighten. This is done to hold the disc on the hub.

9. Thread the piston into the caliper bore clockwise using disc brake driver tool MB9f52 or its equivalent.

To install:

10. Lubricate all sliding and pivot points.

11. Install the brake pads, shims and spring clip to the caliper support.

12. Install the caliper over the brake pads.

➡ **Be careful that the piston boot does not become caught when lowering the caliper onto the support. Do not twist the brake hose during caliper installation.**

13. Lubricate, install and tighten the lower pin.

14. Install the tire and wheel assemblies. Lower the vehicle.

15. Test the brakes for proper operation.

Diamante and 1994–00 Galant

◆ **See Figures 29, 30, 31, 35 thru 47**

❊❊ CAUTION

Brake pads and shoes contain asbestos, which has been determined to be a cancer causing agent. Never clean the brake surfaces with compressed air! Avoid inhaling any dust from brake surfaces! When cleaning brakes, use commercially available brake cleaning fluids.

➡ **Unlike most rear disc brake designs, this system does not incorporate the parking brake system, into the rear brake caliper, therefore, the rear brake system is serviced the same as the front system.**

1. Remove some of the brake fluid from the master cylinder reservoir. The reservoir should be no more than $1/2$ full. When the pistons are depressed into the calipers, excess fluid will flow up into the reservoir.

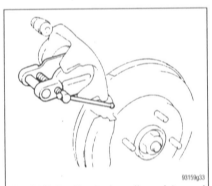

Fig. 34 Retracting brake caliper piston and aligning pad to piston—Mirage

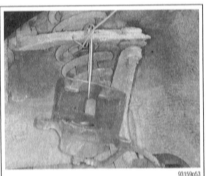

Fig. 35 Use mechanic's wire or a similar device to support the caliper out of the way

Fig. 36 Remove the inner brake pad and . . .

Fig. 37 . . . also the outer pad from the caliper

Fig. 38 Remove the spring clips and replace if necessary

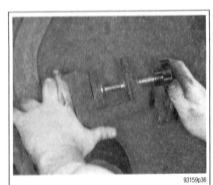

Fig. 39 The caliper piston can be depressed using a special tool, such as this one from Lisle® or . . .

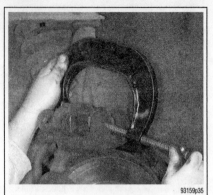

Fig. 40 . . . a large C-clamp will also work to compress the caliper piston

Fig. 41 Thoroughly clean the caliper slides . . .

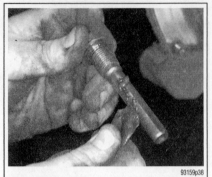

Fig. 42 . . . then make sure to lubricate the caliper slides with a quality lubricant before installation

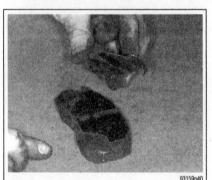

Fig. 43 Remember to remove the shims from the old pads to install on the new pads

Fig. 44 A quality disc brake quiet or equivalent should be applied to the new pads

Fig. 45 Spread the brake quiet evenly over the pad surface . . .

Fig. 46 . . . then install the shim on the pads

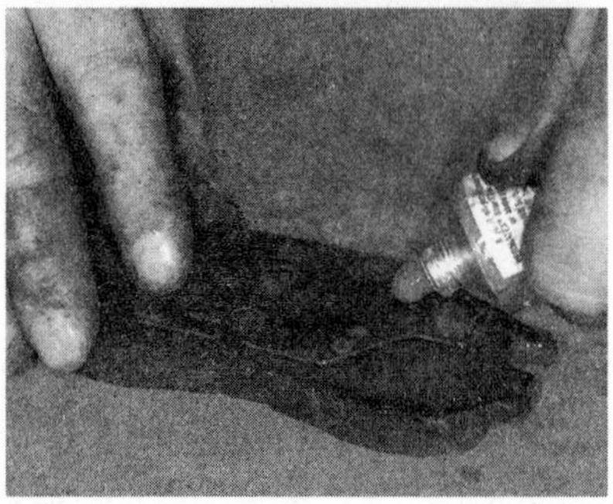

Fig. 47 Apply more brake quiet over the outside of the shim before installing the pads on the vehicle

2. Raise the vehicle and support safely.

3. Remove the appropriate tire and wheel assemblies.

4. Remove the caliper guide and lock pins and lift the caliper assembly from the caliper support. Tie the caliper out of the way using wire.

✳✳ WARNING

Do not allow the caliper to hang by the brake line.

➡On some vehicles, the caliper can be flipped up by leaving the upper pin in place and using it as a pivot point.

5. Remove the brake pads, spring clip and shims. Take note of positioning to aid installation.

6. Install the wheel lug nuts onto the studs and lightly tighten. This is done to hold the disc on the hub.

To install:

7. Use a large C-clamp to compress the piston(s) back into caliper bore.

8. Lubricate slide points and install the brake pads, shims and spring clip onto the caliper support.

9. Install the caliper over the brake pads.

➡Be careful that the piston boot does not become caught when lowering the caliper onto the support. Do not twist the brake hose during caliper installation.

10. Lubricate and install the caliper guide and lock pins in their original positions.

11. Tighten the guide and locking pins to 54 ft. lbs. (75 Nm) on the front, and 20 ft. lbs. (27 Nm) on the rear.

12. Install the tire and wheel assemblies.

13. Lower the vehicle.

✳✳ WARNING

Pump brake pedal several times, until firm, before attempting to move vehicle.

14. Road test the vehicle and check brakes for proper operation.

INSPECTION

▶ See Figures 48 and 49

✳✳ CAUTION

Older brake pads or shoes may contain asbestos, which has been determined to be cancer causing agent. Never clean the brake surfaces with compressed air! Avoid inhaling any dust from any brake surface! When cleaning brake surfaces, use a commercially available brake cleaning fluid.

The disc brake pads have wear indicators that contact the brake disc when the brake pad thickness becomes 0.08 in. (2.0mm) and emit a squealing sound to worn the driver.

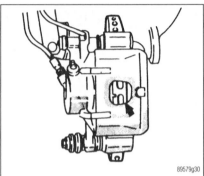

Fig. 48 Inspect front disc pad thickness through caliper body check port

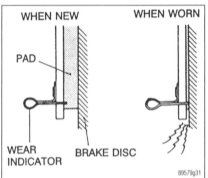

WHEN NEW   WHEN WORN

PAD

WEAR
INDICATOR   BRAKE DISC

Fig. 49 The disc brake pads have wear indicators which will make a squeaking noise when the pads become worn and need to be replaced

Inspect the thickness of the brake linings by looking through the brake caliper body check port. The standard value of the brake pad is 0.39 in. (10mm). The thickness limit of the lining is 0.08 in. (2.0mm).

When the limit is exceeded, replace the pads on both sides of the brake disc and also the brake pads on the wheel on the opposite side of the vehicle. Do not replace 1 pad on a caliper because the wear indicator is hitting, without replacing the other pad on the same wheel as well as the brake pads on the other front or rear wheel, as applicable.

If there is a significant difference in the thickness of the pads on the left and right sides, check the sliding condition of the piston, lock pin sleeve and guide pin sleeve.

Brake Caliper

REMOVAL & INSTALLATION

✳✳ CAUTION

Brake pads and shoes contain asbestos, which has been determined to be a cancer causing agent. Never clean the brake surfaces with compressed air! Avoid inhaling any dust from brake surfaces! When cleaning brakes, use commercially available brake cleaning fluids.

Mirage and 1990–93 Galant

FRONT

♦ **See Figure 33**

1. Raise the vehicle and support safely.
2. Remove the appropriate tire and wheel assembly.

➥**Do not let air into the master cylinder by allowing the reservoir to empty or complete system bleeding will be required.**

3. To disconnect the front brake hose, hold the nut on the brake hose side and loosen the flared brake line nut. With the hose disconnected at the line, remove the brake hose from the caliper.
4. Remove the caliper guide and lock pins.
5. Remove the caliper assembly from the caliper support.
To install:
6. Position the brake caliper onto the caliper support.
7. Install and tighten the guide and lock pins.
8. Reconnect the brake hose.

➥**Use caution not to twist brake hose during installation.**

9. Bleed the brake system.
10. Apply brake pedal and inspect the system for proper operation and no leakage.
11. Install tire and wheel assembly.

REAR

♦ **See Figure 17**

1. Disconnect the battery negative cable.
2. Raise the vehicle and support safely.
3. Remove the appropriate tire and wheel assemblies.
4. Loosen the parking brake cable adjustment from inside the vehicle.
5. Remove the retaining clips, and disconnect the parking brake cable from the rear brake caliper assembly.

➥**Do not let air into the master cylinder by allowing the reservoir to empty or complete system bleeding will be required.**

6. On FWD models, to disconnect the brake hose from the caliper, remove the banjo bolt from the brake caliper.
7. On AWD models, hold the nut on the brake hose side and loosen the flared brake line nut. With the hose disconnected at the line, remove the brake hose from the caliper.
8. Remove the caliper lock pin. Pivot the caliper upward, and slide the caliper assembly from the caliper support.
To install:
9. On FWD models, install the rear brake hose onto the caliper with new washers in place and tighten the brake hose retainer.
10. On AWD models, connect the brake hose to the caliper and tighten the fitting to 9–12 ft. lbs. (13–17 Nm). Then connect the hose at the bracket to the steel line and tighten the fitting to 9–12 ft. lbs. (13–17 Nm).

➥**Do not twist the brake hose during installation.**

11. Install the caliper over the brake pads, making sure stopper grove lines up with pad projection.
12. Lubricate and install the lock pin and tighten to 23 ft. lbs. (32 Nm).
13. Bleed the brake system.
14. Inspect the brake system for leaks and ensure proper operation.
15. Install tire and wheel assemblies.
16. Properly adjust parking brake cable.

Diamante and 1994–00 Galant

♦ **See Figures 50 thru 55**

Unlike most rear disc brake designs, this system does not incorporate the parking brake system into the rear brake caliper. Therefore, the rear brake system is serviced the same as the front system.

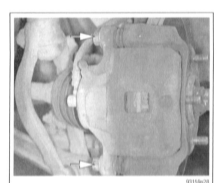

Fig. 50 The brake caliper is mounted to the caliper support with two bolts

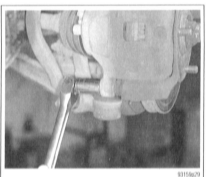

Fig. 51 Remove the brake caliper-to-caliper support retaining bolts

Fig. 52 Grasp the caliper and lift it from the caliper assembly from the caliper support

Fig. 53 Loosen the caliper hose banjo bolt . . .

Fig. 54 . . . then remove the bolt from the fitting

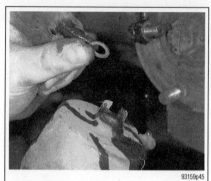

Fig. 55 Make sure that you remove the copper washers and replace them with new ones during reassembly

1. Raise the vehicle and support safely.
2. Remove the appropriate tire and wheel assembly.

➡Do not allow the master cylinder reservoir to empty. An empty reservoir will allow air to enter the entire brake system and complete system bleeding will be required.

3. To disconnect the brake hose on models with a banjo-bolt connecting the brake hose to the caliper assembly, simply remove the bolt at the hose connection. To disconnect the brake hose on all other systems, hold the nut on the brake hose side and loosen the flared brake line nut.

✼✼ CAUTION

Brake fluid contains polyglycol ethers and polyglycols. Avoid contact with the eyes and wash your hands thoroughly after handling brake fluid. If you do get brake fluid in your eyes, flush your eyes with clean, running water for 15 minutes. If eye irritation persists, or if you have taken brake fluid internally, IMMEDIATELY seek medical assistance.

4. Once the hose has been disconnected from the line, remove the brake hose from the caliper.
5. Remove the caliper guide and lock pins and lift the caliper assembly from the caliper support.

To install:
6. Position the caliper onto the caliper support.

7. Install the guide pin and lock pin. Tighten to 23 ft. lbs. (32 Nm).
8. Reconnect the brake hose or install the banjo bolt with new washers.

➡Use caution not to twist the brake hose during installation.

9. Bleed the brake system.

✼✼ WARNING

Clean, high quality brake fluid is essential to the safe and proper operation of the brake system. You should always buy the highest quality brake fluid that is available. If the brake fluid becomes contaminated, drain and flush the system, then refill the master cylinder with new fluid. Never reuse any brake fluid. Any brake fluid that is removed from the system should be discarded. Also, do not allow any brake fluid to come in contact with a painted surface; it will damage the paint.

10. Apply brake pedal and inspect the system for leaks. Ensure proper operation and no leakage.
11. Install tire and wheel assembly. Torque lug nuts to 87–101 ft. lbs. (120–140 Nm).

OVERHAUL

▶ **See Figures 56 thru 63**

➡Some vehicles may be equipped dual piston calipers. The procedure to overhaul the caliper is essentially the same with the exception of multiple pistons, O-rings and dust boots.

1. Remove the caliper from the vehicle and place on a clean workbench.

✼✼ CAUTION

NEVER place your fingers in front of the pistons in an attempt to catch or protect the pistons when applying compressed air. This could result in personal injury!

➡Depending upon the vehicle, there are two different ways to remove the piston from the caliper. Refer to the brake pad replacement procedure to make sure you have the correct procedure for your vehicle.

2. The first method is as follows:
   a. Stuff a shop towel or a block of wood into the caliper to catch the piston.
   b. Remove the caliper piston using compressed air applied into the caliper inlet hole. Inspect the piston for scoring, nicks, corrosion and/or worn or damaged chrome plating. The piston must be replaced if any of these conditions are found.

Fig. 56 For some types of calipers, use compressed air to drive the piston out of the caliper, but make sure to keep your fingers clear

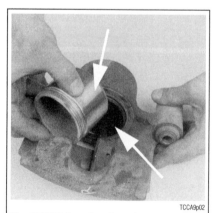

Fig. 57 Withdraw the piston from the caliper bore

Fig. 58 On some vehicles, you must remove the anti-rattle clip

Fig. 59 Use a prytool to carefully pry around the edge of the boot . . .

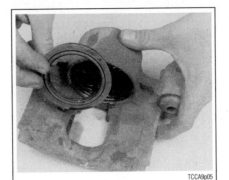

Fig. 60 . . . then remove the boot from the caliper housing, taking care not to score or damage the bore

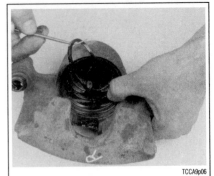

Fig. 61 Use extreme caution when removing the piston seal; DO NOT scratch the caliper bore

Fig. 62 Use the proper size driving tool and a mallet to properly seal the boots in the caliper housing

Fig. 63 There are tools, such as this Mighty-Vac, available to assist in proper brake system bleeding

3. For the second method, you must rotate the piston to retract it from the caliper.

4. If equipped, remove the anti-rattle clip.

5. Use a prytool to remove the caliper boot, being careful not to scratch the housing bore.

6. Remove the piston seals from the groove in the caliper bore.

7. Carefully loosen the brake bleeder valve cap and valve from the caliper housing.

8. Inspect the caliper bores, pistons and mounting threads for scoring or excessive wear.

9. Use crocus cloth to polish out light corrosion from the piston and bore.

10. Clean all parts with denatured alcohol and dry with compressed air.

To assemble:

11. Lubricate and install the bleeder valve and cap.

12. Install the new seals into the caliper bore grooves, making sure they are not twisted.

13. Lubricate the piston bore.

14. Install the pistons and boots into the bores of the calipers and push to the bottom of the bores.

15. Use a suitable driving tool to seat the boots in the housing.

16. Install the caliper in the vehicle.

17. Install the wheel and tire assembly, then carefully lower the vehicle.

18. Properly bleed the brake system.

Brake Disc (Rotor)

REMOVAL & INSTALLATION

✳✳ CAUTION

Brake pads and shoes contain asbestos, which has been determined to be a cancer causing agent. Never clean the brake surfaces with compressed air! Avoid inhaling any dust from brake surfaces! When cleaning brakes, use commercially available brake cleaning fluids.

1993–00 Mirage, Diamante, and Galant

▶ See Figures 64 thru 70

The following procedure is applicable to both the front and rear brakes.

1. Raise the vehicle and support safely.

2. Remove the appropriate wheel.

3. Remove the caliper and brake pads.

Fig. 64 Support the caliper using mechanic's wire or another suitable device. Do NOT let it hang by the brake hose

Fig. 65 Remove the caliper bracket retaining bolts . . .

Fig. 66 . . . then remove the caliper bracket from the vehicle

Fig. 67 There are two threaded holes located on the rotor

Fig. 68 Install a suitable size bolt into the threaded holes

Fig. 69 Tighten the bolts until they force the rotor off of the hub . . .

Fig. 70 . . . then remove the rotor from the hub assembly

4. Support the caliper out of the way using a wire.

5. On some models the rotor is held to the hub by two small threaded screws. Remove the screws and pull off the rotor.

To install:

6. Position the rotor on the hub and install the mounting screws.

7. Install the caliper holder and brake pads.

8. Slide the caliper over the brake pads and tighten the guide pins.

9. Install the wheel and tighten the lug nuts.

✳✳ WARNING

Pump the brake pedal several times before attempting to move vehicle.

1990–92 Mirage

FRONT

1. Loosen the large driveshaft nut while the vehicle is still on the ground with the brakes applied.

2. Raise and safely support vehicle.

3. Remove appropriate wheel assembly.

4. Remove the axle end nut and lock washer.

5. Remove the caliper from its bracket.

✳✳ WARNING

Do not allow the caliper to hang by the brake line.

6. Remove the brake pads.

7. Remove the ball joint and tie rod end from the lower control arm.

8. Use and puller to push the halfshaft through the rotor/hub assembly.

9. Remove the lower strut bolts and remove the assembly from the vehicle.

10. To separate the rotor from the hub assembly, remove the rotor retainer bolts and separate using tool MB991001 or equivalent.

To install:

11. Assemble the rotor and hub. Tighten the nuts to 40 ft. lbs. (54 Nm) and install the assembly to the vehicle.

12. Install the washer so the chamfered edge faces outward. Install the nut and tighten temporarily.

13. Install the ball joint and tie rod end.

14. Install the brake components.

15. Install the wheel and lower the vehicle to the floor.

16. Tighten the axle nut with the brakes applied to a maximum torque of 188 ft. lbs. (260 Nm). Install the cotter pin and bend to secure.

REAR

▶ **See Figure 17**

1. Raise the vehicle and support safely.

2. Remove appropriate wheel assembly.

3. Detach the parking brake connection at the rear caliper assembly.

4. Remove the caliper and brake pads.

5. Support the caliper out of the way using wire.

6. Remove the brake rotor from the rear hub assembly.

To install:

7. Position the rotor on the hub. Install a couple of lug nuts and lightly tighten to hold rotor on hub.

8. Install the caliper holder and place brake pads in holder.

9. Slide caliper over brake pads and install guide pins. Once caliper is secured, the lug nuts can be removed.

10. Reconnect parking brake cable and install wheel(s).

INSPECTION

Using a micrometer, measure the disc thickness at eight positions, approximately 45 degrees apart and 0.39 in. (10mm) in from the outer edge of the disc. The minimum thickness is 0.882 in. (22.4mm) for front rotors or 0.331 in. (8.4mm), with a maximum thickness variation of 0.0006 in. (0.015mm).

If the disc is beyond limits for thickness, remove it and install a new one. If the thickness variation exceeds the specifications, replace the disc or turn rotor with on the car type brake lathe.

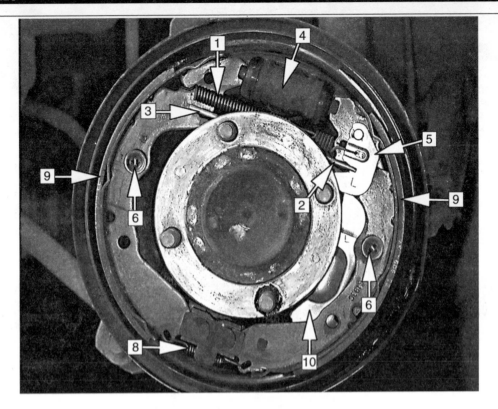

DRUM BRAKE COMPONENTS

1) Shoe-to-lever spring   6) Shoe hold-down spring
2) Shoe-to-shoe spring   7) Shoe hold-down pin
3) Adjuster assembly   8) Retainer spring
4) Wheel cylinder   9) Shoes
5) Adjuster lever   10) Parking brake lever

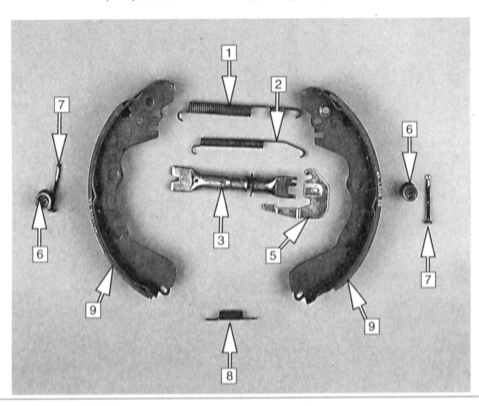

93159p57

Brake Drums

REMOVAL & INSTALLATION

> ❋❋ **CAUTION**

Brake pads and shoes contain asbestos, which has been determined to be a cancer causing agent. Never clean the brake surfaces with compressed air! Avoid inhaling any dust from brake surfaces! When cleaning brakes, use commercially available brake cleaning fluids.

1990–92 Mirage

▶ **See Figure 71**

1. Raise the vehicle and support safely.
2. Remove the wheel and tire assembly.
3. Remove the dust cap.
4. Remove the self-locking nut.
5. Remove the outer wheel bearing.
6. Remove the drum with the inner wheel bearing from the spindle.
7. Remove the grease seal.

To install:

8. To determine if the self-locking nut is reusable:

   a. Screw in the self-locking nut until about $1/8$ in. (3mm) of the spindle is showing.

   b. Measure the torque required to turn the self-locking nut counterclockwise.

   c. The lowest allowable torque is 48 inch lbs. (5.5 Nm). If the measured torque is less than the specification, replace the nut.

9. Lubricate and install the inner wheel bearing.
10. Install a new grease seal.
11. Install the drum to the spindle.
12. Lubricate and install the outer wheel bearing.
13. Tighten the self-locking nut to 108–145 ft. lbs. (150–200 Nm).
14. Install the grease cap.

Galant and 1993–00 Mirage

▶ **See Figures 72, 73, 74, and 75**

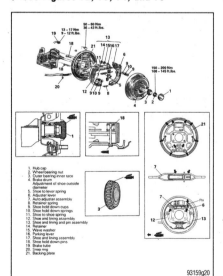

Fig. 71 Exploded view of the drum brakes—1990–92 Mirage

1. Raise and safely support the vehicle.
2. Remove the rear wheel.
3. Loosen the parking brake adjusting nut.
4. Pull the drum from the rear hub assembly. Tap the drum with a soft mallet if necessary.

To install:

5. Install the drum on the rear hub assembly.
6. Install the wheel and adjust the parking brake.
7. Lower the vehicle to the floor.

INSPECTION

▶ **See Figure 76**

1. With the brake drum removed from the vehicle, measure the inside diameter of the hub and drum at two or more locations.
2. The service limit specification is 9.1 in. (231mm).
3. Replace the brake drums and shoe and lining assemblies when the wear exceeds the limit or is badly out of balance.

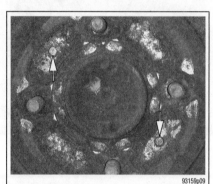

Fig. 72 There are two threaded holes located on the brake drum

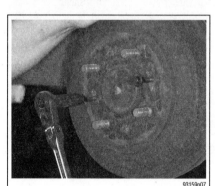

Fig. 74 Tighten the bolts until they force the drum off of the hub . . .

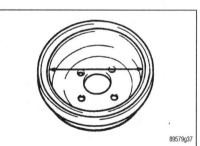

Fig. 76 Measure the inside diameter of the brake drum

Brake Shoes

INSPECTION

▶ **See Figure 77**

> ❋❋ **CAUTION**

Brake pads and shoes contain asbestos, which has been determined to be a cancer causing agent. Never clean the brake surfaces with compressed air! Avoid inhaling any dust from brake surfaces! When cleaning brakes, use commercially available brake cleaning fluids.

1. Remove the brake drum.
2. Measure the wear of the brake lining at the place worn the most. The service limit for replacement is 0.039 in. (1.0mm).

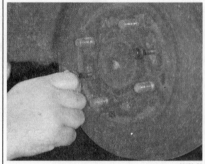

Fig. 73 Install a suitable size bolt into the threaded holes

Fig. 75 . . . then remove the drum from the hub assembly

Fig. 77 Measure the thickness of the lining where it is worn the most

➡When servicing drum brakes, only dissemble and assemble one side at a time, leaving the remaining side intact for reference.

3. Replace the shoe and lining assembly is any located is less than the limit. Whenever the shoe and lining assembly is replaced, be sure to replace the left and right side assemblies as a set to prevent the car from pulling to one side when braking.

4. If there is a big difference between the thickness of the shoe and lining assembly on the left and right sides, check the sliding condition of the wheel cylinder piston.

REMOVAL & INSTALLATION

1990–92 Mirage

♦ See Figure 71

> ❊❊ **WARNING**
>
> **Brake shoes contain asbestos, which has been determined to be a cancer causing agent. Never clean the brake surfaces with compressed air! Avoid inhaling any dust from brake surfaces! When cleaning brakes, use commercially available brake cleaning fluids.**

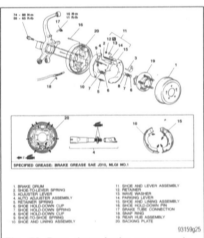

Fig. 78 Rear drum brake components— Galant

1. Raise vehicle and support safely.
2. Remove the tire and wheel assembly.

➡Note the location of all springs and clips for proper reassembly.

3. Remove the brake drum.
4. Remove the front shoe-to-rear shoe spring.
5. Remove the shoe-to-lever spring and remove the adjuster assembly.
6. Remove the shoe hold-down clips and the brake shoes.
7. Disconnect the parking brake cable from the rear shoes by spreading the horseshoe clip apart.
   To install:
8. Thoroughly clean and dry the backing plate. Ensure the backing plate bosses are smooth, so shoes won't bind.
9. Lubricate backing plate bosses, anchor pin, and parking brake actuating mechanism with a lithium-based grease.
10. Remove, clean and dry all remaining parts. Apply anti-seize to the star wheel threads and transfer all parts to the new shoes.
11. Connect the parking brake arm to the appropriate brake shoe.
12. Attach shoes to the backing plate and install all remaining hardware in the reverse order it was removed.
13. Preadjust the shoes so the drum slides on with a light drag and install brake drum.
14. Install a new wheel bearing self-locking nut and torque to 130 ft. lbs. (180 Nm).
15. Install the wheel bearing dust cap and adjust the rear brake shoes.

Fig. 79 Use a pair of pliers or a special brake tool to remove the shoe-to-lever spring

Fig. 81 Remove the auto adjuster assembly

Fig. 82 Remove the lower brake shoe retaining spring

Galant and 1993–00 Mirage

♦ See Figures 78 thru 93

1. Raise and safely support the vehicle.
2. Remove the rear wheels and drums.
3. Remove the lever return spring.
4. Remove the shoe-to-lever spring.
5. Remove the adjuster lever.
6. Remove the auto-adjuster assembly.
7. Remove the retainer spring.
8. Remove the brake shoe hold-down springs and spring cups.
9. Remove the shoe-to-shoe spring.
10. Remove the brake shoes.
11. Disconnect the parking brake cable from the lever on the rear shoe.
    To install:
12. Remove the parking brake lever from the used shoe and install it on the new brake shoe. Make sure the wave washer is installed in the proper direction.
13. Clean the backing plate and lightly apply brake grease to the six shoe support pads.
14. Clean the adjuster assembly and apply brake grease to the threads; do not use more grease than necessary.
15. Connect the parking brake cable to the lever on the rear shoe.
16. Position the rear shoe on the backing plate and install the hold-down spring and pin.
17. Position the front shoe on the backing plate and install the hold-down spring and pin.
18. Position the adjuster assembly between the two shoes.
19. Install the shoe-to-shoe spring.

Fig. 80 Remove the adjuster lever assembly

Fig. 83 Using a suitable hold-down spring tool, compress the hold-down spring and . . .

Fig. 84 . . . remove the hold-down spring and cup assembly

Fig. 85 With the shoes attached by the spring, pull them apart to clear the hub and bearing . . .

Fig. 86 . . . then detach the parking brake cable and remove the shoe and linings from the vehicle

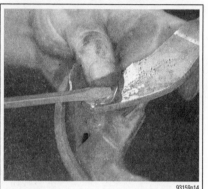

Fig. 87 Use a small prytool to twist open the retainer joint and remove the retainer . . .

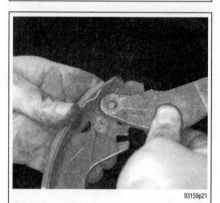

Fig. 88 . . . then remove the parking brake lever from the shoe

Fig. 89 Using a wire brush or other suitable tool, clean the shoe contact points on the backing plate

Fig. 90 Apply a high temp lubricant to the shoe contact points on the backing plate

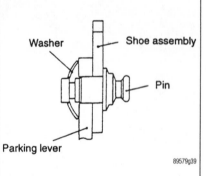

Fig. 91 Proper installation of the wave washer

Fig. 92 A portable cleaning tub made especially for cleaning brakes, like this one from SafetyKleen®, is extremely helpful

Fig. 93 If a cleaning tub is not available, a quality aerosol cleaning solvent can be used

20. Install the retainer spring.
21. Install the adjuster lever.
22. Install the shoe-to-lever spring.
23. Install the lever return spring.
24. Adjust the brake shoes and install the drum.
25. Install the wheel and tire assembly.
26. Lower the vehicle to the floor.

ADJUSTMENTS

The rear brakes are automatically adjusted while driving the vehicle. The brakes are also adjusted each time the parking brake is applied. Manual brake adjustment is only required after the brake shoes or

hardware has been replaced, or the adjuster has been replaced.

1. Remove the brake drum as described in this section.
2. Remove any excessive dust and dirt present on the brakes using the appropriate methods.
3. Using a brake adjustment gauge, measure the inside diameter of the brake drum.
4. Adjust the brake shoes to the same diameter as the drum by placing the brake adjustment gauge on the shoes and turn the adjusting star wheel.
5. Install the brake drum as described in this section.

Wheel Cylinders

REMOVAL & INSTALLATION

▶ **See Figures 94, 95, 96, 97, and 98**

1. Safely raise and support the vehicle.
2. Remove the rear wheel and the drum.
3. Remove the spring on the adjuster lever.
4. Remove the shoe-to-shoe spring.
5. Remove the auto adjuster assembly.

➡**Special flare nut wrenches should be used on all line fittings to prevent damage to the flats on the nut.**

6. Place a drain pan under the wheel to catch the brake fluid and disconnect the brake line from the rear of the wheel cylinder.

7. Remove the wheel cylinder mounting bolts and the wheel cylinder.

To install:

8. Install the wheel cylinder on the backing plate. Tighten the mounting bolts to 7 ft. lbs. (10 Nm).

9. Connect the brake line the wheel cylinder. Tighten the line fitting to 11 ft. lbs. (15 Nm).

10. Add brake fluid to the reservoir and leave the wheel cylinder bleeder screw loose. Brake fluid will start the flow into the wheel cylinder and may save time when bleeding the brake system later.

11. Install the auto adjuster assembly.
12. Install the shoe-to-shoe spring.
13. Install the spring on the adjuster lever.
14. Install the drum and the wheel assembly.
15. Lower the vehicle and bleed the brake system.

OVERHAUL

▶ **See Figures 99 thru 108**

Wheel cylinder overhaul kits may be available, but often at little or no savings over a reconditioned wheel cylinder. It often makes sense with these components to substitute a new or reconditioned part instead of attempting an overhaul.

If no replacement is available, or you would prefer to overhaul your wheel cylinders, the following procedure may be used. When rebuilding and installing wheel cylinders, avoid getting any contaminants into the system. Always use clean, new, high quality brake fluid. If dirty or improper fluid has been used, it will be necessary to drain the entire system, flush the system with proper brake fluid, replace all rubber components, then refill and bleed the system.

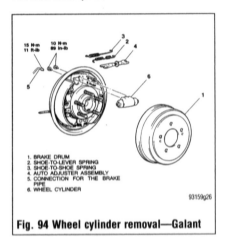

1. BRAKE DRUM
2. SHOE-TO-LEVER SPRING
3. SHOE-TO-SHOE SPRING
4. AUTO ADJUSTER ASSEMBLY
5. CONNECTION FOR THE BRAKE PIPE
6. WHEEL CYLINDER

93159p26

Fig. 94 Wheel cylinder removal—Galant

93159p23

Fig. 95 Use an appropriate size wrench to remove the brake line from the wheel cylinder

93159p25

Fig. 96 When the line is sufficiently loosened, brake fluid will flow out of the fitting

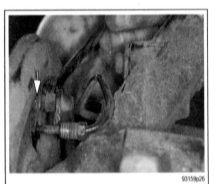

93159p26

Fig. 97 The wheel cylinder is held by two retaining bolts; remove the bolts . . .

93159p27

Fig. 98 . . . then remove the wheel cylinder from the backing plate

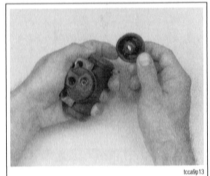

tcca9p13

Fig. 99 Remove the outer boots from the wheel cylinder

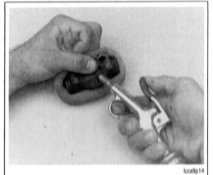

tcca9p14

Fig. 100 Compressed air can be used to remove the pistons and seals

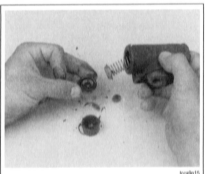

tcca9p15

Fig. 101 Remove the pistons, cup seals and spring from the cylinder

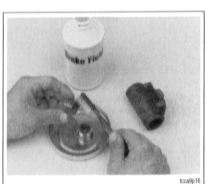

tcca9p16

Fig. 102 Use brake fluid and a soft brush to clean the pistons . . .

1. Remove the wheel cylinder from the vehicle and place on a clean workbench.

2. First remove and discard the old rubber boots, then withdraw the pistons. Piston cylinders are equipped with seals and a spring assembly, all located behind the pistons in the cylinder bore.

3. Remove the remaining inner components, seals and spring assembly. Compressed air may be useful in removing these components. If no compressed air is available, be VERY careful not to score the wheel cylinder bore when removing parts from it.

Discard all components for which replacements were supplied in the rebuild kit.

4. Wash the cylinder and metal parts in denatured alcohol or clean brake fluid.

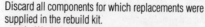

※ WARNING

Never use a mineral-based solvent such as gasoline, kerosene or paint thinner for cleaning purposes. These solvents will swell rubber components and quickly deteriorate them.

5. Allow the parts to air dry or use compressed air. Do not use rags for cleaning, since lint will remain in the cylinder bore.

6. Inspect the piston and replace it if it shows scratches.

7. Lubricate the cylinder bore and seals using clean brake fluid.

8. Position the spring assembly.

9. Install the inner seals, then the pistons.

10. Insert the new boots into the counterbores by hand. Do not lubricate the boots.

11. Install the wheel cylinder.

Fig. 103 . . . and the bore of the wheel cylinder

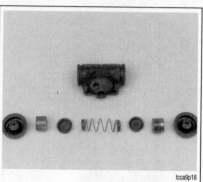

Fig. 104 Once cleaned and inspected, the wheel cylinder is ready for assembly

Fig. 105 Lubricate the cup seals with brake fluid

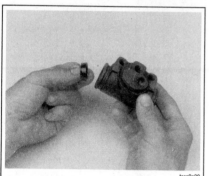

Fig. 106 Install the spring, then the cup seals in the bore

Fig. 107 Lightly lubricate the pistons, then install them

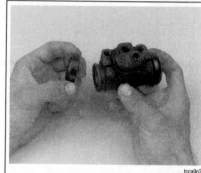

Fig. 108 The boots can now be installed over the wheel cylinder ends

PARKING BRAKE

Cable(s)

REMOVAL & INSTALLATION

Mirage

WITH REAR DRUM BRAKES

➡**If equipped with an air bag (SRS system), be sure to disarm system before starting repairs on the vehicle.**

1. Disconnect the negative battery cable.

2. Remove the screws from the center section and remove the rear part of the console.

➡**If equipped with SRS, when removing the floor console, don't allow any impact or shock to the SRS diagnostic unit.**

3. Remove the rear seat cushion.

4. Remove the center cable clamp and grommet.

5. Raise the vehicle and support safely.

6. At the rear wheel, remove the brake drum and shoes.

7. Disconnect the cable end from the parking brake strut lever.

8. Compress the retaining strips to remove the cable from the backing plate.

9. Unfasten any other frame retainers and remove the cables.

To install:

10. The parking brake cables may be color coded to indicate side. Check the parking brake cables for an identification mark.

11. Install the cable to the rear actuator. Secure in place with the parking brake cable clip and retainer spring.

12. Install the brake shoes and drum.

13. Position the cable and loosely install the retainers.

14. Reattach the parking brake cables to the actuator inside the vehicle.

15. Adjust the rear brake shoes.

16. Tighten the adjusting nut until the proper tension is placed on the cable. Adjust the parking brake stroke using appropriate method.

17. Secure all cable retainers.

18. Apply and release the parking brake a number of times once all adjustments have been made.

19. With the rear wheels raised, make sure the parking brake is not causing excess drag on the rear wheels.

20. Install the floor console and rear seat assembly.

21. Connect the negative battery cable.

22. Check that the parking brake holds the vehicle on an incline.

WITH REAR DISC BRAKES

➡**If equipped with an air bag (SRS system), be sure to disarm the system before starting repairs on the vehicle.**

1. Disconnect the negative battery cable.
2. Remove the screws from the center section and remove the rear part of the console.

➡**If equipped with SRS, when removing the floor console, don't allow any impact or shock to the SRS diagnostic unit.**

3. Remove the rear seat cushion.
4. Loosen the cable adjusting nut and disconnect the rear brake cables from the actuator.
5. Remove the center cable clamp and grommet.
6. Raise the vehicle and support safely.
7. Remove the parking brake cable clip and retainer spring.
8. Disconnect the cable end from the parking brake assembly.
9. Unfasten any remaining frame retainers and remove the cables from the vehicle.

To install:

10. The parking brake cables may be color coded to indicate side. Check the parking brake cables for an identification mark.
11. Install the cable to the rear actuator. Secure in place with the parking brake cable clip and retainer spring.
12. Position the cable and loosely install the retainers.
13. Reattach the parking brake cables to the actuator inside the vehicle.
14. Tighten the adjusting nut until the proper tension is placed on the cable. Adjust the parking brake stroke using appropriate method.
15. Secure all cable retainers.
16. Apply and release the parking brake a number of times once all adjustments have been made.
17. With the rear wheels raised, make sure the parking brake is not causing excess drag on the rear wheels.
18. Install the floor console and rear seat assembly.
19. Connect the negative battery cable.
20. Check console electrical components for proper operation.
21. Road test the vehicle and check for proper brake operation.
22. Check that the parking brake holds the vehicle on an incline.

1990–93 Galant

WITH REAR DRUM BRAKES

1. Disconnect the negative battery cable.
2. Remove the center console as follows:
   a. Remove both side cover panels.
   b. Remove the shifter knob on manual transaxle models. Remove the spacer trim piece on automatic transaxle models.
   c. Remove the switch panel/box and remove the two screws beneath the panel/box.
   d. Remove the radio trim panel.
   e. Remove the radio and tape player.
   f. Remove the console inner panel and remove the two screws for beneath the panel.
   g. Remove the remaining screws from the sides of the console.

h. Remove the console assembly from the vehicle.
3. While pressing downward on the front of the rear seat cushion, release the locking levers and remove the seat cushion.
4. Loosen the cable adjustment at the cable equalizer.
5. Remove the center cable clamp and grommet.
6. Raise the vehicle and support safely.
7. At the rear wheel, remove the brake drum and shoes.
8. Disconnect the cable end from the parking brake strut lever.
9. Remove the snapring securing the cable to the backing plate.
10. Unfasten any other frame retainers and remove the cables.

To install:

➡**The parking brake cables may be color coded to indicate side. Check the parking brake cables for an identification mark.**

11. Install the cable to the rear actuator. Secure in place with the parking brake cable clip and snapring.
12. Install the brake shoes and drum.
13. Position the cable and loosely install the retainers.
14. Reattach the parking brake cables to the actuator inside the vehicle. Tighten the adjusting nut until the proper tension is placed on the cable. Adjust the parking brake stroke using appropriate method.
15. Secure all cable retainers.
16. Apply and release the parking brake a number of times once all adjustments have been made.
17. Adjust the rear brakes and parking brake cables.
18. Check the rear wheels to confirm that the rear brakes are not dragging.
19. Install the center console and rear seat cushion.
20. Connect the negative battery cable.
21. Check console electrical components for proper operation.
22. Check that the parking brake holds the vehicle on an incline.

WITH REAR DISC BRAKES

1. Disconnect the negative battery cable.
2. Remove the center console as follows:
   a. Remove both side cover panels.
   b. Remove the shifter knob on manual transaxle models. Remove the spacer trim piece on automatic transaxle models.
   c. Remove the switch panel/box and remove the two screws beneath the panel/box.
   d. Remove the radio trim panel.
   e. Remove the radio and tape player.
   f. Remove the console inner panel and remove the two screws from beneath the panel.
   g. Remove the remaining screws from the sides of the console.
   h. Remove the console assembly from the vehicle.
3. While pressing downward on the front of the rear seat cushion, release the locking levers and remove the seat cushion.
4. Loosen the cable adjusting nut and disconnect the rear brake cables from the actuator.
5. Remove the center cable clamp and grommet.
6. Raise the vehicle and support it safely.

7. At the rear caliper assembly, remove the parking brake cable clip and retainer spring.
8. Disconnect the cable end from the caliper.
9. Unfasten any remaining frame retainers and remove the cables from the vehicle.

To install:

➡**The parking brake cables may be color coded to indicate side. Check the parking brake cables for an identification mark.**

10. Connect the cable to the actuator at the brake caliper. Secure in place with the parking brake cable clip and retainer spring.
11. Position the cable and loosely install the retainers.
12. Reattach the parking brake cables to the actuator inside the vehicle. Tighten the adjusting nut until the proper tension is placed on the cable.
13. Adjust the parking brake stroke using appropriate method.
14. Secure all cable retainers.
15. Apply and release the parking brake a number of times once all adjustments have been made.
16. With the rear wheels raised, make sure the parking brake is not causing excess drag on the rear wheels.
17. Install the floor console assembly and rear seat cushion.
18. Connect the negative battery cable.
19. Check console electrical components for proper operation.
20. Road test the vehicle and check for proper brake operation.
21. Check that the parking brake holds the vehicle on an incline.

1994–00 Galant

WITH REAR DRUM BRAKES

1. Disconnect the negative battery cable.

✳✳ WARNING

The SRS control unit is mounted beneath the center console. Use care when working with the center console assembly not to impact or shock the control unit.

2. Remove the center floor console assembly as follows:
   a. Remove the shifter knob on models equipped with a manual transaxle.
   b. Remove the shifter trim panel.
   c. Remove the center instrument panel.
   d. Remove the panel box from the console assembly.
   e. Remove the two screws from the center of the console.
   f. Remove the four side panel screws and remove the console from the vehicle.
3. Loosen the cable adjuster nut, then remove the parking brake cable by pulling it from the passenger compartment.
4. Raise the vehicle and support safely.
5. At the rear wheel, remove the brake drum and shoes.
6. Disconnect the cable end from the parking brake strut lever. Compress the retaining strips to remove the cable from the backing plate.

7. Unfasten any other frame retainers and remove the cables.

To install:

8. Install the cable to the rear actuator. Secure in place with the parking brake cable clip and retainer spring.
9. Install the brake shoes and drum.
10. Position the cable and loosely install the retainers.
11. Reattach the parking brake cables to the actuator inside the vehicle.
12. Tighten the adjusting nut until the proper tension is placed on the cable.
13. Adjust the parking brake stroke using appropriate method.
14. Secure all cable retainers. Apply and release the parking brake a number of times once all adjustments have been made.
15. Assemble the interior components which were removed.
16. Adjust the rear brakes and parking brake cables.
17. Connect the negative battery cable.
18. Check the rear wheels to confirm that the rear brakes are not dragging.
19. Check that the parking brake holds the vehicle on an incline.

WITH REAR DISC BRAKES

See Figure 109

Unlike conventional rear disc brake systems, the parking brake operation is NOT incorporated into the brake caliper. This system, uses a separate set of brake shoes, located behind the brake rotor.

1. Disconnect the negative battery cable.

WARNING

The SRS control unit is mounted beneath the center console. Use care when working with the center console assembly not to impact or shock the control unit.

2. Remove the center floor console assembly as follows:
   a. Remove the shifter knob on models equipped with a manual transaxle.
   b. Remove the shifter trim panel.
   c. Remove the center instrument panel.
   d. Remove the panel box from the console assembly.
   e. Remove the two screws from the center of the console.
   f. Remove the four side panel screws and remove the console from the vehicle.
3. Loosen the cable adjuster nut, then remove the parking brake cable by pulling it from the passenger compartment.
4. Raise the vehicle and support safely.
5. At the rear wheel, remove the brake caliper and rotor.
6. Remove the parking brake shoes. Refer to the procedure in this section.
7. Disconnect the cable end from the parking brake strut lever.
8. Compress the retaining strips to remove the cable from the backing plate.
9. Unfasten any other frame retainers and remove the cables.

To install:

10. Install the cable to the rear actuator. Secure in place with the parking brake cable clip and retainer spring.
11. Install the parking brake shoes.
12. Install the brake rotor and caliper assembly.
13. Position the cable and loosely install the retainers.
14. Reattach the parking brake cables to the actuator inside the vehicle.
15. Tighten the adjusting nut until the proper tension is placed on the cable.
16. Adjust the parking brake stroke using appropriate method.
17. Secure all cable retainers.
18. Apply and release the parking brake a number of times once all adjustments have been made.
19. Assemble the interior components which were removed.
20. Adjust the parking brake shoes and parking brake cables.
21. Connect the negative battery cable.
22. Check the rear wheels to confirm that the rear brakes are not dragging.
23. Check that the parking brake holds the vehicle on an incline.

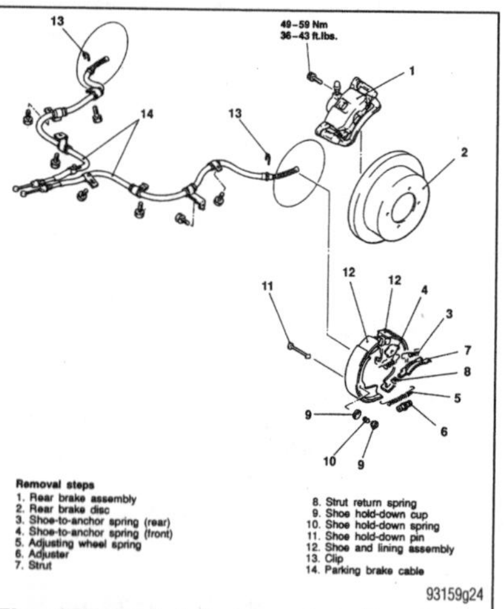
49–59 Nm
36–43 ft.lbs.
Removal steps
1. Rear brake assembly
2. Rear brake disc
3. Shoe-to-anchor spring (rear)
4. Shoe-to-anchor spring (front)
5. Adjusting wheel spring
6. Adjuster
7. Strut
8. Strut return spring
9. Shoe hold-down cup
10. Shoe hold-down spring
11. Shoe hold-down pin
12. Shoe and lining assembly
13. Clip
14. Parking brake cable
93159g24

Fig. 109 Exploded view of parking brake components (with disc brake rear system)—1994–95 Galant

Diamante

Unlike conventional rear disc brake systems, the parking brake operation is NOT incorporated into the brake caliper. This system, uses a separate set of brake shoes, located behind the brake rotor.

1. Disconnect the negative battery cable.

CAUTION

Work must be started after 90 seconds from the time the ignition switch is turned to the LOCK position and the negative battery cable is disconnected.

➡If equipped with an air bag, be sure to disarm it before starting repairs on the vehicle.

2. Remove the center floor console assembly as follows:
   a. Remove the ashtray or console switch panel from the console assembly.
   b. Remove the two screws from the center of the console.
   c. Remove the four side panel screws and remove the console from the vehicle.

➡If equipped with SRS, don't allow any impact or shock to the SRS diagnostic unit when removing the floor console.

3. Loosen the cable adjuster nut, then remove the parking brake cable by pulling it from the passenger compartment.
4. Raise the vehicle and support it safely.
5. At the rear wheel, remove the brake caliper and rotor.
6. Remove the parking brake shoes.
7. Disconnect the cable end from the parking brake strut lever.
8. Compress the retaining strips to remove the cable from the backing plate.
9. Unfasten any other frame retainers and remove the cables.

To install:

10. Install the cable to the rear actuator. Secure in place with the parking brake cable clip and retainer spring.
11. Install the parking brake shoes.
12. Install the brake rotor and caliper assembly.
13. Position the cable and loosely install the retainers.
14. Reattach the parking brake cables to the actuator inside the vehicle.
15. Tighten the adjusting nut until the proper tension is placed on the cable.
16. Adjust the parking brake stroke using appropriate method.
17. Secure all cable retainers.
18. Apply and release the parking brake a number of times once all adjustments have been made.
19. Assemble the interior components which were removed.
20. Adjust the parking brake shoes and parking brake cables.
21. Connect the negative battery cable.
22. Check the rear wheels to confirm that the rear brakes are not dragging.
23. Check that the parking brake holds the vehicle on an incline.

ADJUSTMENT

Mirage

See Figure 110

➡If the vehicle is equipped with rear drum brakes, make certain that the brake shoes are properly adjusted before attempting to adjust the parking brake.

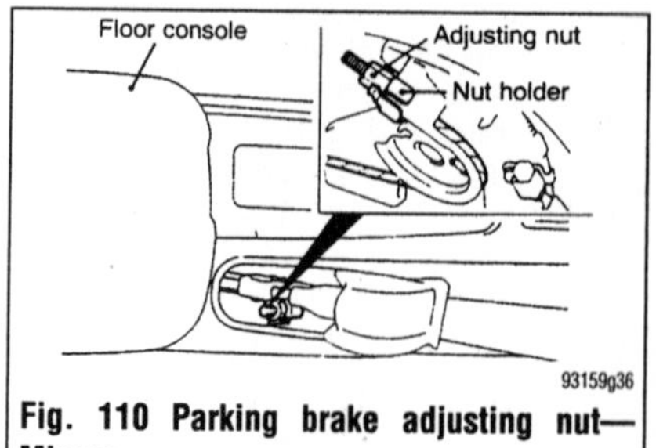
Floor console
Adjusting nut
Nut holder
93159g36

Fig. 110 Parking brake adjusting nut—Mirage

1. Make sure the parking brake cable is free and is not frozen or sticking.

2. Apply the parking brake with 45 lbs. (200 N) of force while counting the number of notches. The desired parking brake stroke should be 5–7 notches.

3. If adjustment is required, access the adjusting nut from inside the floor console.

4. Loosen the locknut on the cable rod.

5. Rotate the adjusting nut to adjust the parking brake stroke to the 5–7 notch setting. After making the adjustment, check there is no looseness between the adjusting nut and the parking brake lever, then tighten the locknut.

➡**Do not adjust the parking brake too tight. If the number of notches is less than specification, the cable has been pulled too much and the automatic adjuster will fail or the brakes will drag.**

6. After adjusting the lever stroke, raise the rear of the vehicle and safely support. With the parking brake lever in the released position, turn the rear wheels to confirm that the rear brakes are not dragging.

7. Check that the parking brake holds the vehicle on an incline.

Galant

1990–93 VEHICLES

♦ **See Figure 111**

1. Pull the parking brake lever up with a force of about 45 lbs. (200 N). The total number of clicks heard should be 5–7 clicks. If the number of clicks was not within that range, the system requires adjustment.

➡**The parking brake shoes must be adjusted before attempting to adjust the cable mechanism**

2. To adjust the parking brake shoes perform the following steps.

a. Remove the floor console, release the lever and back off the cable adjuster locknut at the base of the lever.

b. Raise the vehicle, support safely and remove the wheel.

c. Remove the hole plug in the brake rotor.

d. Remove the brake caliper and hang out of the way with wire. Do not disconnect the fluid line.

e. Use a suitable prybar to pry up on the self-adjuster wheel until the rotor will not turn.

f. Return the adjuster 5 notches in the opposite direction. Make sure the rotor turns freely with a slight drag.

g. Install the caliper and check operation.

3. Once the parking brake shoes have been properly adjusted, adjust the cable mechanism, by performing the following steps:

a. Turn the adjusting nut to give the proper number of clicks when the lever is raised full travel.

b. Raise and support the rear of the car on jackstands.

c. Release the brake lever and make sure that the rear wheels turn freely. If not, back off on the adjusting nut until they do.

1994–00 VEHICLES

1. Pull the parking brake lever with a force of approx. 45 lbs. (200 N) and count the number of notches. Standard value is: 5–7 notches.

✳✳ CAUTION

The 45 lbs. (200 N) force of the parking brake lever must be strictly observed.

2. If the parking brake lever is not the standard value, adjust in the following manner:

a. Remove the inner compartment mat of the floor console

b. Loosen the adjusting nut at the end of the cable rod, freeing the parking brake.

c. With the engine idling, forcefully depress the brake pedal five or six times and confirm that the pedal stroke stops changing. If the pedal stroke stops changing, the automatic-adjustment mechanism is functioning normally, and the clearance between the shoe and the drum is correct.

d. After adjusting the parking brake lever stroke, safely raise and support the rear of the vehicle and with the parking brake lever in the released position, turn the rear wheels to confirm that there is no brake drag.

Diamante

1. Pull the parking brake lever up with a force of about 45 lbs. (200 N). The total number of clicks heard should be 3–5. If the number of clicks was not within that range, the system requires adjustment.

➡**The parking brake shoes must be adjusted before attempting to adjust the cable mechanism**

2. To adjust the parking brake shoes, perform the following steps:

a. Remove the floor console, release the lever and back off the cable adjuster locknut at the base of the lever.

b. Raise the vehicle, support safely and remove the wheel. Remove the hole plug in the brake rotor.

c. Remove the brake caliper and hang out of the way with wire. Do not disconnect the fluid line.

d. Use a suitable prybar to pry up on the self-adjuster wheel until the rotor will not turn.

e. Return the adjuster 5 notches in the opposite direction. Make sure the rotor turns freely with a slight drag.

f. Install the caliper and check operation.

3. Once the parking brake shoes have been properly adjusted, adjust the cable mechanism, by performing the following steps:

a. Pull the parking brake lever up with a force of 45 lbs. (200 N). The total number of clicks heard should be 3–5.

b. Turn the adjusting nut to give the proper number of clicks when the lever is raised.

c. Raise and support the rear of the car on jackstands.

d. Release the brake lever and make sure that the rear wheels turn freely.

Brake Shoes

REMOVAL & INSTALLATION

1994–00 Galant and 1992–96 Diamante

♦ **See Figures 112, 113, and 114**

1. Raise and safely support the vehicle securely on jackstands.

2. Remove the caliper assembly.

3. Remove the rear brake rotor.

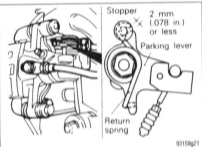

Fig. 111 Parking brake system adjustment points—1993 Galant

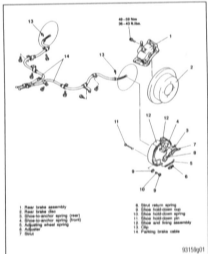

Fig. 112 Exploded view of the parking shoes and related components—1994–00 Galant with disc brakes

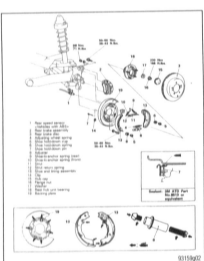

Fig. 113 Exploded view of the parking brake shoes and related components—1992–96 Diamante

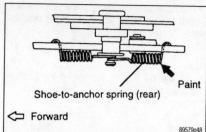

Shoe-to-anchor spring (rear) | Paint

⟸ Forward

89579g48

Fig. 114 Shoe-to-anchor spring installation

➡**When servicing drum brakes, only dissemble and assemble one side at a time, leaving the remaining side intact for reference.**

4. Remove the front and rear shoe-to-anchor springs.

5. Remove the adjusting wheel spring and the adjuster.

6. Remove the strut and the strut return spring.

7. Remove the shoe hold-down cup, spring and pin.

8. Remove the shoe and lining assembly.

9. Unfasten the clips and the retaining bolts, then remove the parking brake cable(s).

To install:

10. Installation is the reverse of the removal procedure.

11. Install the adjuster so the shoe adjusting bolt of the left hand wheel is attached toward the front of the vehicle and the shoe adjusting bolt of the right hand wheel is toward the rear of the vehicle.

12. The load on the respective shoe-to-anchor springs is different, so the spring in the figure has been painted, as shown in the accompanying figure.

1997–00 Diamante

◆ **See Figure 115**

1. Raise and safely support the vehicle securely on jackstands.

2. Remove the caliper assembly.

3. Remove the rear brake rotor.

➡**When servicing drum brakes, only dissemble and assemble one side at a time, leaving the remaining side intact for reference.**

4. Remove the shoe hold-down spring retaining screw.

5. Remove the shoe hold-down spring.

6. Remove the shoe assembly from the backing plate.

7. The installation is the reverse of removal.

ADJUSTMENT

1. Remove the floor console, release the lever and back off the cable adjuster locknut at the base of the lever.

2. Raise the vehicle, support safely and remove the wheel.

3. Remove the hole plug in the brake rotor.

4. Remove the brake caliper and hang out of the way with wire. Do not disconnect the fluid line.

5. Use a suitable prybar to pry up on the self-adjuster wheel until the rotor will not turn.

6. Return the adjuster 5 notches in the opposite direction. Make sure the rotor turns freely with a slight drag.

7. Install the caliper and check operation.

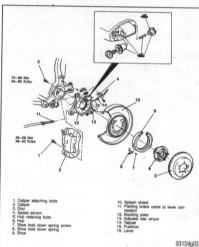

74–88 Nm
54–65 ft.lbs

49–59 Nm
36–43 ft.lbs

1. Caliper attaching bolts
2. Caliper
3. Disc
4. Speed sensor
5. Hub retaining bolts
6. Hub
7. Shoe hold down spring screw
8. Shoe hold down spring
9. Shoe
10. Splash shield
11. Parking brake cable to lever connection
12. Backing plate
13. Adjuster star wheel
14. Tappet
15. Pushrod
16. Lever

93159g03

Fig. 115 Exploded view of the parking brake shoes and related components—1997–00 Diamante

---

ANTI-LOCK BRAKE SYSTEM

General Information

The 4-Wheel Anti-lock Brake System (ABS) is an electronically operated, all wheel brake control system. Major components include the vacuum power brake booster, master cylinder, the wheel speed sensors, the Hydraulic Control Unit (HCU), Anti-lock control unit, a relay, and on the AWD Galant, a G sensor.

The system is designed to retard wheel lockup during periods of high wheel slip when braking. Retarding wheel lockup is accomplished by modulating fluid pressure to the wheel brake units. When the control unit detects a variation in voltage across the wheel speed sensors, the ABS is activated. The control unit opens and closes various valves located inside the HCU. These valves, called dump and isolation valves, modulate the hydraulic pressure to the wheels by applying and venting the pressure to the brake fluid circuits.

PRECAUTIONS

• Certain components within the Anti-Lock Brake System (ABS) are not intended to be serviced or repaired individually. Only those components with removal and installation procedures should be serviced.

• Do not use rubber hoses or other parts not specifically specified for an ABS system. When using repair kits, replace all parts included in the kit. Partial or incorrect repair may lead to functional problems and require the replacement of components.

• Lubricate rubber parts with clean, fresh brake fluid to ease assembly. Do not use lubricated shop air to clean parts; damage to rubber components may result.

• Use only specified brake fluid from an unopened container.

• If any hydraulic component or line is removed or replaced, it may be necessary to bleed the entire system.

• A clean repair area is essential. Always clean the reservoir and cap thoroughly before removing the cap. The slightest amount of dirt in the fluid may plug an orifice and impair the system function. Perform repairs after components have been thoroughly cleaned; use only denatured alcohol to clean components. Do not allow ABS components to come into contact with any substance containing mineral oil; this includes used shop rags.

• The Anti-Lock control unit is a microprocessor similar to other computer units in the vehicle. Ensure that the ignition switch is **OFF** before removing or installing controller harnesses. Avoid static electricity discharge at or near the controller.

• If any arc welding is to be done on the vehicle, the control unit should be unplugged before welding operations begin.

Diagnosis and Testing

◆ **See Figures 116 thru 123**

The diagnosis of the ABS system is rather complex and requires quite a few special tools including scan

tools, special test harnesses and other special and expensive tools. Alternative methods and common sense can be substituted, however, We at Chilton feel that it is beyond the scope of the average do-it-yourselfer. If you experience the amber ANTI LOCK light on in the instrument cluster of your vehicle, check the fluid level in the master cylinder first. Low fluid level will usually illuminate the red BRAKE lamp in the instrument cluster as well as, but not always, the amber ANTI LOCK lamp in the instrument cluster. The low fluid level could indicate a leak, but sometimes just indicates low, worn brake linings that have caused the caliper pistons and wheel cylinders to extend further, and thus using more fluid to exert force on them. Inspect the brake system for hydraulic fluid leaks and also inspect the brake linings for excessive wear.

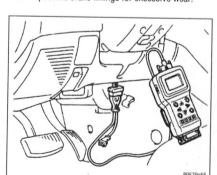

89579g56

Fig. 116 You can connect a scan tool to the data link connector to retrieve ABS trouble codes

Diagnostic trouble code No.	Inspection item	Diagnostic content	Detection conditions
11	Right front wheel speed sensor	Open circuit	A, B
12	Left front wheel speed sensor		
13	Right rear wheel speed sensor		
14	Left rear wheel speed sensor		
15	Wheel speed sensor system	Abnormal output signal	B
16	Power supply system	Abnormal battery positive voltage	A, B
21	Right front wheel speed sensor	Excessive gap or short circuit	B
22	Left front wheel speed sensor		
23	Right rear wheel speed sensor		
24	Left rear wheel speed sensor		
38	Stop light switch system	Open circuit or ON malfunction	A, B
41	Right front solenoid valve system	No response to solenoid valve drive signal	A, B
42	Left front solenoid valve system		
43	Rear solenoid valve system		
51	Valve relay system	Valve relay OFF failure	A, B
53	Motor relay or motor system	Motor relay OFF failure and motor drive failure	B
63	ABS-ECU	Malfunction in ABS-ECU (program maze, etc.)	A, B

Detection conditions

A: During system check immediately after starting
B: When driving

89579g54

Fig. 117 ABS diagnostic trouble code list—1992–96 Diamante

Diagnostic trouble code no.	Inspection item		Detection conditions
11	Front right wheel speed sensor	Open circuit	B, C
12	Front left wheel speed sensor		
13	Rear right wheel speed sensor		
14	Rear left wheel speed sensor		
15	Wheel speed sensor output signal abnormal		A, B
16	Power supply system		A, B, C
21	Front right wheel speed sensor	Short circuit	B, C
22	Front left wheel speed sensor		
23	Rear right wheel speed sensor		
24	Rear left wheel speed sensor		
38	Stop light switch system		B, C
41	Front right solenoid valve (inlet)		
42	Front left solenoid valve (inlet)		B, C
43	Rear right solenoid valve (inlet)		
44	Rear left solenoid valve (inlet)		
45	Front right solenoid valve (outlet)		
46	Front left solenoid valve (outlet)		B, C
47	Rear right solenoid valve (outlet)		
48	Rear left solenoid valve (outlet)		
51	Valve relay		A, B, C
53	Motor relay		B
63	ABS–ECU		A, B, C

Detection conditions

A: During system check immediately after starting
B: While ABS control is not operating while driving
C: While ABS control is operating

93159g04

Fig. 118 ABS diagnostic trouble code list—1997–00 Diamante

The ABS control unit performs system tests and self-tests during startup and normal operation. The valves, wheel sensors and fluid level circuits are monitored for proper operation. If a fault is found, the

Diagnostic trouble code		Diagnostic trouble code	
No.	Scan tool (DRB-II) display letters	No.	Scan tool (DRB-II) display letters
11	FL SPD SENSOR	41	SOL V FRONT L
12	FR SPD SENSOR	42	SOL V FRONT R
13	RL SPD SENSOR	43	SOL V REAR
14	RR SPD SENSOR	51	VALVE RLY
15	SENSOR FAULT	52	MOTOR RLY
22	STOP SW	55	ECU

89579g53

Fig. 119 ABS diagnostic trouble code list—1990–93 Galant

LOCK warning lamp will flash either twice (FWD) or 4 times (AWD) vehicles, in about 1 second with the ignition switch **ON**, then the lamp will turn OFF.

The Diagnostic Trouble Codes (DTC) are an alphanumeric code and a scan tool, such as DRB-III, MUT-II or equivalent diagnostic scan tool, is required to retrieve the codes. Refer to the scan tool manufacturer's instructions for operating the tool and retrieving the codes.

The Data Link Connector (DLC) for the ABS is located under the dash on the driver's side. It is the same connector used for the electronic engine control system.

Hydraulic Control Unit

REMOVAL AND INSTALLATION

The Hydraulic Control Unit (HCU) is located in the engine compartment. It contains the solenoid valves and the pump/motor assembly which provides pressurized fluid for the anti-lock system when necessary. Hydraulic units are not interchangeable on any vehicles. Neither unit is serviceable; if any fault occurs within the hydraulic unit, the entire unit must be replaced.

Diamante

◆ See Figure 124

1. Disconnect the negative battery cable.
2. Remove the splash shield from beneath the vehicle.
3. Use a syringe or similar device to remove as much fluid as possible from the reservoir. Some fluid will be spilled from lines during removal of the hydraulic unit; protect adjacent painted surfaces.

❊❊❊ CAUTION

Brake fluid contains polyglycol ethers and polyglycols. Avoid contact with the eyes and wash your hands thoroughly after handling brake fluid. If you do get brake fluid in your eyes, flush your eyes with clean, running water for 15 minutes. If eye irritation persists, or if you have taken brake fluid internally, IMMEDIATELY seek medical assistance.

4. Lift the relay box with the harness attached and position it aside.
5. Remove the air intake duct.
6. Disconnect the brake lines from the hydraulic unit. Correct reassembly is critical. Label or identify the lines before removal. Plug each line immediately

ABS will be deactivated and the amber ANTI LOCK light will be lit until the ignition is turned OFF. When the light is lit, the Diagnostic Trouble Code (DTC) may be obtained. Under normal operation, the ANTI-

Diagnostic trouble code No.	Inspection item	Diagnosis content
11	Front right wheel speed sensor	Open circuit
12	Front left wheel speed sensor	
13	Rear right wheel speed sensor	
14	Rear left wheel speed sensor	
15	Open circuit in sensor	Open circuit in sensor
16	Drop of battery voltage	Drop of ABS operation voltage
21	Front right wheel speed sensor	Short circuit
22	Rear right wheel speed sensor	
23	Rear left wheel speed sensor	
24	Rear left wheel speed sensor	
25	Both rear wheel speed sensors	Open circuit in both rear wheel speed sensors, short circuit
31	Rotor of front right wheel speed sensor	Chipped tooth of rotor
32	Rotor of front left wheel speed sensor	
33	Rotor of rear right wheel speed sensor	
34	Rotor of rear left wheel speed sensor	
35	Generator	Drop of generator output voltage
41	Front right solenoid valve	No response to solenoid valve drive signal
42	Front left solenoid valve	
43	Rear right solenoid valve	
44	Rear left solenoid valve	
51	Valve relay 1	Detection impossible in OFF condition
52	Valve relay 2	Detection impossible in ON condition
53	Motor relay, motor 1	ON impossible
54	Motor relay, motor 2	OFF impossible
55	Sticking of motor	Motor operation impossible
62	Malfunction inside hydraulic unit	Hydraulic pressure reduction impossible
63	Malfunction inside ABS-ECU	Irregular program, etc.

Fig. 122 ABS diagnostic trouble code list—1993–96 Mirage

Diagnostic trouble code no.	Inspection item	Diagnostic content
11	Front right wheel speed sensor	Open circuit or short circuit
12	Front left wheel speed sensor	
13	Rear right wheel speed sensor	
14	Rear left wheel speed sensor	
15	Wheel speed sensor	Abnormal output signal
16	Power supply system	
21	Front right wheel speed sensor	
22	Front left wheel speed sensor	
23	Rear right wheel speed sensor	
24	Rear left wheel speed sensor	
33	Stop light switch system	
41	Front right solenoid valve (inside)	
42	Front left solenoid valve (inside)	
43	Rear right solenoid valve (inside)	
44	Rear left solenoid valve (inside)	
51	Valve relay	
53	Motor relay, motor	
63	ABS-ECU	

Fig. 123 ABS diagnostic trouble code list—1997–00 Mirage

Diagnostic trouble code no.	Inspection item		Detection conditions
11	Front right wheel speed sensor	Open circuit	B, C
12	Front left wheel speed sensor		
13	Rear right wheel speed sensor		A, B, C
14	Rear left wheel speed sensor		B, C
16	Power supply system		
21	Front right wheel speed sensor	Short circuit	
22	Rear right wheel speed sensor		
23	Rear right wheel speed sensor		
24	Rear left wheel speed sensor		B, C
25	Front right wheel speed sensor	Excessive gap	
26	Front left wheel speed sensor		
27	Rear right wheel speed sensor		
28	Rear left wheel speed sensor		
33	Stop light switch system		B, C
35	Front right wheel speed sensor	Pulse processing (wheel speed input corresponding to a vehicle speed of 300 km/h (186 mph) or more)	B, C
36	Front left wheel speed sensor		
37	Rear right wheel speed sensor		
38	Rear left wheel speed sensor		
41	Front right solenoid valve (inside)		B, C
42	Front left solenoid valve (inside)		
43	Rear right solenoid valve (inside)		
44	Rear left solenoid valve (inside)		
45	Front right solenoid valve (outside)		
46	Front left solenoid valve (outside)		
47	Rear right solenoid valve (outside)		
48	Rear left solenoid valve (outside)		
51	Valve relay	ON impossible	A, B, C
52	Valve relay	OFF impossible	A
53	Motor relay	ON impossible	B
54	Motor relay	OFF impossible	B, C

Detection conditions

A: During system check immediately after starting
B: While ABS control is not operating while driving
C: While ABS control is operating

Fig. 120 ABS diagnostic trouble code list—1994–98 Galant

DIAGNOSTIC TROUBLE CODE NO.	INSPECTION ITEM	DIAGNOSTIC CONTENT
11	Front right wheel speed sensor	Open circuit or short circuit
12	Front left wheel speed sensor	
13	Rear right wheel speed sensor	
14	Rear left wheel speed sensor	
16	Power supply system	ABS-ECU power supply voltage below or above the standard value. Not displayed if the voltage recovers.
21	Front right wheel speed sensor	
22	Front left wheel speed sensor	
23	Rear right wheel speed sensor	
24	Rear left wheel speed sensor	
38	Stoplight switch system	
41	Solenoid valve inside hydraulic unit	Open circuit or short circuit
42	ABS-ECU	
51	Hydraulic unit solenoid valve relay open or short circuit	
53	Malfunction of hydraulic unit	
63	ABS-ECU	

Fig. 121 ABS diagnostic trouble code list—1999–00 Galant

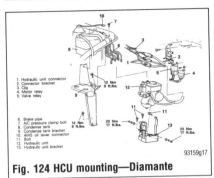

1. Hydraulic unit connector
2. Connector bracket
3. Clip
4. Motor relay
5. Valve relay

6. Brake pipe
7. A/C pressure clamp bolt
8. Condense tank
9. Condense tank bracket
10. 4WS oil lever connector
11. Bolt
12. Hydraulic unit
13. Hydraulic unit bracket

12 Nm
9 ft.lbs.

23 Nm
17 ft.lbs.

23 Nm
17 ft.lbs.

93159g17

Fig. 124 HCU mounting—Diamante

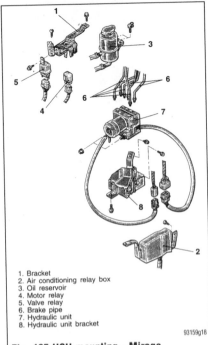

1. Bracket
2. Air conditioning relay box
3. Oil reservoir
4. Motor relay
5. Valve relay
6. Brake pipe
7. Hydraulic unit
8. Hydraulic unit bracket

93159g18

Fig. 125 HCU mounting—Mirage

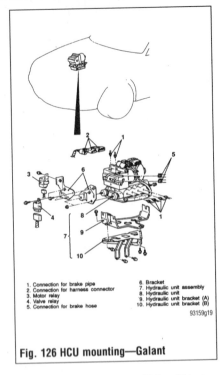

1. Connection for brake pipe
2. Connection for harness connector
3. Motor relay
4. Valve relay
5. Connection for brake hose

6. Bracket
7. Hydraulic unit assembly
8. Hydraulic unit
9. Hydraulic unit bracket (A)
10. Hydraulic unit bracket (B)

93159g19

Fig. 126 HCU mounting—Galant

after removal. It will be necessary to hold the relay box aside to allow wrench access.

7. Detach the wiring harness connections at the hydraulic unit.

8. Disconnect the hydraulic unit ground strap from the chassis.

9. Remove the 3 bolts holding the hydraulic unit bracket. Remove the unit and the bracket.

➡**The hydraulic unit is heavy; use care when removing it. The unit must remain in the up-right position at all times and be protected from impact and shock.**

10. Set the unit upright, supported by blocks on the workbench. The hydraulic unit must not be tilted or turned upside down. No component of the hy-draulic unit should be loosened or disassembled.

11. Loosen the nut holding the bracket to the hy-draulic unit and remove the bracket.

12. Disconnect the external ground wire from the bracket.

To install:

13. Install the bracket if removed.

14. Connect the ground wire to the bracket.

15. Install the hydraulic unit into the vehicle, keeping it upright at all times.

16. Install the retaining nuts and tighten.

17. Connect the hydraulic unit wiring harness.

18. Connect each brake line loosely to the correct port and double check the placement. Tighten each line to 11 ft. lbs. (15 Nm).

19. Fill the reservoir to the MAX line with brake fluid.

20. Bleed the master cylinder, then bleed the brake lines.

21. Secure the relay box in position and install the air duct.

22. Install the splash shield.

Galant and Mirage

♦ **See Figures 125 and 126**

1. Use a syringe or similar device to remove as much fluid as possible from the reservoir. Some fluid will be spilled from lines during removal of the hy-draulic unit; protect adjacent painted surfaces.

✳✳✳ CAUTION

Brake fluid contains polyglycol ethers and polyglycols. Avoid contact with the eyes and wash your hands thoroughly after handling brake fluid. If you do get brake fluid in your eyes, flush your eyes with clean, running wa-ter for 15 minutes. If eye irritation persists,

or if you have taken brake fluid internally, **IMMEDIATELY seek medical assistance.**

2. Remove the splash shield from the left front wheel house or fender area.

3. Remove the coolant reserve tank.

4. Remove the coolant reservoir bracket.

5. Remove the dust shield from below the hy-draulic unit.

6. Disconnect the brake hoses and lines from the hydraulic unit. Correct reassembly is critical. La-bel or identify the lines before removal. Plug each line and each port immediately after removal.

7. Remove the cover from the relay box. Dis-connect the electrical harness to the hydraulic unit.

8. Remove the bolts holding the 3 mounting brackets to the vehicle; remove the unit downward and out of the vehicle.

➡**The hydraulic unit is heavy; use care when removing it. The unit must remain in the up-right position at all times and be protected from impact and shock.**

9. Set the unit upright, supported by blocks on the workbench. The hydraulic unit must not be tilted or turned upside down. No component of the hy-draulic unit should be loosened or disassembled.

10. The brackets and relays may be removed if desired.

To install:

11. Install the brackets and relays if they were re-moved. Tighten the bracket bolts to 16 ft. lbs. (22 Nm).

12. Install the hydraulic unit into the vehicle, keeping it upright at all times.

13. Install the retaining bolts holding the brackets to the vehicle. Tighten the bolts to 16 ft. lbs. (22 Nm).

14. Connect the hydraulic unit wiring harness.

15. Install the cover on the relay box.

16. Connect each brake line loosely to the correct port and double check the placement. Tighten each line to 10 ft. lbs. (13 Nm).

17. Fill the reservoir to the **MAX** line with brake fluid.

18. Bleed the brake system.

19. Install the dust shield and the coolant reserve tank with its bracket.

20. Install the fender splash shield.

21. Check ABS system function by turning the ig-nition **ON** and observing the dashboard warning lamp. Test drive the vehicle and confirm system op-eration.

Anti-Lock Control Unit

REMOVAL AND INSTALLATION

♦ **See Figures 127 and 128**

1. Ensure that the ignition switch is OFF through-out the procedure.

2. For Galant and Diamante models, remove the left side luggage compartment trim panel.

3. For Mirage models, remove the floor console assembly.

4. Release the lock on the bottom of the connec-tor. Detach the multi-pin connector from the control unit.

5. Remove the retaining nuts and remove the control unit from its bracket. The bracket may be re-moved if desired.

To install:

6. Place the bracket in position if it was removed. Install the controller and tighten the retaining nuts.

7. Connect the ground wire to the bracket, if re-moved. Insure a proper, tight connection. The ground must be connected before the multi-pin harness is connected.

8. Attach the multi-pin connector and secure the lock.

9. Install the luggage compartment trim or the floor console.

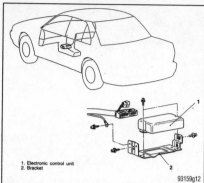

Fig. 127 Anti-lock control unit mounting— Mirage

Speed Sensors

REMOVAL & INSTALLATION

Mirage

FRONT

▶ See Figure 129

1. Disconnect the negative battery cable.

❊❊ CAUTION

Wait at least 90 seconds after the negative battery cable is disconnected to prevent possible deployment of the air bag.

2. Raise and safely support the vehicle.
3. Remove the splash shield.
4. Detach the speed sensor connector.
5. Remove the clips holding the sensor harness.
6. Remove the speed sensor from the bracket.
To install:
7. Install the speed sensor to the bracket and secure with mounting bolt.
8. Install the clips holding the sensor harness.
9. Attach the speed sensor connector.
10. Connect the negative battery cable.

REAR

▶ See Figure 129 and 130

1. Disconnect the negative battery cable.

❊❊ CAUTION

Wait at least 90 seconds after the negative battery cable is disconnected to prevent possible deployment of the air bag.

2. Raise and safely support the vehicle.
3. Detach the speed sensor connector.
4. Remove the clips holding the sensor harness.
5. Remove the mounting bolt and the speed sensor.
To install:
6. Install the speed sensor and loosely tighten the mounting bolt.
7. Install the clips holding the sensor harness.

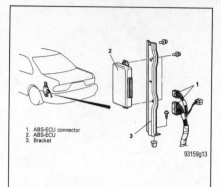

Fig. 128 Anti-lock control unit mounting— Galant and Diamante

8. Install the sensor wire harness and attach the connector.
9. Using a non-magnetic feeler gauge, adjust the sensor air gap so the clearance between the rotor and the sensor is 0.012–0.035 inches (0.3–0.9mm).
10. Tighten the sensor bracket and recheck the clearance.
11. Connect the negative battery cable.

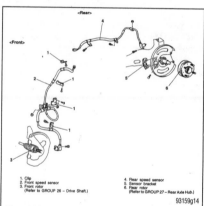

Fig. 129 Front and rear wheel speed sensors—Mirage

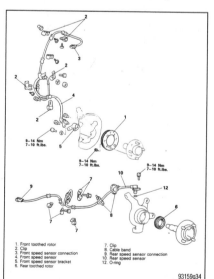

Fig. 131 Wheel speed sensors—1990–93 AWD Galant

Galant

FRONT

▶ See Figures 131 and 132

1. Disconnect the negative battery cable. Wait at least 90 seconds before performing any work.
2. Raise and safely support the vehicle. Remove the necessary tire and wheel assembly.
3. Remove the fender splash shield.
4. Detach the ABS speed sensor connector.
5. Remove the sensor harness clamp bolts and clamps.
6. Remove the ABS speed sensor mounting bolt and the sensor.
To install:
7. Install the ABS speed sensor with its mounting bolt.

➡**The clearance between the wheel speed sensor and the rotor's toothed surface is not adjustable, but measure the distance between the sensor installation surface and the rotor's toothed surface. Standard value is: 1.11–1.12 in. (28.2–28.4mm). If not within specifications, replace the speed sensor or the toothed rotor.**

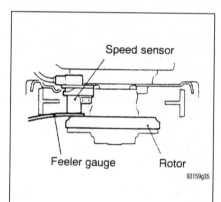

Fig. 130 Adjusting the rear speed sensor air gap—Mirage

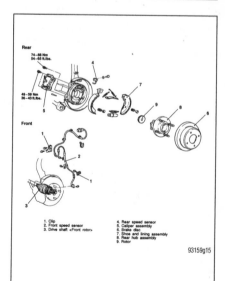

Fig. 132 Wheel speed sensors—1994–00 Galant

8. Reinstall the sensor harness with its clamps and bolts.

9. Reconnect the speed sensor connector.

10. Install the fender splash shield.

11. Reinstall the tire and wheel, safely lower the vehicle, and reconnect the negative battery cable.

REAR

♦ **See Figure 131 and 132**

1. Disconnect the negative battery cable. Wait at least 90 seconds before performing any work.

2. Raise and safely support the vehicle. Remove the necessary tire and wheel assembly.

3. Detach the ABS speed sensor connector.

4. Remove the sensor harness clamp bolts and clamps.

5. Remove the ABS speed sensor mounting bolt and the sensor.

To install:

6. Install the ABS speed sensor with its mounting bolt.

➡ **The clearance between the wheel speed sensor and the rotor's toothed surface is not adjustable, but measure the distance between the sensor installation surface and the rotor's toothed surface. Standard value is: 1.11–1.12 in. (28.2–28.4mm). If not within specifications, replace the speed sensor or the toothed rotor.**

7. Reinstall the sensor harness with its clamps and bolts.

8. Reconnect the speed sensor connector.

9. Reinstall the tire and wheel, safely lower the vehicle, and reconnect the negative battery cable.

Diamante

FRONT

♦ **See Figure 133**

1. Disconnect the negative battery cable.

> ※※ **CAUTION**
>
> **Work must be started after 90 seconds from the time the ignition switch is turned to the LOCK position and the negative battery cable is disconnected.**

2. Raise and safely support the vehicle.

3. Remove the splash shield.

4. Detach the speed sensor connector.

5. Remove the clips holding the sensor harness.

6. Remove the speed sensor.

To install:

7. Install the speed sensor and torque to 9 ft. lbs. (12 Nm).

8. Install the clips holding the sensor harness.

9. Connect the speed sensor connector.

10. Connect the negative battery cable.

REAR

♦ **See Figure 133**

1. Disconnect the negative battery cable.

> ※※ **CAUTION**
>
> **Work must be started after 90 seconds from the time the ignition switch is turned to the LOCK position and the negative battery cable is disconnected.**

2. Raise and safely support the vehicle.

3. Detach the speed sensor connector.

4. Remove the clips holding the sensor harness.

5. On AWD models, remove the cable band.

6. Remove the mounting bolt and the speed sensor with the O-ring.

To install:

7. Install the speed sensor with the O-ring and torque to 9 ft. lbs. (12 Nm).

8. Install the clips holding the sensor harness.

9. Install the cable band.

10. Install the sensor wire harness and connect the connector.

11. Connect the negative battery cable.

G-Sensor

The G-sensors are used only on the AWD vehicles. The rear is mounted in the trunk under the floor mat while the front sensor is under the console assembly. The sensor transmits acceleration and deceleration information to the anti-lock control unit. This data is used in conjunction with individual wheel speed and engine data, allowing the controller to determine the approximate road friction. This friction factor is then used to compute the proper control of the solenoid valves.

REMOVAL & INSTALLATION

♦ **See Figure 134**

1. For the front sensor, remove the console assembly.

2. For the rear sensor, remove the trunk floor mat.

3. Disconnect the G-sensor wiring harness.

4. Remove the cover from the rear sensor. Remove the sensor from the bracket. Remove the bracket if desired.

To install:

5. Reinstall the bracket if it was removed.

6. Install the G-sensor and connect the wiring harness. Tighten the retaining bolts to 8 ft. lbs. (11 Nm).

7. Install the cover on the rear G-sensor.

8. Install the console and/or the trunk floor mat or carpet.

Tone (Exciter) Ring

REMOVAL & INSTALLATION

Front

1. Raise and safely support the vehicle.

2. Remove the wheel and tire.

3. Remove the wheel speed sensor and disconnect sufficient harness clips to allow the sensor and wiring to be moved out of the work area.

➡ **The speed sensor has a pole piece projecting from it. This exposed tip must be protected from impact or scratches. Do not allow the pole piece to contact the toothed wheel during removal or installation.**

4. Remove the front hub and knuckle assembly.

5. Remove the hub from the knuckle.

6. Support the hub in a vise with protected jaws.

7. Remove the retaining bolts from the toothed wheel and remove the toothed wheel.

To install:

8. Fit the new toothed wheel onto the hub and tighten the retaining bolts to 7 ft. lbs. (10 Nm).

9. Assemble the hub to the knuckle

10. Install the hub and knuckle assembly to the vehicle.

11. Install the wheel speed sensor.

12. Install the wheel and tire.

13. Lower the vehicle to the ground.

Rear

EXCEPT AWD GALANT

1. Raise and safely support the vehicle.

2. Remove the wheel and tire.

3. Remove the wheel speed sensor and disconnect sufficient harness clips to allow the sensor and wiring to be moved out of the work area.

➡ **The speed sensor has a pole piece projecting from it. This exposed tip must be protected from impact or scratches. Do not allow the pole piece to contact the toothed wheel during removal or installation.**

4. Remove the hub assembly.

5. Support the hub in a vise with protected jaws.

6. Remove the retaining bolts from the toothed wheel and remove the toothed wheel.

To install:

7. Fit the new toothed wheel onto the hub and tighten the retaining bolts to 7 ft. lbs. (10 Nm).

8. Install the hub assembly to the vehicle. The center hub nut is not reusable. The new nut must be

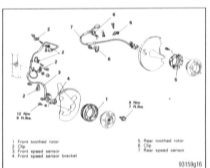

Fig. 133 Wheel speed sensors—Diamante

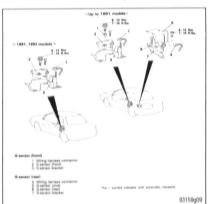

Fig. 134 Front and rear G-sensor mounting—1990–93 AWD Galant

tightened to 144–188 ft. lbs. (200–260 Nm). After the nut is tightened, align the nut with the spindle indentation and crimp the nut in place.

  9. Install the wheel speed sensor.
  10. Install the wheel and tire.
  11. Lower the vehicle to the ground.

AWD GALANT

  1. Raise and safely support the vehicle.
  2. Remove the wheel and tire.
  3. Disconnect the parking brake cable from the caliper.
  4. Remove the speed sensor and its O-ring. Disconnect sufficient clamps and wire ties to allow the sensor to be moved well out of the work area.

➡ **The speed sensor has a pole piece projecting from it. This exposed tip must be protected from impact or scratches. Do not allow the pole piece to contact the toothed wheel during removal or installation.**

  5. Remove the brake caliper and brake disc.
  6. Remove the 3 retaining nuts and bolts holding the outer end of the driveshaft to the companion flange.
  7. Swing the axle shaft away and support it with stiff wire. Do not overextend the joint in the axle; do not allow it to hang unsupported.
  8. Remove the retaining nut and washer on the back of the driveshaft. Use special tool MB 9g67 or equivalent to counterhold the hub.
  9. Remove the companion flange from the knuckle.
  10. Using an axle puller which bolts to the wheel lugs, remove the axle shaft assembly.
  11. Fit the shaft assembly in a press with the toothed wheel completely supported by a bearing plate such as special tool MB 9e60 or its equivalent.
  12. Press the toothed wheel off the axle shaft.
  To install:
  13. Press the new toothed wheel onto the shaft with the groove facing the axle shaft flange.

  14. Install the axle shaft to the knuckle and fit the companion flange in place.
  15. Install the lock washer and a new self–locking nut on the axle shaft. Tighten the nut to 116–159 ft. lbs. (160–220 Nm).
  16. Swing the axle assembly into place and install the 3 nuts and bolts. Tighten each to 45 ft. lbs. (61 Nm).
  17. Install the brake disc and caliper.
  18. Install the wheel speed sensor. Always use a new O-ring.
  19. Connect the parking brake cable to the caliper.
  20. Install the wheel and tire; lower the vehicle to the ground.

Bleeding the ABS System

There is no special procedure to bleed the ABS system. Proceed with the normal brake bleeding procedure located earlier in this section.

BRAKE SPECIFICATIONS
All measurements in inches unless noted

Year	Model		Original Thickness	Brake Disc Minimum Thickness	Maximum Runout	Original Inside Diameter	Brake Drum Diameter Max. Wear Limit	Maximum Machine Diameter	Minimum Lining Thickness Front	Rear	Brake Caliper Bracket Bolts (ft. lbs.)	Mounting Bolts (ft. lbs.)
1990	Galant	F	0.940	0.882	0.003	—	—	—	0.080	—	58-72	16-23
		R	—	—	—	8.000	—	8.100	—	0.080	—	—
	Galant	F	0.940	0.882	0.003	—	—	—	0.080	—	58-72	16-23
	w/rear disc	R	0.390	0.331	0.003	—	—	—	—	0.080	36-43	16-23
	Mirage	F	0.510	0.449	0.006	—	—	—	0.080	—	58-72	16-23
		R	—	—	—	7.100	—	7.200	—	0.040	—	—
	Mirage	F	0.940	0.882	0.003	—	—	—	0.080	—	58-72	46-62
	w/rear disc	R	0.390	0.331	0.003	—	—	—	—	0.080	58-72	16-23
1991	Galant	F	0.940	0.882	0.003	—	—	—	0.080	—	58-72	46-62
		R	—	—	—	8.000	—	8.100	—	0.080	—	—
	Galant	F	0.940	0.882	0.003	—	—	—	0.080	—	58-72	46-62
	w/rear disc	R	0.390	0.331	0.003	—	—	—	—	0.080	36-43	16-23
	Mirage	F	0.510	0.449	0.006	—	—	—	0.080	—	58-72	①
	Solid rotor	R	—	—	—	7.100	—	7.200	—	0.040	—	—
	Mirage	F	0.710	0.646	0.006	—	—	—	0.080	—	58-72	27-36
	Vented rotor	R	—	—	—	7.100	—	7.200	—	0.040	—	—
	Mirage	F	0.940	0.882	0.006	—	—	—	0.080	—	58-72	46-62
	w/rear disc	R	0.390	0.331	0.006	—	—	—	—	0.080	36-43	16-23
1992	Diamante	F	0.940	0.882	0.003	—	—	—	0.080	—	65	54
		R	0.710	0.646	0.003	—	—	—	—	0.080	36-43	20
	Diamante	F	0.940	0.882	0.003	—	—	—	0.080	—	65	54
	Wagon	R	NA	0.720	0.003	—	—	—	—	0.080	36-43	20
	Galant	F	0.940	0.882	0.003	—	—	—	0.080	—	58-72	46-62
		R	—	—	—	8.000	—	8.100	—	0.040	—	—
	Galant	F	0.940	0.882	0.003	—	—	—	0.080	—	58-72	46-62
	w/rear disc	R	0.390	0.331	0.003	—	—	—	—	0.080	36-43	16-23
	Mirage	F	0.510	0.449	0.006	—	—	—	0.080	—	58-72	①
	w/solid rotor	R	—	—	—	7.100	—	7.200	—	0.040	—	—
	Mirage	F	0.710	0.646	0.006	—	—	—	0.080	—	58-72	27-36
	w/vented rotor	R	—	—	—	7.100	—	7.200	—	0.040	—	—
	Mirage	F	0.940	0.882	0.006	—	—	—	0.080	—	58-72	46-62
	w/rear disc	R	0.390	0.331	0.006	—	—	—	—	0.080	36-43	16-23
1993	Diamante	F	0.940	0.882	0.003	—	—	—	0.080	—	65	54
		R	0.710	0.646	0.003	—	—	—	—	0.080	36-43	20
	Diamante	F	0.940	0.882	0.003	—	—	—	0.080	—	65	54
	Wagon	R	NA	0.720	0.003	—	—	—	—	0.080	36-43	20
	Galant	F	0.940	0.882	0.003	—	—	—	0.080	—	58-72	46-62
		R	—	—	—	8.000	—	8.100	—	0.040	—	—
	Galant	F	0.940	0.882	0.003	—	—	—	0.080	—	58-72	46-62
	w/rear disc	R	0.390	0.331	0.003	—	—	—	—	0.080	36-43	16-23
	Mirage	F	0.510	0.449	0.006	—	—	—	0.080	—	58-72	①
	w/solid rotor	R	—	—	—	7.100	—	7.200	—	0.040	—	—
	Mirage	F	0.710	0.646	0.006	—	—	—	0.080	—	58-72	①
	w/vented rotor	R	—	—	—	8.000	—	8.100	—	0.040	—	—
	Mirage	F	0.710	0.646	0.006	—	—	—	0.080	—	58-72	①
	w/rear disc	R	0.390	0.331	0.006	—	—	—	—	0.080	36-43	16-23
1994	Diamante	F	0.940	0.882	0.003	—	—	—	0.080	—	65	54
		R	0.710	0.646	0.003	—	—	—	—	0.080	36-43	20
	Diamante	F	0.940	0.882	0.003	—	—	—	0.080	—	65	54
	Wagon	R	NA	0.720	0.003	—	—	—	—	0.080	36-43	20
	Galant	F	0.940	0.882	0.003	—	—	—	0.080	—	65	54
		R	—	—	—	8.976	—	9.078	—	0.040	—	—
	Galant	F	0.940	0.882	0.003	—	—	—	0.080	—	65	54
	w/rear disc	R	0.390	0.331	0.003	—	—	—	—	0.080	36-43	54
	Mirage	F	0.510	0.449	0.006	—	—	—	0.080	—	58-72	①
	w/solid rotor	R	—	—	—	7.100	—	7.200	—	0.040	—	—
	Mirage	F	0.710	0.646	0.006	—	—	—	0.080	—	58-72	①
	w/vented rotor	R	—	—	—	8.000	—	8.100	—	0.040	—	—
	Mirage	F	0.710	0.646	0.006	—	—	—	0.080	—	58-72	①
	w/rear disc	R	0.390	0.331	0.006	—	—	—	—	0.080	36-43	16-23

BRAKE SPECIFICATIONS
All measurements in inches unless noted

Year	Model		Original Thickness	Brake Disc Minimum Thickness	Maximum Runout	Brake Drum Diameter Original Inside Diameter	Max. Wear Limit	Maximum Machine Diameter	Minimum Lining Thickness Front	Rear	Brake Caliper Bracket Bolts (ft. lbs.)	Mounting Bolts (ft. lbs.)
1995	Diamante	F	0.940	0.882	0.003	—	—	—	0.080	—	65	54
		R	0.710	0.646	0.003	—	—	—	—	0.080	36-43	20
	Diamante	F	0.940	0.882	0.003	—	—	—	0.080	—	65	54
	Wagon	R	NA	0.720	0.003	—	—	—	—	0.080	36-43	20
	Galant	F	0.940	0.882	0.003	—	—	—	0.080	—	65	54
		R	—	—	—	8.976	—	9.078	—	0.040	—	—
	Galant	F	0.940	0.882	0.003	—	—	—	0.080	—	65	54
	w/rear disc	R	0.390	0.331	0.003	—	—	—	—	0.080	36-43	54
	Mirage	F	0.510	0.449	0.006	—	—	—	0.080	—	58-72	①
	w/solid rotor	R	—	—	—	7.100	—	7.200	—	0.040	—	—
	Mirage	F	0.710	0.646	0.006	—	—	—	0.080	—	58-72	①
	w/vented rotor	R	—	—	—	8.000	—	8.100	—	0.040	—	—
	Mirage	F	0.710	0.646	0.006	—	—	—	0.080	—	58-72	①
	w/rear disc	R	0.390	0.331	0.006	—	—	—	—	0.080	36-43	16-23
1996	Diamante	F	0.940	0.882	0.003	—	—	—	0.080	—	65	54
		R	0.710	0.646	0.003	—	—	—	—	0.080	36-43	20
	Galant	F	0.940	0.882	0.003	—	—	—	0.080	—	65	54
		R	—	—	—	8.976	—	9.078	—	0.040	—	—
	Galant	F	0.940	0.882	0.003	—	—	—	0.080	—	65	54
	w/rear disc	R	0.390	0.331	0.003	—	—	—	—	0.080	36-43	54
	Mirage	F	0.510	0.449	0.006	—	—	—	0.080	—	58-72	①
	w/solid rotor	R	—	—	—	7.100	—	7.200	—	0.040	—	—
	Mirage	F	0.710	0.646	0.006	—	—	—	0.080	—	58-72	①
	w/vented rotor	R	—	—	—	8.000	—	8.100	—	0.040	—	—
	Mirage	F	0.710	0.646	0.006	—	—	—	0.080	—	58-72	①
	w/rear disc	R	0.390	0.331	0.006	—	—	—	—	0.080	36-43	16-23
1997	Diamante	F	0.940	0.882	0.003	—	—	—	0.080	—	65	54
		R	0.390	0.331	0.003	—	—	—	—	0.080	36-43	20
	Galant	F	0.940	0.882	0.003	—	—	—	0.080	—	65	54
		R	—	—	—	8.976	—	9.078	—	0.040	—	—
	Mirage	F	0.710	0.646	0.006	—	—	—	0.080	—	67-81	①
		R	—	—	—	8.000	—	8.100	—	0.040	—	—
1998	Diamante	F	0.940	0.880	0.002	—	—	—	0.080	—	54	65
		R	0.410	0.330	0.0023	—	—	—	—	0.039	24	36-43
	Galant	F	0.940	0.880	0.0031	—	—	—	0.080	—	54	65
		R	—	—	—	8.976	9.078	9.078	—	0.040	—	—
	Mirage	F	0.710	0.650	0.0024	—	—	—	0.080	—	36	67-81
		R	—	—	—	8.00	8.10	8.10	—	0.039	—	—
1999	Diamante	F	0.940	0.880	0.002	—	—	—	0.080	—	54	65
		R	0.410	0.330	0.0023	—	—	—	—	0.039	24	36-43
	Galant	F	0.940	0.880	0.0031	—	—	—	0.080	—	54	65
		R	—	—	—	8.976	9.078	9.078	—	0.040	—	—
	Mirage	F	0.710	0.650	0.0024	—	—	—	0.080	—	36	67-81
		R	—	—	—	8.00	8.10	8.10	—	0.039	—	—
2000	Diamante	F	0.940	0.880	0.002	—	—	—	0.080	—	54	65
		R	0.410	0.330	0.0023	—	—	—	—	0.039	24	36-43
	Galant	F	0.940	0.880	0.0031	—	—	—	0.080	—	54	65
		R	—	—	—	8.976	9.078	9.078	—	0.040	—	—
	Mirage	F	0.710	0.650	0.0024	—	—	—	0.080	—	36	67-81
		R	—	—	—	8.00	8.10	8.10	—	0.039	—	—

NA - Not Available

F - Front

R - Rear

① Upper: 39 ft. lbs.
  Lower: 65 ft. lbs.

10

BODY AND TRIM

EXTERIOR

Doors

REMOVAL & INSTALLATION

▶ See Figures 1, 2, and 3

➡ **This procedure applies to both the front and rear doors.**

1. Disconnect the negative battery cable.
2. Support the door, by placing a floor jack and a piece of wood underneath the door.
3. Remove the bolts from the door check arm.
4. Rotate the collar on the main wiring harness connector to unplug it. Unplug any other applicable wiring connectors.
5. Matchmark the location of the hinges on the door.

6. Remove the hinge bolts and remove the door assembly.

To install:

7. Position the door into place and finger tighten the hinge bolts.
8. Align the door with the hinge marks made earlier and tighten the bolts, as follows:
   a. 1990–92 Mirage and 1990–93 Galant: 12–19 ft. lbs. (17–26 Nm)
   b. 1993–96 Mirage, 1994–00 Galant and all Diamante: 16 ft. lbs. (22 Nm)
   c. 1997–00 Mirage: 20 ft. lbs. (27 Nm)
9. Attach the wiring connectors.
10. Attach the door check arm and tighten the retaining bolts.
11. Remove the supporting jack.
12. Connect the negative battery cable.

ADJUSTMENT

Door Alignment

1. Determine which hinge should be loosened to move the door in the desired direction.
2. Loosen the hinge bolts just enough to permit movement of the door with a padded prybar (if necessary).
3. Move the door to the desired position and tighten the hinge bolts, as follows:
   a. 1990–92 Mirage and 1990–93 Galant: 12–19 ft. lbs. (17–26 Nm)
   b. 1993–96 Mirage, 1994–00 Galant and all Diamante: 16 ft. lbs. (22 Nm)
   c. 1997–00 Mirage: 20 ft. lbs. (27 Nm)
4. Repeat the procedure until the door is aligned as desired.

Door Latch Striker

1. Loosen the striker plate retaining bolts.
2. Rotate the striker until the door opens smoothly.
3. Tighten the striker bolts to 9 ft. lbs. (12 Nm).
4. Repeat if necessary.

Hood

REMOVAL & INSTALLATION

▶ See Figures 4, 5, 6, and 7

1. Open the hood and support it by the prop rod.
2. Use a felt tip marker or grease pencil to mark the hinge location on the hood.
3. Disconnect the windshield washer lines running to the hood if any. Detach any necessary wiring connectors.
4. Remove the bolts attaching the hood to the hood hinges. Have a helper support the rear of the hood as the bolts are removed. Without support, the hood will slide off the hinges and hit the upper bodywork.
5. Remove the hood assembly, lifting it off the hood prop.
6. Place the hood out of the work area, resting on its side on a protected surface.

To install:

7. Reinstall the hood by carefully placing it in position and installing the hinge bolts finger tight. Install the hood prop immediately. Move the hood around on the hinges until the matchmarks (felt tip marker) align.

✻✻ WARNING

Take great care to prevent the hood from bumping the windshield. Not only will the hood be damaged, the windshield can be broken by careless installation.

8. Tighten the hinge bolts.
9. Attach the windshield washer lines and any necessary electrical connectors.
10. Align the hood as necessary.

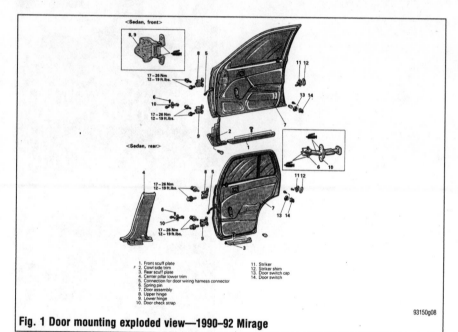

1. Front scuff plate
2. Cowl side trim
3. Rear scuff plate
4. Center pillar lower trim
5. Connection for door wiring harness connector
6. Spring pin
7. Door assembly
8. Upper hinge
9. Lower hinge
10. Door check strap
11. Striker
12. Striker shim
13. Door switch cap
14. Door switch

17–26 Nm
12–19 ft.lbs.

Fig. 1 Door mounting exploded view—1990–92 Mirage

93150g08

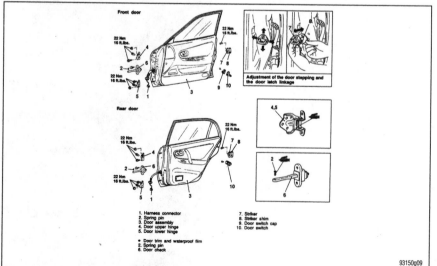

Front door

22 Nm
16 ft.lbs.

Rear door

Adjustment of the door stepping and the door latch linkage

1. Harness connector
2. Spring pin
3. Door assembly
4. Door upper hinge
5. Door lower hinge
6. Door trim and waterproof film
7. Spring pin
8. Door check
7. Striker
8. Striker shim
9. Door switch cap
10. Door switch

Fig. 2 Door mounting exploded view—1994–98 Galant

93150g09

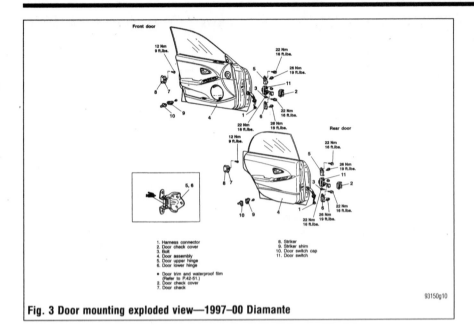

1. Harness connector
2. Door check cover
3. Bolt
4. Door assembly
5. Door upper hinge
6. Door lower hinge

• Door trim and waterproof film
  (Refer to P.42-51.)
2. Door check cover
7. Door check

8. Striker
9. Striker shim
10. Door switch cap
11. Door switch

93150g10

Fig. 3 Door mounting exploded view—1997–00 Diamante

93150p26

Fig. 4 Matchmark the installed position of the hinges on the hood

93550p27

Fig. 5 Detach the washer hoses from the jet nipples . . .

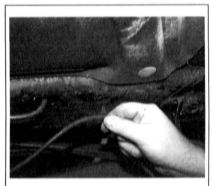

93150p28

Fig. 6 . . . then remove the hose retaining clips from the hood

93150p25

Fig. 7 With an assistant supporting the hood, remove the hinge bolts

ALIGNMENT

1. Close the hood, at least engaging the first latch, and check the hood-to-fender and hood-to-cowl seams and alignment. Re-open the hood and make adjustments as needed to give equal seams all around. When the hood is in final alignment, tighten the hinge bolts.

2. Reconnect the washer lines and any electrical lines which were disconnected.

3. Check the hood latch operation; it should engage easily and smoothly. The latch should release without the use of excessive force. The hood latch mounting bolts may be loosened; the latch can be adjusted left/right or up/down to compensate for the hood striker position.

4. With the hood closed and latched, check the height of the hood. It should sit even with the fender tops; this dimension may be adjusted by turning the hood stops to a higher or lower position. Note that adjusting these stops may require readjustment of the latch to position the hood correctly.

Hatch

REMOVAL & INSTALLATION

1990–92 Mirage

1. Disconnect the liftgate support or strut. The struts are held by either a cross-point screw or a bolt.
2. Disconnect the washer tube running to the glass.
3. Disconnect any necessary wiring harnesses.
4. Close the hatch. From the inside of the vehicle, remove the nuts holding the lid to the hinge. With an assistant, carefully open the lid and remove it from the car.

To install:
5. Fit the hatch into place and install the nuts finger tight.
6. Reinstall the support.
7. Close the tailgate and align it by checking the seam all around. The gap must be equal and even. Align the hatch by moving it on the hinges until correctly placed, then tighten the hinge nuts to 11 ft. lbs. (15 Nm).
8. Attach the electrical harnesses.
9. Connect the rear windshield washer tube. Make sure it is pressed firmly onto the fitting.
10. Check the alignment of the hatch.

ALIGNMENT

Close the hatch and align it by checking the seam all around. The gap must be equal and even. Align the hatch by moving it on the hinges until correctly placed, then tighten the hinge nuts. The final position of the lid may be further adjusted by moving the latch and/or striker on their mounts. When fully closed, the hatch must be flush with the surrounding body panels. Minor adjustments in this dimension may be made by turning the rubber bumpers in or out as needed.

Tailgate

REMOVAL & INSTALLATION

Diamante Wagon

♦ See Figure 8

1. Disconnect the tailgate support.
2. Disconnect the washer fluid tube.
3. Disconnect any necessary wiring harnesses.
4. Have an assistant support the tailgate.
5. Remove the nuts holding the tailgate to the hinge.

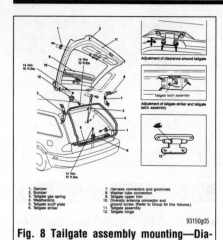

Fig. 8 Tailgate assembly mounting—Diamante Wagon

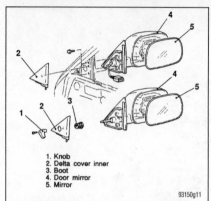

1. Knob
2. Delta cover inner
3. Boot
4. Door mirror
5. Mirror

93150g11

Fig. 9 Outside door mirror mounting—1994–98 Galant shown, others similar

6. Remove the tailgate from the vehicle and place it in a safe place.
7. The installation is the reverse of removal. Tighten the hinge nuts to 10 ft. lbs. (14 Nm).
8. Check the alignment of the tailgate.

ALIGNMENT

To adjust the tailgate, loosen the tailgate hinge-to-body bolts or tailgate latch assembly mounting screws and adjust as necessary.

Trunk Lid

REMOVAL & INSTALLATION

1. Disconnect the negative battery cable.
2. Open the trunk lid. Identify the trunk release cable running from the latch to the body.
3. Disconnect the cable from the latch.
4. Detach any necessary electrical connectors.
5. Outline the position of the hinges on the trunk lid.
6. Support the trunk lid in the open position.
7. If equipped, insert a small prytool into the lock cover slit, remove the lock covers, then remove the trunk lid gas springs.
8. Unfasten the retaining bolts, then remove the trunk lid hinges.
9. Remove the trunk lid from the vehicle
10. Installation is the reverse of the removal procedure.
11. If necessary, align the trunk lid.

ALIGNMENT

1. Close the lid and check both the seam width all around and the closed height. The trunk lid must be flush with the adjacent panels. Minor height adjustments may be made by turning the rubber bumpers on the trunk lid. Additional adjustments require loosening and repositioning of the latch and/or striker.

Outside Mirrors

REMOVAL & INSTALLATION

▶ See Figure 9

1. Disconnect the negative battery cable.
2. Remove the delta cover (the triangular trim cover) from the top of the door panel.
3. On manual mirrors remove the set screw and the adjustment knob.
4. If the mirror is electric, disconnect the wire harness.
5. Remove the mounting nuts and the door trim bracket.
6. Lift the mirror from the vehicle.

To install:

7. Position the mirror on the vehicle.
8. Install the door trim bracket and the mounting nuts.
9. If the mirror is electric, reconnect the wire harness.
10. On manual mirrors, install the knob and set screw.
11. Install the delta cover.
12. Connect the negative battery cable.
13. If electric, cycle the mirror several times to make sure that it works properly.

Antenna

REPLACEMENT

1990–92 Mirage

▶ See Figure 10

➡ The mast may be replaced separately by simply unscrewing it from the base. The fol-

lowing procedure is for replacing the base and cable as a unit.

1. Raise and safely support the vehicle securely on jackstands.
2. Remove the passenger side front wheel.
3. Remove the splash shield inside the passenger side front wheel arch.
4. Remove the center panel (for radio access) and remove the glove box.
5. Remove the right side sill plate and remove the kick panel.
6. If the car has a rear heater, remove the shower duct under the glove box.
7. Carefully remove the PCM. For more details, please refer to Section 4.
8. Remove the radio and disconnect the antenna cable.
9. Release the cable from the bands and clips holding it under the dash.
10. Unscrew the mast from the antenna base.
11. Remove the upper base mounting nut (at the fender) and disconnect the lower bolt holding the mast. Remove the mast and carefully remove the cable.
12. Install the new unit, tightening both the upper nut and lower bolt.
13. Carefully feed the cable into the car and route it to the radio. Engage the cable in the clips and install new retaining bands.
14. Connect the antenna cable to the radio and reinstall the radio.
15. Replace the MPI control unit.
16. Install the heater duct, if it was removed, and install the kick panel on the right side.
17. Install the sill plate. Install the glove box.
18. Install the center panel.
19. Reinstall the wheel arch splash shield. Install the wheel if it was removed. Lower the car to the ground.

1993–00 Mirage

▶ See Figure 11

1. Disconnect the negative battery cable.
2. Remove the antenna base retaining screws.
3. Lift the base and mast assembly up from the roof.
4. Detach the connector for the antenna.
5. The installation is the reverse of removal.

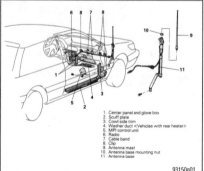

1. Center panel and glove box
2. Scuff plate
3. Cowl side trim
4. Washer duct <Vehicles with rear heater>
5. MPI control unit
6. Radio
7. Cable band
8. Clip
9. Antenna mast
10. Antenna base mounting nut
11. Antenna base

93150g01

Fig. 10 Antenna mounting—1990–92 Mirage

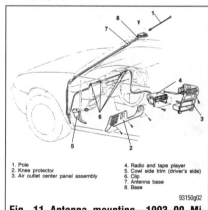

1. Pole
2. Knee protector
3. Air outlet center panel assembly
4. Radio and tape player
5. Cowl side trim (driver's side)
6. Clip
7. Antenna base
8. Base

93150g02

Fig. 11 Antenna mounting—1993–00 Mirage

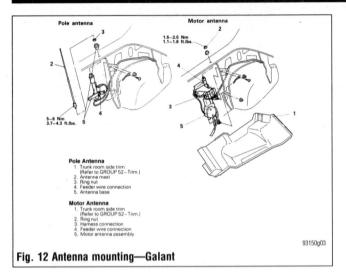

Fig. 12 Antenna mounting—Galant

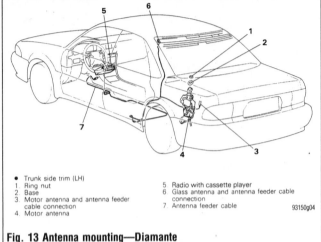

Fig. 13 Antenna mounting—Diamante

Galant and Diamante

◆ **See Figures 12 and 13**

1. Disconnect the negative battery cable.
2. Remove the side trim from the trunk.
3. On a non-power antenna, unscrew the mast.
4. Carefully remove the ring nut from the fender top.
5. Detach the wiring for the electric motor and the antenna cable connection.
6. Remove the nuts and bolts holding the motor to the body, then remove the motor.

To install:

7. Install the new motor and tighten the mounting nuts and bolts.
8. Attach the wiring connectors for the antenna cable and the motor.
9. Install the ring nut and tighten it only to 3 ft. lbs. (4 Nm).

➡**This is little more than finger tight; do not overtighten this nut.**

10. On a non-power antenna, install the mast.
11. Install the trim panels in the trunk.

Fenders

REMOVAL & INSTALLATION

1992–96 Diamante

◆ **See Figure 14**

1. Disconnect the negative battery cable.
2. Remove the front mud guard.
3. Remove the side protector molding.
4. Remove the front side airdam.
5. Remove the retainers and the front splash shield.
6. Remove the parking and side marker lamp assemblies.
7. Remove the front bumper assembly.
8. Remove the retainer bolts along the upper, lower and rear side of the fender.
9. Remove the fender from the vehicle.
10. Apply sealant between the fender and the body panels. This will assure that there are no gaps when the fender is mounted. Install the fender to the

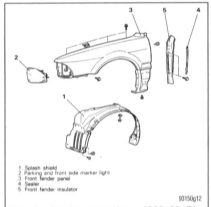

Fig. 14 Fender mounting—1992–96 Diamante

vehicle and tighten all retainer bolts to 4 ft. lbs. (6 Nm).
11. The installation is the reverse of removal.

1997–00 Diamante

◆ **See Figure 15**

1. Disconnect the negative battery cable.
2. Remove the front bumper assembly.
3. Remove the front side airdam.
4. Remove the retainers and the front splash shield.
5. Remove the retainer bolts along the upper, lower and rear side of the fender.
6. Remove the fender from the vehicle.
7. Apply sealant between the fender and the body panels. This will assure that there are no gaps when the fender is mounted. Install the fender to the vehicle and tighten all retainer bolts to 4 ft. lbs. (6 Nm).
8. The installation is the reverse of removal.

1990–93 Galant

◆ **See Figure 16**

1. Disconnect the negative battery cable.
2. Remove the front fender garnish.
3. Remove the side protecting molding.
4. Remove the retainers and the front splash shield.

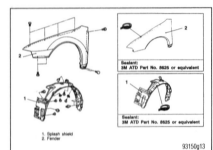

Fig. 15 Fender mounting—1997–00 Diamante

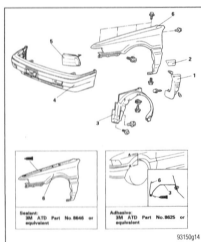

Fig. 16 Fender mounting—1990–93 Galant

5. Remove the front bumper assembly.
6. Remove the turn signal lamp and the combination lamp.
7. Remove the retainer bolts along the upper, lower and rear side of the fender.
8. Remove the fender from the vehicle.
9. Apply sealant between the fender and the body panels. This will assure that there are no gaps when the fender is mounted. Install the fender to the vehicle and tighten all retainer bolts to 4 ft. lbs. (6 Nm).
10. The installation is the reverse of removal.

1994–98 Galant

♦ **See Figure 17**

1. Disconnect the negative battery cable.
2. Remove the stone guard.
3. Remove the retainers and the front splash shield.
4. Remove the radiator grille assembly.
5. Remove the turn signal lamp
6. Remove the headlamp lamp assembly.
7. Remove the header panel assembly.
8. Remove the retainer bolts along the upper, lower and rear side of the fender.
9. Remove the fender from the vehicle.
10. Apply sealant between the fender and the body panels. This will assure that there are no gaps when the fender is mounted. Install the fender to the vehicle and tighten all retainer bolts to 4 ft. lbs. (6 Nm).
11. The installation is the reverse of removal.

1999–00 Galant

♦ **See Figure 18**

1. Disconnect the negative battery cable.
2. Remove the front bumper assembly.
3. Remove the headlamp lamp assembly.
4. Remove the fender side cladding.
5. Remove the stone guard.
6. Remove the retainers and the front splash shield.
7. Remove the hood damper bracket.
8. Remove the retainer bolts along the upper, lower and rear side of the fender.
9. Remove the fender from the vehicle.
10. Apply sealant between the fender and the body panels. This will assure that there are no gaps when the fender is mounted. Install the fender to the vehicle and tighten all retainer bolts to 4 ft. lbs. (6 Nm).
11. The installation is the reverse of removal.

1990–92 Mirage

♦ **See Figure 19**

1. Disconnect the negative battery cable.
2. Remove the radiator grille assembly.
3. Remove the retainers and the front splash shield.
4. Remove the antenna assembly.
5. Remove the side protecting molding.
6. Remove the headlamp lamp assembly.
7. Remove the grille filler panel.
8. Remove the front bumper assembly.
9. Remove the retainer bolts along the upper, lower and rear side of the fender.
10. Remove the fender from the vehicle.
11. Apply sealant between the fender and the body panels. This will assure that there are no gaps when the fender is mounted. Install the fender to the vehicle and tighten all retainer bolts to 4 ft. lbs. (6 Nm).
12. The installation is the reverse of removal.

1993–00 Mirage

♦ **See Figure 20**

1. Disconnect the negative battery cable.
2. Remove the front bumper assembly.
3. Remove the retainers and the front splash shield.
4. Remove the front turn signal lamp assembly.
5. Remove the ornament from the fender.
6. Remove the retainer bolts along the upper, lower and rear side of the fender.
7. Remove the fender from the vehicle.
8. Installation is the reverse of the removal procedure.

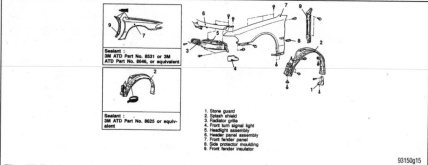

Fig. 17 Fender mounting—1994–98 Galant

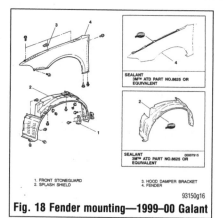

Fig. 18 Fender mounting—1999–00 Galant

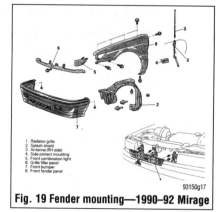

Fig. 19 Fender mounting—1990–92 Mirage

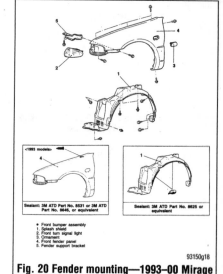

Fig. 20 Fender mounting—1993–00 Mirage

INTERIOR

Instrument Panel

REMOVAL & INSTALLATION

♦ **See Figures 21 thru 31**

For installation of the instrument panel, different types of fasteners were used. During installation, it is important that these fasteners are installed in their original locations. To aid in this, the specific fasteners and their positions are referenced by letters in the exploded views of the instrument panel which follow.

1. Disconnect the negative battery cable.
2. Remove the floor console(s).
3. Remove the plugs and the screws from the knee protector assembly. Remove the assembly from the vehicle.
4. Remove the retainer and the hood lock release handle from the vehicle.

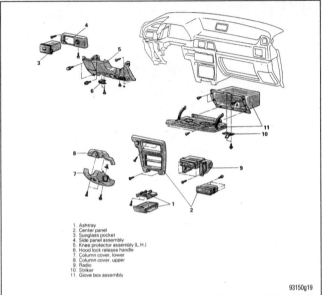

1. Ashtray
2. Center panel
3. Sunglass pocket
4. Side panel assembly
5. Knee protector assembly (L.H.)
6. Hood lock release handle
7. Column cover, lower
8. Column cover, upper
9. Radio
10. Striker
11. Glove box assembly

93150g19

Fig. 21 Exploded view of the instrument panel (1 of 2)—1990–92 Mirage

12. Instrument panel cover, lower
13. Heater control assembly installation screw
14. Meter bezel
15. Combination meter
16. Speedometer cable adapter
17. Combination meter wiring harness connector connections
18. Speaker garnish (R.H.)
19. Speaker (R.H.)
20. Side defroster grille

21. Clock or plug
22. Steering shaft mounting bolt and nut
23. Instrument panel mounting bolts
24. Instrument panel assembly

9 – 14 Nm
7 – 10 ft.lbs.

93150g20

Fig. 22 Exploded view of the instrument panel (2 of 2)—1990–92 Mirage

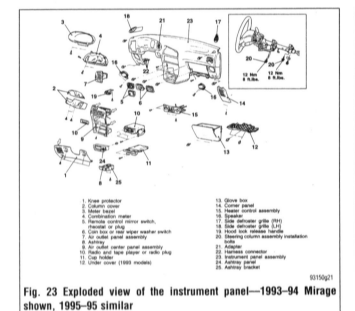

1. Knee protector
2. Column cover
3. Meter bezel
4. Combination meter
5. Remote control mirror switch, rheostat or plug
6. Coin box or rear wiper washer switch
7. Air outlet panel assembly
8. Ashtray
9. Air outlet center panel assembly
10. Radio and tape player or radio plug
11. Cup holder
12. Under cover (1993 models)

13. Glove box
14. Corner panel
15. Heater control assembly
16. Speaker
17. Side defroster grille (RH)
18. Side defroster grille (LH)
19. Hood lock release handle
20. Steering column assembly installation bolts
21. Adapter
22. Harness connector
23. Instrument panel assembly
24. Ashtray panel
25. Ashtray bracket

12 Nm
8 ft.lbs.   12 Nm
8 ft.lbs.

93150g21

Fig. 23 Exploded view of the instrument panel—1993–94 Mirage shown, 1995–95 similar

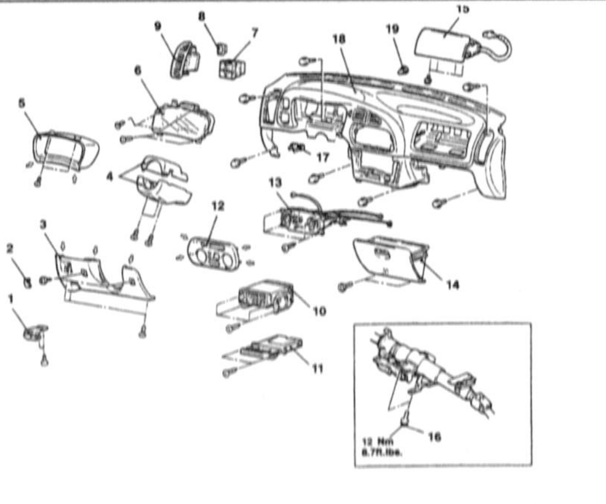

1. Hood lock release handle
2. Knee protector plug
3. Knee protector assembly
4. Column cover
5. Meter bezel
6. Combination meter
7. Door mirror control switch or plug
8. Auto-cruise control main switch, fog light switch or plug
9. Side air outlet assembly
10. Radio and tape player

11. Cup holder
12. Heater control panel
13. Heater control assembly
14. Glove box
15. Front passenger's air bag module assembly
16. Steering column assembly installation bolt
17. Harness connector
18. Instrument panel assembly
19. Grommet

12 Nm
8.7ft.lbs.

93150g23

Fig. 24 Exploded view of the instrument panel—1997–00 Mirage

5. Remove the steering column upper and lower covers.

6. Unfasten the retaining screws, then remove the combination meter (instrument cluster) bezel. Detach the harness connectors as required.

7. Remove the mounting screws, then remove the combination meter (instrument cluster). On some models it is necessary to pull the meter out slightly and detach the electrical connections from the rear of the combination meter.

8. If equipped, disconnect the speedometer cable from the combination meter as follows:

  a. Detach the speedometer cable from the transaxle assembly.

  b. Pull the speedometer cable slightly toward the vehicle interior.

  c. Release the cable lock by turning the adapter to the left or right, and then remove the adapter.

9. Remove the radio trim plate.

10. Remove the radio retainers and the radio from the console. Disconnect the electrical harness and the antenna lead from the radio and remove it from the vehicle.

11. Remove the center air outlet assembly.

12. If equipped, remove the screw retainers from each dial knob on the center cluster. Gently pull the dial knobs from the center cluster panel assembly.

13. Remove the glove compartment by pushing the stoppers toward the rear of the vehicle to unlock them, then remove the glove compartment assembly.

14. Remove the right and left speaker covers. Disconnect and remove the speakers from the instrument panel assembly.

15. Remove the heater control assembly retaining screws and detach the harness connectors and cables. Remove the heater control assembly from the vehicle.

16. Remove any necessary ducts taking note of their orientation.

17. Remove the steering shaft mounting bolts and allow the steering wheel to rest on the front seat cushion. Make sure no harness wires or connections are being pulled or stretched.

18. Remove the instrument panel retaining bolts, label and detach all electrical harness connectors.

19. Remove the instrument panel from the vehicle. Disassemble components as required.

20. Install the instrument panel into the vehicle, reattach all harness connections and install retaining bolts. Before installing bolts, make sure the electrical harness wires were not pinched during instrument panel installation.

21. The installation is the reverse of removal.

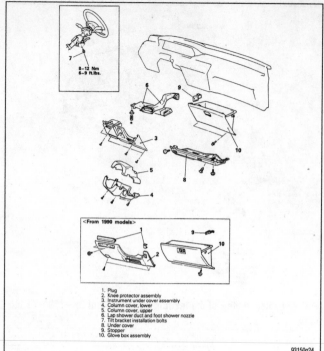

1. Plug
2. Knee protector assembly
3. Instrument under cover assembly
4. Column cover, lower
5. Column cover, upper
6. Lap shower duct and foot shower nozzle
7. Tilt bracket installation bolts
8. Under cover
9. Stopper
10. Glove box assembly

93150g24

Fig. 25 Exploded view of the instrument panel (1 of 2)—1990–93 Galant

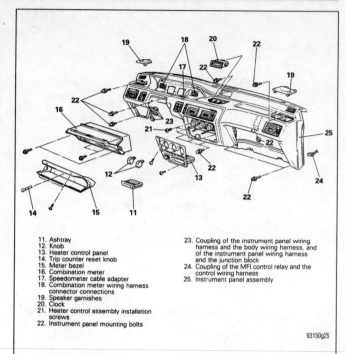

11. Ashtray
12. Knob
13. Heater control panel
14. Trip counter reset knob
15. Meter bezel
16. Combination meter
17. Speedometer cable adapter
18. Combination meter wiring harness connector connections
19. Speaker garnishes
20. Clock
21. Heater control assembly installation screws
22. Instrument panel mounting bolts
23. Coupling of the instrument panel wiring harness and the body wiring harness, and of the instrument panel wiring harness and the junction block
24. Coupling of the MFI control relay and the control wiring harness
25. Instrument panel assembly

93150g25

Fig. 26 Exploded view of the instrument panel (2 of 2)—1990–93 Galant

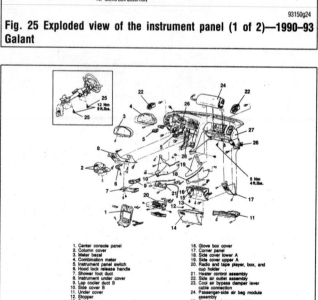

1. Center console panel
2. Column cover
3. Meter bezel
4. Combination meter
5. Instrument panel switch
6. Hood lock release handle
7. Shower foot duct
8. Instrument under cover
9. Lap cooler duct B
10. Side cover B
11. Under cover
12. Stopper
13. Catcher
14. Glove box
15. Glove box striker
16. Glove box cover
17. Corner panel
18. Side cover lower A
19. Side cover upper A
20. Radio and tape player, box, and cup holder
21. Heater control assembly
22. Side air outlet assembly
23. Cool air bypass damper lever cable connection
24. Passenger-side air bag module assembly
25. Steering column assembly installation bolts
26. Harness connector
27. Instrument panel assembly

93150g26

Fig. 27 Exploded view of the instrument panel—1994–98 Galant

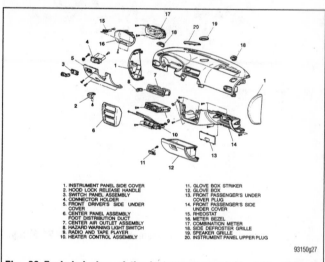

1. INSTRUMENT PANEL SIDE COVER
2. HOOD LOCK RELEASE HANDLE
3. SWITCH PANEL ASSEMBLY
4. CONNECTOR HOLDER
5. FRONT DRIVER'S SIDE UNDER COVER
6. CENTER PANEL ASSEMBLY FOOT DISTRIBUTION DUCT
7. CENTER AIR OUTLET ASSEMBLY
8. HAZARD WARNING LIGHT SWITCH
9. RADIO AND TAPE PLAYER
10. HEATER CONTROL ASSEMBLY
11. GLOVE BOX STRIKER
12. GLOVE BOX
13. FRONT PASSENGER'S UNDER COVER PLUG
14. FRONT PASSENGER'S SIDE UNDER COVER
15. RHEOSTAT
16. METER BEZEL
17. COMBINATION METER
18. SIDE DEFROSTER GRILLE
19. SPEAKER GRILLE
20. INSTRUMENT PANEL UPPER PLUG

93150g27

Fig. 28 Exploded view of the instrument panel (1 of 2)—1999–00 Galant

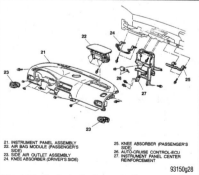

21. INSTRUMENT PANEL ASSEMBLY
22. AIR BAG MODULE (PASSENGER'S SIDE)
23. SIDE AIR OUTLET ASSEMBLY
24. KNEE ABSORBER (DRIVER'S SIDE)
25. KNEE ABSORBER (PASSENGER'S SIDE)
26. AUTO-CRUISE CONTROL-ECU
27. INSTRUMENT PANEL CENTER REINFORCEMENT

93150g28

Fig. 29 Exploded view of the instrument panel (2 of 2)—1999–00 Galant

Floor Console

REMOVAL & INSTALLATION

♦ See Figures 32 thru 39

Rear

1. Disconnect the negative battery cable. If equipped with SRS, wrap the cable in insulated tape, then wait at least 60 seconds before continuing to allow the SRS system time to disable.

✷✷ CAUTION

If equipped with SRS, be careful not to let the console bump against the SRS-ECU during removal and installation.

2. Open the console lid.
3. If necessary, peel back any carpeting on the bottom of the console.
4. Remove the retaining screws from the bottom of the rear floor console.
5. If necessary, remove the screw covers from the front of the console and remove the retaining screws.
6. Lift the console up and remove it from the vehicle.

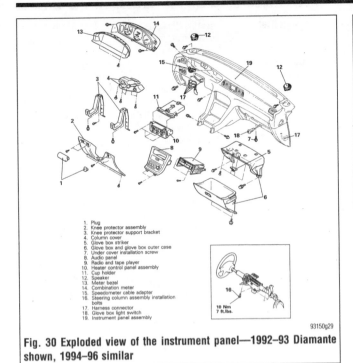

1. Plug
2. Knee protector assembly
3. Knee protector support bracket
4. Column cover
5. Glove box striker
6. Glove box and glove box outer case
7. Under cover installation screw
8. Audio panel
9. Radio and tape player
10. Heater control panel assembly
11. Cup holder
12. Speaker
13. Meter bezel
14. Combination meter
15. Speedometer cable adapter
16. Steering column assembly installation bolts
17. Harness connector
18. Glove box light switch
19. Instrument panel assembly

10 Nm
7 ft.lbs.

93150g29

Fig. 30 Exploded view of the instrument panel—1992–93 Diamante shown, 1994–96 similar

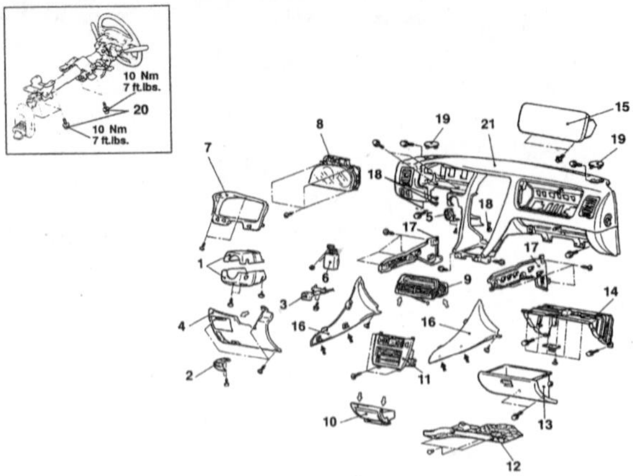

10 Nm
7 ft.lbs.

10 Nm
7 ft.lbs.

1. Column cover
2. Hood lock release handle
3. Parking brake release handle
4. Instrument panel lower cover assembly (LH)
5. Key cylinder panel
6. Instrument panel ECU
7. Meter bezel
8. Combination meter
9. Center air outlet assembly
10. Ashtray
11. Air control panel assembly & audio unit
12. Undercover assembly
13. Glovebox assembly
14. Glovebox outer case
15. Passenger side airbag module
16. Console side cover assembly
17. Floor carpet rear reinforcement
18. Harness connector
19. Plug
20. Steering column mounting bolt
21. Instrument panel

93150g31

Fig. 31 Exploded view of the instrument panel—1997–00 Diamante

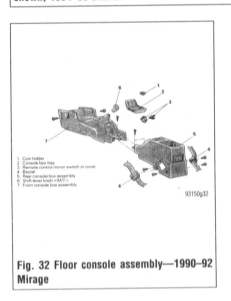

1. Coin holder
2. Console box tray
3. Remote control mirror switch or cover
4. Bezzel
5. Rear console box assembly
6. Shift lever knob <M/T>
7. Front console box assembly

93150g32

Fig. 32 Floor console assembly—1990–92 Mirage

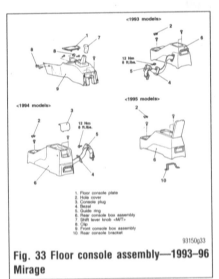

<1993 models>

12 Nm
8 ft.lbs.

<1994 models>

12 Nm
8 ft.lbs.

<1995 models>

1. Floor console plate
2. Hole cover
3. Console plug
4. Bezel
5. Guide ring
6. Rear console box assembly
7. Shift lever knob <M/T>
8. Clip
9. Front console box assembly
10. Rear console bracket

93150g33

Fig. 33 Floor console assembly—1993–96 Mirage

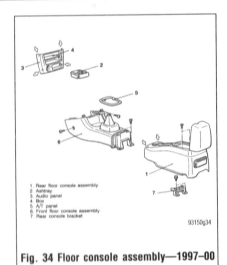

1. Rear floor console assembly
2. Ashtray
3. Audio panel
4. Box
5. A/T panel
6. Front floor console assembly
7. Rear console bracket

93150g34

Fig. 34 Floor console assembly—1997–00 Mirage

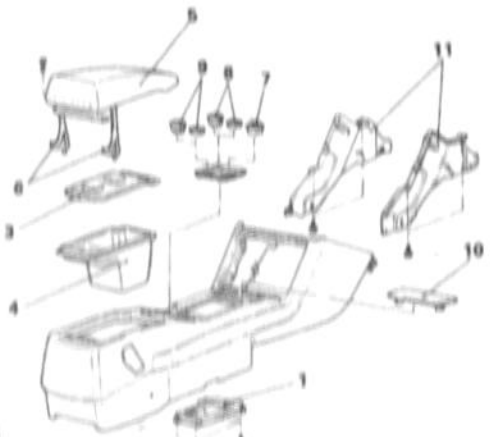

1. Manual transaxle shift lever panel
2. Shift lever boot
3. Cup tray
4. Inner box
5. Lid assembly
6. Stopper
7. Remote controlled mirror switch
8. Power (PWR)/ECONO (ECO) changeover switch or plug
9. Electronic power steering switch or plug
10. Box plate
11. Bracket
12. Bracket (vehicles without audio)

93150g35

Fig. 35 Floor console assembly—1990–93 Galant

SRS diagnostic unit

1. Shift lever knob <M/T>
2. Shift lever boot
3. Box panel
4. Center console panel
5. Front console box assembly
6. Floor console box bracket A
7. Floor console box bracket B

93150g36

Fig. 36 Floor console assembly—1994–98 Galant

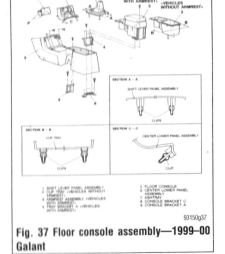

<VEHICLES WITH ARMREST>
<VEHICLES WITHOUT ARMREST>

SECTION A - A
SHIFT LEVER PANEL ASSEMBLY
CLIPS

SECTION B - B
CUP TRAY
CLIPS

SECTION C - C
CENTER LOWER PANEL ASSEMBLY
CLIP

1. SHIFT LEVER PANEL ASSEMBLY
2. CUP TRAY <VEHICLES WITHOUT ARMREST>
3. ARMREST ASSEMBLY <VEHICLES WITH ARMREST>
4. TRAY BRACKET A <VEHICLES WITH ARMREST>
5. FLOOR CONSOLE
6. CENTER LOWER PANEL ASSEMBLY
7. ASHTRAY
8. CONSOLE BRACKET C
9. CONSOLE BRACKET A

93150g37

Fig. 37 Floor console assembly—1999–00 Galant

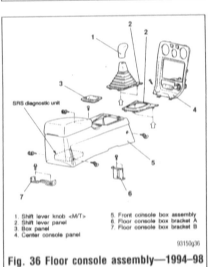

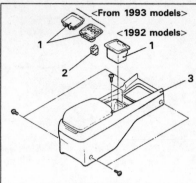

1. Ashtray or floor console switch panel
2. Switch or plug
3. Floor console assembly

93150g38

Fig. 38 Floor console assembly—1992–96 Diamante

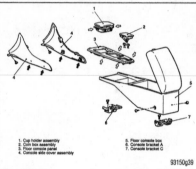

1. Cup holder assembly
2. Coin box assembly
3. Floor console panel
4. Console side cover assembly
5. Floor console box
6. Console bracket A
7. Console bracket C

93150g39

Fig. 39 Floor console assembly—1997–00 Diamante

➠On some models, the seat belts are routed through the console. Carefully slide the belts out of the hole.

7. The installation is the reverse of removal.

Front

1. Disconnect the negative battery cable. If equipped with SRS, wrap the cable in insulated tape, then wait at least 60 seconds before continuing to allow the SRS system time to disable.

✲✲ CAUTION

If equipped with SRS, be careful not to let the console bump against the SRS-ECU during removal and installation.

2. If equipped, remove the rear floor console.
3. If necessary, remove the ashtray and cup holder assemblies.
4. If equipped, remove the carpet inserts from the floor console assembly.
5. On manual transaxle equipped models, remove the manual transaxle shifter knob.
6. On automatic transaxle equipped models, remove the transaxle shift lever trim plate.
7. Remove the screw plugs in the side covers. Remove the retainer screws and the side covers from the vehicle.
8. Remove the front mounting screw cover from the floor console.
9. Label and detach the electrical wire harness connections for the floor console.

10. Remove the retaining screws and the floor console from the vehicle.

To install:

11. Install the floor console in position in the vehicle and secure with the retaining screws.
12. The remainder of installation is the reverse of removal.

Door Panels

REMOVAL & INSTALLATION

◆ **See Figures 40 thru 49**

1. Disconnect the negative battery cable.
2. If equipped with manual windows, insert a shop towel behind the window regulator handle and

93150p03

Fig. 40 Remove the inside door release handle cup retaining screw . . .

93150p03

Fig. 42 Remove the inside pull handle retaining screw cover . . .

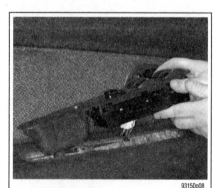

93150p08

Fig. 44 Release the front retaining clips, and lift the handle and switch assembly from the door panel

push the retainer clip outward. Once the clip is removed, remove the window glass regulator handle and escutcheon.

3. If equipped with power windows/locks, remove the escutcheon panel (control panel) and detach the electrical connectors.
4. If equipped, remove the door grip/pull handle mounting screws and the grip from the door panel.
5. Remove the door pull handle cover. Remove the pull handle, if equipped.
6. Remove the door trim panel retaining screws.
7. Pull the door panel gently from the door. The panel is retained by spring clips. To separate the clips from the door, slide a small prytool behind the clip and carefully pull the clip, with the door panel, outward. Try not to bend the door panel or damage may occur.

93150p02

Fig. 41 . . . then remove the inside door release handle cup

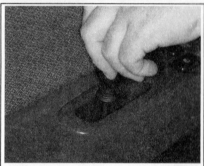

93150p09

Fig. 43 . . . then remove the inside pull handle retaining screw

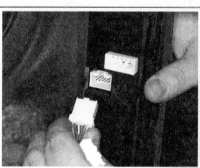

93150p06

Fig. 45 Detach the electrical connectors from the door lock and window switches, then remove the switch plate/handle assembly

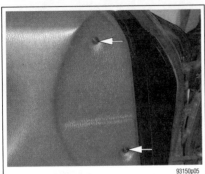

Fig. 46 Remove the two front door panel retaining screws . . .

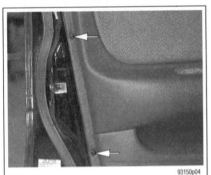

Fig. 47 . . . and also the rear retaining screws from the door panel

Fig. 48 Lift the door panel straight up to unhook it . . .

Fig. 49 . . . then remove the door panel from the vehicle

8. Once all retainer clips are separated, remove the door panel assembly.

9. Carefully remove any retainer clips that remained in the door during panel removal. If damaged, replace the retainer clips.

10. If necessary, remove the waterproof film from the door.

To install:

11. If removed, install the waterproof film from the door.

12. Install and missing or damaged retainer clips into the door panel.

13. Install the door panel onto the vehicle. Push retainers into the holes in the door until they lock into position. If any clips do not lock, replace with new ones.

14. The remainder of installation is the reverse of removal.

Door Handle/Latch Assembly

REMOVAL & INSTALLATION

♦ **See Figure 50**

1. Disconnect the negative battery cable.
2. Remove the door panel.
3. Peel back the weathproofing film from the door.
4. Remove the retaining clip and the lock rod from the handle assembly.
5. Remove the retaining hardware and remove the handle from the door.
6. The installation is the reverse of removal.

Door Lock Cylinder

REMOVAL & INSTALLATION

1. Disconnect the negative battery cable.
2. Remove the door handle/latch assembly.
3. Release locking tab retaining the lock cylinder to the outside handle.
4. Remove the lock cylinder from the outside handle and feed the illumination wire through the opening in the handle.

To install:

5. Route the illumination wire through the handle and install the lock cylinder.
6. Snap the locking tab into place retaining the lock cylinder to the outside handle.
7. Install the door handle/latch assembly.
8. Connect the negative battery cable.

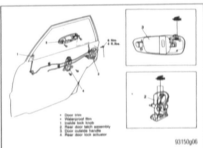

Fig. 50 Common door handle/latch mounting

Hatch/Tailgate/Trunk Lid Lock Cylinder

REMOVAL & INSTALLATION

1. Disconnect the negative battery cable.
2. If necessary, remove any trim in on the underside of the trunk lid, hatch, or tailgate.
3. Release locking tab retaining the lock cylinder to outside handle.
4. Remove the lock cylinder from the trunk lid, hatch, or tailgate.

To install:

5. Place the lock cylinder into the opening on the trunk lid, hatch, or tailgate.
6. Snap the locking tab into place retaining the lock cylinder to the outside handle.
7. If removed, install any trim in on the underside of the trunk lid, hatch, or tailgate.
8. Connect the negative battery cable.

Tailgate/Hatch Handle

REMOVAL & INSTALLATION

1. Disconnect the negative battery cable.
2. Remove the hatch/tailgate trim cover.
3. Remove the retaining clip and the lock rod from the handle assembly.
4. Remove the retaining hardware and remove the handle from the hatch/tailgate.
5. The installation is the reverse of removal.

Door Glass and Regulator

REMOVAL & INSTALLATION

♦ **See Figures 51, 52, 53, 54, and 55**

1. Lower the door glass.
2. Remove the door panel and moisture barrier.
3. Using a non-marring tool and a cloth pad, gently pry the belt molding up and off the door.
4. Remove the inner glass stabilizers.
5. On front doors only, remove the glass guide slider.
6. Support the bottom of the door glass and remove the two mounting bolts holding the glass to the regulator. If the glass is not supported, it will fall into the door when the bolts are removed.

Fig. 51 After the door panel is removed, remove the insulation from the door

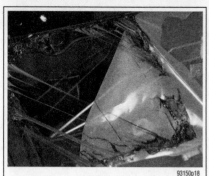

Fig. 52 To access the door components, peel back the plastic weatherproofing

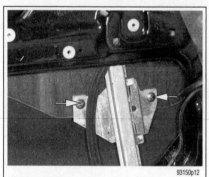

Fig. 53 Remove the door glass-to-window regulator retaining screws

Fig. 54 The regulator is retained to the door by bolts located at the top . . .

Fig. 55 . . . and also at the bottom of the door

7. Remove the door glass by lifting it up and out of the door.

8. Remove the installation bolts holding the regulator to the door.

9. If equipped with electric windows, disconnect the wiring to the window motor.

10. Remove the regulator through the access hole in the door.

To install:

11. When reinstalling the regulator, apply a light coat of multipurpose grease to the moving parts.

12. Install the regulator and tighten the bolts finger-tight.

13. Beginning with the lower left bolt, final tighten the regulator retaining bolts and proceed in a clockwise pattern.

14. Connect the wiring to the window motor, if applicable.

15. Install the window glass. If the vehicle is a hatchback, tighten the rearmost glass mount first. If the vehicle is a sedan, tighten the front bolt first.

16. Operate the window a little bit at a time, checking the fit of the glass in all dimensions and all positions. The window should fit evenly in all channels and operate smoothly throughout its travel. Adjustment is generally not needed, and difficult to perform. If adjustment is necessary, remove the window regulator and elongate the mounting holes in the door. Before this measure is undertaken, check carefully for bent or damaged components.

17. Reinstall the moisture barrier and the door panel.

18. Connect the negative battery cable.

Electric Window Motor

REMOVAL & INSTALLATION

The window motor is an integral part of the regulator assembly. Refer to the door glass and window regulator assembly procedure above.

Inside Rear View Mirror

REPLACEMENT

▶ **See Figure 56**

Remove the inner rear view mirror by loosening the set screw on the mirror stem and lifting mirror off

of the base, which is glued onto the windshield. The installation is the reverse of the removal procedure. If the mirror base falls off of the windshield it can be installed as follows:

1. Scrape the base mounting area with a razor blade to remove the old adhesive.

2. Thoroughly clean the base mounting area.

3. Obtain a mirror adhesive kit. Apply the cleaning compound to the windshield in the area that the base is to be mounted. Allow to dry.

4. Apply the adhesive to both the base plate and the windshield. Install the base to the glass. Hold in position until the adhesive has a chance to set. Make sure the correct side of the base is installed against the glass.

5. Allow around 24 hours for the adhesive to dry completely before installing the mirror to the base plate. This will assure proper adhesion.

Seats

REMOVAL & INSTALLATION

Front Seats

▶ **See Figure 57**

1. Disconnect the negative battery cable.

2. If equipped with power seats and the motor doesn't work, perform the following to slide the seat in order to access the retainers:

   a. Unfasten the bolts that secure the gear box to the left and right ends of the rails.

   b. Remove the gear shaft from the left side. Pull the gear box at the right side toward you, to detach the gear from the side rail.

   c. Use your hand to push the seat to a position where the mounting nuts and bolts can be removed.

3. Remove the seat anchor covers.

4. Detach the electrical connector from the seat, if equipped.

5. Unfasten the seat mounting nuts and bolts, then remove the seat from the vehicle.

To install:

6. Install the seat into the vehicle. Make sure the seat adjusters on both sides of the seat are locked in position.

7. Provisionally tighten the front mounting nuts first. After the front fasteners have been tightened, temporarily tighten the rear seat mounting bolts.

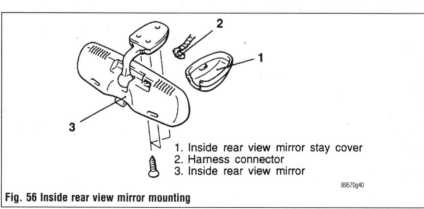

1. Inside rear view mirror stay cover
2. Harness connector
3. Inside rear view mirror

Fig. 56 Inside rear view mirror mounting

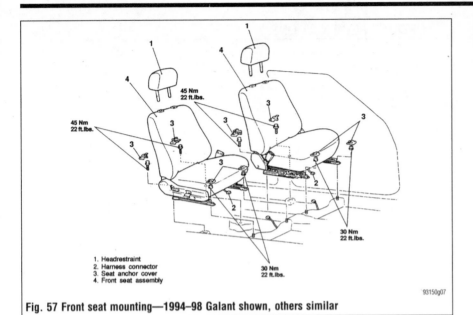

Fig. 57 Front seat mounting—1994–98 Galant shown, others similar

1. Headrestraint
2. Harness connector
3. Seat anchor cover
4. Front seat assembly

93150g07

8. Tighten the front seat mounting nuts to 22 ft. lbs. (30 Nm). Tighten the rear mounting bolts to 33 ft. lbs. (44 Nm).

9. Install the seat anchor covers.

10. If equipped with power seats, attach the electrical harness connector.

11. Connect the negative battery cable.

Rear Seats

SEAT CUSHION

♦ See Figures 58 and 59

1. Locate the release levers on the bottom front of the seat cushion.

2. Grasp the release levers and lift the seat bottom up.

To install:

3. Place the seat cushion into place, and press down to engage the retaining clips.

SEAT BACK

♦ **See Figures 60, 61, and 62**

1. Remove the rear seat cushion.

2. Remove the seat back retaining bolts/nuts and lift the seat back up and remove it from the vehicle.

To install:

3. Place the seat back into place and tighten the retaining bolts/nuts to 16 ft. lbs. (22 Nm).

4. Install the seat cushion.

Power Seat Motor

REMOVAL & INSTALLATION

1. Disconnect the negative battery cable.

2. Remove the front seat assembly from the vehicle.

3. Tag and detach the electrical connector(s).

4. Unfasten the retaining bolts, then remove the power seat motor from the vehicle.

5. Installation is the reverse of the removal procedure.

Fig. 58 The seat bottom is retained by two clips under the front of the seat bottom. Grasp the handles to release the clip . . .

Fig. 59 . . . then lift the seat bottom to remove it from the vehicle

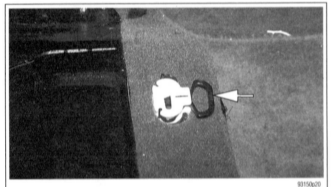

Fig. 60 Remove the seat back retaining bolts on the right and left sides . . .

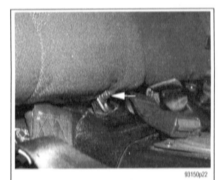

Fig. 61 . . . there are also bolts on the center of the seat back bottom that need to be removed

Fig. 62 Lift the seat back up and remove it from the vehicle

TORQUE SPECIFICATIONS

Components	English	Metric
Antenna nut	3 ft. lbs.	4 Nm
Door hinge-to-door bolts		
1990-92 Mirage and 1990-93 Galant	12-19 ft. lbs.	17-26 Nm
1993-96 Mirage, 1994-00 Galant, and Diamante	16 ft. lbs.	22 Nm
1997-00 Mirage	20 ft. lbs.	26 Nm
Door striker bolts	9 ft. lbs.	12 Nm
Fender retaining screws	4 ft. lbs.	6 Nm
Front seat		
Front retaining nuts	22 ft. lbs.	30 Nm
Rear mounting bolts	33 ft. lbs.	44 Nm
Rear seat back retaining bolts	16 ft. lbs.	22 Nm
Tailgate-to-hinge retaining nuts	10 ft. lbs.	14 Nm

93150c01

11

TROUBLE-
SHOOTING

Condition	Section/Item Number

The following troubleshooting charts are divided into 7 sections covering engine, drive train, brakes, wheels/tires/steering/suspension, electrical accessories, instruments and gauges, and climate control. The first portion (or index) consists of a list of symptoms, along with section and item numbers. After selecting the appropriate condition, refer to the corresponding diagnostic procedure in the second portion's specified location.

INDEX

SECTION 1. ENGINE

A. Engine Starting Problems

Gasoline Engines

Engine turns over, but will not start	1-A, 1
Engine does not turn over when attempting to start	1-A, 2
Engine stalls immediately when started	1-A, 3
Starter motor spins, but does not engage	1-A, 4
Engine is difficult to start when cold	1-A, 5
Engine is difficult to start when hot	1-A, 6

Diesel Engines

Engine turns over but won't start	1-A, 1
Engine does not turn over when attempting to start	1-A, 2
Engine stalls after starting	1-A, 3
Starter motor spins, but does not engage	1-A, 4
Engine is difficult to start	1-A, 5

B. Engine Running Conditions

Gasoline Engines

Engine runs poorly, hesitates	1-B, 1
Engine lacks power	1-B, 2
Engine has poor fuel economy	1-B, 3
Engine runs on (diesels) when turned off	1-B, 4
Engine knocks and pings during heavy acceleration, and on steep hills	1-B, 5
Engine accelerates but vehicle does not gain speed	1-B, 6

Diesel Engines

Engine runs poorly	1-B, 1
Engine lacks power	1-B, 2

C. Engine Noises, Odors and Vibrations

Engine makes a knocking or pinging noise when accelerating	1-C, 1
Starter motor grinds when used	1-C, 2
Engine makes a screeching noise	1-C, 3
Engine makes a growling noise	1-C, 4
Engine makes a ticking or tapping noise	1-C, 5
Engine makes a heavy knocking noise	1-C, 6
Vehicle has a fuel odor when driven	1-C, 7
Vehicle has a rotten egg odor when driven	1-C, 8
Vehicle has a sweet odor when driven	1-C, 9
Engine vibrates when idling	1-C, 10
Engine vibrates during acceleration	1-C, 11

D. Engine Electrical System

Battery goes dead while driving	1-C, 1
Battery goes dead overnight	1-C, 2

E. Engine Cooling System

Engine overheats	1-D, 1
Engine loses coolant	1-D, 2
Engine temperature remains cold when driving	1-D, 3
Engine runs hot	1-D, 4

F. Engine Exhaust System

Exhaust rattles at idle speed	1-F, 1
Exhaust system vibrates when driving	1-F, 2
Exhaust system seems too low	1-F, 3
Exhaust seems loud	1-F, 4

Condition	Section/Item Number

SECTION 2. DRIVE TRAIN

A. Automatic Transmission

Transmission shifts erratically	2-A, 1
Transmission will not engage	2-A, 2
Transmission will not downshift during heavy acceleration	2-A, 3

B. Manual Transmission

Transmission grinds going into forward gears while driving	2-B, 1 2-C, 2
Transmission jumps out of gear	2-B, 2
Transmission difficult to shift	2-B, 3 2-C, 2
Transmission leaks fluid	2-B, 4

C. Clutch

Clutch slips on hills or during sudden acceleration	2-C, 1
Clutch will not disengage, difficult to shift	2-C, 2
Clutch is noisy when the clutch pedal is pressed	2-C, 3
Clutch pedal extremely difficult to press	2-C, 4
Clutch pedal remains down when pressed	2-C, 5
Clutch chatters when engaging	2-C, 6

D. Differential and Final Drive

Differential makes a low pitched rumbling noise	2-D, 1
Differential makes a howling noise	2-D, 2

E. Transfer Assembly

All Wheel and Four Wheel Drive Vehicles

Leaks fluid from seals or vent after being driven	2-E, 1
Makes excessive noise while driving	2-E, 2
Jumps out of gear	2-E, 3

F. Driveshaft

Rear Wheel, All Wheel and Four Wheel Drive Vehicles

Clunking noise from center of vehicle shifting from forward to reverse	2-F, 1
Excessive vibration from center of vehicle when accelerating	2-F, 2

G. Axles

All Wheel and Four Wheel Drive Vehicles

Front or rear wheel makes a clicking noise	2-G, 1
Front or Rear wheel vibrates with increased speed	2-G, 2

Front Wheel Drive Vehicles

Front wheel makes a clicking noise	2-G, 3
Rear wheel makes a clicking noise	2-G, 4

Rear Wheel Drive Vehicles

Front or rear wheel makes a clicking noise	2-G, 5
Rear wheel shudders or vibrates	2-G, 6

H. Other Drive Train Conditions

Burning odor from center of vehicle when accelerating	2-H, 1; 2-C, 1; 3-A, 9
Engine accelerates, but vehicle does not gain speed	2-H, 2; 2-C, 1; 3-A, 9

SECTION 3. BRAKE SYSTEM

Brakes pedal pulsates or shimmies when pressed	3-A-1
Brakes make a squealing noise	3-A, 2
Brakes make a grinding noise	3-A, 3
Vehicle pulls to one side during braking	3-A, 4
Brake pedal feels spongy or has excessive brake pedal travel	3-A, 5
Brake pedal feel is firm, but brakes lack sufficient stopping power or fade	3-A, 6

Condition	Section/Item Number
Vehicle has excessive front end dive or locks rear brakes too easily	3-A, 7
Brake pedal goes to floor when pressed and will not pump up	3-A, 8
Brakes make a burning odor	3-A, 9

SECTION 4. WHEELS, TIRES, STEERING AND SUSPENSION

A. Wheels and Wheel Bearings

All Wheel and Four Wheel Drive Vehicles

Front wheel or wheel bearing loose	4-A, 1
Rear wheel or wheel bearing loose	4-A, 1

Front Wheel Drive Vehicles

Front wheel or wheel bearing loose	4-A, 1
Rear wheel or wheel bearing loose	4-A, 2

Rear Wheel Drive Vehicles

Front wheel or wheel bearing loose	4-A, 2
Rear wheel or wheel bearing loose	4-A, 1

B. Tires

Tires worn on inside tread	4-B, 1
Tires worn on outside tread	4-B, 2
Tires worn unevenly	4-B, 3

C. Steering

Excessive play in steering wheel	4-C, 1
Steering wheel shakes at cruising speeds	4-C, 2
Steering wheel shakes when braking	3-A, 1
Steering wheel becomes stiff when turned	4-C, 4

D. Suspension

Vehicle pulls to one side	4-D, 1
Vehicle is very bouncy over bumps	4-D, 2
Vehicle seems to lean excessively in turns	4-D, 3
Vehicle ride quality seems excessively harsh	4-D, 4
Vehicle seems low or leans to one side	4-D, 5

E. Driving Noises and Vibrations

Noises

Vehicle makes a clicking noise when driven	4-E, 1
Vehicle makes a clunking or knocking noise over bumps	4-E, 2
Vehicle makes a low pitched rumbling noise when driven	4-E, 3
Vehicle makes a squeaking noise over bumps	4-E, 4

Vibrations

Vehicle vibrates when driven	4-E, 5

SECTION 5. ELECTRICAL ACCESSORIES

A. Headlights

One headlight only works on high or low beam	5-A, 1
Headlight does not work on high or low beam	5-A, 2
Headlight(s) very dim	5-A, 3

B. Tail, Running and Side Marker Lights

Tail light, running light or side marker light inoperative	5-B, 1
Tail light, running light or side marker light works intermittently	5-B, 2
Tail light, running light or side marker light very dim	5-B, 3

C. Interior Lights

Interior light inoperative	5-C, 1
Interior light works intermittently	5-C, 2
Interior light very dim	5-C, 3

Condition	Section/Item Number

D. Brake Lights

One brake light inoperative	5-D, 1
Both brake lights inoperative	5-D, 2
One or both brake lights very dim	5-D, 3

E. Warning Lights

Ignition, Battery and Alternator Warning Lights, Check Engine Light, Anti-Lock Braking System (ABS) Light, Brake Warning Light, Oil Pressure Warning Light, and Parking Brake Warning Light

Warning light(s) remains on after the engine is started	5-E, 1
Warning light(s) flickers on and off when driving	5-E, 2
Warning light(s) inoperative with ignition on, and engine not started	5-E, 3

F. Turn Signal and 4-Way Hazard Lights

Turn signals or hazard lights come on, but do not flash	5-F, 1
Turn signals or hazard lights do not function on either side	5-F, 2
Turn signals or hazard lights only work on one side	5-F, 3
One signal light does not work	5-F, 4
Turn signals flash too slowly	5-F, 5
Turn signals flash too fast	5-F, 6
Four-way hazard flasher indicator light inoperative	5-F, 7
Turn signal indicator light(s) do not work in either direction	5-F, 8
One turn signal indicator light does not work	5-F, 9

G. Horn

Horn does not operate	5-G, 1
Horn has an unusual tone	5-G, 2

H. Windshield Wipers

Windshield wipers do not operate	5-H, 1
Windshield wiper motor makes a humming noise, gets hot or blows fuses	5-H, 2
Windshield wiper motor operates but one or both wipers fail to move	5-H, 3
Windshield wipers will not park	5-H, 4

SECTION 6. INSTRUMENTS AND GAUGES

A. Speedometer, cable operated

Speedometer does not work	6-A, 1
Speedometer needle fluctuates when driving at steady speeds	6-A, 2
Speedometer works intermittently	6-A, 3

B. Speedometer, electronically operated

Speedometer does not work	6-B, 1
Speedometer works intermittently	6-B, 2

C. Fuel, Temperature and Oil Pressure Gauges

Gauge does not register	6-C, 1
Gauge operates erratically	6-C, 2
Gauge operates fully pegged	6-C, 3

SECTION 7. CLIMATE CONTROL

A. Air Conditioner

No air coming from air conditioner vents	7-A, 1
Air conditioner blows warm air	7-A, 2
Water collects on the interior floor when the air conditioner is used	7-A, 3
Air conditioner has a moldy odor when used	7-A, 4

B. Heater

Blower motor does not operate	7-B, 1
Heater blows cool air	7-B, 2
Heater steams the windshield when used	7-B, 3

DIAGNOSTIC PROCEDURES

1. ENGINE

1-A. Engine Starting Problems

Gasoline Engines

1. Engine turns over, but will not start

a. Check fuel level in fuel tank, add fuel if empty.

b. Check battery condition and state of charge. If voltage and load test below specification, charge or replace battery.

c. Check battery terminal and cable condition and tightness. Clean terminals and replace damaged, worn or corroded cables.

d. Check fuel delivery system. If fuel is not reaching the fuel injectors, check for a loose electrical connector or defective fuse, relay or fuel pump and replace as necessary.

e. Engine may have excessive wear or mechanical damage such as low cylinder cranking pressure, a broken camshaft drive system, insufficient valve clearance or bent valves.

f. Check for fuel contamination such as water in the fuel. During winter months, the water may freeze and cause a fuel restriction. Adding a fuel additive may help, however the fuel system may require draining and purging with fresh fuel.

g. Check for ignition system failure. Check for loose or shorted wires or damaged ignition system components. Check the spark plugs for excessive wear or incorrect electrode gap. If the problem is worse in wet weather, check for shorts between the spark plugs and the ignition coils.

h. Check the engine management system for a failed sensor or control module.

2. Engine does not turn over when attempting to start

a. Check the battery state of charge and condition. If the dash lights are not visible or very dim when turning the ignition key on, the battery has either failed internally or discharged, the battery cables are loose, excessively corroded or damaged, or the alternator has failed or internally shorted, discharging the battery. Charge or replace the battery, clean or replace the battery cables, and check the alternator output.

b. Check the operation of the neutral safety switch. On automatic transmission vehicles, try starting the vehicle in both Park and Neutral. On manual transmission vehicles, depress the clutch pedal and attempt to start. On some vehicles, these switches can be adjusted. Make sure the switches or wire connectors are not loose or damaged. Replace or adjust the switches as necessary.

c. Check the starter motor, starter solenoid or relay, and starter motor cables and wires. Check the ground from the engine to the chassis. Make sure the wires are not loose, damaged, or corroded. If battery voltage is present at the starter relay, try using a remote starter to start the vehicle for test purposes only. Replace any damaged or corroded cables, in addition to replacing any failed components.

d. Check the engine for seizure. If the engine has not been started for a long period of time, internal parts such as the rings may have rusted to the cylinder walls. The engine may have suffered internal damage, or could be hydro-locked from ingesting water. Remove the spark plugs and carefully attempt to rotate the engine using a suitable breaker bar and socket on the crankshaft pulley. If the engine is resistant to moving, or moves slightly and then binds, do not force the engine any further before determining the problem.

3. Engine stalls immediately when started

a. Check the ignition switch condition and operation. The electrical contacts in the run position may be worn or damaged. Try restarting the engine with all electrical accessories in the off position. Sometimes turning the key on an off will help in emergency situations, however once the switch has shown signs of failure, it should be replaced as soon as possible.

b. Check for loose, corroded, damaged or shorted wires for the ignition system and repair or replace.

c. Check for manifold vacuum leaks or vacuum hose leakage and repair or replace parts as necessary.

d. Measure the fuel pump delivery volume and pressure. Low fuel pump pressure can also be noticed as a lack of power when accelerating. Make sure the fuel pump lines are not restricted. The fuel pump output is not adjustable and requires fuel pump replacement to repair.

e. Check the engine fuel and ignition management system. Inspect the sensor wiring and electrical connectors. A dirty, loose or damaged sensor or control module wire can simulate a failed component.

f. Check the exhaust system for internal restrictions.

4. Starter motor spins, but does not engage

a. Check the starter motor for a seized or binding pinion gear.

b. Remove the flywheel inspection plate and check for a damaged ring gear.

5. Engine is difficult to start when cold

a. Check the battery condition, battery state of charge and starter motor current draw. Replace the battery if marginal and the starter motor if the current draw is beyond specification.

b. Check the battery cable condition. Clean the battery terminals and replace corroded or damaged cables.

c. Check the fuel system for proper operation. A fuel pump with insufficient fuel pressure or clogged injectors should be replaced.

d. Check the engine's tune-up status. Note the tune-up specifications and check for items such as severely worn spark plugs; adjust or replace as needed. On vehicles with manually adjusted valve clearances, check for tight valves and adjust to specification.

e. Check for a failed coolant temperature sensor, and replace if out of specification.

f. Check the operation of the engine management systems for fuel and ignition; repair or replace failed components as necessary.

6. Engine is difficult to start when hot

a. Check the air filter and air intake system. Replace the air filter if it is dirty or contaminated. Check the fresh air intake system for restrictions or blockage.

b. Check for loose or deteriorated engine grounds and clean, tighten or replace as needed.

c. Check for needed maintenance. Inspect tune-up and service related items such as spark plugs and engine oil condition, and check the operation of the engine fuel and ignition management system.

Diesel Engines

1. Engine turns over but won't start

a. Check engine starting procedure and restart engine.

b. Check the glow plug operation and repair or replace as necessary.

c. Check for air in the fuel system or fuel filter and bleed the air as necessary.

d. Check the fuel delivery system and repair or replace as necessary.

e. Check fuel level and add fuel as needed.

f. Check fuel quality. If the fuel is contaminated, drain and flush the fuel tank.

g. Check engine compression. If compression is below specification, the engine may need to be renewed or replaced.

h. Check the injection pump timing and set to specification.

i. Check the injection pump condition and replace as necessary.

j. Check the fuel nozzle operation and condition or replace as necessary.

2. Engine does not turn over when attempting to start

a. Check the battery state of charge and condition. If the dash lights are not visible or very dim when turning the ignition key on, the battery has either failed internally or discharged, the battery cables are loose, excessively corroded or damaged, or the alternator has failed or internally shorted, discharging the battery. Charge or replace the battery, clean or replace the battery cables, and check the alternator output.

b. Check the operation of the neutral safety switch. On automatic transmission vehicles, try starting the vehicle in both Park and Neutral. On manual transmission vehicles, depress the clutch pedal and attempt to start. On some vehicles, these switches can be adjusted. Make sure the switches or wire connectors are not loose or damaged. Replace or adjust the switches as necessary.

c. Check the starter motor, starter solenoid or relay, and starter motor cables and wires. Check the ground from the engine to the chassis. Make sure the wires are not loose, damaged, or corroded. If battery voltage is present at the starter relay, try using a remote starter to start the vehicle for test purposes only. Replace any damaged or corroded cables, in addition to replacing any failed components.

d. Check the engine for seizure. If the engine has not been started for a long period of time, internal parts such as the rings may have rusted to the cylinder walls. The engine may have suffered internal damage, or could be hydro-locked from ingesting water. Remove the injectors and carefully attempt to rotate the engine using a suitable breaker bar and socket on the crankshaft pulley. If the engine is resistant to moving, or moves slightly and then binds, do not force the engine any further before determining the cause of the problem.

3. Engine stalls after starting

a. Check for a restriction in the fuel return line or the return line check valve and repair as necessary.

b. Check the glow plug operation for turning the glow plugs off too soon and repair as necessary.

c. Check for incorrect injection pump timing and reset to specification.

d. Test the engine fuel pump and replace if the output is below specification.

e. Check for contaminated or incorrect fuel. Completely flush the fuel system and replace with fresh fuel.

f. Test the engine's compression for low compression. If below specification, mechanical repairs are necessary to repair.

g. Check for air in the fuel. Check fuel tank fuel and fill as needed.

h. Check for a failed injection pump. Replace the pump, making sure to properly set the pump timing.

4. Starter motor spins, but does not engage
a. Check the starter motor for a seized or binding pinion gear.
b. Remove the flywheel inspection plate and check for a damaged ring gear.

1-B. Engine Running Conditions

Gasoline Engines

1. Engine runs poorly, hesitates
a. Check the engine ignition system operation and adjust if possible, or replace defective parts.
b. Check for restricted fuel injectors and replace as necessary.
c. Check the fuel pump output and delivery. Inspect fuel lines for restrictions. If the fuel pump pressure is below specification, replace the fuel pump.
d. Check the operation of the engine management system and repair as necessary.

2. Engine lacks power
a. Check the engine's tune-up status. Note the tune-up specifications and check for items such as severely worn spark plugs; adjust or replace as needed. On vehicles with manually adjusted valve clearances, check for tight valves and adjust to specification.
b. Check the air filter and air intake system. Replace the air filter if it is dirty or contaminated. Check the fresh air intake system for restrictions or blockage.
c. Check the operation of the engine fuel and ignition management systems. Check the sensor operation and wiring. Check for low fuel pump pressure and repair or replace components as necessary.
d. Check the throttle linkage adjustments. Check to make sure the linkage is fully opening the throttle. Replace any worn or defective bushings or linkages.
e. Check for a restricted exhaust system. Check for bent or crimped exhaust pipes, or internally restricted mufflers or catalytic converters. Compare inlet and outlet temperatures for the converter or muffler. If the inlet is hot, but outlet cold, the component is restricted.
f. Check for a loose or defective knock sensor. A loose, improperly torqued or defective knock sensor will decrease spark advance and reduce power. Replace defective knock sensors and install using the recommended torque specification.
g. Check for engine mechanical conditions such as low compression, worn piston rings, worn valves, worn camshafts and related parts. An engine which has severe mechanical wear, or has suffered internal mechanical damage must be rebuilt or replaced to restore lost power.
h. Check the engine oil level for being overfilled. Adjust the engine's oil level, or change the engine oil and filter, and top off to the correct level.
i. Check for an intake manifold or vacuum hose leak. Replace leaking gaskets or worn vacuum hoses.
j. Check for dragging brakes and replace or repair as necessary.
k. Check tire air pressure and tire wear. Adjust the pressure to the recommended settings. Check the tire wear for possible alignment problems causing increased rolling resistance, decreased acceleration and increased fuel usage.
l. Check the octane rating of the fuel used during refilling, and use a higher octane rated fuel.

3. Poor fuel economy
a. Inspect the air filter and check for any air restrictions going into the air filter housing. Replace the air filter if it is dirty or contaminated.
b. Check the engine for tune-up and related adjustments. Replace worn ignition parts, check the engine ignition timing and fuel mixture, and set to specifications if possible.
c. Check the tire size, tire wear, alignment and tire pressure. Large tires create more rolling resistance, smaller tires require more engine speed to maintain a vehicle's road speed. Excessive tire wear can be caused by incorrect tire pressure, incorrect wheel alignment or a suspension problem. All of these conditions create increased rolling resistance, causing the engine to work harder to accelerate and maintain a vehicle's speed.
d. Inspect the brakes for binding or excessive drag. A sticking brake caliper, overly adjusted brake shoe, broken brake shoe return spring, or binding parking brake cable or linkage can create a significant drag, brake wear and loss of fuel economy. Check the brake system operation and repair as necessary.

4. Engine runs on (diesels) when turned off
a. Check for idle speed set too high and readjust to specification.
b. Check the operation of the idle control valve, and replace if defective.
c. Check the ignition timing and adjust to recommended settings. Check for defective sensors or related components and replace if defective.
d. Check for a vacuum leak at the intake manifold or vacuum hose and replace defective gaskets or hoses.
e. Check the engine for excessive carbon build-up in the combustion chamber. Use a recommended decarbonizing fuel additive or disassemble the cylinder head to remove the carbon.
f. Check the operation of the engine fuel management system and replace defective sensors or control units.
g. Check the engine operating temperature for overheating and repair as necessary.

5. Engine knocks and pings during heavy acceleration, and on steep hills
a. Check the octane rating of the fuel used during refilling, and use a higher octane rated fuel.
b. Check the ignition timing and adjust to recommended settings. Check for defective sensors or related components and replace if defective.
c. Check the engine for excessive carbon build-up in the combustion chamber. Use a recommended decarbonizing fuel additive or disassemble the cylinder head to remove the carbon.
d. Check the spark plugs for the correct type, electrode gap and heat range. Replace worn or damaged spark plugs. For severe or continuous high speed use, install a spark plug that is one heat range colder.
e. Check the operation of the engine fuel management system and replace defective sensors or control units.
f. Check for a restricted exhaust system. Check for bent or crimped exhaust pipes, or internally restricted mufflers or catalytic converters. Compare inlet and outlet temperatures for the converter or muffler. If the inlet is hot, but outlet cold, the component is restricted.

6. Engine accelerates, but vehicle does not gain speed
a. On manual transmission vehicles, check for causes of a slipping clutch. Refer to the clutch troubleshooting section for additional information.
b. On automatic transmission vehicles, check for a slipping transmission. Check the transmission fluid level and condition. If the fluid level is too high, adjust to the correct level. If the fluid level is low, top off using the recommended fluid type. If the fluid exhibits a burning odor, the transmission has been slipping internally. Changing the fluid and filter may help temporarily, however in this situation a transmission may require overhauling to ensure long-term reliability.

Diesel Engines

1. Engine runs poorly
a. Check the injection pump timing and adjust to specification.
b. Check for air in the fuel lines or leaks, and bleed the air from the fuel system.
c. Check the fuel filter, fuel feed and return lines for a restriction and repair as necessary.
d. Check the fuel for contamination, drain and flush the fuel tank and replenish with fresh fuel.

2. Engine lacks power
a. Inspect the air intake system and air filter for restrictions and, if necessary, replace the air filter.
b. Verify the injection pump timing and reset if out of specification.
c. Check the exhaust for an internal restriction and replace failed parts.
d. Check for a restricted fuel filter and, if restricted, replace the filter.
e. Inspect the fuel filler cap vent . When removing the filler cap, listen for excessive hissing noises indicating a blockage in the fuel filler cap vents. If the filler cap vents are blocked, replace the cap.
f. Check the fuel system for restrictions and repair as necessary.
g. Check for low engine compression and inspect for external leakage at the glow plugs or nozzles. If no external leakage is noted, repair or replace the engine.

ENGINE PERFORMANCE TROUBLESHOOTING HINTS

When troubleshooting an engine running or performance condition, the mechanical condition of the engine should be determined before lengthy troubleshooting procedures are performed.

The engine fuel management systems in fuel injected vehicles rely on electronic sensors to provide information to the engine control unit for precise fuel metering. Unlike carburetors, which use the incoming air speed to draw fuel through the fuel metering jets in order to provide a proper fuel-to-air ratio, a fuel injection system provides a specific amount of fuel which is introduced by the fuel injectors into the intake manifold or intake port, based on the information provided by electronic sensors.

The sensors monitor the engine's operating temperature, ambient temperature and the amount of air entering the engine, engine speed and throttle position to provide information to the engine control unit, which, in turn, operates the fuel injectors by electrical pulses. The sensors provide information to the engine control unit using low voltage electrical signals. As a result, an unplugged sensor or a poor electrical contact could cause a poor running condition similar to a failed sensor.

When troubleshooting a fuel related engine condition on fuel injected vehicles, carefully inspect the wiring and electrical connectors to the related components. Make sure the electrical connectors are fully connected, clean and not physically damaged. If necessary, clean the electrical contacts using electrical contact cleaner. The use of cleaning agents not specifically designed for electrical contacts should not be used, as they could leave a surface film or damage the insulation of the wiring.

The engine electrical system provides the necessary electrical power to operate the vehicle's electrical accessories, electronic control units and sensors. Because engine management systems are sensitive to voltage changes, an alternator which over or undercharges could cause engine running problems or component failure. Most alternators utilize internal voltage regulators which cannot be adjusted and must be replaced individually or as a unit with the alternator.

Ignition systems may be controlled by, or linked to, the engine fuel management system. Similar to the fuel injection system, these ignition systems rely on electronic sensors for information to determine the optimum ignition timing for a given engine speed and load. Some ignition systems no longer allow the ignition timing to be adjusted. Feedback from low voltage electrical sensors provide information to the control unit to determine the amount of ignition advance. On these systems, if a failure occurs the failed component must be replaced. Before replacing suspected failed electrical components, carefully inspect the wiring and electrical connectors to the related components. Make sure the electrical connectors are fully connected, clean and not physically damaged. If necessary, clean the electrical contacts using electrical contact cleaner. The use of cleaning agents not specifically designed for electrical contacts should be avoided, as they could leave a surface film or damage the insulation of the wiring.

1-C. Engine Noises, Odors and Vibrations

1. Engine makes a knocking or pinging noise when accelerating
a. Check the octane rating of the fuel being used. Depending on the type of driving or driving conditions, it may be necessary to use a higher octane fuel.
b. Verify the ignition system settings and operation. Improperly adjusted ignition timing or a failed component, such as a knock sensor, may cause the ignition timing to advance excessively or prematurely. Check the ignition system operation and adjust, or replace components as needed.
c. Check the spark plug gap, heat range and condition. If the vehicle is operated in severe operating conditions or at continuous high speeds, use a colder heat range spark plug. Adjust the spark plug gap to the manufacturer's recommended specification and replace worn or damaged spark plugs.

2. Starter motor grinds when used
a. Examine the starter pinion gear and the engine ring gear for damage, and replace damaged parts.
b. Check the starter mounting bolts and housing. If the housing is cracked or damaged replace the starter motor and check the mounting bolts for tightness.

3. Engine makes a screeching noise
a. Check the accessory drive belts for looseness and adjust as necessary.
b. Check the accessory drive belt tensioners for seizing or excessive bearing noises and replace if loose, binding, or excessively noisy.
c. Check for a seizing water pump. The pump may not be leaking; however, the bearing may be faulty or the impeller loose and jammed. Replace the water pump.

4. Engine makes a growling noise
a. Check for a loose or failing water pump. Replace the pump and engine coolant.
b. Check the accessory drive belt tensioners for excessive bearing noises and replace if loose or excessively noisy.

5. Engine makes a ticking or tapping noise
a. On vehicles with hydraulic lash adjusters, check for low or dirty engine oil and top off or replace the engine oil and filter.
b. On vehicles with hydraulic lash adjusters, check for collapsed lifters and replace failed components.
c. On vehicles with hydraulic lash adjusters, check for low oil pressure caused by a restricted oil filter, worn engine oil pump, or oil pressure relief valve.
d. On vehicles with manually adjusted valves, check for excessive valve clearance or worn valve train parts. Adjust the valves to specification or replace worn and defective parts.
e. Check for a loose or improperly tensioned timing belt or timing chain and adjust or replace parts as necessary.
f. Check for a bent or sticking exhaust or intake valve. Remove the engine cylinder head to access and replace.

6. Engine makes a heavy knocking noise
a. Check for a loose crankshaft pulley or flywheel; replace and torque the mounting bolt(s) to specification.
b. Check for a bent connecting rod caused by a hydro-lock condition. Engine disassembly is necessary to inspect for damaged and needed replacement parts.
c. Check for excessive engine rod bearing wear or damage. This condition is also associated with low engine oil pressure and will require engine disassembly to inspect for damaged and needed replacement parts.

7. Vehicle has a fuel odor when driven
a. Check the fuel gauge level. If the fuel gauge registers full, it is possible that the odor is caused by being filled beyond capacity, or some spillage occurred during refueling. The odor should clear after driving an hour, or twenty miles, allowing the vapor canister to purge.
b. Check the fuel filler cap for looseness or seepage. Check the cap tightness and, if loose, properly secure. If seepage is noted, replace the filler cap.
c. Check for loose hose clamps, cracked or damaged fuel delivery and return lines, or leaking components or seals, and replace or repair as necessary.

d. Check the vehicle's fuel economy. If fuel consumption has increased due to a failed component, or if the fuel is not properly ignited due to an ignition related failure, the catalytic converter may become contaminated. This condition may also trigger the check engine warning light. Check the spark plugs for a dark, rich condition or verify the condition by testing the vehicle's emissions. Replace fuel fouled spark plugs, and test and replace failed components as necessary.

8. Vehicle has a rotten egg odor when driven
a. Check for a leaking intake gasket or vacuum leak causing a lean running condition. A lean mixture may result in increased exhaust temperatures, causing the catalytic converter to run hotter than normal. This condition may also trigger the check engine warning light. Check and repair the vacuum leaks as necessary.
b. Check the vehicle's alternator and battery condition. If the alternator is overcharging, the battery electrolyte can be boiled from the battery, and the battery casing may begin to crack, swell or bulge, damaging or shorting the battery internally. If this has occurred, neutralize the battery mounting area with a suitable baking soda and water mixture or equivalent, and replace the alternator or voltage regulator. Inspect, service, and load test the battery, and replace if necessary.

9. Vehicle has a sweet odor when driven
a. Check for an engine coolant leak caused by a seeping radiator cap, loose hose clamp, weeping cooling system seal, gasket or cooling system hose and replace or repair as needed.
b. Check for a coolant leak from the radiator, coolant reservoir, heater control valve or under the dashboard from the heater core, and replace the failed part as necessary.
c. Check the engine's exhaust for white smoke in addition to a sweet odor. The presence of white, steamy smoke with a sweet odor indicates coolant leaking into the combustion chamber. Possible causes include a failed head gasket, cracked engine block or cylinder head. Other symptoms of this condition include a white paste build-up on the inside of the oil filler cap, and softened, deformed or bulging radiator hoses.

10. Engine vibrates when idling
a. Check for loose, collapsed, or damaged engine or transmission mounts and repair or replace as necessary.
b. Check for loose or damaged engine covers or shields and secure or replace as necessary.

11. Engine vibrates during acceleration
a. Check for missing, loose or damaged exhaust system hangers and mounts; replace or repair as necessary.
b. Check the exhaust system routing and fit for adequate clearance or potential rubbing; repair or adjust as necessary.

1-D. Engine Electrical System

1. Battery goes dead while driving
a. Check the battery condition. Replace the battery if the battery will not hold a charge or fails a battery load test. If the battery loses fluid while driving, check for an overcharging condition. If the alternator is overcharging, replace the alternator or voltage regulator. (A voltage regulator is typically built into the alternator, necessitating alternator replacement or overhaul.)
b. Check the battery cable condition. Clean or replace corroded cables and clean the battery terminals.
c. Check the alternator and voltage regulator operation. If the charging system is over or undercharging, replace the alternator or voltage regulator, or both.
d. Inspect the wiring and wire connectors at the alternator for looseness, a missing ground or defective terminal, and repair as necessary.
e. Inspect the alternator drive belt tension, tensioners and condition. Properly tension the drive belt, replace weak or broken tensioners, and replace the drive belt if worn or cracked.

2. Battery goes dead overnight
a. Check the battery condition. Replace the battery if the battery will not hold a charge or fails a battery load test.
b. Check for a voltage draw, such as a trunk light, interior light or glove box light staying on. Check light switch position and operation, and replace if defective.
c. Check the alternator for an internally failed diode, and replace the alternator if defective.

1-E. Engine Cooling System

1. Engine overheats
a. Check the coolant level. Set the heater temperature to full hot and check for internal air pockets, bleed the cooling system and inspect for leakage. Top off the cooling system with the correct coolant mixture.
b. Pressure test the cooling system and radiator cap for leaks. Check for seepage caused by loose hose clamps, failed coolant hoses, and cooling system components such as the heater control valve, heater core, radiator, radiator cap, and water pump. Replace defective parts and fill the cooling system with the recommended coolant mixture.

c. On vehicles with electrically controlled cooling fans, check the cooling fan operation. Check for blown fuses or defective fan motors, temperature sensors and relays, and replace failed components.

d. Check for a coolant leak caused by a failed head gasket, or a porous water jacket casting in the cylinder head or engine block. Replace defective parts as necessary.

e. Check for an internally restricted radiator. Flush the radiator or replace if the blockage is too severe for flushing.

f. Check for a damaged water pump. If coolant circulation is poor, check for a loose water pump impeller. If the impeller is loose, replace the water pump.

2. Engine loses coolant

a. Pressure test the cooling system and radiator cap for leaks. Check for seepage caused by loose hose clamps, failed coolant hoses, and cooling system components such as the heater control valve, heater core, radiator, radiator cap, and water pump. Replace defective parts and fill the cooling system with the recommended coolant mixture.

b. Check for a coolant leak caused by a failed head gasket, or a porous water jacket casting in the cylinder head or engine block. Replace defective parts as necessary.

3. Engine temperature remains cold when driving

a. Check the thermostat operation. Replace the thermostat if it sticks in the open position.

b. On vehicles with electrically controlled cooling fans, check the cooling fan operation. Check for defective temperature sensors and stuck relays, and replace failed components.

c. Check temperature gauge operation if equipped to verify proper operation of the gauge. Check the sensors and wiring for defects, and repair or replace defective components.

4. Engine runs hot

a. Check for an internally restricted radiator. Flush the radiator or replace if the blockage is too severe for flushing.

b. Check for a loose or slipping water pump drive belt. Inspect the drive belt condition. Replace the belt if brittle, cracked or damaged. Check the pulley condition and properly tension the belt.

c. Check the cooling fan operation. Replace defective fan motors, sensors or relays as necessary.

d. Check temperature gauge operation if equipped to verify proper operation of the gauge. Check the sensors and wiring for defects, and repair or replace defective components.

e. Check the coolant level. Set the heater temperature to full hot, check for internal air pockets, bleed the cooling system and inspect for leakage. Top off the cooling system with the correct coolant mixture. Once the engine is cool, recheck the fluid level and top off as needed.

NOTE: **The engine cooling system can also be affected by an engine's mechanical condition. A failed head gasket or a porous casting in the engine block or cylinder head could cause a loss of coolant and result in engine overheating.**

Some cooling systems rely on electrically driven cooling fans to cool the radiator and use electrical temperature sensors and relays to operate the cooling fan. When diagnosing these systems, check for blown fuses, damaged wires and verify that the electrical connections are fully connected, clean and not physically damaged. If necessary, clean the electrical contacts using electrical contact cleaner. The use of cleaning agents not specifically designed for electrical contacts could leave a film or damage the insulation of the wiring.

1-F. Engine Exhaust System

1. Exhaust rattles at idle speed

a. Check the engine and transmission mounts and replace mounts showing signs of damage or wear.

b. Check the exhaust hangers, brackets and mounts. Replace broken, missing or damaged mounts.

c. Check for internal damage to mufflers and catalytic converters. The broken pieces from the defective component may travel in the direction of the exhaust flow and collect and/or create a blockage in a component other than the one which failed, causing engine running and stalling problems. Another symptom of a restricted exhaust is low engine manifold vacuum. Remove the exhaust system and carefully remove any loose or broken pieces, then replace any failed or damaged parts as necessary.

d. Check the exhaust system clearance, routing and alignment. If the exhaust is making contact with the vehicle in any manner, loosen and reposition the exhaust system.

2. Exhaust system vibrates when driving

a. Check the exhaust hangers, brackets and mounts. Replace broken, missing or damaged mounts.

b. Check the exhaust system clearance, routing and alignment. If the exhaust is making contact with the vehicle in any manner, check for bent or damaged components and replace, then loosen and reposition the exhaust system.

c. Check for internal damage to mufflers and catalytic converters. The broken pieces from the defective component may travel in the direction of the exhaust flow and collect and/or create a blockage in a component other than the one which failed, causing engine running and stalling problems. Another symptom of a restricted exhaust is low engine manifold vacuum. Remove the exhaust system and carefully remove any loose or broken pieces, then replace any failed or damaged parts as necessary.

3. Exhaust system hangs too low

a. Check the exhaust hangers, brackets and mounts. Replace broken, missing or damaged mounts.

b. Check the exhaust routing and alignment. Check and replace bent or damaged components. If the exhaust is not routed properly, loosen and reposition the exhaust system.

4. Exhaust sounds loud

a. Check the system for looseness and leaks. Check the exhaust pipes, clamps, flange bolts and manifold fasteners for tightness. Check and replace any failed gaskets.

b. Check and replace exhaust silencers that have a loss of efficiency due to internally broken baffles or worn packing material.

c. Check for missing mufflers and silencers that have been replaced with straight pipes or with non-original equipment silencers.

NOTE: **Exhaust system rattles, vibration and proper alignment should not be overlooked. Excessive vibration caused by collapsed engine mounts, damaged or missing exhaust hangers and misalignment may cause surface cracks and broken welds, creating exhaust leaks or internal damage to exhaust components such as the catalytic converter, creating a restriction to exhaust flow and loss of power.**

2. DRIVE TRAIN

2-A. Automatic Transmission

1. Transmission shifts erratically

a. Check and if not within the recommended range, add or remove transmission fluid to obtain the correct fluid level. Always use the recommended fluid type when adding transmission fluid.

b. Check the fluid level condition. If the fluid has become contaminated, fatigued from excessive heat or exhibits a burning odor, change the transmission fluid and filter using the recommended type and amount of fluid. A fluid which exhibits a burning odor indicates that the transmission has been slipping internally and may require future repairs.

c. Check for an improperly installed transmission filter, or missing filter gasket, and repair as necessary.

d. Check for loose or leaking gaskets, pressure lines and fittings, and repair or replace as necessary.

e. Check for loose or disconnected shift and throttle linkages or vacuum hoses, and repair as necessary.

2. Transmission will not engage

a. Check the shift linkage for looseness, wear and proper adjustment, and repair as necessary.

b. Check for a loss of transmission fluid and top off as needed with the recommended fluid.

c. If the transmission does not engage with the shift linkage correctly installed and the proper fluid level, internal damage has likely occurred, requiring transmission removal and disassembly.

3. Transmission will not downshift during heavy acceleration

a. On computer controlled transmissions, check for failed sensors or control units and repair or replace defective components.

b. On vehicles with kickdown linkages or vacuum servos, check for proper linkage adjustment or leaking vacuum hoses or servo units.

NOTE: **Many automatic transmissions use an electronic control module, electrical sensors and solenoids to control transmission shifting. When troubleshooting a vehicle with this type of system, be sure the electrical connectors are fully connected, clean and not physically damaged. If necessary, clean the electrical contacts using electrical contact cleaner. The use of cleaning agents not specifically designed for electrical contacts could leave a film or damage the insulation of the wiring.**

2-B. Manual Transmission

1. Transmission grinds going into forward gears while driving
a. Check the clutch release system. On clutches with a mechanical or cable linkage, check the adjustment. Adjust the clutch pedal to have 1 inch (25mm) of free-play at the pedal.
b. If the clutch release system is hydraulically operated, check the fluid level and, if low, top off using the recommended type and amount of fluid.
c. Synchronizers worn. Remove transmission and replace synchronizers.
d. Synchronizer sliding sleeve worn. Remove transmission and replace sliding sleeve.
e. Gear engagement dogs worn or damaged. Remove transmission and replace gear.

2. Transmission jumps out of gear
a. Shift shaft detent springs worn. Replace shift detent springs.
b. Synchronizer sliding sleeve worn. Remove transmission and replace sliding sleeve.
c. Gear engagement dogs worn or damaged. Remove transmission and replace gear.
d. Crankshaft thrust bearings worn. Remove engine and crankshaft, and repair as necessary.

3. Transmission difficult to shift
a. Verify the clutch adjustment and, if not properly adjusted, adjust to specification.
b. Synchronizers worn. Remove transmission and replace synchronizers.
c. Pilot bearing seized. Remove transmission and replace pilot bearing.
d. Shift linkage or bushing seized. Disassemble the shift linkage, replace worn or damaged bushings, lubricate and reinstall.

4. Transmission leaks fluid
a. Check the fluid level for an overfilled condition. Adjust the fluid level to specification.
b. Check for a restricted transmission vent or breather tube. Clear the blockage as necessary and check the fluid level. If necessary, top off with the recommended lubricant.
c. Check for a porous casting, leaking seal or gasket. Replace defective parts and top off the fluid level with the recommended lubricant.

2-C. Clutch

1. Clutch slips on hills or during sudden acceleration
a. Check for insufficient clutch pedal free-play. Adjust clutch linkage or cable to allow about 1 inch (25mm) of pedal free-play.
b. Clutch disc worn or severely damaged. Remove engine or transmission and replace clutch disc.
c. Clutch pressure plate is weak. Remove engine or transmission and replace the clutch pressure plate and clutch disc.
d. Clutch pressure plate and/or flywheel incorrectly machined. If the clutch system has been recently replaced and rebuilt, or refurbished parts have been used, it is possible that the machined surfaces decreased the clutch clamping force. Replace defective parts with new replacement parts.

2. Clutch will not disengage, difficult to shift
a. Check the clutch release mechanism. Check for stretched cables, worn linkages or failed clutch hydraulics and replace defective parts. On hydraulically operated clutch release mechanisms, check for air in the hydraulic system and bleed as necessary.
b. Check for a broken, cracked or fatigued clutch release arm or release arm pivot. Replace defective parts and properly lubricate upon assembly.
c. Check for a damaged clutch hub damper or damper spring. The broken parts tend to become lodged between the clutch disc and the pressure plate. Disassemble clutch system and replace failed parts.
d. Check for a seized clutch pilot bearing. Disassemble the clutch assembly and replace the defective parts.
e. Check for a defective clutch disc. Check for warpage or lining thicknesses larger than original equipment.

3. Clutch is noisy when the clutch pedal is pressed
a. Check the clutch pedal stop and pedal free-play adjustment for excessive movement and adjust as necessary.
b. Check for a worn or damaged release bearing. If the noise ceases when the pedal is released, the release bearing should be replaced.
c. Check the engine crankshaft axial play. If the crankshaft thrust bearings are worn or damaged, the crankshaft will move when pressing the clutch pedal. The engine must be disassembled to replace the crankshaft thrust bearings.

4. Clutch pedal extremely difficult to press
a. Check the clutch pedal pivots and linkages for binding. Clean and lubricate linkages.
b. On cable actuated clutch systems, check the cable routing and condition. Replace kinked, frayed, damaged or corroded cables and check cable routing to avoid sharp bends. Check the engine ground strap for poor conductivity. If the ground strap is marginal, the engine could try to ground itself via the clutch cable, causing premature failure.

c. On mechanical linkage clutches, check the linkage for binding or misalignment. Lubricate pivots or linkages and repair as necessary.
d. Check the release bearing guide tube and release fork for a lack of lubrication. Install a smooth coating of high temperature grease to allow smooth movement of the release bearing over the guide tube.

5. Clutch pedal remains down when pressed
a. On mechanical linkage or cable actuated clutches, check for a loose or disconnected link.
b. On hydraulically actuated clutches, check the fluid level and check for a hydraulic leak at the clutch slave or master cylinder, or hydraulic line. Replace failed parts and bleed clutch hydraulic system. If no leakage is noted, the clutch master cylinder may have failed internally. Replace the clutch master cylinder and bleed the clutch hydraulic system.

6. Clutch chatters when engaging
a. Check the engine flywheel for warpage or surface variations and replace or repair as necessary.
b. Check for a warped clutch disc or damaged clutch damper hub. Remove the clutch disc and replace.
c. Check for a loose or damaged clutch pressure plate and replace defective components.

NOTE: The clutch is actuated either by a mechanical linkage, cable or a clutch hydraulic system. The mechanical linkage and cable systems may require the clutch pedal free-play to be adjusted as the clutch disc wears. A hydraulic clutch system automatically adjusts as the clutch wears and, with the exception of the clutch pedal height, no adjustment is possible.

2-D. Differential and Final Drive

1. Differential makes a low pitched rumbling noise
a. Check fluid level type and amount. Replace the fluid with the recommended type and amount of lubricant.
b. Check the differential bearings for wear or damage. Remove the bearings, inspect the drive and driven gears for wear or damage, and replace components as necessary.

2. Differential makes a howling noise
a. Check fluid level type and amount. Replace the fluid with the recommended type and amount of lubricant.
b. Check the differential drive and driven gears for wear or damage, and replace components as necessary.

2-E. Transfer Assembly

All Wheel and Four Wheel Drive Vehicles

1. Leaks fluid from seals or vent after being driven
a. Fluid level overfilled. Check and adjust transfer case fluid level.
b. Check for a restricted breather or breather tube, clear and check the fluid level and top off as needed.
c. Check seal condition and replace worn, damaged, or defective seals. Check the fluid level and top off as necessary.

2. Makes excessive noise while driving
a. Check the fluid for the correct type of lubricant. Drain and refill using the recommended type and amount of lubricant.
b. Check the fluid level. Top off the fluid using the recommended type and amount of lubricant.
c. If the fluid level and type of lubricant meet specifications, check for internal wear or damage. Remove assembly and disassemble to inspect for worn, damaged, or defective components.

3. Jumps out of gear
a. Stop vehicle and make sure the unit is fully engaged.
b. Check for worn, loose or an improperly adjusted linkage. Replace and/or adjust linkage as necessary.
c. Check for internal wear or damage. Remove assembly and disassemble to inspect for worn, damaged, or defective components.

2-F. Driveshaft

Rear Wheel, All Wheel and Four Wheel Drive Vehicles

1. Clunking noise from center of vehicle shifting from forward to reverse
a. Worn universal joint. Remove driveshaft and replace universal joint.

2. Excessive vibration from center of vehicle when accelerating
a. Worn universal joint. Remove driveshaft and replace universal joint.

b. Driveshaft misaligned. Check for collapsed or damaged engine and transmission mounts, and replace as necessary.

c. Driveshaft bent or out of balance. Replace damaged components and reinstall.

d. Driveshaft out of balance. Remove the driveshaft and have it balanced by a competent professional, or replace the driveshaft assembly.

NOTE: Most driveshafts are linked together by universal joints; however, some manufacturers use Constant Velocity (CV) joints or rubber flex couplers.

2-G. Axles

All Wheel and Four Wheel Drive Vehicles

1. Front or rear wheel makes a clicking noise

a. Check for debris such as a pebble, nail or glass in the tire or tire tread. Carefully remove the debris. Small rocks and pebbles rarely cause a puncture; however, a sharp object should be removed carefully at a facility capable of performing tire repairs.

b. Check for a loose, damaged or worn Constant Velocity (CV) joint and replace if defective.

2. Front or rear wheel vibrates with increased speed

a. Check for a bent rim and replace, if damaged.

b. Check the tires for balance or internal damage and replace if defective.

c. Check for a loose, worn or damaged wheel bearing and replace if defective.

d. Check for a loose, damaged or worn Constant Velocity (CV) joint and replace if defective.

Front Wheel Drive Vehicles

3. Front wheel makes a clicking noise

a. Check for debris such as a pebble, nail or glass in the tire or tire tread. Carefully remove the debris. Small rocks and pebbles rarely cause a puncture; however, a sharp object should be removed carefully at a facility capable of performing tire repairs.

b. Check for a loose, damaged or worn Constant Velocity (CV) joint and replace if defective.

4. Rear wheel makes a clicking noise

a. Check for debris such as a pebble, nail or glass in the tire or tire tread. Carefully remove the debris. Small rocks and pebbles rarely cause a puncture; however, a sharp object should be removed carefully at a facility capable of performing tire repairs.

Rear Wheel Drive Vehicles

5. Front or rear wheel makes a clicking noise

a. Check for debris such as a pebble, nail or glass in the tire or tire tread. Carefully remove the debris. Small rocks and pebbles rarely cause a puncture; however, a sharp object should be removed carefully at a facility capable of performing tire repairs.

6. Rear wheel shudders or vibrates

a. Check for a bent rear wheel or axle assembly and replace defective components.

b. Check for a loose, damaged or worn rear wheel bearing and replace as necessary.

2-H. Other Drive Train Conditions

1. Burning odor from center of vehicle when accelerating

a. Check for a seizing brake hydraulic component such as a brake caliper. Check the caliper piston for surface damage such as rust, and measure for out-of-round wear and caliper-to-piston clearance. For additional information on brake related odors, refer to section 3-A, condition number 9.

b. On vehicles with a manual transmission, check for a slipping clutch. For possible causes and additional information, refer to section 2-C, condition number 1.

c. On vehicles with an automatic transmission, check the fluid level and condition. Top off or change the fluid and filter using the recommended replacement parts, lubricant type and amount. If the odor persists, transmission removal and disassembly will be necessary.

2. Engine accelerates, but vehicle does not gain speed

a. On vehicles with a manual transmission, check for a slipping or damaged clutch. For possible causes and additional information refer to section 2-C, condition number 1.

b. On vehicles with an automatic transmission, check the fluid level and condition. Top off or change the fluid and filter using the recommended replacement parts, lubricant type and amount. If the slipping continues, transmission removal and disassembly will be necessary.

3. BRAKE SYSTEM

3-A. Brake System Troubleshooting

1. Brake pedal pulsates or shimmies when pressed

a. Check wheel lug nut torque and tighten evenly to specification.

b. Check the brake rotor for trueness and thickness variations. Replace the rotor if it is too thin, warped, or if the thickness varies beyond specification. Some rotors can be machined; consult the manufacturer's specifications and recommendations before using a machined brake rotor.

c. Check the brake caliper or caliper bracket mounting bolt torque and inspect for looseness. Torque the mounting bolts and inspect for wear or any looseness, including worn mounting brackets, bushings and sliding pins.

d. Check the wheel bearing for looseness. If the bearing is loose, adjust if possible, otherwise replace the bearing.

2. Brakes make a squealing noise

a. Check the brake rotor for the presence of a ridge on the outer edge; if present, remove the ridge or replace the brake rotor and brake pads.

b. Check for debris in the brake lining material, clean and reinstall.

c. Check the brake linings for wear and replace the brake linings if wear is approaching the lining wear limit.

d. Check the brake linings for glazing. Inspect the brake drum or rotor surface and replace, along with the brake linings, if the surface is not smooth or even.

e. Check the brake pad or shoe mounting areas for a lack of lubricant or the presence of surface rust. Clean and lubricate with a recommended high temperature brake grease.

3. Brakes make a grinding noise

a. Check the brake linings and brake surface areas for severe wear or damage. Replace worn or damaged parts.

b. Check for a seized or partially seized brake causing premature or uneven brake wear, excessive heat and brake rotor or drum damage. Replace defective parts and inspect the wheel bearing condition, which could have been damaged due to excessive heat.

4. Vehicle pulls to one side during braking

a. Check for air in the brake hydraulic system. Inspect the brake hydraulic seals, fluid lines and related components for fluid leaks. Remove the air from the brake system by bleeding the brakes. Be sure to use fresh brake fluid that meets the manufacturer's recommended standards.

b. Check for an internally restricted flexible brake hydraulic hose. Replace the hose and flush the brake system.

c. Check for a seizing brake hydraulic component such as a brake caliper. Check the caliper piston for surface damage such as rust, and measure for out-of-round wear and caliper-to-piston clearance. Overhaul or replace failed parts and flush the brake system.

d. Check the vehicle's alignment and inspect for suspension wear. Replace worn bushings, ball joints and set alignment to the manufacturer's specifications.

e. If the brake system uses drum brakes front or rear, check the brake adjustment. Inspect for seized adjusters and clean or replace, then properly adjust.

5. Brake pedal feels spongy or has excessive travel

a. Check the brake fluid level and condition. If the fluid is contaminated or has not been flushed every two years, clean the master cylinder reservoir, and bleed and flush the brakes using fresh brake fluid that meets the manufacturer's recommended standards.

b. Check for a weak or damaged flexible brake hydraulic hose. Replace the hose and flush the brake system.

c. If the brake system uses drum brakes front or rear, check the brake adjustment. Inspect for seized adjusters and clean or replace, then properly adjust.

6. Brake pedal feel is firm, but brakes lack sufficient stopping power or fade

a. Check the operation of the brake booster and brake booster check valve. Replace worn or failed parts.

b. Check brake linings and brake surface areas for glazing and replace worn or damaged parts.

c. Check for seized hydraulic parts and linkages, and clean or replace as needed.

7. Vehicle has excessive front end dive or locks rear brakes too easily

a. Check for worn, failed or seized brake proportioning valve and replace the valve.

b. Check for a seized, disconnected or missing spring or linkage for the brake proportioning valve. Replace missing parts or repair as necessary.

8. Brake pedal goes to floor when pressed and will not pump up

a. Check the brake hydraulic fluid level and inspect the fluid lines and seals for leakage. Repair or replace leaking components, then bleed and flush the brake system using fresh brake fluid that meets the manufacturer's recommended standards.

b. Check the brake fluid level. Inspect the brake fluid level and brake hydraulic seals. If the fluid level is ok, and the brake hydraulic system is free of hydraulic leaks, replace the brake master cylinder, then bleed and flush the brake system using fresh brake fluid that meets the manufacturer's recommended standards.

9. Brakes produce a burning odor

a. Check for a seizing brake hydraulic component such as a brake caliper. Check the caliper piston for surface damage such as rust, and measure for out-of-round wear and caliper-to-piston clearance. Overhaul or replace failed parts and flush the brake system.

b. Check for an internally restricted flexible brake hydraulic hose. Replace the hose and flush the brake system.

c. Check the parking brake release mechanism, seized linkage or cable, and repair as necessary.

BRAKE PERFORMANCE TROUBLESHOOTING HINTS

Brake vibrations or pulsation can often be diagnosed on a safe and careful test drive. A brake vibration which is felt through the brake pedal while braking, but not felt in the steering wheel, is most likely caused by brake surface variations in the rear brakes. If both the brake pedal and steering wheel vibrate during braking, a surface variation in the front brakes, or both front and rear brakes, is very likely.

A brake pedal that pumps up with repeated use can be caused by air in the brake hydraulic system or, if the vehicle is equipped with rear drum brakes, the brake adjusters may be seized or out of adjustment. A quick test for brake adjustment on vehicles with rear drum brakes is to pump the brake pedal several times with the vehicle's engine not running and the parking brake released. Pump the brake pedal several times and continue to apply pressure to the brake pedal. With pressure being applied to the brake pedal, engage the parking brake. Release the brake pedal and quickly press the brake pedal again. If the brake pedal pumped up, the rear brakes are in need of adjustment. Do not compensate for the rear brake adjustment by adjusting the parking brake, this will cause premature brake lining wear.

To test a vacuum brake booster, pump the brake pedal several times with the vehicle's engine off. Apply pressure to the brake pedal and then start the engine. The brake pedal should move downward about one inch (25mm).

4. WHEELS, TIRES, STEERING AND SUSPENSION

4-A. Wheels and Wheel Bearings

1. Front Wheel or Wheel Bearing Loose

All Wheel and Four Wheel Drive Vehicles

a. Torque lug nuts and axle nuts to specification and recheck for looseness.
b. Wheel bearing worn or damaged. Replace wheel bearing.

Front Wheel Drive Vehicles

a. Torque lug nuts and axle nuts to specification and recheck for looseness.
b. Wheel bearing worn or damaged. Replace wheel bearing.

Rear Wheel Drive Vehicles

a. Wheel bearing out of adjustment. Adjust wheel bearing to specification; if still loose, replace.
b. Torque lug nuts to specification and recheck for looseness.
c. Wheel bearing worn or damaged. Replace wheel bearing.

2. Rear Wheel or Wheel Bearing Loose

All Wheel and Four Wheel Drive Vehicles

a. Torque lug nuts and axle nuts to specification and recheck for looseness.
b. Wheel bearing worn or damaged. Replace wheel bearing.

Front Wheel Drive Vehicles

a. Wheel bearing out of adjustment. Adjust wheel bearing to specification; if still loose, replace.
b. Torque lug nuts to specification and recheck for looseness.
c. Wheel bearing worn or damaged. Replace wheel bearing.

Rear Wheel Drive Vehicles

a. Torque lug nuts and to specification and recheck for looseness.
b. Wheel bearing worn or damaged. Replace wheel bearing.

4-B. Tires

1. Tires worn on inside tread

a. Check alignment for a toed-out condition. Check and set tire pressures and properly adjust the toe.
b. Check for worn, damaged or defective suspension components. Replace defective parts and adjust the alignment.

2. Tires worn on outside tread

a. Check alignment for a toed-in condition. Check and set tire pressures and properly adjust the toe.
b. Check for worn, damaged or defective suspension components. Replace defective parts and adjust the alignment.

3. Tires worn unevenly

a. Check the tire pressure and tire balance. Replace worn or defective tires and check the alignment; adjust if necessary.

b. Check for worn shock absorbers. Replaced failed components, worn or defective tires and check the alignment; adjust if necessary.
c. Check the alignment settings. Check and set tire pressures and properly adjust the alignment to specification.
d. Check for worn, damaged or defective suspension components. Replace defective parts and adjust the alignment to specification.

4-C. Steering

1. Excessive play in steering wheel

a. Check the steering gear free-play adjustment and properly adjust to remove excessive play.
b. Check the steering linkage for worn, damaged or defective parts. Replace failed components and perform a front end alignment.
c. Check for a worn, damaged, or defective steering box, replace the steering gear and check the front end alignment.

2. Steering wheel shakes at cruising speeds

a. Check for a bent front wheel. Replace a damaged wheel and check the tire for possible internal damage.
b. Check for an unevenly worn front tire. Replace the tire, adjust tire pressure and balance.
c. Check the front tires for hidden internal damage. Tires which have encountered large pot holes or suffered other hard blows may have sustained internal damage and should be replaced immediately.
d. Check the front tires for an out-of-balance condition. Remove, spin balance and reinstall. Torque all the wheel bolts or lug nuts to the recommended specification.
e. Check for a loose wheel bearing. If possible, adjust the bearing, or replace the bearing if it is a non-adjustable bearing.

3. Steering wheel shakes when braking

a. Refer to section 3-A, condition number 1.

4. Steering wheel becomes stiff when turned

a. Check the steering wheel free-play adjustment and reset as needed.
b. Check for a damaged steering gear assembly. Replace the steering gear and perform a front end alignment.
c. Check for damaged or seized suspension components. Replace defective components and perform a front end alignment.

4-D. Suspension

1. Vehicle pulls to one side

a. Tire pressure uneven. Adjust tire pressure to recommended settings.
b. Tires worn unevenly. Replace tires and check alignment settings.
c. Alignment out of specification. Align front end and check thrust angle.
d. Check for a dragging brake and repair or replace as necessary.

2. Vehicle is very bouncy over bumps

a. Check for worn or leaking shock absorbers or strut assemblies and replace as necessary.
b. Check for seized shock absorbers or strut assemblies and replace as necessary.

NOTE: When one shock fails, it is recommended to replace front or rear units as pairs.

3. Vehicle leans excessively in turns
a. Check for worn or leaking shock absorbers or strut assemblies and replace as necessary.
b. Check for missing, damaged, or worn stabilizer links or bushings, and replace or install as necessary.

4. Vehicle ride quality seems excessively harsh
a. Check for seized shock absorbers or strut assemblies and replace as necessary.
b. Check for excessively high tire pressures and adjust pressures to vehicle recommendations.

5. Vehicle seems low or leans to one side
a. Check for a damaged, broken or weak spring. Replace defective parts and check for a needed alignment.
b. Check for seized shock absorbers or strut assemblies and replace as necessary.
c. Check for worn or leaking shock absorbers or strut assemblies and replace as necessary.

4-E. Driving Noises and Vibrations

Noises
1. Vehicle makes a clicking noises when driven
a. Check the noise to see if it varies with road speed. Verify if the noise is present when coasting or with steering or throttle input. If the clicking noise frequency changes with road speed and is not affected by steering or throttle input, check the tire treads for a stone, piece of glass, nail or another hard object imbedded into the tire or tire tread. Stones rarely cause a tire puncture and are easily removed: Other objects may create an air leak when removed. Consider having these objects removed immediately at a facility equipped to repair tire punctures.
b. If the clicking noise varies with throttle input and steering, check for a worn Constant Velocity (CV-joint) joint, universal (U- joint) or flex joint.

2. Vehicle makes a clunking or knocking noise over bumps
a. A clunking noise over bumps is most often caused by excessive movement or clearance in a suspension component. Check the suspension for soft, cracked, damaged or worn bushings. Replace the bushings and check the vehicle's alignment.
b. Check for loose suspension mounting bolts. Check the tightness on subframe bolts, pivot bolts and suspension mounting bolts, and torque to specification.
c. Check the vehicle for a loose wheel bearing. Some wheel bearings can be adjusted for looseness, while others must be replaced if loose. Adjust or replace the bearings as recommended by the manufacturer.
d. Check the door latch adjustment. If the door is slightly loose, or the latch adjustment is not centered, the door assembly may create noises over bumps and rough surfaces. Properly adjust the door latches to secure the door.

3. Vehicle makes a low pitched rumbling noise when driven
a. A low pitched rumbling noise is usually caused by a drive train related bearing and is most often associated with a wheel bearing which has been damaged or worn. The damage can be caused by excessive brake temperatures or physical contact with a pot hole or curb. Sometimes the noise will vary when turning. Left hand turns increase the load on the vehicle's right side, and right turns load the left side. A failed front wheel bearing may also cause a slight steering wheel vibration when turning. A bearing which exhibits noise must be replaced.
b. Check the tire condition and balance. An internally damaged tire may cause failure symptoms similar to failed suspension parts. For diagnostic purposes, try a known good set of tires and replace defective tires.

4. Vehicle makes a squeaking noise over bumps
a. Check the vehicle's ball joints for wear, damaged or leaking boots. Replace a ball joint if it is loose, the boot is damaged and leaking, or the ball joint is binding. When replacing suspension parts, check the vehicle for alignment.
b. Check for seized or deteriorated bushings. Replace bushings that are worn or damaged and check the vehicle for alignment.
c. Check for the presence of sway bar or stabilizer bar bushings which wrap around the bar. Inspect the condition of the bushings and replace if worn or damaged. Remove the bushing bracket and apply a thin layer of suspension grease to the area where the bushings wrap around the bar and reinstall the bushing brackets.

5. Vehicle vibrates when driven
a. Check the road surface. Roads which have rough or uneven surfaces may cause unusual vibrations.
b. Check the tire condition and balance. An internally damaged tire may cause failure symptoms similar to failed suspension parts. For diagnostic purposes, try a known good set of tires and replace defective tires immediately.
c. Check for a worn Constant Velocity (CV-joint) joint, universal (U- joint) or flex joint and replace if loose, damaged or binding.
d. Check for a loose, bent, or out-of-balance axle or drive shaft. Replace damaged or failed components.

NOTE: Diagnosing failures related to wheels, tires, steering and the suspension system can often times be accomplished with a careful and thorough test drive. Bearing noises are isolated by noting whether the noises or symptoms vary when turning left or right, or occur while driving a straight line. During a left hand turn, the vehicle's weight shifts to the right, placing more force on the right side bearings, such that if a right side wheel bearing is worn or damaged, the noise or vibration should increase during light-to-heavy acceleration. Conversely, on right hand turns, the vehicle tends to lean to the left, loading the left side bearings.

Knocking noises in the suspension when the vehicle is driven over rough roads, railroad tracks and speed bumps indicate worn suspension components such as bushings, ball joints or tie rod ends, or a worn steering system.

5. ELECTRICAL ACCESSORIES

5-A. Headlights

1. One headlight only works on high or low beam
a. Check for battery voltage at headlight electrical connector. If battery voltage is present, replace the headlight assembly or bulb if available separately. If battery voltage is not present, refer to the headlight wiring diagram to troubleshoot.

2. Headlight does not work on high or low beam
a. Check for battery voltage and ground at headlight electrical connector. If battery voltage is present, check the headlight connector ground terminal for a proper ground. If battery voltage and ground are present at the headlight connector, replace the headlight assembly or bulb if available separately. If battery voltage or ground is not present, refer to the headlight wiring diagram to troubleshoot.
b. Check the headlight switch operation. Replace the switch if the switch is defective or operates intermittently.

3. Headlight(s) very dim
a. Check for battery voltage and ground at headlight electrical connector. If battery voltage is present, trace the ground circuit for the headlamp electrical connector, then clean and repair as necessary. If the voltage at the headlight electrical connector is significantly less than the voltage at the battery, refer to the headlight wiring diagram to troubleshoot and locate the voltage drop.

5-B. Tail, Running and Side Marker Lights

1. Tail light, running light or side marker light inoperative
a. Check for battery voltage and ground at light's electrical connector. If battery voltage is present, check the bulb socket and electrical connector ground terminal for a proper ground. If battery voltage and ground are present at the light connector, but not in the socket, clean the socket and the ground terminal connector. If battery voltage and ground are present in the bulb socket, replace the bulb. If battery voltage or ground is not present, refer to the wiring diagram to troubleshoot for an open circuit.
b. Check the light switch operation and replace if necessary.

2. Tail light, running light or side marker light works intermittently
a. Check the bulb for a damaged filament, and replace if damaged.
b. Check the bulb and bulb socket for corrosion, and clean or replace the bulb and socket.
c. Check for loose, damaged or corroded wires and electrical terminals, and repair as necessary.
d. Check the light switch operation and replace if necessary.

3. Tail light, running light or side marker light very dim
a. Check the bulb and bulb socket for corrosion and clean or replace the bulb and socket.

b. Check for low voltage at the bulb socket positive terminal or a poor ground. If voltage is low, or the ground marginal, trace the wiring to, and check for loose, damaged or corroded wires and electrical terminals; repair as necessary.

c. Check the light switch operation and replace if necessary.

5-C. Interior Lights

1. Interior light inoperative

a. Verify the interior light switch location and position(s), and set the switch in the correct position.

b. Check for battery voltage and ground at the interior light bulb socket. If battery voltage and ground are present, replace the bulb. If voltage is not present, check the interior light fuse for battery voltage. If the fuse is missing, replace the fuse. If the fuse has blown, or if battery voltage is present, refer to the wiring diagram to troubleshoot the cause for an open or shorted circuit. If ground is not present, check the door switch contacts and clean or repair as necessary.

2. Interior light works intermittently

a. Check the bulb for a damaged filament, and replace if damaged.

b. Check the bulb and bulb socket for corrosion, and clean or replace the bulb and socket.

c. Check for loose, damaged or corroded wires and electrical terminals; repair as necessary.

d. Check the door and light switch operation, and replace if necessary.

3. Interior light very dim

a. Check the bulb and bulb socket for corrosion, and clean or replace the bulb and socket.

b. Check for low voltage at the bulb socket positive terminal or a poor ground. If voltage is low, or the ground marginal, trace the wiring to, and check for loose, damaged or corroded wires and electrical terminals; repair as necessary.

c. Check the door and light switch operation, and replace if necessary.

5-D. Brake Lights

1. One brake light inoperative

a. PressPress the brake pedal and check for battery voltage and ground at the brake light bulb socket. If present, replace the bulb. If either battery voltage or ground is not present, refer to the wiring diagram to troubleshoot.

2. Both brake lights inoperative

a. Press the brake pedal and check for battery voltage and ground at the brake light bulb socket. If present, replace both bulbs. If battery voltage is not present, check the brake light switch adjustment and adjust as necessary. If the brake light switch is properly adjusted, and battery voltage or the ground is not present at the bulb sockets, or at the bulb electrical connector with the brake pedal pressed, refer to the wiring diagram to troubleshoot the cause of an open circuit.

3. One or both brake lights very dim

a. Press the brake pedal and measure the voltage at the brake light bulb socket. If the measured voltage is close to the battery voltage, check for a poor ground caused by a loose, damaged, or corroded wire, terminal, bulb or bulb socket. If the ground is bolted to a painted surface, it may be necessary to remove the electrical connector and clean the mounting surface, so the connector mounts on bare metal. If battery voltage is low, check for a poor connection caused by either a faulty brake light switch, a loose, damaged, or corroded wire, terminal or electrical connector. Refer to the wiring diagram to troubleshoot the cause of a voltage drop.

5-E. Warning Lights

1. Warning light(s) stay on when the engine is started

Ignition, Battery or Alternator Warning Light

a. Check the alternator output and voltage regulator operation, and replace as necessary.

b. Check the warning light wiring for a shorted wire.

Check Engine Light

a. Check the engine for routine maintenance and tune-up status. Note the engine tune-up specifications and verify the spark plug, air filter and engine oil condition; replace and/or adjust items as necessary.

b. Check the fuel tank for low fuel level, causing an intermittent lean fuel mixtur

e. Top off fuel tank and reset check engine light.

c. Check for a failed or disconnected engine fuel or ignition component, sensor or control unit and repair or replace as necessary.

d. Check the intake manifold and vacuum hoses for air leaks and repair as necessary.

e. Check the engine's mechanical condition for excessive oil consumption.

Anti-Lock Braking System (ABS) Light

a. Check the wheel sensors and sensor rings for debris, and clean as necessary.

b. Check the brake master cylinder for fluid leakage or seal failure and replace as necessary.

c. Check the ABS control unit, pump and proportioning valves for proper operation; replace as necessary.

d. Check the sensor wiring at the wheel sensors and the ABS control unit for a loose or shorted wire, and repair as necessary.

Brake Warning Light

a. Check the brake fluid level and check for possible leakage from the hydraulic lines and seals. Top off brake fluid and repair leakage as necessary.

b. Check the brake linings for wear and replace as necessary.

c. Check for a loose or shorted brake warning light sensor or wire, and replace or repair as necessary.

Oil Pressure Warning Light

a. Stop the engine immediately. Check the engine oil level and oil filter condition, and top off or change the oil as necessary.

b. Check the oil pressure sensor wire for being shorted to ground. Disconnect the wire from the oil pressure sensor and with the ignition in the ON position, but not running, the oil pressure light should not be working. If the light works with the wire disconnected, check the sensor wire for being shorted to ground. Check the wire routing to make sure the wire is not pinched and check for insulation damage. Repair or replace the wire as necessary and recheck before starting the engine.

c. Remove the oil pan and check for a clogged oil pick-up tube screen.

d. Check the oil pressure sensor operation by substituting a known good sensor.

e. Check the oil filter for internal restrictions or leaks, and replace as necessary.

WARNING: If the engine is operated with oil pressure below the manufacturer's specification, severe (and costly) engine damage could occur. Low oil pressure can be caused by excessive internal wear or damage to the engine bearings, oil pressure relief valve, oil pump or oil pump drive mechanism.

Before starting the engine, check for possible causes of rapid oil loss, such as leaking oil lines or a loose, damaged, restricted, or leaking oil filter or oil pressure sensor. If the engine oil level and condition are acceptable, measure the engine's oil pressure using a pressure gauge, or determine the cause for the oil pressure warning light to function when the engine is running, before operating the engine for an extended period of time. Another symptom of operating an engine with low oil pressure is the presence of severe knocking and tapping noises.

Parking Brake Warning Light

a. Check the brake release mechanism and verify the parking brake has been fully released.

b. CheckCheck the parking brake light switch for looseness or misalignment.

c. CheckCheck for a damaged switch or a loose or shorted brake light switch wire, and replace or repair as necessary.

2. Warning light(s) flickers on and off when driving

Ignition, Battery or Alternator Warning Light

a. Check the alternator output and voltage regulator operation. An intermittent condition may indicate worn brushes, an internal short, or a defective voltage regulator. Replace the alternator or failed component.

b. Check the warning light wiring for a shorted, pinched or damaged wire and repair as necessary.

Check Engine Light

a. Check the engine for required maintenance and tune-up status. Verify engine tune-up specifications, as well as spark plug, air filter and engine oil condition; replace and/or adjust items as necessary.

b. Check the fuel tank for low fuel level causing an intermittent lean fuel mixture. Top off fuel tank and reset check engine light.

c. Check for an intermittent failure or partially disconnected engine fuel and ignition component, sensor or control unit; repair or replace as necessary.

d. Check the intake manifold and vacuum hoses for air leaks, and repair as necessary.

e. Check the warning light wiring for a shorted, pinched or damaged wire and repair as necessary.

Anti-Lock Braking System (ABS) Light

a. Check the wheel sensors and sensor rings for debris, and clean as necessary.

b. Check the brake master cylinder for fluid leakage or seal failure and replace as necessary.

c. Check the ABS control unit, pump and proportioning valves for proper operation, and replace as necessary.

d. Check the sensor wiring at the wheel sensors and the ABS control unit for a loose or shorted wire and repair as necessary.

Brake Warning Light
a. Check the brake fluid level and check for possible leakage from the hydraulic lines and seals. Top off brake fluid and repair leakage as necessary.
b. Check the brake linings for wear and replace as necessary.
c. Check for a loose or shorted brake warning light sensor or wire, and replace or repair as necessary.

Oil Pressure Warning Light
a. Stop the engine immediately. Check the engine oil level and check for a sudden and rapid oil loss, such as a leaking oil line or oil pressure sensor, and repair or replace as necessary.
b. Check the oil pressure sensor operation by substituting a known good sensor.
c. Check the oil pressure sensor wire for being shorted to ground. Disconnect the wire from the oil pressure sensor and with the ignition in the ON position, but not running, the oil pressure light should not be working. If the light works with the wire disconnected, check the sensor wire for being shorted to ground. Check the wire routing to make sure the wire is not pinched and check for insulation damage. Repair or replace the wire as necessary and recheck before starting the engine.
d. Remove the oil pan and check for a clogged oil pick-up tube screen.

Parking Brake Warning Light
a. Check the brake release mechanism and verify the parking brake has been fully released.
b. Check the parking brake light switch for looseness or misalignment.
c. Check for a damaged switch or a loose or shorted brake light switch wire, and replace or repair as necessary.

3. Warning light(s) inoperative with ignition on, and engine not started
a. Check for a defective bulb by installing a known good bulb.
b. Check for a defective wire using the appropriate wiring diagram(s).
c. Check for a defective sending unit by removing and then grounding the wire at the sending unit. If the light comes on with the ignition on when grounding the wire, replace the sending unit.

5-F. Turn Signal and 4-Way Hazard Lights

1. Turn signals or hazard lights come on, but do not flash
a. Check for a defective flasher unit and replace as necessary.

2. Turn signals or hazard lights do not function on either side
a. Check the fuse and replace, if defective.
b. Check the flasher unit by substituting a known good flasher unit.
c. Check the turn signal electrical system for a defective component, open circuit, short circuit or poor ground.

3. Turn signals or hazard lights only work on one side
a. Check for failed bulbs and replace as necessary.
b. Check for poor grounds in both housings and repair as necessary.

4. One signal light does not work
a. Check for a failed bulb and replace as necessary.
b. Check for corrosion in the bulb socket, and clean and repair as necessary.
c. Check for a poor ground at the bulb socket, and clean and repair as necessary.

5. Turn signals flash too slowly
a. Check signal bulb(s) wattage and replace with lower wattage bulb(s).

6. Turn signals flash too fast
a. Check signal bulb(s) wattage and replace with higher wattage bulb(s).
b. Check for installation of the correct flasher unit and replace if incorrect.

7. Four-way hazard flasher indicator light inoperative
a. Verify that the exterior lights are functioning and, if so, replace indicator bulb.
b. Check the operation of the warning flasher switch and replace if defective.

8. Turn signal indicator light(s) do not work in either direction
a. Verify that the exterior lights are functioning and, if so, replace indicator bulb(s).
b. Check for a defective flasher unit by substituting a known good unit.

9. One turn signal indicator light does not work
a. Check for a defective bulb and replace as necessary.
b. Check for a defective flasher unit by substituting a known good unit.

5-G. Horn

1. Horn does not operate
a. Check for a defective fuse and replace as necessary.
b. Check for battery voltage and ground at horn electrical connections when pressing the horn switch. If voltage is present, replace the horn assembly. If voltage or ground is not present, refer to Chassis Electrical coverage for additional troubleshooting techniques and circuit information.

2. Horn has an unusual tone
a. On single horn systems, replace the horn.
b. On dual horn systems, check the operation of the second horn. Dual horn systems have a high and low pitched horn. Unplug one horn at a time and recheck operation. Replace the horn which does not function.
c. Check for debris or condensation build-up in horn and verify the horn positioning. If the horn has a single opening, adjust the opening downward to allow for adequate drainage and to prevent debris build-up.

5-H. Windshield Wipers

1. Windshield wipers do not operate
a. Check fuse and replace as necessary.
b. Check switch operation and repair or replace as necessary.
c. Check for corroded, loose, disconnected or broken wires and clean or repair as necessary.
d. Check the ground circuit for the wiper switch or motor and repair as necessary.

2. Windshield wiper motor makes a humming noise, gets hot or blows fuses
a. Wiper motor damaged internally; replace the wiper motor.
b. Wiper linkage bent, damaged or seized. Repair or replace wiper linkage as necessary.

3. Windshield wiper motor operates, but one or both wipers fail to move
a. Windshield wiper motor linkage loose or disconnected. Repair or replace linkage as necessary.
b. Windshield wiper arms loose on wiper pivots. Secure wiper arm to pivot or replace both the wiper arm and pivot assembly.

4. Windshield wipers will not park
a. Check the wiper switch operation and verify that the switch properly interrupts the power supplied to the wiper motor.
b. If the wiper switch is functioning properly, the wiper motor parking circuit has failed. Replace the wiper motor assembly. Operate the wiper motor at least one time before installing the arms and blades to ensure correct positioning, then recheck using the highest wiper speed on a wet windshield to make sure the arms and blades do not contact the windshield trim.

6. INSTRUMENTS AND GAUGES

6-A. Speedometer, cable operated

1. Speedometer does not work
a. Check and verify that the speedometer cable is properly seated into the speedometer assembly and the speedometer drive gear.
b. Check the speedometer cable for breakage or rounded-off cable ends where the cable seats into the speedometer drive gear and into the speedometer assembly. If damaged, broken or the cable ends are rounded off, replace the cable.
c. Check speedometer drive gear condition and replace as necessary.
d. Install a known good speedometer to test for proper operation. If the substituted speedometer functions properly, replace the speedometer assembly.

2. Speedometer needle fluctuates when driving at steady speeds.
a. Check speedometer cable routing or sheathing for sharp bends or kinks. Route cable to minimize sharp bends or kinks. If the sheathing has been damaged, replace the cable assembly.
b. Check the speedometer cable for adequate lubrication. Remove the cable, inspect for damage, clean, lubricate and reinstall. If the cable has been damaged, replace the cable.

3. Speedometer works intermittently
a. Check the cable and verify that the cable is fully installed and the fasteners are secure.
b. Check the cable ends for wear and rounding, and replace as necessary.

6-B. Speedometer, electronically operated

1. Speedometer does not work
a. Check the speed sensor pickup and replace as necessary.
b. Check the wiring between the speed sensor and the speedometer for corroded terminals, loose connections or broken wires and clean or repair as necessary.
c. Install a known good speedometer to test for proper operation. If the substituted speedometer functions properly, replace the speedometer assembly.

2. Speedometer works intermittently
a. Check the wiring between the speed sensor and the speedometer for corroded terminals, loose connections or broken wires and clean or repair as necessary.
b. Check the speed sensor pickup and replace as necessary.

6-C. Fuel, Temperature and Oil Pressure Gauges

1. Gauge does not register
a. Check for a missing or blown fuse and replace as necessary.
b. Check for an open circuit in the gauge wiring. Repair wiring as necessary.

c. Gauge sending unit defective. Replace gauge sending unit.
d. Gauge or sending unit improperly installed. Verify installation and wiring, and repair as necessary.

2. Gauge operates erratically
a. Check for loose, shorted, damaged or corroded electrical connections or wiring and repair as necessary.
b. Check gauge sending units and replace as necessary.

3. Gauge operates fully pegged
a. Sending unit-to-gauge wire shorted to ground.
b. Sending unit defective; replace sending unit.
c. Gauge or sending unit not properly grounded.
d. Gauge or sending unit improperly installed. Verify installation and wiring, and repair as necessary.

7. CLIMATE CONTROL

7-A. Air Conditioner

1. No air coming from air conditioner vents
a. Check the air conditioner fuse and replace as necessary.
b. Air conditioner system discharged. Have the system evacuated, charged and leak tested by an MVAC certified technician, utilizing approved recovery/recycling equipment. Repair as necessary.
c. Air conditioner low pressure switch defective. Replace switch.
d. Air conditioner fan resistor pack defective. Replace resistor pack.
e. Loose connection, broken wiring or defective air conditioner relay in air conditioning electrical circuit. Repair wiring or replace relay as necessary.
2. Air conditioner blows warm air
a. Air conditioner system is discharged. Have the system evacuated, charged and leak tested by an MVAC certified technician, utilizing approved recovery/recycling equipment. Repair as necessary.
b. Air conditioner compressor clutch not engaging. Check compressor clutch wiring, electrical connections and compressor clutch, and repair or replace as necessary.

3. Water collects on the interior floor when the air conditioner is used
a. Air conditioner evaporator drain hose is blocked. Clear the drain hose where it exits the passenger compartment.
b. Air conditioner evaporator drain hose is disconnected. Secure the drain hose to the evaporator drainage tray under the dashboard.

4. Air conditioner has a moldy odor when used
a. The air conditioner evaporator drain hose is blocked or partially restricted, allowing condensation to build up around the evaporator and drainage tray. Clear the drain hose where it exits the passenger compartment.

7-B. Heater

1. Blower motor does not operate
a. Check blower motor fuse and replace as necessary.
b. Check blower motor wiring for loose, damaged or corroded contacts and repair as necessary.
c. Check blower motor switch and resistor pack for open circuits, and repair or replace as necessary.
d. Check blower motor for internal damage and repair or replace as necessary.

2. Heater blows cool air
a. Check the engine coolant level. If the coolant level is low, top off and bleed the air from the cooling system as necessary and check for coolant leaks.
b. Check engine coolant operating temperature. If coolant temperature is below specification, check for a damaged or stuck thermostat.
c. Check the heater control valve operation. Check the heater control valve cable or vacuum hose for proper installation. Move the heater temperature control from hot to cold several times and verify the operation of the heater control valve. With the engine at normal operating temperature and the heater temperature control in the full hot position, carefully feel the heater hose going into and exiting the control valve. If one heater hose is hot and the other is much cooler, replace the control valve.

3. Heater steams the windshield when used
a. Check for a loose cooling system hose clamp or leaking coolant hose near the engine firewall or under the dash area, and repair as necessary.
b. Check for the existence of a sweet odor and fluid dripping from the heater floor vents, indicating a failed or damaged heater core. Pressure test the cooling system with the heater set to the fully warm position and check for fluid leakage from the floor vents. If leakage is verified, remove and replace the heater core assembly.

NOTE: On some vehicles, the dashboard must be disassembled and removed to access the heater core.

GLOSSARY

AIR/FUEL RATIO: The ratio of air-to-gasoline by weight in the fuel mixture drawn into the engine.

AIR INJECTION: One method of reducing harmful exhaust emissions by injecting air into each of the exhaust ports of an engine. The fresh air entering the hot exhaust manifold causes any remaining fuel to be burned before it can exit the tailpipe.

ALTERNATOR: A device which produces AC (alternating current) which is converted to DC (direct current) to charge the car battery.

AMMETER: An instrument, calibrated in amperes, used to measure the flow of an electrical current in a circuit. Ammeters are always connected in series with the circuit being tested.

AMPERE: The rate of flow of electrical current present when one volt of electrical pressure is applied against one ohm of electrical resistance.

ANALOG COMPUTER: Any microprocessor that uses similar (analogous) electrical signals to make its calculations.

ARMATURE: A laminated, soft iron core wrapped by a wire that converts electrical energy to mechanical energy as in a motor or relay. When rotated in a magnetic field, it changes mechanical energy into electrical energy as in a generator.

ATMOSPHERIC PRESSURE: The pressure on the Earth's surface caused by the weight of the air in the atmosphere. At sea level, this pressure is 14.7 psi at 32°F (101 kPa at 0°C).

ATOMIZATION: The breaking down of a liquid into a fine mist that can be suspended in air.

AXIAL PLAY: Movement parallel to a shaft or bearing bore.

BACKFIRE: The sudden combustion of gases in the intake or exhaust system that results in a loud explosion.

BACKLASH: The clearance or play between two parts, such as meshed gears.

BACKPRESSURE: Restrictions in the exhaust system that slow the exit of exhaust gases from the combustion chamber.

BAKELITE[reg]: A heat resistant, plastic insulator material commonly used in printed circuit boards and transistorized components.

BALL BEARING: A bearing made up of hardened inner and outer races between which hardened steel balls roll.

BALLAST RESISTOR: A resistor in the primary ignition circuit that lowers voltage after the engine is started to reduce wear on ignition components.

BEARING: A friction reducing, supportive device usually located between a stationary part and a moving part.

BI-METAL TEMPERATURE SENSOR: Any sensor or switch made of two dissimilar types of metal that bend when heated or cooled due to the different expansion rates of the alloys. These types of sensors usually function as an on/off switch.

BLOW-BY: Combustion gases, composed of water vapor and unburned fuel, that leak past the piston rings into the crankcase during normal engine operation. These gases are removed by the PCV system to prevent the buildup of harmful acids in the crankcase.

BRAKE PAD: A brake shoe and lining assembly used with disc brakes.

BRAKE SHOE: The backing for the brake lining. The term is, however, usually applied to the assembly of the brake backing and lining.

BUSHING: A liner, usually removable, for a bearing; an anti-friction liner used in place of a bearing.

CALIPER: A hydraulically activated device in a disc brake system, which is mounted straddling the brake rotor (disc). The caliper contains at least one piston and two brake pads. Hydraulic pressure on the piston(s) forces the pads against the rotor.

CAMSHAFT: A shaft in the engine on which are the lobes (cams) which operate the valves. The camshaft is driven by the crankshaft, via a belt, chain or gears, at one half the crankshaft speed.

CAPACITOR: A device which stores an electrical charge.

CARBON MONOXIDE (CO): A colorless, odorless gas given off as a normal byproduct of combustion. It is poisonous and extremely dangerous in confined areas, building up slowly to toxic levels without warning if adequate ventilation is not available.

CARBURETOR: A device, usually mounted on the intake manifold of an engine, which mixes the air and fuel in the proper proportion to allow even combustion.

CATALYTIC CONVERTER: A device installed in the exhaust system, like a muffler, that converts harmful byproducts of combustion into carbon dioxide and water vapor by means of a heat-producing chemical reaction.

CENTRIFUGAL ADVANCE: A mechanical method of advancing the spark timing by using flyweights in the distributor that react to centrifugal force generated by the distributor shaft rotation.

CHECK VALVE: Any one-way valve installed to permit the flow of air, fuel or vacuum in one direction only.

CHOKE: The valve/plate that restricts the amount of air entering an engine on the induction stroke, thereby enriching the air:fuel ratio.

CIRCUIT: Any unbroken path through which an electrical current can flow. Also used to describe fuel flow in some instances.

CIRCUIT BREAKER: A switch which protects an electrical circuit from overload by opening the circuit when the current flow exceeds a predetermined level. Some circuit breakers must be reset manually, while most reset automatically.

COIL (IGNITION): Part of the ignition system that boosts the relatively low voltage supplied by the car's electrical system to the high voltage required to fire the spark plugs.

COMBINATION MANIFOLD: An assembly which includes both the intake and exhaust manifolds in one casting.

COMBINATION VALVE: A device used in some fuel systems that routes fuel vapors to a charcoal storage canister instead of venting them into the atmosphere. The valve relieves fuel tank pressure and allows fresh air into the tank as the fuel level drops to prevent a vapor lock situation.

COMPRESSION RATIO: The ratio of the volume between the piston and cylinder head when the piston is at the bottom of its stroke (bottom dead center) and when the piston is at the top of its stroke (top dead center).

CONDENSER: 1. An electrical device which acts to store an electrical charge, preventing voltage surges. 2. A radiator-like device in the air conditioning system in which refrigerant gas condenses into a liquid, giving off heat.

CONDUCTOR: Any material through which an electrical current can be transmitted easily.

CONTINUITY: Continuous or complete circuit. Can be checked with an ohm-meter.

COUNTERSHAFT: An intermediate shaft which is rotated by a mainshaft and transmits, in turn, that rotation to a working part.

CRANKCASE: The lower part of an engine in which the crankshaft and related parts operate.

CRANKSHAFT: Engine component (connected to pistons by connecting rods) which converts the reciprocating (up and down) motion of pistons to rotary motion used to turn the driveshaft.

CYLINDER: In an engine, the round hole in the engine block in which the piston(s) ride.

CYLINDER BLOCK: The main structural member of an engine in which is found the cylinders, crankshaft and other principle parts.

DEAD CENTER: The extreme top or bottom of the piston stroke.

DETONATION: An unwanted explosion of the air/fuel mixture in the combustion chamber caused by excess heat and compression, advanced timing, or an overly lean mixture. Also referred to as "ping".

DIAPHRAGM: A thin, flexible wall separating two cavities, such as in a vacuum advance unit.

DIESELING: The engine continues to run after the car is shut off; caused by fuel continuing to be burned in the combustion chamber.

DIFFERENTIAL: A geared assembly which allows the transmission of motion between drive axles, giving one axle the ability to rotate faster than the other, as in cornering.

DIODE: An electrical device that will allow current to flow in one direction only.

DISC BRAKE: A hydraulic braking assembly consisting of a brake disc, or rotor, mounted on an axleshaft, and a caliper assembly containing, usually two brake pads which are activated by hydraulic pressure. The pads are forced against the sides of the disc, creating friction which slows the vehicle.

DISTRIBUTOR: A mechanically driven device on an engine which is responsible for electrically firing the spark plug at a pre-determined point of the piston stroke.

DOWEL PIN: A pin, inserted in mating holes in two different parts allowing those parts to maintain a fixed relationship.

DRUM BRAKE: A braking system which consists of two brake shoes and one or two wheel cylinders, mounted on a fixed backing plate, and a brake drum, mounted on an axle, which revolves around the assembly.

ELECTRONIC CONTROL UNIT (ECU): A digital computer that controls engine (and sometimes transmission, brake or other vehicle system) functions based on data received from various sensors. Examples used by some manufacturers include Electronic Brake Control Module (EBCM), Engine Control Module (ECM), Powertrain Control Module (PCM) or Vehicle Control Module (VCM).

ELECTRONIC IGNITION: A system in which the timing and firing of the spark plugs is controlled by an electronic control unit, usually called a module. These systems have no points or condenser.

END-PLAY: The clearance/gap between two components that allows for expansion of the parts as they warm up, to prevent binding and to allow space for lubrication.

ENGINE: The primary motor or power apparatus of a vehicle, which converts liquid or gas fuel into mechanical energy.

EXHAUST MANIFOLD: A set of cast passages or pipes which conduct exhaust gases from the engine.

FEELER GAUGE: A blade, usually metal, of precisely predetermined thickness, used to measure the clearance between two parts.

FIRING ORDER: The order in which combustion occurs in the cylinders of an engine. Also the order in which spark is distributed to the plugs by the distributor.

FLOODING: The presence of too much fuel in the intake manifold and combustion chamber which prevents the air/fuel mixture from firing, thereby causing a no-start situation.

FLYWHEEL: A heavy disc of metal attached to the rear of the crankshaft. It smoothes the firing impulses of the engine and keeps the crankshaft turning during periods when no firing takes place. The starter also engages the flywheel to start the engine.

FOOT POUND (ft. lbs. or sometimes, ft. lb.): The amount of energy or work needed to raise an item weighing one pound, a distance of one foot.

FUSE: A protective device in a circuit which prevents circuit overload by breaking the circuit when a specific amperage is present. The device is constructed around a strip or wire of a lower amperage rating than the circuit it is designed to protect. When an amperage higher than that stamped on the fuse is present in the circuit, the strip or wire melts, opening the circuit.

GEAR RATIO: A ratio expressing the number of turns a smaller gear will make to turn a larger gear through one revolution. The ratio is found by dividing the number of teeth on the smaller gear into the number of teeth on the larger gear.

GENERATOR: A device which produces direct current (DC) necessary to charge the battery.

HEAT RANGE: A term used to describe the ability of a spark plug to carry away heat. Plugs with longer nosed insulators take longer to carry heat off effectively.

HUB: The center part of a wheel or gear.

HYDROCARBON (HC): Any chemical compound made up of hydrogen and carbon. A major pollutant formed by the engine as a by-product of combustion.

HYDROMETER: An instrument used to measure the specific gravity of a solution.

INCH POUND (inch lbs.; sometimes in. lb. or in. lbs.): One twelfth of a foot pound.

INDUCTION: A means of transferring electrical energy in the form of a magnetic field. Principle used in the ignition coil to increase voltage.

INJECTOR: A device which receives metered fuel under relatively low pressure and is activated to inject the fuel into the engine under relatively high pressure at a predetermined time.

INPUT SHAFT: The shaft to which torque is applied, usually carrying the driving gear or gears.

INTAKE MANIFOLD: A casting of passages or pipes used to conduct air or a fuel/air mixture to the cylinders.

JOURNAL: The bearing surface within which a shaft operates.

KEY: A small block usually fitted in a notch between a shaft and a hub to prevent slippage of the two parts.

MANIFOLD: A casting of passages or set of pipes which connect the cylinders to an inlet or outlet source.

MASTER CYLINDER: The primary fluid pressurizing device in a hydraulic system. In automotive use, it is found in brake and hydraulic clutch systems and is pedal activated, either directly or, in a power brake system, through the power booster.

MODULE: Electronic control unit, amplifier or igniter of solid state or integrated design which controls the current flow in the ignition primary circuit based on input from the pick-up coil. When the module opens the primary circuit, high secondary voltage is induced in the coil.

NEEDLE BEARING: A bearing which consists of a number (usually a large number) of long, thin rollers.

OHM: The unit used to measure the resistance of conductor-to-electrical flow. One ohm is the amount of resistance that limits current flow to one ampere in a circuit with one volt of pressure.

OHMMETER: An instrument used for measuring the resistance, in ohms, in an electrical circuit.

OUTPUT SHAFT: The shaft which transmits torque from a device, such as a transmission.

OVERHEAD CAMSHAFT (OHC): An engine configuration in which the camshaft is mounted on top of the cylinder head and operates the valve either directly or by means of rocker arms.

OVERHEAD VALVE (OHV): An engine configuration in which all of the valves are located in the cylinder head and the camshaft is located in the cylinder block. The camshaft operates the valves via lifters and pushrods.

OXIDES OF NITROGEN (NOx): Chemical compounds of nitrogen produced as a byproduct of combustion. They combine with hydrocarbons to produce smog.

OXYGEN SENSOR: Used with a feedback system to sense the presence of oxygen in the exhaust gas and signal the computer which can use the voltage signal to determine engine operating efficiency and adjust the air/fuel ratio.

PINION: The smaller of two gears. The rear axle pinion drives the ring gear which transmits motion to the axle shafts.

PISTON RING: An open-ended ring which fits into a groove on the outer diameter of the piston. Its chief function is to form a seal between the piston and cylinder wall. Most automotive pistons have three rings: two for compression sealing; one for oil sealing.

PRELOAD: A predetermined load placed on a bearing during assembly or by adjustment.

PRESS FIT: The mating of two parts under pressure, due to the inner diameter of one being smaller than the outer diameter of the other, or vice versa; an interference fit.

PRIMARY CIRCUIT: The low voltage side of the ignition system which consists of the ignition switch, ballast resistor or resistance wire, bypass, coil, electronic control unit and pick-up coil as well as the connecting wires and harnesses.

RACE: The surface on the inner or outer ring of a bearing on which the balls, needles or rollers move.

REGULATOR: A device which maintains the amperage and/or voltage levels of a circuit at predetermined values.

RELAY: A switch which automatically opens and/or closes a circuit.

RESISTANCE: The opposition to the flow of current through a circuit or electrical device, and is measured in ohms. Resistance is equal to the voltage divided by the amperage.

RESISTOR: A device, usually made of wire, which offers a preset amount of resistance in an electrical circuit.

RING GEAR: The name given to a ring-shaped gear attached to a differential case, or affixed to a flywheel or as part of a planetary gear set.

ROLLER BEARING: A bearing made up of hardened inner and outer races between which hardened steel rollers move.

ROTOR: (1.) The disc-shaped part of a disc brake assembly, upon which the brake pads bear; also called, brake disc. (2.) The device mounted atop the distributor shaft, which passes current to the distributor cap tower contacts.

SECONDARY CIRCUIT: The high voltage side of the ignition system, usually above 20,000 volts. The secondary includes the ignition coil, coil wire, distributor cap and rotor, spark plug wires and spark plugs.

SENDING UNIT: A mechanical, electrical, hydraulic or electromagnetic device which transmits information to a gauge.

SENSOR: Any device designed to measure engine operating conditions or ambient pressures and temperatures. Usually electronic in nature and designed to send a voltage signal to an on-board computer, some sensors may operate as a simple on/off switch or they may provide a variable voltage signal (like a potentiometer) as conditions or measured parameters change.

SHIM: Spacers of precise, predetermined thickness used between parts to establish a proper working relationship.

SLAVE CYLINDER: In automotive use, a device in the hydraulic clutch system which is activated by hydraulic force, disengaging the clutch.

SOLENOID: An electrically operated, magnetic switching device.

SPARK PLUG: A device screwed into the combustion chamber of a spark ignition engine. The basic construction is a conductive core inside of a ceramic insulator, mounted in an outer conductive base. An electrical charge from the spark plug wire travels along the conductive core and jumps a preset air gap to a grounding point or points at the end of the conductive base. The resultant spark ignites the fuel/air mixture in the combustion chamber.

SPLINES: Ridges machined or cast onto the outer diameter of a shaft or inner diameter of a bore to enable parts to mate without rotation.

TACHOMETER: A device used to measure the rotary speed of an engine, shaft, gear, etc., usually in rotations per minute.

THERMOSTAT: A valve, located in the cooling system of an engine, which is closed when cold and opens gradually in response to engine heating, controlling the temperature of the coolant and rate of coolant flow.

TOP DEAD CENTER (TDC): The point at which the piston reaches the top of its travel on the compression stroke.

TORQUE: Measurement of turning or twisting force, expressed as foot-pounds or inch-pounds.

TORQUE CONVERTER: A turbine used to transmit power from a driving member to a driven member via hydraulic action, providing changes in drive ratio and torque. In automotive use, it links the driveplate at the rear of the engine to the automatic transmission.

TRANSDUCER: A device that changes energy from one form to another. For example, a transducer in a microphone changes sound energy to electrical energy. In automotive air-conditioning controls used in automatic temperature systems, a transducer changes an electrical signal to a vacuum signal, which operates mechanical doors.

TRANSISTOR: A semi-conductor component which can be actuated by a small voltage to perform an electrical switching function.

TUNE-UP: A regular maintenance function, usually associated with the replacement and adjustment of parts and components in the electrical and fuel systems of a vehicle for the purpose of attaining optimum performance.

TURBOCHARGER: An exhaust driven pump which compresses intake air and forces it into the combustion chambers at higher than atmospheric pressures. The increased air pressure allows more fuel to be burned and results in increased horsepower being produced.

VACUUM ADVANCE: A device which advances the ignition timing in response to increased engine vacuum.

VACUUM GAUGE: An instrument used for measuring the existing vacuum in a vacuum circuit or chamber. The unit of measure is inches (of mercury in a barometer).

VALVE: Devices that can open or close fluid passages in a hydraulic system and are used for directing fluid flow and controlling pressure.

VALVE CLEARANCE: The measured gap between the end of the valve stem and the rocker arm, cam lobe or follower that activates the valve.

VISCOSITY: The ability of a fluid to flow. The lower the viscosity rating, the easier the fluid will flow. 10 weight motor oil will flow much easier than 40 weight motor oil.

VOLTMETER: An instrument used for measuring electrical force in units called volts. Voltmeters are always connected parallel with the circuit being tested.

WHEEL CYLINDER: Found in the automotive drum brake assembly, it is a device, actuated by hydraulic pressure, which, through internal pistons, pushes the brake shoes outward against the drums.

MASTER
INDEX